The Black Hole of Empire

The Black Hole of Empire

HISTORY OF A GLOBAL PRACTICE OF POWER

Partha Chatterjee

PRINCETON UNIVERSITY PRESS

PRINCETON AND OXFORD

Library of Congress Cataloging-in-Publication Data
Chatterjee, Partha, 1947-
The black hole of empire : history of a global practice of power /
Partha Chatterjee.
p.   cm.
Includes bibliographical references and index.
ISBN 978-0-691-15200-4 (hardcover : alk. paper)—
ISBN 978-0-691-15201-1 (pbk. : alk. paper)
1. Bengal (India)—Colonization—History—18th century.   2. Black Hole Incident, Calcutta, India, 1756.
3. East India Company—History—18th century.   4. Imperialism—History.   5. Europe—Colonies—History.
I. Title.
DS465.C53 2011
954'.14029—dc23   2011028355

British Library Cataloging-in-Publication Data is available

This book has been composed in Adobe Caslon Pro

Printed on acid-free paper. ∞

Printed in the United States of America

10   9   8   7   6   5   4   3   2   1

*To the amazing surgeons and physicians
who have kept me alive and working*

Contents

Illustrations

Preface

This book braids two histories: a little history, and a grand one. The little history is local, tracing the career of the English East India Company's fortified settlement in Bengal from the eighteenth century. In the nineteenth century, Fort William and the city of Calcutta that surrounds it became the capital of the British Empire in India. In the twentieth century, Calcutta also became a major place where nationalist modernity was fashioned and mass politics was organized. The conspiracies, ambitions, alliances, resistances, and confrontations that mark this local history of Fort William and its environs constitute one strand within this book. The grand history, on the other hand, is about the global phenomenon of modern empire from the eighteenth to the twentieth century. This history, I claim, was fundamentally shaped by the unprecedented problems posed by the fact of modern European states ruling over Asiatic and African peoples, shaping in turn the norms and practices of the modern state itself. Modern empire was not an aberrant supplement to the history of modernity but rather its constituent part. It will continue to thrive as long as the practices of the modern state-form remain unchanged. The continuing global history of the norms and practices of empire constitutes the second strand of the narrative.

The two histories come together in this book in the story of the Black Hole of Calcutta, the site of the alleged death by suffocation of 123 Europeans taken prisoner by Nawab Siraj-ud-daulah of Bengal in 1756. There was a time not too long ago when this account was widely known in many parts of the world. Indeed, the phrase "the black hole of Calcutta" was once commonly used to refer to any dark and suffocating place. Yet from 1758, the time of its first telling, the story has gone through many transformations, with each new version drawing a different moral conclusion. The sequence of retellings of the Black Hole story in the last two and a half centuries provides the narrative spine of this book. Around this, I have built a history of the British Empire in India and the nationalist resistance to it as well as a history of the global practices of empire as they have unfolded in the course of the frequently troubled relationship between metropolis and colony, and the changing demands of economic interest, political power, and moral legitimacy. Needless to say, the history of empire is densely entangled with the modern history of political theory, political economy, and international law. These entanglements work through abstract theoretical concepts and normative judgments.

My narrative commitment serves as a constant reminder that empire was not just about power politics, the logic of capital, or the civilizing mission but instead was something that had to be practiced, as a normal everyday business as well as at moments of extraordinary crisis, by real people in real time. The braiding of the two histories around a story line allows me not only to elucidate and reflect on the theories and ideologies of empire since the mid-eighteenth century; I also present rich narratives of numerous events and characters that make up the real history of empire. A historiography driven solely by debates in political theory, economics, or sociology inevitably leads to harnessing evidence of one's sources into a history that is nothing more than the ineluctable passage of the past into the necessary forms of the present. My attention to actual practices of empire as engaged in by real people in real time calls attention to the irreducible contingency of historical events that can never be fully encompassed by conceptual abstractions, just as it also points toward the significance of historical tendencies that never fructified, or developments that were arrested or suppressed. They are important elements of a history of empire as a global practice of power.

Who can tell a story that deals with so many subjects, periods, and locations? Instead of pretending to fill the role of the all-knowing author-as-historian, I have chosen, like poets and chroniclers of old, to disperse the narrative function over a more modest and indeterminate identity—that of the editorial "we." I hope my readers will not grudge being sometimes interpolated into the collective voice of the storyteller.

The entwining of the local and the global around a place—Fort William and the city that grew up around it—has the further effect of highlighting the fact that empire is not an abstract universal category floating around in some transcendental global space. It is embodied and experienced in actual locations. This book is therefore also about places and things in the city of Calcutta—neighborhoods and buildings, technologies and products, monuments and statuary, meeting halls, theaters, and sporting arenas. As we know, modernity was first experienced, in both metropolis and colony, as an urban phenomenon. The modern history of empire was thus lived and acted out in these places—places where that history is sometimes still remembered, and at other times, has been erased from memory. Both acts are part of the continuing history of empire. The story of the Black Hole of Calcutta, for instance, has disappeared from history books today. As we will see, this act of forgetting not only conceals a complex story of collaboration and conflict between colonizers and colonized but also is itself a powerful technique of empire that still forms a part of its repertoire of practices.

Many debts have been incurred in the course of writing this book. The research was carried out in the British Library in London, the libraries of Columbia University in New York, the National Library in Kolkata, the Nehru Memorial Museum and Library in New Delhi, and the Jadunath Sarkar Resource Centre and library of the Centre for Studies in Social Sciences, Calcutta (CSSSC). I am grateful to Malika Ghosh for her valuable research assistance. I am deeply indebted to Abhijit Bhattacharya and Kamalika Mukherjee of the Hitesranjan Sanyal Memorial Archive at the CSSSC for their unstinting help with micro-filmed and photographic material. I am also grateful to Annapoorna Potluri and Rehan Jamil of the South Asia Institute at Columbia University for assisting me with the visual material. Malini Roy, the visual arts curator of the British Library, was immensely helpful in giving me access to the India Office photo-graphs collection. My sincere thanks to Chitta Panda, Ghulam Nabi, and the staff of the documentation section of the Victoria Memorial Hall, Kolkata, for their generous response to my request for digital images of items in their col-lection. Thanks also to Susan Bean for her kind assistance with an image from the Peabody Essex Museum in Salem. Amalendu De and Christopher Pinney have generously given permission to use images from their books. I thank Ran-gan Chakrabarti, Sudipto Chatterjee, Amlan Dasgupta, and Swapan Majumdar for their assistance with sources and information. Gopalkrishna Gandhi kindly arranged for an instructive guided tour of Government House; I am grateful to him for his ever-friendly encouragement.

Dipesh Chakrabarty and two anonymous readers reviewed the first, unwieldy draft of this manuscript, and offered detailed criticisms and comments. I cannot thank them enough for the guidance they provided for the subsequent pruning of the text. Over the last few years, I have presented parts of this book at several academic events: the Danz Lecture at the Center for the Humanities of the University of Washington at Seattle, the Presidential Lecture at the Humani-ties Center of Stanford University, the plenary lecture at the North American Conference of British Studies in Denver, the plenary lecture at the annual con-ference of the Royal Geographical Society and the Institute of British Geogra-phers in London, the B. N. Ganguli Lecture at the Centre for the Study of Developing Societies in Delhi, and in talks at the Shelby Cullom Davis Center at Princeton University, the Center for Indian Studies at the University of Cal-ifornia at Los Angeles, Brown University, and Tsinghua University in Beijing. I have also discussed several chapters during seminars at the CSSSC and Co-lumbia University. I am grateful to all who participated in those conversations.

Of my colleagues in Kolkata, Raziuddin Aquil, Sibaji Bandyopadhyay, Gau-tam Bhadra, Rosinka Chaudhuri, Keya Dasgupta, Pradip Datta, Anjan Ghosh (who, sadly, is no more), Tapati Guha-Thakurta, Bodhisattva Kar, Udaya Kumar, Janaki Nair, Manas Ray, Asok Sen, and Lakshmi Subramanian have been my constant interlocutors as well as sources of support in this research. The gradu-ate seminar that I have jointly conducted with Nicholas Dirks at Columbia for over a decade was the breeding ground for many of the ideas in this book. In New York, I have also had occasions to discuss parts of this book with Gil Anidjar, Talal Asad, Janaki Bakhle, Akeel Bilgrami, Victoria de Grazia, Carol Gluck, Wael Hallaq, Sudipta Kaviraj, Lydia Liu, Mahmood Mamdani, Mark

Mazower, Uday Mehta, Timothy Mitchell, Sheldon Pollock, and David Scott. Of my students at Columbia, I have learned a great deal from the dissertation research of Mireille Abelin, Aparna Balachandran, Ayça Çubukçu, Rahul Govind, Ron Jennings, and Philip Stern. Sonia Ahsan, Ayça Çubukçu, Abhishek Kaicker, and Philip Schofield have made valuable contributions to specific chapters by providing information, translations, and suggestions. Others who have significantly contributed to this volume through conversations with me are Muzaffar Alam, Shahid Amin, Gyan Prakash, V. Narayana Rao, and Sanjay Subrahmanyam.

I am grateful to Fred Appel, Diana Goevaerts, Sara Lerner, and Cindy Milstein of Princeton University Press for ably guiding this manuscript through the process of publication, as indeed I am to Rukun Advani of Permanent Black for doing the same for the South Asian edition. My thanks to David Luljak for preparing the index.

Unless otherwise mentioned, all translations from Indian languages are my own.

CHAPTER ONE

Outrage in Calcutta

THE MYTHICAL HISTORY of the British Empire in the East begins in a black hole. In the evolutionary history of stars, the black hole is a theoretical construct. Scientists tell us that most of the black hole's properties cannot be directly observed. When the core matter of a star cools, contracts, and collapses into a black hole, the space-time around it is so sharply curved that no light escapes, no matter is ejected, and all details of the imploding star are obliterated. An outside observer cannot associate any meaningful sense of time with the interior events, and hence, in the absence of any chronological equivalence, no communication could possibly take place with an inside observer, if there were one. Scientists do, of course, infer the existence of black holes from observing disks of dust or hot gas near the cores of stars, but no actual black hole has ever been observed so far.

The Black Hole of Calcutta has a somewhat similar status in the history of modern empires. Where exactly was it located, and what happened inside it? How do we know anything about the place or event? To answer these questions, we will need to excavate many layers of narrative and doctrine that lie buried under our currently fashionable postimperial edifice of the global community of nations.

THE TRAVELS OF A MONUMENT

Dalhousie Square is the heart of the administrative district of Calcutta, a city whose name is now officially spelled, in accordance with the Bengali colloquial form, Kolkata. Like many other colonial landmarks in the city, Dalhousie Square too was renamed in the 1960s. The new name is mostly used as an acronym on buses and traffic signs: Bi-ba-di Bag. In Bengali, it sounds as though the place has been named after parties in a legal dispute. But in its expanded form, the name is Binay-Badal-Dinesh Bag, which memorializes three daring young men who, on a winter's day in 1930, walked into the Writers' Buildings and shot dead Lieutenant-Colonel Norman Skinner Simpson, the inspector general of prisons, while he was sitting at his desk in his office. The massive red-brick structure of the Writers' Buildings in fact occupies and dominates the entire northern side of the square, throwing a vast crimson reflection on the shimmering surface of the pool at the center. The principal ministries of the provincial government are still housed in the Writers' Buildings, as they were in the days when the British ruled India. On the western side of the square stands one of the more distinctive buildings of colonial Calcutta—the General Post Office (GPO)—built in the classical style with Corinthian columns and a Renaissance dome. On a workday, the bustle around the place is overwhelming, with hundreds of people scampering up or down the white marble semicircular flight of stairs leading up to an elegant domed hall, encircled by dozens of counters. On the pavement, along the tall iron railings of the post office, stand innumerable vendors peddling the most disparate array of goods one can imagine, from food to envelopes and pens to lottery tickets. Hundreds of buses and minibuses swerve around the GPO in or out of Bi-ba-di Bag every few minutes, honking frenetically and belching noxious fumes. No one here has the least suspicion that the city has not always been this way. How can one imagine a Calcutta without Dalhousie Square and the GPO?

An attentive visitor, however, may notice a small plaque high up on the GPO's eastern wall. It says, somewhat obscurely: "The brass lines in the adjacent steps and pavement mark the position and extent of part of the south-east bastion of Old Fort William the extreme south-east point being 95 feet from this wall." The brass lines are difficult to find, but along one of the lower steps there is a strip of what looks like wrought iron running southward for a few yards and then coming to an abrupt stop. There is no further clue here as to the mystery of the fort wall.

Just north of the GPO there is another red-brick public building known as the Calcutta Collectorate, and further north, running all the way to the corner of Fairlie Place, there is a grand nineteenth-century structure—the headquarters of the Eastern Railway. Rather incongruously, a modern building from the 1960s stands in between, housing the Calcutta offices of the Reserve Bank of India. The entire northern and western sections of Dalhousie Square have an unmistakable Victorian look—an aesthetic richness that is rudely spoiled, for the purist, by the monumental banality of the Reserve Bank. There was once a less grand nineteenth-century building at that spot, but it was pulled down in the 1960s. It used to be the Custom House.

The street running west out of the square past the GPO leads to the Hugli River. This is Koila Ghat, literally the Coal Wharf. It is said that the name is a corruption of Killa Ghat, which would associate the place with a fort. Leading south from Dalhousie Square is Council House Street, which runs past the yard of St. John's Church, built in 1787 and serving until 1847 as the city's Anglican cathedral. Before its recent renovation, it was in a poor state of repair for a long time. The churchyard has some of the oldest funerary architecture from British Calcutta, including the mausoleum of Job Charnock, who founded the first English settlement at Sutanuti, and the grave of Vice Admiral Charles Watson,

Figure 1. The Holwell Monument at St. John's Church. *Photo: Abhijit Bhattacharya*

who along with Robert Clive (1725–74) led the British reconquest of Fort William in 1757. Both of these structures are remarkable for their distinctly Islamic styles—a sign that local masons at the time had still not been trained to build according to European designs. More interesting for the present purpose, though, is a monument standing near the churchyard's western wall, surrounded by overgrown shrubs and piles of rubbish.

It is a white marble obelisk on an octagonal base, with inscribed tablets on six of its sides and a floral frieze on the other two. The main inscription reads as follows:

This Monument
Has been erected by
Lord Curzon, Viceroy and Governor-General of India,
In the year 1902,
Upon the site
And in reproduction of the design
Of the original monument
To the memory of the 123 persons
Who perished in the Black Hole prison
Of Old Fort William
On the night of the 20th of June, 1756.

> The former memorial was raised by
> Their surviving fellow-sufferer
> J. Z. Holwell, Governor of Fort William,
> On the spot where the bodies of the dead
> Had been thrown into the ditch of the ravelin.
> It was removed in 1821.

The next tablet displays the names of twenty-seven persons whom John Zephania Holwell (1711–98) originally listed as having died in the Black Hole. Two other tablets list fifty-four additional victims whose names have been "recovered from oblivion by reference to contemporary documents."

The memorial is actually in the wrong place, because this is neither the site of the Black Hole prison nor where the victims' bodies were allegedly thrown. At the base of the monument, there is another inscription:

> This Monument was erected in 1902
> by
> Lord Curzon on the original site of the Black Hole
> (North-West corner of Dalhousie Square)
> and removed thence to the Cemetery of
> St. John's Church, Calcutta in 1940.

We are dealing, then, with two monuments. The original one, by all accounts, stood somewhere on the northwest corner of what was then called the Tank Square, long before James Andrew Ramsay, Lord Dalhousie (1812–60), was memorialized there as an imperial hero. We know from the records that the ruins of the old fort, including the site of the Black Hole prison, were demolished in 1818 when the old Custom House was built. The Holwell monument stood outside the walls of the old fort—that is, somewhere in front of the present Collectorate building.

We also know that the original monument was designed and built, probably in 1760, by Holwell, a survivor of the Black Hole incident, to whom we owe the only detailed narrative of the event. The inscription on the front of the monument then had forty-eight names of those

> who with sundry other Inhabitants,
> Military and Militia to the Number of 123 Persons,
> were by the Tyrannic Violence of Surajud Dowla,
> Suba of Bengal, Suffocated in the Black Hole Prison of Fort William in the Night of the 20th Day of
> June, 1756, and promiscuously thrown the succeeding Morning into the Ditch of the

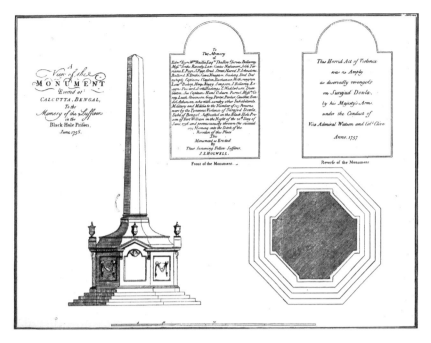

Figure 2. Holwell's plan for his monument and inscription. *Source: Holwell 1774, frontispiece*

Ravelin of this Place,
This
Monument is Erected
by
Their Surviving Fellow Sufferer,
J. Z. HOLWELL.

On the reverse of the monument, the inscription said:

This Horrid Act of Violence
was as Amply
as deservedly revenged
on Surajud Dowla,
by his Majesty's Arms,
under the Conduct of
Vice Admiral Watson and Coll. Clive
Anno, 1757[1]

In 1756, there was no Dalhousie Square, no GPO, and not even the now-nonexistent Custom House. The entire area from Fairlie Place in the north down to Koila Ghat Street in the south, and from Binay-Badal-Dinesh Bag in the east to the Hugli River in the west, which then flowed much further inland than at present, engulfing all of Strand Road, was the location of Fort William, the fortified town that served as the principal settlement of the English East India Company in Bengal. We know this not from any material remains but rather from records preserved in the archives and libraries. Yet to trace the movement of the Black Hole memorial is to unravel the mythical history of empire.

Old Fort William

The center of Calcutta in 1756 consisted of a small fort with earth and ballast bastions and brick walls. It contained the trading hall or factory, warehouses, governor's residence, armory and magazine, barracks, and officers' lodgings of the East India Company. The square bastions at each of the fort's four corners mounted ten guns, and the main east gate had five. The brick curtain walls were about four feet thick and eighteen feet high. Outside the fort, there was a settlement of private British houses, a church, a mayor's court, a hospital, and a playhouse.[2] The small British population apparently lived ostentatiously in spacious town houses built in the European style, often surrounded by large gardens. The much-larger Indian section of the town was to the north, in what was earlier the village of Sutanuti, separated from "White Town" by Indo-Portuguese and Armenian quarters, in addition to another settlement toward the south in the village of Gobindapur.

Calcutta had grown phenomenally in the first half of the eighteenth century, and its total population in 1756 could have been in the region of one hundred thousand.[3] The British population probably numbered no more than four hundred, mostly male—a large portion of whom were soldiers.[4] The Indian population residing in "Black Town" consisted of traders, artisans, and laborers who worked or did business in the flourishing trading center called Bara Bazar, or the Great Market, just north of the fort. Some of the Indian merchants of the town, such as Gopinath Seth, Ramkrishna Seth, Sobharam Basak, or the much-maligned Amirchand (called Omichund in the British sources), were major suppliers of the cotton textiles, silk goods, saltpeter, and other commodities exported by the East India Company and its officers. The Seths and Basaks as well as Amirchand owned property in White Town, which they rented to Europeans. Around 1745, there was a concerted attempt to clearly separate White Town from Black Town. After it was reported that "several Black people having intermixed themselves among the English Houses, and by that means occasion Nusances and disturbances to Several of the English Inhabitants," the order

Figure 3. *Fort William in the Kingdom of Bengal belonging to the East India Company of England*, engraving by Jan Van Ryne, 1754. *Source: Curzon 1925*

went out that "Black People living in Town" must quit.[5] This was followed by instructions from London that "Houses belonging to our Servants or any English must not be sold to Moors or any Black Merchants whatsoever."[6]

The company had held the three villages of Sutanuti, Kalkatta, and Gobindapur as the zamindar, with the right to settle people and collect revenues, starting in 1698. As with its settlement in Fort St. George in Madras, the English company was keen to encourage a local population to take up residence under its protection, engage in trade and husbandry, and contribute to the revenues.[7] In 1717, the company secured a *farman* from Emperor Farrukhsiyar of Delhi to trade without paying customs duties, rent thirty-eight villages adjacent to Calcutta, and mint coins out of its imported bullion. Whether these imperial pronouncements were merely advisory, or whether the nawab of Bengal was required to implement them, remained a matter of dispute. Nawab Murshid Quli Khan allowed the company's goods to be transported without duties, but not those that belonged to the company's officials. Company servants, however, routinely tried to carry out their private trade under the company's seal to evade customs charges. Murshid Quli Khan also refused to allow the company to purchase additional villages, but through the early eighteenth century, several villages were actually acquired under the nominal proprietorship of the company's Indian employees.[8] On the matter of minting coins, the nawab flatly denied permission.

The company's settlement in Calcutta, though, was steadily fortified through the first half of the eighteenth century, sometimes with the permission of the nawab's government, but often without it. The company's directors in London

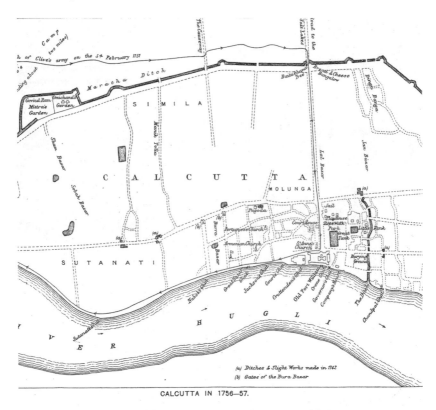

CALCUTTA IN 1756—57.

Figure 4. Section of map of Old Fort William and the town of Calcutta, 1756–57.
Source: Busteed 1888

were always concerned about the need to defend their settlement in Bengal in order to protect their trade. As early as 1700, they were reminding their officials in Bengal that "we have by every Shipping pressed you to make your ffortifications strong enough to discourage or sustaine any attempts of the Moors but in as private a Manner as you can."[9] The instructions were repeated in 1709:

> [Since] the greatest part of our Annuall Exportations are to the Bay our ffort there may be Sufficiently Strengthen'd and made tenable against any attempts of the Moors though they should have any Europeans among them to direct them in their Assaults and therefore we say take all opportunityes to make it so but without noise and as Secretly as you can and be sure colour over your reall intentions by alledging that such a building is to keep out the floods or for Additionall Warehouses to preserve goods from fire or to keep the Walls from falling or any other such reasons as the Case requires which may be true in fact tho' they are not the whole truth.[10]

The private trade of company officials was a matter of much dispute. There is little doubt that for those who chose to sail to India in the company's service, the lure of a fortune acquired in a few years through private trade was the most powerful attraction, because the actual pay was paltry. Writers were paid £5 a year, factors were paid £15, and senior merchants, after at least a decade of service in India, got £40. The average salary and official perquisites for all company servants, including governors, in the period before the battle of Palashi (spelled in the English sources as Plassey) was under £150 annually.[11] Most who came from Britain hated the conditions in Bengal: "They disliked the climate, they disliked the sicknesses that recurred so frequently, they disliked the blacks." But they all looked forward to returning home after ten or fifteen years with enough of a fortune to live "free and independent like a gentleman." This could mean something like £25,000 in savings, which could allow one to live the life of a small squire.[12] Even members of the clergy were not immune. "I am extremely anxious," wrote one young man, "to go as a chaplain on the East India fleet. The stipend is small, only £40, but there are many advantages. The last brought home £3,000."[13]

One variety of private trade, called the "country trade," was the transporting of goods in private British vessels between Indian ports and the Persian Gulf and Red Sea, or China and Southeast Asia. By the 1720s, a large part of India's maritime trade was in private British hands, and Calcutta had overtaken Madras as its principal port. At this time, something like forty private British-owned ships were fitted out from Calcutta each season.[14] It appears that local exporters favored British vessels, mainly because of the speed and dexterity with which they were operated, and the valor with which they were defended. Consequently, Asian traders were prepared to pay the higher freight charges to ensure quick and safe passage.[15] Company officials of all ranks, with the explicit blessings of their seniors, regularly participated in the country trade to make private profits.[16] The directors in London sometimes wrote to their Indian officials to take steps to stop the practice. But the Fort William council responded, "If the Company allowed no private trade, their servants must starve."[17]

The other form of private trade was the participation of the company's officials in the "inland" or internal trade in Bengal. Since they had little capital of their own, company servants would take loans from Indian merchants and use their positions of authority in the company to further their private businesses. This could be done either through company employees stationed in inland factories or via Indian *gumashtas* traveling up-country. In 1723, it was reported that the private trade of company servants in Patna was bigger than the company's own business there.[18] A common practice was to use the company permit or *dastak* to clear private goods through the toll stations. Local officials would retaliate from time to time by seizing the company's goods. After protests and haggling, the goods would be released on payment of a penalty. Sometimes, there would be a face-off, a test of wills. In 1702, when the faujdar (police chief) of Hugli served an order on Calcutta from the nawab's government, the English officials reported to London:

> We found the design was to get money from us, but we resolved to part with nothing choosing rather to spend your Honours money in powder and Shott than to be always giving to every little Rascall, who thought he should do us injury, ... we wrote him word we would not be at a Cowreys Charge, but put our selves in a good posture of defence, mounted severall Guns round the Garrison, Entertained Eight or Ten Europe men more in the Gunners Crew, made up the Company of souldiers, one hunder'd and twenty men, and resolved to make a Stout resistance, the Government hearing of our preparations made no attempt upon the place, altho' we were dayly Alarm'd with severall reports of forces comeing against us.[19]

By 1750, the British position in Bengal became entangled in the extension of European political rivalries in Asia. The aggressive policies of the French governor Joseph François Dupleix of Pondicherry had led to major military and diplomatic successes over the British in south India, and now he was looking to Bengal. In 1751, he was writing to his general, Charles Joseph Bussy: "Nothing can be easier than to humble the pride of that man [Nawab Ali Vardi Khan] whose troops are as worthless as those you already know. By sending to Bengal, Balasore or Masulipatam four to five hundred men ... some light artillery ... that is all you need in Bengal where there isn't a single fort and the whole country lies open to the first glance." He added that "the English and the Dutch are not in a position to give him [Ali Vardi] any help.... I defy them to furnish more than three hundred soldiers."[20]

The British, however, were not slow to pick up the cue. The fiercely competitive spirit of mercantilist rivalry between European nations had long traveled to Asia. In addition, war clouds were looming over Europe. Senior officials of the East India Company were deeply concerned about protecting the future of their lucrative Bengal trade and denying any advantage to the French. Indeed, there is a familiar argument among historians that even though the French were unable to hold on to their initial successes, it was Dupleix who first demonstrated that it was possible for a European trading company to seek political power in India to promote its commercial interests; the British only learned this lesson from the French.[21] The directors wrote to officials at Fort William in 1748:

> Experience having proved no Regard is paid by the French to the neutrality of the Mogul's Dominions, and that were the Countrey Government willing to protect Us, they are not able to do it against the French, who having little to lose, are always prone to violate the Laws of Nations to inrich themselves by plunder.... [Y]ou have

our Orders to make Calcutta as secure as You can against the French or any other European Enemy.… His Majesty will support the Company in whatever they may think fit to do for their future Security; for though a Peace is now making with France, no one knows how long it may last, and when War is broke out, it is always too late to make Fortifications strong enough to make Defence against an Enterprising Enemy, as appears from what happened at Madrass.[22]

Robert Orme, who would later earn his distinction as the official historian of the conquest of Bengal, was advising Clive as early as 1752 to consider toppling Ali Vardi. "The Nabob coming down with all His Excellency's cannon to Hughley, and with an intent to bully all the Settlements out of a large sum of money; Clive, 'twould be a good deed to swinge the old dog. I don't speak at random when I say that the Company must think seriously of it, or 'twill not be worth their while to trade in Bengal."[23]

In December 1752, the company sent out Colonel C. F. Scott as the engineer general to examine and strengthen the fortifications in Calcutta, with special instructions that "keeping our Designs Secret will be the best means of preventing any Troubles and Embarrassments in the carrying them into Execution, which may arise from the Countrey Government."[24] In 1754, the company directors in London sent fifty-nine cannons to Calcutta and suggested that the fort be strengthened, with the permission of Ali Vardi, if it could be obtained, and if not, by bribing his officials. Calcutta began to be further fortified in 1755 without the nawab's permission.[25]

Another matter had often ruffled relations between the provincial government in Murshidabad and the company's settlement in Calcutta. The nawab, needless to say, insisted on his sovereign rights over the territory of the subah of Bengal, including the trading settlements of the French, British, Dutch, and Danish companies. Nevertheless, sometimes there were fugitives who took refuge in Calcutta, and more contentiously, Indian residents of the British settlement or Indian agents of the company over whose property the provincial government made a claim in accordance with the country's prevailing law. The East India Company refused to hand over such persons on several occasions, claiming that it could not "think of subjecting our flag and protection to so much contempt as to abandon our tenants and inhabitants and permit their estates and properties to be seized and plundered."[26]

Ali Vardi, it seems, was well aware of the economic opportunities that had been opened up in Bengal by the European trade. "He used to compare the Europeans," wrote Luke Scrafton, a company official, "to a hive of bees, of whose honey you might reap the benefits, but that if you disturbed their hive they would sting you to death."[27] Ali Vardi was keen to prevent a combination of the British and French against him, and so tried to play one against the other. He also firmly resisted allowing the military fortification of any of the European settlements in his dominion. According to his admiring historian Ghulam Husain Tabatabai, Ali Vardi was apprehensive that after his death, "the hat-men wou'd possess themselves of all the shores of Hindia."[28]

A New Nawab

In March 1756, the eighty-year-old Ali Vardi was fatally ill. A power struggle was brewing in his court in Murshidabad. His grandson Siraj-ud-daulah was known to be Ali Vardi's favorite, but his claims were vigorously opposed by Ali Vardi's eldest daughter, Mihr-un-nisa, better known as Gahsiti Begam. At this time, Krishnadas, the son of Rajballabh Sen, the revenue administrator of Dhaka, accused by the nawab's government of embezzlement, took refuge in Calcutta. Rajballabh was a close confidant of Gahsiti. Siraj took this as a signal that the British were backing Gahsiti's faction in the succession battle.[29] When Ali Vardi died in April and Siraj became the nawab, he immediately demanded from the company the extradition of Krishnadas and a stop to any further fortification of Calcutta. Narayan Singh, the bearer of the nawab's letter, was unceremoniously dismissed by Roger Drake, the governor of Fort William, who then wrote back to Siraj:

> Some enemies had advised His Excellency without regard to truth, that we were erecting new fortifications ... that he must have been acquainted of the great loss our company sustained by the capture of Madras by the French, that there was an appearance of a war between our nations, that, therefore, we were repairing our walls which were in danger of being carried away by the river, and that we were not otherwise erecting new works.[30]

Narayan Singh, humiliated, returned to Murshidabad and complained: "What honour is left to us, when a few traders, who have not yet learnt to wash their bottoms, reply to the ruler's order by expelling his envoy?"[31] Siraj, by all accounts, was enraged. One group in his court advised caution, reminding him that the English were like "flames of fire" and that confronting them might engulf the whole country in a general war. But another group advocated firm diplomacy backed by a show of force.[32] The recent conflicts between the British and French in south India, and the subjugation of the rulers of Hyderabad and Arcot, were known in Murshidabad, and it was reasonable for Siraj to think that he should not allow any of the Europeans to build fortified enclaves in Bengal.[33] In fact, he may even have been keen to nullify the privileges that the British were enjoying in Bengal in comparison with the other European companies and treat all of them on the same footing.[34]

Khwaja Wajid, an Armenian merchant of Hugli who traded with the English company, was appointed as an intermediary. Siraj explained to him that he objected to the strong fortifications in Calcutta, the misuse of the company's dastak that had resulted in huge losses of revenue, and the protection that the British had given to corrupt employees of the nawab's government. On the question of the dastak, Siraj did not raise the issue of its misuse by company servants but rather its illegal sale to Indian merchants—a practice that was apparently quite common.[35] He also wrote to George Pigot, the governor of Fort St. George in Madras, declaring:

> It was not my intention to remove the mercantile business of the Company belonging to you from out of the *subah* of Bengal, but Roger Drake, your *gomasta*, was a very wicked and unruly man and began to give protection to persons who had accounts with the *Patcha* [emperor] in his *koatey* [factory]. Notwithstanding all my admonitions, yet he did not desist from his shameless actions."[36]

Yet Khwaja Wajid's mission came to nothing. Drake would not listen to him and virtually turned him away.

Siraj retaliated immediately. At the end of May 1756, his troops surrounded the English factory in Kasimbazar, not far from Murshidabad, and forced William Watts, the factor, to sign an undertaking pledging that the company would accept the nawab's conditions. None of the company's servants who surrendered were subjected to violence, nor were the company's assets seized. Watts later wrote that "a proof that the Nabob's intent was to accommodate matters, was that he touched none of the Company's effects at Cossimbuzar except the warlike stores."[37]

Drake in Calcutta, however, decided that the nawab was merely creating pretexts for seizing the company's assets and expelling the British from Bengal. He disregarded the repeated suggestions from Watts that he seek some sort of reconciliation with Siraj. Instead, the council at Fort William wrote to Fort St. George asking for reinforcements to be sent immediately:

> We are again to request in the most earnest manner, as you tender the interest of our employers so deeply concerned in this Settlement, as you regard the lives and propertys of the inhabitants, and as you value the honour of our Nation, all of which are now at stake, that you do not on any motive whatsoever neglect to supply us with the number of men we have demanded…. Should you after all we have said and urged upon this head either refuse or delay the reinforcement we have demanded, we hope your Honour &c. will excuse us, if we exculpate ourselves by protesting against you in behalf of our Honourable Employers, for all the damages and ill consequences of such default.[38]

The Fall of Calcutta

On June 16, the nawab, personally leading a force of some thirty thousand soldiers with heavy artillery, arrived in the vicinity of Calcutta. At Fort William, the number of armed men available to defend it was around five hundred, of whom no more than half were European, including soldiers, militia members, and volunteers, with the rest consisting of Armenians, Indo-Portuguese, and Indians.[39]

A council of war met at Fort William. It was suggested that the fort alone should be defended and that all the British houses surrounding the fort should be blown up to allow unrestricted fire on the nawab's troops. But the idea was rejected. The prevailing view seems to have been that Siraj would not really go through with his threats in the face of determined opposition from the British.[40] Instead, to deter the nawab's advance, the bamboo and straw huts of the Indian residents of Gobindapur were set on fire, and then looters plundered Bara Bazar.[41] Drake, the governor, noted later that except for Gobindaram Mitra, a prominent Indian in the company's service, no one in the native part of town offered any help: "They are such a niggardly race of people that we gained no assistance or strength to the place from any of those whose great-great-grandfathers had enjoyed the protection of our flag under which they accumulated what they are now possessed of."[42] All European women as well as the families of the Armenian and Portuguese fighters were given shelter in the fort.

The nawab's forces began an assault on all fronts on June 16. After three days of battle, a majority of the council at Fort William was arguing in favor of abandoning the fort and retreating to the ships anchored in the river. The nawab's troops plundered the town "to such an extent that the rabble of the party gave food and water to their beasts in china vessels.... For three or four days," wrote Yusuf Ali Khan, "the servants attached to the Nawab's cavalry and infantry, and the rabbles of the market, numbering about sixty to seventy thousand men, spared nothing in razing and burning, and looting properties worth lakhs and crores."[43] Morale was desperately low inside the fort, and as Drake, the fort's governor, himself remarked, "Every black fellow who could make his escape" ran away. Thus, even though there were provisions in the fort, there were no cooks, and Drake, in describing how distressing the situation was, noted that "even the Governour had no servant but one slave boy."[44] One officer later commented that "animositys amongst the persons who had the whole command and charge of the garrison in their hands did not contribute a litle to our misfortunes." There was much unruly behavior and drunkenness among the soldiers: "Half of our men in liquor in the fort, no supply of provisions or water sent to those in the houses without, the drum beat to arms three different times on alarm of the enemy's being under the walls, but hardly a man could be got on the ramparts."[45]

On the night of June 18, it was decided that the European women in the fort should be escorted to the boats waiting on the river. But crowds of Indo-Portuguese women and children who had been given shelter in the fort pressed forward to get on board: "It was thought hard to refuse them protection, as their husbands carried arms for the defence of the place."[46] Soon the governor's house and the garrison had been abandoned. When it was discovered that no more than two days' ammunition was left in the stores, there was a demand for a general retreat from the fort. Holwell, in particular, maintained that by retreating to the boats at night, all Europeans as well as the company's treasure could be safely removed before daybreak. No firm decision was reached, though. Amirchand, who had been imprisoned in the fort by Drake on the charge of secretly conspiring with the nawab's party, was asked to write to the nawab seeking terms of negotiation, but Amirchand was in no mood to oblige his captors.[47] In any case, even the Persian writer employed by the company had deserted.

When the nawab's army resumed its assault in the morning, and the ship *Dodaly* arrived up the river below the fort, there was a general desertion. Everyone who could find a place on a boat left. By noon, Governor Drake himself was gone, sailing downstream. Soon there were no more boats available, even though many, including eight members of the council of war, were still waiting in the fort, ready to leave. The expectation was that the company's ship, *Prince George*, waiting upstream, would arrive shortly to pick up the remaining Europeans. Yet at this critical moment, as ill luck would have it, the ship ran aground and would not move. The defenders were stranded in the besieged fort.[48]

The governor having ingloriously deserted, the remaining council members elected Holwell as governor of Fort William. He promised to distribute three chests of the company's treasure among the soldiers if they could hold the fort. But with so many senior officers gone, it was impossible to maintain discipline. Many European soldiers, most of them allegedly Dutch, virtually mutinied, forcing their way into the stores, helping themselves to the liquor, and subsequently deserting in the night.[49] On June 20, after further fighting, Holwell was left with no more than a 150 fighters, demoralized, and "exhausted of strength and vigour."[50] He signaled for a truce. By evening, the fort was occupied by the nawab's troops.

Holwell was brought before Siraj, who expressed much resentment against Drake. The Indo-Portuguese, Armenians, and Indians in the fort were allowed to leave, along with some fifteen Europeans. The remaining Europeans were left in charge of the nawab's guard. At this time, according to one account, some

Figure 5. *Siraj-ud-daulah,* from a contemporary portrait. *Courtesy: © Victoria Memorial Hall, Kolkata*

of the Europeans, apparently under the influence of liquor, misbehaved with the guards, at least one of whom received fatal injuries. It appears that some hostilities continued even after the fort had been taken. When this was reported, either the nawab or one of his officers ordered that the Europeans be confined within the fort. In the process, they discovered a cell, picturesquely called the

Black Hole, which was used by fort officials to lock up unruly Europeans. This was where the European prisoners were held during the night of June 20.

The Aftermath of Defeat

To understand the context in which the first narratives of the Black Hole deaths were produced, we have to travel a few miles downstream from Calcutta, opposite what was then the quite-nondescript rural market of Phalta, where there was a Dutch pilot station for guiding ships sailing up or down the treacherous Hugli River. That is where Drake and those of his colleagues who had decamped waited in their boats, to be joined by Watts and Collet from Kasimbazar as well as Holwell and other survivors of the fall of Fort William. For several months, the East India Company representatives in Bengal operated out of *Dodaly*, surrounded by a small flotilla offshore from Phalta.

The situation there was far from edifying. A week after the fall of Calcutta, the Dutch company in Hugli refused to respond to a request from the *Dodaly* for provisions and clothing: "We have viewed with surprise the presumptuous recklessness of that nation in first bidding defiance to such a formidable enemy as the Nawab, and afterwards, after offering little or no resistance, in abandoning their permanent fortress and matchless colony without making any provision for the few things that were absolutely required."[51] The French in Chandannagar (Chandernagore) were merciless in their condemnation of the English: "Their shameful flight ... covers all Europeans with a disgrace which they will never wipe out in this country; every one curses, detests and abhors them.... In short whatever one may say, these gentlemen, especially Mr. Drake, will never free themselves from such an infamy, and Mr. Drake will never be able to deprive his nation of the right to hang him and all his Council."[52]

The first letter from the council in Phalta to its superiors at Fort St. George, containing the news of Calcutta's fall, did not go out before July 13, more than three weeks after the event, because of difficulties in arriving at an agreed-on version of what had happened.[53] When Charles Manningham was chosen to carry this letter to Madras and report in detail, there was a written protest from some in Phalta who charged that Manningham had deserted his post at Fort William and could not be relied on to give a true account of the events there.[54] Around the same time, Watts and Collet, then in Chandannagar after their release from the nawab's custody, wrote to the council in Phalta, charging: "You incensed the Nabob to come against Calcutta and then deserted the place and fled on board your ships, which in all probability and by all accounts was the occasion of the loss of the place which might have been defended if you had staid, and by which step we are of opinion you abdicated your several stations and are now no longer to be deemed Servants of the Company."[55]

On July 17, Holwell wrote his first letter to Fort St. George from Murshidabad, where he had been taken in custody by the nawab's officers, in which he described the flight of Drake and others as an act of desertion and a "cruel piece of treachery," for which the remaining council members at Fort William had resolved to suspend the deserters, "it being the only just piece of resentment in our power."[56] William Lindsay in Phalta, on the other hand, writing to Orme in Madras, specifically mentioned Holwell in his report on the fall of Calcutta: "Mr. Holwell after the Governor was gone took the charge of the factory. It was much against his inclination being there, two gentlemen having carried away the *budgerow* he had waiting for him. I mention this as I understand he made a merit in staying when he found he could not get off."[57]

In early August, after Holwell's arrival in Phalta, the antagonisms within the council became sharper. Holwell refused to sign any papers relating to the council, because he considered Drake and others, by quitting the fort's defense, to have "divested themselves of all right or pretensions to the future government of the Company's affairs, or the colony." He also maintained that the remaining council members at Fort William had elected him as governor and administrator of the company's affairs, and "the gentlemen at present constituting the Agency" did not have "any just power to divest him" of that appointment.[58] He objected to the expenditure of 64,662 Arcot rupees for costs and damages for *Dodaly*, because, he said, she had abandoned the defense of the company's fort for which she had been commissioned, and hence, no such expenses could be charged to the company.[59] William Tooke, in his detailed narrative of the conquest of Calcutta, described Drake's and Manningham's actions as "something so scandalous and inhuman that it is a reflection upon the nation.... [S]uch an unprecedented affair surely is not to be paralleled among the greatest barbarians, much more among Christians." He also said that in Phalta, "the junior servants' antipathy at last grew so great against some of the Council's ill conduct" that they began to question its authority, causing Drake to drop the designations governor and council, and began calling themselves "agents for the Company."[60]

Another matter that rankled was the charge that the company's treasures held in the fort were stolen. This was a persistent topic in every report that circulated among French officials in India at the time about the capture of the English settlement and factories in Bengal by Siraj. When Holwell surrendered on June 20, 1756, the nawab's soldiers found only fifty thousand rupees in the fort's treasury; Siraj flew into a rage because he was expecting millions.[61] Where had the treasure gone? "It is no longer a matter of doubt," said a French account, "from the way in which Mr. Drake behaved that he had formed a plan with the Commandant of the troops and certain Councillors, and that they had all agreed that these troubles offered an excellent opportunity to appropriate a portion of the wealth confided in their care."[62] Holwell, in his first letter after his release in Murshidabad, mentions that on the evening of June 18, when it was decided that the European women in the fort should be shifted to the boats on the river, it was also resolved to remove the company's treasure and books.[63] He was more specific in his next letter, from Hugli:

> Whether the treasure or books were embarked I cannot say, the late President and Gentlemen below who have assumed the title and authority of "Agents for the Company's Affairs" are the best judges. After the President's departure, I made inquiry after the Sub-Treasurer and keys of the Treasury, but neither one or the other was to be found. I intended on the first recess to have opened the Treasury to have been satisfied in this particular; but that recess never came.[64]

Holwell's language is careful, but the aspersion is unmistakable. Tooke was quite explicit in his allegations:

> What was the reason we could not have acted as politically as they [the French and Dutch], I cannot conjecture. There is certainly some reason to think we acted upon some other scheme…. Indeed could we have resisted the Nabob's forces till succours arrived to us from the Coromandel coast and Bombay, there must have been glorious plunder for some of our Gentlemen in Council, for those in particular of the natives who had received protection of our flag would have been made to pay for it, as also no small contributions raised round about the country; besides the plunder of the river would have been very sufficient to have made a few persons' fortunes …; nay so sure were some of them of success against the Nabob … that vessells were fitted out to make prizes of the enemys ships homeward bound, two of which were taken …; and though the Company had then in the river several small vessells that might have been sent on that expedition they were all put aside, and a vessell sent (which Mr. Drake purchased a very considerable part of) upon the expedition, that the whole plunder might be their own.[65]

This is the backdrop for the first accounts of the Black Hole incident. Brijen Gupta has carefully compiled a full list. There are thirteen such sources that have come down to us, ranging from a mention in a letter written on July 3, 1756, some two weeks after Calcutta's fall, by an anonymous Frenchman of Chandannagar, to Holwell's *Genuine Narrative* written in February 1757. There is one more account—the fourteenth—by John Cooke, who was in the fort at the time of its fall, but who narrated his version of the Black Hole story before a select committee of the House of Commons in 1772, sixteen years after the incident. Gupta shows with impeccable reasoning that Holwell was directly involved in the production of every single one of these narratives—that is, they are not independent pieces of evidence but rather all the result of consultations with Holwell or a reading of his various descriptions of the event.[66] It is to

Holwell's narrative, then, that we must turn, as indeed everyone else has in the last 250 years, for an account of what happened on the night of June 20, 1756, at Fort William.

The "Genuine" Narrative

Though born in Dublin, Holwell came from a London merchant family with education. He was trained as a doctor and traveled to India as a surgeon's mate. In Calcutta, he showed his skills in judicial and revenue administration, and became the mayor and zemindar of the settlement as well as the youngest council member. After his final return to Britain in 1760, he emerged as something of a specialist in Indian affairs, wrote historical and ethnographic tracts, and became a fellow of the Royal Society. He was keen to display his superior moral and intellectual qualities in comparison with the usual run of greedy adventurers who came out to India in the company's service.

He wrote the *Genuine Narrative* on board the *Syren* in February 1757 on his journey back to Britain from Bengal. By then, Calcutta had been recaptured by Clive's army. Holwell was now feeling much better. The sea air had, as he explained in the opening page of the narrative, "had that salutary effect on my constitution I expected; and my mind enjoys a calm it has been many months a stranger to." He had had "leisure to reflect," and since no one who had survived the night when Fort William fell had written down a detailed narrative, he felt it necessary to do so. "The annals of the world," he believed, "cannot produce an incident like it in any degree or proportion to all the dismal circumstances attending it." His account might, he said, offer hope and confidence "to such as may hereafter fall under like tryals, by giving them an instance (and sure a stronger cannot well be given), that we ought never to despair, when innocence and duty have been the causes of our distress."[67]

Holwell's account was composed in the form of a letter to his friend William Davis, and first published in London in 1758 under the title *A Genuine Narrative of the Deplorable Deaths of the English Gentlemen, and Others, Who Were Suffocated in the Black-Hole in Fort William, in Calcutta, in the Kingdom of Bengal; in the Night Succeeding the 20th Day of June, 1756.*[68] By time the narrative was published, Siraj had been defeated in Palashi and killed. Clive and the East India Company were in full charge of political affairs in Bengal.

> Figure to yourself, my friend, if possible, the situation of a hundred and forty six wretches, exhausted by continual fatigue and action, thus crammed together in a cube of about eighteen feet, in a close sultry night, in Bengal, shut up to the eastward and southward (the only quarters from whence air could reach us) by dead walls, and by a wall and door to the north, open only to the westward by two win-

dows, strongly barred with iron, from which we could receive scarce any the least circulation of fresh air.[69]

Holwell and the other European defenders of the fort had been ordered into the Black Hole prison at about 8:00 p.m. by the nawab's guards and forced through the only door. Somewhat improbably, considering the smallness of the room in relation to the numbers that had to be packed inside, "like one agitated wave impelling another, we were obliged to give way and enter; the rest followed like a torrent, few amongst us, the soldiers excepted, having the least idea of the dimensions or nature of a place we had never seen."[70] So begins a tale of innocence.

It was not Siraj, Holwell is careful to point out, who had ordered them to be locked up in that particular room. In fact, the nawab had "repeated his assurances to me, *on the word of a soldier*, that no harm should come to us; and indeed I believe his orders were only general, that we should for that night be secured; and that what followed was the result of revenge and resentment in the breasts of the lower Jemmaatdaars, to whose custody we were delivered, for the number of their order killed during the siege." Before he went in, Holwell had been approached by Leech, the company's smith, who had earlier left the fort and returned through a secret passage, offering to escort Holwell to a boat in which he could escape. "I thanked him in the best terms I was able; but told him it was a step I could not prevail on myself to take, as I should thereby very ill repay the attachment the gentlemen and the garrison had shewn to me; and, that I was resolved to share their fate, be it what it would."[71] Clearly, Holwell was eager to emphasize that he was not a Drake or a Manningham; this was, after all, also a tale of duty.

In his attitude and mental poise, Holwell was utterly different from most of his fellow prisoners as well. They were far too susceptible to "the violence of passions," whereas he knew immediately "that the only chance we had left for sustaining this misfortune, and surviving the night, was the preserving of a calm mind and quiet resignation to our fate." This is the dominant theme of his narrative: not the perfidy of Siraj or cruelty of his guards, but instead the descent of a crowd of ordinary Europeans, placed in a situation of dangerous adversity, into mindless disorder, and his own heroic struggle to retain control and discipline over his body. Soon after they had been incarcerated, Holwell began to entreat them "to curb, as much as possible, every agitation of mind and body, as raving and giving a loose to their passions could answer no purpose, but that of hastening their destruction."[72]

Looking out of the window, Holwell noticed that an old guard "seemed to carry some compassion for us in his countenance." He spoke to him and offered to pay him a thousand rupees the next day if he would arrange to shift half of the prisoners to another room. The guard went away and came back to say that it was impossible. Holwell offered to double the payment, on which the guard went away again and came back to announce that the nawab had gone to sleep and no one dared wake him up.[73]

At this time, Holwell noticed that having perspired profusely, everyone was inflicted by a "raging thirst," which "increased in proportion as the body was drained of its moisture." Holwell could only be a mute witness once again to the folly of his ignorant fellow prisoners, who decided to take their clothes off: "In a few minutes I believe every man was stripped (myself, Mr. Court, and the two wounded young gentlemen by me, excepted). For a little time they flattered themselves with having gained a mighty advantage." Someone suggested that they should sit down on their haunches. "This expedient was several times put in practice, and at each time many of the poor creatures, whose natural strength was less than others, or had been more exhausted, and could not immediately recover their legs, as others did, when the word was given to rise, fell to rise no more; for they were instantly trod to death, or suffocated." When everyone was clamoring for water, the old guard took pity and ordered some skins of water. Holwell instantly knew this would have "fatal effects." "This was what I dreaded. I foresaw it would prove the ruin of the small chance left us, and essayed many times to speak to him privately to forbid its being brought; but the clamour was so loud, it became impossible."[74]

Paradoxically, then, a humane gesture from a prison guard brought on the destruction of a crowd of thoughtless prisoners unable to rise above their animal instincts. "I had flattered myself that some, by preserving an equal temper of mind, might outlive the night; but now the reflection which gave me the greatest pain, was, that I saw no possibility of one escaping to tell the dismal tale." As soon as the water arrived, there was a mad rush for it. Those near the window filled up their hats to the brim, but "there ensued such violent struggles, and frequent contests to get at it, that before it reached the lips of any one, there would be scarcely a small tea-cup full left in them." The insufficient supply of water only increased the thirst. "The confusion now became general and horrid. Several quitted the other window (the only chance they had for life) to force their way to the water, and the throng and press upon the window was beyond bearing; many forcing their passage from the further part of the room, pressed down those in their way, who had less strength, and trampled them to death."[75]

Holwell, however, was "still happy in the same calmness of mind I had preserved the whole time; death I expected as unavoidable, and only lamented its slow approach." In a moment of weakness, he had cried out for water. Such was the "respect and tenderness" that the other prisoners had for him that a full hat of water was brought to him. But there was no relief, and realizing at once that this was no solution, he firmly decided not to drink any more. Instead, "I kept my mouth moist from time to time by sucking the perspiration out of my shirtsleeves, and catching the drops as they fell, like heavy rain from my head and face: you can hardly imagine how unhappy I was if any of them escaped my mouth." Soon he discovered that the man next to him, naked like the rest of the prisoners, was also sucking his sleeve: "After I detected him, I had ever the address to begin on that sleeve first, when I thought my reservoirs were sufficiently replenished; and our mouths and noses often met in the contest." There was a hint of scientific explanation here, because Holwell seemed to be suggesting that unlike the rest of the crowd, he was aware that the salts in his sweat were more useful in his condition than water. "Before I hit upon this happy expedient, I had, in an ungovernable fit of thirst, attempted drinking my own urine; but it was so intensely bitter there was no enduring a second taste, whereas no Bristol water could be more soft or pleasant than what arose from perspiration."[76]

The scene inside the prison was one of violent confusion. The prison guards seemed to find this amusing. Holwell was incensed. "Can it gain belief, that this scene of misery proved entertainment to the brutal wretches without? But so it was; and they took care to keep us supplied with water, that they might have the satisfaction of seeing us fight for it, as they phrased it, and held up lights to the bars, that they might lose no part of the inhuman diversion."[77] For Holwell, it was unforgivable that native eyes should have been allowed to witness the descent of a group of Europeans into a state of natural savagery. All he could do by way of retaliation was to transfer the attribute of "brutality" from his benighted compatriots to the amused Indian prison guards.

By half past eleven (it is unclear how Holwell managed to read his watch so often inside the dark prison cell), "the much greater number of those living were in an outrageous delirium, and the others quite ungovernable." They abused the guards and cursed the nawab.

> They whose strength and spirits were quite exhausted, laid themselves down and expired quietly upon their fellows: others who had yet some strength and vigour left, made a last effort for the windows, and several succeeded by leaping and scrambling over the backs and heads of those in the first ranks; and got hold of the bars, from which there was no removing them. Many to the right and left sunk with the violent pressure, and were soon suffocated; for now a steam arose from the living and the dead, which affected us in all its circumstances, as if we were forcibly held with our heads over a bowl full of strong volatile spirit of hartshorn, until suffocated.[78]

Holwell needed to use some force himself to stay alive, because "from half an hour past eleven till near two in the morning, I sustained the weight of a heavy man, with his knees in my back, and the pressure of his whole body on my head." There was a Dutch sergeant seated on Holwell's left shoulder, and a Topaz— that is, an Indo-Portuguese soldier—leaning on his right. "The two latter I frequently dislodged, by shifting my hold on the bars, and driving my knuckles into their ribs." But by two o'clock, Holwell was so exhausted that he pulled out his penknife, determined to slit open his arteries, "when heaven interposed and restored me to fresh spirits and resolution, with an abhorrence of the act of cowardice I was just going to commit."[79] Soon, though, he passed out.

When day broke, some of the prisoners began to search for Holwell in the hope that he might intercede with the authorities to get them out of the cell. They recognized him by his shirt, buried under a pile of naked dead bodies, and realized he was still alive. In the meantime, the nawab apparently gave orders that the prisoners be released. "But oh! Sir, what words shall I adopt to tell you the whole that my soul suffered at reviewing the dreadful destruction round me? I will not attempt it; and, indeed, tears … stop my pen."[80]

Holwell was taken to Siraj. On the way, one of the guards gave him the friendly advice that he should tell the nawab where the company's treasure was hidden or else he would be blown from the mouth of a cannon. "The intimation gave me no manner of concern; for, at that juncture, I should have esteemed death the greatest favour the tyrant could have bestowed upon me." Siraj noticed Holwell's wretched condition and ordered that a large folio volume be brought in for him to sit on. After a drink of water, Holwell tried to describe to the nawab the terrible suffering that the prisoners had undergone. "But he stopt me short, with telling me, he was well informed of great treasure being buried, or secreted, in the fort, and that I was privy to it; and if I expected favour, must discover it." Holwell disclaimed all knowledge of any treasure. Frustrated, Siraj ordered him to be taken under guard to Murshidabad.

> My being treated with this severity, I have sufficient reason to affirm, proceeded from the following causes. The Suba's resentment for my defending the fort, after the Governor, &c, had abandoned it; his prepossession touching the treasure; and thirdly, the instigations of Omychund in resentment for my not releasing him out of prison, as soon as I had the command of the fort: a circumstance, which in the heat and hurry of action, never once occurred to me, or I had certainly done it; because I thought his imprisonment unjust.[81]

Holwell's trip to Murshidabad as a prisoner was arduous. At every step, he was told that he was no longer the chief of the fort of Alinagar, the name that Siraj had given to the town of Calcutta, and that he must obey. As he and three other English prisoners were paraded down the streets of Murshidabad, the old Begam, Ali Vardi's widow and Siraj's grandmother, apparently noticed and took pity on them, probably interceding with the nawab on their behalf. The prisoners were presented before Siraj the next day. "The wretched spectacle we made must, I think, have made an impression on a breast the most brutal; and if he is capable of pity or contrition, his heart felt it then. I think it appeared in spight of him in his countenance." The nawab ordered that the chains be removed, and that Holwell and his companions be allowed to go wherever they chose. Holwell was told that some of the courtiers had suggested to the nawab that Holwell had enough funds of his own to buy his freedom.

> To this, I was afterwards informed, the Suba replied: "It may be; if he has any thing left, let him keep it: his sufferings have been great; he shall have his liberty." Whether this was the result of his own sentiments, or the consequence of his promise the night before to the old *Begum*, I cannot say; but believe, we owe our freedom partly to both.[82]

A final point must be made before leaving Holwell's narrative. In the course of his description of the chaotic scenes inside the Black Hole prison, Holwell mentioned a certain naval officer called Peter Carey and added in parentheses, almost as an afterthought: "His wife, a fine woman tho' country-born, would not quit him, but accompanied him into the prison, and was one who survived." On the morning of June 21, after Holwell, Court, Walcot, and Burdet were ordered to be sent to Murshidabad, the rest of the prisoners were set free, "except," noted Holwell, "Mrs. Carey who was too young and handsome."[83] Other than this tantalizingly brief clause, not a word more is said about her. Much would be made of Faliceo Maria Carey later.

There is no doubt that Holwell had an ax to grind. The settlement's civil and military leadership had disgracefully abandoned the fort, and Holwell had been left behind to negotiate the inevitable surrender. The temptation would have been overwhelming for him to paint the adversity of his situation and the heroism of his devotion to duty in the most dramatic colors, especially in a tract intended for the company's stockholders and members of the public in Britain. It is also true that to protect himself from charges of inaccuracy and inconsistency, Holwell repeatedly invoked in his rhetoric the fundamental impossibility of representing this "founding trauma."[84]

A careful reader of the narrative, though, cannot but conclude that the predominant theme is not the brutality of the Bengal nawab or his soldiers; it is the value of mental self-discipline and informed moral judgment in coping with unanticipated disaster.[85] In the narrative, the charge of brutality against Siraj is nothing more than a prejudice, assumed as part of the background. The nawab appears impatient and willful perhaps, yet not in any way cruel, and indeed not devoid of compassion. Some of his guards are positively helpful toward the prisoners. Holwell's tract is actually pedagogical, not accusatory. He was writing to establish what may be called elevated principles of moral discipline as self-governance for his own people. What the Indians had seen of Europeans that night in Fort William had destroyed every claim of the civilizational superiority of white Christian nations. The task was, Holwell seemed to be claiming, the moral education of the British people to make them worthy of ruling over Moors and Gentoos steeped in tyranny and depravity. We might say with hindsight that he was calling for the imperial nation to civilize itself before taking on the task of civilizing others. In making this plea, he was somewhat ahead of his times.

RECONQUEST AND MORE

It requires a little effort to orient ourselves to the space-time coordinates of the world of the eighteenth century. If we do it, however, we should not be surprised to discover that with the council in Madras taking several months to decide on the correct version of events, the news of Calcutta's fall did not reach the East India Company directors in London until June 4, 1757, almost a year after the event. Six weeks later, on July 22, 1757, they heard from Holwell, who had just reached London after a remarkably quick voyage of five months, that Calcutta had been retaken. In London, Holwell got involved in the labyrinthine intrigues of the company. He returned to India in 1758 and became the temporary governor of Fort William when Clive left for England in 1760.

It was at this time that Holwell put up his obelisk outside the fort walls to commemorate the Black Hole deaths. There is a painting, done in 1760 and attributed to Johan Zoffany, of Holwell standing in front of the monument under construction, with a plan in his hand, instructing—or perhaps admonishing—a cowering Indian mason. In his *Genuine Narrative*, written when Siraj was still master of Bengal, he had taken care to emphasize that the nawab was not in any way personally responsible for the confinement and treatment of the Black Hole prisoners. On his memorial, however, now that Siraj was vanquished and dead, Holwell inscribed on stone his judgment that a "horrid act of violence" committed by Siraj had been "amply and deservedly revenged" by Watson and Clive. In any case, within months Holwell found himself on the wrong side in the factional wars, and as his letter of dismissal from service was making its way across the seas from London to Calcutta, he himself put in his papers and left for home.[86]

The history of Bengal and indeed India had, by then, taken what would prove to be a decisive turn. This involved not a small amount of scandal, as Nicholas Dirks reminds us.[87] The debates over the loss of Calcutta concluded at Fort St. George with the finding that there was little sense in approaching the Bengal nawab for a compromise. Even if he allowed the English to return to Calcutta, he would probably insist on terms that would rid them of all their privileges and reduce them to a position similar to those of the Armenian traders. And even then, there was no guarantee that the nawab would not flex his muscles again. The decision thus was made in September 1756 to send a royal squadron

Figure 6. *John Zephania Holwell, Governor of Fort William*, platinotype print from painting, probably by Johan Zoffany, 1760. © *The British Library Board. All Rights Reserved. Source: British Library Images (P 587)*

commanded by Admiral Watson, with company's troops led by Colonel Clive—forces that were available in Madras to move against the French in the event of war breaking out in Europe—to retake the company's settlement in Calcutta by force. Clive was instructed to undertake such military operations as would compel the nawab to consent to a treaty "for the best advantage of the Company."[88] The council in Madras wrote to their counterparts in Bengal:

> The mere taking of Calcutta should, we think, by no means be the end of this undertaking; not only their settlements should be restored but all their privileges established in the full extent granted by the *Great Mogul*, and ample reparations made to them for the loss they have lately sustained…. We need not represent to you the great advantage which we think it will be to the military operations … to effect a

junction with any powers in the provinces of Bengal that may be dissatisfied with the violences of the nawab's government, or that may have pretensions to the nawabship.[89]

Clive speculated: "I flatter myself that this expedition will not end with the retaking of Calcutta only, and that the Company's estate in these parts will be settled in a better and more lasting condition than ever."[90]

Interestingly, officials of the French company had come to the same conclusion about the future prospects of European trade in Bengal. Siraj's capture of Calcutta had alarmed Chandernagore to no end: "His army elated with success over the English only waited for orders to fall upon us." Europeans in Bengal, it was noticed, were being treated with contempt. "The Government at Hugli now treats us with unbearable haughtiness, stops the course of our business and cheats us without any pretence in the simplest matters."[91] The conclusion was clear: "If this government continues on its present footing we shall have much to suffer, and commerce will become extremely difficult."[92] As it happened, Britain and France were heading toward a war in Europe that would, in the end, last seven years. Clive knew what he had to do in that event: "The news of a war may … interfere with the success of this expedition. However should that happen and hostilities be committed in India, I hope we shall be able to dispossess the French at Chaʳnagore and leave Calcutta in a state of defence."[93]

Siraj had left Calcutta in charge of his officer Manikchand. The nawab did not make any attempt to pursue Drake and his fleet anchored outside Phalta. It is likely that he expected the English to come to him asking for terms to return to Calcutta.[94] He probably did not anticipate that they would return with a force strong enough to retake the fort. Calcutta was reoccupied by the company's troops on January 2, 1757, without any serious resistance by the nawab's army.

But the intrigues did not cease. The company's agents in Bengal complained to officials in Madras about Clive: "We cannot conceive by what authority you have assumed a right in giving that gentleman the powers you have done, and therein treating us in the light of a subordinate…. [T]he authority and trust invested in us by our Honourable Masters have been highly infringed by your unprecedented conduct."[95] Clive in turn wrote about them: "The loss of private property, and the means of recovering it, seem to be the only object which takes up the attention of the Bengal gentlemen…. [B]elieve me they are bad subjects and rotten at heart, and will stick at nothing to prejudice you…. [T]he riches of Peru and Mexico should not induce me to dwell among them." He also complained about "the mortifications" that he had received "from Admiral Watson and the gentlemen of the squadron, in point of prerogative." Watson had apparently insisted on naming himself the fort's governor, even though Fort St. George had given Clive the responsibility, and it had taken much persuasion to force the admiral to step down.[96]

True to his word, Clive did not stop with the reconquest of Calcutta. Armed with his superiors' permission "to attack Hughly or any other Moors' town, or to make reprisals in the river upon Moors' vessells … and to dispose of the prizes that may be so taken," he immediately proceeded to attack and plunder the nawab's fort at Hugli.[97] The pillage of Hugli by the British forces was massive, and when Khwaja Wajid, the local Armenian merchant, complained about the huge losses that he had suffered, Clive explained: "I do assure you what was done there was not meant against you, but against the city of Hughley in revenge for the ruin of Calcutta. You know very well with what barbarous circumstances the destruction of that place was attended, and it was resolved before we left Chinapatam [Madras] that that city should fall a sacrifice."[98]

During the next few days, even as there were overtures and exchanges of pleasantries between Clive and Siraj, the latter moved his troops to the neighborhood of Calcutta. Hidden behind the mist of a February morning, Clive launched a highly risky surprise attack on the nawab's troops and apparently managed to unnerve him enough to induce Siraj to agree to a treaty, referred to by historians as the treaty of Alinagar, by which he restored all the earlier privileges that the English had enjoyed.[99] He even allowed them to fortify Calcutta and establish a mint there. Siraj did not agree to provide restitution for the British losses in Calcutta, Kasimbazar, and Dhaka, but returned all seized cash and treasure. It is said that Siraj was keen to make peace with the British because of the threat of the Afghan ruler Ahmad Shah Abdali advancing eastward from Delhi, which he had just occupied.[100] In any case, Siraj returned with his troops to Murshidabad.

There is a debate among historians as to who initiated and directed the conspiracy that finally toppled Siraj from the *masnad* at Murshidabad. No one doubts that there was a conspiracy, though. One set of arguments relies on the personal unpopularity of Siraj among many of the powerful figures within the military as well as the landed and financial elite of Bengal. Siraj was said to be arrogant, strong willed, and even vicious in his dealings with those who expected courtesy and respect from a young nawab. Many stories circulated about his cruelty, not only among Europeans, but even in the writings of contemporary Indian chroniclers familiar with the Murshidabad court. There were many powerful people in Bengal, it is said, who would have been happy to see Siraj deposed.

Another set of arguments stresses the importance of the European trade, and its deep connections with the merchant and financial groups in Bengal. The British had powerful allies in the court of Murshidabad who were their collaborators in business, especially the cousins Mahtab Rai and Swarup Chand of the house of Jagat Seth, among the wealthiest bankers in the world at the time, or merchant politicians like Amirchand, Khwaja Wajid, or Khwaja Petrus Arathoon.[101] They were eager participants in the conspiracy to get rid of the thoughtless Siraj, who had struck at the foundations of European trade in Bengal.

Finally, there are those who believe that in spite of all these forces opposed to Siraj, the die would not have been cast without the direct incitement provided by Clive, Watts, Scrafton, and other officials of the East India Company who had made up their minds that the only way they could secure the future of British trading interests in Bengal against the depredations of local rulers as well as French competition was to put a pliable nawab on the throne in Murshidabad. Scrafton so much as said this in a letter to one of Clive's close associates on the eve of the conspiracy: "For God's sake let us proceed on some fixed plan.... Give Mr. Watts a hint of this, the least encouragement, and he will set about forming a party.... How glorious it would be for the Company to have a Nabob devoted to them!"[102]

In the meantime, news reached Bengal that war had broken out in Europe seven months before between the French and British. Clive was determined to attack Chandannagar, but Watson insisted on securing the nawab's permission. Siraj in turn announced he would not tolerate two foreign nations fighting their war within his territories, and to display his impartiality, gave the same privileges to the French in Chandannagar that he had given to the British in Calcutta. Clive began a siege of Chandannagar on March 14. A suitable bribe ensured that Nandakumar Ray, the faujdar of Hugli, would not involve the nawab's troops in defending the French. About a week later, the French surrendered, agreeing to leave Chandannagar and all their factories in Bengal at the disposal of the nawab and Admiral Watson. Fort d'Orleans in Chandannagar was promptly plundered and destroyed by the victorious British troops.

In the middle of April 1757, the conspiracy to oust Siraj began with Yar Lutf Khan, a relatively minor military officer, being pushed by the Jagat Seths as the pretender. Within a few days, however, Mir Jafar, an Arab fortune seeker from Najaf who was then the commander of the nawab's army, became the conspirators' choice. On May 1, British officials at Fort William formally resolved to join the plot:

> The Committee then took into consideration, whether they could (consistently with the Peace made with the Nabob) concur in the measures proposed by Meer Jaffir of taking the Government from Souragud Dowla, and setting himself up.... [T]he Committee were unanimously of opinion that there could be no dependance on this Nabob's word, honour, and friendship, and that a revolution in the Government would be extremely for the advantage of the Company's affairs.[103]

A secret treaty was concluded by Watts, the company resident in the Murshidabad court, with Mir Jafar that set out the terms of his alliance with the British after he became the nawab. This included a military alliance, turning over all French possessions to the British, huge reparations for the losses suffered during Siraj's occupation of Calcutta, and a promise by the future nawab not to build fortifications to the south of Hugli.[104] In addition to the Jagat Seth cousins, Rai Durlabhram Som, the nawab's revenue minister, joined the plot.[105] Amirchand, a key figure through whom the British dealt with members of the nawab's court, was so distrusted by Clive that his name was omitted from the list of beneficiaries in the original copy of the secret treaty with Mir Jafar and only included in a duplicate shown to Amirchand. Appalled by this trickery, Watson refused to sign the false copy, at which point Clive, not one to be impeded by a squeamish conscience, had the admiral's signature forged.[106]

All that remained was a pretext to break the peace with Siraj. On June 13, Clive sent the nawab an ultimatum accusing him of not having observed the treaty of Alinagar and began to move with his forces toward Murshidabad. Siraj marched to meet Clive at Palashi (Plassey), about 150 kilometers north of Calcutta and 50 kilometers south of Murshidabad. The nawab's forces probably numbered around fifteen thousand, while Clive commanded a thousand European and two thousand Indian troops. But the conspiracy ensured that three of the nawab's generals—Mir Jafar, Rai Durlabh, and Yar Lutf—would reduce about two-thirds of his army to the role of silent spectators. The battle lasted from the morning until noon with neither side gaining a clear advantage. At this point, a sudden thunderstorm turned the battlefield into a swamp. Large stocks of gunpowder in the nawab's camp were rendered useless by the rain. The heavy artillery could hardly be moved through the sludge. At around three in the afternoon, Mir Madan, one of the more effective commanders in the nawab's army, was killed. Alarmed, Siraj pleaded with Mir Jafar and Rai Durlabh to save his honor. Both advised him to suspend hostilities until the next morning. Siraj commanded Mohanlal and the other officers to leave their positions. The British troops then began an assault that soon led to a complete rout of the nawab's army. Realizing that all was lost, Siraj himself left the field. The battle was over by the fall of dusk.[107]

The next day, Clive wrote to Mir Jafar: "I congratulate you on the victory, which is yours not mine.… We propose marching to-morrow to compleat the conquest that God has blessed us with, and I hope to have the honour of proclaiming you Nabob."[108] Siraj, meanwhile, had returned to Murshidabad in the darkness of night and left in disguise the next day. Mir Jafar was proclaimed the nawab of Bengal, Bihar, and Orissa on June 29. The following day, Siraj was discovered, brought back to the capital, and brutally murdered under the direction of Mir Jafar's son Miran on July 2, 1757.

WHOSE REVOLUTION?

The Khoshbagh cemetery is across the Bhagirathi River from the town of Murshidabad. A pall of violent death hangs over this austere garden. One enclosure has nineteen graves belonging, it is said, to Siraj's kin, all poisoned to death one night after a feast arranged by Miran. There is the grave, allegedly, of Dan Shah Fakir, a mendicant who recognized the fugitive nawab at the riverside near Rajmahal and handed him over to Mir Jafar's spies. The young man who works as a guide at Khoshbagh feels it necessary to explain that Mir Jafar believed that a fakir who could betray the country's ruler for the love of money could easily be bought over once more to betray the next ruler, so he had him and his family put to death. None of the guide's stories, however, are supported by the official gazetteer, which mentions that most of these unmarked graves belong to unknown members of Nawab Ali Vardi's lineage.[109]

The modest mausoleum at the center of Khoshbagh shelters the grave of Ali Vardi, who had ominously predicted the advent of the hatmen as rulers of the shores of India, but even he could not have known that it would happen so soon after his death. Next to him is buried Siraj, "the last independent ruler of Bengal, Bihar, and Orissa," as the guide says in a voice heavy with emotion. The adjacent graves belong to Lutf-un-nesa, Siraj's wife, and a younger brother, all killed, the guide notes, immediately after the young nawab's death. The history books do not corroborate the details of the guide's narrative. But he is entitled to his dramatic license. Palashi may have been a nonbattle, but the revolutions that followed in Bengal were immeasurably bloody.[110]

Historians have often speculated on the political thinking behind Siraj's actions against the British. It is doubtful that anyone will ever come up with a satisfactory answer, given the fact that Siraj died in his early twenties and held power for just over a year. Yet the popular judgment in Bengal on his successor Mir Jafar is unambiguous. His palace at Jafaraganj in the town of Murshidabad has vanished. All that survives is a massive gate, impressive even in ruin, known in town as *nimakharam deuri*, the traitor's gate.

CHAPTER TWO

A Secret Veil

IT HAS OFTEN been said in the last two centuries that the British acquired the territories of Bengal without ever having planned to do so. The description was turned into a much-repeated aphorism by the historian John Seeley, who remarked in 1883: "Nothing great that has ever been done by Englishmen was done so unintentionally, so accidentally, as the conquest of India."[1] Of course, it is necessary to remind ourselves that when considering large processes such as the rise of modern empires, it is foolish to expect to identify world-historical intentions in the careers of individual politicians or generals. The idea that empires are founded by single figures of rare genius is a prejudice we have carried over from older histories of bygone empires. Modern empires, like modern capitalism and modern nation-states, do not have founders, notwithstanding the persistent desire in certain quarters to claim and celebrate them. Perhaps it is only now, at this juncture at the beginning of the twenty-first century when all three entities—capitalism, the nation-state, and empire—can be subjected to systematic historical critique, that we can see this clearly. It is easier today to argue that we should not expect to read intentions of empire directly out of Clive's letters, the council's proceedings at Fort St. George, or the resolutions of the East India Company directors in London. They must be sought in the complex formations of discourse that shaped, through rules and precedents, precepts and advices, traditions and innovations, the conditions of practice for the strategic move toward conquest and territorial empire.

THE CONQUEST IN HISTORY

What do we know about the discursive formation within which the East India Company made sense of the geographic entity called India in the mid-eighteenth century? What were the strategic possibilities open to its agents in London and India? Fortunately, a mountain of written records on this subject has been available to historians for the last two centuries or more. It is thus possible to sketch out the following outline of the parameters within which Clive had to think and act.

First, there was a clear genealogy of claims of privilege—based on racial and religious difference, going all the way back to the Portuguese—available to

European traders in Asia in the eighteenth century. João de Barros, the Portuguese scholar, had stated the claim in the sixteenth century as follows:

> For even though there does exist a common law which allows all navigators to sail the seas freely ... this law applies only to the whole of Europe and its Christian inhabitants, who have been placed within the fold of the Church of Rome by baptism and by faith, and who are also governed by the Roman law in their polity.... But as regards Muslims and Heathens, who are outside the law of Jesus Christ, ... if these are condemned in their souls, being the principal part of them, their bodies which are animated by their souls cannot plead the privileges of our laws, since the adherents of those creeds are not members of the evangelical congregation, even though they may be our neighbours as rational beings and though they may live to be converted to the true faith.[2]

This was an early, even though quite sophisticated, application of the rule of colonial difference that would contend, many times in the next five centuries, that a normative proposition of supposedly universal validity did not apply to the East because of some inherent moral deficiency of the Oriental. Hugo Grotius did not accept the argument that the East Indies were terra nullius, in which the Portuguese or Spanish ruler could unilaterally claim sovereign powers by the right of discovery or papal authority. He agreed with Francisco de Vitoria, the Spanish theologian who criticized the conquerors' assertion of dominium over Amerindians, that "Christians, whether of the laity or of the clergy, cannot deprive infidels of their civil power and sovereignty merely on the ground that they are infidels, unless some other wrong has been done by them."[3] Yet when Grotius went on to argue that the Dutch must, "by peace, by treaty or by war," maintain their right of trade with the East Indies, for "a common benefit of the human race," his definition of those who had this natural right of free use of the seas for purposes of trade became scrupulously restricted to "the Christian nations." Further, as Richard Tuck has pointed out, Grotius also alleged that individuals, like states, had the natural right to use violence to defend their possessions and punish others for wrongs done to them. This right was derived, Grotius held, from "two precepts of the law of nature":

> First, that *It shall be permissible to defend* [one's own] *life and to shun that which threatens to prove injurious*; secondly, that *It shall be permissible to acquire for oneself, and to retain, those things which are useful for life.*[4]

These two natural rights gave such associations of individuals as trading companies the same rights as the sovereigns of Europe to wage war in order to expand and secure their commerce in the Indies.[5]

John Selden, the English lawyer who sought in 1635 to refute Grotius on the freedom of the seas, contended that in the beginning, the whole world—the land and seas—was owned collectively by all men as a grant from God and that all subsequent rights of private property had arisen through specific agreements among men. He then claimed to cite Hebrew and other Oriental views on warfare to argue that for these people, "neither precedent injury nor safety were necessary for war, but extending empire was a good enough reason."[6] He maintained that unless there were specific agreements between peoples to respect one another's territory, war for the sake of acquiring territory and imperial possessions was entirely legitimate. Tuck calls Selden's perspective "the most extreme defence of war for aggrandizement which had yet been presented by any European theorist," and it is worth noting for our purposes here that he was an important English legal theorist of his time.[7]

Such claims of privilege, whether of the older Spanish and Portuguese vintage, or the new Anglo-Dutch vintage, justified for the first time in the Indian Ocean region the use of armed violence on the seas to assert power over commercial navigation. The Portuguese insisted that Indian vessels could only sail with the *cartaz* or pass purchased from them—a regime enforced, often quite brutally, by Portuguese boats fitted with guns.[8] The change brought about in the character of the seaborne trade in the region was irreversible: all European naval powers—the Dutch, English, and French—continued the Portuguese tradition of supporting their trade with the gunboat. "The arrival of the Portuguese in the Indian Ocean abruptly ended the system of peaceful oceanic navigation that was such a marked feature of the region…. The importation by the Portuguese of the Mediterranean style of trade and warfare, by land and sea, was a violation of the agreed conventions and certainly a new experience."[9] On this particular historical genealogy, the Portuguese precedent cannot be dismissed as merely a bigoted premodern practice later abandoned by the more rational trading practices of the West European companies. On the contrary, as we shall see, through the successive redefinitions of the criterion of colonial difference, it represented a strong line of continuity from the period of Portuguese dominance to that of the maritime and mercantile rivalries between the Dutch, English, and French.

Second, the European companies trading in Asia all decided, contrary to the patterns of international trade between European countries, not just to buy from or sell to local Asian merchants but also to actually set up "factories" surrounded by fortified settlements that were self-governing, asserting a fair degree of sovereignty. Unlike Arab, Iranian, Jewish, or Armenian merchants who learned to deal with local commercial institutions and practices in India, the European companies regarded these institutions as hazardous and unacceptable. They were also deeply suspicious of the intentions of the local "Moorish"

governments toward foreign traders. Hence, the setting up of fortified settlements, generating their own revenues and defended by the force of arms, was
seen by the English East India Company as early as the seventeenth century as
a crucial lesson that it needed to learn from the Portuguese and Dutch.[10] In
1684, for instance, it declared: "Though our business is only trade and security,
not conquest which the Dutch have aimed at, we dare not trade boldly nor
leave great stocks ... where we have not the security of a fort."[11] Even as they
adopted coercive tactics that were quite unprecedented in the trading world of
India, the English merchants invariably felt that they were always the victims
of Moorish tyranny—a form of government that was intrinsically arbitrary and
despotic.[12]

The ideological effect, as Sanjay Subrahmanyam has pointed out, was not
necessarily produced by a real superiority of power, because in the seventeenth
century the English company, representing at best a middle-sized European
power, was trying to negotiate terms with an indisputably larger power, the
Mughal Empire. Yet the discursive framework was one in which representatives
of the English company even in the seventeenth century always described the
Mughal government as constitutionally corrupt and despotic. A particular tradition of political xenology was deeply inscribed within the discursive formation in which this "war of images" was carried out.[13]

Third, the English company did not just attempt to trade in India. It sought—
continually and strenuously—to extract special privileges not enjoyed by the
other European traders. "More than any other European nation trading with
India the English insisted on being exempted from the local customs payments.
The ideological justification for this policy was derived from a mental attitude
which regarded all Asian governments as oriental despotisms intent on extract-
ing the maximum possible gain from merchants."[14] The argument was, in effect, that Europeans had a natural freedom to trade anywhere for profit, and
that if Oriental regulations came in the way, it was legitimate to overcome them
by whatever method was practicable, since Oriental laws had no inherent legitimacy. Thus, for more than a hundred years before Palashi, we find the East
India Company trying to extract—from authorities ranging from the Mughal
emperor himself all the way down to local governors of port cities and market
towns, and using methods that included persuasion, tact, duplicity, bribes, threats,
and sometimes force—differential privileges not enjoyed by other foreign or
local traders. The company frequently succeeded in its efforts. The imperial
farman obtained from Emperor Farrukhsiyar in 1717 made the English company perhaps the most privileged merchant in the whole of India.

Fourth, Clive's campaign in Bengal was not the first time that the company
undertook an aggressive military strategy to defend and expand its trading interests against Indian rulers. There had often existed a "party of war," so to speak,
within the company. In the 1680s, this party, under the leadership of Josiah

Child, was in control. Child argued, clearly and forcefully, that the commercial success of the Dutch in the East Indies was the result of its political strategy of seeking dominion over its coastal enclaves.[15] The English company, too, had to acquire territories in India from which it could raise revenues and gain formal recognition from the Mughal government as a company with the right to trade as a sovereign power. In private communication, Child went as far as to say that

> the first consideration, in my poor opinion, ought to be abstractively what powers a National East India Company ought to have for the public good to hold up against the Dutch and other foreign powers in India; and I say and will maintain it against all mankind by reason and experience, that it ought to be not less than absolute sovereign power in India.[16]

It so happened that Child's policy ended in disaster when in 1690 the Mughals forcibly expelled the English from Surat, Bombay and Hugli. Through the early eighteenth century, Child was castigated in company circles as a dangerous adventurer who nearly wrecked the firm. But that is not to say that his theory was disproved. It was available, ready to be picked up and set into action when the time was propitious.

Fifth, as K. N. Chaudhuri has observed, the corporate structure of the Dutch, English, and French companies trading in the Indian Ocean region, built on the pillars of joint stock capital, a national monopoly protected by the state, and a single integrated business organization stretched out across the seas, was a major innovation in European commerce, and entirely unprecedented in the trading and political world of Asia.[17] This gave the companies cohesion, institutional continuity, and a sense of long-range purpose that was unthinkable for any entity in Asian commerce.

Added to this were the close ties of mutual dependence between the British Crown and the East India Company—a relationship that allowed the company to act at times like a state within a state, at others as the external representative of British sovereignty, and on occasion as even a rival to the British government. Its total trading capital was permanently lent to the British state—after the Bank of England, the company was the second most important creditor of the Crown—which in return gave the company protection against all competitors in the home market, and diplomatic as well as military support against foreign powers, on sea and foreign soil. The company's fortified settlements in India were virtually sovereign enclaves, with governmental and judicial systems organized on English principles, autonomous systems of revenue collection, and a permanent armed force. The company exercised sovereign powers over all British subjects in India, including the power to try and punish under English civil and criminal law, and also to make necessary bylaws. British subjects could reside in India only with the company's permission. The company minted coins

in Bombay in the name of the English king, even though the coins did not circulate much, and in all its settlements exercised its own legal jurisdiction over
Indian residents. It had the right to make war and peace anywhere in the East.
No other private body in Britain could claim "sovereign" powers of this kind.
"In the circumstances it is not surprising to discover that the Company's organizational structure and bureaucratic apparatus shared many of the attributes
of a great department of state."[18]

Finally, in relation to the immediate conjuncture in which Clive worked out
his plans of intervening decisively in Bengal's political affairs, there was the
rivalry between Britain and France. A major constituent here was the discourse
of mercantilism, an economic doctrine proclaimed by many distinguished publicists in both countries in the seventeenth and eighteenth centuries, which argued for the regulation of the nation's economy by the state in order to augment
its power at the expense of other states. This was, in some sense, the economic
counterpart of state absolutism in Europe. Among the many principles of mercantilist economic theory was the idea that trade with other countries must
lead to the acquisition of precious metals as the repository of national wealth.
Another was that trade with the colonies must be the monopoly of the mother
country.

This line of thinking led to the regulation and unification by the state of the
foreign trade of all the European maritime countries—Portugal, Spain, Holland, England, and France. The French overseas trading companies set up in
the mid-seventeenth century under the ministry of Jean-Baptiste Colbert were
state-owned enterprises that became emblematic of classic mercantilist policy.
In England, the trading companies were formed by private enterprise, but were
granted monopoly privileges by royal charter to trade in designated parts of the
world and were incorporated by the state. The regulated companies and British
state developed close relations of mutual dependence, with the state relying on
them as a valuable fiscal source, and the companies seeking political and military support in their competition with other European mercantile powers. As
Eli Heckscher noted in his classic study—an assertion that has been refined and
substantiated by recent historians—it was through fiscal-military means that
the English state regulated the colonial trade to strengthen itself.[19]

Mercantilist doctrine in its pure form advocated the supervision of foreign
trade in the interest of state power. This effectively meant carrying out mercantile wars with rival states. Colbert was the most explicit advocate of this view:
"Trade is the source of finance and finance is the vital nerve of war." In 1670,
he wrote to Louis XIV:

> It seems as if Your Majesty, having taken in hand the administration of your finances,
> has undertaken a monetary war against all European states.... There remains only
> Holland, which still struggles with all its great power.... Your Majesty has founded

companies which attack them [the Dutch] everywhere like armies.... This war, which must be waged with might and main, and in which the most powerful republic since the Roman Empire is the price of victory, cannot cease so soon, or rather it must engage Your Majesty's chief attention during the whole of your life."[20]

Similar ideas prevailed in England too. Child argued that "this Kingdom being an Island, the defence whereof hath always been our Shipping and Sea-men, it seems to me absolutely necessary that Profit and Power ought jointly to be considered."[21] Charles Davenant, an important writer on economic subjects who was for some time involved with the East India Company, was even prepared to sacrifice domestic economic interests for the pursuit of power through foreign trade: "England could subsist, and the Poor perhaps would have fuller Employment, if Foreign Trade were quite laid aside; but this would ill Consist with our being great at Sea, upon which (under the present Posture of Affairs in Europe) all our Safety does depend."[22]

By the mid-eighteenth century, the Dutch had been left behind, and the chief maritime rivalry in Europe, now extended to the Atlantic and Indian oceans, was between France and Britain. As recent historians of Britain have shown, the eighteenth century was when the new identity of a British nation was formed, with Protestantism at its core and enmity with France as its persistent rallying cry.[23] What had begun in the seventeenth century as a fiscal-military instrument of strengthening the absolutist state became, by the time of the Seven Years' War (1756–63), part of a national struggle to acquire overseas colonial territories in order to increase the power of the nation-state at the expense of its rival.

In sum, there was a clear sense in the minds of virtually all the significant figures in the English East India Company in 1756 that the only way to protect the future of European trade in Bengal was to directly influence the center of political authority located in Murshidabad, and that if the British did not do it, sooner or later the French would. It was, as mercantilist theory insisted, always a zero-sum game. What one competitor won, the others lost. There was no possibility of cooperative gains among European traders.

THE AGE OF PLUNDER

"The first fruit of our success," as Scrafton said in his description of the aftermath of the victory in Palashi,

> was the receipt of near a million sterling, which the Soubah paid us on the third of July, and was laden on board two hundred boats, part of the fleet that attended us in our march up, escorted by a detachment from the army. As soon as they entered the

great river, they were joined by the boats of the squadron, and all together formed a fleet of three hundred boats, with music playing, drums beating, and colours flying, and exhibited to the French and the Dutch, by whose settlements they passed, a scene far different from what they had beheld the year before, where the Nabob's fleet and army passed them, with the captive English, and all the wealth and plunder of Calcutta. Which scene gave them more pleasure, I will not presume to decide.[24]

Soon there would follow many more fruits of the revolution in Bengal. With the installation of Mir Jafar in Murshidabad, the fortune seekers in the company's service quickly fanned out into the Bengal countryside in the single-minded pursuit of private gain.[25] Most company servants wanted to be sent outside Calcutta and the traditional factories of the company to, as it were, virgin territories where they could grab a slice of the "inland" trade. Besides, the company's army now virtually became the nawab's army, and its officers were stationed in Murshidabad, Patna, or even further north, where unsupervised by civilian eyes, they could engage in some gainful trade. The more successful private traders would employ ten or fifteen Indians as *gumashta* to visit the outlying markets and buy or sell on their behalf. One estimate says that by 1763, British participation in Bengal's inland trade was worth over five hundred thousand pounds.[26] The first impact was on the nawab's government, which started to incur huge losses in customs dues because the company's dastak was now used without any restraint at all, not only by company servants, but also by their private Indian agents, no matter how distantly related.

But the impact of the company's newly acquired political dominance was not limited to its officers claiming immunity from taxation. They began to use the company's troops to support their private trade against competitors and dictate prices. There are many recorded instances of company agents using armed force to sell their goods at 50 percent above the market price or buy much cheaper than what producers regarded as a remunerative price.[27] Harry Verelst, soon to be governor, declared that when another English trader had sided with a local official of the nawab to hurt Verelst's trade, Verelst had responded by sending the company's troops to protect his own agents. In 1764, the council in Calcutta agreed "that European agents could no longer be trusted to operate outside Calcutta without behaving oppressively."[28]

Yet another consequence of the "revolution" in Bengal was the entry of Europeans into commodity trades that the nawab's government had so long tried to protect. Salt was the most important such commodity. By 1760, two-thirds of all Bengal's salt came under the control of British traders, and in 1765, when the company obtained the position of *diwan* or revenue administrator of Bengal, the entire salt trade was taken over. The scale of some of these private British enterprises is staggering. A certain Archibald Keir was said to have employed 13,000 workers to manufacture 12,000 tons of salt on his behalf in 1762.[29]

William Bolts, a company official, employed 150 Indian agents to manage his private trade, with 20 of them acting as "head gomastas" supervising the rest.[30] Tobacco, betel nut, and opium were also commodities in which the private British presence became overwhelming. In the 1760s, profit margins for British traders in Bengal were two to three times what they could have expected in Britain, and in terms of commodities like salt, betel nut, or tobacco, the rate of profit was routinely 75 percent or more.[31] And it was not merely unsupervised junior officers who indulged in these practices. The abuse began from the top, with senior officials like Verelst and Henry Vansittart leading the way.

Even the supremely malleable Mir Jafar, beholden to the company for his position as ruler of Bengal, was forced to complain about the depredations of the British private traders. Powerful sections among the company officials in Bengal then decided that Mir Jafar must go.[32] He was replaced in 1760 by Mir Qasim, who after obliging his benefactors for the first few months, started resolutely to lay down the law against the abuses of the private traders. He moved his capital north to Munger, proceeded to build a new army, and in October 1762, ordered the boats of European traders stopped for the nonpayment of dues. Governor Vansittart tried to strike a deal with him, promising that private traders would pay customs at 9 percent on all dutiable commodities. But Vansittart's colleagues thought this outrageous, and alleged that the governor had made a private arrangement with the nawab to exempt his own business from taxation. Moreover, it was not so much the rate of duty; the traders were keen above all to ensure that they would no longer be required to submit to the nawab's authority in pursuing their independent ventures. This was what they construed to be the legitimate benefit of their newly acquired power.[33] Curiously, Vansittart himself voiced this attitude best when replying to a critic: "We are men of power, you say, and take advantage of it. Why, man, what is the use of station if we are not to benefit from it?"[34]

Mir Qasim responded by removing duties from all trade carried out by all Europeans. The prospect of an end to their special privileges vis-à-vis their European competitors could only be greeted with hostility by the British. This was the last straw. In June 1763, open clashes broke out between Mir Qasim and the company. Several British trading posts in different parts of Bengal were attacked by the nawab's troops, and some Europeans were killed. Even as Mir Qasim resisted in Bihar, the British decided to reinstall Mir Jafar as the nawab in Murshidabad. Dutiful as ever, Mir Jafar immediately paid out five million rupees as compensation to the company for the damages inflicted by Mir Qasim. The latter's intransigence finally ended with his defeat at the hands of the company's army in the battle of Baksar in October 1764.

Apart from the inflated profits from private trade extracted by not paying taxes or through sheer coercion, a major means of Bengal's plunder in the decade after Palashi consisted of "presents" to company officials from Indians eager to please them. Clive, who regarded himself as morally superior to his greedy and self-serving compatriots in Bengal, appears to have stayed away from private trade, but probably took home the largest fortune of all, consisting mainly of money, jewels, and precious objects gifted to him, often from the government treasury, by prominent people in India. In addition, Clive obtained a personal estate from Mir Jafar within the company's zamindari lands, giving him a lifetime annual income of twenty-seven thousand pounds from the Bengal revenues.

But Clive was not the only one. Everyone of consequence in the company used their position to ask for and receive presents from the Indians they dealt with. Even Holwell, self-proclaimed model of rectitude and devotion to duty, is on record complaining from Britain in 1763 to Nawab Mir Qasim that he had only received fifty thousand rupees of his promised present of two hundred thousand rupees.[35] On obtaining copies of these letters from Holwell, the directors in London were convinced "that Mr. Holwell and others received large sums of the late Nabob Cossim Ally Khan for seating him in the *subahship* by the deposal of Meer Jaffier," and "the lucrative view of individuals had too great a share in bringing it about."[36] It was noted by an official committee in Britain that between 1757 and 1765, presents worth more than two million pounds taken out of Bengal could be actually listed.[37]

A third source of the plunder of Bengal was the series of collusive contracts awarded by the company to favored private traders for the supply of various commodities. This practice was said to have been particularly common in 1772–85, when Warren Hastings was India's governor general. These contracts contributed to the private fortunes of European traders in Bengal at the expense of both the company as well as the primary producer, although Francis Sykes, company resident in Murshidabad and a major beneficiary of the practice, advanced an ingenious argument in its defense:: "Toward the Company I have ever been attentive nor would one sixpence I enjoy ever come into the Company's treasury; the question was this: whether it would go into a black man's pocket or into my own."[38] Defrauding the company in this way was, of course, a major abuse that contributed to the widespread uproar in Britain in the 1770s and 1780s calling for a thorough inquiry into Indian affairs. As Narendra Krishna Sinha has pointed out with a disarming show of naïveté, however, "so far as Indians are concerned it was immaterial whether the wealth was extracted by the East India Company or its servants," even though "from the British point of view there was some difference."[39]

Clive himself appears to have been aware that under the new conditions of its political dominance, the organizational resources of the company were inadequate for imposing the necessary discipline even on its own personnel. The task of governing the population of Bengal was not, at this time, anywhere within the horizon of the company's political thinking—the assumption being that the existing machinery of the nawab's government would take care of the job. In 1759, on the eve of his return to Britain from Bengal, Clive wrote: "But so large a sovereignty may possibly be an object too extensive for a mercantile Company; and it is to be feared they are not of themselves able, without the nation's assistance, to maintain so wide a dominion."[40] When he returned to Bengal in 1765, he found that the abuses had reached such a state that the "name of the English stink in the nostrils of a Jentue or a Mussalman."[41] Clive was indeed quite eloquent on this subject:

> In a country where money is plenty, where fear is the principle of government, and where your arms are ever victorious; in such a country, I say, it is no wonder that corruption should find its way to a spot so well prepared to receive it. It is no wonder that the lust of riches should readily embrace the proffered means of its gratification, or that the instruments of your power should avail themselves of their authority, and proceed even to extortion in those cases where simple corruption could not keep pace with their rapacity.[42]

Clive's efforts at the "cleansing of the Augean stables" did not have much effect other than breed resentment against him among the company's servants, leading to an aborted mutiny by European officers and soldiers along with a failed conspiracy against his life.[43] On the political front, however, Clive quickly followed up the defeat of Mir Qasim and his ally Shuja-ud-daulah of Awadh to conclude an agreement with the Mughal imperial government by which the East India Company was appointed diwan of the provinces of Bengal, Bihar, and Orissa, responsible for collecting the revenues and transferring an annual sum of 2.5 million rupees to the imperial treasury, while keeping the rest to itself. In August 1765, the emperor Shah Alam II, then in Allahabad, personally handed over the proclamation to Clive, promising to "leave the said office in possession of the said Company, from generation to generation, for ever and ever."[44] The emperor was glad, one presumes, to have found someone in effective power to rely on to deliver the vital Bengal revenue to the imperial coffers. But Clive himself was looking far ahead: "We have at last arrived," he wrote in 1765, "at that critical Conjuncture, which I have long foreseen, I mean that Conjuncture which renders it necessary for us to determine, whether we can, or shall take the whole to ourselves.… It is scarcely an Hyperbole to say that the whole Mogul Empire is in our hands."[45]

At this time, there was some debate in Britain on the status of sovereignty in Bengal. The company argued that its right to collect revenues in Bengal was merely a grant from the Mughal emperor who continued to hold sovereign power in the eastern provinces of India. On the other hand, its critics maintained that the grant had been obtained by a prolonged war of conquest carried out by the company in which the British state had provided substantial assistance, and hence the revenues were the spoils of war and should belong to the British Crown. As one participant in the public debate put it, the question was whether the company's acquisitions should be regarded as a "mercantile purchase or acquest by mutual bargain and reciprocal treaty, or the fruit of arms and of terms imposed by conquerors through the terror of military force, and coercion over a naked and defenceless possessor and inhabitants."[46] The government of William Pitt the elder, now Lord Chatham, was keen to assert its claim over the company's possessions in Bengal. But for the company, it was vital to carry on the deception. Even though Clive boastfully referred in Parliament to the Mughal emperor as "*de jure* Mogul, *de facto* nobody at all" and to the nawab of Bengal as "*de jure* Nabob, *de facto* the East India Company's most obedient humble servant," the company insisted that sovereignty in Bengal belonged to the Mughal emperor and his representative the nawab.[47] As it happened, the company did not lack influential supporters in the treasury benches in Parliament. In the end, in May 1767, a compromise was hammered out by which the company agreed to pay an annual sum of four hundred thousand pounds to the British Crown in return for which a decision on the question of sovereign right was postponed indefinitely.[48]

Early Histories of Conquest

Orme (1728–1801) was the first British historian of the conquest of Bengal. He had put together the first archive of the company's papers relating to this period, and on his return to Britain from India, published the first volume of *A History of the Military Transactions of the British Nation in Indostan* in 1763. The second volume, not published until 1778, took the history of the company's advances in India up to the year 1762.[49] Orme tried hard to adopt an objective narrative voice that rose above the disputes and blaming games in which he himself had sometimes been a partisan. He was still not writing the history of an empire, as the title of his work indicates, but rather only the story of the wars in which "the British nation" had become involved in India. Yet he knew what effect his work would have on its readers: "I have wrote one book which comprises the loss of Calcutta, and I have looked forward into the subject far enough to see that the Bengal transactions will not do my countrymen so much honour as they have received from the first volume." He decided not to take the story beyond 1762.

> It is these cursed presents which stop my History. Why should I be doomed to commemorate the ignominy of my countrymen, and without giving the money story, that has accompanied every event since the first of April 1757, I shall not relate all the springs of action, that is I shall be a Jesuitical Historian, two terms which Vol-

taire says are incompatible, for no Jesuit could ever tell a true tale, much less write a true History.

He also predicted in 1767: "Parliament in less than two years will ring with declamation against the Plunderers of the East."[50] Whatever one thinks of Orme as a historian, he was without doubt a perceptive reader of political fortunes.

The nodal event in his history of the Bengal's conquest is, of course, the fall of Calcutta, and the key explanatory element that supplies a narrative logic to it is the character of Siraj. "The disorderly brain of Surajah Dowlah, his excessive cowardice, his tyrannical ideas, and the instigations of his minions, representing Calcutta as one of the richest cities in the world, sufficiently account ... for his inflexible perseverance in a resolution which flattered the pusillanimity and other vices of his own mind." Having driven the British out of Calcutta, he made no effort to ensure that they did not return.

> But there always reigned so much confusion in his mind, that he rarely carried his ideas beyond the perfect appearance of things; and, soothed by the compliments of his courtiers into a belief that the reduction of Calcutta was the most glorious and heroic achievement that had been performed in Indostan since the days of Tamerlane, he imagined that the English nation would never dare to appear again in arms in his country; and, ... he neglected to pursue the fugitives.[51]

Siraj's faults were not unexpected, Orme indicated repeatedly, given the deep moral deficiencies of the people of India. Most of the Indian characters that appear in his account—the nobles and merchants who play a prominent role in Bengal's politics—come out as crafty, devious, and venal. Certainly, the morally dubious methods of Clive and others can hardly be concealed, but they are described as consistent with the way things had to be done in Indian courts in the legitimate pursuit of corporate profit and private fortune, which were the reasons why Europeans had come to India anyway. Orme thus prefaced his account of the discussions in the Fort William committee over the colossal reparations it demanded from Mir Jafar as the price for his elevation to the position of nawab by suggesting "the committee really believed the wealth of Surajah Dowlah much greater than it possibly could be." So it kept adding to the terms that Watts had proposed following his secret negotiations in Murshidabad.

> In this persuasion they increased the restitution to Europeans [in Calcutta] from three to five millions of rupees; but allotted only two instead of three millions to the Gentoos, and only 700,000 instead of one million to the Armenians.... It was then agreed to ask a donation of 2,500,000 rupees to the squadron, and the same sum to the army. A member then proposed that it should be recommended to Mr. Watts, to

ask a donation from Meer Jaffier to each of the members of the committee; and this likewise was resolved.[52]

Orme's account of the fall of Calcutta in June 1756 emphasized the military unpreparedness of the defenders against the overwhelming force deployed by the nawab's army rather than the moral failings of the company's officials. He described a scene of extreme confusion in which Governor Drake, "utterly unexperienced in military affairs," makes his departure without being able to properly communicate his orders to others. Orme also acknowledged the dissensions among the company's men while they waited in Phalta:

> The younger men in the company's service, who had not held any part in the government, endeavoured to fix every kind of blame on their superiors, whom they wished to see removed from stations, to which they expected to succeed. At the same time, the members of the council accused one another, all concurring to lay the severest blame upon the governor.[53]

Given this background, when the expedition was sent out to Bengal, "it would have been absurd," said Orme, "to intrust the re-establishment of the company's affairs to those, who, by their own accounts, had ruined them." It nevertheless was decided to allow Drake and his council to retain their powers in commercial and civil matters as well as give carte blanche in military matters only to Clive. The object was nothing less than a change of government in Bengal that would avenge the ignominy of the defeat at Calcutta, and place the economic fortunes of the company and its servants on favorable and secure foundations.

This is the narrative frame within which Orme described the Black Hole incident. He mainly followed Holwell's account, summarizing it in eight pages and emphasizing the descent of civilized humans into an artificially created state of brutish struggle for survival. "This scene, instead of producing compassion in the guard without, only excited their mirth; and they held up lights to the bars, in order to have the diabolical satisfaction of seeing the deplorable contentions of the sufferers within." When the ordeal was over for Holwell and the other survivors, "the Nabob, who was so far from shewing any compassion for his condition, or remorse for the death of the other prisoners, that he only talked of the treasures which the English had buried; and threatening him with further injuries, if he persisted in concealing them, ordered him to be kept a prisoner." Orme added that "an English woman, the only one of her sex amongst the sufferers, was reserved for the seraglio of the general Meer Jaffier," which needless to say, was a substantial embellishment on Holwell.[54]

It is interesting to note that Holwell himself did not think much of the methods employed to secure the victory in Palashi. In one of his many pamphlet wars carried out after his return to England, Holwell pointed out to Scrafton:

Let it in the first place be remembered that however happy in its consequences the *defeat* at PLASSEY proved to individual sufferers, the means by which it was obtained should rather be forgot, nor should you blazon that defeat with the semblance of a military act of prowess, which was solely owing to the treason and treachery of ROYDULLOB and MHIR JAFFIER, two of SURAJAH DOWLA's generals, the highest in office, as well as in the confidence of their master.[55]

Orme, however, chose not to make this qualification. The reconquest of Calcutta and Siraj's defeat in Palashi were, in his account, a just retribution. Such methods of effecting changes in government, Orme remarked, were routine in India.

Thus perished Surajah Dowlah, in the 20th year of his age, and the 15th month of his reign, by the hands of violence, as his father and grandfather had perished before him; and by means not unlike those that were employed by both his grandfathers to destroy the heir of their benefactor, by whom they, as Jaffier by them, had been promoted from obscurity to the highest ranks of the state.... Tyrant as he was, if he had respected the advice of his grandfather Allaverdy, and not have excited the determination of the Gentoos, at the same time that he was rendering himself dreadful to the principal Mahomedan officers of his court, the English would have found no alliance sufficient to have ventured the risque of dethroning him: but it is probable that the same iniquity of character, which urged him to the destruction of Calcutta, would soon have called forth other avengers of other atrocious deeds.[56]

In sum, Orme's history is one of the barbarity of Indians, the political stupidity of Siraj, and just retribution for his crimes against the English. But the latter are still guided entirely by their private interests, generally considered legitimate by Orme because they were pursuing the interests of commerce. Native politics was vicious and corrupt; Clive and others played that politics, backed by arms, in a way that was entirely appropriate to native conditions. In this, the English were only pursuing their self-interest by putting a pliable nawab in power and driving out the French. There is no conception here at all that they would rule the country better.

Indeed, no matter what the legal quibbles and deals in Parliament, the historical justification of Bengal's conquest that had been worked out among the East India Company officials was the one expressed most elaborately by Orme in his *History*. Unlike the earlier debates over the empire in America, there was no attempt here to apply the Roman law concepts of dominium and imperium. Nor was it possible to claim, in the manner of John Locke, that the British had title to the land in India because they were the first to productively cultivate it. Rather, the historical fiction was that the native inhabitants of India were industrious and skilled manufacturers and cultivators, adept at commerce, but naturally servile and inherently incapable of defending themselves with arms.

Orme lays out this argument clearly in "a dissertation on the establishments made by Mahomedan conquerors in Indostan" inserted as an introduction to his *History*.[57] The native inhabitant of India ("the Hendoo") "shudders at the sight of blood, and is of a pusillanimity only to be excused and accounted for by the great delicacy of his configuration. This is so slight as to give him no chance of opposing with success the onset of an inhabitant of the northern regions." But the Indians had made great advances in manufactures.

> Not content with the presents which nature has showered on their climate, they had made improvements when they felt no necessities. They have cultivated the various and valuable productions of their soil, not to the measure of their own but to that of the wants of all other nations; they have carried their manufactures of linnen to a perfection which surpasses the most exquisite productions of Europe, and have encouraged with avidity the annual tributes of gold and silver which the rest of the world contest for the privilege of sending to them. They have from time immemorial been as addicted to commerce, as they are averse to war. They have therefore always been immensely rich, and have always remained incapable of defending their wealth."[58]

Not surprisingly, they had been conquered and ruled for centuries by warlike Muslim invaders who had imposed a vicious tyranny that was hostile to trade and commerce. "It has been observed," Orme said with beguiling authority, "that all the Mahomedans established in India acquire, in the third generation, the indolence and pusillanimity of their original inhabitants, and at the same time a cruelty of character to which the Indians are at present happily strangers."[59] The British, drawn into the politics of the country to defend their trading interests, had been forced to seize power, and replace the tyrannical Moors in order to protect and promote commerce. There was no promise at this juncture that the British would, under the given conditions, provide better government to Indians.

There are two elements in Orme's account of the conquest of Bengal that would persist in different forms in imperialist histories written in subsequent decades and even centuries. The first is that of the natural servility of the inhabitants of India, who are constitutionally incapable of defending themselves by the strength of arms and therefore are always under the sway of more warlike peoples. This tapped directly into the venerated classical Aristotelian tradition— one that would be transmitted right through the nineteenth century by way of the patrician education imparted by the English universities to generations of imperial civil servants—that spoke of the "natural slavery" of barbarians. It also invoked the more recent European humanist tradition in which the French jurist François Connan could say that "liberty was born with servitude ... there was no one free, when no one was a slave," or Nicole Oresme, yet another French Aristotelian, could argue that it was just to wage war to subjugate those who were naturally servile because such war "does not have a new servitude as its cause"—one was not subjugating a people who were naturally free.[60] Even Charles de Secondat Montesquieu, who was not persuaded by Aristotle's defense of natural slavery, accepted that because of climatic conditions and the historical prevalence of "political slavery,"—that is, despotism—a "very gentle right of slavery" did exist in countries such as India.

> As all men are born equal, one must say that slavery is against nature, although in certain countries it may be founded on a natural reason, and these countries must be distinguished from those in which even natural reasons reject it, as in the countries of Europe where it has so fortunately been abolished.[61]

The idea of slavery based on natural reasons would be easily transmuted later into one that claimed that the imperialist had to defend those who were incapable of defending themselves, or indeed of acting politically.

The second element in Orme is that of the right to retaliate and punish an offending power for injuries caused by its actions. The idea was well established in European legal discourse, even when it was only a trading company that was exercising the sovereign right of punishment. As we have noted before, the Anglo-Dutch tradition of international law, illustriously represented by Grotius, specifically asserted that such a right naturally belonged to individuals and associations of individuals just as it did to hereditary monarchs. This is where the story of the Black Hole would play a crucial role in subsequent histories of empire.

The Modern State and Modern Empires

It is useful here to return to our sketch of the discursive formation in which the debate over the implications of Bengal's conquest took place in Britain in the second half of the eighteenth century. Although Britain (earlier England) had possessed extensive colonial settlements in the Americas and on the Caribbean islands for two centuries, the term "the British Empire" began to be used in public discourse for the first time in the period of the Seven Years' War, when Britain made significant gains over France in winning overseas territories.[62] Now the problems of the old American colonies, on the one hand, and those of the new Indian conquests, on the other, came to occupy the center of British politics. What were the conceptual moorings of these debates that are relevant to our story? We will be somewhat schematic here, but schemes are useful for analytic clarity.

First, the cartographic imagination of political space became, by the mid-seventeenth century, generally accepted among the European powers as the basic technical form of delineation of sovereign boundaries. The Treaty of Westphalia of 1648 is often mentioned in this context as inaugurating the general practice of appending certified maps to territorial agreements between European states. This corresponded with the emerging conception of sovereignty in international law—authoritatively formulated in the eighteenth century by the Swiss jurist Emerich de Vattel—that insisted that there could be only one recognized sovereign power over any bounded territory; if there were more, the territory was disputed. Writing at more or less the same time that Clive was marching toward Palashi, Vattel strongly emphasized the need for states to clearly demarcate the boundaries of their territories, even when these were overseas possessions.

> Since the least encroachment upon the territory of another is an act of injustice, in order to avoid being guilty of it, and to remove all occasion of strife and dispute, the boundary lines of territories should be clearly and precisely determined. If the men who drew up the Treaty of Utrecht had given to this important matter the attention it deserved we would not find France and England in arms to decide in a bloody war the extent of their possessions in America.[63]

The actual delineation of sovereign jurisdictions in the everyday practices of government would, of course, acquire the clarity and intensity we know today only in the nineteenth-century nation-states, if not even later. But the juridical idea of cartographically represented territorial sovereignty was transported by the late seventeenth century to the overseas possessions of the European powers. Working through the mutual recognition by European powers of the territorial boundaries of their colonial jurisdictions, the cartographic representation of national boundaries that is now the foundation of the geographic knowledge of schoolchildren everywhere in the world was universally established by the global spread of modern empires.

Second, among the territories that are known in history as the European overseas empires, we can distinguish three types for our analytic purposes here. One type consisted of the colonies of European settlers in North and South America. At one end of this range were the white settler colonies of farmers, craftspeople, and immigrant workers, of British, French, and later other European origins, of the North Atlantic seaboard. At the other end were the provinces of the Spanish empire, populated by a Creole elite of Spanish origin, a mixed-race (mestizo) group in the middle, and a subordinated indigenous population. The second type was made up of the plantation colonies, with a small group of European settlers owning huge amounts of land, worked by a subordinated population of African slaves. Brazil was the largest colony of this type, but most British, Dutch, and French colonies of the Caribbean shared the same characteristics, as indeed did colonies such as Virginia, the Carolinas, and

Louisiana. These two types—the settler and plantation colonies—were all in the Americas and suggest how deeply the perceptions of early modern Europe's relations with the rest of the world were marked by its American experience. The third type emerged with the Portuguese possessions in the Indian Ocean region in the sixteenth century, but assumed its characteristic historical form in the second half of the eighteenth century with the British and Dutch (and later French) territorial conquests in South and Southeast Asia and Africa. These were lands containing large, dense native populations with old and complex military, political, economic, and cultural institutions over which the new European conquerors claimed suzerainty. Each type of overseas possession posed a different set of problems for modern European political thinking.

From Madrid, the Crown directly administered the Spanish possessions in the Americas via the Council of the Indies, which legislated and governed through correspondence, and acted as the final court of appeal. The American colonies themselves were governed as viceroyalties subdivided into provinces. The doctrinal history of Spain's sovereignty over its American possessions is marked by fierce controversies in the sixteenth century. On one side were humanists such as Juan Ginés de Sepúlveda who insisted that the Spanish monarchy had conquered the Americas in a just war because it had been chosen by God to rule over the Native Americans, whose barbaric customs violated natural law and thus constituted a moral provocation to civilized humanity. The legitimacy of Spanish imperium lay in its responsibility to subjugate the Amerindians and bring them over to civilized Christian ways of living. On the other side were theologians such as Domingo de Soto, Francisco de Vitoria, and most radically, Bartolomé de Las Casas who argued that the Spanish Crown could claim true dominium over the Americas only if the indigenous people could be persuaded to give their consent to Spanish rule.[64]

In Spanish legal theory, the indigenous Americans were full subjects of the Crown and thus could not be enslaved.[65] Several methods were found, however, ranging from serfdom to debt peonage, to force them into the position of a subordinate peasantry. Alongside, there was a cultural project of assimilating the Native Americans into European religion and ways of life. Large sections were converted to Christianity and introduced into the Spanish language. Nowhere was there an indigenous American elite pressing for a share in the colonies' governance. In economic dealings, the Spanish Crown imposed strict monopolistic regulations, characteristic of mercantilist economic doctrine, excluding all foreign merchants and vessels from the trade with the colonies. The Portuguese also sought, by the end of the seventeenth century, to control their colonies directly from Lisbon through viceroys and captains general. Spanish and Portuguese forms of colonial government until the eighteenth century were wholly authoritarian; colonies were the overseas territorial possessions of the Crown and mother country.

The French colonies in the Americas were started by dozens of chartered companies, but by the late seventeenth century all of them became direct royal possessions. The colonies were administered through governors, usually belonging to the French nobility, who were advised and kept in check by intendants, mostly lawyers sent from France who could be relied on to hold the line of metropolitan control. Until the mid-seventeenth century, the colonies also had quasi-legislative councils that could make laws, but in 1763, in a sudden wave of royal absolutism, these powers were abolished. Until the French Revolution, therefore, French colonial administration was royal, centralized, and autocratic.

British and French justifications of dominium over their American possessions did not rely much on the argument of just war. Rather, they preferred the idea of terra nullius, insisting that the American lands they had conquered were, for all relevant purposes, uninhabited because they belonged to no one. In the British case, this was strongly supplemented by Locke's argument that the land truly belonged to those who mixed their labor with the soil. Since Native Americans did not cultivate, the land could not belong to them. The French and British conquerors were, by this claim, colonists, or the first settlers of the vast American lands that they now claimed to possess.[66]

The peculiarity of the English (later British) ideology of empire lay in its reconciliation of a critique of Continental empires as land-based absolutist tyrannies with its own possession of overseas territories. This was achieved by the myth of the "empire of the seas"—a constellation of far-flung territories and outposts held together not by the might of armed forces but rather by commerce, producing, it was maintained, an imperial system that was entirely consistent with the requirements of liberty. English writers in the seventeenth and early eighteenth centuries enthusiastically followed John Selden's arguments in *Mare Clausum* to make the claim that both by fact and right, the English Crown possessed dominium in and imperium over the seas around its realms. This was combined with seventeenth-century republican doctrines, such as that of James Harrington in *Oceana*, which beginning as a criticism of the failure of Oliver Cromwell's protectorate to preserve liberty while expanding its imperium, invoked the Ciceronian idea of a well-ordered republic that could expand—in this case as a maritime empire of colonial settlements—without endangering the liberty of its own citizens.[67]

By the 1730s, Britain and its empire started to be seen as a single political community that was "Protestant, commercial, maritime and free."[68] The idea was, in fact, voiced most powerfully at this time as part of an oppositional rather than official discourse—by merchants' lobbies and libertarian writers who resented the preoccupation of Robert Walpole's government with the European balance of power, and pushed for a more aggressive policy against Spain and France. As Kathleen Wilson remarks: "Empire would be the antidote to aristocratic cultural treason and effeteness, the bulwark and proving ground of the true national character, of national (and middle-class) potency, identity and virtue."[69]

In the mid-eighteenth century, the Caribbean possessions such as Jamaica and Barbados as well as colonies such as the Carolinas, Virginia, and Georgia were the most valuable parts of the British Empire. These were plantation economies owned by European settlers growing tropical crops like sugar and tobacco, produced by the labor of African slaves. The New England and mid-continental colonies of white settlers produced little of use to Britain, and sometimes threatened to compete with it in the coastal Atlantic trade. Their social structures, consisting of white immigrant farmers, craftspeople, and laborers, seemed to replicate those of British society. Several of the colonies on the American continent as well as in the Caribbean were started by chartered companies, which unlike the successful East India Company, folded up quickly, and by the late seventeenth century, their settlements were directly administered by the English Crown. Some colonies like Maryland and Pennsylvania, though, were feudal properties, owned until the American Revolution by English aristocratic families. Thus, even in America, where the validity of indigenous laws and proprietary customs were not even acknowledged by British settlers, there remained a variety of forms by which sovereignty was exercised by the British state. Indeed, it has been argued that while imperium was unitary, dominium was divided, since various proprietors, patentees, and royal governments claimed quite different rights of property over their possessions.[70]

The fact that the colonists were all European settlers and no native political institutions intervened meant that the principles and practices of British constitutional government flowed steadily into the governance of the colonies. Regardless of the particular form of attachment with the British state, all colonies had representative assemblies, elected by eligible white settlers, which made laws that were usually approved by the British Crown if they did not contravene the laws of Parliament. They had British courts that applied English common law and English institutions of local government. By the mid-eighteenth century, even though the American colonies did not have a ministerial system as in Britain, the white colonists exerted considerable powers of self-government through their elected assemblies to put pressure on colonial governors. In the domain of trade, however, relations with the American and Caribbean colonies were rigidly controlled from London to protect the interests of the metropolitan economy. The Navigation Acts ensured that all trade to and from the colonies was carried out exclusively in British vessels, sailing in and out of British ports. It was also a matter of policy to see that the American colonies did not threaten any branch of British industry.

It soon became apparent that if the colonists were to be acknowledged as British subjects with full entitlements to natural and hence legal freedoms, then the modern form of British representative government (and indeed, as Adam Smith would argue, the modern British doctrine of free trade) could hardly be withheld from them. Yet that would require a fundamental resolution of the problem of sovereignty. The contradiction reached a breaking point with the American Revolution.

To continue with our schematic view, then, it would not be overstretching the point to say that with the American and French revolutions at the end of eighteenth century, the political course for colonies of our first type became, for the most part, historically determined. Republican sovereignty in the United States was followed, some three decades later, by the Creole republics of Spanish America. This was also, in essence, the form of transition in Canada through the nineteenth century, even though a fictive form called "dominion" was invented to retain the facade of British sovereignty. The same course lay in store for Australia and New Zealand, settled through the nineteenth century by British colonists who, as in the Americas, found it possible to sweep aside all aboriginal practices of property and governance. If modern empire was only about colonies of the first type—that is, the white settler colonies—its problems were, at least in theory, largely resolved in the political and economic transition to the modern nation-states of Western Europe in the late eighteenth and early nineteenth centuries.

But there were the second and third types. The plantation colonies survived the Creole revolutions as well as the futile Haitian uprising. Even though profound ethical problems were raised in the early nineteenth century regarding the compatibility of slavery with a constitutional government that claimed to protect the legal freedoms of all subjects, this crisis too was averted. In the British colonies, the transition was made from an economy supplied by African slaves to one that imported indentured Indians who had ostensibly entered into voluntary labor contracts.[71] The property and civic freedoms of white colonists as well as the sovereign control of the metropolitan state and economy remained largely intact until the twentieth century—including in the curious case of Jamaica, where the abolition of slavery was followed by colonial self-government only to revert, after the Morant Bay uprising of free black peasants in 1865, to the status of a Crown colony. One could say the same about the Dutch colonies of the Caribbean, and possibly of the French ones too, after considering the marginal modification in the pattern brought about by the policy of assimilation of a small colonized elite into French culture and citizenship. Only in the United States was the second type destroyed in a bloody civil war, and incorporated into the modern nation-state and industrial economy, even though traces of the plantation economy were vividly displayed in discriminatory civic entitlements until the mid-twentieth century, and arguably remains visible in many aspects of political culture in the United States to this day.

But colonies of the third—the Oriental—type posed unprecedented conceptual and strategic problems in the late eighteenth century. There were new compulsions brought about, above all, by what was clearly seen in Britain as a worldwide contest for naval, strategic, and mercantile superiority over the French. But the discursive forms made familiar by colonies of the first and second types provided the initial grid within which the new problem of the Indian territorial acquisitions had to be understood, even as that grid would turn out to be inadequate and, for some, even inappropriate. As we will see, the resultant process was crucial for the emergence of the modern state as we know it today. Had there been no Oriental colonies, the modern state in Europe and the Americas would have undoubtedly looked quite different now.

THE NABOBS COME HOME

In February 1769, in the House of Commons, Clive boasted of his achievements in Bengal on behalf of the British nation:

> The East India Company are at this time sovereigns of a rich, populous, fruitful country in extent beyond France and Spain united; they are in possession of the labour, industry, and manufactures of twenty million of subjects; they are in actual receipt of between five and six millions a year. They have an army of fifty thousand men. The revenues of Bengal are little short of four million sterling a year. Out of this revenue the East India Company, clear of all expenses receives £1,600,000 a year.[72]

Clive was exaggerating; the financial picture was not quite so rosy. Nevertheless, for the previous three years, ever since the news of the company's acquisition of the diwani in Bengal had reached London, India stocks had traded at a volume never before seen in Exchange Alley, not even during the Seven Years' War.[73] Even Edmund Burke (1729–97) was impressed. He complimented Clive in Parliament: "He has laid open such a world of commerce; he has laid open so valuable an empire, both from our present possessions and future operations; he has laid open such manufactures and revenues, as I believe never was laid before any committee in so short words."[74] Clive was a much-celebrated British hero, who in 1761 purchased an Irish estate called Ballykilty and changed its name to Plassey in order to become Baron Clive of Plassey, County Clare, in the Kingdom of Ireland.[75]

The interest of the East India Company and its officials was at this time lodged deep within the structures of British political life. It is said that Indian money first played a big role in the parliamentary elections of 1768. Twenty-three percent of the members of that Parliament owned East India Company stocks, which would have made the company one of the most powerful interest groups in the whole country. Company stocks offered attractive returns, as high as 12.5 percent a year, but many members of Parliament were even keener to take sides in the bitterly fought partisan contests for control of the hugely influential East India Company. Several were prominent members of the elected General Court of the company.[76] Besides, there was the so-called Arcot interest, consisting of a dozen or so members of Parliament whose elections had been financed by former company officials who, after their return to Britain, were still in the pay of the nawab of Arcot, because they, like most company officials in Madras, were private creditors to the nawab.[77] This does not mean, of course, that British politicians, or indeed directors of the company, were particularly knowledgeable about Indian matters; a well-known, if apocryphal, story is that of the director who asked Clive if "Sir Roger Dowlat," the former ruler of Bengal, was actually a baronet.[78] But the financial stakes ensured that there was always a great deal of interest among members of Parliament in participating in debates and committee hearings having to do with India or the company.[79]

In 1769–70, there was a massive famine in Bengal, memorialized forever in the Bengali language in the phrase "the famine of seventy-six," referring to 1176, the year according to the Bengali calendar. Historians estimate that a third of the population of Bengal was killed, making it one of the worst famines in modern history.[80] Its effects did not show up in the company revenues, though, because collections from landowners and cultivators were, according to official reports, "violently kept up to its former standard."[81] Yet it was apparent to all informed observers that there was a massive problem building up with the administration of the conquered province of Bengal. In addition, in 1772, the financial improprieties and incompetence of the East India Company's directors precipitated a huge crisis in London banking circles, in which a dozen leading banks in the city went under and the Bank of England had to struggle to keep the rest afloat. But by then, a major public campaign had been unleashed in Britain against the misrule and corruption of company officials in India along with the menace of the returning "nabobs." After the banking crisis of 1772, the climate was so hostile to the company that most members of Parliament seemed to be "in a humour to hang both Directors and servants."[82]

Early that year, William (Willem) Bolts, a Dutch officer dismissed from the East India Company's service and deported from India, published a book on "the present State of Bengal and its Dependencies."[83] It became something of a sensation. The first edition sold out in a few months and a second edition appeared by the year's end, while extracts were published in journals such as the *London Magazine* and *London Evening Post*.[84] At the same time, Alexander Dow, a Scottish officer suspended from the Bengal army for his alleged involvement in a mutiny against Clive, wrote a three-volume history of India based on

Persian sources, and inserted into his third volume an essay titled "An Enquiry into the State of Bengal with a Plan for Restoring That Province to Its Former Prosperity and Splendour."[85] Bolts and Dow were severe in their condemnation of the way that Bengal was being governed under the company's direction. To top it all, in summer 1772, Samuel Foote, a popular playwright, launched a production at the Haymarket Theatre titled *The Nabob*, lampooning the India-returned moneybags seeking desperately to enter the privileged circles of British aristocratic society. In the climactic scene, Sir Matthew Mite, the nabob, announced: "This is not Sparta, nor are these the chaste times of the Roman republic: Now a-days, riches possess at least one magical power; that, being rightly dispersed, they closely conceal the source from whence they proceeded."[86]

Neither Bolts nor Dow were disinterested observers; both had taken up the pen to join the fierce partisan struggles in the company directed against Clive and his successor, Verelst. But their campaigns managed to bring to the fore of national political debates in Britain the crucial question of the place of the Asiatic colonies in the future British Empire. Bolts spared no effort to suggest that the task of governing the populations of Bengal was the last thing on the minds of company officials: "The loaves and fishes are the grand, almost the sole object." He also identified a possible contradiction between conquest and the interests of commerce: "Views of conquest seem to have so engrossed the attention of this Company, … they appear to have been … regardless of the true commercial interest of the Kingdom." He pointed out the inequity of the company's prohibitions on private trade, "repugnant to the true spirit of mercantile affairs"; it was, he said, "the same thing as telling a man he may have a right to live, but no right to use the means of his profession for acquiring wherewithal to support life." Company officials were "unjustfully imprisoning the natives and black merchants and by violence extorting great sums of money from them," and yet the people of India had no remedy because their local courts had been superseded and the company directors were thousands of miles away. The company was every day only adding "to that dangerous despotism in India which they have long ago assumed."[87]

Dow was more blunt. It was commercial greed, he claimed, that was ruining Bengal; India was, he said following Montesquieu, a country long subjected to despotic rule. But the Orientalist in him prompted Dow to add that it was a mild and benevolent despotism.[88] In fact, if there was at this time in some informed British intellectual circles an appreciation of something like an ancient constitution of the Mughals, as Robert Travers has recently suggested, it is in Dow that one finds its clearest statement.[89] It was conquest by a commercial nation like Britain that had now brought disaster to the country. "Peculiarly unhappy, an unwarlike but industrious people, were subdued by a society whose business was commerce. A barbarous enemy may slay a prostrate foe; but a civilized conqueror can only ruin nations without the sword. Monopolies and an exclusive trade joined issue with additional taxations." Bengal, Dow said, was being drained of its wealth by the policies of the company.

> We may date the commencement of decline, from the day on which Bengal fell under the dominion of foreigners; who were more anxious to improve the present moment to their own emolument, than, by providing against waste, to secure a permanent advantage to the British nation. With a particular want of foresight, they began to drain the reservoir, without turning into it any stream to prevent it from being exhausted.[90]

His economic ideas firmly rooted in the principles of mercantilist theory, Dow identified the main cause of Bengal's ruin in the export of specie from the province by numerous channels opened up and fostered by the company's policies. "The evils of a forced state of society increase. Famine, with all its horrors, ensues, and, by sweeping away some millions of wretched people, gives, to the unhappy survivors, the respite of a few years." Dow painted a picture of complete collapse of the revenue and judicial system: "Men who retained some property in spite of the violence of the times, instead of being protected by British laws, found that they had not even the justice of a despot to depend upon when they were wronged." He added that it was not "the inhumanity of the British governors" that brought about the chaos; "the kingdom suffered more from a total want of system, than from any premeditated design."[91]

The pamphlet war heated up to boiling point. Verelst joined the fray to defend himself against the charges made by Bolts, while a dozen others took up one side or the other.[92] But probably for no other reason than his larger-than-life status, Clive became the center of controversy. Horace Walpole had said of him in 1762:

> For, as this age is to be historic, so of course it will be a standard of virtue too; and we, like our wicked predecessors the Romans, shall be quoted, till our very ghosts blush, as models of patriotism and magnanimity. What lectures will be read to poor children on this area! Europe taught to tremble, the Great King humbled, the treasures of Peru diverted into the Thames; Asia subdued by the gigantic Clive! For in that age men were near seven feet high.[93]

In 1772, however, Clive's virtue and even heroism were seriously questioned, and his stature dragged down by several notches. After contentious hearings in a select committee of the House, a motion was moved in Parliament in May 1773, charging Clive with having abused his powers to illegally acquire £234,000 in Bengal, "to the evil example of the servants of the public." In his defense, Clive told Parliament: "Consider the situation in which the victory at

Plassey had placed me. A great prince was dependent on my pleasure; an opulent city lay at my mercy; its richest bankers bid against each other for my smiles; I walked through vaults which were thrown open to me alone, piled on either hand with gold and jewels! Mr Chairman, at this moment I stand astonished at my own moderation!"[94] After a nightlong debate, Clive was found to have received presents, but was cleared of any criminal wrongdoing. In June 1773, Frederick, Lord North, steered a regulating bill that imposed a limited degree of parliamentary control over the East India Company, including the appointment of a governor-general nominated by the government and approved by Parliament.

Eight years later, though, the controversy resumed with no less a figure than Burke leading the charge in Parliament against the company and its governor-general, Hastings. Through protracted hearings and votes over more than a decade, during which Hastings complained more than once of being "tried by one generation, and … expect[ing] judgement from another," Parliament debated the charges of high crimes and misdemeanors against Hastings, who, claimed Burke, had brought "the British Name and Character" into "great Discredit, Disgrace and Dishonour."[95] Hastings, he said, was "the greatest delinquent that India ever saw."[96] Along with the scores of other company officials who had misused their powers to prey on the "unfortunate and plundered inhabitants of India," Hastings had imbibed Eastern corruption. "This was the golden cup of abominations; this the chalice of the fornications of rapine, usury, and oppression, which was held out by the gorgeous eastern harlot; which so many of the people, so many of the nobles of this land, had drained to the very dregs."[97] The real danger was that Eastern corruption was now making its way into British society. "They marry into your families; they enter into your senate; they ease your estates by loans; they raise their value by demand."[98] This was the dangerous underside of commerce that threatened to destroy virtue. Burke was determined to prevent such a disaster.

In his defense, Hastings invoked difference. India was not Britain, he said; it could not be ruled by British principles. If he had, in his own conduct, deviated from British norms, it was because Indian conditions demanded it. "The whole history of Asia is nothing more than precedents to prove the invariable exercise of arbitrary power…. Sovereignty in India implies nothing else [than despotism] … and these are every where the same from Cabool to Assam."[99] Burke, in his reply, was merciless:

> These Gentlemen have formed a plan of Geographical morality, by which the duties of men in public and in private situations are not to be governed by their relations to the Great Governor of the Universe, or by their relations to men, but by climates, degrees of longitude and latitude…. As if, when you have crossed the equinoctial line all the virtues die.

This was a license for corruption and abuse of power. "My Lords," Burke thundered, "we contend that Mr. Hastings, as a British Governor, ought to govern upon British principles.... We call for that spirit of equity, that spirit of justice, that spirit of safety, that spirit of protection, that spirit of lenity, which ought to characterise every British subject in power; and upon these and these principles only, he will be tried."[100]

In sum, Burke's claim was that Indians had their own ancient constitution, laws, and legitimate dynasties. Even the much-reviled Muslim conquerors of India, Burke noted, "very soon abated of their ferocity, because they made the conquered country their own.... Here their lot was finally cast; and it is the natural wish of all, that their lot should not be cast in a bad land.... If hoards were made by violence and tyranny, they were still domestic hoards; and domestic profusion, or the rapine of a more powerful and prodigal hand, restored them to the people." Yet it was exactly the opposite under British rule.

> The Tartar invasion was mischievous, but it is our protection that destroys India. It was their enmity, but it is our friendship. Our conquest there, after twenty years, is as crude as it was the first day.... Every rupee of profit made by an Englishman is lost for ever to India.... England has erected no churches, no hospitals, no palaces, no schools; England has built no bridges, made no high roads, cut no navigations, dug out no reservoirs. Every other conqueror of every other description has left some monument, either of state or beneficence, behind him. Were we to be driven out of India this day, nothing would remain, to tell that it had been possessed, during the inglorious period of our dominion, by any thing better than the ouran-outang or the tiger.[101]

Government in India under Hastings had become "an oppressive, irregular, capricious, unsteady, rapacious, and peculating despotism."[102] Instead of ruling by true British principles, and respecting the time-tested institutions and customs of the country, Hastings had arrogantly cast them aside in order to introduce British forms with the substance of despotism. "But your Lordships," Burke appealed,

> will shew him that in Asia as well as in Europe the same Law of Nations prevails, the same principles are continually resorted to, and the same maxims sacredly held and strenuously maintained; and however disobeyed, no man suffers from the breach of them, that does not know how to complain of that breach; that Asia is enlightened in that respect as well as Europe; but if it was totally blinded, that England would send out Governors to teach them better; and that he must justify himself to the piety, the truth, the faith, of England, and not justify himself by having recourse to the barbarous tyranny of Asia, or any other part of the world.[103]

In short, empire had to become a sacred responsibility, a patriotic duty answerable to the British nation; it had to become a business not of intrigue and loot but rather of virtue.

Hastings, in turn, insisted that he should be judged not by abstract principles but instead by the consequences of his actions. "Did I," he asked, "act prudently and consistently with the interest of my superiors, and of the people whom I governed?" If he had moved aggressively against local rulers, it was because he believed "that extraordinary means were necessary, and those exerted with a strong hand, to preserve the Company's interests from sinking *under the accumulated weight that oppressed them.*" Pointing out that "the resources of India cannot, in time of war, meet the expenses of India," he reminded the members of Parliament that he could not do "*what every Minister of England has done since the Revolution*—I could not borrow to the utmost extent of my wants during the late war, and tax posterity to pay the interest of my loans." Comparing his performance as an imperial governor with the governance of other parts of the empire, Hastings concluded his defense by asserting that despite the extraordinary situations he faced, he had "maintained the provinces of my immediate administration in a state of peace, plenty, and security, when every other member of the British empire was involved in external wars, or civil tumult."[104]

Hastings was in the end exonerated. But by bringing him to trial in Parliament, Burke, as Nicholas Dirks has argued, "made empire safe for British sovereignty.... [It] was not only no longer threatened by empire, but was simultaneously autonomous from it and yet able to encompass it through its justificatory logic that the good despotism it provided was much better than the bad despotism India had known before conquest."[105]

By this move, a crucial step was taken to resolve the deep theoretical problem posed by Britain's acquisition of a territorial empire in India. The contest with France in the Seven Years' War had spurred on a determined effort in Britain to exercise effective sovereign authority over all its overseas possessions, including Ireland, the Caribbean, the North American colonies, and the newly conquered territories in India. The reluctance of the ruling groups in Britain to concede a suitable measure of representation to the American subjects of the Crown eventually led to revolt and the loss of the thirteen colonies. But an independent and sovereign United States could easily claim to have achieved the conditions of freedom that it had sought within the empire and had been denied. The American Revolution did not produce any crisis for the received tradition of English political theory. On the contrary, it only confirmed its fundamental tenets.

In India, on the other hand, the force of arms had acquired a territorial empire and had then become the means of its permanent defense. This meant ensuring continually expanding sources of territorial revenues to meet the expenses of raising native armies and fighting wars. It also meant—as P. J. Marshall, the premier historian of British ascendancy in India in the eighteenth century, has pointed out—the inclusion, sometime during the Seven Years' War, of the East India Company, a monopolistic trading corporation, into the body of the British state and its emergence as a distinct agency of the British Empire.[106] By the logic of English political theory, it was a certain recipe for tyranny. How could Britain hold its subjects in servitude? And if it did, would not freedom be threatened at home? Burke presented one account of this looming danger. Yet it was also apparent to some perceptive American observers, one of whom said in 1773: "For the future, the story of Lord Clive will be that of every military plunderer.... It begins in blood and plunder, it ends in servility and dependence.... In a few years the two houses will be filled with Omrahs and Subehdars, nurtured in the corruption and despotism of the East. What will be the consequence? We must fall as Greece and Rome have fallen."[107]

The solution was found in the aftermath of the Hastings trial. Imperial Britain was desperately seeking to cope with the loss of the American colonies. Hastings himself had written in 1778: "If it be really true that the British arms and influence have suffered so severe a check in the western world, it is the more incumbent on those who are charged with the interests of *Great Britain* in the east to exert themselves for the retrieval of the national interest." To do this, a benevolent autocracy, accountable to Parliament, had to be established in India—a "*despotick power* [that] is constantly amenable to *impartial* justice." Such benevolent despotism overseas could be domesticated within the empire without threatening liberty at home. "A people secure in their freedom would not be corrupted, as the Romans had been, by exercising autocratic rule in Asia. Men of high principle would be chosen for service in India, who would be accountable to the law and subject to the unremitting vigilance of parliament for any deviation from rectitude."[108]

THE CRITIQUE OF CONQUEST

Virtually canonical in the field of European knowledge in Indian history in the nineteenth century, *The History of British India* by James Mill (1773–1836) was first published in 1817. Mill was a utilitarian and a reformist thinker in the new radical tradition launched by Jeremy Bentham. He shared Bentham's distaste for the "priest-ridden, lawyer-ridden, lord-ridden, squire-ridden, soldier-ridden England," and opposed the conservative political and social ideology—enunciated so eloquently by Burke—that seemed to dominate British public life in the wake of the French Revolution. In his *History*, Mill applied entirely new criteria to write a "judging history" of the depraved and worthless religious and political institutions of India as well as the corrupt and ineffective practices introduced by its new British rulers.[109] His chapter on the capture of Calcutta by Siraj mentions the Black Hole incident, but frames it within a paradigm of social ethics that would have been incomprehensible to the eighteenth-century narrators we have encountered so far.

Mill described the confusion and disorder surrounding the retreat from the fort on June 19, 1756, as bordering on criminal negligence of duty, but something that should have been expected given the lack of proper principles of governance in the East India Company's affairs at the time. After the surrender of the fort, Mill said, following Holwell's narrative, Siraj did not show any cruelty to the British captives.

> When evening, however, came, it was a question with the guards to whom they were intrusted, how they might be secured for the night. Some search was made for a convenient apartment; but none was found; upon which information was obtained of a place which the English themselves had employed as a prison. Into this, without any further inquiry, they were impelled. It was unhappily a small, ill-aired, and unwholesome dungeon, called the Black Hole; and the English had their own practice to thank for suggesting it to the officers of the Subahdar as a fit place of confinement.

In a footnote, Mill here digressed on the subject of British penal practices—a favorite subject of Benthamite reformers: "The atrocities of English imprisonment at home, ... too naturally reconciled Englishmen abroad to the use of dungeons: of *Black Holes*. What had they to do with a *black hole*? Had no *black hole* existed (as none ought to exist anywhere, least of all in the sultry and unwholesome climate of Bengal), those who perished in the Black Hole of Calcutta would have experienced a different fate."[110]

There is little doubt that Mill regarded the "plotting and intrigue" that led to Siraj's overthrow as utterly scandalous. "In manufacturing the terms of the confederacy," he observed, "the grand concern of the English appeared to be money." Once again in a footnote, Mill remarked: "That General, Admiral, and Members of the Select Committee, were alike influenced by a grasping and mercenary spirit is undeniable, and they seized, with an avidity which demanded a lamentable absence of elevated principles, upon an unexpected opportunity of realizing princely fortunes." Mill called the deception against Amirchand "a piece of consummate treachery." When Watts's proposals for the secret treaty with Mir Jafar came to Calcutta,

> the sum to be given to Omichund, even as compensation for his losses, seemed a very heavy grievance to men who panted for more to themselves. To men whose minds were in such a state, the great demands of Omichund appeared (the reader will laugh—but they did literally appear) a crime. They were voted a crime; and so great

a crime, as to deserve to be punished—to be punished, not only by depriving him of all reward, but depriving him of his compensation, that compensation which was stipulated for to everybody: it was voted that Omichund should have nothing. They were in his power, however, therefore he was not to be irritated. It was necessary he should be deceived.... Not an Englishman, not even Mr. Orme, has yet expressed a word of sympathy or regret.[111]

Mill also narrated the trial of Hastings with a detailed account of the charges against him, and bemoaned the fact that instead of a proper judicial examination, the whole process was subjected to the fickle forces of popular opinion: "If his accusers could not prove his guilt, it is still more certain that he [Hastings] has not proved his innocence."[112] It was not so much the moral character of officials like Clive or Hastings that Mill saw as the problem: in fact, it has been suggested that his *History* is "singularly devoid of human interest," because his commitment to utilitarian ethics and enthusiasm for "systems" of law and government made him not "care about the play of human character."[113] He repeatedly traced the problem to the utterly inadequate system of government in India after large territories came under the East India Company's domination.

Mill was a philosophical radical. He did not have any sympathy for Burke's reverence for traditional institutions, whether in India or Britain. But curiously, even as the proponent of the radical reform of government in India, Mill shared Burke's intuition that the scandalous story of the founding of Britain's empire in Bengal should not be retold. Referring to Clive's territorial acquisitions in Bengal, Burke had said at Hastings's impeachment in 1788: "Many circumstances of this acquisition I pass by. There is a secret veil to be drawn over the beginning of all governments. They had their origins, as the beginnings of all such things have had, in some matters that had as good be covered by obscurity."[114]

A similar sense of discomfort appeared through the pages of Mill's *History* dealing with the early years of British rule, relieved only by his frequent admonition that such improprieties were not to be repeated. He also insisted that as long as the correct and universally valid principles of government were followed, it did not really matter whether a country's rulers were native or foreign: "The aversion to a government, because in the hands of foreigners; that is, men who are called by one rather than some other name, without regard to the qualities of government, whether better or worse, is a prejudice which reason disclaims."[115] Mill was here initiating a new mode of argument that would demand that the ethics of colonial conquest should be judged not so much by the motivations but rather by its consequences—a contention that would acquire great importance later in the nineteenth century and still remains an influential historiographical trope. But whether one regarded the story of the British acquisition of the Indian Empire as shameful or a mere happenstance, by Mill's account there was little in it worthy of memorialization.

Figure 7. *A View of the Writers' Building from the Monument at the West End*, aquatint by James Baillie Fraser. *Source: Fraser 1824*

This was the intellectual climate in which Holwell's Black Hole monument was demolished in 1821. Henry Busteed, a major campaigner for the monument's restoration, wrote in 1886 that after looking through all available records, he had been unable to trace the reason. Some thought that the Marquis of Hastings, the governor-general, had ordered its demolition in 1821 because "its continuance had become politically undesirable, either as likely to wound the sensibilities of our native fellow-subjects, or to recall prominently at the seat of Government a hideous disaster to British arms, which it would be wiser to locally bury in oblivion."[116] Others, while acknowledging the speculation that the monument was pulled down because "it was inexpedient to perpetuate the memory of the disaster," insisted that "the most likely reason was to make room for the Custom House."[117] Kathleen Blechynden wrote in 1905:

> The predominant feeling at the beginning of the nineteenth century appears to have been a desire to forget all that was disagreeable in the past, and, in 1821, the monument was taken down, and its commemorative tablet mislaid and lost. The spot which should have been held sacred by every Englishman was occupied by a lamp-post.[118]

It is also likely, though, that the governor-general had nothing to do with the decision, and that it was more the monument's state of disrepair and inappropriate use by local people that created an opinion leading to its demolition.

An early nineteenth-century illustration by James Baillie Fraser that shows the original Holwell memorial set against the background of the then–Writers' Buildings drew the following comment from Evan Cotton, a twentieth-century British historian of Calcutta:

> The obelisk in the last named engraving looks at least 50 feet high and is not surrounded by any railings. It seems in consequence to be the lounging place for lower class loafers of all sorts who gossip squatting around and against it. A barber is seen plying his craft in the favourite posture of these Eastern experts. His back is to the base of the monument, while overhead is stretched his outspread cloth between the upper ledge of the pedestal and three or four stakes. The tent thus improvised shelters the operator and a few of his customers. All this unsightliness may explain why the historic structure had a few years before the date of this engraving disappeared from the City of Palaces, after, as tradition says, it had been struck by lightning.[119]

In any case, we have a report in the *Calcutta Journal* in 1821, edited by the controversial freethinker James Silk Buckingham, announcing: "The monument over the well-remembered 'Black Hole' of Calcutta is at length taken down, and we think should long ago have been demolished."[120]

It stayed that way until the end of the nineteenth century. There was nothing in the city of Calcutta, the capital of the British Empire in India, memorializing the events of the Black Hole.

CHAPTER THREE

Tipu's Tiger

MIRZA SHAIKH IHTISHAMUDDIN (c. 1730–c. 1800) set sail in January 1766 from the port of Hijli, now in the district of Purba Medinipur, several miles downstream from Calcutta. After four days of slow maneuvering through the treacherous currents of the Hugli River, the ship finally entered the Bay of Bengal. Ihtishamuddin was on his way to Vilayet.

He was by no means the first person from his part of the world to undertake the sea voyage to Europe. We know of many sailors as well as domestic servants of both sexes from Bengal who went, or were taken, to Britain in the eighteenth century. Rozina Visram's and Michael Fisher's studies have given us the outline of a social history of these visitors about whom little is otherwise known.[1] Thus, we have shipping records of more than a thousand such Indians in Britain by the end of the eighteenth century showing, for example, that there were among them more women than men. Although more of them came from the Coromandel Coast in the earlier half of the century, by the end of the eighteenth century the flow was mainly out of Bengal. Most were Muslim, a few were Indian Catholics, and there were almost no Hindus.

Unfortunately, ayahs and lascars were not people who wrote anything about their visits, and except for indirect and sometimes fictional accounts, we have no stories about their experiences in the West. The only significant exception is the remarkable Shaikh Din Muhammad, who settled down in Ireland and wrote of his travels in 1794.[2] If we also leave aside the autobiographical letters of Joseph Emin, the Armenian adventurer from Calcutta living in Britain in the middle decades of the century, then Ihtishamuddin's is the earliest journey to Britain by a scholar-bureaucrat from Bengal about which we have a book-length narrative.[3] It tells us many interesting things about the initial responses of the Indian elite to the revolution that had just occurred in the political affairs of Bengal.[4]

A BENGALI IN BRITAIN

Ihtishamuddin came from a family of minor officials. His ancestral home was in the neighborhood now known as Kazipara in the small town of Chakdah in Nadia District. Ihtishamuddin's elder brother Ghulam Mohiuddin was a mufti in Nawab Ali Vardi's court in Murshidabad.[5] Ihtishamuddin himself began his career as an apprentice *munshi* or letter writer in Nawab Mir Jafar's court and continued under Mir Qasim. In 1762, he became a Persian munshi in the East India Company's service. It appears that he was present in the camp of Colonel John Carnac during the fateful battle of Baksar in 1764.

Soon after this, Ihtishamuddin entered the service of Shah Alam II, the Mughal emperor, then residing in Allahabad, and was responsible for preparing the Persian draft of the treaty by which the emperor assigned the office of diwan of Bengal to the company "from generation to generation, for ever and ever."[6] But the emperor kept complaining to Clive that although the company's affairs had been settled to its satisfaction, his interests had been ignored, because the company was doing nothing to provide him with the necessary military assistance to enable him to return to Delhi. Clive, it seems, offered the excuse that none other than the king of England could authorize the company to go to war, which prompted Shah Alam to decide to send an embassy to London consisting of Captain Archibald Swinton, formerly of the East India Company, and Ihtishamuddin as the Persian scribe. Yet Clive had no intention to facilitate direct contact between the two monarchs. He intercepted Shah Alam's letter to the English king and persuaded Swinton to keep quiet about it. Only after arriving in Britain did Ihtishamuddin learn that they were not carrying a letter, there would be no audience with the king, and in effect, they had no mission to accomplish. He was, needless to say, filled with bitterness at the "deep game of deceit" played by Clive.[7]

Ihtishamuddin decided to make the most of his visit to Vilayet, though. He was gifted with a critical faculty and was prepared to question many conventional truisms that he had inherited from his cultural background.[8] While on board the ship, he made a careful study of the different kinds of seagoing vessels used by Europeans, the different winds and how they could be turned to advantage, and above all the compass and navigation charts that allowed European vessels to sail night and day without anchoring. "Truly," he concluded, "the Firanghees have attained astonishing mastery over the science of navigation."[9]

But Ihtishamuddin also got direct evidence of the sharp practices engaged in by senior English officials in their role as private traders. Landing at the French port of Nantes, he noticed that his companions Swinton and Peacock handed over gold, silver, fine clothes, and other valuable goods to transporters, who were supposed to smuggle them into Britain by hiding them inside consignments of fruits and vegetables. All of this, Ihtishamuddin gathered, was a regular practice and French customs officials, suitably compensated, willingly turned a blind eye.[10] There was no reason for Ihtishamuddin to believe that trading methods in the East were any more corrupt than in the West.

"The English had never seen a Hindustani dressed as I was. They considered me a great curiosity and flocked to have a look." At first, Ihtishamuddin was somewhat taken aback by the impression he created, even though he found the hospitality of his English acquaintances warm and kind. He realized quite soon, however, that the English had stereotypical images of India, and he was being made to fit one of them.

> The English had never seen an Indian munshi before, but only lascars from Chittagong and Jahangirnagar, and were consequently unacquainted with the clothes and manners of an Indian gentleman. They took me for a great man of Bengal, perhaps the brother of a nawab, and came from far and near to see me. Whenever I went abroad crowds accompanied me, and people craned their heads out of windows and gazed at me in wonder. Children and adolescents took me for a curious specimen and ran into their houses crying, "Look! Look! A black man is walking down the street!"—at which the elders would rush to the door and stare at me in amazement. Many children and small boys took me for a black devil and kept away in fear.

But soon things changed.

> Within a couple of months, everyone in the neighbourhood became friendly. The fear which some had felt vanished completely, and they would now jest with me familiarly. The ladies of the bazaar approached me and, smiling, said, "Come, my dear, and kiss me!"[11]

Ihtishamuddin's curiosity about new technologies along with the improvements in productive activities and civic life that could be brought about by their application is evident from his appreciative descriptions of streetlights and garbage removal in London, and a new proposal for the piped supply of clean drinking water. He understood the benefits of "labour-saving inventions" such as the water mill, windmill, and "spinning mills where a single operator turns a large wheel whose motion is automatically transferred to about twenty other wheels." He saw the widespread use of watches and clocks in public places, by which "in Vilayet people of all classes keep track of time." Ihtishamuddin was impressed by the public entertainment offered in the theaters, where unlike private concerts in wealthy homes in India, people from all classes could buy tickets and enjoy performances fit for royalty. "Truly, the Firanghees can accomplish great things at little expense." He visited the "great madrasa" at Oxford and after seeing the "model of the universe" in the physics laboratory, was convinced that "the English scientists have much more accurate knowledge of the universe" than scholars in the East. He saw that the technology of printing had made books cheap, so that even the lower orders were able to read, write, and count.

> The wise men of Vilayet say that the acquisition of worldly wealth is necessary to make life pleasant and easy, while education increases one's knowledge and wisdom

and enables one to show the right path to those who seek advice. Worldly riches ought not to be squandered on luxurious living, on fine clothes, choice cuisine and dishes, and on collecting a bevy of singing and dancing women with whom to spend endless days and nights, as the wealthy noblemen of Hindustan are wont to do.[12]

He summed up the normative English lifestyle in the following words: "Till forty the English apply themselves in business and also to travel, and study the wonders and curiosities of the world. Then they return home with their amassed wealth, marry, and live in pleasant retirement with their families." Ihtishamuddin then made the inevitable comparison:

In contrast, the behaviour of Hindustanis fills me with shame and sorrow. Indian parents arrange marriages for their sons when they are still mere boys.... But then men have to leave their wives to seek employment. This is very cruel on the wives. This state of affairs must be age-old, for the ancient literature in Persian as well as in Hindi, Brij and Bengali, is replete with poems expressing women's grief at being separated from their husbands.[13]

Thus, Ihtishamuddin, it would seem, imbibed something of the new bourgeois morality that was becoming dominant among the growing middle classes of Britain in the second half of the eighteenth century. He was also clearly convinced that the new knowledge of science and technology was becoming a potent source of strength that the British could use in reorganizing their own social institutions as well as in dealing with other countries and peoples. Yet there is nothing in his account, completed in 1784–85, long after his return to Bengal, which suggests any recognition of the subordination of his people to a European power. On the contrary, despite his criticism of many of the beliefs and practices that he had grown up with in India, he remained firm in his assertion of the integrity and coherence of his culture and identity. He wore his Indian clothes on the streets of London and Edinburgh, and with the assistance of his Indian servant, observed the ritual rules concerning food and prayers. Indeed, when his servant decided to return to India, Ihtishamuddin too resolved to do the same, despite the protests of his English patron Swinton.

This led to an angry exchange. Swinton, boasting of his knowledge of Muslim customs, insisted that there was nothing in Islam that prohibited a Muslim from relaxing his dietary rules when traveling. Ihtishamuddin retorted, "But I am not compelled to travel." Swinton charged: "So you Muslims think we are filthy eaters." Ihtishamuddin replied that the food of one country was different from that of another and there was no point comparing them. "We should remember in particular that between your manners and customs and ours there is the difference of east and west." Swinton then suggested that his visitor was being hypocritical, because in India he had met many clever people who would proclaim their piety in public, but enjoy forbidden food and drink in private. "Why do you behave like the blockheads of Calcutta? … The only reason I can think of for this is that you are a Bengali, and Bengalis are notorious among Indians for their folly and stupidity." Ihtishamuddin was incensed. Summoning every ounce of cultural pride, he declared: "I am a poor man of Sayyid descent, who has been allured by the prospect of gain to travel to this country. Forlorn and friendless, subjected to continual hardship and unable to help myself, I must patiently wait the issue."[14] Ending a trip lasting nearly two years, he returned to Bengal in November 1768.

Contemporary Indian Histories

If the Black Hole incident played such a dramatic part in the British story of the foundation of the Indian Empire, even when the motivations and modalities of that acquisition were sought to be disavowed, what role did it have in Indian histories of the same period? There are several accounts in Persian by contemporary historians of Bengal that describe the political events of Siraj's brief reign. Of these, Ghulam Husain Salim and Karam Ali did not mention the Black Hole incident.[15] Neither did Ghulam Husain Tabatabai (born c. 1727), the preeminent historian of the period and author of the *Sair al-mut'akhhirin*, who was no admirer of Siraj and who had close contacts with British officials. Indeed, he wrote of Mirza Amir Beg, an officer in the nawab's army, delivering a group of marooned European women in his custody to the flotilla in Phalta by boat. Haji Mustafa, the English translator of the *Sair*, added a footnote to Ghulam Husain's text with the following comment:

> There is not a word here of those English shut up in the Black-hole, to the number of 131, where they were mostly smothered. The truth is, that the Hindostanees wanting only to secure them for the night, as they were to be presented the next morning to the Prince, shut them up in what they heard was the prison of the Fort, without having any idea of the capacity of the room; and indeed the English themselves had none of it. This much is certain, that this event … is not known in Bengal; and even in Calcutta, it is ignored by every man out of the four hundred thousand that inhabit that city; at least it is difficult to meet a single native that knows anything of it; so careless, and so incurious are those people.[16]

It is not true, however, that no contemporary Indian account of Siraj's capture of Calcutta mentions the Black Hole. Yusuf Ali Khan specifically talks about it:

> He [Siraj] confined nearly a hundred Farangis who fell victim to the claws of fate on that day, in a small room and entrusted the management of the Factory to some of

the officers.... As luck would have it, in the room where the Farangis were kept confined, all of them got suffocated and died. And the bodies of others, about twenty or thirty in number, who were killed by the strokes of guns etc. during the days of the siege, were in pursuance of an order thrown into the trenches of the Factory, with the feet of one against the face of the other.[17]

Yusuf Ali, a follower of Mir Qasim, fell into disfavor with Mir Jafar during his second term as the puppet nawab. But he does not appear to have any particular ax to grind in the matter of Siraj.[18] Even though he is the only known Indian chronicler to mention the Black Hole event, he clearly does not blame anyone for it and ascribes it to the accidental circumstances likely during a war.

Two of the first printed Bengali histories, published in the first decade of the nineteenth century under the auspices of the Fort William College in Calcutta, were severely critical of Siraj, and lauded the climate of peace and justice established by the East India Company's rule. Rajiblochan Mukhopadhyay spoke of the tyranny of Muslim rule and emergence of the English as saviors of Hindu dharma.[19] Mrityunjay Vidyalankar discussed the damages inflicted on Calcutta by Siraj's army and generous compensations paid to the residents by the British after his defeat.[20] Yet not once did the two authors mention the Black Hole.[21] A Bengali almanac from 1835–36 providing information on the country's rulers mentioned that Siraj attacked Calcutta and put 143 English prisoners in a small cell; 123 died in the course of the night.[22] By then, Charles Stewart's *History of Bengal* had established a narrative in which the tragedy proceeded "entirely from stupidity, and not from malevolence or cruelty," on the part of the nawab's officers dealing with the prisoners in Old Fort William.[23]

It should be pointed out that none of these contemporary Indian histories have any nationalist agenda in portraying Siraj as a patriotic defender of the country's sovereignty against foreign invaders. On the contrary, they frequently blame him for being arbitrary, thoughtless, and cruel. Yusuf Ali says: "There was never a day when he would not mete out some kind of dishonour and insult to respectable men."[24] Ghulam Husain Salim noted: "Siraju-d-daulah treated all the noblemen and generals of Mahabat Jang [Ali Vardi] with ridicule and drollery, and bestowed on each some contemptuous nick-name that ill-suited any of them.... [N]o one had the boldness to breathe freely in his presence."[25] Ghulam Husain Tabatabai thought Siraj "was ignorant of the world, and incapable to take a reasonable party, being totally destitute of sense and penetration, and yet having a head so obscured by the smoke of ignorance, and so giddy and intoxicated with the fumes of youth and power and dominion, that he knew no distinction betwixt good and bad, nor betwixt vice and virtue."[26] Several stories about his depravity and cruelty circulated among the Hindu landed families of Bengal, especially in connection with his alleged attempt to abduct the widowed daughter of Rani Bhabani of Nator.[27] Still, none of the contemporary

Indian histories described the political revolution brought about by Siraj's defeat and death as just retribution for his mistreatment of the English.

This raises the complex and ambiguous question of the Indian response to the British conquest of Bengal in the eighteenth century—a topic that has been thoroughly clouded by later nationalist mythmaking as well as more recent attempts to exculpate British imperialism. To gain a clearer picture of that period and distinguish between several contradictory tendencies that emerged at the time, it is necessary not to see the late eighteenth century through the powerful but not entirely accurate lenses made familiar in the period of high imperialism in the nineteenth century. We need, in fact, to find other angles of vision.

THE EARLY MODERN IN SOUTH ASIA

In his book *Penumbral Visions*, Sanjay Subrahmanyam proposes the idea of the early modern as a concept for writing comparative history.[28] He points out the usefulness of this notion in questioning the rigid orthodoxies of the Kemalist historiography of the Ottoman Empire, which insisted on a sharp, ideologically prompted break between the medieval and the modern, and suggests that a similar move could be made in South Asian history writing. Specifically, he claims that the period from the fifteenth to the eighteenth century, when looked at from a global comparative perspective, reveals several conditions of potential historical change that are common to many regions of the world.

First, it is an era of unprecedented travel, "discovery," and geographic redefinition. Second, the period sees the heightening of a long-term structural conflict between settled agricultural and urban societies, on the one hand, and nomadic hunter-gatherers and pastoralists, on the other. This is true not only for Asia; the entire history of European conquest and settlement of the Americas can be seen in this way. Third, there is an unprecedented rise in the volume and range of long-distance trade, including the trade in slaves, leading to profound economic, social, and political consequences in most regions of the world. Fourth, an important political effect of all these material developments was the new content provided to the idea of universal empire—in Europe, Ottoman Turkey, Mughal India, and possibly also China. There certainly is the emergence of large polities on several continents on a scale unknown in earlier history. In the European case, especially the English one, it produced that specific early modern combination of representative institutions of government at home alongside the pursuit of imperial possessions and colonial settlements overseas. And fifth—most speculatively—Subrahmanyam hints at the emergence of new literary and artistic forms in many regions of the world that may be seen as a response to these new historical conditions. Whether we can call them the rise of humanism, individualism, or something yet to be named depends, of course, on a much more systematic comparative research agenda than has been attempted so far.[29]

In a similar vein, Sheldon Pollock argues for the usefulness of a notion of early modernity as a means for comparatively studying the intellectual histories of Europe, the Islamic world, India, and China in the period from the fifteenth to the eighteenth century. He offers three "master categories" that one might look for: a new sense of the individual, a new skepticism, and a new historical sensibility. But more generally, he contends that it is not only a matter of establishing a threshold that describes "how various the world was at the moment before what would become the dominant form of modernity—colonial, capitalist, Western—achieved global ascendancy." We can go further with the concept of early modernity:

> Since the material world changed dramatically during the three centuries before this threshold, and changed universally, there is good reason to ask how the systems devised for knowing the world responded—or why they failed to respond—to the world that was changing objectively.... Everyone began to participate in a new world economy, to live in new, larger, and more stable states, to confront a demographic explosion, a diffusion of new technology, vaster movements of people in a newly unified world. How did people experience these transformations in the realm of thought? That is what we need to discover.[30]

Pursuing the question of the emergence of new literary forms in India in the period of early modernity, Velcheru Narayana Rao, David Shulman, and Subrahmanyam have explored the field of history writing.[31] They question the facile but common assumption that there was no history writing in India before the colonial encounter—an assumption, of course, that relegates the rich and complex tradition of Indo-Persian historiography to the category of a foreign branch of knowledge. They suggest that by employing more careful and appropriate techniques of reading, we would be able to identify distinctly historical narratives—factual, bound by secular causal explanations, informed by an awareness of the credibility of sources, and largely having to do with the life of the state—embedded within other nonhistorical literary genres, such as poems, ballads, and works within the larger *itihāsa-purāṇa* tradition, yet marked by discursive signs recognized by the community of readers or listeners. They also assert that from the sixteenth century in southern India, a distinct literati group, which they broadly label the *karanam*, produced these new historical narratives in the languages of southern India as well as Sanskrit and Persian. If history is to be identified as a particularly receptive vehicle of the modern, then their argument is that it had already appeared, at least in the southern Indian languages, well before British rule was established. They close their book with the remarkable example of the *Dupati kaifiyatu* by an anonymous early nineteenth-century karanam author—a text that appears to pass every test of modern historical writing and yet was produced within a tradition outside the disciplinary grid of colonial education.

Christopher Bayly, too, has identified traces of the modern in the practices of Indo-Muslim history writing in the eighteenth century. He locates this tradition within what he calls "an Indian ecumene," characterized by a distinct information order and an indigenous public sphere. Bayly mentions a series of people from official letter writers and spies to scholar-bureaucrats who participated in this information order, and processed the material that went into the production of numerous Indo-Persian histories written in the eighteenth century. He also notes the emergence of certain distinctly "modern" concerns in these histories that appear to come from entirely indigenous sources and not from the promptings of a colonial education. Thus, a historian like Ali Ibrahim Khan who wrote about political events involving the Marathas between 1757 and 1780 was, Bayly says, "an unacknowledged founder of a consciously modern Indian history."[32] Bayly's work has been influential in demolishing the prejudices about the absence of history in precolonial India. Nevertheless, notions such as ecumene and information order lack theoretical clarity and analytic power, while the attribution of a Habermasian public sphere to the literary world of eighteenth-century northern India is too quick. In the absence of meaningful conceptual distinctions, the slide from the precolonial to the era of colonial modernity in the nineteenth century is rendered far too smooth and unproblematic.

The Early Modern as a Category of Transition

The early modern therefore must be conceptually distinguished from the colonial modern in South Asia. The early modern is not necessarily, or not yet (for historians of South Asia), a "period."[33] We will use the term here to characterize elements of thought or practice that have been identified as belonging to early modern historical formations in other regions of the world, in recognition of the broadly similar and frequently interconnected developments in those places in the fifteenth to eighteenth centuries. These elements may be found in different regions of South Asia as innovations that question previously held beliefs and practices, recognize their passing because of the unstoppable sway of the new, or represent novel ways of comprehending or coping with the unfamiliar. They may arise within different social strata—among elite groups or the literati, or among popular classes such as artisans.

The crucial historical point would be to distinguish such elements of the early modern from the recognizable components of the colonial modern. The latter may be dated from roughly the 1830s, achieving its fully developed form in the historical period of the Raj. The reasons are as follows. The Indian economy at this time acquires the form of a characteristically colonial economy: the flow of colonial trade has been reversed from the export from India of textiles and luxuries to the export of primary agricultural products and import of industrial manufactures from Britain, and the structures of colonial agrarian property, revenue, credit, and commodity exchange are fully in place. We should remember, as Kenneth Pomeranz shows, that the "great divergence" between a rapidly growing industrial Europe and a stagnant or backward China and India only began in 1800.[34] Politically, the British power is established as paramount all over the subcontinent—a violent process of warfare, conquest, suppression of rebellion, and unequal treaties—with its associated consequences in terms of the symbols and practices of sovereignty and law that bring about a profound transformation in the character of government and politics. In its conception and ambition, as Radhika Singha demonstrates, the East India Company, from the time it began to carry out the administration of criminal justice in the late eighteenth century, thought of sovereignty as undivided and not just another imperium laid over the segmented political formation.[35] Intellectually, the institutions of colonial education spread from the mid-nineteenth century as the breeding ground of new cultural styles and movements that create the Indian middle classes as well as shape an entire range of nationalist responses to colonial rule. The colonial modern has a recognized shape as a formation and period in South Asian history. It also exerts the full weight of its dominance over all discussions of South Asian modernity after the mid-nineteenth century.

Yet this would leave the earlier period of British rule from the mid-eighteenth century to the 1820s or so open to an exploration of historical possibilities of transition not teleologically predetermined by the ascendancy of the colonial modern. This is the principal justification for invoking the idea of the early modern as an agenda for history writing today. Research driven by this proposal could yield valuable historical resources that suggest the possibility of defining other modernities, or to put it more precisely, other historical sequences of modernity.[36] The argument that such possibilities have been lost in the graveyard of the past is, strictly speaking, incorrect, because most intellectual and cultural forms of modernity in the world have been imagined and comprehended as "discoveries" of the past. The very idea of the Renaissance, for instance, invoked in so many places since the sixteenth century, plays out the notion of a rediscovery of the past, as indeed do the ideas of the Reformation and Revival.

Moreover, within the category of the early modern in South Asia, we need to make a further distinction between an *absolutist* and an *antiabsolutist* tendency. As we will see later in this book, both of these tendencies remained alive through the nineteenth and twentieth centuries, providing some of the discursive and affective resources of modern nationalisms in South Asia, in their colonial as well as postcolonial phases.

Nīti versus Dharma

There is one more background feature that needs to be mentioned before describing the absolutist early modern tendency in eighteenth-century India. Rao and Subrahmanyam have drawn our attention to a genre of writing, mostly in Telugu, that was called nīti literature and, apparently quite self-consciously, distinguished itself from the *dharmaśāstra* literature.[37] Nīti, as explicated in the *Mahābhārata*, consists of the principles of *rājadharma* by which kings were meant to preserve their rule and protect their subjects. In the classical tradition, it was always asserted that nīti must be contained within the broader rubric of dharma. But the nīti literature that Rao and Subrahmanyam cite from the Kakatiya and Vijayanagara periods pays no obeisance to dharma, and appears to claim an autonomous field of application for its principles. Thus, a fifteenth-century Telugu compilation called *Sakala-niti-sammatamu* proclaims the following principles: "If serving a ruler causes incessant pain to the servant, the servant should leave such a master right away"; "He may be rich, born in a good caste, a strong warrior beyond comparison, but if a king is an ignoramus, his servants will no doubt leave him"; "A bad king surrounded by good people turns out to be good, but even a good king is difficult to serve if his advisers are bad."[38] It is hard to imagine principles of this kind in any dharmaśāstra text. Rao and Subrahmanyam also stress that this specific genre of nīti texts was composed and read by the group of scholar-bureaucrats they refer to broadly as the karanam. In other words, these texts comprised a literature on statecraft produced by and for the practitioners of statecraft. They also were composed not in Sanskrit but rather in regional vernaculars such as Telugu and Kannada—another sign of their distance from the canonical body of dharmaśāstra texts.

In northern India, the corresponding group to the karanam was the munshi. They were the practitioners of statecraft, and wrote about its principles in the Indo-Persian genre of *tarikh* or history as well as in instruction manuals for princes called *akhlaq*. Muzaffar Alam points out the characteristic features of the akhlaq literature produced in India in the Sultanate and Mughal periods.[39] The prime consideration here was to formulate principles of rule that would be normative for an Islamic monarch ruling over an overwhelmingly non-Muslim body of subjects. As Alam shows, the crucial quality demanded of such a monarch was not Islamic piety but instead *aqal*—that is, good sense and judgment.

These are disparate pieces of evidence. But they show the availability, in southern as well as northern India, of a set of discursive resources that would contribute to the formations we are calling the *absolutist early modern*.[40]

AN EARLY MODERN HISTORY OF BENGAL

Iqbal Ghani Khan has written about Ghulam Husain's *Sair al-muta'akkhirin*, a work that also occupies a pride of place in Kumkum Chatterjee's discussion of Indo-Persian historiography in the late eighteenth century.[41] Written in 1783–84 by a scholar-bureaucrat resident in Murshidabad, the book has been seen as the most articulate defense of the principles of Mughal governance in a period when the empire was in ruins and the English were firmly entrenched in eastern India. Khan reads it primarily as a contemporary critique of British rule, but one uninformed by a true understanding of colonialism. Chatterjee uses the text to explain the moral world of the Mughal scholar-nobles who saw themselves as vigilant protectors of the polity and advisers to princes. Yet much more can be said of this remarkable work of history.

Although the English translator of the book (a somewhat-mysterious man born in Istanbul who called himself Haji Mustafa and used the self-effacing nom de plume Nota Manus) translates the title as "Review of Modern Times," *muta'akkirin* probably should not be read as having any conceptual load greater than what "recent times" would suggest.[42] But it is a grand history of the decline of empire, beginning with Aurangzeb's death in 1707 and ending in 1782. It is, of course, no more than a coincidence that Ghulam Husain wrote this book almost exactly at the same time as Edward Gibbon was writing about the decline and fall of another empire.

In Ghulam Husain's account, the decline of empire takes the form of the complete erosion of the authority of the emperor as the supreme and sovereign source of policy and statecraft. This is the consequence of the succession of unworthy, immoral, and—sometimes—imbecile monarchs who come to sit on the throne of Delhi after Aurangzeb's death. Even though he was a thoroughbred Mughal gentleman, Ghulam Husain still does not pay even the ceremonial homage to the emperor when he evaluates the monarchical careers of Jahandar Shah, Farrukhsiyar, or Muhammad Shah, not to speak of those who were put on the throne and removed in a matter of days. When the monarch cannot be depended on to make policy, how is the empire to survive? If the empire does not survive, how is the security and prosperity of the people to be protected?

The survival of the state then becomes subject to the profound uncertainties of chance. As far as one knows, the Mughals did not have any equivalent for the playful Roman goddess Fortuna, who was the subject of so much theorizing by historians in Europe from Polybius and Livy to Niccolò Machiavelli. Ghulam Husain cannot but reflect, however, on the element of chance that in the absence of the stable legitimacy of the imperial structure, could play havoc with the fate of the polity and lives of the people. Thus, reflecting on the career of Husain Ali Khan, the younger Sayyid brother, he wrote:

In power he seemed superior to all the Princes of his time, nay; to several that bore a character in history for having bestowed kingdoms and crowns and conquered Empires. Unfortunately neither his power nor his life lasted any length of time. If they had, it is highly probable, that the times which we have the mortification to behold, would not prove so humiliating and so deplorable, as they are; nor had the honour of Hindostan been thrown to the winds; ... But as the morals of the whole nation required the iron hand of correction, it is not surprising that the person and power of that hero should have been only shewn to the world.[43]

The uncertainties of chance could only be brought under control by prudence, wisdom, and knowledge. The monarch could not be relied on to provide such wisdom, for that had become entirely a matter of contingency. Ghulam Husain places a great responsibility here on the class of Mughal scholar-nobles to defend the empire and guide it through the thicket of uncertainties. For him, the heroes of the eighteenth century are the Sayyid brothers, especially Husain Ali and Ali Vardi, Shuja-ud-daulah, and Shitab Rai—none of them legitimate claimants to power, but rather individuals whose personal ability, determination, and political skills made them the polity's defenders. But it is also interesting to note his identification of the flaws in his heroes. On Shuja-ud-daulah's refusal to make peace with the English and decision instead to launch an attack on the province of Bengal, leading to the disaster at Baksar, he said:

> But Shudjah-ed-döulah, equally proud and ignorant, ... [who] had conceived as high an opinion of his own power, as he had an indifferent one of what his enemies could perform, would not hear of peace on those terms; and he thought himself equal to the task of conquering all the three provinces. Indeed he had a numerous army with plenty of artillery, great and small, and plenty of all the necessaries requisite for war; but no knowledge at all about the means of availing himself of so much power.... But now, as soon as fortune has been so favourable to anyone, as to raise him suddenly to power, he from that moment fancies himself a compound of all excellence, ... nay such a man comes at last to think, that asking advice would be detracting from his own dignity, and that deferring to a sensible opinion, would be derogating from his own wisdom, be the adviser, an Aristotle or some superior being.[44]

Still, given the "modern" fact that legitimate successors to the throne could turn out to be disasters for the empire, it was, according to Ghulam Husain, justified that able and wise men should use the methods of warfare and statecraft to seize the state's helm. Perhaps his greatest hero was Ali Vardi. Yet Ali Vardi came to power by treacherously killing the nawab Sarfraz Khan. Ghulam Husain nonetheless defended Ali Vardi on consequentialist grounds:

Upon the whole, although the slaying of his Lord and benefactor's son was unquestionably one of the blackest actions that could be committed, and one of the most abominable events that could happen, yet it cannot be denied that Ser-efraz-qhan had no talents for government, and no capacity for business, and that, had his Government lasted but sometime more, such a train of evils, and such a series of endless confusions would have been the consequence of his incapacity, that disorders without number, and disturbances without end, would have arisen insensibly, and would have brought ruin and desolation on these countries and their inhabitants.[45]

Although Ghulam Husain is detailed and articulate in his explication of the arts of diplomacy, he is also clear about the role of force in statecraft. He did not believe that new laws or practices could be established in a country merely by the power of persuasion. "And, indeed, if the promulgation of new principles depended entirely on argument and reason, why should the Prince of Prophets and Chief of Messengers ... have received order to fight from the Lord of the Creation—he who was confessedly the most eloquent man of his time, whether in Arabia or in Iran?"[46]

An essential element of the arts of controlling the uncertain effects of chance in the political arena was moral conduct. Even though Ghulam Husain maintained the conventional religious forms of piety by asserting the authority of the Koran, he actually seemed to adopt a more consequentialist view of political ethics. Morally correct behavior, he explained, makes it less likely for enemies to find fault with a ruler; hence, a ruler has greater goodwill and support in times of ill fortune. Immoral conduct, on the other hand, is more likely to expedite the consequences of ill fortune. As such, observed Ghulam Husain, the immoralities and cruelties of Ali Vardi's family members hastened the calamities that struck Bengal.

It produced a series of events that proved fatal to that power and dominion, which Aaly-verdy-qhan had been rearing with so much bodily labour, and so much toil; it lighted up a blind fire which soon after these two murders, commenced emitting smoke; and which breaking out in flames at last, destroyed in its progresses all that numerous family; and extending its ravages far and near, consumed every thing in those once happy regions of Bengal.[47]

While Ghulam Husain apparently defends an ethical code established over the long duration of the Mughal state, he is clearly most concerned about the uncertainties in applying that code in a world where the certitudes of authority, loyalty, trust, or well-established precedent—all of those things on which a stable moral order is built—could not be relied on anymore. What is ethical politics in such a world? This, we might say, is the crucial early modern question in Ghulam Husain's history. One of his answers was to claim that whereas the duty of self-preservation must become paramount in such a world, one should not for that reason forget the future consequences of one's present actions. He spoke, for instance, of the noble act of Amir Beg who, after the capture of Calcutta by Siraj, delivered a number of English women to the company's ships several miles downstream. Amir Beg refused a reward that the English offered him, commenting that what he had done was only to be expected from a person of honor. Ghulam Husain then launched into an attack on those Muslims who would lay their hands on other people's properties and honor in times of chaos. "Self-defence only becomes our right; by which it is meant, that if anyone should attack our life, honour or property, and injury is not otherwise to be prevented, we have then a right, nay we are obliged to repel it by whatever means are in our power. This unquestionably is lawful to us; but not, that out of ambition and covetousness, we should, on those accounts, expose to imminent danger both ourselves and the People of God."[48]

Because ties of loyalty and kinship no longer meant anything, it was even more important for a ruler to choose the right officers and advisers. Mir Qasim, for example, was an able administrator who well understood that the English would not countenance his independence and would try to remove him by force. He reasoned that to face up to the English in battle, he would have to adopt their military methods. But he made a great error in choosing Gurgin Khan as his commander, because although the Armenian tried to inject European discipline into Mir Qasim's army, Gurgin himself had never seen battle—and he turned out to be a reckless general.[49]

One of the most memorable and moving stories running through the four volumes is the author's account of his relations with his father, Sayyid Hidayat Ali Khan, who was a senior noble in the Delhi court, but estranged from the author's immediate family. Hidayat Ali became an adviser to Prince Ali Gauhar, later to become Emperor Shah Alam II. In the days following the battle of Palashi, Ghulam Husain was in the court of Ram Narain, the governor of Patna, while Ali Gauhar was approaching Bengal from Allahabad with the imperial army. Ram Narain sent Ghulam Husain as his emissary to persuade the prince to make peace with the English. Ghulam Husain met with his father, arguing that since he knew that the imperial army was badly led and provisioned, it would be prudent of him to persuade Ali Gauhar to make peace, or at least for Hidayat Ali to leave the imperial camp. Hidayat Ali rejected the suggestion outright, maintaining "that to this day the house of Timur has never been faithless to any one." As events unfolded, the old Mughal noble became aware that the traditional practices of trust and loyalty had collapsed. Ghulam Husain tried to instruct his father in the new morality of politics, but without success. While Ghulam Husain rapidly adapted himself to the new world in which English arms and diplomatic maneuver had become unstoppable, old Hidayat Ali slowly receded into retirement, bitterness, and oblivion.

Ghulam Husain's understanding of European political and military motives was not naive. He well understood the hostilities between the English and French in Europe and America, and how they were being played out in India. What greatly impressed him, however, was how even in their enmity, the English and French displayed mutual respect toward each other. Thus, he spoke admiringly of the courtesy shown to the French general Jean Law after his surrender to the English and the boorishness of the Indian soldiers who were completely unable to appreciate this gesture toward a defeated officer.[50] Ghulam Husain also knew a great deal about the factional fights among the East India Company officials in Calcutta, although all his information must have been hearsay.

The third volume of the *Sair* contains the frequently discussed passages in which Ghulam Husain summarized his evaluation of English rule in Bengal. He was fully convinced that fighting the English with traditional Indian methods of warfare was futile: the large Indian armies were, he said, like "cities in motion"—slow, undisciplined, and unaccustomed to command. Here was perhaps the greatest technical advantage that the English had—one that was recognized by both European and Indian observers. Indeed, we know that the East India Company's directors in London were urging their officials in Bengal as early as 1765 to prevent "letting any European officers or soldiers enter into the service of the country government," and "discourage as far as in your power all military improvements among them." They thought that "the progress that the natives make in the knowledge of the art of war, both in Bengal and on the Coast of Choromandel is become a very alarming circumstance."[51] But Ghulam Husain went a step further in suggesting that English military superiority was the result of the many new sciences that they had acquired. He mentioned Muhammad Husain Fazal, who had traveled to England and returned to Murshidabad, but unfortunately, he said, no one there was interested in the new knowledge that he had brought back.[52] Needless to say, this echoes the observations of Ihtishamuddin, who incidentally, was writing down his memoirs of Britain at almost exactly the same time that Ghulam Husain was writing his history.

Ghulam Husain noted, though, that given "the faithless character of the times," the English were deeply suspicious of Indians. They were intent on assuming direct management of the affairs of state without the assistance of Indians. But the result was likely to be unfortunate. The English would not have a sufficient knowledge of the country and its practices, and could even be misled by ill-chosen and malevolent Indians. Therefore, while English institutions were often admirable, their greatest defect was that the English themselves did not converse with Indians, and so were secluded and isolated from the people they ruled.

Ghulam Husain noticed a significant contradiction in the English political institutions as he saw them in Calcutta. Clive, he remarked, had absolute power; no governor had ever had such power in India. This was the key to his rapid success. Yet soon the council in Calcutta was divided into parties and factions, and the process of decision making by consultation and vote, with directions being sought from London, became so slow that the business of government was completely stalled, making it impossible for ordinary people to get remedies. Interestingly, Ghulam Husain offered an admiring account of Haidar Ali as a ruler who had acquired absolute power and was training his troops in European methods of warfare.[53] One can see here not only a characteristic early modern moment where the collapse of empire and older forms of political virtue led to a search for a new defense of the state but also the modality of that new statecraft, which is strongly absolutist, indicating a preference for decisive leadership in the face of an unstable and uncertain political world.

If this is one side of Ghulam Husain's political theory—the search for a wise, valorous, knowledgeable, and strategically adept prince with absolute powers (even if that prince is devoid of any traditional legitimacy) who will defend the state as the precondition for peace and order, and the security and prosperity of the people—there is also a contradictory side. This appears as a defense of old-fashioned Mughal principles, but already contains the germ of something else.

In the third volume of the *Sair*, Ghulam Husain outlined a theory of government for India.[54] He talked of the natural conditions that made India a country where the comforts and riches of life were easy to acquire. This, he said, made the goal of government simply the maintenance of the conditions for the ease and prosperity of the inhabitants. All governments in India have been premised on conquest, but all the conquerors had been absorbed into the established structures of rules and institutions. Even the dogmatic Aurangzeb did not meddle with these established practices. After his death, even when the monarchs were personally worthless, the institutions carried on as before. There is a hint here of something like an "ancient constitution," which Ghulam Husain believed lay at the core of government in India, regardless of dynasties and regimes. The difficulty with the English, as he viewed it, was that they were either ignorant of these established rules or paid scant respect to them. As a result, the people could not get the protections and benefits that they expected from government. Interestingly, if Ghulam Husain was here defending a Mughal political tradition, it is not the theory of imperial sovereignty but rather the function of government in "looking after" the people. It is in looking after the people that Ghulam Husain found the English to be failing.

The contradiction between a desire for a new absolutist state and a respect for the ancient constitution also surfaced in Ghulam Husain's deep suspicion and disapproval of the class of zamindars.[55] Historians have seen in the rise of zamindars and other intermediaries in the eighteenth century a major structural change in the social formation in many regions of India.[56] Ghulam Husain considered them clear threats to the empire's viability, and constant dangers to both nobility and peasants. The centralizing impetus in him would curb the autonomy and power of the zamindars; he was thus critical of the English for not realizing this. On the other hand, the English appeared to recognize the power of the zamindars because they had traditional authority over the localities.

Ghulam Husain, of course, discussed the wealth that the English were carrying back with them from India. In some ways, this made them like Nadir Shah or the Abdalis. Iqbal Ghani Khan makes much of this as the first Indian analysis of the "economic drain" introduced by British colonial rule.[57] The drain here consisted of the "presents" demanded by company officials from Indians who sought their protection or favors. Ghulam Husain is entirely right in identifying this as a corrupt practice of government, and it was already being criticized as such in Britain. On the other hand, Khan's criticism of Ghulam Husain as someone who failed to perceive the true nature of colonialism seems hugely anachronistic. It is doubtful that the colonial economy of the mid-nineteenth century was even conceivable in the 1780s.

Rather, Ghulam Husain seems extremely perceptive in identifying the *political* elements of English rule that already made the new rulers of eastern India radically different from all previous ones. They did not know, and were making few efforts to learn, the country's languages. The new rulers had abandoned the age-old practice of granting audiences and making themselves directly approachable to their subjects. Their new judicial procedures were slow, cumbersome, and largely incomprehensible to the people. They preferred to import all the necessities and luxuries of their life from their own country, thereby depriving local producers of the patronage of their rulers, and also making the gulf between the rulers and their subjects a permanent one. In short, Ghulam Husain plainly saw, within two decades of the foundation of British rule in India, that unlike earlier conquerors, these rulers would not adapt themselves to the customs of the country but instead try to change local practices to suit their own interests.

This is the most significant aspect of Ghulam Husain's evaluation of the first two decades of British rule—his understanding of the potentially radical nature of the changes that the English were introducing in the institutions of law, sovereignty, and government. Ghulam Husain certainly did not regard the English as one more Indian player in a game whose rules had been framed by Indians, as some recent British historians would have us believe.[58] On the contrary, the absolutist principles that he appeared to be endorsing as a response to the emergent situation in India in the late eighteenth century could suggest, in opposition to his own declared allegiances, the possibility of direct resistance to British power.

Tipu as an Early Modern Absolute Monarch

> Who could have imagined in the wildest of dreams about the history of India that Tipu, the brilliant son of a man named Hyder Ali, who had started off as an ordinary soldier in the army of the ruler of Mysore, might do such things which could stun and startle history itself. This was the reason why history could not preserve the details of his family background having been unaware of the activities of Tipu.
>
> — Mohammad Ilyas Nadvi, *Tipu Sultan*, 2004

That is how a recent Urdu biography of Tipu Sultan (1749–99), written by a scholar from a major Islamic seminary in Lucknow, explains the fog surrounding the antecedents of the remarkable ruling house of Mysore founded by Haidar that ran from 1761 to 1799. A great deal of what is claimed on this subject is either myth or conjecture. What we do know with relative certainty is that Haidar was the son of a soldier of fortune, who although resolving not "to remain like foxes lurking in the holes and corners of obscurity," went through many vicissitudes in life.[59] Haidar's childhood was spent in circumstances that were quite humble, and he did not get any education. Entering the Mysore army as a cavalry officer, he soon formed his own corps, armed with flintlocks and bayonets, and backed by European gunners. Involving himself in the politics of the Wodeyar court of Mysore, Haidar eventually displaced Nanjaraj, the prime minister, made the raja a prisoner in his own palace, and took over power in 1761. He expanded the territories of the Mysore state by subjugating a series of local chiefs (called *palaiakarar*) in the Kannada and Tamil regions.

Haidar came into confrontation with the British in 1767–69; the war ended with the British suing for peace—the first time they would do so with an Indian power. The reason was Haidar's superior cavalry, which paralyzed the British army on a hilly terrain. His soldiers too were a new breed: "I never saw black troops behave so bravely as Hyder's," wrote a captain of the company's army; "all his foot were led on by Europeans."[60] Haidar is supposed to have commissioned a caricature on the signing of the treaty, showing the governor of Madras and his council kneeling before him.[61]

By the late 1770s, he had a sizable army of some twenty-eight thousand horse, fifty-five thousand foot soldiers, a number of experts in firing rockets and a few hundred French soldiers. Even though, according to Bussy, one of his French officers, Haidar was contemptuous of these French soldiers because of "their shameful cupidity," he appreciated their value in his confrontation with the British.[62] Haidar put together a confederacy with the Marathas and the nizam of Hyderabad to challenge the rising British power in southern India. In 1780, he defeated a British force under the command of Colonel William Baillie in Pollilur and seized Arcot. A French officer in Haidar's army wrote: "There is not in India an example of a similar defeat [of a British army]."[63] The scene of the battle of Pollilur is depicted in a grand mural commissioned by Tipu, still visible at the Dariya Daulat palace in Srirangapattana, in which, as Janaki Nair has shown, the victorious prince was already projecting an alternative vision of political authority to the defunct Mughal order.[64] But in 1781, the British managed to break up the confederacy and defeat Haidar's forces in three battles.

Haidar's genius, for which, as we have seen, he earned the admiration of Ghulam Husain, lay in his skilful adoption of European military techniques in order to stand up to the apparently unstoppable ascendancy of the British. In his role as a ruler, however, Haidar was doubtless an autocrat, but he did not innovate, preferring instead to leave intact the existing institutions of governance in the territories he conquered. The only significant element of economic reorganization he introduced was the attempt to collect land taxes directly from the cultivator rather than through local feudatories.[65]

When Haidar died in 1782, his son Tipu was a young man in his early thirties who had already made a reputation as a general of great courage and ability. Trained by French officers, he had led his troops to victory against a British contingent on the banks of the Coleroon River in 1782. Succeeding his father, Tipu first made peace with the British in 1784. But after declaring himself *padshah* (a title used in India by the Mughal emperor), he sent out diplomatic missions to secure political alliances with Turkey and France. His letter to Sultan Abdul Hamid of Turkey shows that Tipu had a perfectly clear idea of the historical threat posed by the British power in India:

> As a result of the revolution of fortunes and chances of events, the Timurid Empire in Hindustan has become very weak since long; and no powerful or resolute scion of the family has sat on the throne (for sometime past). Consequently, villainous Christians who were in the ports of India in the garb of traders and intent upon creating trouble and chaos, with the connivance of some of the commanders who were unmindful of their duty and were engrossed with falsehood, brought under their domination the vast territories of Bengal and half of the territories of the Deccan. They let loose floods of tyranny over the masses of the people in general and began attacking the honour of the followers of Islam in particular.[66]

In his mission to Louis XVI, he asked for ten thousand French troops to fight the English in India. He also suggested that the French monarch "out of his ancient regard would dispatch some persons skilled in every art," especially cannon founders, shipbuilders, manufacturers of chinaware, glass and mirror makers, engineers, mechanics, gold-plating experts, and so on.[67]

Neither of these missions was successful, but Tipu's enmity with the British grew rapidly. When he attacked Travancore, a British ally, in 1789, it led to war with the East India Company. For two years, Tipu held his own against the British forces until Charles, Lord Cornwallis, laid siege to Tipu's capital. Hostilities were ended in 1792 by the Treaty of Srirangapattana, in which Tipu surrendered half his territories, paid thirty million rupees, and handed over two of his sons—Abdul Khaliq, age eight, and Muiz-ud-din, age five—as hostages to the British. Tipu continued his efforts to seek military help against the British from the revolutionary government in France, though. He proposed to "the *sardars* of the French nation" that there be friendship "between the *Khuda-dad Sarkar* and the Nation of the *Sarkar*, and the French nation," and that ten thousand French soldiers and thirty thousand *habashi* (negro) soldiers, along with ships of war, be sent to India.

> Happy moment! The time has come when I can deposit in the bosom of my friends the hatred which I bear against these oppressors of the human race. If you will assist me, in a short time not an Englishman shall remain in India: you have the power and the means of effecting it, by your free Negroes, with these new citizens (much dreaded by the English) joined to your troops of the line, we will purge India of these cursed villains.[68]

Generals representing the Directory corresponded with "*Citoyen* Sultan Tipu," promising friendship but no specific military assistance. Napoléon Bonaparte wrote to "our greatest friend Tipu Sahib" from Cairo:

> You have already been informed of my arrival on the borders of the Red Sea with an innumerable and Invincible Army, full of the desire of delivering you from the Iron yoke of England.
>
> I eagerly embrace this opportunity of testifying to you the desire I have of being informed by you, by the way of Muscat and Mocha, as to your Political Situation. I would even wish you could send some Intelligent Person to Suez or Cairo, possessing your confidence, with whom I may confer.[69]

The letter never reached Tipu, because British agents intercepted it in Jeddah. Most historians agree that there was little serious intention among the French generals of the time to launch a campaign across the Indian Ocean.[70] But for Richard Wellesley (1760–1842), governor-general, the intercepted letters came as a godsend. He had already drawn up his plans for invading Tipu's territories; now he had his reason.[71] Emphasizing the alarming possibility that Napoléon's forces in Egypt might head toward India and join up with their ally in Mysore,

Wellesley stormed Tipu's capital in Srirangapattana in 1799. Fighting along-side his troops, Tipu was killed in battle.[72]

Irfan Habib has recently elaborated the argument that Haidar and Tipu were modernizing rulers.[73] Haidar's modernizing efforts were largely confined, Habib says, to introducing European techniques and discipline into his army. In this, he was something of a pioneer; several other Indian rulers such as the Nizam of Hyderabad, the Maratha general Mahadji Scindia, and later Ranjit Singh of Punjab followed his example. Tipu's efforts at "modernization" were more comprehensive, even though, Habib notes, his "intellectual horizons ... remained restricted to the old inherited learning." There is no evidence that Tipu had any conception of the new theoretical sciences or enlightened phi-losophy of the West. Thus, despite his many modernizing projects, concludes Habib, "Tipu and his Mysore were ... still far away from a real opening to mod-ern civilization."[74] As we have argued above, a simple characterization of his regime as modernizing does not get us far enough. We need to make finer distinctions within the category of the modern in order to locate the tendency more precisely in historical time as well as evaluate the discursive resources that the tendency created for future use.

Burton Stein has made the argument for regarding Tipu's regime in Mysore as a case of military fiscalism—the form of centralized revenue organization of the national state that emerged in early modern Western Europe principally as an instrument for conducting wars against foreign powers.[75] It involved, in the main, the elimination of tribute-paying petty lordships and their replacement by state officials collecting taxes directly from producers. The "system" that Tipu introduced in the territories of the Mysore state insisted on the responsibility of village heads to keep up full production on village lands and maintain com-plete records; required collectors to give separate receipts to each cultivator for each installment of the land tax, which had to be collected in cash; encouraged cultivation on wastelands, and the introduction of commercial crops such as sugarcane, sericulture, and timber for military and commercial use; brought revenue-free lands owned by religious establishments into a regime of full rev-enue collection; urged revenue officials to themselves engage in trade and bring barren lands into cultivation; initiated irrigation works under state auspices; and established gun foundries and saltpeter factories under state ownership.[76]

On the commercial side, his system introduced state trading in valuable com-modities such as sandalwood, silk, spices, coconut, rice, sulphur, and elephants. It set up state-owned *kothis* or trading houses in neighboring territories, on the western coast as far north as Kutch, and in Madras, Pondicherry, Hyderabad, and Muscat. These trading houses were to be run by trained officials operating with capital advanced by the state. The sultan was to exercise close supervision over the activities of these kothis. Following the example of the European mer-cantilist powers, he sought to impose a state monopoly on foreign trade, prohibiting private traders from importing any foreign commodities except horses, elephants, mules, camels, and guns, and banning all trade contacts with Chennapattana (Madras), the seat of British power in south India. In fact, he virtually imposed a blockade on all trade between Mysore and the British. Tipu also tried to obtain lease rights (*ijara*) in the port of Basra from the *Qaisar-i Rum* (the Ottoman sultan), so that he could, like the European powers, establish trading "factories" and dock his ships there during the rainy season in India; in exchange, he was prepared to offer similar rights to Ottoman traders in one of his ports on the western coast.[77] Finally, the central treasury provided funding for the construction of seagoing merchant and naval vessels. It is clear that Tipu's efforts at economic reorganization were prompted by a conscious understanding of the sources of European dominance. As he explained to his ambassadors: "The Christian nations who dominate the world today have been able to do so only because of their mastery over trade and industry. The good kings of Islam could promote their religion only by paying attention to these factors."[78]

In addition, there is the remarkable political fact that on being rebuffed by the imperial court in Delhi, Tipu began to use the title padshah for himself, mint coins on his own without mentioning the Mughal emperor, send embassies to the sultan of Turkey and king of France, and thus claim the status of sovereign.[79] His neighboring rulers such as the nizam of Hyderabad or Maratha Peshwas would grant him nothing more than a grudging address of nawab. The court of Shah Alam II insisted that he could only get a rank subordinate to the nizam, who was the viceroy of all southern India. But Tipu claimed to have founded a *Saltanat-i Khudadad*, a kingdom given by God. It is said that Tipu sought and obtained from the Ottoman sultan Salim, in the latter's capacity as caliph, confirmation of his claim to sovereignty over the kingdom of Mysore.[80] There appears to be no record of such a document, though, and Habib argues that Tipu considered the sultan of Turkey as an equal and not a superior.[81] Interestingly, the same embassy that went to Turkey was expected to continue its journey to France and Britain, and Tipu instructed his envoys to complain to the king of the English about the atrocities and oppressions that were being committed in India by the people of his nation, and demand the return of the fort of Tiruchirapalli that had been treacherously taken from the Mysore ruler by the English in collusion with their ally Muhammad Ali, the *amil* (revenue collector) of the Carnatic (that is, the nawab of Arcot).[82] All this evidence suggests that Tipu represented probably the strongest example of the early modern idea already encountered in Ghulam Husain of legitimacy deriving not necessarily from lineage or recognition but instead from the sheer personal ability of a monarch to hold effective power and sustain the polity.

Absolutist monarchies always have this strongly "decisionist" character, where sovereignty lies precisely in the *personal* power of the monarch to make decisions, without regard for traditional rules or precedent, and without being bound by any "ancient constitution," for that is the power required to preserve the state. Carl Schmitt has pointed out that this decisionist character derives from the mythology of the omnipotent God, as in Thomas Hobbes's Leviathan.[83] This insight provides an angle to consider Tipu's repeated invocation of his faith in Islam. Tipu minted coins not in his own name but rather by declaring God as the all-powerful sovereign, Muhammad as his Prophet, and Haidar—that is, Ali—as the hero of Islam. As Habib has remarked, this gave an aura of religious militancy to his reign that was entirely absent in Mughal imperial politics in the eighteenth century.[84]

The attempt to explain Tipu's many actions in relation to Muslims, Hindus, and Christians in terms of a consistent ideology has led to much confusion, with some accusing him of being a hateful fanatic, and others emphasizing that he made numerous grants to Hindu temples and promoted Hindu officials to senior positions in his government. It is possible, however, to argue that in the strategic aspects of his politics, Tipu was not a zealot at all but instead entirely pragmatic, dealing with Christians and Hindus both within and outside his kingdom according to the dictates of policy. But, on the claim to legitimacy of his personal authority and the sovereign foundation of his state, he needed to assert with the fullest force of conviction that his was a kingdom given by God himself, to further the cause of Islam, and that there were no limits to his absolute authority except those that God might choose to impose on him. This was a new, almost revolutionary political claim, unknown in the traditional culture of Mughal politics.

Tipu was also far more interventionist in the reform of social practices than other Indian rulers, whether Hindu or Muslim. He prohibited the consumption of liquor and intoxicants in his kingdom; he banned prostitution and the employment of female slaves in domestic service (even though we find him instructing his envoys to Turkey to purchase "five or six fair-faced slave girls from among Turks, Arabs or Mughals").[85] Tipu tried to stop polyandry in Malabar and Coorg, decreed that Malabar women could not go outside their homes without covering the upper half of their bodies, and ended human sacrifice at the Kali temple in Mysore. In order to control wasteful expenses on festivities, he ordered that a village should not spend more than 1 percent of its wealth on charities and festivals.[86]

The distinctness of the Mysore regime in late eighteenth-century India was very much noticed by British officials of the East India Company. Indeed, their perception of Haidar and Tipu as fearsome and formidable enemies was undoubtedly shaped by the idea that they were quite unlike other Indian rulers, and more like ambitious and energetic rulers in the Western world. An anonymous article in the *Annual Register* of 1783 published from London concluded that Haidar was "one of the first politicians of his day, whether in Europe or Asia. He was so far from being naturally cruel, that he differed in that respect from all the eastern conquerors of whom we have any knowledge."[87] Innes Munro, an ex-captive in Haidar's prison, compared him favorably with Frederick the Great of Prussia.[88] Edward Moor, who served in the company's army in Mysore in 1794 and later became an Indological scholar, claimed that if one did not "choose to be carried away by the torrent of popular opinion," one would "find the same excuse for the restlessness of Tippoo, as for that of any other ambitious sovereign; and on the subject of his cruelties, venture to express a doubt whether they may not possibly have been exaggerated."[89] And Thomas Munro, later to become governor of Madras, wrote in 1790:

> [Mysore, has] the most simple and despotic monarchy in the world, in which every department, civil and military, possesses the regularity and system communicated to it by the genius of Hyder, and in which all pretensions derived from high birth being discouraged, all independent chiefs and Zamindars subjected or extirpated, ... and almost every employment of trust or consequence conferred on men raised from obscurity, gives to the government a vigour hitherto unexampled in India.... The character of vigour has been so strongly impressed on the Mysore government by the abilities of its founders, that it may retain it, even under the reign of a weak prince, or a minor.... Tippoo supports an army of 110,000 men, a large body of which is composed of slaves, called Chailies [*chela*], trained on the plan of the Turkish janizaries, and follows with great eagerness every principal of European tactics ... and he is, with all of his extraordinary talents, a furious zealot in a faith which founds eternal happiness on the destruction of other sects.[90]

In his analysis of Tipu's regime, Stein acknowledges Tipu's success in intensifying the penetration of money and markets into the Mysore economy, and simultaneously bringing economic institutions under greater state control through fiscal methods and state trading. But Stein argues that the political shell of "patrimonial sultanism" that Tipu continued to hold was incompatible with the new economic tendencies he sought to promote.[91] Before Stein, Asok Sen had compared Tipu's regime with the absolute monarchies of Europe operating in accordance with the political-economic ideas of mercantilism.[92] In a somewhat similar vein to Stein, Sen finds that the changes introduced by Tipu in the agricultural, commercial, and industrial economy, although often radical, were insufficient to create the conditions for industrial capitalism of the kind already inaugurated in England. Mere "originality of will and purpose" of a brave and able sultan could not accomplish this task. Nikhiles Guha, in his 1985 monograph on Tipu's Mysore, also emphasizes the limited nature of the changes brought about by the ruler: they were marked by greater efficiency rather than by genuine innovation. It was more appropriate to regard Tipu "as a successful instance of the personalised monarchy that had prevailed for long in India."[93] Guha maintains that along with the regime of Muhammad Ali in Egypt in the early nineteenth century, Tipu's Mysore contained few potentialities for the development of industrial capitalism.

Intriguingly, because of their focus on state formations, and hence on the long-term structural conditions for historical transition, none of these historians regarded the contingent outcomes of the military confrontations between Tipu and the British as significant in determining the fate of military fiscalism or mercantile absolutism in India. Stein, on the contrary, made a strong argument that the military-fiscalist methods introduced by Tipu were in fact continued under the East India Company's administration in the nineteenth century, while Sen suggests that absolutist methods, relying solely on a state bureaucracy to bring about a social transformation, were bound to fail if autonomous productive initiatives did not emerge from civil society.

This contention, from the mid-1980s, cannot be left hanging. More can and needs to be said today about the absolutist early modern in South Asian history. In particular, if we can get rid of the idea (easier now than it was twenty-five years ago) that historical transitions to modernity everywhere must follow some familiar trajectories already witnessed in Europe or North America—that military fiscalism or mercantile absolutism must, for instance, lead to an English-style industrial revolution—then we would be better able to appreciate the continued relevance, both discursive and affective, of the absolutist early modern in the colonial and postcolonial history of South Asia.

Specifically, we can list the following elements of the absolutist early modern tendency in eighteenth-century India that are relevant in evaluating the historical potentialities of change in the so-called Orient, before European dominance, and with it the forms of colonial modernity, became irresistible. These are components that allow for a comparative discussion of regimes such as Muhammad Ali's Egypt, Ottoman Turkey in the period of reforms, and not least, Japan after the Meiji restoration.

First, in the context of the search by European powers for aggressive commercial expansion and territorial conquests in the East, the absolutist early modern tendency shows a new and greatly heightened awareness of the state sovereignty question. Rulers who may be said to represent this tendency were more conscious than others before them of the need to assert, against foreign challengers, their sovereign jurisdiction over their territories, fortifications, and economic resources. Second, such rulers became conversant with a new way of comparing their powers with that of others, observing the "sources" of the superiority of others, and trying to emulate them in order to match their powers. Third, they identified novel ways of deploying the means of power through new techniques of discipline, especially in the sphere of military technologies and personnel. Fourth, in order to strengthen their military and fiscal resources, these rulers began to use the state's sovereign powers to intervene in and change political, economic, and social institutions, sometimes in radical ways. They produced states that were not only autocratic but also absolutist and interventionist. Finally, the absolutist early modern tendency responded to the new historical conditions of uncertainty and instability not by reasserting a conservative dogma of dynastic legitimacy but rather by stressing the personal qualities of effective and decisive leadership displayed by the prince. The absolutist element in this early modern tendency was, in this sense, not an element of conservative restoration; it was potentially revolutionary.

THE TIGER OF MYSORE

> When Tippoo vowed to raise the Crescent's fame,
> And on the holy war Fate seemed to frown;
> He, Sultaun-like, preferred a deathless name,
> And left an earthly—for a Martyr's—crown.
> —J. B. Gilchrist, "Miscellaneous Correspondence," 1802

This is the epitaph on Tipu's grave, composed by the poet Shabbir, and here translated by Gilchrist, professor of Urdu at Fort William College in Calcutta. It reminds pilgrims and visitors to the Gumboz mausoleum in Lalbagh in Srirangapattana, where Tipu is buried next to his father, Haidar, that of all the princes of India in the second half of the eighteenth century, Tipu was the one who chose to stand his ground against the British and fight to the death. The inner walls of the mausoleum are entirely covered in the tiger-stripe or *babri* design that Tipu had made his own—a design that appeared on his jackets, turbans, and handkerchiefs, on the bindings of books from his library, and as watermarks on his paper. The tiger motif was ubiquitous on the uniforms and weapons used by his soldiers, and on Tipu's coins, flags, and throne. An enduring curiosity for more than two hundred years has been the mechanical tiger—now displayed in the Victoria and Albert Museum in London—which can be seen devouring a British soldier while emitting snarls, to the accompaniment of the victim's wails.[94]

There has been much speculation on the sources of this choice of the tiger motif by Tipu and its intended meaning.[95] Some have claimed that it invokes Ali, the fourth caliph and son-in-law of the Prophet. Mohammad Moienuddin has argued that Tipu consciously adopted the tiger design because it was the mount of Chamundeswari, the presiding deity of the kingdom of Mysore.[96] Even though its use was not unprecedented among Indian rulers, it was unusual, and there is no question that the sign came to be identified with Tipu to such an extent that even in his lifetime, British writers started to refer to him as the Tiger of Mysore—an appellation that has stuck to this day.

If strength, vigor, and determination are the qualities that characterized Tipu's absolutism, the tiger motif captured it perfectly. But as Linda Colley has

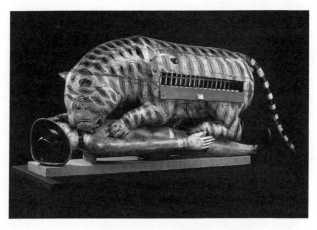

Figure 8. *Tipu's Tiger,* carved wooden effigy containing an organ, captured 1799. *Photo:* © *Victoria and Albert Museum, London*

suggested, "For the British, the tiger evoked India most tellingly at this stage because it was dangerous, beyond knowing, and beyond control."[97] In fact, it was during the wars against Tipu in the 1790s that a decisive shift took place in the British public perception of the empire in India. The doubts, ambiguities, unease, and soul-searching that distinguished the reception of the returning "nabobs," or impassioned accusations of venality, deception, and tyrannical rule that flew around in the early years of the proceedings against Hastings, were now gone. The British nation stood united in support of the campaigns, first of Cornwallis, and later of Wellesley, against "the cruel and relentless enemy; the intolerant bigot or furious fanatic; ... the sanguinary tyrant."[98]

P. J. Marshall carefully documents this shift in public perception. Fed by official as well as private reports, the war in Mysore from 1790 to 1792 received wide coverage in the British press. This was soon followed by several books, illustrated with maps and battle plans, claiming to be histories of the war. Opinion was, with negligible exceptions, unanimous in support of Cornwallis. "Enthusiasm," writes Marshall, "was virtually unalloyed."[99] The popular sentiments can be gauged from some of the songs that circulated in Britain at this time:

> Now d'ye see the queer chief would have fain made us bellow,
>> But for gallant Cornwallis, that fine British fellow;
> While Tippoo made sure how, to kill us and eat us,
>> With half of his kingdom we made him to treat us.[100]

A widely publicized episode, memorialized in prose, verse, paintings, and prints as well as on ceramics, medallions, and all varieties of knickknacks, was the taking of Tipu's sons as hostages by Cornwallis and his kind treatment of the young boys—behavior that was in dramatic contrast with the alleged cruelty of Tipu's earlier treatment of British prisoners. But the popular songs leave some doubt as to whether there was not a more pervasive sentiment of revenge in British hearts:

> Drink a health to brave Cornwallis, and all his valiant men,
>   And to all bold commanders who strive their country's rights to gain,
> And Tippoo's two sons, as Hostages we have got,
>   Should they arrive in England, who knows what may be their lot.[101]

The matter of Tipu's cruelty had a special place in the popular representation of him as the incarnation of Oriental brutality. One pamphlet asserted: "He, among other moderns of the same character, may be said to be a living example of Eastern barbarity. Even his father, the implacable Hyder Ali Khan, has been exceeded by him in acts of the most unparalleled cruelty; his savage manners yielding only to the baseness and malignity of his heart."[102] But as Kate Teltscher has shown, this representation evolved in a curious way. It began with a published accusation by a British soldier that in attacking the fort of Anantpur in Bidanur in 1783, the company's troops had engaged in unscrupulous massacre, pillage, and rape of women. The lower ranks had gone berserk, indulging in a murderous orgy of brutality and lust. When Tipu recaptured the fort, he was equally ferocious and retaliated by executing British prisoners.

These charges were officially refuted by the company's directors, opening the way to a virtual deluge of accounts of the cruelties faced by British captives in Tipu's prisons. Well over a thousand British soldiers were prisoners in Mysore.[103] Many had been circumcised, given Muslim names, made chelas or slaves in Tipu's army, and assigned the task of instructing the Mysore soldiers in the European-style drill. As James Bristow, a former prisoner in Mysore, put it in an account that was widely reprinted and read: "We were obliged to perform an office, which, however small the benefit we took care the practitioners should derive from it, could not but cause the deepest affliction, when we reflected they were the detested enemies of our country whom we were compelled to instruct in that very art which would prove destructive to our countrymen."[104] Other British prisoners were chained in heavy irons and condemned to hard labor.[105]

Why did Tipu act in this way? The reason, according to these captivity narratives, lay in the fact that he was the extreme manifestation of that well-known type—namely, the Oriental despot—who treated his own subjects with untold harshness and cruelty, and not surprisingly, dealt with prisoners from foreign lands with even greater savagery. His behavior also was aggravated by his religious fanaticism; he nursed an implacable hatred for the infidel Christian, as documented by the large volume of his orders and writings that started to circulate in English translation. Even his innovative schemes of government were ridiculed as the self-obsessed, power-crazy fancies of a tyrant. Yet there was without doubt the lurking fear that by diligently learning the secrets of European supremacy, Haidar and Tipu were threatening to become much like European powers themselves. Could that be allowed to happen? The thought had to be banished as soon as it appeared. How could a barbaric Oriental tyrant become a rival to British power? As Chris Bayly observes: "By the early 1790s it had become clear that the Company could never coexist with such more vigorous Indian regimes which sought to face down European power with its own weapons, exclusion of rivals from trade and a strong mobile army."[106]

The idea that the wars in Mysore were a national cause was not only a popular sentiment among people generally in Britain. When Philip Francis asked in Parliament, "Let us know, once, for all, whether a war in India is a national war or not," the answer was "an unequivocal yes." Several royal regiments had been added to the company's troops, strengthening "the impression in the public at home that the Mysore war was indeed a national one fought for national objectives, not a local Indian one in which the arms of the state were helping the Company to further its own particular interests." The revelation that Tipu was in secret correspondence with revolutionary France gave further fuel to the argument that in helping the company's authorities in India to move against him, the British government was actually dealing with the nation's enemies. Indeed, as Marshall concludes: "Old-style eighteenth-century 'patriotism,' which had been libertarian ... was giving way to a more authoritarian nationalism in which monarchy and army and, as the Mysore War demonstrated, empires of conquest overseas, were becoming integral parts."[107]

Yet the celebration of Cornwallis's moderation and humanity also emphasized another element that would henceforth become an integral part of the new imperial ideology that would dominate the nineteenth century. Glimmerings of this new sensibility can be noticed even in some of the captivity stories that came out of Mysore. William Thomson, for instance, compiled many such tales in his widely read book of 1788. In marked contrast to Holwell's account of the Black Hole, in which most British prisoners descended to the level of brutes, Thomson presented stories that "exhibit human nature in an amiable light."

> The Narrative of what happened to our men under confinement with the Barbarians, is not only affecting, but in some measure instructive.... The sensibility of our captive countrymen and friends was powerfully excited, and the energy of their minds called forth in most ingenious contrivances to beguile the languor of total inoccupation, to supply conveniencies and comforts, and, on some occasions, to elude a sudden

massacre. The strength of their sympathy with one another; … the longing of circumcised Europeans and slave-boys, though in the enjoyment of unconstrained exercise and air and all the necessaries of life, to join their countrymen in irons and exposed to assassination and poison; … their anxiety to make some pecuniary recompense to such of the poor natives as had treated them with kindness, &c.[108]

The diaries and letters of the European prisoners revealed how ingeniously and assiduously they kept up secret communications among themselves, exchanging news, devising stratagems, and keeping up their spirits.[109] "When you wish to answer this," said one clandestine message, "or at any other time to write to us, let the signal be, the putting a handkerchief over your turban, whilst at drill on the parade."[110] To become a great imperial power across the world, the British at this time needed to persuade themselves that they were "a virtuous, striving and devoted people," that they were "good men, and therefore incapable of bad deeds." As Colley notes: "The rewriting of Mysore captivity ordeals from the 1780s onwards was one of the ways in which—very much with official sponsorship—the British military overseas was repackaged for improved domestic consumption."[111] Correspondingly, in marked contrast to Clive's or Orme's rhetoric, the British would henceforth be depicted as having invaded Mysore, in Marshall's words, "not as conquerors but as liberators of the mass of the population from the tyranny of Tipu. The annexation of new territories would be an act of benevolence, not of ambition."[112]

But this was political rhetoric appropriate for an expanding national public in Britain. Military historians, writing for the political elite, instead were careful to underline the legal and strategic implications of the Mysore victory. "To the free and uncontrolled exercise of the right of conquest," wrote Mark Wilks, British political resident in Mysore after the restoration of the Wodeyar court, and an inveterate critic of Tipu and his regime, "no obstacle existed in the internal state of the country." There was no question of allowing a son of Tipu to claim even a ceremonial right of succession. The reason was political:

The interests, the habits, the prejudices and passions, the vices, and even the virtues of such a prince, must have concurred to cherish an aversion to the English name and power, and an eager desire to abet the cause of their enemies. A hostile power would have been weakened, not destroyed: and a point of union for every hostile machination would have remained in the centre of the English possessions.[113]

Tipu's sons were taken away in captivity to Vellore, and after some time to the even more secure surroundings of Calcutta, where they would live and die under direct imperial surveillance.

Were Indian writers of the time persuaded by these new imperial claims? Mirza Abu Taleb of Lucknow and Murshidabad, who visited Britain in 1800–

1801, almost immediately after Tipu had been killed and his regime dismantled, was well informed of the war in Mysore and witnessed a stage production in Dublin called *The Capture of Seringapatam*. Abu Taleb thought that it was Tipu's secret correspondence with the French, and especially the threat of Napoléon's army landing on the shores of India, that alarmed the British.

> Tippoo either was ignorant of the power of the English *nation*, and judged of their strength and ability by the wars in which he had formerly been engaged with them, at a time when the councils of the English were not united; or imputed their *moderation* on a former occasion to some less worthy motive: he therefore would not listen to this salutary exhortation, but boldly determined on hostility; and, led on by his own destiny, instead of pursuing his father's mode of warfare, that is, by laying waste the country, and harassing the English with his cavalry and repeated skirmishes, he foolishly tried his strength in a general engagement; and when defeated, shut himself up in the fortress of Seringapatam; where he vainly hoped to resist people, who, by their contrivances, would scale the heavens, if requisite.[114]

Viewing these events from Britain at the turn of the century, Abu Taleb was certain that British dominance could never be successfully challenged head-on. He therefore was not surprised by the rapidity of Tipu's fall. Nevertheless, he seemed to believe there was another mode of challenging Britain that the Mysore ruler had been unwise to ignore.

> Had Tippoo acted with common prudence, he should have entrusted the defence of Seringapatam to one of his generals, and remained with his army outside; where, by cutting off the supplies of the English, and frequently harassing them, he might have prolonged the siege; and, at all events, could have retreated to some other part of his territories, and continued the war: but he had too much pride to leave his family and wealth in a fortress invested by the enemy, and resolved rather to die in defence of what he considered his honour.[115]

Abu Taleb had many other things to say about British power, as we will discuss in the next chapter. But his understanding of the failure of Tipu's frontal resistance clearly indicates that he did not think that the absolutist path to modernity had any future in India. Coping with the British challenge, he was sure, would require other strategies. Along with a new generation of Indian intellectuals who were coming into close contact with modern Western ideas and institutions, Abu Taleb was looking for new possibilities.

Meanwhile, in Britain there were a few dissenting voices among writers and artists who did not join in the nationalist chorus against the threat of revolution as well as godlessness represented by France and its allies. Yet they had little influence. Burke, who had a great deal to say about the company's misadventures in India, "did not much approve of the war" against Tipu, but did not say anything about it because he was too dependent on the government ministers in his campaign against Hastings.[116] In 1757, however, the year of Palashi and before he had begun his political career, Burke had written a philosophical essay on the distinction between the sublime and the beautiful in which he had brought up the example of dangerous tropical animals:

> We have commonly about us animals of a strength that is considerable, but not pernicious. Amongst those we never look for the sublime: it comes upon us in the gloomy forest, and in the howling wilderness, in the form of the lion, the tiger, the panther, or rhinoceros. Whenever strength is only useful, and employed for our benefit or our pleasure, then it is never sublime; for nothing can act agreeably to us, that does not act in conformity to our will; but to act agreeably to our will, it must be subject to us; and therefore can never be the cause of a grand and commanding conception.... In short, wheresoever we find strength, and in what light soever we look upon power, we shall all along observe the sublime the concomitant of terror, and contempt the attendant on a strength that is subservient and innoxious.[117]

After Tipu's fall, his terrifying tiger remained, in the British imagination, a grand and commanding conception. In the scheme of empire, though, it had to be subjected to Britain's will. It could become an exotic creature to be kept in an English menagerie. Already in 1785, the following advertisement appeared in the *Calcutta Gazette* seeking to persuade potential buyers that Bengal tigers were a bargain:

> Two elegant young Royal Tigers, male and female, vary tame and playful, and would answer the purpose of sending to Europe. The lowest price is 800 Sicca Rupees. Their expenses in victualling are very trifling; they now cost two annas per day, and they are very fat and in good order.[118]

Or else the tiger could be hunted. Thus, while Tipu's tiger was displayed as an object of morbid curiosity in a London museum, in India the animal became the ubiquitous sign of imperial manliness in the form of a carcass lying under the boot of the British shikari. The fearsome tiger had been made subservient and innocuous. In its place, the power that would now lay down the law in the Orient was that of the British lion—rampant.

THE MYSORE FAMILY IN CALCUTTA

The Esplanade in Calcutta now runs west to east from the gate of Raj Bhavan, the residence of the governor of West Bengal, to Lenin Sarani, still popularly

Figure 9. *Lord and Lady Curzon after a Hunt*, photograph by Deen Dayal, 1902. © *The British Library Board. All Rights Reserved. Source: British Library Images (592(1) Photo 5)*

known as Dharmatala Street. Raj Bhavan was previously known as Government House and was built by Lord Wellesley in the early nineteenth century, in the style of a grand English stately home, as the official residence of the governor-general of India. The Esplanade was constructed in the 1770s to mark the outer periphery of the new Fort William. At the point where the Esplanade gives way to Dharmatala Street, which is also where Chowringhee (now officially called Jawaharlal Nehru Road) crosses them from north to south—that is to say, flippantly, where Lenin meets Nehru, at one of the busiest, noisiest, and most chaotic intersections in the city—stands a mosque, of modest size, but strikingly elegant and dignified, provided one is lucky enough to find a suitable angle of vision. That is not easy, because the mosque is surrounded on all sides by stalls where clothes, stationery, posters, calendars, and DVDs are on sale.

If one peeps inside, one might get a glimpse of a black banner hanging above the steps leading up to the prayer hall. On the banner is inscribed, in English:

> AMERICA BRITAIN AND ISRAIL
> ARE THE CHIEF OF TERRORIST

Another banner says somewhat obscurely in English:

> BLOOD OF INNOCENT PEOPLE OF
> LEBONAN WILL BRING THE COLOUR

The Urdu slogan below makes it clear that "will bring the colour" is a bizarrely literal translation of the Hindustani phrase *rang layegi*, meaning "will transform," "will turn the tables," or more emphatically, "will accomplish wonders." The mosque is popularly known as "Tipu Sultan's mosque," although the connection is somewhat distant. Next to the gate is an inscription, mostly hidden behind piles of T-shirts and denim jackets. It reads as follows:

> This Musjid was erected during the Government of Lord Auckland, G.C.B., by the Prince Gholam Mahomed, son of the late Tippoo Sultan, in gratitude to God and in commemoration of the Honorable Court of Directors granting him the arrears of his stipend in 1840.

The irony could not have been more telling. A mosque that goes by the name of Tipu Sultan was built by his son in the heart of British Calcutta to acknowledge the granting by the East India Company's government of arrears of stipend due to him under the terms of settlement imposed on his family after the British conquest of Mysore. Ghulam Muhammad, Tipu's eleventh son, was the most prominent member of the Mysore family in Calcutta. He was on familiar terms with senior British officials and was nominated to serve on various public bodies. He visited Britain and other countries in Europe in 1854–55, and soon after was knighted for his philanthropic services. When he died in 1872, the *Englishman* of Calcutta remarked: "A staunch Muhammadan, consistent follower of the Prophet, Gholam Muhammad was nonetheless a most loyal subject to the Queen." The obituary noted that the assassination a few months before of the viceroy Joseph, Lord Mayo, at the hands of an Afghan political convict in the Andaman prison settlement had greatly affected Ghulam Muhammad. "Night and day he lamented the premature end of his greatest friend.... At his age the sad end of his greatest benefactor was continually preying upon his mind, and eventually produced a condition of nervous excitement which interfered materially with sound sleep. Upon this dengue supervened."[119]

But it took a long time before Tipu's descendants, banished to Calcutta, were recognized as loyal subjects of Queen Victoria. After the fall of Srirangapattana in 1799, Colonel Arthur Wellesley, the future Duke of Wellington, was given the responsibility of removing the family of the dead sultan to the fort of Vellore, ninety miles south of Madras. Along with their considerable entourage, the Mysore party confined in Vellore numbered some three thousand people. In 1806, a mutiny broke out among the company's troops stationed at Vellore; it was alleged that two of Tipu's sons—princes Muiz-ud-din and Mohi-ud-din—provided direct encouragement. It was then decided to remove the Mysore family once more—this time a thousand miles away to Calcutta. Tipu's begams, sons, daughters-in-law, grandchildren, and other close relatives, numbering fifty-two, were sent to the swampy and largely uninhabited village of Rasapagla, south of the city, where they were accommodated in four houses. Muiz-ud-din, who along with his brother Abdul Khaliq had been the two sons taken hostage by Cornwallis in 1792, was imprisoned in the Calcutta jail because of his supposed link with the Vellore mutiny. The English lawyer William Hickey, who was allowed to visit Muiz-ud-din in prison, later declared that picking on him "as the object of peculiar severity was most cruel and unjust ... the suspicions raised against Moiz oo Deen and the other princes, originated in the Government of Madras, the members of which had propagated such report with the double view of quieting the minds of the people in general, and in order to pacify the remains of His Majesty's 69th Regiment, which continued in a state of dreadful insubordination." The imprisoned prince complained bitterly of not being allowed the use of writing materials. Hickey arranged for these, "taking special care that he neither received any written address from any person whomsoever nor should send any letter or writing to any person whatsoever."[120] It was not before spending fourteen years in jail that Muiz-ud-din was allowed to join the rest of his family.

Members of the exiled family were given allowances, to be paid out of the state revenues of Mysore. Even today, their descendants are paid stipends from funds provided by the government of Karnataka. But the exiles were also put under strict regulations and surveillance. They were to "refrain from every attempt or design hostile to Government, to the tranquillity of the country." They were not to "quit their habitation, in order to make visits, or from any other reason, without the previous approbation of the Superintendents." The most remarkable prohibitions were as follows:

> That they shall not attend processions, or other public ceremonies, on the occasion of religious festivals, or domestic events, which are usually celebrated in a public way.
>
> That they shall effect no splendour or display in their way of life at home, or elsewhere, calculated to attract public notice, but shall enjoy the personal comforts and accommodation provided for them, with as much privacy as possible.
>
> That they shall avoid as much as possible all intercourse with other families, and generally with natives of India; that all letters, either written or received by them and their families, shall be subject to the inspection of the officers of Government.
>
> That no persons shall be invited or received into their families from the coast, without the previous consent of Government, and finally, that they be regulated in these and all other particulars of their conduct and behaviour, by the advice of the gentlemen appointed to superintend their affairs.[121]

With the passage of time, the Mysore family did come to acquire a presence in the city of Calcutta, especially in the southern section that is now known as Tollygunge.[122] They built some splendid houses and mosques—notably the Shahi Masjid and Zohra Begam Masjid, both constructed in a Dakhani style unknown in eastern India; the Khas Mahal, which now houses a law college; the Nach Kothi, which is currently a high school; and the Bara Mahal and Pul Pahar, which still house, among numerous tenants and squatters, Tipu's heirs. Several streets in the area bear names of prominent family members. Notwithstanding the early prohibition on processions, the Muharram *julus* starting from the Mysore family quarters in Tollygunge became a regular feature of the city's calendar of spectacles. The settlement around the mosque is now little more than a shabby slum, and the city's newspapers periodically carry stories of descendants of the Mysore sultan earning a living by driving a rickshaw or even begging on the streets. There is no longer any trace of royal splendor or elegance left here, no more than the decrepit remains of the clock tower gate that once marked the entrance to the family estate and from which—Ghari Ghar—the local bus stop gets its name. Frayed it may be, but the presence of Tipu's heirs can still be observed in Calcutta.

Still, the British attempt to sever all connections between the exiled family and their kin and followers in Mysore appears to have succeeded. In the Gumboz mausoleum in Srirangapattana, attendants speak movingly about Tipu's last stand. He became a *shahid*, they say. His sons? They were captured by the British and—they continue, in complete sincerity—were taken away and secretly killed. They all became martyrs. Exile a thousand miles away was, after all, little else but death.

CHAPTER FOUR

Liberty of the Subject

THE BRITISH FORT in Calcutta was badly damaged by the siege of 1756 and its aftermath. Siraj, having renamed the city Alinagar, even had a mosque built inside the fort walls. The decision was made, soon after its recapture by the British in 1757, to abandon the old fort and build a new one. Captain Robert Barker, who would later rise to be commander in chief of the Bengal Army under Hastings, prepared a plan for a new fort on slightly raised ground to the east of the old fort, noting that since most of the structures there were "houses of no consequence and black people's huts," clearing the area for new construction would not pose too many problems.[1]

But Barker's plan was dropped—it is said, because of opposition from Clive. The story is credible, since the alternative plan was substantially more ambitious, and it is unlikely that it could have been adopted by the council in Calcutta, against the explicit advice of the company's directors in London, without Clive's encouragement. The new plan involved the resettlement of the inhabitants of the village of Gobindapur located south of the town, because that is where Clive argued the fort should be built. Strategically, the new Fort William would be primarily defended against attacks from the river, and naturally protected by forests to the east and south.

THE NEW FORT WILLIAM

Relocating the inhabitants did not pose as much of a problem as might have been expected, due to the plentiful funds made available by the new nawab, Mir Jafar, as restitution for the damages inflicted on Calcutta by Siraj. The propertied families of Gobindapur, including not only the well-established Seths and Basaks but also the newly emergent Debs, Ghoshals, and Tagores, were handsomely compensated. Nabakrishna Deb took his large establishment to Shobhabazar. Gokul Ghoshal moved south to Khidirpur to build a new mansion.[2] Nilmani Tagore resettled in Pathuriaghata, just north of the Great Bazar of Sutanuti, from where a branch of the family would later move further north to Jorasanko to become one of the most celebrated families in the cultural life of modern India.[3] It is not known to what extent those inhabitants of Gobindapur who did not come within the protected circles of rich patrons were also compensated.[4] The flourishing market of Gobindapur moved to the village of Chetla to the south.[5]

Little survives in Calcutta's public memory today of Gobindapur's evacuation. The new Fort William still functions as the headquarters of the Eastern Command of the Indian Army, and the surrounding grounds are the focus of much anxiety for environmentalists, who treat them as a pristine patch of grass gifted to the city by Mother Earth. That the Maidan was a densely populated village 250 years ago has been wholly forgotten. Forgetfulness is a necessary attribute not only of modernizers but also of its critics.

The clearing of Gobindapur was quick and free of trouble. The actual construction of the fort, however, came up against numerous difficulties and took almost twenty years to complete. Captain John Brohier arrived in Calcutta in July 1757, sent by the company's directors in London to plan and supervise the construction.[6] He laid out elaborate plans for new fortifications. In December 1759, we find the council of Bengal writing to the directors in London: "We are sorry to inform Your Honours that the expence of the new citadel is likely to prove much heavier than was at first expected."[7] A year later, the directors were complaining: "The expense of the fortifications at Fort William already amount to an excessive sum, and if completed upon the extensive plan, adopted contrary to our original intentions, will be immense."[8]

But Bengal in the aftermath of Palashi was rife with corruption. The Brohier story is typical of the times. In April 1760, the directors in London were asking why Brohier, who had apparently "relinquished his trust," had been readmitted into the company's service and was continuing to direct the fort's rebuilding.[9] In January 1761, the council in Calcutta wrote to London about "great Frauds committed in carrying on the new Works by a combination of those who were employed upon them." None other than Holwell, then governor, had "try'd to discover to what length and by whom they had been carried on," and concluded that Brohier and his assistant John Louis, along with two Portuguese writers and two Indian banians, had embezzled more than five hundred thousand rupees. Brohier was put under arrest, but on being released on parole, had jumped bail and was still absconding.[10] The council, however, tried to reassure the directors that "the Body of the place [the fort] is almost compleated excepting the Gateways which are the business now in hand."[11]

Back in London, the directors were thoroughly skeptical of the inquiries carried out by Holwell's council. "We must observe," they responded, "that your Enquiry and Proceedings are too Superficial as we cannot imagine the Banians could without the Privity or even Consent of their Masters be guilty of such gross Frauds, and there is the greatest reason to believe that if you had gone deeper therein you might have found some of our own Servants the principal Plunderers." The directors issued a further admonition to their representatives in Bengal: "We do declare that we expect and positively direct if our Servants employ Banians or Black People under them, they shall be accountable for their Conduct and make good whatever the Company may be wronged of by such Banians or Black People." The council in Bengal was asked to "resume the Enquiry."[12]

The records tell us nothing more of any inquiry, yet meanwhile, a new problem had appeared. Already in 1759, orders had been passed that peons were to be sent "into the pergunnahs" to round up eight thousand coolies to work on the fort's construction.[13] "The method of obliging the Farmers of the Purgunnahs to supply Coolies for the new Works was found to be attended with great Difficulties…. [T]he violent Methods the Farmers were obliged to use with the Tenants caused much Complaint & must if continued have been greatly detrimental to the Produce of the Lands."[14] To tackle the problem of overpayment and pilferage, an Indian banian was appointed for every hundred coolies and a European was assigned to every thousand, "to muster them as a check on the banians, and see that all the Portuguese and peons do their respective duties."[15] In 1762, Captain Antoine-Louis Henri Polier was appointed to supervise the construction.[16]

Polier was a young Swiss engineer, one in a succession of European experts in military technology who were at this time being employed by the East India Company—confirming the fact that the science of fortifications and land warfare was, in the eighteenth century, more developed on the Continent than it was in Britain, and that there were more experts from European countries available for hire across the world. Polier was to have quite a remarkable career as a military engineer in the company, and later in the kingdom of Awadh, retiring as a fabulously wealthy person in a château in Provence, playing the role of a Jacobin fellow traveler, only to die tragically in 1795 at the hands of peasant bandits.[17]

Building the new Fort William in Calcutta was one of his early assignments; during this period, he also drew a wonderful panoramic view of the fort from the river.[18] Given the continued shortage of laborers, Polier was empowered to seize all the bricklayers of Calcutta, but even this coercive tactic did not work. The newly achieved dominance of the East India Company over political and commercial affairs in Bengal clearly had turned Calcutta into something of a boomtown, and those in the building trades were in huge demand. Even the hundred or so bricklayers expressly sent to Calcutta from Britain to work on the new fort deserted to take up jobs with private employers. The directors in London were losing their patience: "The main body of the fort it may be necessary to finish, but no more of the out-works are to be done than are absolutely necessary."[19] By 1766, Polier had moved on, earning a commendation from the company in recognition of his services in rebuilding the fort.[20]

In 1768, it was ordered that "no person wherever residing within the Company's limits or under their protection, should commence new buildings of any kind in and about Calcutta ... and that all workmen registered as engaged upon buildings already in hand should be seized for public service." On express instructions from London, the work of constructing the ravelins, ditches, and glacis was given out to contractors rather than kept under the direct charge of company staff.[21] The directors also declared that they were "extremely solicitous to have the Governor reside and Company's Business carried on there [within the fort] entirely instead of having the different Offices dispersed about the Town in the manner they are at present."[22] As it happened, this instruction was never followed.

Yet the problem of the supply of skilled laborers persisted. The company's resident at the nawab's court in Murshidabad and the faujdar of Hugli were asked to send workers.[23] In June 1770, about ten thousand workers were assembled, largely by force, but within four months, more than half had fled. Incidentally, this was when a devastating famine was ravaging Bengal, so that the labor shortage could not have been because employment was plentiful. The directors finally decided that enough was enough and specific budgetary limits had to be set: "We hereby peremptorily direct that you do not, on any pretence whatsoever, expend, in one year, more than to the amount of one hundred thousand pounds on the fortifications, cantonments, buildings and works.... [W]e strictly enjoin you to confine your view to the completion of the new fort and such works as are most immediately necessary for the security of our settlements."[24] The new fort was put to partial use in 1773, and the fortifications were at last completed in 1781. The entire construction was estimated to cost two million pounds.[25]

In the context of eighteenth-century military thinking, the design of the new Fort William was innovative. As events unfolded in Bengal after Palashi, it became clear that the British settlement in Calcutta would face no military threats from local political powers. The only real menace would be an attack on the riverfront from armed vessels belonging to a rival European power. The fort was therefore designed mainly to withstand an assault from the Hugli River flowing past its western walls. Unlike forts that are built on a high plateau to command the surrounding country, the new Fort William was placed in a bowl created by a natural depression. The battlements and buildings within the fort did not rise above the thickly wooded high grounds on the periphery. Thus, an enemy approaching up the river or from the surrounding country was not allowed to get a clear sight line to train their guns at any specific structure within the fort.[26]

The Dutch admiral John Splinter Stavorinus, visiting Calcutta in 1768, noted that there were bombproof barracks in the fort for ten thousand people, and if all the works were mounted with cannon, there was room for six hundred pieces of artillery. "No ship can pass up or down the *Ganges* without being exposed to the fire of this fort.... This nation [the British] have thus so firmly rooted themselves in *Bengal*, that, treachery excepted, they have little to fear from an European enemy, especially as they can entirely command the passage up and down the river."[27]

Louis de Grandpré, a French army officer who apparently defected and offered his services to the East India Company to plan an invasion of Mauritius, came to Calcutta in 1794 and later published a detailed description of the military features of the new Fort William.

> The citadel of Calcutta is an octagon…. [Since] the citadel can only be attacked by water, the river coming up to the glacis, it was merely necessary to present to the vessels making such attempt a superiority of fire, and to provide the means of discovering them at a distance, in order to disable them the moment they should arrive within cannon-shot. These purposes have been attained by giving the citadel towards the water the form of a large salient angle; the faces of which enfilade the course of the river…. Exclusively of these, the interior of the fort is perfectly open, and offers nothing to the sight but superb grass-plots, gravel walks planted occasionally with trees."[28]

In fact, instead of presenting an imposing appearance of overwhelming military dominance, the new fort at Calcutta actually tried to hide its considerable strategic power in a subtle and calculated posture of invisibility. Eliza Fay, writing in 1780, especially remarked on the difference between the new Fort William and Fort St. George in Madras. The latter, she said, was so full of buildings and residences that it looked like a town, whereas the former was truly a military garrison. She was also struck by the way "the slopes, banks, and ramparts, are covered with the richest verdure," and claimed that she "never saw a more vivid green than adorns the surrounding fields"—the grounds that would come to be called, simply, the Maidan of Calcutta.[29]

The fort's octagonal shape, with salient angles, surrounded by large open grounds on three sides, has given it a strange iconic representation on Calcutta's maps—like some giant tropical flower. Until today, for two and a half centuries since it was built, the new Fort William has never seen battle. It has never come under attack. The hundreds of guns on its walls have never fired at an enemy target. As the headquarters of the Eastern Command of the Indian army, the fort continues to have an inconspicuous presence in the public life of the city, broken only by stray incidents of unruly behavior by soldiers in the streets or bars. Its existence is registered only in the extensive public use made of the surrounding grounds—the largest open space in the city, and the principal venue for sports, amusements, and in the recent age of postcolonial democratic politics, meetings. If a key tactic of the modern regime of power is to hide the state's capability to use its means of sovereign armed force, then the British colonial power was able to develop this method in its imperial capital from an early period in its history.

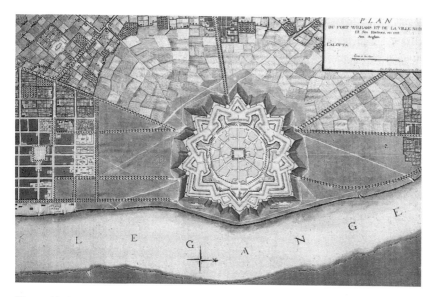

Figure 10. *Plan of Fort William and the Black Town and Its Surroundings, Belonging to the English, Calcutta*, by Lafitte de Brassier, 1779. *Courtesy: Centre for Studies in Social Sciences, Calcutta*

THE EARLY PRESS IN CALCUTTA

It is known that there was a Jacobin Club in Srirangapattana, consisting of about sixty members drawn from among the French soldiers and artisans living in Tipu's capital. We have a report on one of its celebrations in 1797, at which the tricolor was hoisted and the club's president, François Ripaud, asked of his audience: "Citizens! Do you Swear Hatred to all Kings except Tippoo Sultaun the Victorious, the Ally of the French Republic, War against all Tyrants and love towards your country, and that of Citizen Tippoo?" "Yes," came the answer. Addressing the members of the Jacobin Club, Citoyen Tipou said, "Behold my acknowledgement of the Standard of your country, which is dear to me, and to which I am allied, it shall always be supported in my Country, as it has been in the Republic, my Sister!"[30]

These radical and republican sentiments did not, however, travel to other places in India. With the end of Tipu's regime, Mysore could no longer be a source of Jacobin ideas. When radical thoughts of political liberty sprung up in the new British Indian capital of Calcutta, their sources and idioms were more familiarly English. They posed very different problems for the British authorities.

The English-language press began in Calcutta in 1780.[31] By the turn of the century, there were a dozen or so periodicals, mostly weeklies, with several hundred subscribers each among the European residents of Bengal.[32] The first journal, *Hicky's Bengal Gazette*, became an immediate sensation. Owned and edited by James Augustus Hicky, an Irishman who came to India as a surgeon's mate, the weekly *Gazette* started as a place where readers could get information on various commodity prices in the Calcutta markets, sales and auctions, the arrival and departure of ships as well as fires, thefts, and accidents in the city, and where traders and stores could advertise their goods. Soon its columns became a lively forum for the letters and poems of its correspondents. But when Hicky tried to liven up the proceedings by commenting on the goings-on among the East India Company's senior officials, he got into trouble. He was accused of engaging in salacious gossip and scandalmongering, and bringing into disrepute the governing authorities of the colony. Some of Hicky's comments were, without doubt, risqué, but by no means outrageous by the standards of the popular press in Britain at the time. Thus, for example,

[NEWS.] We hear that several amorous Heroes of the Martial Band having been lately foiled in their attacks upon some of the newly arrived Beauties have retired to Barrackpore from the Field of Love, and are seeking Comforts in the Arms of Mars in recompence for the pleasures they were denied in the arms of Venus.[33]

But it was his campaign against what he claimed to be the abuse of power by Governor-general Hastings, in collusion with Elijah Impey, chief justice of the Supreme Court, that brought the wrath of the authorities on him. Some of his allegations were hidden behind metaphoric and at times rather lurid allusions. Hence:

CUTCHERY INTELLIGENCE. *A Real Fact.* Some Days ago the Sardar Bearer of the Right Hon. Sir Elija Impey Knight Lord Chief Justice of these Realms was taken before Thomas Motte Esq., one of the Justices of Peace for the Town of Calcutta, being detected in the fact of committing the Horrid Crime of Beastiality with a Favorite female Goat belonging to the Hon'ble Warren Hastings Esq., the Governor General &c. notwithstanding the Horrid Nature of the Crime and his being actually taken in the fact, he was sentenced to receive only 10 stripes, and to be imprison'd for a short time in the Cutchery, a place of confinement.

The fellow pleaded that He conceived the intimacy subsisting between the Families and his Master being a Great Man, gave him a Priviledge to commit the said Crime of Beastiality with impunity.[34]

In November 1780, on instructions from Hastings, when Hicky was refused permission to circulate his journal by post, he printed the following soliloquy:

To print—or not to print—that is the question. Whether it is nobler for a man to suffer the threats and anger of the S—p—e C—n—l [Supreme Council] or to defy them and the B—d of C—m—e [Board of Commerce], and by opposing tease them! But to stop to print—no more—and by that step to end all squabbles, and the thousand cursed plagues a printer's heir to—'tis a consummation by cowards to be wished.[35]

The order meant that the paper could not circulate anymore beyond the vicinity of Calcutta. It was a major financial blow for Hicky. In an address to the public, he announced:

> He [Mr. Hicky] has now but three things to lose, his *Honour*, in the support of his Paper, his *Liberty*, and his *Life*, the two latter he will hazard in defence of the former, for he is determined to make it the scourge of all schemers and leading tyrants, should they illegally deprive him of his Liberty, and confine him in a jail, He is determined to Print there with every becoming spirit, ...
>
> And let them see that he is a *Freeman* of the first *City* in the *British Empire*, ... and that he has a power, to print a News paper that no East India Company nor the King their Master can wrest out of his hands it is beyond the prerogative of the British Crown to invest the Company or their servants with such a power.[36]

This was, enunciated perhaps for the first time in a British colony in the East, a classic antiabsolutist statement of the innate and inalienable liberty of the freeborn British subject. Little did Hicky realize that the Eastern colony would turn out to be an exception, even for that hallowed universal right. Irked by his defiance, Hastings brought a series of libel charges against Hicky, who was then imprisoned in June 1781 because he was unable to furnish the large sum set for his bail. Undaunted, Hicky continued to write from jail and kept the paper going. His printing types were seized in October 1781, and he was forced to defend himself without a lawyer's assistance. When the jury acquitted him in Impey's court, the chief justice carried out a second trial with another jury and sentenced him to jail.[37] On release from prison, Hicky spent the rest of his life in extreme poverty, without a means of livelihood.[38] He died in 1802 on board a ship to China and was buried at sea.[39] It is not without significance that the publisher and editor of the first printed newspaper of British India suffered a fate such as this.

Hicky's trial has been, unfortunately, long mired in the numerous stories of scandal and intrigue that form the staple of the literature on eighteenth-century Calcutta. It has not been sufficiently recognized that apart from pointing to the frivolous tastes and petty enmities of the company's officials, the episode also signified certain enduring problems with the principles of government that would be instituted in an Eastern colony under British rule. In his study of the

Bengal Gazette's contents, Tarun Mukhopadhyay has pointed out some of these constitutional and political issues.[40] First, by printing the texts of parliamentary debates on India, Hicky's *Gazette* created a direct connection between the public sphere in Britain and the new, growing public in British India for the first time. When the *Bengal Gazette* published the attack in Parliament by Charles Fox against "the unparalleled misapplication of the public treasure" by Hastings, it provided a hitherto-unprecedented means to mount a *public* opposition in Bengal to the governor-general's policies, as distinct from the criticisms made by his opponents, such as Philip Francis, within the chambers of the company's administration.[41]

Second, Hicky opened his columns to complaints about appointments and promotions in the company's army, and allegations of corruption in the awarding of contracts for supplying the army with provisions. He published anonymous letters as well as essays by people in the armed forces condemning "the tame and spiritless submission" by their officers to the civil authorities.[42] Hicky was, of course, a resolute defender of the power of British arms in India, whether directed against the French or the various Indian rulers. But after the defeat of the company's army at the hands of Haidar, he turned his ire against generals such as Hector Munro. Indeed, he railed against what he saw as a cabal of Scottish officers who were both nepotistic and incompetent:

> The CARNATIC might have been saved from ravage; the City of Arcot and the CAR-
> NATIC have been shamefully lost by the same confused blunders and pusillanimity of
> the SCOTCH JUNTO, who Rule everywhere on the coast as well as everywhere else in
> India, *Monopolise* every post of profit and have brought the Company's affairs into
> greater disgrace than ever known in the memory of man.[43]

Third, as distinct from the pamphlet wars carried out in Britain, Hicky's *Gazette* offered the first forum in Bengal where the government's policies could be publicly debated. Hicky launched a fierce criticism of Hastings's conduct of the war against the Marathas and dealings with Chait Singh of Benares. He described Hastings's revenue-farming methods of tax collection as "the most destructive scheme that could have been devised.... [W]hat can [they] end in but the districts, once flourished and populous being transformed into deserts?"[44] Hicky did not spare the judiciary either: using the ploy of a serialized "Japan Journal," ostensibly portraying the doings of ministers and "mandarines" in the Tokugawa court, Hicky lashed out against the "venality, obstinacy in unjust undertakings, and barefaced corruption" in the judiciary of Madras and Bengal. Put in prison and faced with a hostile judge in Impey, Hicky even resurrected from the past the case of Maharaja Nandakumar Ray, executed by the same Impey, supposedly on instructions from Hastings, for forging a document. Hicky decided to reprint in his *Gazette* the observations of Alexander

Macrabie, the sheriff of Calcutta, made six years previously, soon after Nanda-kumar's hanging:

> We first committed a successful forgery on a native of Bengal [Amirchand], and glorified in it, though it occasioned his death. Soon after we sent our English judges to establish English laws in that country, and with a justice peculiar to wise and in-nocent men, a retrospective view of past crimes is taken, and a native of the country, who knew nothing of English laws, is hanged for a crime which we had triumphed in committing. Clive was made a Peer in England though he committed in Bengal the same crime, for which we hanged Nundcomar.[45]

The critique of conquest, as we will see, would remain a subterranean, though persistent theme in the antiabsolutist early modern tendency in Bengal in the late eighteenth and early nineteenth century—a blot from the past that every now and then, would threaten to surface in order to remind both rulers and subjects of the violent and unjust foundations of empire.

Fourth, Hicky's *Gazette* was probably the first newspaper in India to give rise to a movement and an association to direct it. This was the agitation in early 1781 against the so-called Bye-laws for the town of Calcutta that em-powered the newly appointed commissioners and surveyor to assess all houses, shops, and lands, and impose taxes on them. Hicky not only opposed the by-laws but also urged that an association be formed and public meetings held:

> With association they [free English subjects] had it always in their power to main-tain the independence in which they were born and to compel the body whom they had entrusted with their rights, to do them justice; but without association they must fall a sacrifice to that corruption which had given the Crown an influence unknown in any former period in our history.[46]

The point that Hicky was at pains to emphasize was that those who had been authorized to impose taxes had acquired their powers by fiat, not because they represented the colony's subjects. In fact, he highlighted the relation between taxation and representation with a directness that was clearly reminiscent of the American colonists. "The spirit of the constitution requires full and fair representation of the people; on that, and that alone, depends the right of taxa-tion, if then the people are unfairly or imperfectly represented, or not repre-sented at all, that right falls to the ground."[47] If "the spirit of *Magna Carta*" was still alive, he said, their grievances would be looked into, "but if Law and Justice are annihilated—if the British Constitution is destroyed from its foundation—if Liberty is irrevocably lost—Every Englishman should join in the sentiment of Cato, *Indifferent is my choice to live or die.*"[48]

Over the next two decades, as the number of publications increased, the government maintained its attempts to control their contents and opinions, even though there were no press laws as such. William Duane, an American of Irish origin, who edited the *Bengal Journal*, got into trouble in 1791 by publishing an erroneous story on the rumored death of Lord Cornwallis in the Maratha wars. Duane apparently lost his job, but soon started his own *Indian World*, which became a success.[49] His political views were too radical and invectives too sharp, however, for the authorities' liking. In 1794, his house was twice raided and searched, in retaliation, alleged Duane, "for matters that had appeared in my paper relative to the enormous abuses and peculations of the [Supreme] Court."[50] He sought an audience with John Shore, the governor-general, but on his arrival at Government House, was arrested and, Duane later claimed, "cast into the famous or infamous Black Hole of Calcutta."[51] Duane was put on board the next ship to Europe, and his considerable property in Calcutta was confiscated. Shore remarked that Duane's paper had "assumed a licentiousness too dangerous to be permitted in this country."[52] Arriving in Britain, Duane tried to protest his deportation by appealing to the House of Commons.

In the end, his career actually prospered, because on his return to the United States in 1796, Duane collaborated with Benjamin Bache, Benjamin Franklin's grandson, in publishing the *Aurora* of Philadelphia, and in 1798 became its editor. The *Aurora* was the organ of what would soon become the Republican Party, campaigning against George Washington and the Federalists for subverting the true republican principles of the revolution. When Washington retired from the presidency in 1797, Duane wrote: "If ever there was a period for rejoicing, this is the moment.... When a retrospect is taken of the Washington administration ... it is a subject of the greatest astonishment that a single individual should have cancelled the principles of republicanism of an enlightened people just emerged from the gulph of despotism, and should have carried his designs against the public liberty so far as to put in jeopardy its very existence."[53] He accused President John Adams of conspiring to establish a monarchy, and in response, Adams wrote privately: "Is there anything evil in the regions of actuality or possibility, that the *Aurora* has not suggested of me? The matchless effrontery of this Duane merits the execution of the alien law. I am very willing to try its strength upon him."[54] Duane was in fact charged twice under the Sedition Act and once actually jailed as a British subject for contempt of court.[55]

His radical republican opinions, including his support for the French republic and hostility toward Britain, not to speak of his combative style, invited opposition, and at one time he was apparently defending sixty or seventy libel suits. During the administrations of Jefferson and Madison, though, Duane received many official favors. He was a strong supporter of Bolivian independence, and on retiring, undertook a triumphant tour of Colombia, where he was hailed as a friend of the revolution.[56] If Shore, back in Britain as Lord Teign-mouth, knew of Duane's career in the United States, he would have congratu-lated himself on his foresight in bundling him out of Calcutta before he could cause too much trouble.

Relations between government and the press in Bengal at this time have been summed up as follows:

> If the person intending to start a paper was already *persona non grata* with the Gov-ernment or with influential officials, he was deported forthwith. If a newspaper of-fended and was unrepentant, it was at first denied postal privileges; if it persisted in causing displeasure to the Government, it was required to submit part of or the en-tire newspaper to precensorship; if the editor was "incorrigible," he was deported.[57]

Wellesley began his tenure as governor-general with a clearer, even more severe plan to prevent public criticism of official actions. While the conflicts of the British power with various Indian states expanded in the south, west, and north of the country, Wellesley was much irritated by the growing pretensions of the nonofficial European community, especially in Bengal, to judge and criticize the government. "I am resolved," he declared, "to encounter the task of effecting a thorough reform in private manners here, without which the time is not too distant when the Europeans settled at Calcutta will control the Government, if they do not overturn it."[58]

Lurking behind the demands for greater freedom of the press, he saw the specter of the United States, where colonists had demanded control over and finally overthrown the imperial power. Determined to prevent such a possibil-ity emerging in Bengal, in 1799 Wellesley oversaw the framing of the first set of press regulations. They were drastic, authorizing censorship, prohibiting vir-tually all critical discussion of the political and military activities of the govern-ment, including reprinting such material from the British press, and threaten-ing deportation to Europe as the punishment for offenders.[59] The penalty was applied in a few cases, until a loophole was discovered: if an Indian-born per-son, often a Eurasian, was declared the printer, the regulations could be avoided, since an Indian-born person could not be deported. In 1818, this loophole was plugged by a new set of regulations that abolished censorship, but put the onus of conforming to the rules on the author or editor.

Historians of the early press in India have usually narrated the story of the periodic tightening and relaxation of government control as one dependent largely on the ideological leanings of senior officials. Shore, Adam, and Welles-ley were authoritarian, and thus imposed harsh controls; Lord Hastings, Charles Metcalfe, and William Bentinck were more liberal and eased restrictions. But the basic issue concerning freedom of the press in the Eastern colony was al-ready posed in clear terms at this time, and remained invariant through all the phases of loose and tight control. Everyone endorsed the principle of freedom of the press, yet most officials stressed the exceptional situation of British rule in India, which demanded that the public airing of critical opinions be controlled by government. John Malcolm defended the press regulations on the ground that "as long as the necessity exists for the maintenance of absolute power, it is far better for the State and individuals, that it should be exercised to prevent than to punish such offences."[60] W. B. Bayley asserted that British government in India was "substantially and necessarily despotic," and that its stability depended on "the cheerful obedience and subordination of the officers of the Army, on the fidelity of the Native Troops, on the superior character and power of the Government.... The liberty of the Press, however essential to the nature of a free state, is not consistent with the character of our institutions in this country or with the extraordinary nature of our dominion in India."[61] Political leaders in Britain were in general horrified by talk of a free press in India. During a debate in Parliament on the subject in 1811, one member raised the image of Santo Domingo—that is, the Haitian Revolution—while another feared the extermination of the English population, massacred by natives in revolt.[62] On the other side, Lord Hastings believed that the administration ought to be responsive to public opinion, and for that reason, the press should not be forced into a position of hostility toward the government:

> That Government which has nothing to disguise, wields the most powerful instrument that can appertain to Sovereign Rule. It carries with it the united reliance and effort of the whole mass of the governed—and let the triumph of our beloved Country, in its awful contest with Tyrant-ridden France, speak the value of a spirit to be found only in men accustomed to indulge and express their honest sentiments.[63]

The issues were laid bare in the so-called Buckingham affair. Buckingham, following a checkered career as an adventurer in Egypt and Palestine as well as a sailor in the Indian Ocean, arrived in Calcutta in 1818 and started the *Calcutta Journal*. The paper was attractively produced and expertly managed, and soon became a success. It was seen as the organ of the expatriate British business community in Bengal, led by John Palmer, supporting free trade and the abolition of the East India Company's monopoly. Buckingham's radical political views immediately got him into trouble with the authorities and also other newspapers voicing Old Tory opinions. Buckingham declared that the whole of Asia should be opened to unrestricted competitive trade, and that it was his duty "to admonish Governors of their duties, to warn them furiously of their faults, and to tell disagreeable truths."[64] He repeatedly argued that since in the absence of a representative legislature, government in India was essentially irresponsible, a free press was the only means of public scrutiny and the solitary check on its absolute powers. He often quoted Malcolm on this point, since

Malcolm had contended that *because* the rule of the company in India was necessarily absolute and could not be effectively checked from Britain, a free press would go some way in imposing accountability on the company's officials.

> The nature of our possessions in India makes it necessary that almost absolute power should be given to those intrusted with governments in that quarter; and there cannot be a better or more efficient check over these rulers, than that which must be established by the full publicity given to their acts, and the frequent discussion of all their principles of rule.... I am confident that every effort made to repress such discussion, is ... but a direct approximation to the principles of that ORIENTAL TYRANNY which it is, or ought to be, our chief boast to have destroyed.[65]

Buckingham was particularly scathing on deportation as a punishment for violation of the press regulations. "Transmission for offenses through the press," he emphasized, "is a power wholly unknown to the law. Irresponsible power is nowhere to be found acknowledged in the Law or Constitution of England.... The more the monstrous doctrine of transmission is examined, the more it must excite the abhorrence of all just minds."[66] *The Bengal Harkaru*, a Tory paper at this time, dubbed him "Ali Baba" and penned the following doggerel:

> Ass is *Gudda, Ahmuq* is a Fool,
> Liberal *Azad*, and *Alut* a Tool;
> *Ally* a Prophet is, *Babu* a Sire,
> And *Ali Baba* is a Red Hot Radical on Fire![67]

After repeated skirmishes with officials and rival newspapers—some leading to libel suits, and others to inconclusive duels on the swampy fields of Ballygunge—matters came to a head in 1822. Buckingham had relished the battles in court, and indeed got the better of his opponents. He always insisted that the press could only be judged in the courts and not by executive action, since it was bound only by English law and nothing else.[68] But now Chief Secretary John Adam decided that Buckingham belonged to a "mischievous set," and was "the most malignant, the most active and daring of the party."[69] Adam was keen to deport Buckingham, yet was restrained by Lord Hastings—one of the governor-general's last acts before returning to Britain. George Canning, who also held liberal views, was to succeed Hastings. Unfortunately for Buckingham, Robert Stewart, Lord Castlereagh, the British foreign secretary, decided at this time to commit suicide, and as a result, Canning, then undersecretary, had to take charge of the department and Adam was named the acting governor-general of India.

Adam lost no time in ordering that Buckingham be sent home from India. Speaking as the highest British official in India, he denied that "a community constituted like the European Society of India" had any right to exercise control over the government and its officers: "It must not be supposed, that the perpetual assaults on the character and respectability of Government,... are not calculated to shake greatly that salutary confidence in its justice and integrity, and that habitual deference for its authority and judgment which, with advertence to the anomalous structure of our power in this country, it is so essential to preserve unimpaired."[70] *John Bull*, the loudest conservative paper of Calcutta, was more direct. No public criticism of government officials could be legitimate in India, it declared. "We maintain that the PUBLIC interests are in no way concerned in any appointments under this Government ... and this simply because the persons filling those offices are not servants of the PUBLIC; but of the East India Company."[71] Buckingham, in his last address to the public before being sent home, lashed out against "that un-English, and I would say *inhuman* principle of making any man subject to instant ruin at the mere caprice and arbitrary pleasure of another."[72]

Once back in Britain, Buckingham persisted in his condemnation of the arbitrary powers of the East India Company in India. He tried to influence opinion in Britain by launching a pamphlet war. There were, he said, no institutions in the company's dominions in India that were independent of the ruling power, and hence "no constituted bodies, of any description, who have the *right* of addressing the government in the collective form of '*we!*'" As a result, "in no country might the Press be *such* a powerful SAFETY-VALVE as in India." He then pointed to the real political danger:

> We may, perhaps, for some time longer, terrify the less advanced and more timorous Hindoos into submission to demands so extremely unreasonable as this.... But how long can it be supposed that we shall be enabled to intimidate the HALF-CASTE population into such absurd acquiescence? ... Every state having colonies forgets that the growth of new and prosperous dependencies, and the increase of Creole populations, are not to be measured by the same *time-standard* that marks the improvements of older people.... In a thriving colony, twenty or thirty years do as much work as a century in an old country.[73]

For twelve years, Buckingham kept up his campaign to seek compensation for his deportation and loss of property. He started a new journal, the *Oriental Herald* (London), organized meetings and publications in his cause, and even won a parliamentary seat from Sheffield. He succeeded in getting a House resolution recommending that compensation be paid to him, but the company would not budge. Interestingly, Buckingham himself did not think that his treatment, or the issue of the free press in India, had anything to do with the ideological divisions between the Tories and Whigs.

It was by a Whig Governor-General [Lord Hastings] that all India, as well as my-self, was deluded by false promises, made only to be broken—It was by a Whig Member of Council [Adam] that I was banished without trial …—It was by a Whig Administration that the justice of my claim was admitted …—and, to make the end correspond with the beginning, it is by a Whig Government that I have been de-serted and abandoned.[74]

Realizing that the government of Lord John Russell would not push his case against the company, Buckingham resigned from Parliament, complaining bit-terly about the liberal leaders of Britain: "The very persons who were the first to lift the cup of hope to my lips, have been the first to dash it to the ground."[75]

Antiabsolutist demands for the liberty of the subjects of the British Crown quickly found their limits in India. Even freeborn Englishmen could not enjoy those liberties there, because unlike the American colonies or Canada, India was not a settler colony: the principal task of government here was to rule over the natives, and its fundamental character, no matter how attenuated by liberal sentiments or rhetoric, was at core absolutist and authoritarian. The English principles of liberty, based on universal principles of reason, would always have to seek grounds for exception in India.

It might seem that these debates over civic freedoms were entirely confined to the expatriate European community in Bengal. This is not quite the case. First of all, many of the printers and editors of the early English-language newspa-pers were Indian born—a fact that opened up a gap in the governmental pro-cedures designed to keep the press under control, because such alleged offenders could not be deported. Of the nine English newspapers that began publishing in Bengal in the 1820s, at least two were edited by Eurasians—Monte de Ro-zario of the *Columbian Press Gazette* and H.L.V. Derozio of the *Kaleidoscope*.[76] Between 1829 and 1855, as many as thirty English newspapers were owned by Indian proprietors.[77] In 1835, Dwarakanath Tagore was the proprietor of two of the main English-language papers—*John Bull*, now called the *Englishman*, and the *India Gazette*.[78] The liberal reformist journal *Bengal Herald*, published by Robert Montgomery Martin, had among its associates Indian reformers such as Rammohan Roy, Dwarakanath, and Prasanna Kumar Tagore, and when it got into trouble with the government in 1829, transferred its ownership to Nilratan Haldar.[79] By 1833, leading Indian reformers such as Krishna Mohan Banerjee, Prasanna Kumar Tagore, and Rasik Krishna Mallik were publishing their own English-language journals.[80]

Second, by the 1820s, there were some Indian-language newspapers in print in Bengal—in Persian, Bengali, Urdu, and Hindi. The owners and editors of these papers were also concerned about the possible effects of official regu-lation of the press. Following Buckingham's expulsion in 1823, a petition was presented to the Supreme Court on behalf of Rammohan Roy and five other prominent native inhabitants of Calcutta protesting that the press regulations were against the laws of England. The court rejected the petition, arguing that India was not a free country and thus the institutions of a free country did not apply in this case: "A free press might follow, but it could not precede, a free constitution."[81]

Buckingham's cause, it might seem, was vindicated in 1835 when Governor-general Metcalfe passed a new Press Act enabling the largely free circulation of opinion in print. But this meant that the rule of colonial difference would only be applied elsewhere, by using a different criterion. Welcoming the proposal for a new act, the *Englishman* of Calcutta maintained that its freedoms should be restricted only to European proprietors and editors, "because we feel perfectly satisfied that an unrestrained Press in the hands of designing, talented, and dissatisfied natives in the interior might become a very mischievous instrument."[82] By the late 1850s, when the agitations against indigo farming would sweep the Bengal countryside, vigorous policing would be imposed on the Indian-language press, leading finally to the infamous Vernacular Press Act of 1878. In the second half of the nineteenth century, the idea of a free press would exist in India only to the extent that the language of opinion was English. Everything else was subject to the rule of colonial difference and liable to be declared as exceptions to the universal principle of liberty.

The Strength of Constitution

Mirza Abu Taleb Ispahani's account of his visit to Vilayet is somewhat marred by the tedious recounting of his meetings with members of the English nobility.[83] During his stay in London from 1800 to 1802, he seems to have made a place for himself in the social life of the upper classes. But Abu Taleb also spent many pages of his book describing the political and social institutions of English life, not because he wanted to show off his familiarity with them, but instead because he felt it necessary to discuss them seriously with both his Indian and British readers. He thoroughly appreciated the worth of British political institutions—that the powers of the monarch were limited by those of Parliament, for instance, or that the ministers needed to carry the support of a majority of Parliament to stay in office. He admired the fact that every British subject had the right to be tried by a jury, even though he also observed that in actual practice, the judges frequently exercised their influence to direct a jury toward a particular decision.[84]

Yet the most striking invention, in Abu Taleb's view, was that of the printing press: "By its aid, thousands of copies, of any scientific, moral, or religious book, may be circulated among the people in a very short time; and by it, the works of celebrated authors are handed down to posterity, free from the errors and imperfections of a manuscript." Moreover, the newspapers, "read by all ranks of people," gave detailed news of war and politics, the price of grain, and books and entertainment, including, he added somewhat coyly, insertions announcing that "the *Prince Abu Taleb*" would be attending this or that event, resulting in large crowds thronging to see "*the Persian Prince*."[85] He much liked the clubs and literary societies.[86] The education of boys in England, he thought, was "admirably adapted to render them honourable, courageous, and capable of enduring hardships," while that of girls tended "to render them accomplished, rather than to endue them with philosophy." Making the inevitable comparison, he remarked: "I have often seen an English child of five years old possess more wisdom than an Asiatic of fifteen."[87]

Like Ihtishamuddin before him, Abu Taleb marveled at the new machines and intricately coordinated methods of manufacture that he saw, and described them at length:

> On entering one of the extensive manufactories in England, the mind is at first bewildered by the number and variety of the articles displayed therein: but, after recovering from this first impression, and having coolly surveyed all the objects around, every thing appears conducted with so much regularity and precision, that a person is induced to suppose that one of the meanest capacity might superintend and direct the whole process.[88]

He had no doubt that "the common people here enjoy more freedom and equality than in any other well-regulated government in the world. No Englishman, unless guilty of a breach of the laws, can be seized, or punished, at the caprice or from the gust of passion of the magistrate: he may sometimes be confined on suspicion, but his life cannot be affected, except on positive proof."[89]

Abu Taleb also offered many criticisms of English practices. These ranged from uncomfortable beds to an expensive and needlessly complicated legal system open to much abuse. Even though he appreciated the spirit of liberty among the common people of England—leading them to "frequently hiss and reproach any nobleman or gentleman they dislike," or publicly portray them in caricature—he noticed as well that "this equality is more in appearance than in reality, for the difference in the comforts of the rich and of the poor is, in England, much greater than in India. The servants are not at liberty to quit their master without giving proper warning, and, in general, they are as respectful in their behaviour as the slaves of Hindoostan."[90] He also did not approve of the effects on the lower classes of the lack of faith in religion and "great inclination to *falsafa* [philosophy]," which he equated with atheism. The consequence was, he believed, a total lack of honesty, barely held in check by the fear of the penal system.[91]

In addition, Abu Taleb took an interest in the intricacies of political economy. He was concerned by the British government's enormous national debt, whose burden fell mostly on the middle classes, and suggested that all the major creditors be summoned before Parliament and told that there was a risk of imminent revolution such as in France that would lead inevitably to the cancellation of the entire national debt. It therefore would be wise for the creditors to accept a compromise and settle for a partial cancellation, which would allow the government to somewhat lighten the burden of taxes on the middle classes.[92] This was probably the first and last time, at least until our present postcolonial age, that an Indian would offer advice on British political economy.

Spending most of his days in England with the upper classes, Abu Taleb also thought that they had an excessively luxurious style of living, and wasted too much of their time in "sleeping, eating, and dressing." He felt that the English had an unwarranted contempt for the customs of other nations as well, "although theirs, in fact, may be much inferior." These defects, however, were not necessarily disastrous in their consequences:

> Many of these defects, or vices, are not natural to the English, but have been ingrafted on them by prosperity and luxury: the bad consequences of which have not yet appeared, and, for two reasons, may not be conspicuous for some time. The first of these is the strength of constitution, both of individuals and of the Government.... The second reason is, that their neighbours are not exempt from these vices, nay, possess them in a greater proportion.[93]

Abu Taleb was also not greatly persuaded by the inflexible procedures and mechanical impersonality of the English legal system. "I was disgusted to observe that, in these courts, law very often overruled equity, and that a well-meaning honest man was frequently made the dupe of an artful knave; nor could the most righteous judge alter the decision, without transgressing the law." Considering the effects of transporting this legal system to the British courts of India, Abu Taleb echoed Ghulam Husain before him in picturing the miserable plight of those Indians who had the misfortune of getting involved with these courts, whether as plaintiffs, defendants, or witnesses. "In Calcutta, few months elapse that some respectable and wealthy man is not attacked by the harpies who swarm round the courts of judicature." They do this "by frightening people with the terrors of the English law.... These circumstances are all very distressing to a native of India, unacquainted with the English laws and customs, and many of them, rather than have the trouble and run the risk, willingly pay a sum of money.... The hardships and inconveniences that witnesses also suffer, when summoned to Calcutta, are so great, that no man in India will now give voluntary evidence in any case."[94]

Abu Taleb's critical ethnography of Britain was entirely free of any sense of civilizational inferiority. His appreciation as well as criticism of the practices of his British hosts was that of a peer. This quality was most apparent in his little essay containing a "Vindication of the Liberties of the Asiatic Women." Abu Taleb's arguments were set out there in the spirit of a friendly rivalry in a debating society of equals, with none of the defensiveness, rancor, or resentment that would mark such defenses of Indian social practices in the late nineteenth century. For example, in dealing with the charge that Asiatic women do not have the freedom of choosing their own husbands, he gently reminded his readers that "in Europe this liberty is merely nominal, as, without the will of the father and mother, the daughter's choice is of no avail." In the spirit of scoring debating points, he asserted that Asiatic women in effect have greater control over their husband's properties and businesses than do women in Europe, exercise full command over the domestic space and servants, and have complete charge of their daughters even after a divorce. He even added, a little facetiously, that by subtly manipulating the culturally accepted practices of showing indifference toward, or even impatience with, the dependence of their husbands on their services and favors, the women of Asia were able to exercise effective power over their men in daily life. In complete contrast with the tracts on women that would be written in India later in the nineteenth century, Abu Taleb's text showed no signs of anxiety about the practices of his own culture, and thus promoted no agenda for either conserving or reforming them.[95]

Yet he did seem to be strongly drawn by the new sciences, the flood of mechanical innovations, and the orderly spirit of industrial organization. In contrast with what we described earlier as the absolutist tendency in the late eighteenth century, though, Abu Taleb evidenced a clear preference for the constitutional limitation of the relative powers of the sovereign, his ministers, and Parliament. This is underscored by his strong disapproval of what he believed was the arbitrary tyranny of the viziers of Turkey. Although he had much greater familiarity with the intellectual and cultural foundations of the Ottoman principles of government, Abu Taleb's account of his visit to Istanbul, and his journey through the Ottoman territories to the holy cities of Karbala and Najaf, indicate that he was, at least on theoretical grounds, persuaded by the superiority of the British constitutional forms.[96] Even though the ever-present fear of imperial power ensured that there were no serious rebellions against Ottoman rule, Abu Taleb clearly saw that people lived in an atmosphere of far greater freedom in Britain. But he does not offer the thought that such institutions might be successfully implanted in the Orient.

That situation was about to change. Soon there would be a few Indians, only a generation younger, who would imagine that possibility.

The Making of Early Modern Citizens

It has been sometimes suggested, with an air of nostalgic celebration, that there was a certain moment in the late eighteenth and early nineteenth centuries when, despite the conflicts of the European powers with the various Indian states, it was possible for Europeans and Indians to mix socially, adopt each other's languages and habits, establish friendships, and even enter into conjugal relationships. William Dalrymple, for example, waxes eloquent on the cultural openness and curiosity of Europeans in India that allowed even company officials and military commanders to go native in the eighteenth century, before British colonialism imposed a regime of racial arrogance and intolerance in the nineteenth century.[97] More careful scholars have shown, however, that this story is both simplistic and misleading. Maya Jasanoff describes how even in the eighteenth century, instances of prominent European men adopting an Oriental lifestyle and cohabiting with Indian women tended to occur more at "the edge of empire," away from the seats of British power in Calcutta or Madras.[98] Moreover, Durba Ghosh points out that even when cultural lines were crossed, there was a clear recognition of racial and gender hierarchies. Europeans going native were, more often than not, careful to hide these transgressions from their families in Europe, and in the disposal of their property and inheritance, eager to satisfy the conventional norms of European respectability. Ghosh concludes that "the building blocks of colonial ideologies of racial superiority and moral probity were in formation from the middle of the eighteenth century onward, prior to the development of scientific racism."[99]

To give just one example of the racial and gender hierarchies that girded the attitudes of even the most sensitive and adventurous of the eighteenth-century cross-culturalists, here is an extract from the famous journal of Hickey, the lawyer, whose house in Calcutta, shared with his Indian mistress Jamdani, was a center of social life for British gentlemen of the city at the turn of the nineteenth century. Following Jamdani's death, after a period of mourning, Hickey wrote:

> My friend, Bob Pott, now consigned to me from Moorshedabad a very pretty little native girl, whom he recommended for my own private use. Her name was Kiraun. After cohabiting with her a twelvemonth she produced me a young gentleman whom I certainly imagined to be of my own begetting, though somewhat surprized at the darkness of my son and heir's complexion; still, that surprize did not amount to any suspicion of the fidelity of my companion. Young Mahogany was therefore received and acknowledged as my offspring, until returning from the country one day quite unexpectedly, and entering Madam Kiraun's apartments by a private door of which I had a key, I found her closely locked in the arms of a handsome lad, one of my *kit-muddars* with the infant by her side, all three being in a deep sleep, from which I

awakened the two elders. After a few questions I clearly ascertained that this young man had partaken of Kiraun's personal favours jointly with me from the first month of her residing in my house, and that my friend Mahogany was fully entitled to the deep tinge of skin he came into the world with, being the produce of their continued amour. I consequently got rid of my lady, of her favourite, and the child, although she soon afterwards from falling into distress became a monthly pensioner of mine, and continued so during the many years I remained in Bengal.[100]

Race, class, and gender—all the hierarchies are firmly in place here at this moment of openness and cultural sympathy.

Yet there was a more public and political domain where the idea of the citizen-subject—educated, enlightened, responsible, and conscious of his freedoms—was beginning to take root across racial lines. In the next chapter, we will take up the question of Creole modernity and the possibility of its emergence into a republican nationalism in nineteenth-century India, following the model of the Creole revolutions in the British and Spanish empires in the Americas. Here, let us introduce one key element in the rise of that formation—namely, the new private institutions of schooling of boys and young men that flourished in Calcutta before the officially regulated system of colonial education was firmly established starting in the 1830s. Since European missionaries were generally discouraged in British Bengal in the early nineteenth century—the influential Baptist missionaries operated from Srirampur (or Serampore), a Danish enclave—the first schools teaching English and the rudiments of a modern European secondary curriculum were set up by expatriate entrepreneurs. While much of the education was aimed at disseminating practical skills, such as bookkeeping or draftsmanship, rather than fostering elevated intellectual tastes, it is nevertheless remarkable how certain radical, nonconformist modes of thought made their way into the life of Calcutta through these institutions.

Two figures were particularly notable. One was the Scottish watchmaker turned educationist David Hare (1775–1842), celebrated as key to the successful rise of the Hindu College as the premier institution of higher education in Bengal. A revered and much-loved figure among the Bengali elite of the city in his lifetime, after his death in 1842, he was turned into an iconic character by Pearychand Mittra's biography and, most influentially, Sibnath Sastri's history of the nineteenth-century "renaissance."[101] Hare was a close friend of Rammohan Roy, and by most accounts, a thorough nonconformist and freethinker. He joined several liberal causes of his day, including the campaign against the press regulations. His practice of education, it was noted, was "conducted on the principle of excluding religion" in general and the Christian missionaries in particular, even as his role in educating Indians was acknowledged, although "with deep regret, ... his inveterate hostility to the Gospel, produced an unhappy effect on the minds of the native youths ... by inducing a general scepticism, the melancholy consequences of which will long continue to be apparent."[102] Denied a final resting place in the city's Christian cemeteries, Hare was buried on the grounds of Hindu College. His grave and statue, shorn of all religious insignia, are still respectfully preserved, even though they are hidden behind the outdoor bookstalls that line the walls of Presidency College and Hare School on College Street.

But Hare's schools and Hindu College were meant for Hindu, mostly Bengali, students. The remarkable fact about David Drummond, another Scottish nonconformist, now quite forgotten, was that his Durrumtollah Academy had European, Eurasian (then usually called East Indian), and Indian students in the same class. Drummond took up the profession of school teaching soon after his arrival in Calcutta in 1814, and on taking charge of the academy, turned it into the most prominent English school in the city, especially by his innovative introduction of public examinations and theatrical performances.[103] His most celebrated student was Henry Derozio (1809–31), but the list of prizewinners from his school between 1817 and 1825 had, among the Tydds, Sinclairs, Turnbulls, and Bennetts, a fair sprinkling of De Silvas, Da Costas, Pintos, and Pereiras, and quite remarkably, Hurry Doss Bose, Kissen Chunder Dutt, Ramdhone Ghose, Groodoss Muckerjee, Dayal Chund Day, Goupal Kissen Deb, Radha Madhub Burrall, and other Bengali Hindus.[104] Awarding a prize to Haridas Bose in 1821, Drummond said, "In you we have an omnipotent confutation of that impious doctrine which would make colour the test of intellect. That blasphemy is now leaving the world; and man over all the earth begun to be considered as solely the child of circumstances."[105] Drummond's rational skepticism, undoubtedly drawn from the Scottish Enlightenment thinkers of the late eighteenth century, is known to have had a strong formative influence on the young Derozio.[106]

Celebrated by later historians as the mentor of the Young Bengal movement, Derozio's short and tempestuous life has long been the stuff of romance. As a teacher at Hindu College from 1826 to 1831, he attracted a following of some of the brightest young men from elite Bengali Hindu families in and around Calcutta. Derozio himself was a radical freethinker, openly espousing his preference for the philosophical stance of Epicurus and the revolutionary enthusiasm of Percy Bysshe Shelley. He imbibed in his students not merely the radical philosophical spirit but also the fearless pursuit of a lifestyle that did not conform to established religious conventions. The reaction was swift and decisive. Accused of promoting licentiousness and atheism, Derozio was forced to resign his position at Hindu College, only a few months before his untimely death at the age of twenty-two.

The charge against him and his followers that has stuck through the ages is that of youthful excess: "*Beef and Burgundy*' was their watchword, and *no here-*

after their shibboleth.... Who does not remember the enormities they used to commit almost every night on their return from Mr Hare's school, where the late Mr Derozio then delivered a course of lectures on Metaphysics?"[107] Notwithstanding the charge of extremism, Derozio's political position, as expressed in his poetry as well as prose writings, seems entirely consistent with the republican spirit of liberty that we have identified as belonging to an early modern antiabsolutist formation. He was a passionate supporter of the Greek war of independence and penned several poems on the subject. He wrote on the abolition of the slave trade:

> Blest be the generous hand that breaks
> > The chain a tyrant gave,
> And, feeling for degraded man,
> > Gives freedom to the slave.[108]

Referring to an incident of the brisk sale of a thousand copies of Thomas Paine's *Age of Reason* shipped to Calcutta by an American publisher, a correspondent of a Calcutta journal asked: "Now to what else can we attribute this predominant desire on the part of the educated natives to read the work and imbibe the principles of Paine but to the general growth and progress of infidelity?" The source was Derozio's invidious influence on his students. "Paine's 'Age of Reason' was not known to the young *illuminati* of the College, before it was introduced to their notice by the late Mr Derozio."[109] Admiring student Pearychand Mittra, however, put the same point differently: "He used to impress upon his pupils the sacred duty of thinking for themselves ... to live and die for truth."[110] Even as he condemned the burning of the *sati* as a detestable and inhuman act, Derozio, like Rammohan, did not at first favor its legal prohibition because he thought it would injure the religious feelings of millions of Hindus. But after Bentinck's promulgation, he celebrated the abolition of the practice.[111] Derozio's initial resistance was clearly prompted by an antiabsolutist stance that did not favor the state's meddling in the religious freedoms of its subjects. Like other radicals of the time, he was also a supporter of free trade and the settlement of Europeans in India, and wrote editorials on these subjects in the *East Indian*.

Derozio's most lasting contribution was in producing the first generation of young Indians schooled in the antiabsolutist spirit of reason and liberty. Tarachand Chakrabarti, Krishna Mohan Banerjee, Ramgopal Ghosh, Pearichand Mitra, Rasik Krishna Mallik, Radhanath Sikdar, Ramtanu Lahiri, and Sibchandra Deb all played prominent roles in the public life of Bengal in the succeeding decades, even after the dream of equal republican citizenship was shattered.

OTHER EARLY MODERN INSTITUTIONS

Before further pursuing the rise of a republican citizen public in Calcutta in the early nineteenth century, however, it is necessary to leave the elegant White Town springing up around the Maidan of the new Fort William. In White Town, neoclassical white became the dominant architectural style of the public buildings and private residences built for Europeans along the Esplanade and Chowringhee. It was an attempt to consciously insert the signs of imperial grandeur and rational order into a landscape of tropical disorder and excess.[112] But in the so-called Black Town of the northern part of the city, with its labyrinthine lanes and huge mansions surrounded by slumlike settlements of huts and shanties, things were quite different. The most familiar reminder of imperial power heard there, as the literary Night Owl notes in his sketches, was the daily firing of the gun from Fort William, marking the morning, noon, and evening hours, and signaling the new regime of clock time.[113]

The new Bengali neighborhoods in the north of the city saw the emergence in the early nineteenth century of certain distinctly urban forms of sociality that must also be called early modern. These early modern forms were different from the traditional social structures prevalent in rural Bengal, or the urban institutions and practices prevalent in the precolonial cities of northern India. But more significantly, they were also different from the characteristically colonial forms of urban modernity that have become more familiar from the second half of the nineteenth century. Let us follow the distinctions.

Of historians of Calcutta, S. N. Mukherjee has noticed the peculiar features of the new urbanity that began to emerge in the city in the first three decades of the nineteenth century, even though he did not draw the conceptual distinction that we are making.[114] Mukherjee pointed out, first, the new institutional form of the association, called societies or associations in English, or in their Bengali equivalents, *sabha* or *samiti*. The most famous of the early sabhas were the Atmiya Sabha set up in 1815 by Rammohan and the rival Dharma Sabha patronized principally by the Deb family of Sobhabazar. But there were many other societies and associations that followed. These were, of course, associations of wealthy and propertied elite groups, but they were now of mixed caste and even religious composition, based on free membership, and acting as debating societies, organizations of social reform and education, and promoters of causes and even political agitation.

Second, while some of these societies were floated by reformers who held unorthodox religious views, or espoused the breaking of taboos and social conventions, many were also run by highly orthodox people who nevertheless used the new associational form to launch campaigns and create new institutions in the city. It was a group of such orthodox leaders who, in 1817, teamed up with European officials and professionals to start the Hindu College, which was to have a profound role in the spread of modern Western education in eastern India. Indian elites and nonofficial Europeans also combined to create the societies that spread the new schools and produced the new textbooks in the 1820s and 1830s.

Third, as we have already seen, it was in these decades that the new Indian press, in English as well as the Indian languages, established itself as a political weapon, campaigning for social, religious, and political causes, criticizing the government, and frequently bringing down the wrath of the colonial authorities. Here too it is significant that Indian elites along with European merchants and professionals often joined hands to criticize the colonial government. There is no doubt that Calcutta in the early nineteenth century, then inhabited by about two hundred thousand people, developed a new social space for the activities of an urban public, mixed in its racial, religious, and caste composition, and led mainly by the city's wealthy businesspeople, that sought to claim and protect the rights of the public against the ruling authorities, headed by the governor-general and his council.

The second new institutional feature in this period was the emergence of parties, each led by a wealthy Bengali magnate. The parties were called *dal*, which is exactly what they are called today, although in the early nineteenth century there was obviously nothing resembling the political parties we are familiar with now. Once again, Mukherjee has studied the phenomenon closely.[115] He notes that between 1820 and 1850, there were five major parties—led, respectively, by Radhakanta Deb, Ashutosh Deb, the Tagores, Biswanath Motilal, and Kalinath Munshi—and several minor ones. Upper-caste people led most of the parties, even though in some cases their entry into the ranks of the ritually elevated castes was recent, and clearly influenced by the exercise of power and financial inducements. Individuals belonging to ritually low trading and artisan castes, such as the Subarnabanik, Tili, and Tanti, ran some of the other parties. But party membership was quite mixed in its caste composition, and it was common for ritually superior Brahmins to accept the leadership of a ritually inferior Kayastha, Tili, or Subarnabanik party leader. In all cases, the chief qualification for becoming a party leader was wealth and political access to the ruling British authorities. Membership in these parties was voluntary, and people were known to leave a party to join a rival one. One could also leave to start a party of one's own.

Mukherjee explains that the function of the *dalapati* or party leader carried traces of the traditional functions of kingship. Thus, the leader was supposed to enforce the rules of religion and caste among party members, punish offenders and reward the meritorious, and settle disputes over property, inheritance, and marriage. The leader had the power to ostracize those who seriously violated religious or caste injunctions, and members were prohibited from maintaining any social relations with the ostracized family. The party leader also took over another erstwhile-royal function: patronizing scholarship and the arts. Many significant publishing ventures of the period, including journals, dictionaries, and translations of Sanskrit classics along with new genres of popular music and theater, were organized and promoted by the leading magnates in the city, usually in a spirit of mutual competition. There was a hint of sovereign power in the regular use of armed retainers to keep the urban poor under control as well. Artisans and other service groups in the city were under the patronage of wealthy magnates, who frequently used force to collect rents, evict recalcitrant tenants, and prevent disorder during public festivals.

It is easy to read a carryover of older social forms associated with landlords in rural Bengal in the activities of these early nineteenth-century parties and leaders. But the elements of novelty should not be missed. None of the urban magnates could claim even a figment of traditional political legitimacy, either by lineage or military power. Even as they adopted and flaunted many of the Persianate styles of the northern Indian aristocratic culture, the forms of power they exercised and institutions they built in the city were quite innovative. Thus, Radhakanta Deb, who emerged as leader of the conservative Dharma Sabha, defending orthodox religious practices and opposing the reform efforts of Rammohan and his followers, used the early modern form of the civic association to fight, within the representative organs of government in India and Britain, Bentinck's social legislation. Yet he also used the civic association, often in collaboration with Europeans, to promote the spread of Western education among Hindus. His architectural additions to the family mansion in Sobhabazar, especially the Natmandir built in 1840, used the fashionable neoclassical style to entirely original effect—to produce a theater-like space that could serve the ritual function of Durga Puja, secular function of a public meeting, and amusement space for a nautch party, which he frequently threw for his European guests.[116]

Even for ordinary inhabitants of Calcutta, it was widely observed that life in the new city was different from anything that had been previously experienced. *Kalikātā kamalālay*, written in 1823 and possibly the first text of urban sociology in India, divided the propertied (*biṣayī*) urban population into four classes: the wealthy of extraordinary fortune (*asādhāraṇ bhāgyaban*); those holding important positions, such as diwan or *mutsuddi*, with European patrons; *madhyabitta* or middling householders; and *daridra athaca bhadra*—that is, poor but respectable persons.[117] The author, Bhabanicharan Bandyopadhyay (1787–1848), a scholarly Brahmin, had made a career for himself as both a *sircar* (manager) to various British patrons and the editor of the journal *Samācār candrikā*. He was a leading figure, on the conservative side, in the new urban public life of debate and social campaign.[118] His book, he said in his preface, was addressed to visitors to Calcutta from rural areas and small towns who found the ways of the new city utterly incomprehensible. Bhabanicharan's burden was to show

Figure 11. Copy of *Samācār candrikā*, 1831. *Courtesy: Centre for Studies in Social Sciences, Calcutta*

that there was indeed an ethical way of living in the city, despite the fact that it was in many ways different from the traditional practices of the countryside.

"Kalikata," he observed, "is nourished by the deep but undrinkable waters of money [*mudrā*]. Furious activities send out streams of money in different directions, to different countries. The tide ebbs and flows without end along these rivers of money."[119] Yes, wealth and political power, he admitted, had much greater importance in Kalikata than in other places, but no one confused the new secular order of social status with the traditionally prescribed ritual order of precedence that was still respected, even if kept separate. The novelty of life in Calcutta lay in the unprecedented opportunities of social mobility that it offered. Lowly peddlers and shopkeepers could become wealthy aristocrats in the course of a single generation. Similarly, respectable people fallen on bad times could afford to take up menial or disreputable occupations because of the anonymity that the city offered. There were, in short, greater freedom and greater equality than in the traditional order. The new city was a place of social churning, and perhaps a place of the emergence of new moral norms too. Bhabanicharan provided the first elaborate description of the new politics of the dal. Scholar that he was, he noted the plethora of new Persian and English words that had entered the everyday Bengali language spoken in Calcutta. He defended the new practice, saying that there was nothing wrong in it as long as the language of religious ritual was kept uncontaminated.[120]

This was not the same response that would come later in the nineteenth century, when a more articulate project for constructing a national culture would be formulated. If Bhabanicharan's works do not, as Swati Chattopadhyay has correctly remarked, "present a full-fledged nationalist consciousness," it is because, situated within the early modern form of civic associations, often of mixed composition, he did not have the conceptual apparatus for separating the material and spiritual—the inner and outer—domains of culture that only the political conditions of a fully developed colonial state could supply.[121] Although he was cognizant of the elements of novelty in his present, Bhabanicharan's thought does not possess that confident projection into the future that is characteristic of modernity's consciousness of time.

Finally, there is the interesting evolution of the public space of the neighborhood or *para (pāḍā)* in nineteenth-century Calcutta. As with several other social concepts, a genealogy can be found for the para in the patterns of village settlements in Bengal, but it acquired quite new meanings in Calcutta's urban context. Once again, Chattopadhyay has helped us by noticing, for one, that the urban para was a territory of roughly one-quarter by one-half mile, easily walkable from one corner to another, and usually gaining a distinct identity from a physical feature such as a *bāgān* (garden) or *pukur* (pond), or an economic activity like a *bājār* (market) or the settlement of a particular group of craftspeople or traders. Second, the boundaries of a para were not fixed, and could, somewhat like the concept of a community, expand or contract depending on which set of activities or practices were being invoked in relation to the para. A para school thus might have a different catchment area from the group of residents expected to contribute to the para Durga Puja.

The important historical point, however, is that this form of the para evolved through the nineteenth century. In the early decades of the century, the para in Calcutta appears to have received its identity from one or two wealthy magnates, who from their large mansions dominated the neighborhood, settled tenants, extracted rents, kept the peace, and patronized most public activities and amusements. What might have happened if this territorial space of flexible boundaries had acquired an administrative form in municipal government remains an intriguing counterfactual question. But with the imposition in the latter half of the century of the colonial governmental form of municipal wards and police stations as the basic administrative units of the city—units that bore no relationship to the para's social form—the latter developed precisely as an alternative public space to that administered by the colonial authorities. The para became the site of a complex network of institutions catering to the educational, religious, cultural, and indeed moral life of neighborhood residents. By the turn of the twentieth century, this nationalist cultural project, conceived as a project of self-regulation outside the colonial state's control, would be directed, at the microterritorial level of the urban locality, by a new middle class.

But we are jumping ahead of our story. The early modern forms of sociality in the Bengali neighborhoods of Calcutta in the early nineteenth century necessarily have a quality of indeterminacy in terms of their historical possibilities. This is because there were not too many well articulated or conceptually credible historical projects that can be discerned within the developments taking place in the so-called Black Town—except, that is, for one significant movement. In the early nineteenth century, one small group of reformist Bengali leaders did attempt to use the articulation of the civic associations of mixed membership with the processes of government to make a clearly formulated case for a powerful early modern political idea—the antiabsolutist demand for free and equal citizenship. To describe this attempt along with its unfortunate fate it is necessary to turn to the careers of Rammohan Roy and Dwarakanath Tagore.

CHAPTER FIVE

Equality of Subjects

RAMMOHAN (1772/1774–1833) was one of the first Indians to make use of the new print medium in order to emerge as a public figure. His first tract—*Tuhfat-ul muwahhiddin*—was printed in Murshidabad in 1804, and distributed "in order," said Rammohan himself at the end of his text, "to avoid any future change in the book by copyists."[1] It needed more than ordinary courage for a young man of thirty, entirely unknown in the world of letters, to announce in the prefatory paragraph written in Arabic of a Persian work that he was setting out to demonstrate that "falsehood is common to all religions without distinction."[2] But this was no Enlightenment tract in the style of a Voltaire, even though Kishorichand Mitra, one of Rammohan's first biographers, claims that a few years later, the latter did publish a Bengali essay under an assumed name in which "the tomfooleries of the Hindu mode of worship are held up to merited ridicule and contempt."[3] In any case, it is certain that Rammohan was still not very familiar with the corpus of modern European philosophical writings when he wrote the *Tuhfa*. Instead of being a denunciation, the slim book is a rigorous logical examination of what might be called "natural religion," as contrasted with the doctrines and practices of various established religions and sects.

The Falsehood of All Religions

Rammohan made the bold argument that most people come to acquire a faith in religious rituals and doctrines merely by the force of upbringing and habit.

> The fact is this, that each individual on account of the constant hearing of the wonderful and impossible stories of his by-gone religious heroes and hearing the good results of those assumed creeds of that nation among whom he has been born and brought up, ... acquires such a firm belief in religious dogmas that he cannot renounce his adopted faith although most of its doctrines be obviously nonsensical and absurd.... [H]ence, it is evident that a man having adopted one particular religion with such firmness, his sound mind after reaching the age of maturity with acquired knowledge of books, without being inclined to make enquiries into the truth of the admitted propositions of so many years, is insufficient to discover the real truth.[4]

Yet the established religions also find support from the *mujtahid* or doctors of religion who claim, for instance, that the legendary deeds of the founders of religions are known from traditions that preserve the testimony of those who had witnessed those deeds. The difficulty is, said Rammohan, that "whether such a class of people [of eyewitnesses] existed in ancient times, is not known to the people of the present time through the medium of external senses or experience; rather it is quite obscure and doubtful." So one has to rely on the evidence of a second class of people who can vouch for the truthfulness of the first class, and then a third class of people who can vouch for the truthfulness of the second, and so on down to the present. "It is clear that men of sound mind will hesitate to reckon that class of people who co-exist with them, to be a truthful people to whom falsehood cannot be imputed, especially in matters of religion."[5] Tradition therefore cannot be a reliable test for judging the truth of the legends claimed by religions.

Similarly, there are stories of miracles. "It is customary with common people labouring under whims that when they see any act or thing done or found, beyond their power of comprehension, or for which they cannot make out any obvious cause, they ascribe it to supernatural power or miracle." But those of "sound mind and judgment" know that by patient insight and inductive reason, the true causes of such apparently inexplicable matters can indeed be discovered. And what still remains unexplained, noted Rammohan with an astonishing gesture of rational modesty, must be subjected to the following question: "Whether it is compatible with reason to be convinced of our own inability to understand the cause or to attribute it to some impossible agency inconsistent with the law of nature? I think our intuition will prefer the first." Religions also encourage a belief among the common people in the afterlife, so that "for the fear of punishment in the next world and the penalties inflicted by worldly authorities, [they] refrain from commission of worldly deeds." This only means, though, the perpetuation of "hundreds of useless privations regarding eating and drinking, purity and impurity, auspiciousness and inauspiciousness, etc."[6]

Rammohan also questioned the belief in revelation and prophets. If "the existence of all things in creation, whether good or bad, are connected with the Great Creator, without any intermediate agency," then what is the status of the prophets? If the sending of prophets and God's revelation to them are immediate acts of God to instruct people in the true path to salvation, they must be deemed to be quite redundant, because it is surely unnecessary for God to use an intermediary. On the other hand, if they are not immediate acts of God, then one must ask how it is to be established that the testimony of the intermediary is truthful, for it would require a series of intermediaries to keep up the prophetic tradition. "Hence, advent of prophets and revelation, like other things in nature, depend upon external causes without reference to God, i.e., they depend upon the invention of an inventor."[7]

This explains as well why the pronouncements of different prophets, all claiming to echo the word of God, are so different. Rammohan found little merit in the contention, put forth by some mujtahid, that just as common people must approach a king through ministers and officers, so must they approach God through intermediaries, or indeed just as the laws of different kings are so varied and change over time, so are the instructions of the prophets so different. In a devastating sweep of logic and rhetoric, Rammohan declared:

> My reply to this argument is that the ruling or government of the true God, who according to the belief of the followers of religions is acquainted with the particular state of every particle and who is Omniscient and to whom the past, present and future times are equally known and under whose influence hearts of mankind can be turned to whatever He wishes, and Who is provider of visible and invisible causes of everything and Who is far from having any particular object of His own interest and Who is free from whims; has no analogy with the rulings or governments of human beings, whose wisdom is defective and incapable of understanding the end of every action and who are liable to errors and mistakes and whose actions are mixed with selfishness, deceit and hypocrisy.[8]

He believed, and accordingly asserted, that it was possible to discover the truth from among the mass of untruth that the religions of the world offered.

> There is always an innate faculty existing in the nature of mankind that in case any person of sound mind, before or after assuming the doctrines of any religion, makes an enquiry into the nature of the principles of religious doctrines, primary or secondary, laid down by different nations without partiality and with a sense of justice, there is a strong hope that he will be able to distinguish the truth from untruth and the true propositions from the fallacious ones, and also he, becoming free from the useless restraints of religion, which sometimes, become sources of prejudice of one against another ..., will turn to the One Being who is the fountain of the harmonious organization of the universe, and will pay attention to the good of the society.

But it is inevitable, noted Rammohan, that such seekers of truth will find themselves in a minority. And those who are the followers of the established religions will always claim that they represent the majority. Still, "it is admitted by the seekers of truth that truth is to be followed although it is against the majority of the people." In any case, all religions were, in the beginning, religions of the minority.[9]

Rammohan concluded his tract with the following classification:

> In short, the individuals of mankind with reference to those who are deceivers and those who are deceived and those who are not either, amount to four classes.

Firstly—A class of deceivers who in order to attract the people to themselves wilfully invent doctrines of creeds and faith and put the people to troubles and cause disunion amongst them.

Secondly—A class of deceived people, who without inquiring into the fact, adhere to others.

Thirdly—A class of people who are deceivers and also deceived, they are those who having themselves faith in the sayings of another induce others to adhere to his doctrines.

Fourthly—Those who by the help of Almighty God are neither deceivers nor deceived.[10]

It would be later suggested quite convincingly that Rammohan's religious ideas in his mature years, after his familiarity with European writings and debates with Christian scholars, came close to something like deism. It is thus interesting that Obaidullah El Obaide, sitting down in 1883 to translate Rammohan's text, should gloss *muwahhid* as "deist."[11] Yet this rendering, arguably, is unwarranted, because when he wrote the *Tuhfa*, Rammohan was probably unaware of the various schools of post-Reformation Christianity and could not have consciously intended to dedicate his tract to deists. When it was included in the 1906 edition of the *English Works of Raja Rammohun Roy*, Obaidullah's translation of muwahhiddin was changed, in the title as well as the text, to the much more literal "believers in one God."[12]

We also know that this early expression of Rammohan's uncompromising rationalism was not a product of British colonial education. Lant Carpenter, who met Rammohan in England and wrote one of the first biographical notes on him after his death in 1833, observed that when the young Rammohan went to learn Arabic and Persian, "his masters at Patna set him to study Arabic translations of some of the writings of Aristotle and Euclid; it is probable that the training thus given strengthened his mind in acuteness and close reasoning, while the knowledge which he acquired of the Mahommedan religion from Mussulmen whom he esteemed, contributed to cause that searching examination of the faith in which he was educated."[13] As an explanation of Rammohan's extraordinary rationalism, this is clearly insufficient. Rammohan's demonstration of the falsehood of all religions could hardly have emanated from a schoolchild's study of Euclid's geometry or Aristotle's logic. In any case, lessons on these texts were by no means unusual in many well-established madrasas of eighteenth-century India, and Patna in particular was famous for the madrasa established there by Saif Khan, although we do not know if that is where Rammohan went to study.[14]

Besides, Rammohan's critique in the *Tuhfa* went far beyond the condemnation of Brahmanic ritualism—indeed, Rammohan's own ancestral religion is barely mentioned in the text—and called into question some of the principal aspects of Islam and Christianity, such as revelation, the prophetic tradition, miracles, afterlife, and so forth. What was the discursive space in which such a critique might have appeared? Unfortunately, the scholarship on this early phase of Rammohan's religious thought is so scanty that we have little to go on. All we know is that Rammohan was well acquainted with the Persian scholars at Fort William College and the Qazis of the Sadar Diwani Adalat, the highest civil court in Calcutta.[15] We also know that at the turn of the nineteenth century, Calcutta was quite a remarkable place of scholarship and debate among a new group of Muslim intellectuals, such as Tafazzul Husain Khan, the translator of Isaac Newton's and other European scientific works into Arabic, Abdul Latif Shustari, the commentator on British social life in India, and Abu Taleb Ispahani, who returned to Calcutta from his trip to Europe in 1803.[16]

In an influential lecture delivered in 1924, Brajendranath Seal noted that Rammohan was "learned in Mohammadan Law and Jurisprudence, and versed in the polemics of all the 63 schools of Mohammadan Theology." Further, "the free thought and universalistic outlook of the Mohammadan rationalists (Mutazza'lis of the 8th century), and Mohammadan Unitarians (the Muwahhidin) were among the most powerful of the formative influences on the Raja's mental growth."[17] More recently, Dilipkumar Biswas, the most eminent among later Rammohan scholars, agrees that all the arguments of the *Tuhfa* emerged out of debates in Islamic theology and logic.[18] Ajit Kumar Ray has suggested that Rammohan's critique was derived from a study of the *Dabistan-i-mazahib*, the seventeenth-century treatise on comparative religion written most probably by a Zoroastrian scholar, and a text widely circulated in scholarly circles in India in the eighteenth century.[19] Ajit Ray also notes that Rammohan was probably personally acquainted with the editor of the first printed Persian edition of the *Dabistan*, Nazar Ashraf of the Sadar Diwani Adalat in Calcutta.[20]

We also have one other inkling into the discursive network in which Rammohan developed his critique. There is an extant copy of a booklet titled *Jawab-i-tuhfatul muwahhiddin*—printed in Calcutta probably around 1820—that appears to have been written by a Muslim friend and admirer of Rammohan.[21] This *Jawab* was a refutation of the charges leveled against Rammohan by a group of Zoroastrians (whose original tract has not been found). The mystery is that the *Tuhfatul muwahhiddin* has no specific references at all to the Zoroastrian religion. What was it that provoked the Parsi scholars to attack Rammohan? Ajit Ray believes that it might have been another work by Rammohan called the *Manazaratul adiyan*, which he mentioned in the *Tuhfa* and which too has never been found, that was probably written as a tract on comparative religion, in the form of the *Dabistan-i mazahib*, and may have contained specific criticisms of Zoroastrian doctrines.[22] Biswas points out that the *Jawab* is proof that Rammohan's early religious writings in Persian remained a matter of lively public debate among intellectuals of different communities as late as

1820.[23] It certainly shows that regardless of the exceptional character of his views, Rammohan had his interlocutors, both hostile and friendly, among scholars who were not the products of British colonial education.

Later, when engaging in polemics with Hindu scholars defending the orthodox Brahmanic doctrines and practices, Rammohan immediately seized the advantages afforded by the emergent print culture by scrupulously citing page and line numbers when referring to his opponents, and insisting that they do the same rather than incorrectly attributing statements and views to him. This was a new practice in intellectual or sectarian exchanges in India. But in the style or form of their assertions, Rammohan's polemical writings in Bengali and Sanskrit stayed well within the familiar practices of traditional debate. He participated in vigorous hermeneutic discussions, arguing about the interpretation of a particular statement from a canonical source, or citing one canonical authority against another. He also employed sharp and complex logical tools, familiar in Indian logic, to highlight inconsistencies and absurdities in his opponents' contentions.

Thus, debating with Mrityunjay Vidyalankar, the renowned pundit of Fort William College, on the topic of idol worship, he pointed out that material representations of *īśvara*, like all material objects, are subject to creation, decay, and destruction. How could īśvara, who is without beginning or end, and untouched by processes of decay, be represented by such material objects? If it was thought that īśvara, being omnipotent, could assume a material form at will, Rammohan answered that this would imply that the Brahma could be the cause of Brahma's own destruction, because a material form, being necessarily finite in its duration, was contradictory to the *svarūpa* or innate character of īśvara. But nothing that is subject to possible destruction can be Brahma or īśvara. Hence, to hold that īśvara could assume a material form leads to a *viparyaya* or logical contradiction. If the learned pundit argued that of visible forms, only those made of the five elements were subject to change and destruction, but the nonmaterial form of īśvara could nevertheless become visible through the powers of yoga, then Rammohan's reply was that only the pundit's devoted disciples could be expected to believe that their master possessed the power to see a nonmaterial form not made out of any physical element. If it was further claimed that just as a rope lying on the ground could produce the image of a snake, so could an idol produce the image of īśvara in the mind, Rammohan's cutting retort was that just as sensible people realize, on closer observation, that they were mistaken in thinking that the rope was a snake, so should every person of sound mind accept that the image of īśvara produced by a clay or stone idol is a false image.[24]

In another polemic with a Vaishnava scholar, Rammohan maintained that the Vedanta is incompatible with the Krishna of the *Bhāgavat purāṇa*, because it is evident to every person of judgment that the shameful and immoral antics of Krishna with the *gopī* women of Vrindavan cannot be squared with any section or verse of the Vedanta.[25] In other polemical tracts, Rammohan utilized numerous arguments to show the absurdity of ritual prohibitions on eating meat and drinking liquor along with strictures against social interactions with the *yavana* (Muslim), *mleccha* (European), and Sudra.[26] Many of the most orthodox Brahmins of the day, he remarked, wore clothes made by Muslims, accepted employment with Europeans, explained classical Sanskrit texts in journals read by Europeans, and attended receptions after scrubbing their teeth with Muslim-made powder and sprinkling their shawls with Muslim-made perfume. On what grounds could they claim to excommunicate someone who, in search of knowledge, studied the philosophy of the Yavanas or discussed scientific discoveries with Europeans?[27]

Rammohan's principal interest in his polemical writings was rational argument and scholarly debate—to explore the ground and logical consistency of religious doctrines.[28] His central concern was to demonstrate, first, that there was a multiplicity of practices, and doctrines by which they were justified; second, that these were followed largely by the force of habit and upbringing; and third, that their doctrinal justifications were entirely arbitrary and inconsistent. Consequently, there could be no legitimate ground for religious or social authorities to impose sanctions or penalties on those who chose not to follow the prescribed practices. But despite the heated controversies that his writings generated, Rammohan kept his polemics well within the ambit of scholarly disputation. Only in the case of the immolation of widows did he actually engage in a public campaign to stop the supposedly religious practice, and even then, to the perplexity of many of his later admirers, he initially advised Governor-general Bentinck against a legal ban, because Hindus might conclude that the English, having won political supremacy, were now intent on imposing their own religion on the country.[29]

Rammohan's critique of religion and his own unorthodox doctrines could, we are arguing, have emerged from within a discursive space of scholarly debate that was available in India at the turn of the nineteenth century and that was not shaped by the forces of colonial education. As we have shown, his critique led Rammohan to lay down the rational ground for rejecting conventional religious doctrines and practices, even though he himself did not, other than refusing to participate in the *pūjā* of idols, give up the customary practices of Brahmanic daily life. But as is well known, Rammohan did not stop there. He went on to transform this freedom of belief into the legal-constitutional form of the individual subject's right to liberty. This could not have happened without Rammohan's association with the emergent public sphere in Bengal of free traders and freethinkers, as described earlier. The association of nonofficial Europeans, mixed-blood Eurasians, and the new urban Indian elite of Calcutta produced a novel, even if unstable and short-lived, early modern formation seeking to assert the freedoms of the subject against arbitrary and absolute power. The moment is distinctive, and its historical significance is lost by forcibly dragging it into other historical narratives of liberalism or nationalism. It deserves to be studied on its own merits.

THE COLONIZATION OF BARBAROUS COUNTRIES

Rammohan's faith in the generative role of British rule and colonial capital has been subjected to close examination as well as sharp criticism since the 1970s. In particular, three essays by Asok Sen, Sumit Sarkar, and Barun De are regarded as landmarks in this critical scholarship.[30] They were joined by Arabinda Poddar in a set of lectures delivered in 1981.[31] They all pointed to the period from 1772 (or 1774) to 1833, Rammohan's lifetime, as decisive for the foundations of the new colonial economy in Bengal: the permanent settlement with landlords, opening up of Bengal to British industrial imports, destruction of indigenous manufacturing, perpetuation of insecure subsistence farming and rack-renting, and quasi-monopoly of British agency houses over the commercial and financial sectors—in short, all those classic features of colonial exploitation, underdevelopment, and poverty.

While all this was going on, Rammohan, along with his younger contemporary Dwarakanath, collaborated in business ventures with these private trading and financial houses, and offered full-throated support to the demand for free trade and settlement of European capitalists and professionals in India. In this, Rammohan and Dwarakanath were often opposing company policy, and thus not entirely popular among officialdom in India. They believed, all too innocently, that these measures would lead to a flourishing economy and the progressive enlightenment of the Indian people.

"Rammohun's zeal for alliance with the forces of the English industrial revolution," concludes Sen, "looks particularly naïve and misdirected.... [L]ater history can only appreciate the element of self-defeating irony in Rammohun's plea for European colonization to induce foreign capital, skill and enterprise into his motherland."[32] Sarkar saw in Rammohan's career a steady retreat from the radical nonconformism of the *Tuhfa* period to the repeated compromises of his later years along with a growing unwillingness to break with the past. He notes that Rammohan "somehow managed to combine an impressive interest in and sympathy for liberal and nationalist movements in England, France, Naples, Spain, Ireland and even Latin America with a fundamental acceptance of foreign political and economic domination over his own country." Rammohan "visualized a dependent but still real bourgeois development in Bengal in

Figure 12. *Rammohun Roy,* oil on canvas, by Rembrandt Peale, 1833. *Photograph courtesy of the Peabody Essex Museum, Salem, Massachusetts*

close collaboration with British merchants and entrepreneurs."[33] Poddar contends that Rammohan's commitment to rationalism and freedom was fatally marred by his inexplicable faith in the emancipating mission of British rule.

This contradiction in Rammohan has vexed historians because it resists every attempt to place him at the beginning of nationalist modernity in India. And nowhere is the problem more sharply posed than in the question of the settlement of Europeans in India.

The 1820s was a period of accelerated emigration of people from Britain to North America. Toward the other pole, Australia was emerging as the destination for another stream of migration, theorized in political economy by Edward Wakefield, who spoke of the possibility of a middle-class empire, based on the colonization of foreign lands combined with the employment of British capital and labor that could not be used at home.[34] Private traders in India were also vociferous at this time in demanding the removal of restrictions on land purchases by Europeans and the setting up of new agricultural enterprises in the countryside. The argument was taken up in England by the politically influential members of the so-called Clapham sect—the group of Evangelical campaigners, including William Wilberforce and Charles Grant, who were now keen to extend their antislavery movement to the task of ending barbarism and bringing enlightenment to India. They suggested that this could be achieved by opening India to Christian missionaries and British settlers with skill and capital.

According to the then-prevailing policy, shipwrights, coach makers, and mechanics were allowed into India in numbers limited to "what may be sufficient for the initiation and improvement of the natives in the useful arts. The latter are known to be great adepts in imitation, and their frugal habits render it impossible for Europeans to rival them in pursuits where success depends chiefly on the cheapness of manual labour." The East India Company "had strong objections to European menial servants of either sex going to India. They are generally found themselves to require the service of natives, over whom they are prone to tyrannize, whilst, in point of comparative usefulness, they rank far below the native servants." The company also looked at applications from commercial speculators "with considerable jealousy," because "a general compliance with them would afford a wide opening for the indiscriminate resort of Europeans to India."[35]

When Buckingham resumed his journalistic career in England, his *Oriental Herald* became an important organ for voicing the demand for opening up India to European settlement. In the first volume of the journal, Buckingham asserted that Europeans should be allowed to buy land in India: "The possession of the land is the key-stone of the arch, on which the whole superstructure of increased wealth depends; for unless British subjects are allowed to be proprietors of land, no large agricultural surplus can ever be raised for the use of England."[36] He got such luminaries of French political economy as Jean-Charles-Léonard de Sismondi and Jean-Baptiste Say to argue the case. "An Englishman has no *Right* to live in British India," complained Sismondi. "He is only *tolerated* there; no Englishman can buy lands there in his own name, because the Company has determined not to suffer the Colonization of India...."

This strange power, as contrary to British Liberty, as to the dignity and honour of the nation, was conferred on the Company when as yet it had only factories in India.... But now," he concluded, "it is time to change the policy."[37]

When Say, in his essay, made the comment that "India is not, properly speaking, a colony; that is, the English have never driven out nor destroyed the aborigines," Buckingham could not restrain himself from inserting an editorial note:

> It is by no means necessary that the settlement of the English in India should lead to the immediate extermination of the Indians themselves, unless it be supposed, that when the English came among them, the country was already peopled up to the utmost capacity to bear.... [I]s it not desirable, on the score of happiness to the human race, that 100 millions of ignorant, superstitious, indolent, and enslaved beings, should be replaced by the same number of intelligent, reasonable, active and free men? Is it better for humanity, that the United States of America should be peopled as it is; or that the Cherokees and the Chickasaws should come back again, and let their wig-wams be erected in the ruins of the Capitol at Washington, and their dismal swamps replace the elegant and healthy squares of Philadelphia? Either the colonization of barbarous countries is a good or an evil. If it be a good, we ought immediately to encourage it in India;—if an evil, North America should give back her population to Great Britain—South America should pour her republican children into the lap of her bigoted and besotted mother, Spain—and India herself should yield her train of English adventurers, ... their arts, their sciences, and their intellectual attainments, by which alone they made their conquests and retained them.

And as if this burst of purple rhetoric was not enough, Buckingham went on to emphasize:

> The great agent by which both [Islam and the Hindu religion] would be made to disappear more rapidly than by any other, would be by the immediate and extensive Colonization of India by Englishmen.... The Continent of America, though discovered but yesterday, (to speak comparatively,) is more powerful, more wealthy, more virtuous, and more happy, than the Continent of Africa, which contained the Egyptians, the earliest civilized nation of which we have any record.... Let Asia be but colonized as America has been, and she will soon be as great, as virtuous, and as happy.[38]

It is crucial to mention that there was a new urgency in these 1820s' and 1830s' arguments about the economic transformation of India that was entirely missing in the colonial debates of the eighteenth century. Unlike the earlier faith in Indians' agricultural, manufacturing, and commercial skills, which needed to be turned into a source of profit for British trade, it was now being alleged that Indian agriculture and manufacturing were stagnating at levels far below the standards prevailing in other countries, and more important, could not hope to improve without the injection of European capital and technology. John Crawfurd, who acted as a spokesperson in the British Parliament for the merchants of Calcutta, proclaimed that every article of foreign trade produced by Indian agriculturists and manufacturers—cotton and cotton manufactures, woolens, sugar, tobacco, raw silk, and coffee—were of inferior quality. Only indigo was an exception because it was the product of British enterprise and knowledge.

> The whole productions of Indian industry that are abandoned to the exclusive man-agement of the natives ... are inferior to the similar productions of every other tropi-cal country; they are not only inferior to the productions of British colonial industry, but to those of French, Dutch, and Spanish, even to those of Portuguese industry; they are in every case also inferior to the corresponding productions of Chinese industry.

Continuing, Crawfurd made the inevitable comparison with the other colonial world:

> The indigenous products of India have been transferred to America, and there, under the direction of European skill, they far surpass, in goodness and quantity, those of their original country.... Have the Indians retaliated upon the American colonists? Where is our Indian annatto? Where is our Indian cocoa,—our Indian vanilla? ... In whatever direction we turn our eyes, the effects of Indian imbecility and the baleful consequences of European exclusion are equally conspicuous.[39]

The debate gathered steam in 1832 when the East India Company's charter came up for renewal in Parliament. The old guard of the company's establish-ment in India was firmly opposed to the settlement there of Europeans. Mal-colm thought that "their superior pretensions, and the place they occupied in the community, combined with difference of habits and religion, would be likely to create feelings of jealousy and hostility in the minds of the natives."[40] Mountstuart Elphinstone predicted that as in "all regular colonies," the settlers and a new half-caste population would foster "contempt and dislike for blacks."[41] James Grant Duff, soon to distinguish himself as the historian of the Marathas, was more forthright: "I cannot see how the British nation could sanction unrestricted intercourse without danger to the permanency of its own dominion, and injustice to the natives.... If we give way to clamour and soph-istry on this great question, shall we not justify the character for selfishness with which we shall be branded?"[42] As a matter of fact, however, the number of Europeans resident in India at this time, not counting company officials and military personnel, was extremely small—less than 2,000, of whom 1,595 lived in Bengal.[43]

Those who opposed the proposal, in India as well as Britain, pointed to three dangers: a large body of European entrepreneurs, exercising their superior skills and privileges, could oppress their Indian tenants and employees, and thus incite hostile feelings among the native population; alliances between European men and Indian women would produce a large population of mixed blood whose loyalties would be uncertain; and a large settler population with a distinct sense of its interests and rights could become a potent source of political opposition to the colonial government. Advocates of the colonization cause vigorously disputed these claims. Crawfurd argued that the Muslims had conquered and ruled over India, yet "still the Hindoos held, after so many centuries of rude dominion, by far the larger portion of the land.... This is rather a strong case. It may be rationally asked, will one of the most civilized and humane of the nations of Europe, in a civilized age, act a worse, or a weaker part than the semi-barbarians of Persia and Tartary, in a very barbarous one?" Regardless, the Hindus were by innate nature a submissive people. "We hold our Indian empire by the power of the sword.... [The Indian] army is the smallest in the world in proportion to the population of the country.... The population of India, then, instead of being difficult, is more easy to retain in subjection than that of any other country existing, and, probably, than any country that has ever existed in the records of history."[44] As for the mixing of races, it was remarked that the practice was rare, and even with an influx of European settlers, the number of mixed progeny was likely to remain minuscule.

Although conservative opinion within the company administration was strongly opposed to the entry of Europeans into the Indian countryside, the government now had at its head a small group of liberal reformers armed with the theories of utility and fired by the spirit of Evangelicalism. They joined the battle on the side of change. Metcalfe declared: "I have long lamented that our countrymen in India are excluded from the possession of land, and other ordinary rights of peaceable subjects.... [T]hose restrictions impede the prosperity of our Indian empire, and of course their removal would promote it." He added, with a characteristic citation of the utilitarian agenda:

> The only objection that strikes me to the spread of a British Christian population in India, is the existing discordance of the laws by which our English and our native subjects are retrospectively governed. This objection will no doubt in time be removed, and the sooner the better, by laws equally binding on both parties, in all concerns common to both, and leaving to all their own suitable laws, in whatever peculiarly concerns themselves alone.[45]

The most powerful voice was that of the governor-general, though. In a carefully composed minute that did not conceal its liberal inspiration, Bentinck refuted every objection and unhesitatingly argued for the settlement of Europeans in India:

> It would be infinitely advantageous for India to borrow largely in arts and knowledge from England.... To question this is to deny the superiority which has gained us the dominion of India: it is to doubt whether national character has any effect on national wealth, strength and good government: ... it is to hold as nothing community of language, sentiment and interest, between the Government and the governed: ... it is to tell our merchants and our manufacturers that the habits of a people go for nothing in creating a market, and that enterprise, skill and capital, and the credit which creates capital, are of no avail in the production of commodities.

Most interesting was his response to the contention that a British settler population in India might become the hotbed of demands for self-government, as had happened in the American colonies.

> But it may be said that the danger lies in the union of the British settlers with the natives of the country; ... It assumes, however, a vast change to have occurred in the frame of society, such as can scarcely be looked for in centuries to come; I might almost say a vast improvement, which would imply that the time had arrived when it would be wise in England to leave India to govern itself.[46]

Perhaps in centuries to come, thought Bentinck, yet self-government under the leadership of a body of British settlers as the culmination of empire—once again, implicitly, going by the American precedent—was not an unworthy future for a liberal to imagine.

John Rosselli, in his Bentinck biography, maintains that the liberal governor-general believed that "India would attain nationality by becoming British"—in other words, "a kind of Indian Canada or United States"—and that his vision of India was that "of a tropical America haloed with the glory of a regenerated Mughal Empire."[47] It is important to appreciate that such an imagined future seemed possible, at least to some liberal minds, at this brief moment in history. It is equally significant to assert that it would be utterly wrong to read in Bentinck's remark a prescient anticipation of India's history as it actually unfolded over the next century and more. To show this, we need to return to Rammohan and his position on the colonization question.

Citizens of Character and Capital

Rammohan's enthusiasm for various liberal causes is well known. His friend William Adam said of him: "Love of freedom was perhaps the strongest passion of his soul—freedom not of the body merely, but of the mind—freedom not of action merely, but of thought."[48] In the early 1820s, in Calcutta, Rammohan celebrated the brief successes of the constitutionalists in Portugal and Spain.[49] In 1823, he published an article in his Persian newspaper that was strongly critical of the extractions of English landlords and the taxes imposed by the British state in Ireland.[50] He was an ardent supporter of the July revolution of 1830 in France. On his voyage to England, Rammohan is said to have been so excited at the sight of two French frigates at the Cape of Good Hope that, despite nursing an injured leg, he insisted on visiting the boats in order to salute the tricolor.[51] Louis Philippe generously reciprocated his sentiments during Rammohan's visit to France in 1832–33, when the French monarch accorded him a lavish reception worthy of an ambassador of state. Rammohan keenly watched the progress of the reform bill in the British Parliament in 1832, and vowed that if the legislation were defeated, he would "renounce [his] connection with this country [Britain]."[52] It was whispered that his political preferences were thoroughly republican, but knowing "that his republican sentiments would not find very general acceptance,—he spoke cautiously in mixed society, on political subjects."[53]

During the negotiations over his journey to Britain as an emissary of the Mughal ruler (whom the British now called merely the king of Delhi), Rammohan described himself in his letters to the Mughal court as "the humblest of the subjects of his Britannic Majesty" who lived "fearlessly under the protecting influence of the British laws of justice." He was accepting his assignment, he said, out of his "feelings of commiseration for the indigent condition of the illustrious House of Taimur."[54] But when the East India Company officials objected to his representing himself as the accredited envoy of Akbar II, Rammohan agreed to travel as a private individual.[55]

It was bold—one might even say audacious—for Rammohan to claim that he was a subject of the British monarch, because given the ambiguity over sovereignty in India, it was entirely unclear, both legally and politically, whether a native Indian was a British subject in the same sense that expatriate British traders or professionals were. Even more interesting is the fact that while in Britain, Rammohan was apparently struck by a suggestion he heard at a gathering that since he was born within the British dominions, he was a British subject and was "entitled to all the privileges of a native of Great Britain." He made inquiries on whether he was eligible for election to Parliament, and it seems even Bentham was interested in supporting the idea, although nothing came of it in the end.[56] What remains indisputable, however, is Rammohan's determination, even against the declared position of the company's government in India, to represent himself directly as well as on behalf of India's native inhabitants to the British government as a subject of the British Crown.

Rammohan was one of the first Indians to use the press as a vehicle for public communication. In 1821, he launched the *Brahmunical Magazine* in

English and *Saṃbād kaumudī* in Bengali, and in 1822, the *Mirat-ul-akhbar*, a weekly in Persian that, he explained, was a language "understood by all the respectable part of the Native Community." His intention was "to communicate to the Rulers a knowledge of the real situation of their subjects ... and put the people in possession of the means of obtaining protection and redress from their Rulers."[57] As a matter of fact, the *Mirat* was the first printed Persian journal in the world, and had a readership, according to Rammohan's own statement, consisting of "kind and liberal gentlemen of Persia and Hindustan."[58] When the press regulations were imposed in 1823, Rammohan refused to apply for a license, claiming it was below the dignity of any person of honor to supplicate before an official and voluntarily swear to abide by the rules promulgated by the authorities, and instead closed down the *Mirat*.[59]

Rammohan's defense of the freedom of the press is, of course, a classic statement of the liberal position on the subject.[60] In an appeal to the king in council on behalf of the natives of Calcutta, he clearly announced that the restrictions imposed on the press in Bengal in 1823 were "an invasion on our civil rights," indicating "a total disregard of the civil rights and privileges of your Majesty's faithful subjects." He repeated the familiar liberal arguments on the merits of a free press, and recalled that "a Free Press has never yet caused a revolution in any part of the world" because it afforded people the opportunity to voice their grievances and have them redressed. But he also asked the crucial question: Must India be an exception to the universal principle? "While therefore the existence of a free Press is equally necessary for the sake of the Governors and the governed, it is possible that a national feeling may lead the British people to suppose, that in two points, the peculiar situation of this country requires a modification of the laws enacted for the control of the Press in England." These two points were the possibilities, first, that some people might instigate hostilities between the people of India and Britain, and second, that they could disturb relations with neighboring countries. Rammohun held that neither of these were credible dangers.

The interesting twist that Rammohan supplied to his liberal defense of the free press lay in his belief that even under Mughal rule, the privileges of the native inhabitants of the country were respected.

The abolition of this most precious of their privileges, is the more appalling to your Majesty's faithful subjects, because it is a violent infringement of their civil and religious rights.... [U]nder their former Muhammadan Rulers, the natives of this country enjoyed every political privilege in common with Mussulmans, being eligible to the highest offices in the state, entrusted with the command of armies and the government of provinces and often chosen as advisors to their Prince, without disqualification or degrading distinction on account of their religion or the place of their birth.... Although under the British Rule, the natives of India, have entirely lost this political consequence, your Majesty's faithful subjects were consoled by the more secure enjoyment of their civil and religious rights which had been so often violated by the rapacity and intolerance of the Mussalmans.[61]

Given the fact that Indians were entirely excluded from the organs of government of their own country, how could the British ensure that the inhabitants of a country "situated at the distance of several thousand miles" were well governed? Either by allowing a free press that could publicly discuss the failings of the government, or by instituting an independent and neutral commission, "composed of gentlemen of intelligence and respectability," which could supervise government activities and suggest methods of redress. Rammohan also remarked that even the Mughal rulers had their *akhbar-nawis* or news writers and *khufia-nawis* or confidential correspondents to keep themselves informed of popular opinion.[62] He disagreed, therefore, both on the grounds of principle and the pragmatic tactics of governance that India must be treated as an exception to the universal applicability of the freedom of the press.

Rammohan also stridently objected to the exclusion of Indians from the jury in the Calcutta courts. "Any Natives, either Hindu or Mohamedan, are rendered by this Bill subject to judicial trial by Christians, either European or Native, while Christians, including Native Converts, are exempted from the degradation of being tried either by a Hindu or a Mussulman juror, however high he may stand in the estimation of his Society." By this, he alleged, the British were "introducing religious distinctions into the judicial system of the country."[63] It would "stir up a spirit of religious intolerance," he warned, "in a now harmonious though mixed community."[64] He organized a petition against the jury bill in 1826 supported by more than two hundred signatories, both Hindu and Muslim.[65]

In his suggestions for the reform of the Indian judicial system, Rammohan made a similar plea for granting a more equal place to Indian judges. Given the inexperience of European judges in India, and their ignorance of the local languages and customs, the attempt should be made, he said, "to combine the knowledge and experience of the native with the dignity and firmness of the European." This goal could be achieved by appointing an Indian mufti or assessor to every civil court in British Bengal. The mufti would hold office for life and have a seat with the European judge on the bench. "They should be responsible to the government as well as to the public for their decisions, in the same manner as the European judges." In case of a difference of opinion, the European judge might have a casting vote, but the muftis should also have the right to record their dissent.[66]

Thus, even as he upheld the prevailing liberal doctrines about the freedoms of the citizen-subject, Rammohan also insisted that all citizens be treated equally, regardless of race or religion. His ideas on who qualified as proper citizens in this sense certainly were constrained by the dominant liberal opinions of the day. He often referred to such citizens as "men of privilege and respectability"— only men, not women, but also men with education, property, and a capacity to engage in responsible public activity.[67] Rammohan's views, then, were liberal, but not democratic in the twentieth-century sense. But within the early modern formation of a citizen public that emerged in Calcutta in the early nineteenth century—one that comprised nonofficial Europeans, mixed-blood Eurasians, and elite Indians—Rammohan was adamant about the equal status and participation of all.

His proposal for the settlement of Europeans in India needs to be evaluated in this context. In his submission to the Select Committee of the House of Commons in 1832, Rammohan listed several advantages that he thought would result. European settlers would, he said, "introduce the knowledge they possess of superior modes of cultivating the soil and improving its products," as had happened with indigo. The Europeans, being more "aware of the rights belonging to a liberal Government, would obtain from the local Governments, or from the Legislature in England, the introduction of many improvements in the laws and the judicial system; the benefit of which would of course extend to the inhabitants generally." They would establish schools in India to teach the English language along with European arts and sciences. By communicating with Indians, they would "gradually deliver their minds from the superstitions and prejudices which have ... disqualified them from useful exertions." Finally, with the example of America on his mind, Rammohan also brought up another possibility:

> If, however, events should occur to effect a separation between the two countries [Britain and India], then still the existence of a large body of respectable settlers, consisting of Europeans and their descendants, professing Christianity, and speaking the English language in common with the bulk of the people ... would bring that vast Empire in the east to a level with other large Christian countries in Europe, and by means of its immense riches and extensive population, ... may succeed sooner or later in enlightening and civilizing the surrounding nations of Asia.[68]

The principal danger that Rammohan apprehended from the settlement of Europeans was that they might "assume an ascendancy over the aboriginal inhabitants, and aim at enjoying exclusive rights and privileges, to the depression of the larger, but less favoured class." The remedy, he suggested, was to restrict immigration for the first twenty years to "educated persons of character and capital" who would be "less disposed to annoy and insult the natives." He was emphatic, as before, that the laws and judicial system apply equally to all races and religions, without discriminating between Europeans and Indians. "The enactment of equal laws, placing all classes on the same footing as to civil rights, and the establishment of trial by jury (the jury being composed impartially of both classes), would be felt as a strong check on any turbulent or overbearing characters amongst Europeans." Rammohan also considered the "probable danger" that "if the population of India were raised to wealth, intelligence, and public spirit, by accession and by the example of numerous respectable European settlers, the mixed community so formed would revolt (as the United States of America formerly did) against the power of Great Britain, and would ultimately establish independence." Nevertheless, he argued, "the Americans were driven to rebellion by misgovernment." Like the people of Canada, "the mixed community of India, ... so long as they are treated liberally, and governed in an enlightened manner, will feel no disposition to cut off its connections with England."[69]

Rammohan was prepared to imagine a Creole republic in India, consisting of European settlers and their descendants as well as an expanding body of Indians qualified to exercise the functions of responsible citizenship. Yet in his version of this imagined community, Europeans and Indians would have a position of full equality as citizen-subjects. His views in this regard were not entirely consonant with those of other liberals of his time.

The conservative opinion within the Indian administration was, as I noted earlier, strongly opposed to the settlement of large numbers of Europeans in India. James Grant Duff was scornful of Rammohan's viewpoint: "I would recommend that the natives themselves be consulted on the subject, not such natives as have acquired English, and, for that circumstance, just enough of knowledge to be convinced by the last pamphlet or magazine they may have read, but persons following different avocations, retired statesmen, or sound-headed practical men."[70] Others read in Rammohan's perspective a warning against the indiscriminate immigration of Europeans: "[It is] highly necessary for the well-being and contentment of the community, and the maintenance of respect for the Government and the national character, that any general and promiscuous admission of European settlers should on no account be permitted. On this point my views and opinions are most perfectly in unison with those so perspicuously expressed by Rammohun Roy."[71]

Even within his own camp of free traders, there were many who felt betrayed by the qualifications that Rammohan had added to his endorsement of the case for European settlement. The *India Gazette* and *Bengal Hurkaru*, the most outspoken organs of the free trade and colonization lobby in Calcutta, were disappointed. The former alleged that Rammohan's statements in Britain were "not only self-contradictory" but also "inconsistent with those he had been induced publicly and formally to express in Calcutta."[72] The latter saw in his qualified stance an attempt to placate the zamindars of Bengal as well as the company's administration: that part of his statement, the *Bengal Hurkaru* claimed, "seems almost dictated in Leadenhall Street by Mrs. Company herself, at whose tea-table, we suppose, such non-sense was exclusively allowed now-adays."[73] And judging from the resolute refusal of the expatriate European community to submit itself to Indian jurors and judges, it is unlikely that Rammohan's insistence on equality in the judicial system gladdened the hearts of many of his free trader allies.

The difficulties that historians have faced in fixing Rammohan's place in the history of modern India stem primarily from the attempt to put him at the origin of a linear narrative of nationalist and democratic modernity. The critics of the 1970s, by pointing out Rammohan's naive and misplaced faith in the transforming role of British settlement and enterprise in India, questioned the historical role of the so-called Bengal renaissance. In response, his admirers are still trying to retrieve his reputation as the father of Indian modernity by emphasizing that he was not an unqualified supporter of India's colonization.[74] The debate disappears, however, if we are prepared to place Rammohan within a short-lived early modern antiabsolutist formation that appeared in the early nineteenth century. This structure was liberal and capitalist, but neither nationalist nor democratic in the sense in which Indian modernity would develop subsequently. Rammohan occupied a distinct position within this racially mixed configuration, demanding a degree of equality between races and religions that was not necessarily shared by others within the formation.

Dwarakanath, as a disciple of Rammohan, joined him in most of these public activities and continued them after the latter's death. He too was a campaigner for the free press, and in the 1830s, became the proprietor of the *India Gazette*, soon to merge with the *Bengal Hurkaru* and *Englishman*, the two most important English newspapers of Calcutta, staffed by British journalists and voicing liberal opinions critical of the company's administration. But in this period, Dwarakanath had also emerged as a business entrepreneur, setting up his own companies and managing agencies in partnership with British merchants.

Despite all the talk of importing British capital, there was actually little British investment in India before the second half of the nineteenth century. British private trade was conducted with Indian capital, advanced by so-called banians, at varying rates of interest. Dwarakanath broke this pattern by floating companies with British partners. A few others, like Motilal Seal, Ramgopal Ghosh, Rustomjee Cowasjee, or Ashutosh Day, followed in his wake. But in the early 1840s, Dwarakanath was the leading merchant of the city, whether British or Indian, and Carr, Tagore, and Company, formed by Dwarakanath with nine British partners, was the leading agency house.[75] He launched new ventures in shipping and coal mining, in partnership with British engineers and traders, and made an unrealised attempt at starting a railway company. Dwarakanath was also a leading figure in the Union Bank, which once again had a multiracial board. The bank collapsed in 1847, a year after Dwarakanath's death

in London, following a series of fraudulent and criminally irresponsible transactions by a group of leading European merchants in collusion with senior East
India Company officials, proving once more that contrary to the confident pronouncement of Thomas Babington Macaulay the temptation to plunder the
riches of the Orient was still part of the ethos of the British expatriate.[76] The
fall of the Union Bank marked the end of British-Indian corporate partnership
in Bengal.

Like Rammohan, Dwarakanath too was a vigorous champion of free trade
and the settlement of European businesspeople in India, and consequently, was
a critic of the conservative lobby within the East India Company. During his
first visit to Britain in 1842–44, he was expected to represent the case of the
Bengal merchants. When, apparently overwhelmed by the generosity of the reception given to him by the East India Company directors, Dwarakanath spoke
of Clive and Cornwallis as having gone out "to benefit India by their counsels
and arms," and having done it "not in the expectation of a requital—not in the
hope of anything whatever in return, but from the mere love of doing good,"
even his friends in India were scandalized.[77] They thought that such fawning
behavior detracted from his role as a member of the opposition to the company
establishment. The *Bengal Hurkaru* laced its comments with an extraordinary
mix of sarcasm and irony:

> Well done Dwarky! The company must have winced under this. England, says the
> independent Hindoo merchant, took possession of India and her resources—not in
> the hope of anything in return—oh! of course not—Oh!—no—but from pure and
> genuine philanthropy. It was a most disinterested act on the part of our countrymen;
> they did not wish to gain anything; they would have been shocked at the very name
> of profit; they left England full and returned empty; careless of self; they spent vast
> treasures upon the amelioration of the people of India, and got nothing in return—
> Oh!—no—of course not. They took nothing away from India—Oh! no—not a pice—
> not a cowry—they came and took possession of the country from the mere love of
> doing good!—What a felicitous comment upon our appropriation of the continent
> of India. The irony, coming from the mouth of a Hindoo, must have told with terrify-
> ing effect....
>
> Dwarkanauth, we are sure, must have laughed in his sleeve at this effect, which
> this bit of clap-trap, artfully laid, produced upon the sober citizens of London.... It
> does Dwarky great credit—only, perhaps, it was a little bit too severe, especially at
> the tail of the turtle, and salmon, and venison, the champagne and the cold punch.[78]

This speech by Dwarakanath was probably a lapse, because he made efforts
later to undo the damage. Yet another occasion when his position—this time
a principled one—puzzled many of his friends was on Macaulay's proposal in
1836 to take away the privilege that Europeans in the Bengal countryside en-

joyed of directly approaching the Supreme Court in Calcutta and instead put them under the same legal system with Indians in the company's courts. This was a basic reform that the utilitarians had been urging for India—to remove the multiplicity of legal systems and govern everyone by the same set of laws—and it was a demand that Rammohan had supported as well. Defending the reform, Macaulay alleged: "We proclaim to the Indian people that there are two sorts of justice—a coarse one, which we think good enough for them, and another of superior quality, which we keep for ourselves."[79] Macaulay insisted that these double standards had to go.

Dwarakanath, however, joined the expatriate British nonofficials in opposing Macaulay's "black act." His reasoning was interesting. The company's directors, he claimed, wanted to "rule India with absolute power." "They have taken all which the Natives possessed; their lives, liberty, property and all were held at the mercy of Government and now they wish to bring the English inhabitants of the country to the same state! They will not raise the Natives to the condition of the Europeans, but they degrade the Europeans by lowering them to the state of the Natives." The privileges of the English were the freedoms they enjoyed as British subjects. Now the company, "desirous of exercising absolute and despotic power in this country," was bent on taking away even those residual freedoms. "The natives have hitherto been slaves; are the Englishmen therefore to be made slaves also? This is the kind of equality the government are seeking to establish."[80] Dwarakanath was taking a consistently antiabsolutist position—one that demanded not the mere equality of status of all subjects shorn of all rights but rather the equality of all in their freedoms. Ironically, given the overtly expressed stake of the nonofficial European community in their racial privileges, Dwarakanath's argument came across as so much fancy dressing for an acceptance of the racial superiority of Europeans.

The Unsung End of Early Modernity

In a recent essay, Bayly rightly emphasizes Rammohan's role in the emergence of constitutional liberalism in India. He also shows that this development is connected to a global trend in demanding liberal institutions in many parts of the European and colonial world.[81] Nevertheless, despite claiming to abjure historical teleologies, Bayly cannot resist being drawn into a progressive narrative of liberal constitutionalism, because his description does not record the fact that the life of this liberal formation was cut short almost as soon as it was born. The same must be said about the assertion that the enthusiasm for Rammohan among radical liberals in Britain demonstrates that "colonial encounters were not always about the construction of difference" and "far more inclusive notions of political citizenship" were possible.[82]

This supposedly inclusive liberal spurt was doomed not only because British rule would be established on new imperial foundations in the subsequent decades of the nineteenth century, rejecting the antiabsolutism of the early modern liberal formation and putting in place an authoritarian regime of colonial modernization. It was also doomed because the history of liberalism itself, accompanying the hegemonic growth of industrial capital and spread of democratic politics in the metropolitan countries, would discover the institutions and ideologies for constructing a dual structure of liberalism at home and authoritarian rule in the colony. This would become an integral part of the global history of the liberal democratic state in the nineteenth and twentieth centuries.

Just as the absolutist early modern formation, exemplified by Tipu in Mysore, was interrupted by the colonial modern, so was the antiabsolutist early modern. There can be no linear history of liberalism in India from the battles in the early nineteenth century over a free press or the right of Indians to sit on a jury to the liberal-democratic constitution of the republic of India in 1950. This history is broken by the long period of colonial modernity and the nationalist response to colonial tutelage. There lies the significance of the conceptual distinction we have drawn between the early modern and the colonial modern in the domain of the political. Hence, although Derozio's best-known poem, originally untitled, is now easily read as perhaps the earliest invocation of the Indian nation deified, one should remember that Derozio's "native land" evoked in him a very different nationalism:

> My country! In thy day of glory past
> A beauteous halo circled round thy brow,
> And worshipped as a deity thou wast,—
> Where is that glory, where that reverence now?[83]

Notwithstanding the strikingly similar imagery, Derozio's nation was not reimagined in the Indian nationalism of the turn of the twentieth century. His early modern national formation, inspired by the American examples he knew, or perhaps by that of the Greek war of independence, died a quick death. It was evident that equal citizenship irrespective of race or religion was unlikely to be realized. And the other alternative—national independence, regardless of race or religion—was too lofty a demand to be openly voiced. Barely ten years after Derozio's death, his student Sarada Prasad Ghosh was remonstrating with his comrades: "You do not, like the brave and noble minded American, aspire so high as to free yourself from the yoke of British sway.... [Y]ou only desire to be freed from the tyranny and oppression of the local government of this country."[84] The realities of colonial rule under conditions of modern empire were beginning to sink in.

The change in the character of the public sphere is shown dramatically by the history of a single institution: the Town Hall of Calcutta. This elegant neo-classical building, recently restored—situated in the heart of the administrative district, a stone's throw from Government House and just south of the present location of the Black Hole monument in St. John's churchyard—was opened in 1813. It became the favorite place for grand banquets, balls, and public meetings of the Europeans of the city. But in the 1820s and 1830s, with the emergence of a new antiabsolutist public of mixed racial composition, the Town Hall took pride of place as the venue for some of the most memorable public meetings of the period, such as those in 1823 in protest against the strangling of the press or the one in 1829 supporting the settlement of Europeans. From the late 1830s, though, with the Europeans protesting bitterly against Macaulay's proposals for judicial reform, dubbing them the Black Acts, the Town Hall became a contested space. Racially mixed meetings were now a rarity. In 1861, when leading Indians of the city such as Ramgopal Ghose, Jatindra Mohan Tagore, and Asgar Ali Khan wanted to meet to contest certain racial remarks made by a Supreme Court judge, they decided that the Town Hall was no longer their place and instead assembled in the Natmandir of Radhakanta Deb's mansion in Shobhabazar, deep inside Black Town.[85]

By postulating a linear narrative from the early nineteenth century to the nationalist and democratic movements of the twentieth century, the hopeful projects of Rammohan or the Derozians can only seem foolhardy, or else even more ignobly, a fall from radical promises to shameful compromise. In 1973, following his critical study of Rammohan, Sumit Sarkar made a similar point in relation to the Derozians.[86] If, however, one recognizes a rupture between the early modern formation and the later history of colonial-nationalist modernity, one would have to make a different assessment. The early modern antiabsolutist political tendency we have described referred to a historical formation. Discursively, it was able to offer a body of theoretical concepts, canonical authorities, arguments, and evidences that were used by writers, publicists, and agitators from all three social components of this formation—namely, nonofficial Europeans, Eurasians, and members of the new Indian elite. Institutionally, it constituted a distinct public sphere of antiabsolutist campaign, once again through associations of mixed racial composition. Within the logic of this formation, the politics of Rammohan, Dwarakanath, or the early Derozians made perfect sense. But the formation was crushed even as it was being built. Its impact on the next phase of the historical development of colonial empire was reduced to insignificance.

Still, for Indian history, just as Tipu posed the question of state sovereignty as the precondition for the productive organization of national society, so did Rammohan and the Derozians pose the question of the freedoms of the citizen-subject. None of them could answer those questions, which instead would find their historically effective answers more than a century later, after much struggle and bloodshed. To examine that history, it is necessary to first understand the new imperial formation of the later nineteenth century.

When Rammohan died in Bristol in 1833, he was buried on the grounds of the house where he was staying during his fatal illness. The home changed hands in 1843. Dwarakanath, who was in England at the time, arranged to have Rammohan's grave shifted to Arnos Vale cemetery and had a structure built over it. It is a templelike edifice, with a veritable jungle of conical *shikhara* spires over a canopy supported by eight outer and four inner columns. Surrounded by crosses, obelisks, and ornate gravestones, its strangeness is both stark and solitary. In 2002, Arnos Vale cemetery was marked for acquisition by the city council. All office buildings and the crematorium located within the cemetery were boarded up, and signs were posted: "KEEP OUT! UNSAFE BUILDING!" A police warning outside the gate said: "MOTORISTS! Thieves Operate in This Area." There were also a few stickers pleading "SAVE ARNOS VALE."

In the end, Arnos Vale was saved. Rammohan still rests under his outlandish canopy. An endowment from the Kolkata Municipal Corporation is now meant to ensure that the grave of one of Calcutta's most illustrious citizens is kept in good order in Britain.

Dwarakanath's grave in Kensal Green cemetery in London, on the other hand, is virtually forgotten. His memory as a free-spending hedonist, in cahoots with European private traders and indigo planters, is something of an embarrassment for nationalist modernity. His most famous grandson, Rabindranath Tagore, on getting custody of the family papers, is said to have made a bonfire of Dwarakanath's correspondence.[87] Early modernity in India does not sit easily with the nationalist modern.

CHAPTER SIX

For the Happiness of Mankind

THE BLACK HOLE OF CALCUTTA would probably have been forgotten had it not been for the essayist's skills of Thomas Macaulay (1800–1859).

Macaulay was of Scottish descent, but his family was Anglican and lived in London. His father, Zachary, was a leading Evangelical missionary, a member of the so-called Clapham sect, and a close associate of William Wilberforce in the antislavery movement of the early decades of the nineteenth century. Thomas distinguished himself as a student at Cambridge, was then called to the bar, and soon emerged as a notable writer by virtue of a forceful criticism of James Mill's utilitarian theories of government—a youthful exuberance that later somewhat embarrassed him.[1] It was said of him that he was, from a young age, hostile to abstract and speculative thinking. A critic of Macaulay has remarked: "In every academic system there is the inherent danger that amongst its prizemen it may produce scholars of wide reading, tenacious memory, and correct expression who may be fundamentally unintellectual. I hope it is not disloyal to add that this is a danger to which Cambridge scholarship, with its fine traditions of soundness and accuracy, is especially liable."[2]

Macaulay was elected to Parliament in 1830. Looking for a position with a decent salary, he sought an appointment in the East India Company, and in 1834 became a member of the governor-general's council and president of the Law Commission. He was in India for only four years, but left a profoundly lasting impression on the structure of colonial education and law in British India.

Returning to England in 1838, he began a literary career as an essayist and historian that would earn him great fame as well as adulation as a Victorian liberal. His *History of England*, appearing in five volumes between 1848 and 1855, was a publishing sensation, and has become a prime example of the Whig interpretation of history.[3] Macaulay's literary and historical essays, first collected in a volume in 1843, were also widely read. "It is doubtful indeed whether any collection of essays has had a greater effect upon the critical standards of ordinary English readers than had Macaulay's, both for his own and for succeeding generations."[4]

Of course, later critics have been largely dismissive of his literary merits, pointing to the very fact of his popularity and influence as evidence that he stood for all that was shallow and vulgar in the early Victorian period. Matthew Arnold's devastating condescension is typical:

> As soon as the common Englishman, desiring culture, begins to choose for himself, he chooses Macaulay. Macaulay's view of things is, on the whole, the view of them which he feels to be his own also; the persons and causes praised are those which he himself is disposed to admire; the persons and causes blamed are those with which he himself is out of sympathy; and the rhetoric employed to praise or to blame them is animating and excellent. Macaulay is thus a great civilizer.[5]

A. L. Rouse made the same point when he said that Macaulay's essays were "incomparable for young people who are just beginning to take an interest in things of the mind."[6] Indeed, from John Ruskin, Matthew Arnold, and Thomas Carlyle to the present day, critics have regarded Macaulay as a prime ideologue of the liberal middle class of Victorian Britain—progressive, confident, morally superior, self-righteous, and smug.

In 1840, Macaulay published an essay on Clive in the *Edinburgh Review*—a review, in fact, of Malcolm's biography—that was read by every schoolchild who knew English for the next hundred years. Along with the piece on Hastings, the two "India essays" by Macaulay were by far the most popular of his writings.[7] They were widely read in British schools. The British Library has more than twenty separate editions, published between 1891 and 1931, of the essay on Clive, with introduction and notes, meant for high school and university students preparing for examinations. Some of the typical questions that students were told to expect were as follows: "What is Macaulay's opinion of Clive's transactions with Omichund?" "What important changes have taken place in the government of India since Macaulay published the *Essay on Clive*?"[8] "Why is Clive regarded as one of our great Empire builders?"[9] "On what moral grounds can you justify annexation by a more civilized neighbour?" "How does our Empire in India differ from any other system of rule previously set up there?" "'The white man's burden.' What is meant by this phrase?"[10]

THE FOUNDING OF A MYTH

Macaulay's essay on Clive turned the Black Hole story into "a founding myth of empire."[11] When Holwell's monument was pulled down in 1821 in Calcutta's Tank Square, there was, as noted before, a Burkean consensus on drawing the veil over the sordid story of the conquest of Bengal. By 1840, the mood had definitely changed.

"I have always thought it strange," began Macaulay in his essay on Clive, that, while the history of the Spanish empire in America is familiarly known to all the nations of Europe, the great actions of our countrymen in the East should, even among ourselves, excite little interest. Every schoolboy knows who imprisoned Montezuma, and who strangled Atahualpa. But we doubt whether one in ten, even among English gentlemen of highly cultivated minds, can tell who won the battle of Buxar.... Yet the victories of Cortes were gained over savages who had no letters, who were ignorant of the use of metals, who had not broken in a single animal to labour.... The people of India, when we subdued them, were ten times as numerous as the Americans whom the Spaniards vanquished, and were at the same time quite as highly civilized as the victorious Spaniards.... It might have been expected, that every Englishman who takes any interest in any part of history would be curious to know how a handful of his countrymen, separated from their home by an immense ocean, subjugated, in the course of a few years, one of the greatest empires in the world. Yet, unless we greatly err, this subject is, to most readers, not only insipid, but positively distasteful.[12]

Macaulay's work was tragic biography and heroic history. The Black Hole played the crucial part in it. India in the mid-eighteenth century, he wrote, was "tainted with all the vices of Oriental despotism," with a succession of rulers "sunk in indolence and debauchery, ... chewing bang, fondling concubines, and listening to buffoons." The Mughal Empire, "powerful and prosperous as it appears on a superficial view, was yet, even in its best days, far worse governed than the worst governed parts of Europe now are."[13] Macaulay thus introduced here an entirely new mode of argument that claimed to compare the quality of government in different countries of the world and evaluate them on a common scale. It was, as we will see later in this chapter, based on a set of analytic techniques developed by Bentham, following his utilitarian theory of government. By the time Macaulay was writing his essays, this comparative mode of evaluating governments was being widely adopted to justify European intervention in other parts of the world. Macaulay's was one of the first and most influential of such interpretations of empire. Inspired by this new historical sensibility, he asked the question that no other historian of India had asked before him: "In what was this confusion to end? Was the strife to continue during centuries? ... Was another Baber to descend from the mountains, and to lead the hardy tribes of Cabul and Khorasan against a wealthier and less warlike race?"[14]

It is interesting that in narrating the historical answer here, Macaulay implied that a purposeful and stable resolution of the disorderly conditions in India in the mid-eighteenth century could only have come from a European power, because it was Dupleix, the French governor of Pondicherry, who first "clearly saw that the greatest force that the princes of India could bring into the field would be of no match for a small body of men trained in the discipline, and guided by the tactics, of the West." But despite having invented the necessary arts, "both of war and policy," it was not Dupleix and the French who were to found the new Indian Empire.

> The situation in India was such that scarcely any aggression could be without a pretext, either in old laws or in recent practice. All rights were in a state of utter uncertainty; and the Europeans who took part in the disputes of the natives confounded the confusion, by applying to Asiatic politics the public law of the West, and analogies drawn from the feudal system. If it was convenient to treat a Nabob as an independent prince, there was an excellent plea for doing so. He was independent, in fact. If it was convenient to treat him as a mere deputy of the Court of Delhi, there was no difficulty; for he was so in theory.[15]

Finding a legally tenable reason for intervention in India, Macaulay suggested, was not a problem for a European power, because there were, in effect, no binding legal constraints. The only problem that remained was to judge the moral legitimacy of conquest.

This was when an utterly unexpected and wholly providential chain of events unfolded in Bengal.

> The Castilians have a proverb, that in Valencia the earth is water and the men women; and the description is at least equally applicable to the vast plain of the Lower Ganges. Whatever the Bengalee does he does languidly. His favourite pursuits are sedentary. He shrinks from bodily exertion; and though voluble in dispute, and singularly pertinacious in the war of chicane, he seldom engages in a personal conflict, and scarcely ever enlists as a soldier.... There never, perhaps, existed a people so thoroughly fitted by nature and by habit for a foreign yoke.

Siraj, their ruler, "one of the worst specimens" of the Oriental despot, "hated the English" and resolved to plunder them. "His feeble and uncultivated mind," Macaulay pointed out, "was incapable of perceiving that the riches of Calcutta, had they been even greater than he imagined, would not compensate him for what he must lose, if the European trade, of which Bengal was a chief seat, should be driven by his violence to some other quarter." He attacked Fort William. "Then was committed that great crime, memorable for its singular atrocity, memorable for the tremendous retribution by which it was followed."[16]

Turning Holwell's narrative into a story of the criminal savageries of Oriental rulers, Macaulay made Siraj the chief perpetrator of a horrible brutality. "Nothing in history or fiction ... approaches the horrors which were recounted by the few survivors of that night." Having ordered the forced confinement of the unfortunate prisoners at sword point, the despot was unavailable for the rest of the night for any appeals because he was "sleeping off his debauch." In the morning, he treated the survivors "with execrable cruelty." "Holwell, unable to walk, was carried before the tyrant, who reproached him, threatened him, and sent him up the country in irons," and other survivors, "still bowed down by the sufferings of that great agony, were lodged in miserable sheds, and fed only with grain and water." And the mysterious Mrs. Carey, now referred to as "one Englishwoman [who] had survived that night," was, according to Macaulay, "placed in the harem of the Prince at Moorshedabad."[17]

What happened next? When news reached Madras of the atrocities that had taken place in Calcutta, it "excited the fiercest and bitterest resentment. The cry of the whole settlement was for vengeance." It was immediately decided that an expedition would be sent to Bengal with Clive at the head of the land forces. What followed, we might observe quite accurately, is history. And needless to say, Clive was its leading and most successful figure. "But it is also unquestionable," admitted Macaulay, "that the transactions in which he now began to take a part have left a stain on his moral character."[18]

It is to history that Macaulay turned in judging Clive. His actions had to be evaluated by their merits as "policy"—that is, by their historical consequences. Macaulay argued that James Mill was wrong in deducing from Clive's behavior in India that he was deceitful by nature; that is not how he had behaved with other Englishpeople. Rather, "the great difference between Asiatic and European morality was constantly in his thoughts." Clive therefore "considered Oriental politics as a game in which nothing was unfair," and although "an honourable English gentleman and a soldier," no sooner was he "matched against an Indian intriguer than he became himself an Indian intriguer, and descended, without scruple, to falsehood, to hypocritical caresses, to the substitution of documents, and to the counterfeiting of hands."

> He knew that the standard of morality among the natives of India differed widely from that established in England.... He seems to have imagined, most erroneously in our opinion, that he could effect nothing against such adversaries, if he was content to be bound by ties from which they were free, if he went on telling truth, and hearing none, if he fulfilled, to his own hurt, all his engagements with confederates who never kept an engagement that was not to their advantage.[19]

These were Clive's reasons for resorting to the sordid intrigues leading up to the "revolution" of 1757. Yet Macaulay was careful to make distinctions between ends and means. "The odious vices of Surajah Dowlah, the wrongs which the English had suffered at his hands, the dangers to which our trade must have been exposed, had he continued to reign, appear to us fully to justify the resolution for deposing him. But nothing can justify the dissimulation which Clive stooped to practice."[20] For instance, his dealings with Amirchand: "...Clive was more than Omichund's match in Omichund's own arts. The man, he said, was a villain. Any artifice which would defeat such knavery was justifiable." But Admiral Watson was unwilling to be a party to the deceit. "... Clive was not a man to do anything by halves. We almost blush to write it. He forged Admiral Watson's name."[21]

As the armies prepared for battle at Palashi, Siraj, imagined Macaulay, "sat gloomily in his tent, haunted, a Greek poet would have said, by the furies of those who had cursed him with their last breath in the Black Hole." In the opposite camp, Clive had called a council of war, at which a majority voted against fighting. Clive "retired alone under the shade of some trees, and passed near an hour there in thought. He came back determined to put everything to the hazard, and gave orders that all should be in readiness for passing the river on the morrow."[22] It is well known what happened the next day at Palashi, where the fate of India was decided.

Macaulay claimed not to judge Clive's actions by "any rigid principles of morality." "Indeed," he said, "it is quite unnecessary to do so; for, looking at the question as a question of expediency in the lowest sense of the word, and using no arguments but such as Machiavelli might have employed in his conferences with [Cesare] Borgia, we are convinced that Clive was altogether in the wrong, and that he committed, not merely a crime, but a blunder." Once again, Macaulay was here introducing a "policy" argument that was entirely new, and hence quite anachronistic for Clive's political world.

> That honesty is the best policy is a maxim which we firmly believe to be generally correct.... The entire history of British India is an illustration of the great truth, that it is not prudent to oppose perfidy to perfidy, and that the most efficient weapon with which men can encounter falsehood is truth.... English valour and English intelligence have done less to extend and to preserve our Oriental empire than English veracity.... Had we acted during the last two generations on the principles which Sir John Malcolm [Clive's biographer] appears to have considered as sound, had we as often as we had to deal with people like Omichund, retaliated by lying and forging, and breaking faith, after their fashion, it is our firm belief that no courage or capacity could have upheld our empire."[23]

The "policy" that Macaulay was enunciating here was, of course, relevant to an imperial power that was concerned with the acceptability and permanence of its position as rulers of a colonized country—a relevant concern in Macaulay's time, but one that was far removed from those that motivated Clive. As we will see, though, Macaulay was also applying a method of moral evaluation of historical events that was fundamentally anachronistic.

Clive did accumulate huge personal wealth in India. In fact, Macaulay suggested, "no Englishman who started with nothing has ever, in any line of life, created such a fortune at the age of thirty-four." Not all of it was acquired by scrupulous means, even though, Macaulay added, many of the later charges against Clive were malicious and unfair, and had Clive been utterly greedy, given his opportunities, he could have made far more. But aside from his military and financial successes, it was Clive's role as an empire builder during his final years in Bengal to which Macaulay attaches the greatest importance. "The power of the Company, though an anomaly, is in our time, we are firmly persuaded, a beneficial anomaly. In the time of Clive, it was not merely an anomaly, but a nuisance." It did not follow any rational principles of governance; there were no proper systems of administrative control. It was a virtual free-for-all. "The India House was a lottery-office, which invited everybody to take a chance, and held out ducal fortunes as the prizes destined for the lucky few." It was no surprise, therefore, that after Palashi, when the company became the supreme power in Bengal, its officials stopped at nothing to satisfy their urge to make a quick and large treasure.

> Enormous fortunes were thus rapidly accumulated at Calcutta, while thirty millions of human beings were reduced to the extremity of wretchedness. They had been accustomed to live under tyranny, but never under tyranny like this. They found the little finger of the Company thicker than the loins of Surajah Dowlah.... That government, oppressive as the most oppressive form of barbarian despotism, was strong with all the strength of civilisation.... Even despair could not inspire the soft Bengalee with courage to confront men of English breed, the hereditary nobility of mankind, whose skill and valour had so often triumphed in spite of tenfold odds.[24]

Not only was the country devastated by plunder and misrule; the company's own house in Bengal was turned into a cesspool of corruption and intrigue. When Clive returned to Bengal for the last time in 1765, he began, Macaulay claimed, "one of the most extensive, difficult, and salutary reforms that ever was accomplished by any statesman." He stopped the practice of receiving presents and tried to set limits on the private trade of company servants. Needless to say, he came up against fierce resistance from vested interests within the company. Yet from Clive's last term as governor of Bengal, Macaulay declared, "dates the purity of the administration of our Eastern empire." Now, "a great quantity of wealth is made by English functionaries in India; but no single functionary makes a very large fortune, and what is made is slowly, hardly, and honestly earned."[25] Government in India had been reformed.

Macaulay insisted that this was the perspective from which to judge Clive's life. The evaluation had to be historically relative. The truth was that history gave such people "a more than ordinary measure of indulgence," because they had to be judged not as their contemporaries judged them but rather "as they will be judged by posterity. Their bad actions ought not indeed to be called good;

but their good and bad actions ought to be fairly weighed; and if on the whole the good preponderate, the sentence ought to be one of not merely acquittal but instead approbation. Not a single great ruler in history can be absolved by a judge who fixes his eye inexorably on one or two unjustifiable acts." In other words, on balance, the historical consequence must determine one's judgment of a great statesperson's career. The best judgment of contemporaries, moreover, ought to foresee that consequence. "History takes wider views; and the best tribunal for great political cases is the tribunal that anticipates the verdict of history." The tragedy of Clive's life was that his contemporaries failed to see what he had accomplished for posterity.

> If in India the yoke of foreign masters, elsewhere the heaviest of all yokes, has been found lighter than that of any native dynasty, if to that gang of public robbers, which formerly spread terror through the whole plain of Bengal, has succeeded a body of functionaries not more highly distinguished by ability and diligence than by integrity, disinterestedness, and public spirit, ... the praise is in no small measure due to Clive. His name stands high on the roll of conquerors. But it is found in a better list, in the list of those who have done and suffered much for the happiness of mankind.[26]

It is important to note the new set of contrasts that Macaulay introduced, and put in two separate lists: conquest, valor, courage, skill, ability, intelligence, and capacity, on the one side, and honesty, veracity, purity, integrity, disinterestedness, and public spirit, on the other. The contrast was between the business of war and the business of government. Both were part of the activities of the state, but they adopted different practices and demanded different aptitudes. Macaulay's claim was, of course, that Clive possessed both sets of qualities in abundance. It could also be argued that in the mid-eighteenth century, his abilities as a military commander and political tactician were crucial in ensuring British supremacy over both the French and the various Indian powers. But judged in terms of the historical impact of Clive's military victories, his merits as a conqueror, Macaulay insisted, must take second place to his abilities as an administrative reformer. The progress of history had made the establishment of good government in India a matter of far greater significance than the providential acquisition of territories. On balance, then, Clive's moral improprieties as a conqueror can be condoned, because he was the one who initiated the process of putting the Indian government on rational, stable, and honest foundations.

Macaulay was enormously stretching the point. No historian today will agree that the structure and practices of administration that prevailed in India in the 1840s were the results of Clive's efforts of 1765. Still, Macaulay succeeded in laying down a story line of British rule in India that would become paradigmatic of all justificatory histories of modern empire right down to the present day. The myth went something like this. Oriental governments were tyrannies that even at their best, were worse than the worst governments of Europe. Siraj, one of the worst Oriental despots, not only oppressed his own people but also laid siege to the English trading settlement of Bengal, treated English prisoners with unspeakable cruelty, caused them to be suffocated to death inside a prison, and sent the sole surviving Englishwoman into his own harem. Outraged, the English, "the hereditary nobility of mankind," retaliated by force, and under Clive's able leadership, deposed Siraj and put their own nawab on the throne. Uninformed by good principles of government, the English traders merely made their own fortunes while the country was laid to waste. Once again led by Clive, however, the institutions of government in British India were slowly reformed. Though still authoritarian and paternal, the state now sat far more lightly, securely, and happily on the people than at any time in India's history.

At last, empire was safe from its own infamous origins. The secret veil could now be lifted. Clive's history could be taught to British schoolchildren as a fable of moral instruction, to instill pride in their hearts not merely for the valor of their compatriots but also for the selfless service they were rendering to the people of the empire.

THE UTILITY OF EMPIRE

Macaulay is chiefly remembered in Indian history for his famous 1835 "Minute on Education" in which he defined the objective of colonial education through the medium of the English language as one intended to produce "a class who may be interpreters between us and the millions whom we govern—a class of persons Indian in blood and colour, but English in tastes, in opinions, in morals and in intellect." But the bulk of his work in Calcutta as a member of the East India Company's government concerned the reform of legal institutions in India.[27] Living with his sister in a house that later became the site of the exclusive Bengal Club, in the fashionable new White Town coming up along Chowringhee, south of Park Street, Macaulay devoted his energies to the rational reorganization of the clumsy, expensive judicial system and the codification of the law.

In his classic work on the subject, Eric Stokes has amply detailed the immense debt that Macaulay owed to the principles enunciated by Bentham, the founder of utilitarianism.[28] Let us recount the main points. Macaulay did not believe in a general renovation of society on the basis of an abstract universal theory, nor was he drawn to the idea of a planned, centralized, bureaucratic state pictured in many of Bentham's writings. Nevertheless, he was strongly persuaded by the Benthamite notions that law must be clear, unambiguous, certain, and widely publicized, that legal redress must be cheap and swift, that evidence must be judged not only on the basis of its consistency and logic but also on the manner in which it is orally delivered, and that there should be as many courts of primary jurisdiction as possible yet only a single court of appeal. Following these guiding principles, Macaulay produced a brand-new penal code for India, and fought passionately to bring uniformity into the judicial system, regardless of racial distinctions, and have mostly Indian judges appointed to the district courts while restricting European judges to the courts of appeal.

Macaulay's reformist zeal, as we have seen, provoked much opposition among Europeans in India, and his proposals were only partially accepted—some long after his departure from India. But it was not so much in the details of his suggestions that Macaulay was beholden to Bentham; it was, as Stokes has remarked, more in their "design and informing spirit."[29] Indeed, Macaulay's proposals for judicial reform in India were examples of a completely new way of thinking about the government of colonies—one that was primarily enabled by the conceptual apparatus provided by Bentham and utilitarianism. It is through these instruments that empire was fitted out, in the early decades of the nineteenth century—and only then—with a set of flexible and finely calibrated global practices.

After enormous neglect for almost a century, owing largely to the difficulty in accessing his works, Bentham's political and social thought is currently going through a new evaluation. It is now apparent that the influential assessments of his work by John Stuart Mill, and later, Elie Halévy, Leslie Stephen, and Werner Stark, were often simplistic and misleading. Thus, Bentham's alleged authoritarianism, expressed in his preference for strong and decisive executive powers, and late espousal of democracy both deserve more complex treatment. It is clear that he was a principled supporter of the extension of suffrage to women, even though he thought that prevailing opinion would not allow it. Most crucially, he was neither for the emancipation of all colonial peoples nor uniformly against it. Bentham instead developed a differentiated and nuanced view on the subject, distinguishing between different types of colonies, and recommending different policies toward each.[30] The last point needs closer attention.

Bentham's lifelong aversion to the abstract notion of natural rights, and his dismissal of the French Declaration of the Rights of Man as unintelligible and false, are well known. "Scarce an article," he said about the famous declaration, "which, on rummaging it, will not be found a true Pandora's Box. Were this to be taken for the standard, not a law, good or bad, past, present, or future—real and imaginable—that would not find its condemnation in some part or other of this tabernacle of the laws of nature. Not a law ever has been or would be passed here or any where against which insurrection would not be the most sacred."[31] Consistent with this position, he rejected, early in his intellectual life, the claim of the rebels in the British American colonies that there could be no taxation without representation, arguing that property was not a natural right but rather a creation of state law, and that the sovereign authority could legitimately demand the payment of taxes as a duty of its subjects in return for the guarantee of security.[32] Later, however, when he became convinced that the "governing few" needed to be kept under check by the expressed will of the many, he turned into an enthusiastic supporter of the United States as the best working example of representative democracy.[33]

In 1793, he addressed a plea to the National Convention of revolutionary France with the slogan "Emancipate Your Colonies!" He repeated much the same appeal in a statement intended for the constitutional reformers in Spain in 1822 titled *Rid Yourselves of Ultramaria*. Again, his plea was not based on any natural right of self-determination but rather on considerations of utility for both the metropolitan power and its colonized subjects. He reminded the French that they had supported the rebels in the British colonies of America because it was wrong for one nation to hold another in subjection: "How would you like a Parliament of ours to govern you, you sending six members to it?"

> You will, I say, give up your colonies—because you have no right to govern them, because they had rather not be governed by you, because it is against their interest to be governed by you, because you get nothing by governing them, because you can't keep them, because the expence of trying to keep them would be ruinous, because your constitution would suffer by your keeping them, because your principles forbid your keeping them, and because you would do good to all the world by parting with them....
>
> If hatred is your ruling passion, and the gratification of it your first object, you will still grasp your colonies. If the happiness of mankind is your object, and the declaration of rights your guide, you will set them free.[34]

As the Bolivarian revolutions began their victorious journey in the Spanish Americas, Bentham pointed out to Spanish liberals that despotic government in the colonies would not only be contradictory to the liberal principles of the new Spanish constitution. There would be a serious risk that those despotic tendencies would travel back and threaten liberty at home. Bentham commented: "By planting in those unseen regions, with or without original design … a necessary despotism, the reimportation of which into your Peninsula would, of all your imports from thence, be the most assured."[35]

But these were all colonies of an "advanced" type of society, meaning, needless to say, that they were effectively colonies of European settlers. Even as Bentham argued for their emancipation from imperial rule, he was also making the apparently contradictory suggestion that if there were uncultivated lands overseas, then to relieve the pressure of overpopulation in European countries, it was rational to colonize those overseas territories. In fact, he was supporting the assertions advanced early in the nineteenth century by Edward Wakefield for British settlers' colonization of the penal colonies of South Australia. If one notices the distinction that Bentham was making between types of colonies, then, of course, one would see that within his system, there is really no contradiction between the two claims.[36]

When discussing India, Bentham defined a third type of colony. He introduced the problem of East India in his 1793 address in which he wanted France to emancipate its colonies.

> You know how things are changed there—the power of Tippoo is no more.—Would the tree of liberty grow there, if planted? Would the declaration of rights translate into *Shanscrit?* Would *Bramin, Chetree, Bice, Sooder,* and *Hallachore* meet on equal ground? If not, you may find some difficulty in giving them to themselves. You may find yourselves reduced by mere necessity to what we should call here a practical plan. If it is determined they must have masters, you will then look out for the least bad ones that could take them; and after all that we have heard, I question whether you would find any less bad than our English company. If these merchants would give you any thing for the bargain, it would be so much clear gain to you: and not impossible but they might.[37]

Bentham, curiously, was using utilitarian grounds to maintain that France might profitably sell its Indian possessions to the English East India Company, since rule by Europeans would be less burdensome to Indians than rule by their own princes.

In general, Bentham's view was that colonies were expensive for the home country and oppressive to the colonies. Colonies with so-called advanced societies, such as the French, British, and Spanish colonies in the Americas, should be emancipated. Yet since the key principle was not emancipation, drawn from some abstract conception of natural right, but utility, the matter could not end there. If, for instance, overpopulation in the country of origin could be relieved by the settlement of colonists in uninhabited or uncultivated lands, such as in Australia, then the principle of utility would favor the colonization of such territories. Or to take another example, if the laws and political or religious institutions of a country such as India or Egypt made the oppression of the people under their native rulers far worse than that under British governors, then it was certainly advisable to keep the country under British rule, since that would provide greater opportunity for the welfare and progress of the people.[38]

The conceptual basis for these comparisons and typologies was provided by a new theoretical system that could presumably enable a sufficiently trained and informed person to become "legislator of the world." In his *Principles of*

Morals and Legislation, published in 1789, Bentham declared that the methods and standards of legislation he was proposing were "alike applicable to the laws of all nations."[39] More interestingly for us, in an early essay, "The Influence of Time and Place in Matters of Legislation," Bentham offered the following method:

> Referring every thing to this standard, I inquire what are the deviations which it would be requisite to make from this standard in giving to another country such a tincture as any other country may receive without prejudice from English laws. I take my own country for the standard.... The problem, as it stands at present, is—the best possible laws for England being established in England, the variations which it would be necessary to make in those of another given country in order to render them the best laws possible with reference to that other country.

In providing an instructive case, Bentham chose a country that presented "as strong a contrast with England as possible."

> Such an example we seem to have in the province of Bengal. Climate, face of the country, natural productions, present laws, manners, customs, religion of the inhabitants, every circumstance on which a difference in the point in question can be grounded, as different as can be.... To a lawgiver, who having been bred up with English notions, shall have learnt how to accommodate his laws to the circumstances of Bengal, no other part of the globe can present any difficulty.[40]

But Bentham also insisted that "human nature was everywhere the same," and different countries did not have "different catalogues of pleasures and pains." Then why should the same laws not hold good for all countries? Because the things that caused pleasure or pain were not the same everywhere. "The same event ... which would produce pain or pleasure in one country, would not produce an effect of the same sort, or if of the same sort, not in equal degree, in another." For instance (undermining, like his follower James Mill, the force of moral outrage invoked by this incident), "a night's confinement in the prison called the Black hole in the hot climate of Calcutta was productive of the most excruciating torments, proved fatal to nearly all the persons who were confined in it. In a winter's night in Siberia, the same number of persons might perhaps have undergone a confinement of the same length in a similar space, without any very remarkable inconvenience." These grounds of variation were not all of the same kind, though. Some were physical, such as the climate or the nature of the soil, and these were invariant and insurmountable. Others, no matter how difficult or inexpedient, were subject to intervention and change, such as "the circumstances of government, religion, and manners."[41] Different sets of laws would be appropriate for different circumstances. Further, by the application of appropriate laws, the mutable circumstances could be subjected to the forces of change.

Bentham thought of these variations as amenable to more or less precise qualitative and quantitative comparison—that is, they were all subject to some common measure.

> [The legislator] should be provided with two sets of tables. Those of the first set would exhibit a number of particulars relative to the body of laws which has been pitched upon for a standard ...: for example, a table of offences, tables of justifications, aggravations, extenuations, and exceptions; a table of punishments; a table of the titles of the civil code; a table of the titles of the constitutional code, and so on. Those of the other set will be: a general table of the circumstances influencing sensibility; tables or short accounts of the moral, religious, sympathetic and antipathetic biases of the people for whose use the alterations are to be made; a set of maps, as particular as possible; a table of the productions of the country, natural and artificial; tables of the weights, measures and coins in use; tables of the population, and the like. These tables, if a man would work with accuracy, he should have not metaphorically, but literally and materially, before his eyes.[42]

One can almost imagine here an anticipation of the statistical handbooks of social indicators with which any undergraduate of the twenty-first century would be able to rank the countries of the world according to standards of living, mortality rates, governance quality, human development, and dozens of other evaluative criteria. Unlike in the writings of eighteenth-century historians and travelers brought up on Montesquieu, cultural difference is no longer incommensurable. Rather, it can now be seen in terms of its consequences, plotted as deviations from a standard and hence normalized. All deviations between states are comparable according to the same measure; states can be divided into ranks and grades.

Moreover, once normalized, deviations could be tracked over time: the deviation of a state from the norm could close or widen. A country thus could conceivably over time enter the grade of advanced societies or drop out of it. Bentham himself explained, in the "Time and Place" essay, that he was taking England as a standard only partly because he had a preference for it; the chief reason was that it was the country with which he had had "the best opportunity to be informed."[43] Presumably, therefore, another advanced country could just as well have been chosen as the standard for this conceptual exercise. Besides, as Ian Hacking has shown, the statistical elaboration of the idea of normality in the nineteenth century could retain a sense of the normal as the right and the good as well as the empirically existent mediocre, in need of improvement.[44] In sum, law and governance in the whole world could become the subject of a science of comparative government as well as the object of interventions for "improvement." Practices of government could now be set against a common measure and hence normalized on a global scale.

The significance of this conceptual innovation for the emergence of the new practices of empire in the nineteenth century has not been adequately stressed. We see the ideas elaborated for the first time in Bentham and his utilitarian theories of legislation. But these formal properties of the comparative method would become part of the background assumptions of several different tendencies and schools of thought on the subject of empire, including many that had no truck with the baggage of utilitarianism as a political philosophy.

As a matter of fact, Bentham's nuanced answer to the colonial question facing European empires laid the ground for a conceptual distinction between sovereignty and government that would prove to be of great importance in later justifications of empire in the nineteenth and twentieth centuries. Sovereign power was certainly a necessary means for good government. Yet only in the case of countries with an advanced type of society—that is, those that had achieved a standard that was normatively desirable—could sovereignty be congruent with self-government. For the rest, it was indeed desirable for good government that the sovereign power be held not by inhabitants of the country but rather by others more capable of providing good government. The criterion was, of course, the consequentialist one of the quality of actual results delivered by government.

Bentham's own policy prescriptions for his extreme contrasting case of Bengal were cautious and gradualist. Thus, in that country, a man wanting to see the face of "a married woman from the higher class of Mahometans or Gentoos" would cause injury, but Europeans would be quite insensible to such a thing. A Brahmin might be outraged by an outcaste's touch. "A prejudice so strong, though altogether unjust and ferocious, would require great forbearance on the part of the legislator.... But it would be better to yield to it altogether for a time than uselessly to compromise his authority, and expose his laws to hatred." Once again, the relevant principle was that of utility: "Changing of a custom repugnant to our manners for no other reason than such repugnancy, is not a benefit. The satisfaction is for a small number, the pain for many."[45]

Nevertheless, the variations in laws and institutions made necessary by the inferiority in physical as well as cultural conditions must themselves be thought of as changeable. The question must be asked:

> Which is likely to be the greater evil? the evil depending upon such inferiority, or the evil, if any, which might be produced by the measures requisite to remove the other? the evil of the disease, or the evil of the remedy? This question is complicated, and includes many others; the evil of the remedy is, perhaps, likely to be but temporary; while the evil of the disease, and thence the benefit of the remedy, is likely to be perpetual.

There had to be, in other words, a future horizon to the comparisons of utility on the basis of which policy choices were to be made. The objective in the longer term was improvement, closing, as far as possible, the difference between England and Bengal. "This difference ... would depend in good measure upon a certain inferiority which at present there appears to be in Bengal, with respect to the form of government on the one hand, and the national manners on the other: insomuch that were the time ever to come, when such inferiority should disappear, the reasons for the difference between the institutions would become less forcible, and perhaps vanish altogether."[46]

Bentham also had little doubt as to who could be a "legislator of the world"—the epithet bestowed on him by José del Valle, the Guatemalan leader with whom he was in correspondence, and whom Bentham wanted to introduce to Rammohan as a kindred liberal reformer from the colonial world.[47] Even for "nations professing liberal opinions," Bentham thought a foreigner's codification of the laws was preferable, because it would be less influenced by "sinister interests and affections."[48] For countries like India, where rule by European governors was far less oppressive for its people than rule by their own princes, it went without saying that the best laws would be made, at least for the time being, by a suitably qualified European. In a widely cited remark whose authenticity has been questioned, Bentham is said to have prophesied, not without a mischievous sense of irony: "[James] Mill will be the living executive—I shall be the dead legislative of British India. Twenty years after I am dead, I shall be despot."[49]

Once again, it is worth underlining the significance of Bentham's construction of a theory of comparative government for the global practices of empire ever since. It provided a set of conceptual and analytic resources whose value has far outlasted the limited influence of utilitarianism as a political philosophy.[50] Notwithstanding Bentham's exaggerated confidence in the ability of his method to supply exact solutions to policy problems, what it did mark out was a field of debate over policy questions, identifying the criteria by which such discussions might be settled, emphasizing in particular the sorts of empirical evidence that would be relevant and admissible, and laying down that, above all, the merits of laws and policies were to be judged by their social consequences. The history of empire in the nineteenth and twentieth centuries would see many deliberations over direct and indirect rule, the degree to which indigenous institutions should be retained or replaced, and which classes in indigenous society were best suited to be the allies of empire and which its most likely enemies. Most of these debates would be carried out within the conceptual parameters first articulated in Bentham's comparative and universal scheme of legislation.

Bentham's typology of colonies also created another global paradigm. If constitutionally established representative government were now to be recognized as the universally valid normative standard, then the universally valid and legitimate exception would be some form of enlightened despotism. Despotism is unlimited and arbitrary power, unconstrained by constitutional rules. In this sense, it was often distinguished in the classical literature of the seventeenth and eighteenth centuries from absolutism, which was unlimited power but legitimately constituted within certain fundamental laws. The form of government recommended for European colonies in the East was absolutist in that while it did not recognize any limits to its sovereign powers within the occupied territory, it did claim to be constituted by and function within certain fundamental laws. But it was despotic in its foundational assumptions, since the authority that was to lay down those fundamental laws was arbitrarily constituted and in no way responsible to those whom it governed. As Leonard Krieger, a rare recent scholar to defend the theory of enlightened despotism, has pointed out, however, when despotism purports to be enlightened, it places a constraint on itself and promises to itself to be responsible: it becomes limited by and responsible to enlightened reason. When that happens, there is effectively no difference between despotism and absolutism. Despotism has to justify its actions to itself by their consequences. It becomes "conditionally constituted" because it is "conditionally operative." Indeed, it functions by "elevating the relative measurement of government by result into a steady principle."[51]

Beginning with its formal espousal by eighteenth-century cameralists such as Johann Heinrich Gottlob Justi and Joseph von Sonnenfels, and by physiocrats such as François Quesnay and Anne-Robert-Jacques Turgot, enlightened despotism was variously supported, Krieger claims, by Voltaire and Denis Diderot, and explicitly, even if ambiguously, advocated by Claude Adrien Helvétius, Comte de Mirabeau, and Baron d'Holbach. Even Immanuel Kant, he notes gleefully, desperately strove to unite "the idea of human right" with the actuality of "human morals," and ended up recommending governments "to govern autocratically and yet also to administer constitutionally."[52]

The idea of enlightened despotism found its proper theoretical place (even though it was not called by that name) within Bentham's universal scheme of comparative government, where it was explicitly connected to the prevalence in a specific country of inferior laws, institutions, and manners, recommended as a corrective and transitional arrangement, justified on the basis of political realism, and subjected to evaluation in terms of its consequences. Bentham's scheme was universal, but accommodated the widest possible range of variations in circumstances, identifiable by empirical methods, and allowed for the greatest degree of flexibility in the making of appropriate laws and policies. The universally valid and desirable norm that recognized the capacity of the many to look after their interests was that of representative government. Yet the circumstances in many or perhaps most countries made it necessary to suspend that norm. The exception would have to be an appropriate variety of despotism, limited and informed by enlightened reason. It would indeed become a familiar refrain among liberal disciples of Bentham in the nineteenth century that while India could not have a free government, she might have the next best thing—a firm and impartial despotism.

The Morality of Empire

Stokes dramatically described the setting in which the reform of colonial government took place in India at the beginning of the nineteenth century as "the battle of the two philosophies." The reformers were convinced that the ideas and institutions that were transforming European societies, and had been proved to be both theoretically valid and historically progressive, must be implanted on Indian soil. The so-called Cornwallis system in eastern India, consisting of a permanent settlement with zamindars as the hereditary proprietors of the land with an obligation to pay an annual revenue that was fixed in perpetuity, was largely derived, as Ranajit Guha has shown, from physiocratic ideas.[53] Utilitarian commentators such as James Mill along with his followers in India such as Bentinck and Macaulay were not adherents of physiocracy, and were far more persuaded by the political economy of Adam Smith and the doctrines of free trade. Mill, in particular, was an open critic of the permanent settlement with a native aristocracy. Still, imbued with Benthamite ideas, they became the major proponents of progressive reform of Indian legal and social institutions. Their opponents within the company administration were figures like Munro, Malcolm, and Elphinstone who were thoroughly skeptical of abstract theoretical systems, and suspicious of attempts to alter ancient institutions that were deeply rooted in the history and culture of an alien civilization. In their political conservatism, dressed up in India as paternalism, reformist liberalism encountered, as Stokes remarks, "the spirit of Burke."[54]

Liberal imperialism in the early nineteenth century had three components. "Free Trade was its solid foundation. Evangelicalism provided its programme of social reform, its force of character, and its missionary zeal. Philosophic radicalism gave it an intellectual basis and supplied it with the science of political economy, law, and government."[55] But as the century progressed, and many little debates raged and were quelled, the battle of the two philosophies seemed to dissolve imperceptibly in an unannounced truce. Paternalism, the insignia of the conservative school at the century's start, became the ubiquitous sentiment of imperial rule over colonized peoples, not only in India, but all over the globe too. The most sophisticated theoretical statement of this position was made midcentury by one of the leading liberal thinkers of all time, John Stuart Mill, who spent almost his entire professional life writing dispatches to India from the East India Company offices in London. The best form of government for dependent colonies such as India, Mill announced, was a vigorous and paternal despotism.

Scholars, most notably Jennifer Pitts and Shankar Muthu, have recently advanced the notion that the late eighteenth century saw a deep and sustained critique of the ideas as well as practices of overseas empire from the philosophers of the Scottish and French Enlightenment.[56] Pitts goes on to argue that the "turn to empire" took place in the second and third decades of the nineteenth century, when the nuanced and ambivalent statements of Smith or Bentham were mutilated and simplified by their followers, such as James and John Stuart Mill, to serve the purposes of a new imperial idea of civilizational superiority and universal progress.

According to Pitts, Smith thought that holding colonies under political domination was a burden, and the solution was either complete emancipation or complete political and economic integration. Since it was unrealistic to expect any country to voluntarily give up its colonies, Smith favored the integration of the American colonies with Britain. As for territories largely populated by non-Europeans, Smith, like his Scottish contemporary Adam Ferguson, employed a theory of stages of social development, from hunting, pastoral, and agricultural societies to commercial society, to describe and understand social institutions in unfamiliar cultures and civilizations. But, Pitts asserts, Smith did not flaunt the moral superiority of European society and was not judgmental about other cultures. Instead, his stage theory of civilization tended toward a certain functionalist understanding of the relation between beliefs or practices, and their structural location in a social context. He thus would not condemn the practice of infanticide or polygamy as simply barbaric but instead try to explain why it might make sense to those who practiced it in a particular social situation. Besides, even though his theory of social development implied an order of succession of social stages, it was a "natural" one, driven by an internal historical dynamic. Given Smith's view of human action as necessarily limited by imperfect knowledge and subject to unintended consequences, he did not, Pitts maintains, have anything resembling the idea of progress as social engineering that would dominate imperial projects in the nineteenth century.[57]

Bentham too, at least in his later years, says Pitts, was strongly in favor of the emancipation of settler colonies, as evidenced in his appeals to France and Spain. His sense of realism, however, told him that some form of European political control over India would have to continue for some time to come. But he was not a "crusading legislator" in the same way that many of his followers were in India. He was willing to appreciate the value of native institutions and practitioners in their own contexts, arguing, for instance, that "the Cawzee and the Bramin" were more likely to judge rightly than an ill-informed English judge. Pitts claims that the Mills, father and son, distorted Bentham's subtle comparative distinctions by asserting a simple divide between civilized and barbaric societies, denying to the latter any legitimate agency in their own governance and declaring the universal superiority of Western civilization.[58]

There is a sharp focus on subjective motivations and attitudes in Pitts's study of Burke, Smith, Bentham, and the Mills that is not of immediate interest to the present inquiry into the discursive formations of empire in the nineteenth century. The attention here must go less to character studies and more to the genealogical delineation of concepts and arguments that opened up the possibility for the formulation of imperial policies and practices. Hence, for our purposes, the functionalist anthropology embedded in Smith's theory of the stages of social development or Bentham's utilitarian theory of comparative government must be seen as having prepared the discursive ground for the practices of imperial policy later in the nineteenth century.

There was in fact a difference between Smith and Bentham, on the one hand, and the Mills, on the other, on the question of the overseas empire. It was the difference between empire as *technique* and empire as *ideology*. There is no doubt that Smith and Bentham were not imperial ideologues; indeed, it would be correct to say that ideologically, they were opposed to empire, identifying it with the entrenched interests of the few as against those of the many. Yet they provided, as we have tried to demonstrate, the basic *technical* apparatus of concepts and theories with which *all* imperial practices would henceforth be ideologically justified.

The conceptual foundations of the liberal ideology of empire in the mid-nineteenth century have been laid bare in Uday Singh Mehta's pathbreaking study.[59] There are, first, the apparently obvious exclusions listed by Locke in his universalist anthropological assumptions about reason and human nature. Lunatics and idiots were permanently unable to exercise their reason, and children temporarily so; as such, they could not be part of the political community that was to express its consent for government.[60] This seemingly innocuous and minimal anthropological assumption would cast a massive shadow over later claims that the backward peoples of overseas colonial territories were, by their "nature," as irrational as lunatics or as immature as children, and so must be brought under the protective care of superior and rational people. The strategy here was to exclude, by an appeal to nature, a mass of humans from the universal space of natural right. The second strategy was the utilitarian one of measuring cultural deviations to hold that certain peoples were, at least at the present time, incompetent to manage their own political affairs and so were best governed by others. The two critical deviations, Mehta shows, that were alleged to be empirically observable, were inscrutability and civilizational infantilism.[61]

Inscrutability "designates an unfathomable limit to the object of inquiry without implicating either the process of inquiry or the inquirer."[62] The object, in this case the Oriental, appears mysterious and unpredictable to the observer not because of any deficiency in the methods of observation or the structure of understanding employed by the latter but rather because of some inherent deficiency in the character of the former. Orientals seem inscrutable because they do not think or behave according to the familiar patterns of human reason. Inscrutability is, in other words, a variant of lunacy or idiocy; Orientals talk and behave strangely because, like the lunatic or idiot, they are incapable of reasoned speech or action. This supposedly empirical claim about the inscrutable Asiatic (or African) is based, as Mehta says, on "a crude descriptive fiat." Nevertheless, the voluminous literature produced in the nineteenth century by European travelers, administrators, novelists, and anthropologists relentlessly built up this image of the peoples of Asia and Africa as, by their very nature, inscrutable, and therefore excluded from the domain of humans capable of exercising their reason in political matters.

The second strategy of exclusion was even more commonly employed. It was to mine the literary, philosophical, and scientific texts along with the religious, cultural, and political practices of an entire civilization for its supposed deficiencies, and to pronounce it as infantile. The basic argument was almost ridiculous in its simplicity—so ridiculous, indeed, that nationalist ideologues and postcolonial scholars of the twentieth century were astonished that anyone could have been duped by this hallowed literature of imperial apologetics. To some extent, this explains the fury of outraged criticism that greeted Edward Said's *Orientalism* when it was published in 1978—the main charge being that the critique of Orientalism as a mode of Western thought was much too reductionist.[63] Writing after the moment of decolonization, Said was well positioned to uncover the utterly simple structure of the moral justification of nineteenth-century imperial power. This rationalization of paternal despotism over morally infantile subjects acquired its political grounding, applicable globally, in the comparative theory of government inaugurated by Bentham.

There were several specific variants in which this moral argument was packaged. One used the language of Burkean trusteeship, another invoked the image of Plato's guardians; and a third was, of course, guided by Benthamite considerations of utility. Some of the most passionate pleas for stern paternalist education were made by Evangelicals, just as later there would be anthropologists demanding the paternal protection of primitive tribal cultures against the destructive tide of modernity. But common to all of them was the affirmation of a simple relation of paternal power of mature and responsible adults over vulnerable and unthinking children. As Raghavan Iyer, writing in the first flush of postcolonial self-assertion, put it: "Like every despotism, it [imperial rule] was based on the principle that everything had to be done for the [colonized] people as they could do nothing themselves."[64]

Once again, John Stuart Mill remains the most instructive because sophisticated advocate of the liberal ideology of empire. Criticisms of his writings as arrogantly Occidental and racially prejudiced, while doubtless true, do not, as we shall see, disturb the robustness of the liberal ideological structure that he put up. His policy dispatches on Indian affairs, dealing mostly with the East India Company's relations with the various Indian princely states, have been recently researched.[65] They reveal, not surprisingly, that Mill was caught between two tendencies that pulled in opposite directions: the conservative school that wanted to preserve the old aristocracy and the traditional literate classes of India; and the reformers, now fired by Evangelical zeal, that wanted to govern according to universally valid true principles, and thus to tolerate neither the barbaric practices that abounded in that country nor their many benighted propagators.

Turning his back on his father's reformist legacy, in the 1830s Mill came under the intellectual influence of the Romantic movement, especially that of Samuel Taylor Coleridge, and on Indian subjects took advice from Horace Hayman Wilson, who after a distinguished career in India, had returned to become the first professor of Sanskrit at Oxford. Wilson was a leading figure among the Orientalists who opposed the spread of English education in India, arguing instead that Western knowledge would be best transmitted by grafting it on to classical learning and propagating it through India's traditional learned classes. Mill echoed Wilson in 1836 in a draft dispatch that was never sent to India in which Mill maintained that the new class of English-speaking Bengalis would be of little value in disseminating useful knowledge, and that the traditional "men of letters by birth and profession" should not be alienated by the British educational policy in India.[66]

Given his Romantic leanings, Mill was sympathetic in his early years to Johann Gottfried von Herder's idea that each national culture had unique qualities and should not be compared by the same standard. In his professional capacity in India House, the London headquarters of the East India Company, Mill was specifically required to deal with the Indian princely states within an evolving framework of indirect imperial rule. But his involvement in the administration of empire led him, as Lynn Zastoupil shows, to retreat from his early sympathies, and argue, for instance, that only a few Indian states had ancient political traditions that deserved to be treated as nationalities and most were unworthy of preservation.[67] He also contended that relations between civilized and barbarian peoples could not be governed by international law, since "barbarians have no rights as a *nation*."[68] On Awadh, a major state that was the focus of many imperial debates in the mid-nineteenth century, Mill changed his position several times. In 1834, he took such a dim view of native rule in Awadh that he virtually recommended direct administration by the company: "To permit the continuance of misgovernment of so flagrant a kind is to participate in it."[69]

In the 1840s, though, he took up a middle ground between the reformers and the defenders of the princely states. Mill appeared to think that only the Rajput states had truly ancient "national" governments, and that "foreigners" ruled most other states in India. He therefore was reluctant to tamper with the Rajput states. But on Awadh, when the clamor for annexation became irresistible in the 1850s, Mill defended the idea as a moral obligation to intervene on behalf of the state's hapless people.[70] The point to note, for the present purposes, is that all of these policy options were available within the comparative framework of government with which Mill worked. Each option was backed by a knowledge claim, presumably based on good empirical information, about the relative position of a particular government within a normalized comparative order along with the expected costs and benefits of each policy alternative.

Nadia Urbinati has observed that Mill, like Locke before him, thought of paternal despotism over non-European peoples as directed toward the future autonomy of the subjected, not for the benefit of the rulers. But like children, dependent peoples could not be the agents of their own education. Hence, Mill insisted, the natives ought not to be allowed to run their own despotic governments when they were under the protection of European powers. Legitimate despotism had to be paternal, not political.[71] Mill nonetheless carried the argument about the illegitimacy of political despotism in another direction, which was to have a profound influence on the modern practices of empire.

Mill always thought that it was wrong for the people of one country to hold the people of another in subjection. Thus, the legitimate despotism of paternal protection and guidance of a European power over non-European peoples must not be the *political* despotism of the former over the latter. Mill wanted to mark a clear distinction between the administrative functions of government and the political ones. The administration of paternal despotism over backward native peoples required, Urbinati says, "skilled persons with specialized training, an instrumental and impersonal rationality, an apolitical sense of responsibility that was relative to specific tasks, and a disciplined judgment that could follow direction and abide by hierarchical procedures."[72] This task could only be performed by a specialized and trained bureaucracy. Most crucially, it ought not to be brought under the purview of the deliberative procedures of the political process in the metropolitan country. Deliberative politics follows an exchange of opinion and persuasive process that is the opposite of bureaucratic judgment; it can only be carried out as a practice of self-government, not of government over others. Paternal despotism over non-European peoples therefore was best left to a bureaucracy of experts with specialized knowledge. The general electorate of the metropolitan country was unlikely to have either sufficient knowledge or sufficient tolerance of other peoples to be able to make political decisions on how they ought to be governed. To return to a distinction we made earlier in the context of Bentham, while sovereign power, for the sake of good government in India, should not belong to the inhabitants of that country, for the same reason it also should not belong to the British people. Effective sovereign power in a paternal despotism should vest in a body of trained experts.

It has been sometimes alleged that in making this theoretical claim, Mill was only engaging in some special pleading on behalf of his employers, the East India Company, which in the mid-nineteenth century was under enormous pressure at home to relinquish its governing role over India in favor of direct government under the Crown and Parliament. Whatever its motivation, Mill's argument left a deep mark on the evolving practices of modern empire by providing the ground for treating colonial policy as a separate, specialized domain of metropolitan government. The pressures of democratic accountability would force all liberal imperial powers of the nineteenth and twentieth centuries to bring colonial governance under some sort of parliamentary control. Yet it would always retain its character as a sphere ruled by experts who would both demand and enjoy a degree of autonomy from supervision by an ignorant and uncomprehending metropolitan public along with its elected representatives. In fact, as Charles Maier has recently pointed out, "the domestic victim of empire is not necessarily democracy but the control of war and peace by traditional legislatures."[73]

If we remember this feature of liberal democracy from the mid-nineteenth century, we should not be surprised, as Bernard Porter has claimed to be, by the general ignorance among Britons of the time about the empire, or by the wide gulf that seemed to separate domestic from colonial policy.[74] The liberal justification of paternal despotism in the colonies explains how, alongside the growing power of the bourgeoisie and the extension of the suffrage in British domestic politics, colonial government in the nineteenth century was run, at the highest levels of viceroys and governors by scions of the aristocracy and lower down by men from the upper middle classes, with a university education in the classics, usually from Oxford, suffused by a patrician spirit of virtue that had by then largely disappeared from British public life. As Lord Curzon (1859–1925) of Balliol and All Souls remarked, no one educated at Oxford in his day could fail to be an imperialist.[75] The young men from the upper classes who were trained in the university for careers in diplomacy and the colonial services were certainly not ignorant about the empire. As one Oxford graduate wrote in 1893, "For every ten books which our fathers read about India we read 1000."[76] That is why liberals and radicals could justify a paternal authoritarianism for the colonies with such moral fervor, and why the empire's frequently arbitrary policies could even be concealed from an allegedly uninformed metropolitan public opinion.

Describing Mill's concept of paternal despotism, Urbinati has suggested that his basic question always was: How can despotism be ended?[77] This provided to his thought the core liberal ideas of individual perfection and social progress everywhere in the world. But unlike many enthusiastic reformers, Mill was acutely aware of the deep foundations of despotism in tradition and habit, and saw the need for a prolonged effort to change the way people thought and lived. Paternal despotism for backward peoples was, for him, a pedagogical project that had to have a horizon where it would no longer be needed. The trouble is, as Urbinati herself admits, Mill did not offer any criterion by which it could be determined that protected subjects had reached the age of maturity when they could be left to manage their own affairs.[78] If they were not to participate in the paternal care of their own people, because that would amount to political despotism, how were they to signal their readiness to assume adulthood? By rebelling against their guardians? Would not such violent self-assertion, however, merely reinforce the charge of immaturity and irrationality? There is no answer in Mill's liberal theory of empire, except the implicit and enduring assumption that only the wise guardians could decide when their wards might be safely emancipated. As we will see, this is a problem that would continue to haunt liberal imperialism.

THE MYTH REFURBISHED

As the Boden Professor of Sanskrit at Oxford, Wilson was a towering figure among British Indologists. He had been secretary of the Asiatic Society of Bengal for many years, and had supervised the translation and publication of a large body of Sanskrit literary and religious texts.[79] Back in Britain, he continued to argue against the policy of English-language education in India, stressing his belief that by an appreciation of the irrationalities of some of their practices, Hindus learned in their own scriptures would come to embrace enlightened, even Christian virtues. He had, as we have noted before, some influence on Mill in educating him on Indian affairs, telling him perhaps of the ancientness of some of the political institutions of the Hindu kingdoms and undoubtedly emphasizing the continued tyrannical rule of foreign Muslim conquerors. It is entirely possible that Mill had a hand in engaging Wilson to revise his father's canonical history of India.

The fifth edition of James Mill's *History* was published in 1858, with each page ornamented with long editorial footnotes by Wilson. It was like a parallel commentary on Mill's text—correcting, supplementing, and interpreting it for a new imperial age. Virtually every detail in the *History* was subjected to Wilson's scrutiny. We want to focus on only one aspect here, since it is relevant to our story of Bengal's conquest. While Mill, as we have seen in chapter 2, was unsparing in his criticism of the greed and chicanery of the company's officials in Bengal, Wilson felt it necessary to include his own corrective note: "In [Mill's] statement some very material circumstances are omitted, which palliate, if they do not justify the deception that was practiced." Wilson then mentioned Amirchand's threat to disclose the plot to dethrone Siraj.

> There may be a difference of opinion, on this subject, and it would have been more for the credit of the European character, that however treacherously extorted, the

promise should have been performed, the money should have been paid; but there can be no doubt, that in order to appreciate with justice the conduct of Clive and the Committee, the circumstance of Omichund's menaced treason should not be kept out of sight.[80]

Mill's comments on the responsibility of British penal practices for the Black Hole tragedy clearly incensed Wilson. He inserted a long note of his own:

> The spirit in which this transaction is noticed, in this and the preceding note, as well as in the text, is wholly unjustifiable. It extenuates a deliberate act of wanton cruelty by erroneous assumptions and inapplicable analogies. The Black Hole was no dungeon at all; it was a chamber above ground—small and ill-aired only with reference to the number of persons forced into it, but affording abundant light and air to many more than it had ever lodged under the English administration.... Had a dozen or twenty people been immured within such limits for a night, there would have been no hardship whatever in their imprisonment, and in all probability no such number of persons ever was confined in it. The English, then, in the objectionable sense in which the author chooses to understand the "Black Hole," never had such a prison.... There is no doubt some gross exaggeration in the anecdote, but a case of inadvertency, however culpable, is no set-off against deliberate persevering barbarity. Even if the excuse of inconsiderateness might be urged for driving the prisoners into a space so utterly inadequate to their numbers, there was abundant opportunity to correct the mistake, when it was seen what suffering it occasioned.

Wilson then added what would now become the authorized historical gloss on the event.

> The whole transaction admits of no defence: it was an exemplification of Mohammedan insolence, intolerance, and cruelty; and in contemplating the signal retribution by which it has been punished, a mind susceptible of reverence, though free from superstition, can scarcely resist the impression, that the course of events was guided by higher influences than the passions and purposes of man.[81]

The tyranny of Muslim conquerors had been brought to an end by an act of divine providence that had placed the Indian people under British paternal care.

Wilson and Macaulay had been implacable rivals in the great education debate of the 1830s. On the historical significance of the foundation of the Indian Empire, though, they were unanimous. A mythical history of empire as moral progress had been founded.

CHAPTER SEVEN

The Pedagogy of Violence

Lord Dalhousie, governor-general of India, stood in front of the northern windows of the council chamber on the upper floor of Government House. The outer walls around the great mansion had still not been lined with the tall, thickly leaved trees that now provide it with an air of seclusion, even though it is situated in the middle of the city's busiest office district. Looking north across Tank Square, Dalhousie could see the bamboo scaffolding put up by masons working on the new facade and extension of Writers' Buildings. Beyond the offices of the Bengal government was the squalor and bustle of Black Town, and further past that, as he may have envisioned, lay stretched out the fertile plains of Upper India, soaked in the monsoon rains. Those territories were very much on his mind that August morning of 1855, because the day's agenda for discussion in the governor-general's council included the contentious topic of Awadh. The demand was being made from liberal and Evangelical quarters for the East India Company to annex the kingdom. Dalhousie was not inclined to concede.

It was not that he lacked sympathy for the liberal or Evangelical causes. Echoing the best liberal sentiments of the day, he once wrote in his diary:

> We govern India now with a limited despotism, because India is wholly incapable of governing itself, and we are wise in so doing. But we cannot, and we ought not, to anticipate that the condition of India and its population shall for ever stand still, and that it shall be in all time coming as wholly incapable of being admitted to a share of the government of itself, in union with its British conquerors, as it avowedly is at the present time![1]

That happy eventuality still lay in some obscurely perceptible future. Dalhousie's problem was immediate. It was one of correctly applying the right legal and moral norms to a policy.

The Law of Nations in the East

We have seen in the previous chapter how the emergence in the early nineteenth century of a normative framework of comparative government created

Figure 13. Government House before 1870, photograph. *Source: Curzon 1925*

two senses of the norm: as the empirically prevailing average, and as the desired standard to be achieved. Using the first meaning, any given society or government could be measured against others, and placed on a scale signifying its *deviation* from the empirically prevailing norm. Then, using the second sense, a suitable policy could be formulated for such a deviant case so that, if necessary, the universally desirable normative practice is suspended and a practice of *exception* applied until such time as its conditions came closer to the desired norm. Countries that were above the global empirical norm would then set the universally desirable standard, but the practices associated with those standards might not be considered appropriate for countries where the predominant standards were much lower. An exception therefore would be made for those countries, and suitable policies applied such that their standards could be improved. With a general improvement in standards in several countries, the globally prevailing empirical norm could also be expected to rise and come closer to the universally desirable one.

The two senses of the norm thus encoded a new political strategy of relating the normative to the empirical. The norm-deviation structure would establish the empirical location of any particular social formation at any given time in relation to the empirically prevailing average or normal. The corresponding normative framework could then provide, by means of a norm-exception structure of justification, the ground for the application of "policy" to intervene and bring the empirical average closer to the desired norm. Normalization was the theoretical key to this political strategy.

The practices of modern empire developed in the nineteenth century amounted to a new educational project of normalization—that is, disciplining. The techniques ranged between two types: a *pedagogy of violence*, and a *pedagogy of culture*. While culture increasingly became the preferred method, including legal reform, reform of social and economic institutions, and the spread of Western-style education, it concurrently was asserted that the proper conditions for cultural pedagogy may often have to be ensured by the use of imperial force. The history of imperialism since the nineteenth century is fundamentally characterized by debates over the degree, sequence, combination, and points of application of the pedagogical techniques of violence and culture.

The normative considerations involved questions of both morality and law. Occupying a central place in these debates of imperial policy was the concept of sovereignty. In each case where the issue came up of whether or how much to intervene, the application of moral as well as legal norms required a determination of the existence and quality of sovereignty. The striking fact, even though largely unacknowledged until quite recently, is that the evolving practices of imperial power in the Americas, Asia, and Africa had a profound effect in shaping the so-called law of nations, and defining the place within it of the modern sovereign nation-state.

In earlier chapters, we looked at the changing discursive conditions in the sixteenth- and seventeenth-century debates about the moral and legal propriety of the European conquest of the Americas, and those in the eighteenth century about the British territorial acquisitions in India. Broadly speaking, the shift is from the discussions between the scholastics and humanists in the earlier period, to the natural law theorists of the later period. In the legal domain, Grotius's ideas governed the acquisition of territory in India in the eighteenth century, while Montesquieu largely shaped the moral-political arguments. In the nineteenth century, alongside the emergence of utilitarian reasoning in political affairs, the legal domain was marked by the rise of positivism. John Austin was the foremost proponent here, with his ideas becoming posthumously influential in the latter half of the century.

The shift from natural law to legal positivism was distinguished by the devaluing of universal natural law assumptions, which were taken to be principles of morality rather than of law, and an emphasis on the empirical evidence of legal acts executed by sovereign state authorities. In domestic society, only the positive law made by a sovereign state could qualify as proper law. In the field of international law, this definition raised a problem, articulated by Austin himself: absent a globally sovereign state, there could not be, properly speaking, any international *law*. Yet this fundamentalist objection was circumvented by the claim that the body of extant international law consisted of specific acts, such as treaties, conventions, agreements, and so forth, entered into by sovereign states. Even though there were voices, such as that of Henry Maine, that suggested international law should be looked on as customary rather than positive law, the general desire was to ground the law of nations on the solidly empirical and positive foundation of the acts of sovereign states.[2]

But who were these sovereign states whose legal transactions with other sovereign states could produce a body of positive international law? Some scholars maintain that the mutual treaties and agreements between these sovereign states were based on certain shared premises, and had, over the years, produced a set of mutually recognized and accepted principles of international transaction. In other words, what otherwise might be called customary had been actually incorporated into a body of positive international law, because those sovereign states in fact constituted an international society, or perhaps a "family" of nations. As Antony Anghie points out, "Despite positivist preoccupations with sovereignty doctrine, ... 'society' and the 'family of nations' is the essential foundation of positivist jurisprudence and the vision of sovereignty it supports."[3]

In his landmark study on the subject, Charles Henry Alexandrowicz argued that before the nineteenth century, legal relations between European powers and states in India and Southeast Asia existed "on a footing of equality." The former acknowledged the sovereignty of the latter and even adopted, or at least tried to fit into, the legal practices that prevailed in interstate relations in the region. The Europeans were aware that there were different classes of sovereigns in the East, ranging from suzerains like the emperor of China or Mughal emperor, to minor sovereigns who were otherwise vassals of a suzerain, to vassals on the borderline of sovereignty and nonsovereign feudal status. Some of the treaties between Europeans and Indian rulers were declared to be transactions between sovereigns, even when they were only concluded between their local representatives, such as, for instance, the treaty of 1547 between the kings of Portugal and Vijayanagara. Of course, the European powers always sought preferential privileges from Eastern rulers in matters of trade and even extracted various territorial concessions. Yet "a great number of treaties originating from the pre–nineteenth century period were either equal treaties, or, if they were unequal or imposed transitory or permanent burdens on the contracting Rulers, they did not necessarily result in the suppression of their sovereignty or remove them from the orbit of the natural family of nations."[4] Even when Indian rulers effectively surrendered territory to the East India Company in the eighteenth century, as in Bengal or the Carnatic, or in the Maratha territories, they did so as sovereign powers through treaties.

The situation changed drastically in the nineteenth century when, with the adoption of legal positivism in place of natural law theories, the sovereign status of Eastern rulers came to be doubted, and the family of nations comprising the proper subjects of international law was restricted only to the countries of Europe and the new republics of the Americas. Paradoxically, therefore, as Alexandrowicz remarks, the domain of the law of nations in the nineteenth century "shrank to regional dimensions though it still carried the label of universality."[5]

While this claim might seem persuasive from a strictly legal point of view, the change in legal regimes makes better sense if one places it within the changing political context of relations between nineteenth-century European powers and Eastern rulers. We have already alluded in earlier chapters to the profound transformations brought about in social and political discourse in Europe, and in Britain in particular, with the Industrial Revolution. The world in the nineteenth century as seen from Europe was quite different from how it looked in the eighteenth. The attraction of Asian and later African territories as sources of raw material for European industry, land for European commercial agriculture, and markets for European industrial manufactures had become overwhelming.

Added to this was the expansion through the nineteenth century of the balance-of-power system of Europe to include within its scope the territories of virtually the entire globe. The classical structure had developed a mechanism, through territorial transfers and shifting alliances, to prevent the emergence of a single dominant power or coalition in Europe. Thus, the relative strengths of the system's core players—Britain, France, Austria, Russia, and Holland (replaced by Prussia after 1815)—were frequently adjusted by territorial acquisitions at the expense of minor powers (the partitions of Poland in the late eighteenth century being the most notorious example), and in the case of the maritime powers, by overseas territories. The Napoleonic Wars did, of course, push this diplomatic system into a crisis, but when the crisis was over, the conservative restoration of the principles of legitimate sovereignty returned the structure to its previous methods of adjustment of the balance of power. Hence, even though France was contained by the peace of 1815, it was not punished and was allowed to retain most of its overseas possessions. Indeed, all of the core powers of Europe, including France, had more in 1815 than they did in 1790. Overseas territories actually became the chief means for maintaining the European balance in the nineteenth century, reaching egregious limits in the partition of Africa at the Berlin colonial conference of 1884–85.[6]

Moreover, with the rising tide of democratic and nationalist movements in central and eastern Europe, resonating with the threatening revolutionary rhetoric of the natural rights of peoples and nations to self-government, the discursive shift in the legal domain from natural law to positivism made good conservative sense. This was the political background to the changing significance of the law of nations in the nineteenth century. The European powers became the only proper subjects of the purportedly universal law of nations because the entire world was now properly the object of European power.

The effect of this shift on the Indian subcontinent becomes dramatically clear from a chart prepared by Michael Fisher showing the annexation of territory by the East India Company.[7] Until 1799, the bulk of the company's territory, mostly in Bengal and the Carnatic, was not quite annexed since de jure sovereignty still lay with various Indian rulers. During Wellesley's term as governor-general, a new aggressive policy was implemented, not always endorsed by the British government or the company's directors in London. From 1799 to 1806, in Mysore, Awadh, and the Maratha country, the company annexed some 135,000 square miles (nearly 350,000 square kilometers) of land—the size, Fisher notes, of reunited Germany today. Indeed, over Wellesley's period in office, the company annexed 50,000 square kilometers of territory every year.[8]

Annexations continued through the early nineteenth century. Lord Hastings, governor-general from 1813 to 1823, proclaimed the legal doctrine of "paramountcy," by which the company's authority as the paramount power superseded that of all Indian rulers and bestowed on it the right to annex their territories if, in its view, there were sufficient grounds to do so. Malcolm, writing in 1826, supplied a logic of inevitability to the annexation process:

> The truth is, that the day on which the Company's troops marched one mile from their factories, the increase of their territories and their armies became a principle of self-preservation.... [I]t was a vain attempt to endeavour to stop altogether, the career of a state, which was rising rapidly into greatness under the influence of causes that were irresistible in their force, and which it was not possible to control.

By that time, despite acknowledging the material benefits of territorial expansion in the form of increased revenue and commerce, the principal justification for annexation became the plea that the people living under various Indian rulers needed to be protected from misgovernment. Malcolm made this argument too:

> To men tired out as they were with wars and contentions, and who, from the repeated conquests to which they had been subjected, were lost to all feeling of national pride, the very permanency of usurpation was a blessing; and it was natural for them to forget their prejudices against their European masters in the contemplation of that superior regard to justice, good faith, and civilization, by which they saw their rule accompanied.[9]

The consideration that the people wanted and deserved better government, it would be asserted in the nineteenth century, could trump all prior legal provisions of treaties and override the objections of the rulers whose presumed rights of sovereignty had been replaced by the paramount power assumed by the British.

It is here that the history of European territorial acquisitions in Asia and, later in the nineteenth century, Africa would pose conceptual problems for the law of nations. Even though in the course of their imperial advance European powers such as Britain had entered into various treaties and agreements with Oriental rulers and chieftains, were the latter really to be regarded as sovereign entities? To admit this would be to acknowledge that the family of sovereign nations that was the source of international law included such non-European members. On the other hand, to deny them any sovereign authority would imply that the treaties they had entered into with European powers had no legal standing. The problem, as we shall see, dogged imperial policy in India in the nineteenth century.

The solution was devised, once again, by reference to the new comparative scheme of normalization of governmental attributes. It allowed European jurists to make a basic distinction between civilized and uncivilized nations. By virtue of this, the family of nations that constituted the proper subject of international law could be restricted to only the civilized nations of Europe and white settler nations of the Americas. John Westlake, the doyen of British scholarship on international law in the nineteenth century, defined this "society of states" as the Europe that was born in classical Greece and Rome, consolidated in Westphalia, and now included European and American states plus "a few Christian nations such as the Hawaiian Islands, Liberia and the Orange Free State."[10]

As for the uncivilized peoples of the rest of the world, some had no state formations or legal regimes at all, while others had rulers who were arbitrary, and whose laws were shaped by religions and cultures that did not value the underlying precepts that had produced the law of civilized nations. The uncivilized nations could not be regarded as proper subjects of international law. Westlake, writing at the end of the nineteenth century, was clear on this point. Sovereignty was a purely European concept, and native chiefs in Africa could not be said to have transferred something of which they had no concept. "International law has to treat natives as uncivilized. It regulates, for the mutual benefit of the civilized states, the claims which they make to sovereignty over the region and leaves the treatment of the natives to the conscience of the state to which sovereignty is awarded."[11] By the nineteenth century, then, the proper subjects of international law had become restricted to the "civilized nations"; it was for *their* mutual benefit that international law was supposed to regulate the transactions between nations.

Was this a shift that had been brought about by a discursive transformation from universalist natural law doctrines to legal positivism? Martti Koskenniemi, who does not give much credence to the theory of change in legal regimes, holds that in the nineteenth century, appeals to universalist values did not disappear. Nor was the universalist humanism of the natural law doctrines of Grotius and Emerich de Vattel, "a secular variant of the Christian view of a single god," an impediment to excluding the non-European subject by emphasizing its radical difference according to some purely European standard.[12] Even when non-European nations were regarded as capable of engaging in acts of sovereignty, the proper subjects of the law of nations were always the European states. If there was a change in the discursive practices of law, it took place entirely *within* a purely European discourse.[13]

The distinction between civilized and uncivilized nations, however, still left unanswered the question of whether the treaties entered into by the former with the latter were legally valid. One response was to resort to the flexibility afforded by the normalized scheme of comparison between nations, suggesting that there were different degrees of sovereignness among uncivilized states. These degrees translated into different kinds of treaties between European and non-European states, ranging from trade agreements to cession of territory. Each of these transactions implied a certain amount of capacity by the uncivilized state to engage in international transactions. The acquisition of territory by European powers could take place by the cession of territory by treaty, annexation, or conquest.

In the nineteenth century, the concept of the protectorate also emerged by which a backward state would, through its legal consent, be brought under the control of an imperial power without the latter taking on the burden of administration. Imperial practices in Asia and, later, Africa thus imparted the qualities of variation and complexity to the positivist concept of state sovereignty. This enabled, for instance in 1856, the inclusion of Ottoman Turkey in an international peace conference, and later in the century the recognition of Japan, Siam, Persia, and China as occasional members of the family of sovereign nations. Not only that, these imperial practices brought out the conceptual obverse of the idea of sovereignty: it was necessary for an entity—that is, an uncivilized nation—to first possess sovereignty precisely in order to be able to give it up through a valid legal agreement with a civilized European power. Lassa Oppenheim, writing his canonical text in the early twentieth century, revealed some bewilderment when he observed: "Cession of territory made to a member of the family of nations by a State as yet outside that family is real cession and a concern of the Law of Nations, since such State becomes through the treaty of cession in some respects a member of that family."[14] Anghie correctly concludes: "The development of the idea of sovereignty in relation to the non-European world occurs in terms of dispossession, its ability to alienate its lands and rights."[15]

Further, these earlier treaties could not be discarded all of a sudden, not because of any consideration for the sensibilities of Oriental or African rulers, but rather because of the restraint of legal practice they placed on mutual relations *between* the European powers. To allow the validity of these treaties to lapse would introduce a dangerous instability into the relations and practices that had been established among the various European powers themselves in Asia and Africa. Anghie notes: "It was precisely the fear of disputes over title to colonial territories among European powers that inspired the Conference of Berlin in 1884–5. Consequently, the non-European world had to be located in the positivist system, not merely for purposes of control and suppression, but to prevent its ambiguous status from undermining European solidarity."[16] Not surprisingly, this feature once more confirmed the virtually exclusive centrality of the European powers to the family of nations that made international law in the nineteenth century.

By the mid-nineteenth century, the legal concept of the protectorate had arisen, so that "one state could acquire complete control over another ... without necessarily assuming the burden of its administration.... [I]t was this feature of the protectorate which favoured its extensive adoption by European Powers in the spread of their dominion."[17] Although control of internal affairs was left to the native ruler, that function could be taken over by the protecting power either because of a provision in the treaty or because the native ruler was incapable of providing good government. The grounds for such intervention, though, were left vague and undefined, affording the paramount power a considerable range of strategic flexibility in framing its policies toward the so-called protected states. As William Lee-Warner, an official dealing with the Indian princely states, observed:

> There is paramount power in the British Crown, of which the extent is wisely left undefined. There is a subordination in the native states, which is understood but not explained. The paramount power intervenes only on grounds of general policy, where interests of the Indian people or the safety of the British power are at stake.[18]

Once again, even within the ostensibly positivist framework defined by the concept of undivided sovereignty, the law of nations in the East had to proceed by keeping sovereignty flexible and undefined, and therefore subject to policy rather than to fixed legal principle.[19]

Surveying the history of relations between the Indian princely states and the British, Barbara Ramusack concludes that the decision of whether and how far to intervene in the affairs of native states was always flexible, contingent, and dependent on specific understandings of the imperial interest, and not bound by rigid conceptions of either legal or moral principle.[20] This would, as we will soon see, become a major resource in the practices of modern empire in the twentieth century.

The history of European imperialism in Asia and Africa thus reveals a general feature of the history of international law itself. It would be said in the latter half of the twentieth century that with the rivalry between the two superpowers, the United States and the Soviet Union, in extending their control and dominance over every part of the globe, the field of international law was taken over by policy in place of law: the so-called diplomatic school, which preferred flexible principles and case-by-case negotiated settlements, won over the legal school, which demanded firm principles of law and permanent international institutions of adjudication. The superpowers began to use the language of law to justify their political acts of foreign policy.[21] The history of the law of nations on the Indian subcontinent in the nineteenth century almost exactly prefigures the history of international law in the second half of the twentieth. Until the eighteenth century, relations between the European powers and Oriental states appear to have largely conformed to the restraints imposed by the concept of sovereignty enshrined in Europe since the Peace of Westphalia in 1648 and theorized in the eighteenth century by Vattel. This was because the European presence in India was either distinctly inferior in terms of power compared to the Indian states or, as in the eighteenth century, Europeans dealt with the Indian states within a certain balance-of-power framework. The law of nations as developed in Europe was quite reasonably suited for such a structure.

By the early nineteenth century, British power started to be projected in India as hegemonic. Other powers, whether European or Indian, were no longer serious competitors in the region. There was no reason left to abide by the constraints imposed by a law of nations designed to maintain the balance of power. Law was now mobilized to further the policy objectives of the paramount power. Indeed, our exploration of the legal and policy debates over British relations with the Indian states in the nineteenth century, and survey of the technical instruments they produced for a dominant power to exercise control over other putatively sovereign entities, allows us to offer a general definition of modern empire that covers most examples of imperial power in the world in the last two centuries. *The imperial prerogative*, one could say, *lies in the claim to declare the colonial exception.*

It is, of course, a claim whose effectiveness and legitimacy were open to negotiation. In the nineteenth century, the principal site where such claims were put forward and sometimes challenged was that of the so-called family of civilized nations, mainly consisting of the major European powers. In a related sense, these claims also had to be negotiated within domestic political formations in the imperial countries. Only in a peripheral and utterly subsidiary sense were they discussed with the people of subordinated states, even though, as we have seen, they were frequently invoked as justifications for imperial intervention—in the form of "alibis," as Karuna Mantena has shown.[22]

Besides, the privilege of declaring the colonial exception here applies to relations between a sovereign power and other political entities whose sovereignty has to be recognized even if only for them to surrender that sovereignty, whether wholly or partially. A variety of techniques certainly are developed, but all involve a determination that the universal principles that apply to relations between sovereign states cannot apply in this exceptional case, because for one reason or another the entity does not deserve the full status of, or has lost its legitimacy as, a proper sovereign state. It is this criterion that limits the concept of modern empire to the domain of inter*national* relations, confirming the historical process over the last two hundred years of the nation-state's normalization as the standard form of the modern state. Instances of declaring the exception within contexts that are taken to belong to the sphere of the domestic politics of states are not, in this sense, colonial-imperial. This is the definition of modern empire that arises from its history over the last two hundred years.

It is somewhat ironic that the universalism of legal forms enshrined in international law precisely in order to prevent the emergence in the eighteenth and nineteenth centuries of a hegemonic power in Europe should now, starting in the late twentieth century, be recognized and criticized as the mark of imperialism. The critique began with Carl Schmitt, despised and marginalized as a Nazi sympathizer, who in 1950 bemoaned the passing of the traditional global order based on the *jus publicum Europaeum* and its replacement by, on the one hand, US hegemonism, cloaking the pursuit of its imperial interests with the moral rhetoric of war on behalf of humanity, and on the other hand, the anticolonial forces purporting to fight imperialism, but using the same moral appeal to humanity. Schmitt firmly believed that appeals to humanity in the field of politics could only be a deception, since humanity as such did not correspond to any political entity on earth and could never be a proper political subject. The traditional international public law of war and peace, a purely European concept, had developed a set of universal principles based on territorial jurisdictions that were intended to restrain states from imposing the domination of one over the others. The new moralism of wars on behalf of humanity had ended that regime of law. Henceforth, wars would be moral, unrestrained, and total.[23]

The critique was picked up by the realist theorists of international relations, led by Hans Mongenthau, who regarded power in pursuit of the national interest as the principal driving force of world politics and conceded only a minor role to international law in facilitating the resolution of disputes that did not involve fundamental conflicts of national interest. Thus, moralism on one side and realism on the other combined to undermine the *formal* structure of international law that had provided, even in an age when there were no supranational legal institutions, the source of compelling arguments that could restrain the actions of states with respect to one another. Koskenniemi, among contemporary legal scholars, has clearly identified the resultant antiformalism as contributing to two kinds of imperialism. One is the rational imperialism that assumes that the particular preferences of an authoritative power either constitute or exactly correspond to the universally desirable norm, and that all deviant preferences are morally flawed or the result of ignorance, and as such are devoid of legitimacy. The other is the cynical imperialism that upholds a universally desirable norm, but does not believe that it has been fully realized by any na-tion, thereby making all particular preferences imperfect and flawed, and yet in bad faith proceeds to justify the acts of the authoritative power by invoking that universal norm.[24] The two variants of "empire's law" have replaced the classical law of nations.

Returning to Dalhousie's predicament in 1855, it is apparent exactly how empire's law was made to replace the law of nations on the Indian subcontinent in the nineteenth century. Schmitt would not have flinched if he heard this story, since he did not think that the Indian states were ever the proper subjects of the law of nations: it was legitimate and rational, he would have said, for the stability of the European states system that Britain should bring under its domain the control of that part of the world. But in order not to succumb to nationalist sentiments of outrage or nostalgia, it is important to also recall that the effective erasure in the nineteenth century, under British imperial auspices, of the law of nations from the territorial space of the Indian subcontinent was essential for the imagining of undivided national sovereignty in the twentieth.

In fact, the second half of the nineteenth century was when, as Manu Gos-wami has shown, the territory of subcontinental India, *including* the princely states, effectively consolidated under British paramountcy, began to be geograph-ically envisioned as a national space, with a map, borders, and physical and human resources that could be claimed for economic and political assertion by an Indian nation.[25] When in 1947, Vallabhbhai Patel, the home minister of newly independent India, proceeded to cajole and sometimes coerce the hun-dreds of Indian princes, hitherto under British "protection," to integrate their territories with those of the Indian state through treaties of accession, from the formal viewpoint of the law of nations his acts were no less imperialist.[26] Whether they were of the rational or cynical variety may, of course, be a matter of interpretation.

DALHOUSIE AND PARAMOUNTCY

By the 1840s, even the East India Company directors in London were per-suaded that their territorial reach in India should be extended to better consoli-date and expand British interests in the region. The colonial economy of India was by then taking its characteristic shape under conditions of rapid industrial growth in Britain.[27] Private European entrepreneurs were seeking opportunities for profit making in the frontier zones outside the relatively regulated domains of the company's territories. The company's interests too were now actively en-gaged further east as far as China, where armed conflict broke out in 1839–42 over the British trade there in Indian opium. Besides, the security of the com-pany's Indian possessions became a concern with growing fears of Russian dominance along the northern frontier. British officials in India looking to increase the company's lands were now much more likely than before to receive the approval of their directors in London.

Dalhousie is famous in British Indian history for achieving the largest territorial expansion under a single governor-general. Between 1848 and 1856, he annexed, as Fisher reminds us, 250,000 square miles (680,000 square kilometers), representing a quarter of the company's entire lands in India, and clocking an annual rate of 85,000 square kilometers, which was equivalent to acquiring an Austria every year.[28] And yet, reading the records of this period, the postcolonial historian is likely to be somewhat perplexed by the endless debates that dominate colonial decision making under Dalhousie, especially over legal jurisdiction, treaty obligations, and internal sovereignty. If it was true, as the first generation of nationalist historians of the 1950s concluded, that nineteenth-century Indian princes wore the regalia of statehood only at the sufferance of the British and that their presumptions of sovereignty were no more than an empty shell, then why were the annexations of Dalhousie so contentious?[29] One of the perennial dangers in treating history as the ineluctable path to the decisive construction of the present is that we overlook, in this case, the real constraints and possibilities that made the mid-nineteenth century a moment of critical historical transition in India. Unless we tune ourselves to the discursive shifts that took place in nineteenth-century international law and diplomacy, we will miss what the fuss was all about.

The received orthodoxy among colonial officials in the 1840s was noninterference in the internal sovereignty of the Indian states. Lee-Warner, Dalhousie's biographer and an expert on the princely states, explained the relevant considerations as follows:

> The Company's servants knew that the so-called states were not nationalities, but heterogeneous populations under dynasties, or even upstarts of foreign races.... [T]he experience of the Pindari campaigns compelled [Lord Hastings] to break down the ring-fence, and to fill the map of India with protected states. He took from them the reality of international life. He deprived them of the rights of making war or of contracting engagements with their neighbours.... Thus, one of the full attributes of sovereignty, which in the aggregate gave to their possessor an international status or a position of independence, namely internal sovereignty, was alone left to the protected princes of India, and an excessive importance was attached in 1847 to the obligations imposed on the protecting power by its promises to avoid interference into the domestic affairs of its allies.[30]

Most residual signs of earlier assumptions of equal sovereignty between the British and Indian powers were erased, however. The earlier treaties, for instance, provided for the office of the British resident in the protected Indian state in return for a *vakil* or diplomatic representative of the prince posted in Calcutta. By the 1830s, the sending of vakils was actively discouraged and finally ended.[31] The sovereignty of Indian states under conditions of British paramountcy, even though a valid legal category, was decidedly residual in practice.

Dalhousie nevertheless was keen to find room, even within those limitations, to expand the company's territories. He discovered it in the so-called doctrine of lapse. The first test case came early in his term of office—in the western Indian state of Satara in 1848, when the ruler died without leaving behind a son. Dalhousie annexed the state, and defended his action by declaring that "the British Government is bound not to put aside or neglect such rightful opportunities of acquiring territory or revenue as may from time to time present themselves, whether they arise from the lapse of subordinate states by the failure of all heirs."[32] His logic here was purely strategic: "I cannot conceive it possible for any one to dispute the policy of taking advantage of every just opportunity that presents itself *for consolidating* the territories that already belong to us, by taking possession of states which may lapse *in the midst of them....* By incorporating Sattarah with our possessions we should acquire continuity of military communication, and increase the revenues of 'the state.'" He would repeat the argument in 1853, when he annexed Nagpur by applying this doctrine:

> It would render continuous several British provinces, between which foreign territory is now interposed.... It would place the only direct line of communication which exists between Calcutta and Bombay almost within British territory, whereas the road now passes for a considerable distance through foreign states.... To sum up all in one sentence, the possession of Nagpore would combine our military strength, would enlarge our commercial resources, and would materially tend to consolidate our "power."[33]

In 1849, he annexed Punjab, which was nominally ruled by the minor Dalip Singh, on the charge of disloyalty, since the Sikh chieftains had allegedly sought the assistance of the Afghans in resisting the paramountcy of the British.

The strategic vision that impelled these acts was described by Edwin Arnold, the celebrated narrator of Buddha's life, but here in his less-known role as defender of Dalhousie's policies:

> One dominant passion has shown itself palpably, driving the great and able man possessed of it to the very verge of conventional justice, generosity, and good faith, and sometimes not a little beyond those boundaries.... Lord Dalhousie had, in fact, deliberately conceived the idea of a homogeneous Indian peninsula, with the British sovereign for sole Seigneur, the native princes for pensioned peers, and the native zemindars, officers, public servants, and employés, replaced by "young gentlemen from Haileybury."[34]

Even as he was possessed by this radical imperial vision, though, Dalhousie was mindful of the legal constraints that he needed to respect. He regarded the absence of natural heirs as a strategic opportunity; disloyalty was surely an offense that had to be punished by the paramount power, although such a thing was unknown in international law. But he balked at intervention in internal sovereignty. The test case was presented in 1851, when a clamor was raised in official circles to annex Hyderabad for the alleged misrule of the nizam. Dalhousie resisted.

> The acknowledged supremacy of the British power in India ... entitles it to interfere in the administration of the Native princes, if their administration tends unquestionably to the injury of the subjects or of the allies of the British Government. But I recognise no mission confided to the British Government which imposes upon it the obligation, or can confer upon it the right, of deciding authoritatively on the existence of Native independent sovereignties, or of arbitrarily setting them aside whenever their administration may not accord with its own views.[35]

Dalhousie, it seems, was particularly sensitive to public opinion in Britain, and wary of doing anything that might be construed there as having violated international obligations and good faith. "The passion for approval and consent," Arnold observed, "visible in his last anxious act, was conspicuous at every stage of his career; and sprang from something deeper than vanity in one who had witnessed the omnipotence of the popular will, preparing in 1848 to shake the powers of earth."[36] Dalhousie was also reminded by friends and advisers from Britain of the need to keep British public opinion in mind before embarking on bold imperial initiatives. Charles Wood, having returned to England after a long Indian career, wrote to Dalhousie in 1854 on the subject of Awadh, which would soon come to occupy center stage in Indian politics:

> Take Oudh by a voluntary surrender.... I am not at all averse to the operation, and only am anxious that it should be skilfully performed—skilfully, I mean, in reference to public opinion here—for I am not at all afraid of your not doing it skilfully on Indian ground. One cannot nowadays disregard public opinion, and the Court of Directors is by no means a popular body.[37]

The annexation of Awadh would test the political skills and legendary fortitude of Dalhousie to their limits.

Awadh under British Protection

Awadh at the end of the eighteenth century was a kingdom comprising the greater part of the Gangetic plains, roughly equal in size to and possibly greater in population than Great Britain. It had emerged as an independent principality through the eighteenth century with the decline of the Mughal Empire. In the second half of the century, as British power rose in Bengal and expanded to the frontiers of Awadh in the north, the ruling nawabs were forced into various treaties with the British that allowed the East India Company special privileges in matters of the trade and recruitment of soldiers to its army, but the internal sovereignty of Awadh was protected. In 1775, when Nawab Shuja-ud-daulah died, the British claimed new privileges. "Assuming, with calculated cynicism," as Michael Edwardes described the move, "that the death of the Nawab cancelled the agreements entered into with him, the Calcutta Council insisted on negotiating a fresh treaty with his successor. By it, the nawab became a puppet in the hands of the Governor-General, and the State of Oudh a dependency of the East India Company."[38] From this time, a British resident was appointed to the court of Awadh to represent the company's supervisory authority. Awadh also became a substantial supplier of raw cotton, textiles, indigo, and opium to British Bengal.[39]

Wellesley's expansionist zeal found a major target in Awadh. In 1798, he declared: "I am satisfied that no effectual security can be provided against the ruin of the province of Oude, until the exclusive management of the civil and military government of that country shall be transferred intact to the Company."[40] In the end, despite Wellesley's desire to annex the whole of the kingdom, Awadh was partitioned in 1801, and large parts of its territory were ceded to the company. Arthur Wellesley, later to be celebrated in world history as the Duke of Wellington, defended his brother's action:

> For some years previous to 1798 apprehensions had been entertained that Zemaun Shah, the King of Caubul, would carry into execution an old and favourite plan of the Affghan government to invade Hindustan.... Towards the close of the year 1799 the Governor-General called upon the Nabob of Oude to dismiss his expensive, useless, and dangerous troops, and to fill their places by increased numbers of the Company's troops.... [When he said that he was unable to meet the financial burden] a treaty was concluded ... by which, in commutation of the subsidy, and for the perpetual defence of his country, the Nabob ceded to the Company the territory of Rohilcund, the Dooab, and Gorruckpoor....
>
> By the whole of this arrangement the Company gained,
>
> 1st. The advantage of getting rid of a useless and dangerous body of troops stationed on the very point of their defence, and ready at all times to join an invading enemy:
>
> 2ndly. The advantage of acquiring the means of placing upon this weak point additional numbers of the British troops, and thereby increasing its strength, and the general security of the provinces in their rear:
>
> 3rdly. Ample territorial security for the regular and perpetual payment of these funds for the support of their military establishments in Bengal:

4thly. By the introduction of their own system of government and management into the countries ceded to them and the employment of their own servants in the administration, they secured the tranquillity of those hitherto disturbed countries, the loyalty and happiness of their hitherto disaffected and turbulent inhabitants; and, above all, they acquired the resources of those rich but hitherto neglected provinces for their own armies, in case of the recurrence of the necessity for military operations upon that frontier.[41]

Military person that he was, Wellington put the imperial argument here in the most matter-of-fact terms possible: the partial annexation of Awadh in 1801 was made necessary by the needs of security (two hundred years ago, it was still Afghanistan), restoration of order, deployment of troops, and resources to pay for it all. There was no argument about coming to the rescue of oppressed people.

In the early decades of the nineteenth century, Awadh was practically governed by a dual authority. The nawab's administration was crippled by the constant interference of the British resident. Most historians agree that under this "system of meddling," the nawabs and their ministers were left with little initiative or responsibility: "A corrupt administration was guaranteed by the presence of the Company's troops."[42] It was later alleged that the Awadh rulers stopped ruling, and retired into a life of wine, women, and poetry. Yet Thomas Metcalf writes: "Indolence was the only appropriate response to the situation in which the princes of Oudh were placed: in which they could not be overthrown but could not act effectively in either the old way or the new."[43]

But there was never any question about the Awadh rulers' loyalty to the British. In 1819, the British decided to upgrade the status of the Awadh ruler from a nominal subordinate of the emperor in Delhi to a sovereign king, thereby diminishing even further the already-marginal authority of the Mughal throne. The coronation was held in Lucknow, the capital city of Awadh, accompanied by a twenty-one gun salute and *God Save the King*. Regardless of this legal fantasy, however, the British hardly took the trappings of Awadh royalty seriously. Their officers insisted on sitting, as opposed to standing, in the royal presence. They would move around the city in palanquins and have umbrellas held over them—both considered privileges of the local aristocracy. When the governor-general Charles, Lord Hardinge, visited Lucknow in 1847, the king of Awadh was made to wear English patent leather boots to establish parity of status, instead of following the local tradition of visitors removing their shoes when in the king's presence.[44]

As mentioned before, the prudent view until the 1840s in British circles was not to interfere in the internal affairs of the subsidiary Indian allies, because that was both the letter and spirit of the treaties that the British had signed with them, and also because constant interference tended to sour relations without bringing any permanent benefits. Francis, Lord Moira (later Lord Hastings), governor-general in 1813, reminded John Baillie, a particularly pushy and arrogant resident in Awadh, that "the Resident should consider himself as the ambassador from the British Government to an acknowledged sovereign; a respectful urbanity and a strict fulfilment of established ceremonials should thence be preserved by the Resident towards His Excellency."[45]

Still, the policy of noninterference also made the British presence in these dependencies utterly anomalous. British officers complained that the company's troops were being asked to protect a corrupt and oppressive native administration. Indeed, the British power was becoming an accomplice in the perpetration of countless crimes and immoralities. This view of the imperial mission was voiced with great fervor by the liberal Evangelical movement.

The Evangelicals in the 1840s had two main items on their agenda for the Indian Empire: the spread of English education among Indians, and the further opening of India to Christian missionaries. They had, as we have seen, powerful proponents within the company establishment in officials like Grant. In their minds, the duties of Evangelical Christianity were wonderfully married, in a blissful ménage à trois, to thriving commerce as well as progressive social reform. As Grant put it:

> In considering the affairs of the world as under the control of the Supreme Disposer, and those distant territories ... providentially put into our hands ... is it not necessary to conclude that they were given to us, not merely that we might draw an annual profit from them, but that we might diffuse among their inhabitants, long sunk in darkness, vice and misery, the light and benign influence of the truth, the blessings of well-regulated society, the improvements and comforts of active industry? ... In every progressive step of this work, we shall also serve the original design with which we visited India, that design still so important to this country—the extension of our commerce.[46]

The Evangelical tone was particularly shrill among the nonofficial British population of India—merchants, missionaries, and newspaper editors. They were obsessively focused on the dissolute lifestyles of Indian princes. It was virtually axiomatic for them that the Indian nobility was immoral and incapable of good government. Charles Jackson, a defender of Dalhousie's policies, wrote: "But what hope could be entertained of any Indian prince brought up in the purple—of his becoming anything but an indolent, sensual, and tyrannical sovereign?" Citing a report on the last ruler of Nagpur, he continued:

> A distaste for business and low habits seem the distinguishing features of his temperament.... [H]is natural inclination has led him, when unchecked, to absorb himself in the society of low followers, in the sports of wrestling, kite-flying, and cards, in singing and dancing, and in the intercourse of his dancing-girls.... A concubine, by name Janee, is spoken of as having led the Rajah into confirmed habits of drinking

about eight years since, so that now, when not ill, his drinking exceeds a bottle of brandy a day.[47]

Arnold, professor for several years in Poona before becoming a journalist in Britain and editor of the *Daily Telegraph*, commented: "It has no great bearing, indeed, on our right to annex Oudh, that their Kings took their pleasure in the stud-yard, and pandered at once to the passions of he-goats and their own; or that they laid aside the sceptre to catch cats."[48] The brazen circularity created by these assumptions and prejudices is best exemplified by Henry Elliot's methodological preface to his immensely influential compendium of extracts from the chronicles of Muslim rule in India:

> In Indian Histories there is little which enables us to penetrate below the glittering surface, and observe the practical operation of a despotic government.... If, however, we turn our eyes to the present Muhammadan kingdoms of India, and examine the character of the princes, we may fairly draw a parallel between ancient and modern times.... We behold kings, even of our own creation, slunk in sloth and debauchery, and emulating the vices of a Caligula or a Commodus.[49]

In 1850, the *Delhi Gazette* put the following challenge to the government: "What we contend for is, that our countrymen should either govern Oudh or abandon its rulers to their fate. As it is, we are powerless for good and unwilling accomplices in evil. We do infinite and perpetual wrong, because some of our nation in times past made treaties which it is immoral to observe."[50]

There was little doubt in British opinion in India about the superiority of British rule. But there was a serious debate in the mid-nineteenth century about the legality as well as morality of the annexation of Indian kingdoms. Henry Lawrence, for instance, an imperial hero of the first rank, was what could be described as a fundamentalist Christian, yet he was firmly against annexations. In an anonymous article in the *Calcutta Review* in 1845, he wrote: "Let the government of the country be taken over, but let the administration of the country be as far as possible native. Let not a rupee come into the Company's coffers. Let Oudh at last be governed, not for one man, the king, but for him and his people."[51]

Interestingly, Karl Marx, writing in 1853 from London as a correspondent for the *New York Daily Tribune*, was scathing in his remarks about the objections of English radicals such as John Bright and Richard Cobden to the annexation of Indian states:

> The final absorption or annexation of these native States is at present eagerly controverted between the Reformers who denounce it as a crime, and the men of business who excuse it as a necessity. In my opinion the question itself is altogether improperly

put. As to the native *States* they virtually ceased to exist from the moment they became subsidiary to or protected by the Company....The conditions under which they are allowed to retain their apparent independence are at the same time the conditions of a permanent decay, and of an utter inability of improvement.... It is, therefore, not the native *States*, but the native *Princes* and Courts about whose maintenance the question revolves. Now, is it not a strange thing that the same men who denounce "the barbarous splendours of the Crown and Aristocracy of England" are shedding tears at the downfall of Indian Nabobs, Rajahs, and Jagheerdars, the great majority of whom possess not even the prestige of antiquity, being generally usurpers of very recent date, set up by English intrigue! ... If [the princes] are good for any thing, it is for exhibiting Royalty in its lowest stage of degradation and ridicule.... The English money-lenders, combined with the English Aristocracy, understand, we must own, the art of degrading Royalty, reducing it to the nullity of constitutionalism at home, and to the seclusion of etiquette abroad. And now, here are the Radicals, exasperated at this spectacle![52]

THE ROAD TO ANNEXATION

In 1847, Wajid Ali Shah became king of Awadh. He was an accomplished poet in Urdu and Persian; his intelligence, aesthetic sensibility, and wit were much admired by the sophisticated elite of Lucknow. Curiously, Dalhousie became governor-general of India in the same year. One cannot think of a starker contrast between two characters in the same play. Dalhousie was a fervent Presbyterian and is said to have carried self-discipline to the point of self-mortification. He was haughty, imperious, autocratic, and quick-tempered, resented opposition and demanded absolute obedience.[53] His industry and devotion to work was legendary. He was also thoroughly convinced of the superiority of British rule over that of any of the Indian rulers. An admiring biographer portrayed Dalhousie's attitude in the following words:

> He knew too much of the native princes and courts of his day to cultivate their goodwill at the expense of their ungoverned subjects. His sympathies went with the suffering people, not with their weak, vicious, idle, pleasure-loving masters. Policy and justice alike impelled him to give the former a fair chance, wherever possible, of bettering their lot by a change from Native to British rule.[54]

But Dalhousie was careful to pick his way skillfully through the thicket of laws and conventions. In 1849, he appointed Colonel William Sleeman as the resident in Awadh with the express instruction to provide him with a detailed report on the state of administration in the kingdom. Sleeman was already a much-decorated officer who had made his mark by suppressing "thuggee"—the depredations of fearsome gangs of armed robbers all over northern India. With his puritan sensibilities, he detested the court of Lucknow: "Such a scene of intrigue, corruption, depravity, neglect of duty, and abuse of authority, I have never before been placed in, and hope never again to undergo.... Lucknow is an overgrown city, surrounding an overgrown Court, which has, for the last half century, exhausted all the resources of this fine country."[55] Dalhousie, in the meantime, had already made up his mind that Awadh must be brought under the company's direct supervision, even though he was opposed to outright annexation. Within days of sending Sleeman to Lucknow, he was writing to a friend: "I have got two other kingdoms [in addition to Punjab] on hand to dispose of—Oude and Hyderabad. Both are on the high road to be taken under our management—not into our possession; and before two years are over I have no doubt they will be managed by us."[56] This distinction between management and possession would soon become a key point of policy debate within the imperial establishment.

Sleeman's report was a total indictment of the administration of Awadh and particularly its ruler, Wajid Ali, who he depicted as "a crazy imbecile in the hands of a few fiddlers, eunuchs, and poetasters." Later published in two volumes, Sleeman's diary takes one through the different districts of Awadh, and details stories of rampant crime, bribery, extortion, fraud, infanticide, suttee, insecurity of life and property, a predatory army, and an unresponsive government.[57] He declared that "the King's ambition seems to be limited to the reputation of being the best drum-beater, dancer, and poet of the day. He is utterly unfit to reign."[58] He strongly recommended that the East India Company assume the administration of Awadh:

> The treaty of 1837 gives our Government ample authority to take the whole administration on ourselves, in order to secure what we have often pledged ourselves to secure to the people; but if we do this we must, in order to stand well with the rest of India, honestly and distinctly disclaim all interested motives, and appropriate the whole of the revenues for the benefit of the people and royal family of Oude.

At the same time, he added a warning:

> Were we to take advantage of the occasion to *annex* or *confiscate* Oude, or any part of it, our good name in India would inevitably suffer; and that good name is more valuable to us than a dozen of Oudes. We are now looked up to throughout India as the only impartial arbitrators that the people generally have ever had, or can ever hope to have without us; and from the time we cease to be so looked up to, we must begin to sink.... [In Oude] the giant's strength is manifest, and we cannot "use it like a giant" without suffering in the estimation of all India.... We must show ourselves to be high-minded.[59]

Sleeman was both optimistic and confident that the people of Awadh would welcome British administration with open arms.

> There is not, I believe, another Government in India so entirely opposed to the best interests and most earnest wishes of the people as that of Oude now is; at least I have never seen or read of one. People of all classes have become utterly weary of it.... All, from the highest to the lowest, would, at this time, hail the advent of our administration with joy; and the rest of India, to whom Oude misrule is well known, would acquiesce in the conviction, that it had become imperative for the protection of the people.[60]

It is worth pointing out here that Sleeman was strongly suspicious of those Evangelical liberals who were keen to annex every piece of territory in India.

> There is a school in India, happily not yet much patronised by the Home Government nor by the Governor-General, but always struggling with more or less success for ascendancy. It is characterised by impatience at the existence of any native State, and its strong and often insane advocacy of their absorption—by honest means, if possible—but still, their absorption. There is no pretext, however weak, that is not sufficient, in their estimation, for the purpose; and no war, however cruel, that is not justifiable, if it has only this object in view.[61]

He repeatedly referred to this doctrine as "Machiavellian" and thought that the Baptist missionaries, through their newspaper the *Friend of India*, were influencing opinion in Britain, since similar views were being expressed in articles published in the *Times* of London.[62]

It was later alleged that "Colonel Sleeman was the emissary of a foregone conclusion." An anonymous book, attributed to Samuel Lucas but probably the work of Captain Robert Bird, sometime assistant to Sleeman and later an advocate of the deposed Wajid Ali, described the Sleeman report:

> He affected to inspect and make a report, but the character of his report was determined for him *before* he entered Oude. He professed to examine, but he was under orders to sentence; he pretended to try, but he was instructed simply to condemn.... Moreover, the Colonel accomplished this feat at the cost of the Oude Government, and its royal family were charged three lakhs of rupees for the expenses of this very tour, which undermined their authority, diminished their revenue, and was the principal source of the charges afterwards brought against them.[63]

As it happened, before Dalhousie could do anything with Sleeman's document, there were troubles in Burma, recently conquered and annexed by the British, and it was not until late 1854, when the Burmese wars ended, that he could turn his attention again to Awadh. By then, Sleeman had left Lucknow because of bad health (and probably, unendurable moral outrage). Dalhousie now sent another Scotsman, Colonel James Outram, to Lucknow to give him an updated report. Outram knew nothing of northern India and did not have even a smattering of Persian, the language in which all official work was carried out in Awadh. He did the best he could: he simply recycled Sleeman's report.[64]

Its substance was as follows. The king was "guided by low and incapable advisors, eunuchs, fiddlers, and songsters." The treasury was exhausted, and the troops and establishments were in arrears. The courts were notoriously venal: "Justice is openly bought and sold ... [A]ll subordinate judges are equally and notoriously corrupt." The "frontier" police was the only efficient public institution, but only because it was commanded by British officers. The Awadh army, by contrast, presented an "appalling picture." No new roads had been built since Sleeman's account of 1849. "But," remarked Outram, "while public works of utility are so scant throughout Oude, the capital itself boasts of a greater display of palaces and tombs than any other city in India.... [V]ast sums are lavished ... on His Majesty's new palaces, gorgeous and extensive as they are."[65]

He finished his report with some long tables listing all crimes reported in the districts of Awadh between 1848 and 1854, and inferred, without any statistical justification, that they were on the increase. Outram concluded:

> The condition of Oude is, as I have shown, most deplorable. And it has been my painful duty to demonstrate that the lamentable condition of the Kingdom has been caused by the very culpable apathy and gross misrule of the sovereign and his Durbar.... It is, therefore, peculiarly distressing to me to find that, in continuing to uphold the Sovereign power of this effete and incapable dynasty, we do so at the cost of 5,000,000 of people, on whose behalf we are bound to secure—what the Oude Government solemnly pledged to maintain—"such a system of Government as shall be conducive to their prosperity, and calculated to secure to them their lives and property."

He also anticipated a possible question, though:

> It may be naturally supposed that the people of Oude, if so greatly oppressed as has been represented, would emigrate to the neighbouring British districts, which it does not appear from the replies I have yet received from the Magistrates.... But the condition of the people of Oude cannot fairly be tested by the extent of emigration; for, as stated by Major Troup, "although shamefully oppressed, they are much attached to their country."[66]

One more piece of evidence, we might note, of the moral infancy of the people of India.

The anonymous author of *Dacoitee in Excelsis,* while calling for a parliamentary inquiry into the truth behind the annexation of Awadh that had been "carefully and ingeniously concealed from the British people," described Outram's report as something culled out of "old and suspicious materials, prefaced with an acknowledgement of his own inexperience."The account showed "how falsely a pretended care for a native race can be made the excuse for thwarting their inclinations, while appropriating their substance; and how, consulting our own objects alone, we can enforce a revolution to which they were adverse, and can thrust upon them our rule because we coveted their rupees." A sovereign prince was now being asked to defend his private life before the English public. "The fact is, that this unfortunate gentleman has been the object of constant espionage; his private amusements have been watched and reported, and he has lived as it were in a cage of clear glass open to the constant inspection of inquisitive Residents."[67] Outram's report, however, was sufficient for Dalhousie's purposes.

In June 1855, Dalhousie prepared a memorandum declaring: "The Government of Oude has been notorious for its abuse of power, for gross misrule, and for the oppression of its subjects." But his advice was cautious: "I, for my part, ... do not advise that the Province of Oude should be declared to be British territory." Instead, he recommended that the king of Awadh "should be required to vest the exclusive administration of the civil and military government of Oude and its dependencies in the hands of the Company," although for this, the governor-general said, "the King's consent is indispensable.... It would not be expedient, or right, to endeavour to extract this consent by means of menace or compulsion."[68] The contorted logic was patently obvious: the king would be "required" to give up the administration, but only by his "consent." In other words, he was being asked to affirm his sovereignty by voluntarily giving it up.

Dalhousie was clearly thinking of critics in Parliament and the public, because he added: "The measure, if it be assented to, will doubtless be assailed by those who are ever on the watch to attack the policy of the Indian Government."[69] He had been warned of this by the president of the company's board of directors: "Any plan which approaches to annexation of Oudh will, I have reason to believe, excite a violent opposition from some active parties in this country."[70] Hence, a show had to be made for the sanctity of treaty obligations. Arnold later explained Dalhousie's memorandum:

> Without admitting the ridiculous doctrine, that because Vattel laid it down that "a treaty implied equal sovereign rights," the Company and the Nawabs should be regarded as equal powers, these pages not only admit, but claim, that as regards those arrangements or orders which were called treaties, and issued to the Oudh princes to sign, the Company owed veracity and good faith in return for its vassal's obedience.[71]

AWADH ANNEXED

Yet Dalhousie still had to convince the members of his own council. This was his predicament in August 1855. The weakness of his argument was pointed out by council member John Peter Grant: "On comparing the two plans, it will be found that they differ only in this, that the first plan [annexation] involves no political fiction, whilst the second plan [the king's consent] does involve one."[72] Grant made no secret of his understanding of the moral issues involved in this matter.

> I have always thought our long neglect of our obligations towards the people of Oude, a great moral error.... No one, I believe, maintains that a policy of permanent non-interference would be justifiable. If a man brings his elephant into a crowd, and, having the power to prevent him, does not interfere to prevent him for trampling the people to death, the judge will hang that man exactly as if he had put the people to death with his own hand; and nothing that can be said in favour of a policy of non-interference will suspend execution of the sentence.[73]

It is unclear what exactly Grant meant by the elephant analogy. Presumably, he was referring to the British propping up of the Awadh monarchy, in which case he was talking about the problem of controlling Frankenstein's monster—a theme familiar from the history of twentieth-century international alliances. James Dorin, another council member, asserted bluntly that the paramount power had an unlimited right of interference, irrespective of treaties, if it wanted to put an end to the oppression of native princes.[74] Supreme Court chief justice Barnes Peacock explored the legal angle and decided that annexation would be legally justified. "If a Treaty entered into by two countries be broken by one of them, the injured nation has the option either to consider the Treaty at an end, or to uphold it, and insist upon the performance of it, and, if necessary, to resort to force for that purpose." Citing Vattel, he concluded that under international law, it was right to go to war against Awadh.[75]

As many as four members of the governor-general's council disagreed with Dalhousie's "consent" option and favored outright annexation. In the meantime, "public" voices emphasizing the moral duties of empire were reaching a crescendo. The Lucknow correspondent for the *Englishman* wrote: "Everyday that the annexation of this misgoverned country is delayed, another day of suffering is added to the lot of hundreds, nay thousands, of one of the finest races of Hindustan."[76] Around this period, a book titled *The Private Life of an Eastern King* appeared in London, purporting to be the diary of a European in the court of Nasir-ud-din Haidar in the 1830s, and detailing the excesses and depravity of the Awadh monarch and his courtiers. A patent forgery, the book nonetheless drew outraged comments from the English press. The *Edinburgh*

Review demanded: "Are we to be deterred from doing our duty to those millions by a morbid fear that we shall be charged with cloaking ambition and greed under a pretence of humanity?"[77] An anonymous article in the *Calcutta Review* by a European visitor to Lucknow was almost apoplectic with anger:

> We saw a great deal, but I am sick of all this. I have been listening all day to stories, some of them backed by irrefutable evidence, any one of which would make the House of Commons quiver with indignation. What is the misgovernment of Naples compared with this? I doubt if Tiberius or Caligula were a bit worse either in cruelty or debauchery, than the Nasir-ud-din; and the present man is as bad, though of a feebler energy.... "Why is not indigo grown?" said I. "Well," said he [a man of Lucknow], "it has been tried, two Englishmen tried it. One was murdered, and the other had to fly. You see, there is no security of life and property here." I heard, too, one little statistical fact, that will give you some idea of the state of morals. There are upwards of one hundred houses in Lucknow, all taxed and registered, and inhabited not by women but by men. Was Gomorrah worse? Such is life in Lucknow.[78]

Surrounded by this clamor, the court of directors in London wrote to the council in Calcutta to say that unless it was a "virtual certainty" that the king would accede to the transfer of his administration, he should not be offered any alternative and Awadh should be annexed by force if necessary.[79]

Goaded by his superiors, and faced with a timetable that required him to relinquish his post and return to Britain by March, Dalhousie was compelled to throw legal caution to the winds. He decided to offer the king of Awadh a new treaty, under which he would sign away his kingdom or face removal by force. Even though he had changed his earlier position, Dalhousie had no qualms about what he was doing: "I believe the work to be just, practicable, and right. With that feeling on my mind, and in humble reliance on the blessing of the Almighty, I approach the execution of the duty gravely; and not without solicitude, but calmly and altogether without doubt."[80] On February 4, 1856, with British troops from Kanpur advancing to the gates of Lucknow, Outram met Wajid Ali. According to the official report, "His Majesty turned towards the Resident and said, 'Why have I deserved this? What have I committed?'" When the resident explained the options, the king

> gave vent to his feelings, in a passionate burst of grief, and exclaimed: "Treaties are necessary between equals only: who am I, now, that the British Government should enter into Treaties with?"... Uncovering himself, he placed his turban in the hands of the Resident, declaring that, now his titles, rank, and position were all gone, it was not for him to sign a Treaty, or to enter into any negotiation.... He touched on the future fate which awaited his heirs and family, and declared his unalterable resolution to

seek in Europe for that redress which it was vain to find in India. The Resident ... assured His Majesty that at the expiration of three days, unless His Majesty acceded to the wishes of the British Government, the Resident would have no alternative but to assume the government of the country.[81]

On February 7, Outram sent a message to Calcutta announcing that "the King had declined to execute the treaty." Not surprisingly, he found a European conspirator behind this unexpected act of boldness on the part of an effete Oriental:

> The King has been encouraged and sustained in his resolution to adopt a course of negative opposition and passive resistance, by the advice, I am told and believe, of Mr. Brandon, a merchant at Cawnpore, whose antecedents of meddling mischievousness are well known to his Lordship in Council. This individual assures His Majesty that, if deputed to England as his Agent, he will, without a doubt, obtain his restoration.[82]

That day, British troops entered Lucknow as Outram issued a proclamation announcing the king's removal and the assumption of power by the East India Company. A few days later, Wajid Ali, along with his family and servants, was transported to Calcutta to spend the rest of his life there as a virtual prisoner. In his trail came a song that would for some time be remembered and sung in musical soirees among Calcutta's Bengali elite:

> The traitors have so unsettled the kingdom
> That his highness has to go to London!
> In every house the women weep.
> The pavestones weep on every street.[83]

Dalhousie put it on record that he had been prompted by the opinion of the court of directors in London and members of his own council in Calcutta to abandon his previous position, instead adopting "the more peremptory course."[84] Privately he wrote: "So our gracious Queen has five million more subjects and £1,300,000 more revenue than she had yesterday. As a present object, it would have been better that a treaty had been signed, for an amicable agreement would have looked best. But as regards the future, it is much better as it is. We shall have to bear a much less heavy charge, and we are entirely free prospectively."[85]

The author of *Dacoitee in Excelsis* asked: "And now that this result has been attained, by the violation of treaties, with signal ingratitude, and not without some taint of perfidy,—now that the Oude people have been liberated and are kept enfranchised by an overwhelming force, to what extent can we show that they are our debtors, or that the substitution of our authority has been a boon or advantage to them?"[86] More than a hundred years later, analyzing the annexation of Awadh, John Pemble would observe:

> If Evangelicalism provided the emotional impulse, liberalism provided the dogma and moral justification for annexation, for it preached that British institutions were those best calculated to promote the happiness of the Indian people. It also provided an illusion of popular mandate, and this was an essential condition of action in an age morbidly sensitive to the political dangers of offending Indian opinion.... [The liberals] sincerely believed not only that annexation was good for the people of Oudh, but also that it was what they wanted. The truth is that Indian opinion was quite different from what the British imagined it to be.[87]

IMPERIALISM: LIBERAL AND ANTILIBERAL

A little more than a year after the annexation—in May 1857—all of northern India broke out in the most widespread and violent revolt in British India's history. Awadh was at the center of the rebellion, locally led by one of the wives of the deposed king, various landlords and chiefs, and a mysterious Islamic preacher.[88] For ten months, Lucknow and much of the countryside around it were in rebel hands. Henry Lawrence, who had advised against annexation and was appointed to succeed Outram in Lucknow, died during a rebel attack on the besieged residency. Later, critics in the British Indian establishment would attribute the so-called Indian mutiny to the Evangelical zeal of the liberals.[89] The second half of the nineteenth century in India was dominated by a conservative colonial ideology that shied away from social intervention, and preferred to rule through local chiefs and power brokers, anticipating the form of indirect rule that would become the theory of British colonialism in Africa.[90]

It is important to consider this antiliberal turn in imperial ideology in the late nineteenth century, since it hinges crucially on the distinction made in the previous chapter between imperial ideology and the techniques of imperial practice. The hardening of imperial attitudes in Britain is usually dated from the Indian Mutiny of 1857 and the Morant Bay rebellion of 1865 in Jamaica. They led to a strong critique, not only of liberal pretensions of improving native institutions to bring them up to the level of those of civilized nations, but also of the alleged sentimentality of the liberal pedagogical project of culture. Thus, James Fitzjames Stephen, just returned from service in India, famously remarked in 1883 that British power in India

> is essentially an absolute government, founded, not on consent, but conquest.... It represents a belligerent civilization, and no anomaly can be more striking or so dangerous, as its administration by men, who being at the head of a Government founded

on conquest, implying at every point the superiority of the conquering race, of their ideas, their institutions, their opinions and their principles, and having no justification for its existence except that superiority, shrink from the open, uncompromising, straightforward assertion of it, seek to apologize for their own position, and refuse, from whatever cause, to uphold and support it.[91]

Alfred Lyall, another distinguished civil servant from India, accused the liberal pedagogical project of disseminating "ideas of abstract political right, and the germ of representative political institutions … in a country where local liberties and habits of self-government have been long obliterated or have never existed." Western education in India, he alleged in 1884, was leading to discontent, disaffection, and political instability.[92]

The most nuanced and theoretically sophisticated imperialist critique of the liberal view of empire was made, as Karuna Mantena has argued, by Henry Sumner Maine.[93] Taking the universal evolutionary scheme of social formations away from the speculative realms of philosophical anthropology in which Scottish Enlightenment writers like Hume, Smith, and Ferguson had placed it, and inspired by the discoveries of comparative philology about the evolution of the Indo-European languages, Maine grounded his studies in a new science of comparative jurisprudence that looked closely at the evolution of law and property in the ancient societies of Europe and India. His key idea was that law in ancient society operated not through the legislative acts of sovereign lawmakers but rather via customary practices. For India, therefore, he criticized Orientalist scholars and British judges for their reliance on the canonical texts of Brahmanic law, and looked instead at the ethnographic records of the actual practices of social regulation at the level of villages, kinship groups, and communities. His principal theoretical claim was that most ancient societies, including those that were part of large tax-extracting empires, reproduced themselves within their local structures of customary institutions, with only slow incremental changes. A centralized imperial state such as the Roman Empire was exceptional, because it chose to legislate according to its own, often-abstract principles, thus hastening the breakdown of local customary practices.

Nevertheless, the evolution of social formations was a universal historical tendency. The Indian evidence persuaded Maine that even within largely self-regulating village communities, there was a slow transition from relations based on customary status to those of contract, leading to the decay of kinship-based communal property and the gradual emergence of private property. An especially interesting aspect of Maine's argument is his suggestion that this—admittedly slow—dynamic of the emergence of private property was immanent in the social formation and did not (as with Marx's Asiatic mode of production, for instance) need the violent intrusion of an external force such as a modern capitalist imperial power to dissolve it.[94]

Based on this theoretical foundation of evolutionary anthropology, Maine proposed certain dicta of imperial policy that were directly opposed to those of liberal imperialism. In fact, throughout his career in India and later in his lectures at Oxford, Maine kept up a torrent of criticism of liberal and utilitarian prescriptions on the Indian Empire. His primary charge was that by seeking to introduce progressive legislation in order to "civilize" native society, liberal utilitarianism had brought the traditional institutions of village India into a rapid and deep crisis. Colonial officials sought to legislate into existence overnight what might have arisen slowly over centuries of historical evolution. Most significantly, blinded by their utilitarian spectacles, these officials failed to see that landed property in most of India was communal, premised on complex collective rights defined by caste and kinship. Impelled by their dogma, they had legislated new titles to land based on absolute private property. The result was catastrophic. Traditional society, a complex whole consisting of the structurally balanced sum of their parts, faced imminent collapse.

Contrary to the much-vaunted mission of liberal imperialism to improve native society, Maine contended that the only legitimate reason for empire was to halt as far as possible the destruction of the traditional society of India. The idea must be not to artificially transform but rather to protect the character and integrity of native society. The ruinous effects were already far advanced. "It is by the indirect and for the most part unintended influence that the British power metamorphoses and dissolves the ideas and social forms underneath it; nor is there any expedient by which it can escape the duty of rebuilding upon its own principles that which it unwittingly destroys." Hence, since every act of colonial intervention would necessarily result in the hastening of traditional society's collapse, the wisest policy was to bank on continuity and interfere as little as possible. "In the existing state of authority and opinion I can see no rule to follow, except to abide by actual arrangements, whether founded or not on an original misconstruction of native usage, I say let us stand even by our own mistakes. It is better than perpetual meddling.[95]

Maine's antiliberal analysis of the ends of empire supplied, Mantena suggests, the ground for the theories of indirect rule that would dominate imperial policy in India in the latter half of the nineteenth century and especially in Africa in the twentieth. In India, indirect rule, involving the preservation, as much as possible, of local customary institutions and traditional authorities, was remedial, trying to minimize the damage already done to native society. But in the frontier regions outside the borders of traditional agrarian society, such as the forest areas of central India, or hill regions of the northeast and northwest, inhabited by "tribal peoples," the British colonial power came to see itself in the special role of protector of the local tribal communities against planters and traders, both European and Indian, seeking to entangle the childlike tribal into the vicious webs of commerce, credit, and marketable property.[96] Similarly in

Africa, indirect rule, involving the decentralization of power to tribal chiefs who would administer their local societies according to customary law, was thought of as preemptive, aiming to forestall the destruction of traditional native society besieged by the forces of modernity.[97] The preservation of native society from disintegration became, as Mantena puts it, the new alibi of empire.

It is important to clarify where the difference lies between this later antiliberal view of empire and the earlier liberal or utilitarian vision. The difference is in the structures of justification, which in turn is based on different comparative theories of social formations and different assessments of the efficacy of state policy in changing institutions. The liberal and antiliberal perspectives gave rise to different ideologies of empire. Yet they shared a common universalist framework within which *all* social formations everywhere in the world could be compared and evaluated, albeit within complex processes of historical evolution. Thus, Maine's portrayal of traditional Indian society explicitly insisted that its functionality and coherence were entirely related to its specific place in the evolution of ancient societies, and that in the universal comparative scheme, the institutions of the modern West were, without doubt, normatively superior.[98]

Moreover, despite his hostility to Benthamite projects of universal enlightenment, Maine strongly favored the codification of Indian law, because in the absence of credible native institutions, British judges needed a rational code that they could follow rather than fall back on half-baked and inappropriate principles of English common law.[99] The antiliberal ideology of empire therefore fully endorsed the normalized comparative scheme of social formations and governments, upheld the normative superiority of modern Western institutional practices, and like all modern imperial forms of power, rationalized the suspension of those normative standards and declared the colonial exception. Specifically, instead of rushing to close the deviation of the colonial society from the superior norm, it advocated a gradual and balanced process of change in which the imperial power had to hold the balance and make the decisions, because otherwise native society would collapse.

Despite the rise of antiliberal imperial ideologies in the late nineteenth century, liberal imperialism did not die out. In fact, Gladstonian liberals fought against the hardheaded conservatives, and tried whenever they could to further the liberal agenda by extending representative institutions to sections of the Indian elite and introducing progressive laws, such as those against child marriage. Mantena speaks of these two opposed tendencies as "oscillations *internal* to the structure of imperial ideology," brought about not by doctrinal necessity but rather by "a relation of political entailment."[100] What this means, according to our analysis here, is that different techniques of imperial governance were proposed and adopted according to changing assessments of the political situation, with all such techniques being available within the range of practices invented and authorized by the exercise of modern imperial power. Given this, as we have seen in this chapter, the wide array of practices of dealing with native sovereign entities—ranging from complete noninterference, to varying kinds and degrees of interference, to outright annexation—were all developed in India by the mid-nineteenth century within the paradigm of imperial paramountcy. Each of these methods could be adopted, with appropriate ideological justifications, to fit the specific requirements of the exercise of imperial power.

Further, as is clear from the dramatic impact of the midcentury revolts in India and Jamaica, the choice of imperial techniques was crucially shaped by the assessment of indigenous tendencies of collaboration and resistance. The politics of empire, in other words, operated within a *relation of forces* consisting of imperial as well as indigenous elements. In an influential argument, Ronald Robinson and John Gallagher state that there was no "grand design" behind late Victorian imperialism; both expansion and consolidation in the decades leading up to World War I were prompted by the need to protect existing strategic possessions, preempt rival imperial powers, and respond to the developing political situations in the colonies. Decisions were ad hoc, and justifications in terms of economic or political reasons were supplied after the fact.[101] David Fieldhouse supplemented the argument by claiming that the economic needs of the metropolis had little to do with the expansion of empire in the late nineteenth century and that it was the political situation in the peripheries that determined imperial policy.[102]

Following these interventions, there has been a major tendency among historians to treat imperialism from the late nineteenth century as driven by an "official mind" that is pragmatic, seeking immediate solutions to practical problems and wholly devoid of ideology. This "reluctance to discover a concerted imperial agenda," Charles Maier has pointed out, "is one of the attributes of liberal and sometimes apologetic history."[103] Our analysis, in line with Mantena's discussion of Maine and indirect rule, suggests that this apparently nonideological strategy is one that was available, along with various ideologically loaded ones, *within* the range of techniques of imperial practice developed in the nineteenth century. The specific choice was frequently the function of the particular configuration of relations between imperial and indigenous forces in a specific colony.

Indeed, conservative writers like Maine and Stephen, writing in the aftermath of the extension of suffrage in Britain, honed their arguments against liberal imperialism by purporting to anticipate the response from those who had to be governed. Maine warned against "that extreme form of popular government which is called Democracy" as dangerous even for Britain and complained that the British Constitution was "insensibly transforming itself into a popular government surrounded on all sides by difficulties."[104] Stephen asserted that coercion was a fact of history, and that no civilization or religion had ever been founded except by command. "There is a period ... at which discussion takes the place of compulsion, and in which people when they know what is good for them generally do it.... [N]o such period has as yet been reached anywhere."[105]

The ideological difference between these views and those of the liberals in the late nineteenth century lay in their identification of the universal norm for the most desirable form of government. While the liberals thought that representative government on a wide and possibly universal franchise was best, conservatives such as Maine or Stephen believed that it was enlightened representative government guided by an intellectual aristocracy and protected against the vicissitudes of popular politics that ought to be upheld. Both positions would have maintained that this universal norm could not be applied to overseas colonies in Asia and Africa, even though liberals might have said that with sufficient tutelage, representative institutions might be established in some of them in the future, while Maine or Stephen would probably have said that such a future was utterly inconceivable.

When imperialism did become a matter of popular enthusiasm in Britain in the 1890s, it was Egypt and Africa that emerged as the new focus.[106] Following internal political resistance, indirect rule was replaced by the annexation of Egypt in 1882; an anti-British rebellion in Sudan was suppressed some years later with considerable violence. Curiously, the largest number of Mutiny novels was published in Britain in the 1890s, more than thirty years after the event.[107] Many of the strategic and moral arguments justifying the imperial project, whether from a liberal or antiliberal position, that would be used to mobilize democratic opinion had already been played out decades before in India.[108]

What is remarkable is how many of the same arguments, including the Evangelical fervor, axiomatic assumption of the mantle of civilization, fig leaf of legalism, intelligence reports, forgeries and subterfuges, and hardheaded calculations of national interest, remain exactly the same at the beginning of the twenty-first century. The global techniques of empire sharpened in the days of British paramountcy in India continue to shape the practices of empire today. An entire set of worldwide practices ranging from the equal sovereignty of nation-states and noninterference in their internal affairs to claims of paramountcy are visible—all of them techniques developed in imperial theaters in the nineteenth century. The formula "democracy at home, despotism abroad" is perfectly applicable now in the context of the realist discourses of national interest; the liberal Evangelical creed of taking democracy and human rights to backward cultures is still a potent ideological drive; hence, the instrumental use of that ideological rhetoric for realist imperialist ends is entirely available, as evidenced in Iraq in 2003.[109] Eight months after the "liberation" of Iraq, Lieutenant Colonel Nathan Sassaman, a battalion commander in the US occupying forces, was reported as saying: "With a heavy dose of fear and violence, and a lot of money for projects, I think we can convince these people that we are here to help them."[110] Even today, the pedagogy of violence must often precede the pedagogy of culture.

A Chimerical Lucknow

Proceeding south from Fort William along the Hugli River, and passing through the virtually defunct Kidderpore docks and shipbuilding yards, one comes on the congested and polluted Garden Reach neighborhood. Unless one belonged here, few citizens of Calcutta would have any reason to visit this part of the city. Garden Reach emits the whiff of crime and gangster power. Given its proximity to the docks, it has long been a center of smuggling, pilferage from the warehouses, and strong-arm management of dock labor by contractors and union leaders. Garden Reach in recent years has also become known as the heart of a huge proliferation of sweatshops for the informal-sector garment industry, employing tens of thousands of people.

The only indication that this grimy neighborhood might have seen more elegant and prosperous times comes from the Sibtainabad Imambara, which though only a modest structure reminiscent of the far more stately and opulent style of Nawabi Lucknow, is nonetheless impressive in its rundown surroundings. Inside lie buried the mortal remains of Wajid Ali, the last nawab of Awadh. A few neighborhood shops proclaim with subdued pride that the street in front is now called Wajid Ali Shah Road—a recent nationalist appropriation of the nawab's memory.

When Wajid Ali chose exile from his kingdom rather than sign a humiliating treaty with the British, his intention was to go all the way to London to seek justice. After he reached Calcutta with an entourage of about a thousand, including thirty-seven wives and many of his favorite courtiers, his doctors advised that his health would not stand up to the long sea journey.[111] So the king's mother, brother, and heir apparent sailed for Britain to make Wajid Ali's case with Parliament and Queen Victoria. Wajid Ali was given four houses with a large open area on the riverbank in Garden Reach, across from the Botanical Gardens. The area was then locally called Muchikhola, but subsequently became known by the Hindustani name Matiya Burj. Only a few months after his arrival in Calcutta, the revolt broke out in Awadh, with the rebels putting his ten-year-old son Mirza Birjis Qadir on the throne and declaring the child's mother, Begam Hazrat Mahal, one of Wajid Ali's wives who chose to stay behind in Lucknow, as regent. The British authorities in Calcutta decided not to take any risks and interned Wajid Ali within Fort William.

Whatever chances the queen mother of Awadh might have had to find a sympathetic ear in London were effectively ended by the revolt of 1857. Realizing the hopelessness of her mission, she decided to return home over land, only to die of an illness in Paris. Following the uprising's suppression, Wajid Ali was allowed to return to Matiya Burj. Thus far, he had refused the pension that the British had offered him. Now, with all hopes dashed of being restored to his throne, Wajid Ali, on a monthly allowance of a hundred thousand rupees, turned his attention to building a second Lucknow.

The most graphic account we have of this settlement is from the historian and novelist Abdul Halim Sharar, who grew up in Matiya Burj in the 1860s as part of the exiled Awadh court.[112] The houses that had been given to Wajid Ali by the British government in Garden Reach were encircled by large stretches of land about a mile from the riverbank, and with a perimeter of six or seven miles. There he built scores of homes for his wives and courtiers—Sharar named seventeen of them, adding "there were several other houses the names of which I have forgotten.… [A]ll these houses, in their separate settings, were so decorative and trim that no one could help admiring them. Surrounding them were gardens and lawns set out in geometrical design with such engineering skill that those who beheld them marvelled at the King's talent and sense of proportion."[113] Wajid Ali also constructed an excellent zoo and aviary, with strange and beautiful animals and birds from many countries, besides collecting thousands of snakes in captivity—perhaps the first time this had ever been attempted, thought Sharar, because European visitors were amazed to see the collection.[114] An entire township developed outside the royal estate, enclosed by a high wall, filled with fine shops, craftspeople, and houses of the royal staff. Sharar estimated that the second Lucknow at Matiya Burj had a population of some forty thousand people, whose incomes were derived from the activities of Wajid Ali's estate, even though his allowance was only a hundred thousand rupees a month.[115]

It is remarkable how the sustained circulation of Wajid Ali's image as a dissolute Oriental prince given to poetry, music, and sexual pleasure—a depiction perpetuated by the iconic painting in which he appears wearing a transparent *angrakha* with his left nipple exposed—has thoroughly obliterated the traces of his quite-remarkable achievements as an early modern cultural figure. A study by Kaukab Qadir Mirza shows that his patronization of the fine arts, both in Lucknow and Calcutta, was not merely as a royal connoisseur but also as an active innovator and participant.[116] His Pari-khane became the hub of a major center of dance and music training in Matiya Burj. Wajid Ali himself became a recognized sitar player, trained by Qutb Ali Khan of Rampur, and a dance teacher, taking as many as 43 of the 216 dance students under his wing in the year 1877–78.[117] It has been suggested that had Wajid Ali not taken up *kathak* as a dancer and teacher, the dance form may have never emerged as a secular art. His role in giving a distinct shape to the *thumri* as a musical genre is, of course, acknowledged. Less appreciated perhaps is his influence in making Calcutta a modern center of the cultivation of Hindustani classical music: its popularity among the city's middle class in the late nineteenth century seems to be directly related to artists patronized by Wajid Ali's circle in Matiya Burj.[118]

But there are other remarkable aspects to his creative personality. As a prince in Lucknow, he took a great interest in the English theater in Kanpur, and developed the stage form of *rahas* for dramatic performances scripted and produced by him on the *rāsalīlā* theme of Krishna and the milkmaids, with realistic sets and illusion effects created through ingenious lighting. In Calcutta, between 1858 and 1862, in his Rahas Manzil, he produced three performances of a rahas focused on Radha. Wajid Ali's distinctive talents as an architectural designer are only now receiving scholarly recognition.[119] The Qaisar Bagh in Lucknow, in particular, was an outstanding example of the hybrid genre, much reviled by the British in the nineteenth century, combining European and Indian designs with great elegance—an effort in which Wajid Ali played an active part.[120] After his banishment to Calcutta, Wajid Ali re-created the style in Matiya Burj, as evidenced by a set of photographs of the Shah Manzil, Rahas Manzil, and Mirza Manzil taken before their demolition after Wajid Ali's death.[121] He was also a serious naturalist, and there is proof that his interest in collecting animals and birds was not prompted by the idle curiosity of a vain monarch. He set up the Matba Sultani, a royal publishing house, which put out numerous titles between 1860 and 1885, most of which were distributed free. His library in Calcutta was, not surprisingly, spectacular, but his most recent biographer notes that of the collection, only two hundred books, mostly on medicine and religion, can now be found.[122]

Wajid Ali was no nationalist. Nor did history give him the chance to be an absolutist modernizer. Yet it is worth reflecting on his vision of the innovative cultivation of the arts, through the creation by state patronage of authoritative institutions of training in the performance disciplines, adopting new forms and techniques from European practices, but preserving the integrity of the indigenous genres. This would become the agenda, from the late nineteenth century, of cultural nationalists in India. The field of Hindustani music would see the virtual invention of classical music as a modern institutionalized discipline in which the cultured middle-class citizen could be trained to be an enthusiast as well as a performer.[123] As we will see in the next chapter, theater producers in the late nineteenth century, especially in Calcutta and Bombay, would make it their mission to insert the forms and methods of European theater into Indian genres of dramatic performance, heavily dependent on music and dance, to produce a modern popular theater for urban audiences. After independence, the project of promoting the modern secular arts would be handed over to the postcolonial state, through national music, dance, and theater academies and the state-owned radio. The genealogical location of Wajid Ali in this narrative of the emergence of modern Indian national culture needs to be rediscovered.

The British government reclaimed Wajid Ali's property in Calcutta barely three days after his death in 1887. Weeks later, all of his possessions were auctioned off. His houses, dancing halls, and libraries were razed to the ground in a matter of days. The massive late Victorian headquarters of the Bengal Nagpur (now South Eastern) Railway was erected on the reclaimed grounds of Garden Reach. The ruthless alacrity with which the physical traces of the former monarch's presence in Calcutta were obliterated suggests that the spirit of retribution that marked the quelling of the revolt in Awadh in 1858 was still alive in Calcutta thirty years later. There are almost no traces left in Matiya Burj today of an entire township modeled on Lucknow. The memory of Wajid Ali in Calcutta is recounted mostly in the spirit of lament that marked his many *masnavi* composed in exile. Sharar, once a resident of Matiya Burj at its most resplendent, set the tone:

> From the time of the King's arrival in Calcutta, a second Lucknow had arisen in its neighbourhood…. There was the same bustle and activity, the same language, the same style of poetry, conversation and wit, the same learned and pious men, the same aristocrats, nobles and common people. No one thought he was in Bengal: there was the same kite-flying, cock-fighting, quail-fighting, the same opium addicts reciting the same tales, the same observance of Muharram, the same lamentations at the recital of *marsiya* and *nauha*, the same Imam Baras and the same Kerbala as in former Lucknow…. How could this beautiful and entrancing scene ever be destroyed! But alas, fate destroyed it and destroyed it so completely that it might never have existed.[124]

But the idea of re-creating a little monarchy of refinement and sophistication on the outskirts of British Calcutta was an illusion. Sharar revealed this even in his nostalgic remembrance:

> If you stood on the bank of the river you obtained a most wonderful view. Ships going to and from Calcutta passed in front of you and as they did, dipped their standards in salute to Fort William; people, however, thought they were being dipped in salutation to the King.[125]

Only in the subsequent age of nationalism would the people discover the illusion.

CHAPTER EIGHT

The Pedagogy of Culture

IT IS NOT DIFFICULT to date when Indian opinion began to be voiced against the calumny of the Black Hole. There is evidence from the 1870s, when a series of textbooks were published on Bengal's history. The model for these Bengali books was the *Outline of the History of Bengal* by John C. Marshman, a Baptist missionary closely associated with the newspaper *Friend of India*. In it, Marshman described the "massacre of the Black Hole" as an "atrocity that keeps the event fresh in the memory of men in all countries," even though Siraj "knew nothing of this deed of darkness, till the next morning."[1] But the Bengali versions often deviated from the prescribed script. A school text from 1872, for instance, spoke of Siraj's tyranny, but after declaring that he was not responsible for the Black Hole incident, went on to say that although betrayed by Mir Jafar, Siraj's other generals fought valiantly: "If this battle had continued for some time, then Clive would surely have lost. But fortune favoured the English, and weakened by the betrayal of Mir Jafar, the Nawab was defeated and Clive was victorious."[2] Resort to conspiracy and force did not end with the British victory in Palashi. In the period before and after Clive, stated the same book by Kshetranath Bandyopadhyay, "the English committed such atrocities on the people of this country that all Bengalis hated the name of the English."[3]

Another textbook on the history of India published in 1870 mentioned Clive's intrigues: "Most people criticize Clive for these heinous acts, but according to him there is nothing wrong in committing villainy when dealing with villains." The author also speculated on the political condition that might have foiled the British conquest of India: "If this country had been under the dominion of one powerful ruler, or if the different rulers had been united and friendly towards one another, then the English would never have become so powerful here and this country would have remained under the Musalman kings. Perhaps no one in this country would have ever heard of the English."[4] Yet another book from 1876 opened with this preface by the author: "I have written this book for those who have been misled by translations of histories written in English." It ends with the following conclusion: "Having come to India as a mere trader, the East India Company became through the tide of events the overlord of two hundred million subjects, and the shareholders of the Company, having become millionaires and billionaires, began to institute the laws and customs of foreign peoples. In no other country of the world has such an unnatural event taken place."[5]

The Contradictions of Colonial Modernity

The liberal vision for India had imagined that with Western-style education and rational governance, a class of Indians would emerge that would be culturally equipped to participate as equals in governing the country. Things turned out rather differently. While education in English did produce a new class trained to appreciate the virtues of modern Western civilization, it was impossible, given the realities of power under alien colonial rule, to create the institutional conditions under which Europeans and Indians could engage in public life as equal citizens. We have already discussed the unfortunate fate of Rammohan and Dwarakanath's liberal hopes. The egalitarian partnership that was impossible to achieve in the world of capital could hardly materialize in the realm of government. Indians were admitted into the bureaucracy, because their services were necessary, but only in subordinate positions largely relegated to the districts. Even when, from the 1860s on, Indians were allowed into the higher civil services after having passed the examinations as graduates of British universities, they were not appointed to the top positions, and questions were raised, as in the Ilbert Bill controversy, on whether they could have jurisdiction over the European population living in India.[6] By the mid-nineteenth century, British liberalism had, as we have seen, incorporated the idea into its doctrinal body that colonial government must, for good reasons, be the despotism of the advanced few over the backward many.

The realization that there could not be a civil society of equal citizens regardless of race and color did not turn the emerging middle-class Indians away from Western education. On the contrary, they took on the task of spreading the opportunities of education in English to larger sections of the propertied and literate classes. It is not often understood that despite its policy initiatives in the matter of liberal education, the colonial government had a quite limited role in the actual spread of English-language education in India in the second half of the nineteenth century. Between 1881–82 and 1901–2, during which time only one new government college was set up in all of India, the number of private colleges with government aid increased from 21 to 55, and that of private unaided colleges went up from 11 to 53. The growth of English secondary schools in the same period shows a similar trend: government schools increased from 562 to 696, private aided schools went from 1,080 to 1,573, and private unaided schools increased from 491 to 828.[7] Most of this expansion of education in the private sector was in Bengal. Government high schools in Calcutta had 1,750 students in 1883, whereas the city's unaided schools had 8,088 students.[8] Some of the older private schools were run by European missionaries, almost always with government aid, while the unaided schools and colleges were invariably set up and run by Indians. In 1881–82, of the 23 arts colleges in all of India in the private sector, only 5 were managed by Indians, with the rest belonging to foreign missionary organizations; by 1901–2, Indians ran 42 colleges, compared to 37 operated by missionaries.[9]

On the whole, the expansion in higher education was most rapid in Bengal. In 1901–2, Bengal had 44 colleges, government and private, compared to 40 in Madras, 26 in the United Provinces, and 10 in Bombay.[10] Literacy in English increased in Bengal by 100 percent between 1891 and 1901, by 50 percent in the next decade, and by 50 percent again in the following one. In 1921, while 18 percent of the population was literate in Bengal, 3.4 percent was literate in English.[11] The remarkable fact that one-fifth of all literate persons in Bengal were able to read English points to the dominance of the new English schools and virtual demise of other forms of schooling. It also highlights the bilingual character of the new literati. By 1918, with 27,000 students, the University of Calcutta was the largest university in the world, and the proportion of literate people taking full-time university courses was the same as in the United Kingdom.[12]

But the proliferation was only in the liberal arts. Just as official policy on vocational education was merely to train Indians for the lower grades of the government's technical services, so also was there a lack of enthusiasm among Indians to initiate professional or technical education. There seemed to be little demand for it. In 1901–2, compared to 140 arts colleges in India with some 17,000 students, there were 30 law colleges with about 2,700 students, and only 4 colleges each for medicine and engineering.[13] Not surprisingly, the bulk of the university graduates were employed in government service, education, and law: out of 1,378 graduates of the University of Calcutta between 1858 and 1881, 44.48 percent were in legal occupations, 25.91 percent in government service, and 23.66 percent in teaching; this left a mere 6 percent in other occupations.[14]

Of course, the colonial government did influence the course of modern education in India in other ways, most notably by shaping the contents of what was to be taught in schools and colleges. Introducing Western education in India did not mean the replication of a course of instruction that might have been offered at a British school or university. Much thought and effort was given in the nineteenth century to designing suitable content for Western education under colonial conditions. The emphasis was on providing a general humanistic education; advanced classes in the sciences were unavailable until the turn of the twentieth century. Religious instruction was carefully avoided, but in its place an entire academic discipline was invented for teaching English literature as the formative spiritual influence on a colonized elite.[15]

The consequences were far-reaching, and frequently unintended, for the development of the new literary and aesthetic disciplines in the modern Indian languages.[16] It is not without significance, for instance, that the most articulate proponents of the new national spirit in the literary sphere of Bengal should have emerged from *within* the colonial bureaucracy stratified by a racial hierarchy.

The great figures of literary nationalism in late nineteenth-century Bengal—Hemchandra Bandyopadhyay, Dinabandhu Mitra, Nabinchandra Sen, Rameschandra Dutt, and above all Bankimchandra Chattopadhyay—all devoted their professional lives to careers in the colonial bureaucracy. In their literary lives, they were the first nationalists.

THE CITY AND THE PUBLIC

The city is the place of the colonial modern. That was where the new Indian middle classes, through their encounter with colonial rule, created the institutions as well as modes of thought and practice that would characterize nationalist modernity. Still, the emergence of the colonial modern was also accompanied by a split in the urban public sphere. Unlike the earlier period when there were many institutions and initiatives in which European and Indian residents of cities were partners, the second half of the nineteenth century saw the drawing of strong, socially enforced dividing lines between the British rulers and their Indian subjects. The new institutions of nationalist modernity, correspondingly, were founded on what was defined as a separate domain of national culture from which the alien rulers were excluded.[17]

It is important to stress, however, that these racial dividing lines between rulers and ruled were kept in place not by publicly declared rules of segregation. There was no apartheid system in the cities of colonial India. On the contrary, the civic regulations and urban institutional structures were based on what Patrick Joyce has called "the rule of freedom," with the qualification that it was subject to another rule—the rule of colonial difference.[18] The rule of freedom justified the deployment of the new, more liberal techniques put in place in British cities in order to govern urban populations, and make them more healthy, peaceful, and productive. This is the liberal project that produced detailed urban censuses and maps, new systems of piped water supply, underground sewers, garbage removal and disposal of the dead, public libraries and publicly supervised school systems, avenues and parks, street lighting and public transport, and elected municipal government. All of these techniques were applied in the city of Calcutta in the second half of the nineteenth century. Yet the rule of colonial difference ensured that the difference between White Town and Native Town was known and observed by all residents, that official maps or directories specified the individual details of every house and its residents in the European wards and only large classes of population in the native wards, and that schools for European or Eurasian students and those for "native" students were supervised by different boards.

The criteria by which the colonial could be declared the exception to the universal rule were diverse. Sometimes it would be the difference between public and private, so that clubs or swimming pools could be reserved for whites

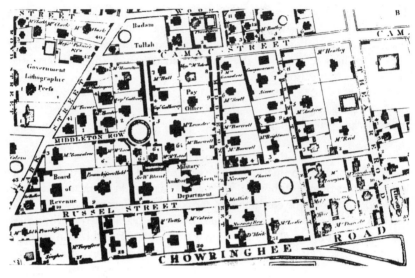

Figure 14. An area of European habitation in South Calcutta, 1825, from a map prepared by J. A. Schalch. *Courtesy: Centre for Studies in Social Sciences, Calcutta*

only because they were regulated by rules made by private associations. In other cases, dress, demeanor, or even suspicious behavior could allow the police to prevent most classes of the native population from walking down specific streets or appearing in public places frequented by Europeans. An 1821 order, for instance, stated that

> considerable inconvenience is experienced by the European part of the community who resort to the Respondentia [now Strand Road] from the crowds of Native work-men and Coolies who make a thoroughfare of the Walk. His Lordship is pleased to direct that Natives shall not in future be allowed to pass the Sluice Bridge ... between the hours of 5 and 8 in the morning and 5 and 8 in the evening.[19]

This was no blanket segregation; only a rule of exception purporting to apply to particular population groups for specific time periods. For example, when work began in 1859 on an underground sewerage system for Calcutta, White Town in the city's south was the first to get it.

> It has been hinted that the Europeans acted somewhat selfishly in commencing these works in their own quarter of the town. But it was pointed out ... that the prevailing winds being from the South, every improvement in the European quarter

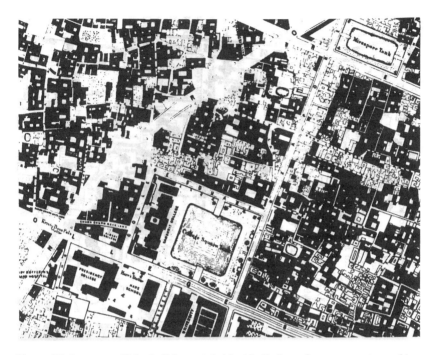

Figure 15. A section of North Calcutta inhabited by Indians, from a map prepared by the Survey of India, 1887–94. *Courtesy: Centre for Studies in Social Sciences, Calcutta*

benefits the whole Town, whereas the same cannot be said of improvements in the Northern division.[20]

One of the most significant developments in the urban history of late nineteenth-century Calcutta was the extension of the rule of freedom into Black Town. This was a classically colonial process in which the moral project of modernity was wrested from the hands of the alien rulers by the new nationalist elite. Sumanta Banerjee has described the process by which a vibrant popular street culture was suppressed and tamed in the Calcutta of this period to produce the genteel urban high culture of the new Bengali middle class.[21] In the early decades of the century, the streets served as an open marketplace. Peddlers and beggars jostled with gamblers and prostitutes. All roads and open spaces were potential sites of public entertainment. Religious festivals were observed by processions, music, ritual performances, and public revelry on the streets. Rijaluddin, a Malay traveler from Penang, described the streets of Calcutta in 1810 as full of entertainers such as snake charmers, puppeteers, gymnasts, trapeze artists, and fakirs showing tricks with monkeys, goats, and bears. He also observed that men of all races—English, Portuguese, French, Dutch, Chinese, Bengali, Burmese, Tamil, and Malay—frequented the brothels and drinking houses.[22] The Night Owl's satirical sketch from the midcentury depicts the brothel districts as places where it was impossible to tell the respectable man from the lowborn one, because everyone wore the same fashionable clothes.[23]

By the 1860s, however, the campaign was on to cleanse the streets of these noisy, obscene, and allegedly barbaric forms of entertainment. A guidebook published in 1886 warned rural visitors to the city that although the streets of Calcutta were open equally to all members of the public, those straying on to the carriageway were liable to get a crack of the whip from a passing coach, and unsuspecting men relieving themselves on the roadside might have to spend the night in a police lockup.[24] The authorities sought to ban popular festivals with performances such as body piercing and swinging from hooks. Pantomime floats with ribald and satirical singing were removed from the streets, and brothels and liquor shops were put under strong surveillance. This was not merely the work of a colonial government driven by the Evangelicalism of a civilizing mission. The new Bengali middle class was equally keen to create a moral order of genteel civility, cleansed of the coarseness and vulgarity of the popular street and marketplace culture.

The New Bengali Theater

English theater came to Calcutta as early as the eighteenth century. Several playhouses opened over the years; most were short-lived, and all were run by expatriate amateurs. Even in the early decades of the nineteenth century, female parts were played by male actors because actresses were not allowed on stage. "The Court of Directors ... feared that handsome actresses in India might arouse a spirit of intrigue among the junior servants of the [East India] Company; and doubtless in those days, when English women were so scarce, the advent of actresses would have created a great stir and possibly led to scandal."[25] By the 1830s, though, there were a few theaters with professional actors and actresses, some with professional experience in Europe. Apart from British officials and businesspeople, even Indian notables of the city, such as Dwarakanath Tagore, participated in the management of these theaters.[26] Although William Shakespeare's works and Italian opera were performed from time to time, the staple was light comedy and farce.[27] There was still the odd protest by clergypersons who regarded the theater as a "house of evil," and were concerned that "the colonial population of Calcutta, a comparatively late element in its society, [was] growing up in irreligion, dissipation, and gross immorality."[28] But no one took much notice of these feeble remonstrations.

By midcentury, with the spread of English education among Indians in the city and the strong emphasis in the curriculum on English literature, Bengali young men with a college background began to be attracted to the English playhouses. Theater was expensive. As Amritalal Bose, one of these Bengali audience members explained, a ticket could cost as much as sixteen rupees, which was more than a month's salary for most office employees, and a drink of brandy and soda from the bar cost four rupees.[29] But they still went. Brought up on a fare of the *jatra*—open-air performances in the round on mythological and devotional themes—or on the song, dance, and pantomime of popular street culture, the new class of Indian men educated in the Western style started to dream of entirely new expressive possibilities in the tightly framed drama of the proscenium stage.

In 1848, there was apparently a minor sensation when it was announced that James Barry of the Sans Souci Theatre was producing Shakespeare's *Othello*, with "a native gentleman" playing the Moor of Venice, and Mrs. Anderson, daughter of the city's most famous actress, in the role of Desdemona. There was a commotion on opening night in front of the theater on Park Street, with coaches and buggies going in all directions, and people muttering "By Jove! Barry and the Nigger will make a fortune!" Yet the gates were shut, and rumors flew that Barry was drunk, Othello struck himself with his own sword, or Desdemona had eloped with an army general. The next day, it was revealed that three of the actors who were army officers had been forbidden by their commanding officer to perform and that the police were waiting to arrest Barry if he did not stop the show. The brigadier who issued the order apparently did not approve of his officers appearing on stage with a native actor in the company of European actresses.

Barry was an enterprising man, however. In two weeks, he had replaced the army officers with new actors. *Othello* opened to mixed responses. The *Bengal Hurkaru* was both polite and patronizing:

> If the indulgent approval of the audience is to be taken as a criterion of success, Baboo Bustomchurn Addy can have no cause to complain. Unquestionably there is ample room for improvement, little reason to despair. Experience will do much, for, deprived of good models as the student has hitherto been, we are bound to make every allowance, and to look with favourable eyes upon this dramatic offshoot of the native body.

The *Englishman* was less charitable: "In the delivery ... the effects of imperfect pronunciation were but too manifest. This was to be expected, but not to the extent it occurred. Scarcely a line was intelligible." On a later performance, the *Englishman*'s criticism was damning: "Whether our Native friend judged wisely or well in selecting so difficult a task we will not venture to discuss but that he failed, in every sense of the word, both in conception and execution, we think everybody present must admit."[30]

Fortunately or unfortunately, this was possibly the last time that an Indian actor played a leading part in a theater for Europeans in Calcutta.[31] We say fortunately because instead of killing the enthusiasm of educated Bengalis for the stage, the sad experience of Baishnabcharan Addy only confirmed their conviction that they had to have their own public theater. After several short-lived amateur playhouses, the first professional proscenium theater for Bengali plays opened in Calcutta in 1872.[32] Amritalal, one of the pioneers, described in his memoirs how meticulously they studied the city's English theaters in order to replicate the details of sceneries, props, lighting, orchestra, and even the number of folds on the curtain. The only thing the Bengali public theater did not have was a bar.[33]

By the late 1870s, there were four or five theaters in the northern, entirely Indian part of the city, competing with one another for the patronage of a Bengali-speaking public. The average price of a seat was a rupee in the front stalls and eight annas (half a rupee) in the rear—still expensive, but affordable for a large section of the city's residents and visitors prepared to splurge a little for a special evening's entertainment.[34] Soon it would become a regular feature of the city's life for canvassers to distribute handbills on the street announcing a new play, and horses and carriages to line up late into Saturday night in front of the theaters on Cornwallis Street and Beadon Street.

This expansive character of the theatergoing urban public was significant. The Bengali public theater was created by and for the new English-educated Bengali middle class because it could not find a place in the English theater of the city. At the same time, the new audience was much wider than the educated middle class itself, including as it did poorer residents and visitors to the city who had never been to school along with a large number of women from middle-class homes who had no formal education. Indeed, in deference to the prevailing norms of gender segregation, most theaters reserved the entire balcony section for women and children, hidden behind latticed screens until the houselights were dimmed and the scene opened, and provided female ushers to communicate with the men of their families sitting in the stalls.[35] Of the different forms of cultural production that were deployed in this period to spread modernity and nationalism, therefore, the theater certainly had a far broader reach than either the novel or newspaper.

Even though the Bengali public theater was consciously modeled on the European stage, the differences in the nature of the urban public quickly moved it into aesthetic and technical directions that were quite different from those of modern European theater. Historical romance became the most popular of the many adaptations of Western dramatic genres, with many Shakespearean motifs being freely employed, even though Shakespeare's plays themselves did not prove to be successful.[36] Satire and farce were also popular; Molière and English comedy hall routines were mixed with the pantomime and street performance genres of Calcutta's urban popular culture. A new genre was the mythological, adapted for the proscenium stage from the devotional *yātrā* performances of Bengal's traditional Vaishnava sectarian culture. Most genres, even the historical romance, wove the device of song and dance into their narrative structure.

On the first anniversary celebration of the National Theatre in 1873, the dramatist Manomohan Basu reminded his audience: "In this country, we cannot accomplish anything at any time at any place without singing a song." The elimination of song and dance from the new theater, he thought, would be too radical an innovation. "We are moderates," he announced. "We would like to reduce the frequency of songs in the traditional jatra performances, modify their manner of singing and incorporate them into the appropriate narrative form of the theatre."[37] His advice was heeded. The Calcutta theater—like the Parsi theater of Bombay and later forms of Indian popular cinema—succeeded in developing an entirely new language of dramatic narration that employed the song as a crucial rhetorical device.[38]

Several of the new theatrical genres were used to spread the message of social reform and nationalism. Theater's power in reaching a wide urban public was palpable. Within four years of the launching of the first Bengali public theater, the colonial government enacted a law to give itself the right to prohibit any dramatic performance that in its opinion, was "scandalous, defamatory, seditious, obscene or otherwise prejudicial to the public interest." The immediate provocation seems to have been a lampoon aimed against a Bengali notable who had invited the visiting Prince of Wales to his house in Calcutta and introduced him to the women of the family. Senior police officials Stuart Hogg and Richard Lamb were also caricatured in a skit titled *The Police of Pig and Sheep*.

The Bengal government was eager to put a stop to such attempts to ridicule figures of British authority. Thomas Baring, Lord Northbrook, the viceroy, first promulgated an ordinance in February 1876 to empower the Bengal government to take action against such performances, and after deliberation, the Dramatic Performances Act, applicable all over British India, was passed in December 1876.[39] The law was frequently used. Leading theater personalities such as Upendranath Das and Amritalal Bose of the Great National Theatre of Calcutta were arrested, and only acquitted after an appeal to the High Court. In turn, the theater developed new methods of deception and subterfuge, often cloaking its message of anticolonial nationalism in an anachronistic historical plot or inserting fervidly patriotic songs into a benign romance.[40]

Another borrowing from the European stage had radical social implications. The Bengali public theater introduced female actors. These women were drawn from among the professional singers and dancers living in the city's brothels. This remarkable pedagogical project, which did not meet with universal approval, involved gentlemen producers training their illiterate actresses to play the sophisticated heroines and mythological goddesses featured in the new theater. Manomohan poured scorn on the project: "At last prostitutes have been accorded public and equal rights with respectable men in respectable society. At last the eyes and ears of the Bengali audience have been gratified and the new universal ethic of society, like the newly laid sewers of Calcutta, has acquired both fragrance and speed."[41] This time, though, his admonition was ignored. Despite the stigma of their origins, actresses of the Calcutta stage often found fame, money, and even a certain recognition as professional artists—in itself a new, entirely urban occupational category.

It is also worth recalling that possibly the single most significant event that legitimized the presence of actresses in a theater for the respectable public was the visit by Ramakrishna Paramahamsa, the new spiritual celebrity among the Calcutta *bhadralok* (respectable people), to a performance of *Caitanyalīlā* by Girishchandra Ghosh (1844–1912) at the Star Theatre in 1884. Ramakrishna's unstinting endorsement of Binodini playing the role of Chaitanya, the sixteenth-century founder of Bengali Vaisnavism (in itself a bold move since it emphasized the androgynous aspect of the saintly figure), went a long way in establishing public theater's place in the cultural life of the new middle class.[42] Ramakrishna has remained the patron saint of the Calcutta stage to this day. Every theater in the city still has a picture of him and his wife, Sarada, tucked away in a backstage alcove.

The Calcutta theater is a good example of the strategic politics of the emerging nationalist elite of a colonial city. Denied equal participation in a racially divided civil society, the nationalist elite proceeded to carve out a separate public cultural sphere for itself. But in doing so, it also hoped to reach out to a wider urban public, educate it in its new and sophisticated tastes, and persuade it to listen to the new doctrines of social reform and nationalism. Of all the means employed by the Indian nationalist elite to create a base of mass support in the cities, the theater was one of the most effective.

SHEDDING A TEAR FOR SIRAJ

Nabinchandra Sen (1847–1909) came from the eastern district of Chittagong and graduated from the University of Calcutta in 1867. Between 1868 and 1899, he held various posts in the provincial civil and judicial service in different districts of Bengal, Bihar, and Orissa. He began to publish his poetry from a young age, and in 1875 made a big splash with his book-length dramatic poem *Palāśīr yuddha*.[43] His crowning poetic achievement was the trilogy *Rai-*

Figure 16. Nabinchandra Sen, photograph. *Source: Sen 1959*

batak (1886), *Kurukṣetra* (1893), and *Prabhās* (1896), based on the story of Krishna. But his narration in scintillating verse of the battle of Palashi still remains his most popular work. In 1875, soon after its publication, Nabinchandra's *Palāśīr yuddha* was staged by the New Aryan Theatre, an amateur company that included Girishchandra. In 1877, the National Theatre produced it in a new adaptation by Girishchandra, who himself played the role of Clive (and Binodini that of Britannia).[44] The poem's popularity, in print and on stage, did not diminish for quite some time. It was revived by Amarendra Datta at the Minerva Theatre in 1895 and the Classic Theatre in 1897.[45] A major boost to its circulation was provided when, soon after its publication, it was selected as a text for the study of Bengali literature in high schools.[46]

The first canto of the poem opens dramatically over Murshidabad. The night sky is somber, lit up from time to time by snakelike streaks of lightning. It is as if the damsels of heaven, curious to watch the fate of Bengal, are peering out of the skies only to bang the windows shut in horror at the sight of Siraj's depredations. The frightened stars have hid behind the clouds. Below, the trees stand still, as if carved in stone; not a single wave disturbs the waters of the Ganga. The world waits in silence as it hears the angry voice of destiny send shudders through the heart of the sinful nawab. The sprawling mansion of the Jagat Seths, renowned the world over for their fabulous wealth, is also dark and silent—no glittering chandeliers, no strumming of the sitar, no jingling anklets on the dancers' feet. Only a thin sliver of light has escaped from the inner chamber of the family temple. Inside, five of the most powerful figures of Bengal are deep in thought. Ensconced in secrecy, they are considering a proposal to depose Siraj.

Breaking a long spell of silence, Mir Jafar speaks out. "I cannot do it," he declares.

> Treachery is sin. Besides, what will we achieve by removing the nawab? Exchange one slavery for another? Who will defend us if another Nadir Shah were to invade India and this time not stop at Delhi but come all the way to plunder Bengal? If you can rule Bengal by yourselves, then go to war against the nawab. But why this trickery? I admit that Siraj is unruly and cruel. But is it not possible to capture and tame even the fiercest tiger or the most venomous snake? Let us end this evil conspiracy.

To this, Jagat Seth replies in a voice laced with sarcasm:

> Thus speaks a minister to the nawab! Isn't this why Bengal can never unite behind a cause? Perhaps the minister has never felt a thorn prick his foot, which is why he can laugh when an arrow has pierced my heart. The blood boils in my veins when I think of what the nawab has done to me. Dressed in the clothes of a *begam*, he entered the women's apartments of my house and blackened the reputation of my family. From that day, I have made this vow: even if the whole world—why, even if the gods themselves—were to favour Siraj, I will wipe out the stain on my family's name with his blood. My heart burns in a raging fire of vengeance. I will take my revenge, even if I have to do it alone. Revenge, revenge, revenge—I have nothing else to offer.

Raja Rajballabh follows:

> One would not have imagined that a human heart was capable of such misdeeds—until Bengal saw what its nawab could do. From the day he came to the throne, he has pursued me as his enemy. If the English had not given them refuge, I would have lost my son and family. I still shudder to think how Siraj tortured to death the prisoners in Calcutta's *andhakūp* [black hole]. Yet he has barely crossed adolescence: imagine what he will be like when he is fully grown. If you don't destroy him now, or

at least take out his fangs, he will torment Bengal for the rest of his life. My advice is this: with the help of the English, let us get rid of the youngster and ask the good general Mir Jafar to take the throne.

Maharaja Krishnachandra of Nadia, one of Bengal's most powerful zamindars, agrees with Rajballabh.

The nawab is an intemperate and thoughtless young man, raised in sinful indulgence, surrounded by lowly rascals. Think of how the revered and beloved Ali Vardi, now departed, defended Bengal against the dreaded Marathas; how just and unbiased he was in dealing with his subjects. Now, on his throne, sits a vile dog. We spend listless days and sleepless nights, worrying about our lives and property. So let us, with the aid of the English, remove this blot on the Muslim rulers of this land and seat the general on the throne of Bengal. The British lion is here to avenge the outrage of the Black Hole. It used to be said that there were no greater soldiers than the French; now Clive has banished the French from Bengal. If the commander of Bengal's army were to join his forces with those of Clive, the craven young man will be blown away like a blade of grass.

This time the four men concur. Krishnachandra turns his head and asks, "We wish to know the opinion of the Rani." Behind a screen, secluded from the men, sits a woman, Rani Bhabani of Nator, statuelike, her eyes vacant and unblinking. Slowly, she begins to talk:

You have painted the nawab in the blackest of colours. But I know he is far blacker than that. Yet, I say as a woman, I do not approve of this cowardly conspiracy against him. I cannot understand how the Maharaja has assented to it. Look once at the picture of India today. The Mughal power has eclipsed. I hear the French have been defeated by Clive in the south. Here in Bengal, the British flag flies from the French fort. Now Clive is eyeing the throne of Bengal. If you aid him, his powers will grow unchallenged. There will be such a conflagration that all the waters of the Ganga will not suffice to put it out. The English will not stop with Bengal. They will then turn to Maharashtra. We are poised at a moment of revolution. With the decline of Yavana rule, will the ruler of Maharashtra become the ruler of India? Or will a revolution in Bengal spur on the British to conquer the rest of the country? Why do you want to invite in the crocodile by digging a canal? Why set fire to your own house? Yes, the Yavanas are a different *jāti*, but they have lived here for more than five hundred years. Their relations with the Aryas are no longer of conqueror and conquered; there are bonds of love between them. Hindus serve in the highest positions in their army, their treasury, their ministry. On the other hand, we hardly know the English and their strange ways. Legend has it that they are born of monkeys in the wombs of demons. They came in the garb of merchants and now they shake the world with their armed force. Do you not remember the warning of the old Nawab Ali Vardi? If you give them a chance, the British will take over the whole of India.

She pauses for a moment. "So what is the Rani's opinion, you ask? My opinion is not to dethrone the dissolute Siraj. Rather, if oppression is indeed insufferable, dress for battle and wield your swords to defend the freedom of Bengal. That is the way to save Mother Bengal—by your swords—not by retreating into the alleys of conspiracy and servitude." As Rani Bhabani finishes, the skies are illuminated with lightning and the clouds roar with thunder.

The scene shifts in the second canto to the Katwa riverbank, where the British troops are crossing the Bhagirathi. From a distance, the boatloads of red-jacketed soldiers look like a garland of hibiscus flowers floating on the river. On the shore, the roll of drums and call of bugles announce the British confidence in the power of their arms. But if we look at each soldier, one at a time, we see a myriad of emotions reflected on their faces. One is thinking of the woman he left behind whose lips he may never kiss again; another, a father, weeps silently for the little daughter back home; some ponder the fabulous riches that might be their war booty; others contemplate rising in the army; and still others think of returning home to a life of comfort and peace. All are seduced by the chimera of hope, just as (notes the poet in a gesture of self-reflexive candor) the narrator weaves his story in verse in the hope—who knows?—of achieving immortal fame.

Away from the tumult of the riverbank, Clive sits alone under a tree, troubled by conflicting thoughts. Sometimes his face reddens with the anger so common among the British, only to be replaced the next moment by a deep pallor of dejection. "I have defied the advice of my war council," he says to himself. "If I lose, not only do I sink, all of these men sink with me. Why, even the British power sinks with me, and with it the sun of British glory. My only hope now is Mir Jafar. But the Yavanas are deceitful cowards. How can I trust his word? What if the wily Omichand poisons his ear? The secret agreement will be tossed into a pool of human blood. The killings of the Black Hole will be repeated. All hopes of untrammelled profits and an obedient British ally in Bengal will be dashed. The French will rise again in the south." But the downcast look soon vanishes. "Now that the die is cast," he seems to suggest, so "why think of what might have been? Twice in my life did I hold the hand of fate to my head; twice I failed to end my life. Surely, I am not to die in the hands of some cowardly nawab. I have the duty of avenging the Black Hole murders by bringing upon him the fury of British retribution. Of course, I will be victorious."

Suddenly a heavenly music strikes, and the skies light up with a thousand suns. A wondrous female figure descends in a halo of brightness. Her breasts half uncovered, her arms white as snow, her thighs as if cut from clear quartz, her face lit by a million Kohinoors, the angelic figure asks Clive, "What is it that frightens you, son?" The waters of the Ganga inch closer to hear her words, and the setting sun stops for a moment on the horizon. "I am the goddess of England's fortune," the divine voice continues.

> When I sensed your thoughts—wavering, irresolute—I decided to come down to earth to tell you that this is the moment when England's star will rise. In a few years from now, half of the world will come under the British realm. No blood will be shed any more in golden India by the Marathas or the Mughals or the fearsome French. No second Babar will come down from the north to start a dynasty. No hordes of invaders will spring from the mountains to plunder the wealth of Delhi. Do not be surprised, son, when I tell you that you are the source of that historic power. The wheel of India's fate is in your hands: it is for you to turn it. I have brought for you from the temple of destiny the future map of India—look at it. The rapid waters of the Irrawaddy border the east; the five arms of the Indus police the west. In the middle lies a dominion, painted in red, larger than twenty Britains. I will put you on the throne; all of India will bow their heads before you. All of its kings will encircle you like planets. As long as the British rule impartially, their dominion will remain unharmed. That is the great principle of politics that the Yavana has forgotten, which is why the sword of destiny now hangs, on the thin thread of justice, over his head. Unable to endure the Yavana's oppression, the people of Bengal have sought your protection. Remember that above all rulers and all kings, there is impartial justice personified, the power that moves the sun and the stars and gifts rich and poor, white and dark alike. Do not think of material gain. Waiting in front of you is the test of destiny.

Just as suddenly, the heavenly figure is gone. Clive wakes up, as if from a dream. Someone is saying to him, "The troops have crossed the river. They are waiting for your orders, sir." In a flash, Clive runs down the riverbank and jumps into the boat waiting for him. The sailors pull their oars and break into song: "Victory, victory, victory to Britain."

The third canto brings us to the fields of Palashi, where the immoral Yavanas surrendered their liberty. The feeble Bengali must visualize that scene with the help of his Imagination. Sneaking past the guards, she must tiptoe, warily, into the nawab's camp. Tell us, dear Imagination, in a hushed tone: What do you see of that sad scene from a hundred years ago?

Siraj is seated on a golden throne, surrounded by dozens of beautiful women. They are dancing under the chandeliers, accompanied by ecstatic music. Yet the nawab's mind is somewhere else. In a nearby camp, the conspirators huddle. Shame on you, Raja Krishnachandra! Shame on you, Umichand! And you, Rai Durlabh, the traitor, the eternal blot on the Bengali's name! Had you not laid this mean trap and instead had the courage to rebel against the undeserving tyrant, would your memories have been blackened as they are today? But wait; has the nawab got wind of your plans? Why else is he so distracted? A half-undressed dancer holds the cup of wine to his lips and sings. From a distance, suddenly, comes the sound of cannon fire. Startled, the young nawab throws down his smoking pipe and runs to a window. Through the darkness of the night, he can see the flares from the enemy camp lighting up the horizon. Tomorrow's battle, he knows, will decide his fate. If he loses, will his subjects care? After all, they will have a new ruler for the old one; the throne of Bengal will not stay empty. Or has Mir Jafar instructed his troops not to fight? Has he conspired with Clive? Why else should the English dare to pit their tiny force against my massive army? It was a mistake to believe Clive's words. Yet who would have thought the English were such liars?

A man approaches the nawab. Is this the assassin sent by Mir Jafar? Terrified, Siraj runs for cover, only to realize that it is his own attendant. Still quivering like a leaf, the nawab sits down and says to himself, "Let me write to Clive, offering him my kingdom in exchange for my life." He snatches pen and paper, starts to write, and then quickly stops. "What if," he thinks, "having grabbed my throne, he still puts me to the sword? How can I trust Clive?" The nawab falls on his back, utterly exhausted by fear and anxiety. "No, there is only one thing left to be done. Go to Mir Jafar, give him my crown, my sceptre, my sword, fall at his feet and beg for mercy." He drags himself toward the door of the tent, but stumbles and falls. A woman holds him in her arms. It is the nawab's young wife. Caressing him, she calms him down. Siraj passes into a fitful sleep, with one frightening dream following another—a wailing widow on whom he had forced himself; the pregnant woman whose womb he had ordered to be cut open; Husain Quli Khan, vowing vengeance in tomorrow's battle. And who were these other phantoms? A crowd of Englishmen, victims of the Black Hole, crying out: "We come for retribution. The English are as fearsome in death as they are in life." Siraj shakes in his sleep as his wife holds him close to her.

The fourth canto opens with a sunrise filled with sadness. The fate of India will be sealed today in the mango groves of Palashi. The vultures and crows sit still on the treetops, waiting patiently. All at once, the British war drums strike up and the bugles sound, sending shivers across the battlefield and stirring the waters of the Ganga. The call is met by a fierce war cry from the nawab's camp. The battle is on. Cannons roar, swords are unsheathed, and the soldiers, some on horses, others on foot, rush at each other. "Forward, forward!" shouts Clive, egging on his troops. And then, as if from nowhere, a cannonball strikes Mir Madan. He falls off his horse. "Hurray! Hurray!" yell the English. Confused by the fall of the officer, the nawab's troops begin to scatter. "Stop!" demands Mohanlal. "Whether Yavana or Kshatriya, if you leave the battle field today, there is no place in India where you can escape. You will be hunted down and killed." Turning to Mir Jafar, he says,

General, shame on you! Look at your soldiers, standing there like wooden puppets. Do you not realize that the liberty of Bengal is at stake? Do you think the British will stop with this battle and hand back the throne to the Yavanas? You are a fool to think so! These are not mere traders. They will enslave both Yavanas and Hindus. Both will lose their freedom. If we lose this battle, we will all be enslaved for ever. So I say to you Yavanas, don't throw away your precious treasure of liberty. And to you Kshatriyas I say, let us show the English the best of Arya valour. Turn around and resume the charge!

Inspired, the soldiers return to battle. It is a ferocious clash. Soon the British are on the verge of defeat when, all of a sudden, the clarion sounds and the order goes out, "Soldiers, stop! The nawab commands that the battle be resumed tomorrow at dawn!" The troops come to a standstill, swords still held in midair. They stand there, like a giant rock at the edge of a cliff. And then, as if to push the rock over the precipice, the English soldiers rush at the nawab's army. The swords come down, some on the back, some on the neck, and some on the chest. The Yavanas fall on the ground like drops of rain. Sending shivers across the battlefield and stirring the waters of the Ganga, the British announce their victory.

As he lies on the ground, his body ripped into countless bleeding gashes, Mohanlal watches the sun go down. "Stop for a moment, don't go down just yet," he implores.

For with you vanishes the freedom of India. And as you rise on another sky, half-way across the world, fortune smiles on the British. Indians have never seen the British sun, nor had the English, until the other day, seen the stars on the Indian sky. But tomorrow, Britain will rise as the sun over India. That sun will not set soon. Indeed, will it ever set? Only the future can tell. Now, as you go down, the last hopes of India's freedom sink into darkness. So perhaps it's best that you go. Go, and never come back to the sky of Bengal. India will have to do without your light. The sun of India's glory will not return. Indeed, the battle of Palashi is not the end of our woes; it is only the beginning. This white cloud that has formed over this battle field will soon spread all over India, unleashing fierce storms, overturning hallowed thrones and ancient kingdoms. And then, once the storm has blown over, there will reign peace in India. But that will be the peace of the prison. For those who love liberty, freedom in hell is more pleasurable than servitude in heaven. I know the Yavanas were often tyrants. But scattered in that memory of oppression, were there not moments of nobility, of beauty, still cherished in history? But what is the use now of remembering those treasures of happiness? Soon, both Murshidabad and Delhi will become the ruins of Yavana glory.

So stop, dear Imagination! Do not recall any further the scene at Palashi where the hopes of Indians sank into oblivion. With blood gushing out of his wounds, Mohanlal closes his eyes.

In the fifth canto, the city of Murshidabad is decked for celebration. Idlers gather on street corners, talking about the battle of Palashi. In his palace, the new ruler of Bengal, Bihar, and Orissa sits with his opium pipe, eyelids drooping, surrounded by flatterers. Enjoy the moment while it lasts, Mir Jafar, because it will not last long. Your fate is in the hands of the English merchants who will soon make the throne of Bengal a commodity to be bought and sold in the market. In another palace is Miran, now prince. The wine is flowing; the women are at his service. A guard walks in stiffly, looking like the messenger of death. "The women in Siraj's harem," he announces, his voice choking with remorse, "have been put to death. They all drowned in the Bhagirathi. Their cries are still ringing in my ears. As they gasped for the last time, one of them shouted, 'Miran will be struck by lightning: I foretell this.'" Outside, one can hear the sound of "Hip, hip, hurray!" The British soldiers in their lodgings are celebrating their victory.

In one of the former nawab's palaces, locked in a room, is a young woman. She runs from one door to another, banging on them with her fists. We have met her before in the nawab's camp in Palashi. She is Siraj's begam, now held at the pleasure of Miran. Not far from her, in a dungeonlike room, is a man lying prostrate at a soldier's feet. Is this Nawab Siraj-ud-daulah, whose very name struck terror in the hearts of the people of Bengal? There he is, begging for mercy at the feet of Muhammadi Beg, his own officer. Is that the sword of destiny hanging over him, waiting to punish him for his countless misdeeds? But the sword is in the hand of his servant, sworn to the pledge of loyalty to his sovereign. Stop! Think for a moment before you commit this ghastly act of treachery! There is Siraj, full of remorse, begging for his life. Is that not punishment enough? How could he harm anyone if he rots in prison? Could you not spare his life?

It's of no use. The sword comes down on Siraj's neck; his head falls to the ground, and a torrent of blood gushes out of his neck. In that flood is swept away the last hopes of Bengal's freedom.

On the Poetic and Historical Imaginations

By all accounts, Nabinchandra's *Palāsīr yuddha* was a great literary success. It gained further popularity with Girishchandra's stage adaptation and, above all, its selection as a text to be read in high schools. But as Rosinka Chaudhuri has documented, its portrayal of Muslim rule and the British conquest of Bengal elicited criticism even in some of the early book reviews.[47] The loudest objections were raised by those voicing Hindu revivalist views. One of them complained directly to Nabinchandra:

In *Palāśīr yuddha*, the Muslims lost Bengal. Why should the Hindus be moved by that? Indeed, why should Mohanlal grieve? Is it because he was a servant of the Muslims? You are a Hindu, how can you accept that? And by putting those words of regret in Mohanlal's lips, have you not shown disloyalty to the British government? … I do not understand why the Hindu's heart should be swayed by emotion at the thought of the battle of Palashi. Is it because a few Hindus handed Bengal over to the English? If that is the case, do you really believe that if the English had lost at Palashi a Hindu kingdom would have been established in Bengal or India?[48]

The matter became a controversy in the Text Book Committee in 1895–96, at the end of which Nabinchandra submitted a revised version of the school edition of *Palāśīr yuddha*, which was approved for inclusion in the reading list.[49] Despite this, the charge of "disloyalty" would not go away easily. Nabinchandra was informed in 1899 by the government of "the objectionable nature of several passages" in *Palāśīr yuddha* and was told that he would "be held responsible for the elimination of those passages from any future Edition of that book."[50] Soon he realized that his promotion was in jeopardy. When he appealed to John Woodburn, the lieutenant governor of Bengal, the latter shot back, "You have not seen the reports that I have seen. You do not know what I know. You say you have a grievance against Government. But Government has a greater grievance against you. So long [as] I remain Lieutenant Governor, there is absolutely no chance of your promotion. Good bye!"[51] Nabinchandra was no revolutionary. At that time, twenty-three years after its publication, *Palāśīr yuddha* had sold more than a hundred thousand copies, and Nabinchandra's annual royalty from the book was more than a thousand rupees. A salaried man on the verge of retirement, he could not afford to be defiant. He changed all of the so-called objectionable passages, secured his promotion to the higher grade, and immediately retired.[52]

The changes did make a difference.[53] The reference in Rani Bhabani's speech to inviting in the crocodile by digging a canal was dropped, as was the saying that the English were born of monkey fathers and demon mothers. In the fourth canto—in the introduction as well as Mohanlal's dying speech—the characterization of the battle was hugely altered by changing *bhārat* to *yaban*, thus shifting its historical significance from the demise of India's freedom to merely the fall of Muslim power. The last two lines of the poem describing Siraj's execution were reworded, from "In that flood was swept away the last hope of Bengal's freedom" to "The light in the room went out. India's last hope turned into a dream." Sensing the hostility of both the colonial government and at least a section of the dominant Hindu-revivalist opinion in Bengal's literary circles, Nabinchandra undoubtedly chose to deaden the critical impact of his poem on the officially circulated reading of the battle of Palashi.[54]

He would soon realize that he could not win. The reason why *Palāśir yuddha* attracted such popular acclaim was precisely because it gave voice to a new sense of disapproval among Bengal's middle classes of the British claim to legitimate sovereignty over India. In doing so, it also gestured, even if only rhetorically, to the possibility that Bengal under Siraj, although badly governed, was at least sovereign, and therefore free, and had a state where even though the ruler was a Muslim, Hindus nonetheless enjoyed positions in the highest echelons of government. Compared to that, under British colonial rule, both Muslims and Hindus were equally excluded from participation in government. The newly established Indian National Congress, in which Nabinchandra took an active interest, was already making the same argument. Nabinchandra too was trying to craft a new rhetoric of Hindu-Muslim fraternity. Thus, even though he chose the Hindu general Mohanlal as his voice, negating at one stroke the charge that the Hindus had gifted Bengal to the British while simultaneously reserving the position of natural leadership of the new national formation for the Hindus, he still showed him grieving for the loss of India's freedom (even in the poem's altered version), and declaring that after five centuries of living side by side, the Muslim had been naturalized into the affective bonds of an adopted kinship. But this, it would soon be claimed, was not nearly enough.

Muslim critics had often complained about the unfair portrayal of Siraj in Nabinchandra's *Palāśir yuddha* and, by implication, Muslim rule as a tyranny. But soon a formidable critic emerged in the person of historian Akshaykumar Maitreya (1861–1930). In a book-length work serialized in 1895–96, Akshay-kumar launched what would become a determined nationalist rebuttal of the official British origin story of the empire in Bengal.[55] In the process, he directly attacked Nabinchandra for his uncritical acceptance of motivated British ac-counts, leading to a historically false depiction of Siraj's character and a com-plete misreading of the significance of the battle of Palashi.

Akshaykumar was at the forefront of a new movement of writing Indian history in the "scientific" manner, emphasizing the critical study of archival documents, and copiously footnoting his books and articles in order to cite his sources.[56] Operating from the district town of Rajshahi where he earned a liv-ing as a lawyer, he started *Aitihāsik citra*, a historical journal, and founded the Varendra Research Society, a learned society and museum that played a major role in the archaeological, numismatic, and textual study of the early history of Bengal. Akshaykumar published extensively in important Bengali periodicals of the time, writing history in a prose that was analytic and argumentative at the same time as it was passionate and frequently lyrical. He also wrote histori-cal articles in English in *Bengal Past and Present* and the *Modern Review*.[57]

His study of *Sirājaddaulā* was an exercise in rescuing the memory of the unfortunate nawab from the infamy that had been heaped on him by his ene-mies, both Indian and foreign. As he went about his task, Akshaykumar would

Figure 17. Akshaykumar Maitreya, photograph. *Source: Maitreya 1982*

lay down some of the lasting foundations of nationalist anticolonial historiography. One of his major themes was the critique of European prejudices about the Indian character—the Muslims as tyrannical and dissolute conquerors, and the Hindus as weak, wily, and corrupt survivors, always in need of a protector. This perspective allowed him to turn the tables on the British rulers and subject the moral character of eighteenth century trader-conquerors, supposedly infused with the Christian spirit of honesty and humility, to a searching test. "Immorality led to the fall of the Roman empire; immorality also gave birth to the Indian empire. Those who believe," continued Akshaykumar, his pen dripping with irony, "that god's will can produce nectar out of poison will find a shining example in our history."[58]

The other theme was located within the terrain of realist politics—*rājadharma*—following principles that were true worldwide among all states.[59] Here Akshaykumar carried out an examination of specific interests and capacities, particular powers and ambitions, putting Europeans and Indians on the same plane, and produced an explanatory account of why certain powerful Indian interests collaborated with the British to topple Siraj, ultimately paving the way for British dominance over all of India. By countering the charge that Siraj was feeble-minded or perverse, and asserting that he was pursuing perfectly credible and legitimate goals in defending the interests of his state, Akshaykumar was in fact establishing for nationalist politics the concept of state sovereignty as an attribute that ought to apply equally to all nations. His *Sirājaddaulā* must be regarded as one of the founding texts of the nationalist historiography of modern India.[60]

Given that his form was biographical, Akshaykumar first based his description of Siraj's character on the psychological facts of the monarch's childhood. Siraj was a spoiled child—willful, obstinate, given to tantrums, and always managing to get what he wanted. The person to blame for this was his doting grandfather. Yet Siraj was by no means stupid, and indeed often showed signs of precocious intelligence. In his adolescence, he fell into bad company. He became addicted to alcohol and women. Again, despite many complaints, Ali Vardi did nothing to correct his ways. Siraj took a keen interest in military affairs, though, accompanying his grandfather on his many expeditions against the Maratha raiders. He also displayed a penchant for decisive action—having Husain Quli Khan peremptorily killed, for instance, when stories began to circulate of his affair with Gahsiti Begam. As Ali Vardi became old and weak, various persons representing many powerful interests started to jostle in order to make a bid for the throne of Bengal. Siraj himself turned into a rebel, only to be disarmed and pardoned by his grandfather. As he lay dying, Ali Vardi extracted a promise from his grandson that he would stop drinking; all evidence suggests, says Akshaykumar, that Siraj kept his word. In the murky politics leading to the "revolution" in Bengal, Siraj never resorted to trickery or subterfuge, but instead often accepted at face value the pledges made by his untrustworthy courtiers and the British. In fact, in a deft polemical move, Akshaykumar turned Macaulay's biographical study of Clive on its head to suggest that if the English hero, unruly and violent in his adolescence, grew up to be a greedy and deceitful man, then by comparison it had to be admitted that Siraj outgrew his early depravities to become a determined and principled political actor.[61]

Akshaykumar insisted that by the time he came to power, Siraj had a fairly clear idea of the threats to Bengal's sovereignty. Power in the kingdom was then effectively wielded by a group of major zamindars and bankers. Even though Ali Vardi had made known his preference for Siraj as his successor, the zamindars, in collaboration with the Jagat Seths, would have backed Nawazish Muhammad, husband of Gahsiti, Ali Vardi's second daughter. But this possibility was removed with the death of Nawazish in 1756. The zamindars knew that

Siraj would not agree to be a pliable nawab: all the signs indicated that he was intelligent, purposeful, and perhaps even headstrong enough to seize the reigns of the state.

Moreover, he clearly had a particular distaste for the British, seeing in them an aggressive ambition that he did not see in the other European traders in Bengal. He regarded the British as a potential threat to sovereignty, objecting principally to their fortifications in Calcutta, misuse of the privilege of exemption from customs duties, and harboring of fugitives wanted by the government for violations of the law. But the animosity was tempered by political considerations, as was apparent in Siraj's decision not to pursue the British fleeing Calcutta after the town and fort were overrun by his forces. He was obviously expecting the British to negotiate for fresh terms for their return to Bengal. He might also have avoided the confrontation in Palashi had he given in to the British demand to hand over the French officials to whom he had given refuge after the British sacked Chandannagar. Yet Siraj refused to engage in duplicity, preferring instead to test the British on the battlefield, and given the overwhelming preponderance of forces in his favor, who could reasonably say that he was wrong?

Akshaykumar portrayed Siraj as an absolutist ruler fighting to defend the sovereignty of the state, which he believed was the precondition for peace and prosperity in his kingdom. A diligent student of Ghulam Husain and other eighteenth-century historians, Akshaykumar seems to have imbibed something of the late Mughal scholarly sensibility that yearned for the defense of the state by a skillful and decisive prince.[62] At the turn of the twentieth century, however, he was also influenced by the examples of Otto von Bismarck's Germany and a resurgent Japan; his historiographical tastes were shaped by the new Rankean school of positivist history as well as the economic theories of Friedrich List's historical school. His understanding of Bengal's eighteenth century was strongly inflected by a consideration of the historical possibility of an absolutist and mercantilist alternative to British conquest of the kind we discussed earlier in the case of Mysore. In *Sirājaddaulā* as well as his later work *Mīr Kāsim*, Akshaykumar appears to uphold a political ideal of royal absolutism as the principled defense of unified state sovereignty that was concurrently the defense of the economic sovereignty of the incipient nation in a time of increasing international commerce.[63]

By contrast, the conspirators against Siraj were each motivated by specific interests: "the Jain Jagatseth, the Musalman Mirjafar, the Baidya Rajballabh, the Kayastha Durlabhram, the usurer Umichand, the vengeful Manikchand—none of them had ties of blood or friendship with the other; only the pursuit of their selfish interests drove them to back one another in the combination."[64] Opposed to these narrow interested views of the battle of Palashi, as indeed the interested views of British writers, the popular memory in Bengal of the battle, stated Akshaykumar, is preserved at the grave of a nameless soldier of Siraj's army, which has now become a shrine in Palashi where peasants offer *shirni* every Thursday in devout remembrance of his martyrdom.[65] This observation conveyed a nationalist sentiment that in its invocation of historical memory as preserved in popular practice, was very much in tune with the spirit of Swadeshi that would sweep the intellectual and political world of Bengal in the first decade of the twentieth century.

Judged from this new ideological standpoint, Nabinchandra's *Palāśīr yuddha* would be accused of being insufficiently nationalist. Akshaykumar kept up a running criticism of Nabinchandra's poem throughout his *Sirājaddaulā*, accusing him of gross historical error, and refusing to accept the plea, made by Nabinchandra in the original version of *Palāśīr yuddha*, that the poet's path was smooth and unencumbered by historical facts (*niṣkaṇṭak*: literally, devoid of thorns).[66] Akshaykumar not only showed that Nabinchandra was keen to cloak his poetic re-creation of a historical event with supposedly authentic historical references but also that these references were all drawn from histories of Bengal written by British writers—Charles Stewart, John Marshman, and most galling of all, Macaulay. Why did Clive sit under a tree, debating whether or not to go against the advice of his war council, until goddess Britannia as Divine Providence appeared before him, except for the fact that Macaulay depicted the scene that way in his essay? Why on the eve of the battle was Siraj shown surrounded by dancing girls pouring wine into his glass, when there was no such description in contemporary historical sources? Was the scene not reminiscent of Stewart's depiction, following Ghulam Husain, of Shaukat Jang, Siraj's rival claimant to the throne of Bengal, before the decisive battle of Nawabganj where he was defeated by Siraj's forces? Why did Jagat Seth accuse Siraj of having entered his house in a female disguise and molesting the women of his family when, in actual fact, the Jagat Seth family had no such memory? Rather, it was Sarfraz Khan, Ali Vardi's predecessor, who was rumored to have done something like this.

It would seem that in his eagerness to portray Siraj as the worst example of the Oriental tyrant, Nabinchandra collected assorted instances of the depravity of Muslim rulers and heaped them all on poor Siraj. Why indeed was Siraj visited in his nightmares by the victims of the Black Hole, other than the fact that Macaulay suggested this was what a Greek poet might have imagined in a similar situation? "It would have been better," said Akshaykumar, "if the poet had trusted his own imagination, for then it would not have been shaped in every detail by the mould supplied by Macaulay." To Nabinchandra's plea that he was writing poetry, not history, Akshaykumar retorted, "But not everyone knows that Nabin Babu's *Palāśīr yuddha* is 'not history.'" The school edition, in its preface, advertised its merits as "the history of Bengal of the period in verse." The poet's depiction of historical characters, insisted Akshaykumar, could not claim to be innocent of historical facts. In this respect, "the battle of Palashi as written by Macaulay is also poetry, not history."[67] Such poetry, Akshaykumar was proposing, was motivated history, and Nabinchandra should have been more aware of this trap.[68]

Attacked by the new patriots, Nabinchandra evaded the charge of distorting history by declaring that he had only written poetry, not history, but in private, virtually pleaded guilty. Writing in 1906 to his friend Girishchandra after reading the latter's new play *Sirājaddaulā*, the poet said: "You are both more able and more fortunate than me. When I wrote *Palāsīr yuddha*, our only sources were the accounts left by Siraj's enemies."[69] He went on to mention Akshaykumar's accusations and maintained: "My reading then consisted of Marshman. But I was probably the first Bengali to shed a tear for poor Siraj."[70]

Akshaykumar's intervention in the academic domain of history writing would have important effects in the popular domain of the circulation of nationalist rhetoric and images, and later, as we will see, even in the political domain of mass agitation. Backed by the authority of scholarship and analytic reasoning, the nationalist narrative of the Black Hole, the battle of Palashi, and the British conquest of Bengal would now become irresistible in its determination to sweep away the canards as well as misrepresentations perpetrated by British colonial writers. By comparison, Nabinchandra's poetry would appear as timid, half-hearted, and compromised in its patriotism.

But the colonial pedagogy of English literature would have an unintended consequence when the new literati mounted its productions on the public stage for a popular audience. Despite the criticism he faced for the literary and historical shortcomings of his work, Nabinchandra did accomplish something that would be of lasting significance in the subsequent efforts to popularize the nationalist story of British colonial rule. He devised some of the key rhetorical and performative resources that would be used by later playwrights on the Palashi theme, such as Girishchandra, Kshirodprasad Vidyavinode, and Sachindranath Sengupta. Nabinchandra was bold enough to introduce a theme of recent history, filled with local and foreign characters engaged in transformative historical events, but narrated in the familiar metrical and rhymed forms of *payār* and *tripadī*. The novelty of *Palāsīr yuddha* was its content—not something from the Puranas or the great epics but instead an event of modern history—full of foreign names and sounds rendered into easily recited verse. The popular success of *Palāsīr yuddha* could be attributed in no small measure to the fact that it lent itself to easy, often dramatic elocution in a traditional and familiar meter.[71]

Second, his characterization of Siraj on the eve of the battle, while depicting him as a depraved oppressor, nevertheless humanized him by making him weak and indecisive, overcome by fear, ready to surrender even before the battle had begun, and finally being consoled by his wife. Bankimchandra himself described Nabinchandra's character portrayals as flat and wooden.[72] The Siraj created by

Nabinchandra was no hero of Shakespearean tragedy; he was not, as Akshay-kumar would have liked to see, the incipient early modern absolutist monarch, schooled in the practices of power, hemmed in by petty yet vicious conspirators, and ultimately giving his life in defense of his kingdom. Nabinchandra's Siraj was more like the feeble Bengali the poet had imagined ruminating on the disaster that befell the nation—understanding its importance, but utterly lacking the capacity to affect the course of history. From the turn of the twentieth century, nationalist intellectuals like Akshaykumar would refuse to accept this subject position. Paradoxically, though, it would remain a persistent motif in the popular culture of nationalism, as we will see later in Girishchandra and Sachin Sengupta's *Sirājaddaulā*.

Third, while critics have pointed out that Nabinchandra's forte lay more in lyricism and the vivid evocation of scenes rather than in the structural design of dramatic action and form, and while the poet himself was somewhat dismissive of *Palāśīr yuddha* as an early and immature work, it is his only poetical composition that was adapted for the stage and saw lasting popularity. The apparent contradiction is great, since it gestures toward a new chasm in Bengal's public culture between the high and the popular. Literary scholars have insisted that *Raibatak-Kurukṣetra-Prabhās*, designed as a new interpretation of the Mahabharata for modern times, was the crowning achievement of Nabinchandra's poetic career.[73] Today, copies of the so-called Krishna trilogy can be found in a few old libraries, where only the rare dissertation writer reads them. *Palāśīr yuddha*, by contrast, for all its lack of formal sophistication and dramatic panache, remains part of the received literary tradition handed down through textbooks and amateur elocution. As Girishchandra would find out through his attempts to popularize the new proscenium theater, the certitudes of European high theater were not necessarily applicable to the popular aesthetic domain. It was a crucial lesson that the new English-educated Bengali dramatist would have to learn in his efforts to produce material for a new popular public culture.

The one-dimensional and stiff characters of *Palāśīr yuddha* along with the absence of dramatic tension apparently were not barriers to its popular enjoyment. In one of his letters to Girishchandra, Nabinchandra mentioned that in the first edition of *Palāśīr yuddha*, he had Siraj's wife sing a doleful song on hearing of her husband's execution. Bankimchandra, in his review, had criticized this device as unrealistic and unduly sentimental, and Nabinchandra subsequently dropped the song from future editions. "But you were always stubborn," wrote Nabin to Girish in thinly veiled admiration. "I see [in your play *Sirājaddaulā*] that you have followed that same dubious path."[74] Indeed, it is remarkable how often Nabinchandra employed the device of the song in his narrative poem. He puts a martial song in the choral voice of British sailors, for example, and has a British soldier singing of his beloved Carolina on the battle's eve. As we know, the song was at this time emerging as an integral element of the modern popular narrative in Indian theater, and was adopted later in the cinema. Despite all the criticism, *Palāśīr yuddha* must be counted as having produced some of the building blocks of the popular nationalist theater in Bengal.

Fourth, Nabinchandra also provided the key elements of the rhetoric of Hindu-Muslim fraternity that would ring out so loudly in the days of the Swadeshi movement. This was not the fraternity premised on the abstract citizen-subject, grounded in homogeneous and equal citizenship, and then handed down as the liberal ideal of civic nationalism, most exemplarily since the French Revolution. Rather, it was based on Hindus and Muslims as constituting distinct communities that were nonetheless bound by the solidarity of naturalized kinship. Both Rani Bhabani and Mohanlal describe it eloquently in *Palāśīr yuddha*, in terms that would be used by Girishchandra and Kshirodprasad in their historical plays written in the Swadeshi period.

SIRAJ AND THE NATIONAL-POPULAR

When Nabinchandra attended a performance of *Palāśīr yuddha* at the National Theatre in 1877, he is said to have remarked to Girishchandra: "I see you can turn even the multiplication tables into riveting drama." Not to be outdone, the producer-actor replied: "I can, but only if you write the multiplication tables."[75] Underlying this friendly game of mutual congratulation was an unstated compact between two creative artists who had, each in his own way, journeyed into a world of popular dramatic narration that was not structured by the aesthetic rules of classical Sanskrit or Greek dramatics, or indeed modern Western dramatic literature of the high canonical kind. They were acknowledging each other's role as practitioners of the drama of the national-popular.

Girishchandra, acclaimed in his lifetime in the popular press of Bengal as a playwright surpassing even Shakespeare, has received scant praise from academic critics of Bengali drama for whom the line of canonical dramatists jumps from Madhusudan Dutt and Dinabandhu Mitra in the mid-nineteenth century, to Rabindranath and the modernist progressives of the twentieth century, bypassing entirely the enormously successful popular theater of the commercial stage in Calcutta of the late nineteenth and early twentieth centuries. Jogendranath Gupta, delivering the Girish Lectures at the University of Calcutta, mentioned the excessive adulation of Girishchandra earlier in the century, but also noted that the playwright was already nearly forgotten in the 1950s.[76] It was as if the very popularity of the public theater was the telltale sign of its shortcoming as true art. The critical analysis of Girishchandra's plays too has generally proceeded by identifying the aspects in which they have deviated from the norms of high dramatic art by conceding to prevailing popular tastes. It was left to Utpal Dutt, himself an enormously successful actor-producer-playwright of the late twentieth century, to point out the immensely significant contributions of Girish as the pioneer actor-producer-playwright of the anticolonial stage.[77] Dutt's observations are better appreciated by taking them out of the mechanical frame of Marxist class analysis into which he rather ham-handedly squeezes them, and understanding Girishchandra as the producer-playwright of a new national-popular mode of dramatic narration.[78]

Girishchandra's *Sirājaddaulā* was first performed at the Minerva Theatre in September 1905, a month after the Swadeshi agitation was launched and a month before the official proclamation of the partition of Bengal.[79] Historians of the Calcutta stage are all agreed that the production's timing was perfect. Given the prevailing political excitement, *Sirājaddaulā* became one of the greatest commercial successes of the Bengali stage, leading Girishchandra to write and produce a sequel, *Mīr kāsim*, in June 1906 that also reaped "fabulous sums of money."[80] The average takings per night for *Sirājaddaulā* on its first run amounted to seven hundred rupees, while those for *Mīr kāsim* exceeded a thousand rupees—a record at the time.[81] Minerva Theatre made unheard-of profits, enabling it to repay its large debts and still end up with a considerable surplus.[82] The Palashi theme was clearly evocative of a certain prevailing spirit, since Kshirodprasad, another successful playwright, had also begun writing a play on Siraj, but on hearing that Girish was about to stage a production on the subject, changed his focus to the period after the battle of Palashi. His play *Palāśīr prāyaścitta* (Penance for Palashi) was produced at the Star Theatre in August 1906.[83]

Girishchandra's *Sirājaddaulā* and *Mīr kāsim* were explicitly based on the new historical research of Akshaykumar and other nationalist historians.[84] Clearly, Girish had resolved not to tread the dubiously smooth path taken by his predecessor Nabinchandra.[85] Both of Girish's plays were peopled by scores of historical characters and were rich in historical detail. Like Akshaykumar, Girish too identified what he thought were the key political antagonisms of the period: a clique of zamindars and bankers seeking to strengthen their hold on power, and willing even to collude with a dangerously ambitious foreign force to thwart a prince determined to defend the sovereign independence of the state. But Akshaykumar's was a scholarly exercise; Girish had to find ways to reach a public that was not in the habit of reading history books.

He did this by devising theatrical techniques for giving voice to a popular commentary on historical events. As Dutt observes, a major theme in both *Sirājaddaulā* and *Mīr kāsim* is money—the pursuit of fortune as the principal motivation of the East India Company officers, and the willingness of Indian officials and merchants to buy and sell both private and state interests in exchange for money.[86] In *Sirājaddaulā*, the money theme was used as a moral peg of popular criticism in several scenes: the riotous song of the looting mob (depicted by a troupe of chorus girls) on the eve of the nawab's invasion of Cal-

Figure 18. Surendranath (Dani) Ghosh in title role in *Sirajaddaula*, 1905, photograph.
Source: Ghosh 1969

cutta; the blatantly crude attempts by Holwell to persuade his prisoner Umichand to write a letter on his behalf to the nawab; the division of spoils, planned before the battle and executed after the victory at Palashi, and the fraudulent exclusion of Umichand; and as we will see, numerous remarks by Karim Chacha, who was created by Girish to provide a running commentary on the doings of the rich and famous from the plebeians' perspective. It is stretching the point to find in this, as Dutt does, an incipient criticism of capitalism. Rather, it is a critique of the mysterious powers of money, which seen from the world of those who do not have it, seems to be able to bring about the most unlikely alliances and achieve the most impossible outcomes.

Perhaps the fundamental problem in narrating the battle of Palashi and its consequences in terms of popular reason was its sheer implausibility. How could a large kingdom under a skilled and determined monarch succumb to a foreign power with an utterly insignificant force at its command? How could the entire Mughal order of state power suddenly collapse and come under the control of alien merchants? It was a mysterious history, inexplicable in terms of the ordinary and familiar rules of causality. It could only be explained as some extraordinary forces working through their human agents.

Girishchandra employed this element of popular reason most strikingly and controversially through the character Zahara, a fictional creation meant to be the widow of Husain Quli Khan, one of Siraj's victims. This character has been generally condemned by literary critics for her very unreality. Her presence in the most improbable places at the most impossible moments, making her in fact the principal dynamic agent moving the plot toward its tragic conclusion, has been roundly condemned as a cheap theatrical device unworthy of a major national dramatist. But if we regard her as a dramatic signifier designed specifically to perform what is rationally impossible, then realism is hardly what we should expect. Instead, in both her appearance and words, Zahara, soaked in the *zahr* (poison) of vengeance, explicitly presents herself as an unnatural force, quite different from the other historical characters pursuing their mundane ambitions. In this she is also able to connect with another pervasive belief in popular consciousness that cataclysmic events in both the natural and human worlds are beyond human reasoning: their causes are necessarily unknown. In her context, Zahara is not an implausible character for the national-popular. She in fact may even be thought of as Girishchandra's answer to Macaulay's Divine Providence.

This truth about Zahara is revealed most tellingly in the play when Karim, pretending to be a ghost on a tree, proposes to her, a fellow ghost, to spend a night of love with him (II, 6). Karim points out, with startling irony, that despite all her efforts at skillfully bringing about the ruin of Siraj, her name would never appear in the history of Bengal—Clive, Mir Jafar, and all the other agents she had cleverly manipulated would get all the credit. "The pages of history will be filled by the ink with which the names of traitors are inscribed; you or I will not find a place there" (V, 5). Girishchandra's gestures toward the national-popular were profoundly self-conscious in revealing their artifices.

The failure of literary critics to appreciate the difference posed by the popular mode of dramatic narrative is well exemplified by Kshetra Gupta's analysis of *Sirājaddaulā*.[87] Gupta criticizes Girishchandra for failing to hold on to a tight plot structure that would rigorously indicate the sequence of historical causation, and for straying into peripheral episodes and irrelevant scenes merely to feed the desire of some sections of the audience for emotional excitement. After scrutinizing the entire play scene by scene, Gupta comes to the conclusion that nineteen of the thirty-six scenes of the five-act work were irrelevant to the plot and should have been excised. Similarly irrelevant are the songs, ten in number (few if judged by the standards of the hugely successful mythological plays produced by Girishchandra), which only hold up the action and pander to sentimentality. Girishchandra, Gupta says, also defies rational causality, whether natural or historical, by introducing magical and implausible actions to move the plot forward. Needless to say, the character Zahara takes the brunt of this criticism: she is said to have been created in order to provide the cheap sensation that a maniacal woman, driven raving mad by the desire for revenge, can supply on stage.[88] The political message of Swadeshi too, Gupta alleges, is mostly supplied as declamations in the mouths of characters such as Siraj, Mohanlal, or Mir Madan. At such moments, they appear to be political leaders of the modern Swadeshi movement, which to follow the rules of historical realism, is utterly anachronistic.[89]

Girishchandra's characters are flat, says Gupta; they show no inner contradictions. Siraj is no tragic hero, since his contradictoriness is only that of having transformed himself from his early immoral ways to that of a responsible ruler. It does not create any deep psychological conflict within him, and its superficiality is indicated by the frivolous way in which Karim Chacha, the authorial voice in the play, can dismiss its significance:

KARIM: When was a great deed ever accomplished by deliberation? ... Our master just deliberates while the English conspire. If instead of deliberating, he had shouted his orders, things would have been different. All those fangless snakes would have slithered back into their holes. (III, 4)

KARIM: The kid just became confused. If I could have tossed a couple of drinks into him at Palashi, your treachery would have come to nothing, and Clive too wouldn't have shouted "Hip hip hurray!" (V, 4)

Indeed, Siraj's contradictoriness does not lead to bold deeds, and their tragic defeat. It only confirms the futility of human action and the inevitable triumph of destiny. Some mysterious superhuman force scripted the results of Palashi long before anything happened in Murshidabad or Calcutta, and there was nothing that poor Siraj could have done to stop it. We may feel some pity for him, says Gupta, but his life, as dramatized by Girishchandra, is not the stuff of great tragedy.[90]

The character of Karim Chacha, ostensibly following the path of the *vidū-ṣaka* in Sanskrit drama, is not as uninvolved in the proceedings as the classical model and is indeed a commentator speaking on behalf of the author addressing the audience.[91] He seems to have full knowledge of history as it has unfolded since the dramatized events of 1756–57, and often refers to it in the form of prophecies about the future, even though this is anachronistic for a character participating in eighteenth-century affairs. But the ironical mode of Karim's pronouncements does not seem to Gupta to carry any deep insight into either the human character or colonial condition. On the contrary, they are cheap devices to evoke laughter.[92]

Gupta's observations are, on the whole, not incorrect when judged from the standpoint of the canons of historical tragedy in the high Western tradition. Still, precisely for that reason, they are accurate indicators of why *Sirājaddaulā* was so successful in communicating with the national-popular in the age of Swadeshi. The point can be grasped more firmly when we consider a contemporary criticism of Girishchandra's dramaturgy. In the first decade of the twentieth century, Dhananjay Mukhopadhyay (Byomkes Mustafi's pseudonym) launched a trenchant criticism of the prevailing styles of acting, set design, costumes, choreography, makeup, and other aspects of Calcutta's public theater.[93] One of his main complaints was that Girish had introduced "a new style of acting" that was a throwback to the days before the birth of the modern stage in Bengal and entirely contrary to the style he had himself followed in producing Dinabandhu's plays in the 1870s. His actors would now address the audience directly, violating the first principle of stage acting that actors, when immersing themselves in the dramatic action, must become oblivious to the audience's presence. When a group of characters made an entrance, they would file in and stand in line. When speaking sotto voce, some would even walk up to the front of the stage, throw the line at the audience, and return to their earlier positions. Not even Ardhendu Mustafi, Girish's associate from his early days in the theater, had been able to correct these faults. The defect became particularly painful because Girish always made his actors stand on stage, no matter what the scene; even Siraj or Mir Qasim holding a council would be shown standing with their courtiers.[94]

Furthermore, Girishchandra taught his actors to speak their lines, even when in prose, in a songlike intonation. To the discerning member of the audience, Dhananjay claimed, this was excruciatingly monotonous. Girish was also not averse to introducing a vulgar variety of humor into his plays on elevated subjects, such as the banter between Karim and Zahara in *Sirājaddaulā*. "It should have been borne in mind," wrote Dhananjay with some irritation, "that the members of a nawab's *darbar* [court] don't exactly behave like the Nikari Muslim fisher folk of Bagbazar [the neighborhood where Girishchandra lived]." Girish paid little attention as well to ensuring that the costumes of his historical characters accurately reflected the context and period. Like the rest of the public theaters of Calcutta, he allowed his stage managers to fit up emperors, courtiers, princesses, and chorus girls with the same sets of costumes owned by the company, regardless of the nationality or period. The dancing girls, for instance, always wore ballroom gowns, whether they were entertaining Rana Pratap, Siraj-ud-daulah, or Ali Baba.[95]

Dhananjay's complaint was quite clear. The modern theater of Bengal had emerged to cater to the cultural needs of the educated middle class. Now it was being overwhelmed by the demand to satisfy the tastes of a lower grade of spectators—those who had not yet acquired the cultivated sensibilities of the true public. Sadly, Girishchandra, a pioneer of the new theater, had surrendered to this trend. "Even the Indian *nāṭyaśāstra* did not recognize the right of all—whether respectable or lowly, educated or unlettered, cultivated or crude, knowledgeable or ignorant—to enter the theatre. In these days of equality and freedom, and enticed by the goddess of wealth, the modern theatre is not prepared to heed that sound advice."[96] In short, Dhananjay objected to Girishchandra's innovations precisely because they violated the canons of the high theater in order to pander to the popular.

THE DRAMATIC FORM OF THE NATIONAL-POPULAR

These criticisms, whether from the first part of the twentieth century or the last, of Girishchandra's nationalist plays say enough in their negative depiction to offer an idea of why they were so successful in striking a chord in the popular domain. Let us elaborate further. Girish, who had earlier successfully developed the mythological and devotional drama for the modern stage, using a modified version of the new blank verse introduced by Madhusudan and a vast array of songs mostly composed in traditional styles, had to employ prose in dealing with modern political history. But in *Sirājaddaulā*, he frequently had his tragic hero speak in verse in his soliloquy, intimate and emotional scenes with his grandmother or wife, or declamations on patriotic duty. Even in engaging with the subject of politics, therefore, Girish was eager to utilize the familiar rhetorical power of dramatic verse to reach the popular on the affective register. In this, he was consciously introducing, as Utpal Dutt also points out, techniques borrowed from the traditional jatra into the proscenium theater.[97]

Second, he maintained a line of popular commentary by periodically introducing a troupe of dancers, sometimes male and sometimes female (the text of the play calls them "citizens"), who remark on political events in songs composed in the style of the popular *kabigān* and *saṅg* performances of early nineteenth-century Calcutta. Girish, in other words, put "the people" directly on stage, even in a play dealing with the high politics of nobles and foreign merchants.

Third, the character of Siraj served as the crucial signifier unifying and embodying the diverse elements of "the people-nation," and distinguishing them from its enemies—namely, the greedy foreigners and treacherous nobles. Even though Girishchandra took great pains to portray Siraj as having transformed himself from a depraved young man to a mature ruler, and showed Dan Shah Fakir, a corrupt preacher, as the chief purveyor of the canards about Siraj's misdeeds, including the Black Hole incident, he still employed the same narrative techniques used by Nabinchandra to present Siraj as a vulnerable and familiar hero—a loving husband and father, a respectful grandson, fearful and indecisive at moments of crisis, prepared even to hand over his crown to his enemies for the sake of peace in Bengal. Indeed, Siraj became the principal voice of the people-nation, cutting across religious and class divisions, and unified by its opposition to the danger represented by the foreign power and its native allies.

> SIRAJ: Hindu and Musalman—
> Come, let us forgive each other;
> Let us forget the old histories; …
> Beware—
> Do not give the Firangi the slightest room,
> For this much is certain—
> Their thirst for conquest is endless.…
> Abjure the Firangis as enemies;
> The alien Firangis are not our kin,
> They are self-seeking—all they want is control of the state.
> So prepare for battle. (I, 5)

This is without doubt a political speech inspired by the spirit of Swadeshi, but the anachronism is perfectly compatible with the conventions of popular narrative performance. Siraj's message of Hindu-Muslim fraternity, based on separate but equal participation in state affairs, is also consistent with the idea of "composite patriotism" current at the time of Swadeshi. The Hindu-Muslim theme, we know, could be deployed in the nationalist theater of this period to produce ambiguous meanings. Stories of Rajput or Maratha resistance to the Delhi sultanate or the Mughal Empire could be read in a straightforward way as Hindu resistance to Muslim rule. It could also be read, provided one was able and willing to recognize the ploy, as a coded way of talking about Indian resistance to British rule. Girishchandra's *Chatrapati śibājī* (1907) could be viewed as open to such alternative readings. But *Sirājaddaulā* and *Mīr kāsim* left no room for ambiguity.

Karim Chacha's character is a dramatic innovation. He is both an authorial voice as well as the voice of "the people." But he is more than just an observant commentator, because at crucial moments, he also participates in the historic events unfolding around him. In an audacious move, Girish used a popular legend that claimed that Dan Shah Fakir recognized Siraj, in disguise, by his jeweled shoes, which the defeated nawab had forgotten to remove in his hurry to escape. Girish actually had Karim exchange clothes with Siraj and send him on his way. This device made it possible for Girish to write a hilarious scene in which Karim, decked out in nawabi finery, is utterly ignored by both nobles and commoners. When Siraj is caught and executed, Karim exclaims:

KARIM: ... I didn't quite comprehend the significance of footwear. I thought the nawab would find it hard to walk in my rough shoes. Now I see that the insignia of headgear is being replaced by that of footwear. Now the difference between the respectable and the lowly will be marked not by their turbans or clothes but by their shoes. (V, 4)

Karim is referring here to the well-known European disinclination to conform to the elaborate Indian system of gradation of headgear by social status, preferring instead to wear their hats, and their aversion to the removal of shoes in the presence of a higher authority.

To introduce an action of comic irony bordering on the slapstick in the final scenes of a historical tragedy was immensely risky. It worked because Karim had been effectively constructed as an outsider in the affairs of the *darbar*, but one who embodied the element of the popular. In a sense, therefore, Karim also implicates the audience in the action of those final scenes. It is significant that whereas Zahara's interventions, representing as it were the hand of destiny, successfully bring about Siraj's downfall, those of Karim, trying to save the nawab from his enemies, fail miserably. The people may fight, yet they are ineffective in stopping the course of malevolent fate. If there is a genre of tragedy in the national-popular, its form is not that of modern bourgeois tragedy as known in the Western tradition.

Irony is a major rhetorical mode utilized by Karim in his comments on political events. Perhaps the most famous of them—to the point of having passed into common parlance without anyone ascribing the source—is his exclamation when the conspirators, seeking to precipitate a confrontation with the British, advise Siraj to attack Calcutta once again after Clive had retaken the town. In an aside, Karim says: "*Elomelo ka're de mā, luṭepuṭe khāi* [Oh Mother, turn everything topsy-turvy, so I can plunder to my heart's content]." When Mir Madan asks him if he wants disorder in the country, he shoots back:

KARIM: ... Why, was I not born in Bengal? Am I not crafty? Don't I know how to fill my own pocket? Don't I seek my own well-being? Why should I care for the well-being of others? I was born in Bengal, so my own good is good enough for me. (II, 4)

His final pronouncement on this subject, however, has no trace of irony: "Only the maker of our destiny can bring peace to Bengal. The old Bengal will not do any more; Bengal has to be built anew" (II, 4). Once again, Girishchandra was announcing a political project for Swadeshi Bengal.

In the final act, when the new nawab, Mir Jafar, orders his execution for treason, Karim says:

KARIM: Of course you'll execute me, but won't you put my body on an elephant and take it around town? Let me act out the full role of nawab.

MIR JAFAR: What? Still being sarcastic? Traitor!

KARIM: I have no monopoly on treason. In fact, I am only an ugly duck here among royal swans. If there was a punishment for treason, a procession of heads would have rolled by now.

MIR JAFAR: Impale him!

CLIVE: Er, considering our presence here, I suggest you change that punishment.

MIR JAFAR: Sahib, I accept your request. But this traitor is fit to be impaled on the stake. Go and execute him.

KARIM: Uncle, you've given me high honours. If I have surpassed you in treachery, then my performance deserves to be congratulated. [*to Clive*] My salute, sahib, you are a mighty man. Not just Bengal, all of India will belong to you.

CLIVE: [in English, completely missing the irony] *Thank you for your good wishes.* (V, 6)

Even as *Sirājaddaulā* inscribed the division between the nation as people and its foreign enemies, Girishchandra also made a subtle hegemonic move that frequently has not been noticed. He introduced an English woman, Mrs. Watts, who is first shown pleading with Siraj's wife for the release of her husband, an East India Company official who had been imprisoned by the nawab. She then appears again when, following Mir Jafar's coming to power, his son Miran is holding Lutf-un-nesa, Siraj's wife, captive and proposing to her to enter his harem.

Mrs. Watts enters in haste with two English soldiers

MRS. WATTS: *Oh! you lecherous villain! Soldiers, do your duty!*

FIRST SOLDIER: [*seizing Miran*] *You rascally nigger!*

SECOND SOLDIER: *Oh you hell-hound!*

MIRAN: [*bound*] But I am the prince—the prince.

MRS. WATTS: *Hold your silly tongue, you brute!* Flaunt your rank somewhere else. I am an English woman. These two are *English soldiers.* Do you know that those who have given your father the throne can take it away from him? [*to Lutphunnisa*] Begam sahib, don't be afraid. I am here now. You had freed my husband once, and I had promised to repay your debt. An English woman never breaks her *promise.* Come with me and have no worries. (V, 2; emphasis in English original)

A host of power-laden relations are engaged with in this scene. Mrs. Watts is the representative of an imperial power, unashamed of its racial superiority and prepared to assert its might to protect the weak, especially women, from tyrannical Oriental men. But she is also able to establish a more personal affective bond of sisterhood with the oppressed Oriental woman—something that is beyond the reach of British male officials.

This aspect is highlighted in the last scene of the play when Mrs. Watts accompanies Lutf-un-nesa to Siraj's grave.

Mrs. Watts: Begam sahib, I have come to put flowers on your husband's grave. I will join you today in praying for him. As long as I am in this place, I will come with you to light the lamp on his grave.

Lutf: Memsahib, I will remain indebted to you all my life. I can never repay that debt. All I can do is pray to my god that you live happily with your husband for all your life.

Mrs. Watts: Begam sahib, you saved my husband, but I could not save yours. I will always live with that regret. I offer flowers to your husband with tears in my eyes. (V, 7)

This is the moment when—famously or notoriously, depending on one's taste—Lutf-un-nesa breaks into a mournful song as the curtain comes down on the stage. It is a remarkable final scene for a nationalist play of the Swadeshi era to have an Englishwoman, the wife of a conspiring East India Company official, offering flowers at the grave of Siraj, allegedly the chief perpetrator of an atrocity that triggered the act of retribution that was the battle of Palashi. The nationalist opposition to empire was clearly seeking to enlist the support of at least a section of even the British people. It is important that this portion was marked in its gender as feminine.

On the subject of the visual aspect of nationalist theater, it is difficult to say much since there is so little visual documentation of Girishchandra's theater. Could we hypothesize that Karim Chacha's commentary acquired its popular significance because it was spoken, in the flesh, by Girishchandra Ghosh, the premier actor, producer, and playwright of his time, who acted in that role—that, in other words, the commentary came not from a fictional character called Karim but rather from Girishchandra giving voice to the sentiments of the people of Bengal? We cannot, unfortunately, settle that question at this time.

What we do know, however, is that in the early decades of the twentieth century, the success of Girishchandra and Kshirodprasad's plays gave rise to a formulaic genre of nationalist drama in the public theater. Once again, our guide here is a critic of the surrender of the commercial stage to the low popular. In 1933, Apareschandra Mukhopadhyay, for some time a close associate of Girish, penned a critique of the nationalist theater:

After *Sirājaddaulā*, there was a veritable flood of historical plays on the Bengali stage. This flood led to some financial gains for the theatre, but it is undeniable that it considerably muddied the pure springs of literature. Historical truth, the integrity of historical characters—these have quietly made their exit from the so-called historical plays. The craving for *sensation* has lowered the literary form of drama to such depths that one is ashamed to recall that story.... This search for sensation and unmerited applause has led many a historical dramatist in the last several years to produce low *melodrama*.

Apareschandra further elaborated on this formulaic melodrama:

A model, like a shoemaker's last, was soon devised for the easy production of historical plays: one side will attack India and the other will resist; a wild woman, in despicable imitation of Zahara ... will sing a patriotic song; whether dramatically justified or not, someone will pull the sword from a general or king and loudly declaim on the duty to liberate the country; someone may, if needed, sing a *kīrtan* as though one was performing the funerary rites for Bharat Mata; some gangster-like characters will appear in a scene, shooting from their pistols at a group of oppressors molesting a woman; the poor hero, not knowing what to do, will either hang himself or turn raving mad and pull out the hair from his wig.[98]

Even in this savage caricature, one gets a sense of the form of the run-of-the-mill nationalist play that would be routinely produced on the Calcutta stage in the years following the Swadeshi movement. The image of pistol-shooting fighters on the side of the oppressed clearly updates the historical context to the early 1930s. Despite his distaste for the formulaic historical melodrama, though, Apareschandra acknowledged that had these plays not brought in the crowds, many public theaters in Calcutta would have shut down.[99]

SURVEILLANCE AND PROSCRIPTION

In 1875, a young man named Sarat was taking a stroll in the Eden Gardens of Calcutta. It was something of a privilege, he thought to himself, because any day the powers that be could decide that between the hours of five and seven, only white people would be allowed in the park. Suddenly, turning to the south, he exclaimed:

SARAT: There, straight ahead, is the fearsome bastion of Fort William, a palpable insult to Bengal. It seems to be shouting out at the cowardly Bengali: "Beware! Never harbour the desire to be free, or if you do, never say it aloud. Those who built me have subdued the entire planet; they are world conquerors; they have thunder and lightning at their command. If you come to me like a craven dog or an obedient slave, you are welcome. But never dare to approach me as a rebel in arms, because if you do, it will take only a moment for your angry blood to turn cold." [*sighs*] Fort William! Had we not been selfish and given only to the satisfaction of our senses, and instead if we could have made even a minimal claim to being called human, then we would not have had to endure your arrogant words. You would have been razed to the ground a long time ago—not a single brick would have stayed in place."[100]

Such bold words would not be uttered subsequently on the Calcutta stage for several decades. Upendranath Das, the creator of the fictional Sarat in the play *Śarat-sarojinī*, was arrested in 1876 for his next production at the Great National Theatre—*Surendra-binodinī*—on the charge of obscenity, even though the real provocation was his depiction of a British official as a rapist.[101]

With the passing of the Dramatic Performances Act later that year, the public theater was effectively barred from using overtly subversive political messages. Theater owners were reluctant to take the risk, if only for commercial reasons, of incurring the wrath of the law. Even though the act did not give the police specific powers to examine scripts and censor them before they were performed on stage, "the moral effect" of the legislation had legitimized this practice. The commissioner of police reported in 1910 that he "requires the production before him of the manuscript of all newly published plays, and he has not found any difficulty in inducing managers and authors to do what he wants."[102] Girishchandra's *Sirājaddaulā* had to go through a lengthy and stringent censorship before the police approved it for the stage in 1905.[103] His *Mīr kāsim* and *Chatrapati śibājī* as well as Kshirodprasad's *Palāśir prāyaścitta* and *Nandakumār* all had their first runs, usually of twenty-five weeks each, in their officially approved versions in the period 1905–7, the early years of the Swadeshi movement.[104]

The rise of the armed revolutionary movement in Bengal, accompanied by the realization that the use of the dramatic form for political purposes had spread far beyond the confines of the public stage in Calcutta, prompted an official reassessment of the situation along with a demand for greater legal powers of surveillance and prohibition. If one considers the average ticket sales from a successful production such as *Sirājaddaulā*—about seven hundred rupees per night—and puts the average price of a ticket at one rupee, then the total number of people who actually saw a performance of the play during its run at the Minerva Theatre could not have exceeded twenty thousand. But then, a successful play would be reenacted from its printed text by local troupes and amateur enthusiasts in district towns and even villages, using a variety of enclosed and open spaces with makeshift stages located in public buildings, schools, or the private mansions of landlords, often on occasions such as religious festivals. Merely controlling performances in the public theater was proving to be inadequate. A further problem was posed by what British officials referred to as the "gag": the practice of actors interpolating lines that were not part of the scripted dialogue. Even surprise visits by the police during performances were not a sufficient deterrent.[105]

Besides, the political jatra had become a dangerous new phenomenon—a product of the Swadeshi agitation. Previously confined to devotional and mythological themes, this traditional dramatic form had been excluded from the purview of legal regulations. During the Swadeshi years, however, the jatra had turned political, and playwright-performers such as Mukunda Das introduced into it new historical themes, frequently inspired by the Calcutta theater, to spread the message of anticolonial nationalism. Officials inferred that with the press and public theater under control, "the performance of dramatic plays with a seditious tendency by theatrical companies and so called 'Jatra' parties would probably be more extensively resorted to as a means for the dissemination of seditious doctrines."[106]

All these considerations led to a demand within official circles for a tightening of the law. Officials also stressed that the political situation had changed since 1905–6 with the rise of the revolutionary groups. Many of the "most mischievous" plays had been allowed to be staged in the period 1902–7. Now, though,

> the manner in which they are staged, the temper of the audiences who go to see them, and the double meaning which is intended to be and doubtless is attached by them to the historical and various other allusions contained in the plays, might render it inadvisable to allow their production at the present day.... [E]very one knows what the allusions are intended to convey and accepts them accordingly.[107]

Officials, in other words, had to admit that a rapidly widening public had been created by the Bengali theater that was conversant with the codes and protocols of the new historical drama deployed in the service of anticolonial nationalism. The political danger that this posed was most anxiously pointed out by the loyalist press of Bengal. The *Indian Nation* wrote in 1910 on the "Native Theatre":

> These places of amusement are the favourite resort of the ne'er-do-wells and idlers, whose feelings are played upon by gross caricatures of English life and society and by misrepresentations of certain historical incidents connected with the establishment of British rule in India.... The atmosphere of Bengali Theatres is peculiarly calculated to warp the judgement of emotional youths whose mental wardrobe is of the scantiest.... This is a subtle danger which cannot be lost sight of in a scheme for the suppression of sedition, and a stricter censorship of the urban stage seems called for in the present situation.[108]

After an extended debate at the highest echelons of the government in Bengal, in which the view prevailed that additional police powers would not necessarily be of much use against the strategy of evasion and subterfuge adopted by the so-called seditious elements, the authorities devised a somewhat-duplicitous strategy of their own. The government of Eastern Bengal and Assam had announced in January 1911 that it was prohibiting six plays—namely, *Sirājaddaulā*, *Mīr kāsim*, and *Chatrapati* by Girishchandra, *Palāśīr prāyascitta* and *Nandakumār* by Kshirodprasad, and *Karmaphal* by Manamohan Goswami. In February 1911, the government of Bengal ordered that its police could seize copies of these plays and prevent their performance on the strength of the neighboring province's laws.[109]

Perhaps the annulment of the partition of Bengal was being foreseen. In June 1911, Hardinge, the viceroy, was writing to London: "The results anticipated ... have not been attained. The political power of the Bengalis has not been broken.... On the contrary, they have become more powerful and certainly more troublesome." Unless the partition of Bengal was modified, "we must, I fear, be prepared for a recrudescence of revolutionary crime."[110] When the province of Bengal was reconstituted at the end of 1911, the laws of Eastern Bengal and Assam, unless specifically repealed, became those of Bengal.

The list of prohibited plays got longer with the years. In 1932, a dramatization by Kshetramohan Mitra of Nabinchandra's *Palāśīr yuddha* for the Natya Niketan theater was prohibited by the police on the grounds that it was "of an objectionable nature and likely to excite feelings of disaffection to the Government established by law in British India."[111] It is hard to guess how the poet might have reacted to this judgment on his most popular work; he had, mercifully, passed away several years previously, in 1909.

CHAPTER NINE

Bombs, Sovereignty, and Football

FOLLOWING THE DEMOLITION of Holwell's monument in 1821, there was nothing in the city of Calcutta to physically commemorate the Black Hole event. Given the enormous discursive circulation of the story in the second half of the nineteenth century, this lack was seen as something of an anomaly. In 1883, Roskell Bayne, an engineer working on the foundations of the East Indian Railway's new office building northwest of Dalhousie Square, discovered some walls that appeared to have been part of the old Fort William. In 1891–92, Charles Robert Wilson, professor of history at Presidency College in Calcutta, studied some further excavations at the spot, and comparing the finds with an old plan of the fort from 1753, identified the site of the Black Hole at a location adjacent to the General Post Office. But in measuring the site, Wilson was puzzled that the actual dimensions of the Black Hole prison were smaller than what was shown in the 1753 plan. He concluded that the old plan was faulty.[1]

In 1908, Busteed, an official of the Calcutta Mint and historian of Calcutta, produced evidence that a storage space may have been created along the prison's eastern wall between 1753 and 1756, thus explaining the discrepancy between the plan and the excavated site. The latter revealed that the Black Hole was not eighteen feet square, as suggested by Holwell, but eighteen feet by fourteen feet, ten inches.[2] Clearly, the practice of historians was now responding to new demands for the scientific veracity of their evidence and arguments. They could no longer afford to deal with the facts in the cavalier manner of a literary dandy like Macaulay.

Busteed also began what could be called a new campaign for a suitable monument to remind the inhabitants of the capital city of British India of the Black Hole tragedy. In his history of eighteenth-century Calcutta, first published in 1888, Busteed wrote two detailed chapters recounting once more, this time from original documents, the story of Siraj's storming of Fort William and the Black Hole calamity. Defending the reliability of Holwell's narrative against the malice shown by his detractors in the company, Busteed used it to correct the unjustified charges made by Orme and Macaulay against Siraj. It was "beyond dispute," Busteed declared, "that the Nawab had nothing to do with the measures adopted for securing those who fell into his power." The guards "were careless as to the dimensions—indeed, they probably were as ignorant of what these really were, as the throng were whom they were driving in." The nawab

Figure 19. Snuffbox belonging to Warren Hastings with portrait of Mrs. Carey, a Black Hole survivor. *Photo: Pratap Sinha. Courtesy: © Victoria Memorial Hall, Kolkata*

also did not order Holwell and three other prisoners to be taken to Murshidabad, and actually treated them with kindness when they were brought before him. Busteed concluded: "His [Siraj's] short life is said to have been fruitful in vice and crime. Very probably it was. But writers ... have dwelt on these, and have kept out of sight the few good acts which might fairly be shown, not in exculpation, but in mitigation of damages. So true is it that 'men's evil manners live in brass; their virtues we write in water.'"[3]

Busteed also investigated the story of Mrs. Carey, supposedly the only woman among the Black Hole prisoners. He produced an account from 1799 that described Mrs. Carey, then fifty-eight years old, as a lady "of a size rather above the common stature, and very well proportioned; of a fair Mesticia colour, with correct regular features, which give evident marks of beauty which must once have attracted admiration." This source also suggested that she was possibly not the only woman among the prisoners; there may have been one or two others. Busteed dismissed another allegation made against Siraj: "The relegation to a harem, which tradition assigns to the fate of Mrs. Carey, rests on no substantial basis."[4] Indeed, Busteed discovered that Mrs. Carey married again, continued to live in Calcutta, and died in 1801. To add further color to her historical memory, there is the curious fact that the Victoria Memorial Hall in Calcutta displays to this day a snuffbox that is said to have belonged to Warren Hastings and bears a little gilded portrait of "Mrs. Carey, a survivor of the Black Hole."[5] There is rich irony in the knowledge that Mrs. Carey, allegedly sent to the nawab's harem in Murshidabad, also found her way on to Hastings's snuffbox.

Writing of Holwell's monument in the first edition of his book, Busteed remarked:

> One would have thought that every Englishman in Calcutta would have regarded the monument's preservation as a personal trust. Yet it was allowed to go to ruin, and its demolition was so effectually completed, that no knowledge survives of what became even of its inscription marble.... Calcutta has been allowed to be without any commemorative structure, or sculptured tablet of any kind, sacred to those few "faithful found among the faithless," whose memory their fellow-sufferer, who best knew their deservings, wished and tried to honour.[6]

The New Memorial

Curzon read Busteed's book while sailing to India to assume the viceroy's office in 1898 and was, one suspects, struck by the anomaly of the lack of a monument to the memory of the Black Hole incident.[7] The turn of the century was also when a group of British scholars working in Bengal got together to promote the new "scientific" methods of positive history. Curzon's presence in Calcutta, and his active efforts to uncover and preserve the country's neglected historical sites and monuments, provided a fillip to these scholars to collect the documentary sources and start writing a new academic history of British rule in Bengal. Curzon was also the patron of the Calcutta Historical Society, founded in 1907 with Evan Cotton as president and Walter Firminger as editor of its journal, *Bengal Past and Present*.[8]

Curzon took a special interest in memorializing the Black Hole. After working for two years on the collected records, in 1901 he created a space alongside the General Post Office, paved it with black polished marble, and fenced it with low iron railings. The inscription on the adjacent wall announced that the site of the Black Hole was below:

The pavement marks the exact breadth of the prison, 14 feet 10 inches,
    But not its full length, 18 feet,
About one-third of the area at the North end being covered
    By the building on which this tablet is fixed.[9]

He also had brass lines laid to locate the walls of the old fort and plaques put up to mark various spots within it. To complete a tour that was meant to be both instructive and spiritually uplifting, Curzon also had wooden models constructed of the old fort and the Black Hole prison.[10]

In 1902, Curzon had a new monument built, partly at his personal expense, as a replica of Holwell's obelisk, and set it up on the northwest corner of Dalhousie Square.[11] The obelisk was made by a British firm from Sicilian marble and shipped to Calcutta. Curzon decided "it would be undesirable to reproduce either the reference to Siraj-ud-Dowlah in the larger inscription (which was historically untrue, as well as inexpedient) or the brief record of British vengeance in the shorter inscription." He also modified Holwell's list of victims in light of new research, and instead of the forty-eight names on Holwell's original monument, inscribed those of sixty Black Hole victims, including Eleanor Weston, who Busteed suggested had died in the prison. Further, Curzon

Figure 20. Site of Black Hole. *Source: Curzon 1925*

Figure 21. Arrival of Lord Hardinge as viceroy in Dalhousie Square, November 1910. © *The British Library Board. All Rights Reserved. Source: British Library Images (592(1) Photo 7)*

inscribed another list of twenty-one "who were killed or died of their wounds either immediately before the Black Hole or after."[12] Confidently riding the global wave of high imperialism, the British rulers once more installed the memory of their early victimhood in India, this time without laying blame or celebrating the retribution. The mood now was heroic: as Busteed commented, quoting John Kaye on the British disasters during the 1857 revolt, "The heroism of failure is often greater than the heroism of success."[13]

THE SCRAMBLE FOR EMPIRE

In the meantime, the world was witnessing a furious race among the great powers for the acquisition of overseas colonial territories. In Europe, this was primarily provoked by the rapid rise of unified Germany as an industrial and military power. Germany made a determined bid from the 1880s onward to secure colonial possessions in order to find "a place in the sun" as a great power alongside Britain and France. This led to the notorious "scramble for Africa" with Britain occupying Egypt in 1882, Somaliland in 1884, Nigeria in 1886, and East Africa in 1889, and France taking Tunisia in 1881, followed in rapid succession by the Ivory Coast, Dahomey, Lake Chad, Niger, and Equatorial Congo. Most of northern and southern Africa having been taken, Germany attacked the middle and occupied the Cameroons, Togoland, South West Africa, and parts of East Africa. Italy, not to be left behind, founded colonies in Eritrea and part of Somaliland, while King Leopold of Belgium took Congo as a personal trust. Most of these acquisitions were diplomatically ratified by the Berlin colonial conference of 1884–85. By 1890, the kingdom of Ethiopia and republic of Liberia remained the only independent territories in Africa. The Western powers had held only 25 percent of Africa in 1878; on the eve of the First World War, they had 90 percent—with France holding the largest chunk, Britain the second largest, and Germany, Italy, Belgium, and Portugal controlling roughly equal shares.[14]

But the imperial scramble took on an entirely new dimension with the entry of Japan and the United States as contenders for colonial possessions in East Asia and the Pacific. Japan, which too had industrialized and militarized rapidly in the last decades of the nineteenth century, made a strong bid in the 1890s for the last great colonial reservoir left in the world, seizing Formosa, Korea, and parts of Manchuria from China. This led Russia to occupy Port Arthur and Talien, and prompted the other colonial powers—France, Britain, and Germany—to carve out their spheres of influence along the coasts of China. The United States also became an imperial power in the Pacific when it occupied the Philippines and Guam as well as annexed Hawaii in 1898.

While diplomats in Europe still tried to use the familiar techniques of balance of power to "contain" Germany, it was clear that with the rise of two new non-European powers—Japan and the United States—and the virtual exhaustion of available colonial territories, the technique of balanced additions to each great power at the expense of lesser powers and colonies would no longer work. The global imperialist system had become an inherently unstable zero-sum game.[15] Writing in 1916, Vladimir Ilyich Lenin described the global political picture quite accurately:

> The colonial policy of the capitalist countries has *completed* the seizure of the unoccupied territories of our planet. For the first time the world is completely divided up, so that in the future *only* redivision is possible, i.e. territories can only pass from one "owner" to another, instead of passing as ownerless territory to an "owner."[16]

Looked at from this angle, a war to redivide the colonial world was inevitable. Hence, despite the tendency to see World War I as one more European conflict, the paradigm of the European balance of power had clearly lost its relevance, as was shown by the nature of the peace agreements drawn up in Versailles in 1919. Germany was required to surrender more than twenty-five thousand square miles of territory and nearly seven million inhabitants in Europe, and had to give up all its colonial possessions. In other words, Germany was eliminated from the ranks of the great powers. The Austrian and Ottoman empires were dismantled as well to create new nation-states in central Europe and mandated colonial territories in the Arab world. In Asia and the Pacific, Japan and the United States began a new rivalry for imperial domination.

In large parts of the world, therefore, the range of informal techniques of imperial control that had been developed in the mid-nineteenth century was apparently abandoned in favor of direct annexation of territory. Viewed from the economic motives of modern imperialism, John Gallagher and Ronald Robinson famously portrayed these earlier techniques as "the imperialism of free trade," which advocated "trade with informal control if possible; trade with rule if necessary."[17] What were the new compulsions for modern industrial economies to look aggressively for overseas colonial possessions? Interestingly, the surge in imperialism also produced a parallel surge in critical theories of imperialism.

Joseph Schumpeter, in two articles published in Germany in 1919, denied that imperialism had anything at all to do with the modern capitalist economy. Rather, it was "the objectless disposition on the part of a state to unlimited forcible expansion," a tendency carried over from their absolutist pasts by the remnants of the feudal classes that still held some power in the modern states of Europe. Imperialism was an atavistic and irrational psychological force that was wholly opposed to the rational politics of modern bourgeois liberalism. Even though he produced a great many examples from centuries of European history, Schumpeter obviously had in mind the proximate instance of Prussian militarism leading up to World War I.[18]

John Hobson, a radical liberal journalist whose experience of the Anglo-Boer War turned him into a bitter critic of modern imperialism, initiated the most influential line of argument that linked a new phase of capitalist development in Western Europe to the scramble for colonial territories. In a book published in 1902, he contended that the sudden expansion of British colonial territories was the direct result of growing overseas investments fueled by financial circles that faced a saturation of the home market. This in turn was caused by the class structure of British society in which the huge share of profits in the hands of a small layer of capitalists led to "oversavings" and the lack of expendable income among the mass of workers led to "underconsumption." Imperialism was the result of the financial plutocrats of capitalist society seeking new territories for capital investment.[19] Hobson did not think imperialism was a necessary consequence of capitalism. If the lopsided division of national wealth could be shifted toward the working class, the home market would expand and the truly liberal principle of noncoercive relations between peoples would prevail. Hobson's polemical thrust was aimed at the clamor raised by politicians such as Joseph Chamberlain who claimed that imperial profits were essential for the British people's well-being. Hobson thought that colonies were a drain on British taxpayers, and profited only the financial investors and speculators.

Apparently unaware of Hobson's work, in 1910, Rudolph Hilferding, an Austrian Marxist who later became Germany's finance minister in the Weimar period, published an analysis of imperialism in which he identified the dominance of finance capital in the form of monopolies and cartels as a new as well as necessary stage of capitalism. Finance capital was opposed to free trade, and demanded a strong national state to protect its home market and aggressively seek colonial markets for the export of capital and monopoly trade. The assertively militarist imperial policy was thus essential to keep up the profits of national finance capital and maintain its competitive edge.[20]

In 1913, Rosa Luxemburg picked up the theme of underconsumption leading to falling profits in the home market, but did not connect it to a specific stage of monopoly finance capital. She instead contended that it was inherent in Marx's scheme of reproduction of capital that the "unrealized surplus value" in capitalists' hands could only be turned into productive investment by continually bringing the means of production available in the noncapitalist parts of the world under the sway of capital. Hence, capital needed to penetrate noncapitalist sectors of production not only in its so-called primary stage of accumulation but even more so in its mature stage. The competitive acquisition of colonial territories represented the process of the continuing accumulation of capital.[21]

Lenin did not agree with Luxemburg that the annexation of colonial territories was inevitably bound up with the process of capitalist accumulation itself. Writing from his exile in Switzerland in 1916, he returned to the feature of finance capital highlighted by Hobson and Hilferding, and without necessarily attributing it to the underconsumption thesis, claimed that the merging of banking and industrial capital had created new financial oligarchies that had taken the advanced economies into the monopoly capital stage. International monopolistic associations now were engaged in exporting capital rather than commodities and sharing the world among themselves. The occupation of colonial territories having been completed, what was happening under imperialism was the redivision of the world among the biggest capitalist powers.

Lenin admitted that a part of the profits earned by monopoly capital in the colonial theaters was being transferred to a privileged section of the working class, turning it into a chauvinistic supporter of militaristic imperialism. But this could only be a temporary staving off of capitalism's crisis in its highest stage, in which it faced the prospect of devastating imperialist wars.[22] Lenin, of course, famously connected the class struggle in capitalist countries with the anti-imperialist struggles of national liberation in the colonies and semicolonies.

Arguing against the Marxist orthodoxy that regarded nationalist movements as unworthy of support because of their bourgeois character, Lenin declared the solidarity of the Soviet republic and Communist International with the anti-imperialist movements in the colonial world.[23]

These contending theories of imperialism in the early years of the twentieth century were, therefore, attempts to explain the phenomenon of aggressive competition for colonial possessions that occurred in a particular phase of development of the Western European capitalist economies. (It is not clear that the claims applied to the United States or Japan, for instance, and examples from those countries were rarely used.) As specific explanations for this phase of imperialism, there was much in these arguments that was persuasive. The role of bankers and mining interests in pushing British colonial policy in South Africa was well known. The key position of large banks within the cartels and trusts that dominated German industry of the day was also a new phenomenon, although nothing on the same scale existed in Britain or France. It is also apparent that there was a rapid rise in the export of capital from the major economies of Europe, but—significantly—it did not necessarily go to the new colonies. For instance, 75 percent of the British capital exported in 1913 went to the United States, Canada, Latin America, Australia, and New Zealand, and only about 10 percent each to India and South Africa. French capital exports were mostly to Russia and other countries of Europe, and only 9 percent to its colonies. In terms of German capital exports, 13 percent went to its colonies and the rest elsewhere.[24]

Of course, even if actual capital exports were not large, the colonies did serve as sources of crucial raw materials, particularly minerals (not only metals but also petroleum, which was emerging as a critical source of energy), and reserve markets and investment destinations when the need arose, especially in a situation where colonial territories all over the world were being exhausted. Moreover, political control often ensured that the returns on investments in colonial countries were guaranteed, as with British private investment in the Indian railways. These theories emphasizing the *necessary* connection between monopoly finance capital and imperialism could not, on the other hand, account for the fact that Switzerland or the Scandinavian countries, while having similar corporate structures and exporting large amounts of capital, did not appear to have a need for colonies. Significantly, these were also advanced capitalist economies that were not among the world's great powers.

Of these theorists of the economic motives behind the scramble for colonies, Lenin had the sharpest focus on the political grounds of imperialism. The old reasons for colonial rule had not gone away, he said. Rather, "to the numerous 'old' motives of colonial policy, finance capital had added the struggle for the source of raw materials, for the export of capital, for spheres of influence, ... economic territory in general."[25] In 1919, he further clarified: "To maintain that there is such a thing as integral imperialism without the old capitalism is merely making the wish father to the thought.... Imperialism is a superstructure on capitalism.... There is the old capitalism which in a number of branches has grown to imperialism."[26] The rise of monopoly finance capital had provided a new edge to the global competitive rivalries of the great powers. Given this, the struggle against capitalism must join with the national struggles in the colonial and semicolonial countries to attack the worldwide chain at its weakest links.

What most of these theories of imperialism seem to have underestimated was the ability of the emerging capitalist global order to adjust to political resistances, and modify accordingly its own governmental structures and policies. Following World War I, processes were begun that in the course of the twentieth century, would fundamentally transform the global imperial order.

THE NORMALIZATION OF THE NATION-STATE

The early decades of the century initiated another global process that has not been sufficiently noticed and remarked on: the normative acceptance over a wide spectrum of political opinion of the nation-state as the universally normal, legitimate form of the modern state. The process is indicated by the espousal of the right to self-determination of nations by two leaders holding entirely opposed ideological views on most things. Both Woodrow Wilson and Lenin argued from their own political forums that this was a right that legitimately belonged to all peoples that had formed themselves as nations. Wilson insisted that it was, in fact, one of the moral principles that had emerged victorious out of the world war and tried to institutionalize it in the League of Nations. Even though Wilson was mostly thinking of the nationalities of Europe that had been parts of the Austrian and Ottoman empires, and believed that the so-called backward peoples of Asian and African colonies needed to go through a period of tutelage under Western supervision, the potential force of his idea of self-determination could not be limited by his personal intentions.[27] As far as Lenin was concerned, he made the right of self-determination of nations an express goal of the Communist International and incorporated it as a constitutional principle within the emerging Soviet federation.[28]

There are two dimensions along which the nation-state came to be normalized in the League of Nations era. One was that of sovereignty. There was a general presumption that the locus of sovereignty everywhere in the modern world was the nation-state. Among the League members were countries such as Albania, Bulgaria, Czechoslovakia, and Hungary that until recently, were part of the Ottoman and Austrian empires; Ireland, which was a British colony until the Irish Free State was created in 1921, and India, which was still a British colony; and those within the British dominions like Canada, Australia, New

Zealand, and South Africa. Thus, despite the fact that their sovereign status was to some degree ambiguous, they qualified as members because they were seen to be actual or potential nation-states.

Most interesting, of course, was the status of the so-called mandated territories. These were the Arab provinces of the Ottoman Empire and the former colonial possessions surrendered by Germany. These territories were mandated to individual member states, under the supervision of the Permanent Mandates Commission, in order to facilitate their transition to self-governing states. Article 22 of the League Covenant noted that these territories were "inhabited by peoples not yet able to stand by themselves under the strenuous conditions of the modern world," and declared that "the tutelage of such peoples should be entrusted to advanced nations who, by reason of their resources, their experience or their geographical position, can best undertake this responsibility ... as Mandatories on behalf of the League."[29] It was the old liberal colonial project, now brought under the management of an international organization and hence subjected to a single juridical order. The old debate between liberal and conservative strands of imperial ideology were not necessarily resolved but rather incorporated within the international order by differentiating between different types of mandates.

Who had sovereignty over the mandated territories? Not the mandatory powers because they were only given the task of administering the territories. Instead, sovereignty was, as it were, held in abeyance until such time that the people of the territory acquired the capability to govern themselves. Until then, it remained latent in the potential nation-state.[30] The goal of independent national sovereignty was explicitly declared for the so-called A Mandates—that is, the British mandates of Palestine and Mesopotamia (which in fact became the independent Republic of Iraq in 1932) as well as the French mandate of Syria (including Lebanon)—while self-government was left somewhat ambiguous for the B and C mandates—the former German colonies of Africa and the Pacific—because the mandatory powers—namely, South Africa, Australia, and New Zealand (which wanted to annex those territories)—refused to accept ultimate independence as the objective of their mandates. The recognition of national sovereignty by the League of Nations as the goal of what was in effect colonial trusteeship was a major step in the global normalization of the nation-state. What the mandatory powers were asked to do was nothing less than *create* the conditions of sovereignty that would turn the mandated territories into normal nation-states. Not only that, but by grading the mandates into A, B, and C types according to the level of social development, the League suggested

> that sovereignty existed in something like a linear continuum, and that every society could be placed at some point in the continuum, based on its approximation to the

ideal of the European nation-state.... [T]he Mandate System ... acquired the form of a fantastic universalizing apparatus that, when applied to any mandated territory, ... would be directed to the same ideal of self-government and, in some cases, transformed sufficiently to ensure the emergence of a sovereign state.[31]

Besides sovereignty, the other dimension along which the national form of the state was normalized was that of governmental practices. Here the Permanent Mandates Commission tried to initiate a major effort to devise, by using comparative empirical methods, a general administrative science that could help in framing suitable governmental policies according to a people's level of social and economic development. The classification of mandates acknowledged the qualitative difference between the social formations of Mesopotamia, Syria, Lebanon, and Palestine, governed for centuries within a sophisticated bureaucratic empire, and the predominantly tribal African societies of Cameroon, Togoland, Ruanda-Urundi, and Tanganyika, and even more so, the "primitive" societies of New Guinea or Samoa. But by organizing the production of massive sets of standardized information on the economic and social institutions of the mandated populations, the League brought them within a single comprehensive conceptual scheme in which they could all be described comparatively as having different degrees of "stateness."

Anghie explains that economic development in particular dominated the field of social policy under the Permanent Mandates Commission.[32] This was in tune with a new disciplinary turn, noted by Timothy Mitchell in the case of Egypt, toward the construction of "the economy" as a separate and specific object of knowledge, and the rise of a new technopolitics in colonial government subject to "the rule of experts."[33] Indeed, the production and classification of information as well as the devising of administration manuals for the mandated territories suggests the image of a great Benthamite legislative factory devising "the best possible laws" for the peoples of the world, according to the specific abilities and needs of each, yet all tending toward the same universally desirable norm.

The standardization of governmental procedures across the globe was also greatly accelerated in the League era by the new international organizations it created—namely, the International Labor Organization, the Health Organization, and the Commission for Refugees. With varying degrees of effectiveness, these bodies tried to put in place governmental technologies of caring for the basic needs of safety, health, and habitation of populations in all member countries, and making this the normal responsibility of modern states. By doing so, it inaugurated a major process of international supervision of standard governmental practices worldwide—something that would become a feature of biopolitical practices in the late twentieth century. In addition, by creating the

Permanent Court of International Justice, the League introduced the first institutional step in erecting a judicial framework for the legal monitoring of the activities of sovereign nation-states.

Much has been said of the ineffectiveness and indeed failure of most of these efforts of the League of Nations. Nevertheless, despite the shortcomings in realizing its goals, the normative strength of the technical practices introduced by the League was shown by the fact that most of them were taken up once more after World War II under the rubric of the United Nations. This time, the formal end of colonial rule and actual universalization of the nation-state form were near at hand. The anti-imperial struggles had by then scored major victories in many parts of the colonial world. A new world order grounded on the universal principle of noninterference in national sovereignty was about to be founded.

Violence and the Motherland

The year 1905–6 was a crucial moment in Bengal: two new political tendencies were inaugurated in the politics of nationalism. The first was the Swadeshi movement, arguably the first modern mass movement of Indian nationalism, launched with the immediate objective of undoing the partition of the province of Bengal into two parts. The second was the rise of secret groups committed to assassinations and armed insurrection. For the next four decades, the activities of these armed groups would constitute a political movement in itself, at a tangent to the main body of Congress nationalism, which remained officially wedded to the doctrine of nonviolence. The revolutionary movement nonetheless was often ideologically and sometimes organizationally entangled with the Congress.

The history of "terrorism" in British Bengal is well documented. The series of official reports on the armed nationalist groups, beginning with F. C. Daly's report of 1911 to those by R.E.A. Ray in the late 1930s, is richly detailed, meticulous, and frequently brilliantly analytic, testifying to the seriousness with which the colonial establishment took the terrorism threat. Most of the confidential official accounts, based on police intelligence, are now publicly available.[34] In addition, a large collection of autobiographical and reminiscence literature has appeared, written by participants in the movement, many of whom spent long years in prison. The secondary historical literature on the subject is also significant, along with the large body of textbook and popular literature. Most of the facts about so-called terrorism are, in other words, fairly well known, not only to scholars, but to a wide public in Bengal too.

The first phase of the movement ran from 1907 to 1918. The standard histories describe this period in terms of the activities of two organizations: the

Jugantar group, located mainly in western Bengal, and the Anushilan group, with its center in Dacca in the east. As a matter of fact, the so-called Jugantar Party was not a single organization at all but rather a loose confederation of several groups acting with considerable autonomy; it was given this name by the government, because of the leading public role played by the newspaper *Yugāntar* in the first two years of the movement. Much of the early activities of these groups consisted of meeting in secret societies, starting gymnasiums and recruiting young men to revolutionary work. Had the Swadeshi movement not acquired the force it did in 1905–6, it is likely, as Sumit Sarkar has suggested, that these organizations, born out of a desire for greater nationalist militancy, would have died quickly.[35] But the revolutionaries took up the mass campaigns of Swadeshi with enthusiasm, and in at least two districts—Midnapore and Dacca—they were the principal organizers of the popular movement.

Within the mainstream of the Swadeshi movement too, it was the so-called Extremist wing of the Congress led by Aurobindo Ghose and Bepin Chandra Pal that attracted a lot of attention for its call to militant action instead of sterile speeches. The English daily and weekly *Bande Mataram*, edited by Aurobindo, and the Bengali weeklies *Yugāntar*, published without the name of an editor, and *Sandhyā*, edited by Brahmabandhab Upadhyay, gained considerable circulation and created a lot of excitement. The *Bande Mataram*, for instance, was clear about the political stance and objective of the struggle:

> The "Moderate" Indian politician aspires to be an Imperial citizen.… His loyalty draws him towards the Empire and his politics draws him towards self-government and the resultant is self-government within the Empire.… To include India in a federation of colonies and the motherland is madness without method. The patriotism that wishes the country to lose itself within an Empire which justifies its name by its conquest … is also madness without method. But to talk of absolute independence and autonomy—though this be madness, yet there is method in it.[36]

It was also quite forthright in characterizing these methods:

> The old gospel of salvation by prayer was based on the belief in the spiritual superiority of the British people—an illusion which future generations will look back upon with an amazed incredulity.… We do not acknowledge that a nation of slaves who acquiesce in their subjection can become morally fit for freedom.… Politics is the work of the Kshatriya and it is the virtues of the Kshatriya we must develop if we are to be morally fit for freedom. But the first virtue of the Kshatriya is not to bow his neck to an unjust yoke but to protect his weak and suffering countrymen against the oppressor and welcome death in a just and righteous battle.[37]

Hence the claim that colonial rule was not to be judged by the quality of its governance; it was illegitimate because of what it was—rule by a foreign power.

The new movement is not primarily a protest against bad Government—it is a protest against the continuance of British control; whether that control is used well or ill, justly or unjustly, is a minor and inessential consideration. It is not born of a disappointed expectation of admission to British citizenship,—it is born of a conviction that the time has come when India can, should and will become a great, free and united nation. It is not a negative current of destruction, but a positive, constructive impulse towards the making of modern India.... Its true description is not Extremism, but Democratic Nationalism.[38]

The *Bande Mataram* was also insistent in pointing out that the moral force of democratic nationalism had swept nineteenth-century Europe and was now becoming a universal idea all over the world. Thus the new pretensions of imperialism:

The idea that despotism of any kind was an offence against humanity, had crystallised into an instinctive feeling, and modern morality and sentiment revolted against the enslavement of nation by nation, of class by class or of man by man. Imperialism had to justify itself to this modern sentiment and could only do so by pretending to be a trustee of liberty, commissioned from on high to civilise the uncivilised and train the untrained until the time had come when the benevolent conqueror had done his work and could unselfishly retire.... These Pharisaic pretensions were especially necessary to British Imperialism because in England the Puritanic middle class had risen to power and imparted to the English temperament a sanctimonious self-righteousness which refused to indulge in injustice and selfish spoliation except under a cloak of virtue, benevolence and unselfish altruism.[39]

To fight this imperialism that pretended to be benevolent, it was necessary first to create a vanguard of revolutionaries united into an institution:

What is needed now is a band of spiritual workers whose *tapasyā* [spiritual quest] will be devoted to the liberation of India for the service of humanity.... The organisation of Swaraj can only be effected by a host of selfless workers who will make it their sole life-work.... One institution is required which will train and support men to help those who are now labouring under great disadvantages to organise education, to build up the life of the villages, to spread the habit of arbitration, to help the people in time of famine and sickness, to preach Swadeshi. These workers must be selfless, free from the desire to lead or shine, devoted to the work for the country's sake, absolutely obedient yet full of energy.[40]

The influence of this vanguard was not to be judged by the money it raised or arms it collected. The struggle against the despotism of force always began by the sowing of an idea:

Thought is always greater than armies, more lasting than the most powerful and best-organised despotisms.... The idea or sentiment is at first confined to a few men whom their neighbours and countrymen ridicule as lunatics or hare-brained enthusiasts.... The attempt to work [that idea] brings them into conflict with the established power which the idea threatens and there is persecution. The idea creates its martyrs. And in martyrdom there is an incalculable spiritual magnetism which works miracles. A whole nation, a whole world catches the fire which burned in a few hearts; the soil which has drunk the blood of the martyr imbibes with it a sort of divine madness which it breathes into the heart of all its children, until there is but one overmastering idea, one imperishable resolution in the minds of all beside which all other hopes and interests fade into insignificance and until it is fulfilled, there can be no peace or rest for the land or its rulers.... Each despotic rule after the other thinks, "Oh, the circumstances in my case are quite different, I am a different thing from any recorded in history, stronger, more virtuous and moral, better organised. I am God's favourite and can never come to harm." And so the old drama is staged again and acted till it reaches the old catastrophe.[41]

Bande Mataram's call for self-sacrifice in the cause of the nation was phrased in the most stirring rhetoric:

Regeneration is literally re-birth, and re-birth comes not by the intellect, not by the fullness of the purse, not by policy, not by changes of machinery, but by the getting of a new heart, by throwing away all that we were into the fire of sacrifice and being reborn in the Mother. Self-abandonment is the demand made upon us. She asks of us, "How many will live for me? How many will die for me?" and awaits our answer.[42]

It is noteworthy that these conditions created by the broader political struggle of anticolonial nationalism provided the frontier of possibilities for the more militant, violent actions of the revolutionary groups. This entailed both ideological possibilities, involving a critique of the currently prevailing conditions and the imagining of alternative political futures, and strategic and organizational possibilities, including recruiting cadres, building and maintaining organizations, planning and executing militant actions, finding a base of popular sympathy and support, and keeping up activists' morale. Actual and active links between the armed groups and the broader movement, in the form of direct coordination of activities or shared leadership, were not necessarily frequent, even though official agencies were always eager to allege such links. But both groups participated in the same anti-imperialist and nationalist discourse, drew from the same stock of historical memory, often used the same arguments, and ultimately contributed to each other's successes and failures.

EARLY ACTIONS

The first serious "terrorist" act occurred in Bengal in December 1907, when an attempt was made in Midnapore to blow up a train carrying Governor Andrew Fraser. A mine had been laid, and it exploded when the train passed, producing twisted rails and a huge crater, but miraculously, the train was not derailed and the governor escaped unhurt. Some laborers employed by the railway were charged and convicted for having assisted in the effort, but the real authors of the plot were not discovered at this time.

In April 1908, a bomb was thrown at a carriage in Muzaffarpur town in Bihar, killing two European women. The real target was District Judge Douglas Kingsford, who in his earlier posting as a magistrate in Calcutta, had become a hated figure in nationalist circles because he had ordered the flogging of political agitators for defying the police.[43] Khudiram Bose, aged eighteen, was arrested the next day as he was on the run, while Prafulla Chaki, only a year older, when cornered in a gun battle with the police, shot himself to death. It transpired that the two had mistaken the carriage for one that belonged to Kingsford. Khudiram was tried, sentenced, and hanged in Calcutta in August 1908. Khudiram and Prafulla became the first martyrs of the new movement.

The Muzaffarpur bombing immediately led to searches in a house in Maniktala in eastern Calcutta that had been under scrutiny for some time. The police found a stock of arms, ammunition, and chemicals for making bombs, and soon arrested the key figures of the group that had planned the bombing as well as the train wrecking. Barin Ghose, the younger brother of Aurobindo, confessed in order, he said, to save those not already incriminated and "to place the details of our workshops before the country so that others may follow in our footsteps."[44] The next day, Aurobindo too was arrested and charged in the Alipore conspiracy case—the first major trial of a revolutionary group in Bengal.

As the trial proceeded, a former comrade of one of the accused, who had turned approver or state's witness, shot him dead inside the prison, while Asutosh Biswas, the government prosecutor, was killed outside the court. Judge Charles Brailsford sentenced Barin Ghose and Ullaskar Datta to death, and another seventeen to banishment to the Andaman Islands for periods varying from life to seven years. On appeal, the sentences were reduced, and ten of the accused were sent to the infamous Cellular Jail on the Andamans. The case against Aurobindo failed. The Anglo-Indian press alleged that this was because he had studied at Cambridge with Brailsford. Soon after his release, Aurobindo, fearing he would be arrested again, made his way to the French enclave of Chandernagore and subsequently retired forever from political life to Pondicherry.[45]

For the next few years, even though there were not many significant attacks on British targets in Bengal, the revolutionary organizations spread quickly, especially in the districts of eastern Bengal. A list compiled in 1912 by the police intelligence branch of those suspected of being members of secret groups in the

different Bengal districts included more than 800 names along with information on the activities and associations of each person.[46] The list of persons connected with revolutionary groups in Bengal who were actually convicted in
court on various charges added up to 651 at the end of 1920.[47] There was no
doubt that the call to take up arms to rid the country of its foreign rulers held
a great attraction for young men from educated upper-caste Hindu families.

The networks also extended outside Bengal. Hemchandra Das Kanungo,
closely associated with Barin's group, went to Paris in 1906–7 to make contact
with socialist and anarchist revolutionaries, and returned with instructions
on making bombs and maintaining underground organizations.[48] In northern
India, Rashbehari Bose was a key organizer, setting up branches in different
cities, attempting to incite a mutiny within the army, and planning the spectacular bomb attack in 1912 on the viceroy's ceremonial procession in Delhi.
Lord Hardinge, the viceroy, though badly injured, survived the attack. Rashbehari escaped and spent the rest of his life in exile in Japan.

With the outbreak of the world war, some Bengal revolutionaries set up a
plan to import a shipload of German arms by sea. Narendra Bhattacharya was
sent for this purpose to Batavia; he would later become famous in the international Communist movement under his assumed name of M. N. Roy. Jatin
Mukherjee, better known as Bagha, and four others made their way to the
Orissa coast to receive the arms. The plot was discovered by British intelligence:
"It became evident that a definite plot was on foot, under German instigation
and backed by German money, with the co-operation of seditious Indians, to
smuggle arms into India, with the ultimate object of creating a rising against
the British administration."[49] Bagha Jatin's group was intercepted by armed
police and, after a gun battle, surrendered. Bagha Jatin died from his wounds to
become one of the most celebrated martyrs of the movement.

In Bengal itself, a couple of attempts were made in this early phase to assas-
sinate senior British officials, including Governor Fraser; both efforts were attributed to the Anushilan Samiti and both failed. Otherwise, the list of "terrorist outrages" compiled by the police in the period up to 1917 is dominated by
robberies at private homes of wealthy and not-so-wealthy Indians (in a bid to
collect funds for procuring arms), the killing of dozens of Indian police personnel, mostly of low rank, and a few murders of activists suspected of betraying
the cause.[50] These incidents, far more numerous than the few spectacular strikes
against the alien rulers, are not surprisingly largely forgotten in the memorialized history of the revolutionary movement in Bengal.

Strategies and Tactics

There is a trend in the historical literature to characterize this early phase of terrorism in Bengal as an amateurish, almost infantile effort to organize an armed

struggle for national liberation. Hemchandra Kanungo, after spending twelve years in prison in the Andamans, launched a scathing attack in his memoirs on the movement's leadership, ideological and organizational preparedness, and indeed seriousness of purpose.[51] He alleged that the leaders never grasped the importance of adopting proper methods of prolonged secret organization and instead sought quick publicity. As a result, the revolutionary groups were easily infiltrated by the police and their plans thwarted. There was not enough emphasis on rigorous and scientific training in the use of arms, which was why so many of their actions were unsuccessful. Curiously, he placed responsibility for this on the unwillingness of the Indian leaders to learn from the experiences of revolutionaries in other countries. He condemned the Extremist leaders for taking the easy route to rouse the people into political action by instilling in them a cultural hatred of Europeans, often by stoking their religious prejudices. Writing in the late 1920s, Hemchandra was utterly pessimistic about the prospects of Indian freedom. He was enthusiastic neither about Gandhian non-cooperation nor the revolutionary armed struggle, and blamed the indolence, fatalism, irrationality, and ignorance of the "national character."

Later historians have largely agreed with his judgment, at least on the ineffectiveness of the early revolutionary efforts. Amales Tripathi, who was in general appreciative of the role of the Extremists, concluded:

> The Bengal Extremists looked to the idealized "people" and impatiently expected them to rise. When they did not (which was only natural), despair led some of the Extremists to the path of individual terror. They thought, again mistakenly, that through terror it would be "easy to bring the ideas of revolution home to the common people."[52]

Sumit Sarkar, the historian of the Swadeshi movement, has a similar evaluation:

> Taken as a whole, it is difficult to avoid the conclusion that revolutionary terrorism was a heroic failure. The British were certainly badly frightened, as shown by the intensity of repression, but their administration was never in any real danger of collapsing. The bombs took far greater toll of Indian subordinates than of their white overlords.... [L]acking a peasant base, the revolutionaries could never rise to the level of real guerrilla action or set up "liberated areas" in the countryside. As for the average educated Indian, he derived vicarious satisfaction from the deeds of the heroes, and watched and admired—from a distance.[53]

This assessment is entirely reasonable if one takes "revolutionary terrorism" as one particular organized form of nationalist struggle, contending with other forms such as liberal constitutionalism, Gandhian noncooperation, or agrarian agitation. There is no doubt that the contemporary debates were framed as being between these rival forms of political action. Modern Indian historiography has, for the most part, followed that framework by continuing to evaluate the relative successes and failures of those competing tendencies. But if all these movements are regarded as components of a single formation of anticolonial nationalism, linked to each other by complex discursive and organizational connections, then any judgment on "successes and failures" would no longer be so straightforward. Thus, even the apparent failure of one tendency, judged by its own terms, might produce the effect, through unforeseen discursive possibilities, of enabling the success of another tendency. Historians of nationalism have become far more aware in the last two decades, following the pathbreaking work of Benedict Anderson, of the subtle yet powerful working of the nationalist imagination, enabled by the print, visual, and aural media, in forging large anonymous communities.[54] The early history of revolutionary terrorism in Bengal needs to be seen from this more recent analytic perspective.

It is not true to say that the Bengal leadership at this time had no conception of the broader political context and horizon of the different elements of armed resistance to colonial rule, or that it was ignorant of or uninterested in the historical experiences of other nationalist struggles. In fact, if one takes the weekly *Yugāntar* as a platform where the intellectual leaders of the Extremist movement such as Aurobindo, Bhupendranath Dutt, Sakharam Ganesh Deuskar, and Debabrata Bose came together with revolutionary activists such as Barin Ghose and Upendranath Banerji, then one finds considerable discussion on the history of revolutionary struggles in Europe, the Americas, and Asia as well as the specific strategies and tactics of modern warfare, including guerrilla war. In particular, three examples from recent history were repeatedly explored: the unification of Italy as a successful case of nationalist armed struggle against imperial rule (Giuseppe Mazzini's life was held up as exemplary), the continuing struggles in Ireland as an instance of armed anticolonial resistance, and the military successes of Japan as a demonstration of what could be achieved with sovereign nationhood. There was also a fair amount of discussion on guerrilla tactics in the Anglo-Boer War.[55]

In each case, the lesson drawn was the moral legitimacy and historical viability of nationalist armed resistance:

> Revolutionaries have the right to destroy the established ruling authority. When the social body is sick and decrepit, when a flood of oppression sweeps the whole country ... then if the subjects seek to destroy the oppressive ruling power, surely it must be hailed as a sign of their humanity and vitality. A nation that lacks the spirit of sacrifice and valour might think that begging for favours is the best way to deal with the situation, but countries like Italy or Japan would be ashamed to suffer such an indignity.[56]

When foreign rulers such as the English accuse all Indians of sedition, it is a meaningless charge.... When Russia and Japan in their recent war tried their utmost to destroy each other, neither accused the other of sedition.... England has occupied India by deception.... Hence there is no legality in her occupation of India; indeed, at every step one finds the grossest injustice and immorality.... So if the entire nation desires to end its subjection and become free no matter what, then whose demand is right in the eyes of justice—that of the English or of the Indians? We must say that no ruler has the right to shackle the desire for freedom—there is simply nothing else to be said.[57]

In fact, once the goal had been declared as complete and sovereign independence, and not some form of representative government within the British Empire, it was historical knowledge that told the Extremist leaders that such an objective had been never reached without armed conflict—from the struggle for independence in North and South America to the unification of Italy. Upendranath Banerji told the story of a holy man from Gujarat who came to the Jugantar Party hideout in Maniktala and tried to persuade the young men there that national independence could be achieved without bloodshed. The revolutionaries were incredulous. "Has that ever happened?" they asked. Upendranath thought the idea was little more than a tale from the Arabian Nights.[58]

Yugāntar published two long serialized tracts on modern war strategies— one called "War is the Law of Creation," and the other "The Theory of Revolution."[59] The first, clearly based on military manuals, contained long and detailed discussions on modern guns (the Mauser rifle and Howitzer cannon were particular favorites) and shells (including shells that release shrapnel and poisonous gases), trench warfare, sharpshooters, storming parties, engineers, lines of communication, and several installments on guerrilla tactics.[60] The second serialized tract dealt with the moral justification of revolutionary movements ("This is the law of creation. All created things must decay with time. They must be destroyed and recreated with new life.... Revolution is the true basis of peace. A peace induced by decay is no peace; indeed, it is a sickness."), the collection of arms from home and abroad, the collection of funds, temporary conditions of unrest caused by revolutionary upheavals ("inevitable, but that is no reason to desist from doing what is ultimately good for the country"), the shaping of public opinion through newspapers, literature, music, theater, and secret meetings, and the methods of removing an oppressive regime.[61] The series ended by proclaiming:

It could be asked: what is the point in destroying the previous regime if the intention is to set up another centralized power in the same place? The answer is: the power that stands as an obstacle to the moral, spiritual, economic, physical and mental progress of the entire country must be destroyed and replaced by a ruling power that will actively support and facilitate such progress. That is the reason and objective of the revolution.[62]

This can only be seen as one of the earliest statements of an idea that would become dominant in the Indian national movement as a whole: establishing an independent, sovereign nation-state as a condition for all-round national development.

If there was a more specific theory behind these early attempts at armed revolution, it was one that could be called the theory of exemplary action. A favorite argument that was frequently cited in the literature of the day was the huge disparity between the small number of British officials and soldiers in India and the millions over whom they ruled. *Yugāntar* quoted a British visitor as saying:

> An Indian once said to a friend of mine: "It is very extraordinary that the British should maintain their hold of India; for there are so few of you and so many of us that if you could all be collected together in one spot, and each of us were to take a pinch of dust between his thumb and forefinger and sprinkle it upon you, you would all be buried under a mountain a mile high."[63]

Given this disparity, the claim went, if even a small fraction of Indians could be motivated to actively resist the British military superiority, then British rule would become unviable.

> If even one-tenth of the people of the country feel in their hearts the pain [of subjection], then when the English seek to test their strength by deploying their soldiers, the unarmed resistance will turn violent, causing a huge conflagration. Out of that sacrificial fire will emerge the goddess, promising protection; on her forehead will be written in burning letters—LIBERTY.[64]

The operative part of the strategy was thus to initiate a series of assassinations of British officials by a few brave revolutionaries prepared to sacrifice their lives to break the climate of fear and hopelessness.

> Hundreds of thousands of people die every year in this country from epidemics and famine. Do we not have ten thousand sons of Bengal who are prepared to embrace death in order to avenge the humiliation of the motherland? The English in this country number no more than 150,000. How many English officials are there in each district? If you are determined, you can put an end to English rule in one day.... Give up your lives by first taking lives. Sacrifice your life at the altar of liberty. The worship of the goddess will not be complete without the sacrifice of blood.[65]

IGNITING THE IMAGINATION

It is interesting that even when historians have characterized the efforts of the terrorists as a failure, they have remarked on the effect their actions had on the nation's morale. Tripathi wrote:

> They might be wrong. But as Yeats asked about the Easter risers:
> > "And what if excess of love
> > Bewildered them till they died?"
> And was such sacrifice altogether in vain? The land brooded over the Martyr's memory.... [I]ts imagination was stirred to its depths and the apathy of centuries disturbed.... When Gandhi gave his call to a more arduous struggle, more arduous because it was non-violent, India was ready.[66]

It is not clear at all from this account, however, why the failed actions and deaths of a few individuals should have such a miraculous impact on millions of Indians of the next generation. Ramesh Chandra Majumdar, who spent several pages defending the moral and strategic reasons given by the revolutionaries for their actions, concluded:

> The revolutionaries galvanized the political consciousness of the country in a way that nothing else could, and left a deep impress upon all the subsequent stages of our political advance. They really commenced the national struggle for freedom as we conceive it today.... Even today when we think of the true national movement for freedom, our minds fly back, at one leap, clear over half a century, to those who conceived their country as Mother-goddess and worshipped her with their own lives as offerings.[67]

But other than mentioning the popular songs about Khudiram's execution or the thousands joining Kanailal Datta's funeral procession after he was hanged, Majumdar does not explain why the actions of the revolutionaries of 1908 should make them the pioneers of the political movement of Indian freedom.

The problem lies in trying to measure the linear impact of the so-called terrorist movement, defined by a distinct ideology and strategy, in comparison with other competing movements. Instead, if one looks for the horizontal spread achieved by certain events in facilitating the imagination of a political community called the nation, one might better appreciate the historical effects and significance of the early revolutionary movement in Bengal. Consider the following description from official sources of the funeral procession of Kanailal Datta, one of the accused in the Alipore conspiracy case, who along with fellow accused Satyen Bose, killed their former comrade Naren Gossain in prison after Naren turned approver. Kanai's hanging on November 10, 1908, was announced in the press.

> An extraordinary scene was witnessed at Kalighat at the time of the cremation of Kanai, whose body after the execution was made over to his relations for disposal. Crowds thronged the road, people pushing past one another to touch the bier. The body was strewn with flowers and anointed with oil. Many women, to all appearances of a highly respectable class, followed the funeral procession wailing, while men and boys thronged round shouting "Jai Kanai"! This Kanai Lal Dutt was a person of humble origin, a weaver by caste.... He gloried in the deed he had committed and went to his execution without flinching. After the cremation his ashes were being sold in Calcutta, as much as Rs. 5 an ounce being paid by some enthusiasts. It is believed that the supply was made to suit the demand, and that the vast amount of ashes sold in Calcutta as the ashes of Kanai Lal Dutt was fifty times the genuine amount that ever existed. This affair had a most pernicious effect on the minds of the youths of Bengal; so much so that in the following January, Lalit Mohan Ganguli, ... on being arrested ... made a false confession to having murdered Sub-Inspector Nanda Lal Banerji. He subsequently admitted that he had made this false confession because it was the dream of his life to have a funeral like Kanai Lal Dutt's.[68]

How are we to understand this event? Kanai had been guilty of shooting to death a former comrade who had betrayed the cause and whose evidence would be used against the accused. Did that make Kanai a popular hero? There was some skillful plotting involved in smuggling a revolver into the prison and arranging to meet the approver, who was kept isolated from the other prisoners, but that was not why the people revered him.[69] It was, everyone said, his self-lessness—volunteering to do the job in order, possibly, to lighten his comrades's sentences by eliminating Naren, who would then become unavailable to testify against them in court. Kanai knew, of course, that he would never be able to escape and that a death sentence was inevitable. Yet not once did he break down or repent, repeating several times during his trial that if the situation arose, he would do it again. It was the patently disinterested honesty of his act, and the fact that he was punished with death for it, that made him an object of reverence. Stories about Kanai's resolution in the face of interrogation, threats, and inducements circulated in the Bengali press after court reporters managed to learn about them from the accused in the Alipore conspiracy case.[70]

On the morning that he was to be hanged, there were hundreds waiting outside the prison gate even before daybreak. The funeral procession is said to have been the largest Calcutta had seen until then.[71] Furthermore, even as people tried to make sense of this extraordinary set of events in terms of traditional notions of heroism or martyrdom, the reason behind Kanai's death appeared as something completely novel. "He died for the country," people said. Yet what

Figure 22. *The Hanging of Khudiram*, chromolithograph, c. 1940. *Courtesy: Christopher Pinney*

was this entity called the country that could claim the sacrifice of a young life and turn thousands of unrelated people into a single community of mourners? It is at such moments of shared experience that the nation as an imagined community is born.

It is relevant to add that the colonial government was quick to learn from this incident.

> After the wild scene attendant on the funeral of Kanai Lal Dutt, the Government disposed of the bodies of persons executed for political murders, inside the jail wall, and all demonstrations of the kind were prohibited. This has doubtless put a stop to the determination that existed in many youthful minds to make an end like Kanai.[72]

Or take the famous song about Khudiram's execution that began to circulate soon after his death and became one of the most widely sung nationalist verses in Bengal. Khudiram's execution had been a great sensation, and Valentine Chirol, reporting in the *Times* of London, noted that Khudiram had become "a martyr and a hero. Students and many others put on mourning for him and schools were closed for two or three days as a tribute to his memory. His photographs had an immense sale, and by-and-by the young Bengalee bloods took to wearing *dhotis* with Khudiram Bose's name woven into the border of the garment."[73] The song was truly a folk creation, because in spite of the intense historiographical attention to the details of the revolutionary movement in Bengal, no one has been able to name its author.

> Bid me farewell, mother, just once; I'm off on a trip.
> With a smile on my lips, I'll wear the noose; all of India will watch....
> Saturday at ten: the judge's court was bursting with people.
> For Abhiram it was transportation, for Khudiram death by hanging....
> After ten months and ten days, I'll be born again at my aunt's.
> If you don't recognize me then, mother, look for the noose around my neck.[74]

An imputed kinship, a son like him in every home, any ordinary boy who could become extraordinary in death and be born again in another ordinary home—such is the nation, consisting of innumerable ordinary people united by an imagined kinship. Once again, the nation is a community born out of mourning, with thousands of anonymous persons sharing their grief over a young man's death. Why grief? Because of the sheer unselfish disinterestedness of Khudiram's violent act and the retribution as punishment exacted for it by the colonial government.

Khudiram's attempt at assassination failed, because he chose the wrong target. He expressed his regrets in court for having killed two innocent women, but announced that if he were to get a second chance, he would go after Kingsford again. Unlike the judgment of historians, the popular imagination appears to have been captivated by the amateurishness of the whole attempt: its youthfulness, lack of careful calculation, and unwillingness to weigh costs and benefits—in short, its remoteness from the world of professional politics. It is this that explains the sudden, perceptible expansion of the boundaries of "the nation" in the period following the early revolutionary activities—something that could never have been achieved by the cumulative addition of constituencies by the organized politics of nationalist mobilization.

Indeed, the violent actions of the early revolutionaries and their "sacrifice" brought about by the inevitable retributions exacted by the state constituted that catastrophic moment when the law-preserving violence of the colonial regime was shown up for what it was: a myth. "Far from inaugurating a purer sphere," Walter Benjamin has observed, "the mythical manifestation of immediate violence shows itself fundamentally identical with all legal violence, and turns suspicion concerning the latter into certainty of the perniciousness of its historical function, the destruction of which thus becomes obligatory."[75] Why did Khudiram or Kanailal, pure of heart, guided by nothing other than love for their compatriots, have to die at the gallows? What could be more unjust than that? The answer was: they had to die because the law of the colonial regime was the manifestation of a fundamental system of injustice. Their sacrifice was a reminder to the nation that the system of colonial injustice had to be destroyed:

> This very task of destruction poses again, in the last resort, the question of a pure immediate violence that might be able to call a halt to mythical violence. Just as in all spheres God opposes myth, mythical violence is confronted by the divine.... If mythical violence is law-making, divine violence is law-destroying.... Mythical violence is bloody power over mere life for its own sake, divine violence pure power over all life for the sake of the living. The first demands sacrifice, the second accepts it.[76]

It is curious that when, more than a decade after the first actions of the Bengal revolutionaries, Gandhian activists launched their nonviolent campaign to break the laws of the colonial state, they invoked the same rhetoric of sacrifice. Nonviolent noncooperation was, in fact, an insistent invitation to the colonial power to use its law-preserving violence in the most immediate way possible—by inflicting injury on the bodies of the agitators. Congress volunteers were bound by the pledge of sacrifice, offering their bodies to the state's violence. Even when the state refused to inflict harm on the body, Gandhian nonviolence could employ the extreme technique of the fast unto death, making the imperialist state complicit in the destruction of the lives of its colonized subjects. The myth of legitimacy of legal violence is thus broken; the nation is galvanized into a collective desire for the destruction of the colonial state.

Contrary to the reasoned arguments of historians about the strategic efficacy of armed versus peaceful methods of anti-imperialist struggle, popular memory seems to judge the heroes and martyrs of both movements by the same criterion of sacrifice. This is what explains the indiscriminate coexistence of terrorists and Gandhians in the hagiography of popular nationalism—in songs and theater, textbooks and children's literature, calendar prints and portrait galleries, and street names and statuary. Looking at the popular prints of nationalist heroes circulating in the bazaars of small-town India, Christopher Pinney found that armed revolutionaries such as Khudiram or Bhagat Singh appeared to attract as much reverence as Mahatma Gandhi or Jawaharlal Nehru.[77] It is the same indiscriminate memory that Shahid Amin encountered in his research in Chauri Chaura, where Congress volunteers and police personnel, arsonists and victims, all now participate equally in the remembered struggle for freedom in which they had all sacrificed their lives.[78] "Forget your quibbles about strategies and tactics, about ends and means," the popular nationalist imagination seems to say. "In the greater narrative of the nation, they are irrelevant, confusing and misleading us into fruitless debates, and succeeding only in hiding what was really at issue—namely, the fundamental illegitimacy of the legally constituted order. That is what we all wanted to destroy and replace by a new constituent power—ourselves."

FOOTBALL AS A MANLY SPORT

Elizabeth Kolsky highlights the widely prevalent, but rarely researched phenomenon of everyday white violence in colonial India.[79] In particular, she details the violent behavior of white employers against their servants, white soldiers against Indian civilians, and white planters in frontier territories such as Assam. The rule of law seldom provides a remedy for such daily violence. The point needs to be borne in mind as we shift focus here to another activity that became popular on the grounds of Fort William: football.

Like many other things British and urban, soccer, or "association football," to use its proper name, appeared in Calcutta soon after its emergence in British cities. Being a largely working-class sport in Britain, it was played in the late nineteenth century by British soldiers stationed in India as well as Europeans and Eurasians in the railway, police, and other services. It was also adopted enthusiastically by rapidly growing numbers of Indians, who started neighborhood football clubs in cities like Calcutta. The best white teams played against one another on the sprawling grounds of Fort William in the center of the city. The Indian teams played barefoot in sundry open spaces in the native quarters.

An argument has been made that the "games ethic" of Victorian public schools became a useful pedagogical tool for disciplining a colonized middle class into civilized citizens of the empire.[80] From the late nineteenth century, European schoolteachers and missionaries tried to introduce the game among Indian students in schools and colleges as part of a general effort to inculcate physical training along with the moral lessons of hard work, team spirit, and obedience to authority. In the case of Bengal, there was the additional consideration of instilling "manliness" among a people long regarded by the British as cowardly, effeminate, and physically weak. In the context of the new sociobiological theories of race, the physical deficiency of the Bengalis was, not surprisingly, linked to the backward practices of their culture, such as their sedentary habits, poor diet, and child marriage.

The new Bengali middle class smarted under these accusations. In the political arena, it bitterly contested the charge that the English-educated Bengali was physically or culturally incapable of carrying out with equal distinction the public responsibilities then vested exclusively in Europeans. From the Ilbert Bill controversy of 1883–84 to the agitations over the Age of Consent Bill in 1891, organizations of educated Bengalis publicly disputed the allegation of cultural backwardness. On the flip side, however, these accusations triggered within the *bhadra* (respectable) upper-caste Hindu community of Bengal an internal movement of social reform that included a scathing self-criticism of the effete culture of the Calcutta *babu*, the promotion of new norms of conjugal family life, and the inculcation of new habits of bourgeois self-discipline. It is in this light that educated Bengali men in the late nineteenth century took to physical training in gymnasiums, wrestling arenas, and football clubs. The games ethic, in other words, was appropriated by the Bengali middle class and turned into an instrument for matching up to the power of the British.[81] From the point of view of imperial pedagogy, the introduction of football into Bengali society therefore had unintended effects.

We have already mentioned in previous chapters that several arenas of colonial civil society were split along racial lines in the second half of the nineteenth century. Businesses, schools and colleges, clubs and literary societies, and spaces of entertainment were, as if by mutual consent, segregated into separate arenas where Europeans and Indians often pursued the same activities of modern economic and cultural life without coming together in the same institutions. This divide was also an important condition that enabled the nationalist formulation of an independent cultural project of Indian modernity that would not be a mere imitation of the West. We have shown in the previous chapter how the separation and subsequent emergence of a nationalist theater marked the history of the Calcutta stage.

The arena of sports was something of an exception to this colonial history. Here too, the sporting clubs were quite strictly segregated on racial lines. But from quite early on, perhaps rather serendipitously, a competitive domain was created where European and Indian teams met as rivals. This opened up a sphere of public life in the colonial city that was mixed yet deeply racialized.

In 1889, a Trades Cup was launched, presented by "the trading Community of Calcutta"—meaning the European business houses—and organized by the Dalhousie Football Club, to be played for "by bonafide Football Clubs only."[82] The Sovabazar Club, patronized by the influential Deb family of Sobhabazar, was the only Indian team that was allowed to compete. It lost in the first round. In 1892, though, Sovabazar defeated East Surrey Regiment by two goals to one in an early round of the Trades Cup; it was the first time an Indian team beat a British military team on the Calcutta Maidan. In 1893, the Indian Football Association (IFA) was started to run an IFA Shield tournament along the lines of the English FA Cup. Each year, two or three Indian teams were allowed to play, even though Indians had no place in the association itself.

It is important to appreciate the strategic location of this new arena of competitive sport in the public space of the colonial city. The IFA Shield was played on the *gader mâth* or fort grounds, supervised by an association of white clubs and white referees. The competitors were mostly British regimental teams from different military stations all over India. But because it was an open tournament, Indian clubs also had the right to compete. The rule of freedom, in other words, had to apply. As always, it was subject to the rule of colonial difference as well. In this case, the criterion invoked was a limit on the number of local teams that could play without curtailing the number of visiting teams and thereby jeopardizing the "all-India" character of the tournament. For several years, only two or three Indian teams from Calcutta were allowed to participate in the IFA Shield.

The Maidan at the turn of the twentieth century was generally not a place where Indian residents of Calcutta would venture; it was for all practical purposes reserved for the recreation of Europeans only. So when Indians began to flock to the football grounds to watch the progress of one or the other team from the northern quarters, they must have felt the thrill of having transgressed a protected zone of power.

There was something else about the domestication of football on the soil of Bengal that involved its basic techniques and had a great impact on its cultural significance well into the early decades of the twentieth century. Most Indian footballers, even those appearing at the highest competitive levels of the time, played barefoot, without the aid of boots. This partly had to do with the way most of them were introduced to the game as young boys—football, after all, demanded no equipment other than a ball and some open space. It also had to do with the fact that unlike Europe, where shoes or boots were the usual everyday footwear, most people in Bengal wore sandals that did not cover the whole foot. One can easily imagine Bengali schoolboys discarding their slippers (if they were wearing them at all) before running excitedly on to a football field.

Interestingly, players developed technical skills of dribbling, passing, shooting, and the sliding tackle that fully utilized the flexible movements of the bare foot, including the toes. Yet this also entailed a grievous technical flaw. Players with bare feet had little chance against booted ones on a slippery surface. This was a particularly critical drawback for players in Calcutta, where competitive football was played during the monsoon months of June, July, and August. Football lore in the city is replete with stories of how the prospects of an Indian club pitted against a British side were dashed by a heavy afternoon downpour, just as there are tales of fervent prayers at the Kali temple in Kalighat or Thanthania being answered by the goddess providentially delaying the showers until after the final whistle was blown.

Football actually is especially well suited to the competitive exercise of controlled collective violence. It is a contact sport in which physical stature and strength play a significant part, even though speed and skill are just as important. But it is above all a team sport that lives on the continuously coordinated movements of all twenty-two players and the ball, and thus requires the mental

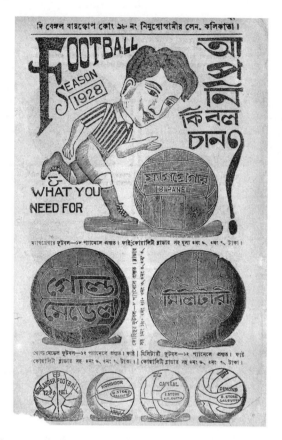

Figure 23. Advertisement for football. *Source: P. M. Bagchi's Panjikā 1331, 1924–25. Courtesy: Centre for Studies in Social Sciences, Calcutta*

powers of strategic thinking and execution. The deployment and movement of forces belonging to the two sides across the territorial space of the football field, with each side defending a citadel that the other is trying to penetrate, easily lends the game to the analogy of field warfare. It is hardly startling, then, that not only when national teams are playing against one another but also in club football, the support for rival teams so often tends to break along ethnic lines. Without resorting to functionalist theories of ritual violence as a social safety valve or means of letting off steam, it is nonetheless crucial to appreciate the cultural significance of what is going on in a game of football watched by thousands of rival supporters.

It is with all of this allegorical baggage that football came to be seen as a manly sport. In the context of Bengal, where Indian players generally played barefoot against British players wearing boots, the question of manliness acquired a somewhat-special significance. There was added manliness, as it were, in a barefoot player coming out the winner against a crunching tackle from a booted player, stealing the ball with a deft flick of the toes, or slicing through the defense with a series of magical feints and dribbles. This manliness, in short, was the ability to prevail over a technologically superior opponent by sheer courage, skill, and cleverness.[83]

The sentiment was well summed up by the legendary Samad, who played mostly for the Eastern Bengal Railways and Mohammedan Sporting in the 1920s and 1930s. His loping runs down the left flank and mesmerizing dribbling skills made him a mythical hero of the Maidan. Migrating to East Pakistan after the country's partition, he came back to the Maidan once in 1962 to watch a game. All the players were now wearing the regulation football boots. On being asked for his comments, Samad said, "It wasn't a bad game, but it could just as easily have been played by women."[84]

FOOTBALL AND NATIONALISM

The turning point in the history of Calcutta football, and some say the history of nationalism itself in Bengal, was the astonishing victory in the IFA Shield final of 1911 of Mohun Bagan, a club located in the northern part of the city, over the East Yorkshire Regiment. The club had been patronized by some eminent Bengali professional families, such as that of the lawyer Bhupendra Nath Basu, a moderate politician who held important government offices and later became president of the Indian National Congress. His nephew, Sailen Basu, who was a junior officer in the British Indian army, became the club's secretary in 1900, and tried to drill its middle-class Bengali players, many of them college students, into the rigors of physical training, gymnastics, and tactical lessons to which army footballers were used. The team began to see success in several local tournaments, winning the Trades Cup three times in a row between 1906 and 1908 after defeating local European and Eurasian sides. In 1909, Mohun Bagan was allowed entry into the IFA Shield, but lost in the first round, doing only slightly better the next year by moving as far as the second round.

Nothing spectacular could have been expected from Mohun Bagan, therefore, when it won the first round of the 1911 tournament. Fortunately, the weather was mostly dry and sunny in July that year, except when Mohun Bagan met Rangers for a place in the quarter finals. Notwithstanding the soggy field, Mohun Bagan managed to cling on to a two-to-one lead, thanks to a superlative effort by goalkeeper Hiralal Mukherjee, who saved as many as three penalties. When the club beat Rifle Brigade by a solitary goal from Bijaydas Bhaduri and went into the semifinals of India's premier football championship, the city suddenly woke up to the fact that history was about to be made. Thousands crowded to watch Mohun Bagan play the Middlesex Regiment to a one-to-one draw, and bitterly complained afterward that the army team's equalizer was gained by their forwards rushing on goalkeeper Hiralal, knocking him down, and pushing the ball into the goal with their hands. In the replay, however, Mohun Bagan scored a resounding victory by three goals to nil, helped by an unfortunate injury to the Middlesex goalkeeper Pigot.

July 29, 1911. The match was supposed to start at 5:30 p.m. but the crowds began to assemble starting in the morning. Special trains ran between Burdwan and Howrah, and extra boats ferried passengers across the river to Calcutta. The western side of the Calcutta Football Club grounds had white stands for its members—all Europeans—while temporary green stands were put up on the northern side for spectators with tickets priced at two rupees (they were selling for fifteen rupees on the day before the match).[85] The total capacity inside could not have been more than four or five thousand. Outside the fencing on the eastern side, opportunist entrepreneurs had set up rows of shipping boxes arranged like galleries going up to ten or twelve feet. On the southern side, people were standing on top of parked bicycles, and behind them were rows of people on the sloping glacis of Fort William, known to generations of football watchers on the Maidan as "the ramparts." There were, it was reported, perhaps eighty to a hundred thousand people that day in and around the football grounds, most of whom had no chance of seeing anything of the game.[86] Still, they were informed of the game's progress by kites in the sky bearing the latest score. Several city newspapers had temporary telephone lines installed on the grounds so that the result could be immediately reported to their offices—the first time this had been done for a sports event in Calcutta.

After a goalless first half (of twenty-five minutes, which was considered sufficiently punishing on a tropical summer afternoon), a hush descended on the assembled multitude when Jackson put East Yorks in the lead. But five minutes before the final whistle, the crowd exploded when skipper Shibdas Bhaduri, after frequently switching positions with his look-alike brother Bijaydas to confuse the opponents, made a run down the left to equalize. Then, with barely a minute left, "Slippery" Shibdas, as he came to be known among white players and journalists, dribbled through the defense once more, and facing a solitary Cressey in goal, kept his head and passed the ball to the unmarked Abhilash Ghosh, who drove home the winner.[87]

The scenes that followed had been never seen before on the Calcutta Maidan. People went delirious, not knowing how to react to something so unprecedented. "Hats, handkerchiefs, umbrellas and sticks were waved," reported *Amrita Bazar Patrika*, while Reuters added in a dispatch for British newspapers that the Bengalis in the crowd tore off their shirts and waved them.[88] The Mohun Bagan players were taken on an open carriage in a procession to the north of the city.

Figure 24. Cartoon on the 1911 IFA Shield final by unknown artist. *Source: Arbi (1955) 2002, 128*

A group of Muslim young men joined the procession at Harrison Road with a large brass band. All the way up Cornwallis Street, women blew conch shells and showered flowers on the players from the balconies.

The Reuters report on the game published in the *Times* of London remarked: "The absence of all racial feeling was noticeable. The European spectators were good humoured, and the Bengalis cheered the losing team." But the *Times* correspondent added: "The Bengal papers claim that the success is a proof of the physical potentialities of their race."[89] Indeed, in an editorial titled "The Immortal Eleven," *Amrita Bazar Patrika*, the leading nationalist daily, first emphasized the need for racial amity:

> May God bless the Immortal Eleven of Mohan Bagan for raising their nation in the estimation of the Western people by their brilliant feat on Saturday last.... The

victory is no doubt ours and that in the line of physical culture wherein the Bengalees at any rate were so long held to be lamentably deficient.... But if we are to be true to Hindu instinct and culture such triumphs should not at all be exploited for other ends than establishing the best of relations between the two races. These are divine events meant for facilitating the harmonious working of two great peoples by curbing to a certain extent the pride of the one and contributing to the growing self-consciousness of the other.

It then pointed to an implication that was directly political:

We must also ask the attention of the Government to the moral of this incident. Is it not high time that they did some thing to give full play to the developing physical powers of our countrymen? Should those materials be allowed to rust unused? ... We hope that the incident ... will lead the Government to review their estimate of Indian capacity even in the matter of defending the Empire when the need arises.[90]

The demand, if indeed it was one, was put mildly, well within the recognized boundaries of the discourse of loyalty to the empire.

As a matter of fact, when the need did arise barely three years later with the outbreak of World War I, Indians were heavily recruited to defend the British Empire, and sent out by the thousands to war in the Middle East and Europe. But in 1911, still the heyday of high imperialism, the cultural discourse of racial stereotypes was alive and kicking. The *Statesman*, a daily identified with the British community of Bengal, offered this retort to the *Amrita Bazar* suggestion that Bengalis had demonstrated their capacity to be good soldiers:

It is much more desirable that the Bengalis themselves should perceive that, when physical energy has been developed by healthy sports, the effect ought to be to divert the attention of the most promising young men of the country from sedentary pursuits to out-door occupations which are at present not agreeable to them.... [I]t will be strange if young men who have undergone the stimulating discipline of football and cricket do not feel the attraction of the career offered by farming and other industries which demand physical strength and endurance.[91]

Amrita Bazar Patrika was incensed:

Why does our contemporary evade the point and raise a side-issue? What we contended was that when the Indians can display such excellence in English manly games, which require not only physical endurance but such qualities as strong will, intrepid courage and powers of organisation, they might as well be utilised in the battle-field.

The editorial pointed out that the Bengalis were physically strong a hundred years ago, and Gilbert, the first Lord Minto, had described them in 1807 as "tall, muscular, athletic figures, [and] perfectly shaped."

> Where is now this race ...? And how did they manage to make themselves such fine specimens of humanity? The reasons are not far to seek. In those days the people had their national games.... Every village at that time had its gymnasium and it was a religious duty with its male inhabitants, young and old, to spend their evenings ... in physical culture. They had not to attend courts as litigants and lawyers ... or to drive quills in Government or mercantile offices.... They had enough of food; the prices of all necessary articles were cheap; fish, milk and vegetables more than abundant; they had good drinking water and malaria and cholera were unknown.
>
> There are those who attribute the physical deterioration of the race mainly to early marriage. But be it noted that the fine race of whom Lord Minto spoke in such rapturous terms, were the fruits of that system of marriage. The eleven of the Mohan Bagan Foot Ball Team are we believe also the products of such marriage....
>
> We cannot help repressing a smile at the proposal of the "Statesman" that, Indians, including, we believe, the Mohan Bagan Team, ... should take to agriculture. Do English youths who distinguish themselves on the play ground ultimately turn into agriculturists? ... No, Mr. "Statesman," they deserve a better career than that of hewers of wood and drawers of water.[92]

Amrita Bazar Patrika's glorification of the health and well-being of Bengal's rural people before the advent of British colonialism ravaged the villages was, of course, a familiar theme in the discourse of the Swadeshi movement. The defense of child marriage too was part of the conservative Hindu revivalism that had emerged in the late nineteenth century against liberal attempts to persuade the colonial government to reform Hindu marriage laws. Yet in the aftermath of Mohun Bagan's victory, the initial anxious plea for racial harmony followed by this exchange of barely disguised racial slurs betrayed the presence of a suppressed discourse that the civic space of public debate was not allowed to articulate, but that had free rein on the public field of competitive sport.

It is difficult to elaborate on this with the help of the usual sources that historians use precisely because the public archive in print does not document any evidence of this submerged discourse. But there is enough experiential evidence familiar to many to suggest that things might be said or gestured by fans, almost entirely male, at a football match that would never be allowed in a civic forum. The sporting arena, in other words, even though a public space sometimes inhabited by masses of people, is a rather special public domain not entirely subject to the rules that govern public political discourse, even when sporting loyalties may be deeply implicated in political affiliations.

This is why the question of manliness and race became such a touchy issue in relation to football in the years following Mohun Bagan's victory in the IFA Shield tournament. For the next two decades, while the club maintained its position as the leading Indian football team in the city, it failed to win another trophy, whether the IFA Shield or Calcutta League Championship. Football legend is replete with stories of how Mohun Bagan was the victim of unfair scheduling by an association dominated by white clubs and, above all, biased match supervision by white referees. The club itself, patronized by leading zamindars and loyalist politicians, was always ready to play by the rules and rarely complained about any of these decisions. Nevertheless, the submerged discourse among Mohun Bagan supporters left no room for doubt that the club's misfortunes were entirely due to the arrogance and envy of the British ruling race. As if to compensate, Indians made special heroes of players such as Gostho Paul (dubbed "The Chinese Wall" for his sturdy defensive skills) and Balai Chatterjee who had the physical strength and courage to challenge British regimental players while not giving an inch even when unfairly tackled.

Rakhal Bhattacharya, a sports journalist who first published his history of Calcutta football in 1955, revealed these subterranean currents of racial feeling:

When someone from my own kin [jāt-bhāi] makes your life hell on the football field, then whether you are an armed soldier or the big boss in my office, you must be inferior to me, or at least in no way superior. You can no longer get away with your tricks here. Even if your kin-brother the referee overlooks your villainy, you cannot but be wary of Gostho Paul or Balai Chatterjee. If you try any of your smart tricks with them, with one lightning kick as lethal as a striking viper, they'll send you to hospital or, who knows, perhaps even to hell. And needless to say, you know our Samad. When he twirls his moustache, blows his nose at you and starts his mesmerizing run, all you will do is dance to his tune like a bunch of monkeys.... And that's not the end of it. Don't forget us. When I am sitting in the galleries, there is no rein on my voice and tongue. The torrent of abuse will scare away the ghosts of your forefathers. You are the big boss only when you are in the office; your soldiers can beat and kick me only after I step out of this ground. But when I occupy these stands assigned for my race [svajāti], I am free, oblivious of all restrictions.[93]

In 1929, there was a crisis of sorts over a match between Mohun Bagan and Dalhousie in the Calcutta League. A goal was awarded against Mohun Bagan when goalkeeper Santosh Dutt, in the view of the referee Cameron, leaned over the goal line with the ball while making a save. This caused much resentment among the Mohun Bagan supporters. A few minutes later, when Williams and Dutt both went up for an aerial ball in front of the goal, there was contact between the two players. Williams fell down and had to be carried off the field with, it was later confirmed, a fractured jawbone. Cameron was seen

Figure 25. Spectators at 1928 IFA Shield final between Calcutta Football Club and Dalhousie, photograph. *Source: Arbi (1955) 2002, 17*

speaking to Dutt, at which point the crowds rushed on to the grounds and attacked the officials. A group of army men watching the match used their sticks to beat back the crowds, and rescue the referee and linesmen. There was much pelting of stones, and it was alleged that the Dalhousie Club tent on the Maidan was vandalized.

At a meeting of the IFA council the next day, Thomas Lamb, the president, "deplored the conduct of the Indian section of the spectators as still lacking in true sporting spirit.... He depicted a gruesome picture of a Calcutta racial riot had the Europeans chosen to retaliate." Lamb warned that if such unpleasant incidents occurred again, the Calcutta Football Club, the premier European team of the city, would refuse to play against Indian teams. The meeting then suspended Santosh Dutt for two years on the evidence of MacLaren, the linesman belonging to Dalhousie, even though the referee Cameron was not sure if Dutt had indeed deliberately hit Williams.[94]

The cat had been set among the pigeons. The Indian clubs decided enough was enough and refused to turn up for their remaining league matches. An Indian member of the IFA council was reported as saying, "A feeling of racial hatred was prominent in what Mr Lamb said."[95] A meeting of 600 representatives of 71 Indian football clubs decided "to completely dissociate from the IFA and to take immediate steps to form an Indian association."[96] The IFA council at this time had 8 representatives for 14 European clubs and 4 for 140 Indian clubs. Amid rumors of closed-door negotiations, it was claimed "that Indian clubs will submit to no settlement which will not offer them an equality of status with their Anglo-Indian fellow sportsmen."[97] Finally, at the mediation of Nripendra Nath Sircar, advocate general to the government, a solution was found to the crisis. Lamb expressed regret for his remarks, and a pair of additional seats were provided in the IFA council for Indian clubs.[98] Dutt's suspension was also lifted. Soon after, European supremacy in the IFA ended altogether, and the council was reconstituted with 7 members each representing the European and Indian clubs.

There is little doubt that the 1911 football victory was widely read as more than just a sporting event. Coming at the same time that the partition of Bengal was undone and the province reunited after mass agitations, and following the unprecedented rise of the armed revolutionary movement, it certainly provided a spurt to the public airing of political grievances focused on the racial divide between the rulers and the ruled. A curious glimpse is afforded into this submerged strain in the everyday public life of the period by the following, somewhat trivial incident. A week after the IFA Shield final of 1911, F. A. Roberts, a European passenger on a suburban train, was charged with assaulting Albert Bose, a Bengali passenger. It appeared that Bose was conversing with another Bengali when Roberts barged in and punched Bose. The judge of the Serampore Police Court asked if the conversation was about the recent football match. On being told that it was not, he found Roberts guilty of assault and fined him five rupees.[99]

Was there a more direct political message, concerning the issue of sovereignty, that was also drawn from the result of this remarkable game of football? It is impossible to tell, because every answer is liable to be framed by the anachronistic perspective of hindsight. But Sudhir Chatterjee, the left fullback of the victorious Mohun Bagan team and its only player to play in boots, and who later became a doctor of divinity and right reverend of the Anglican Church, was fond of recounting the story of an elderly Brahmin who approached him that memorable evening during the celebrations as the players were being led away from the grounds. After congratulating him, the old man said, "Well, this job is done." And then, pointing to the Union Jack flying above Fort William, he asked, "But when will you take care of that?"[100]

OFFICIAL RESPONSES

British colonial officials in Bengal were startled by the sudden emergence of revolutionary secret societies actually planning and carrying out armed attacks on selected targets. The similarity in tactics with revolutionary groups in Europe led to the Bengal revolutionaries initially being called "anarchists" and "nihilists"; the term terrorist came into circulation much later.[101] As soon as it became clear that the authorities were faced not with a few stray incidents but instead a continuing political movement, though, they also had to cope with the entirely unprecedented fact that these "crimes and outrages" were being committed not by rebel warlords, insurgent peasants, or habitual criminals but rather by young men from educated, propertied, and socially respected families—by young men who were precisely the products of modern Western education. For British authorities, this posed a completely new set of problems in dealing with political resistance to the empire. The official literature, both public and confidential, on terrorism in Bengal is particularly interesting for this reason.

The point was made most strikingly in the report of the Rowlatt committee set up in 1918 to look into the phenomenon of "sedition" in India. The committee collected figures that showed that of 186 persons convicted for, or killed in, terrorist activities in Bengal between 1907 and 1917, no less than 135 were from bhadralok occupations, and as many as 165 were upper caste.[102] "The circumstance that robberies and murders are being committed by young men of respectable extraction, students at schools and colleges, is indeed an amazing phenomenon the occurrence of which in most countries would be hardly credible."[103] Then why was it happening in Bengal? Needless to say, the explanation was sought in the specific political and cultural influences on the lives of Bengalis belonging to this class.

The initial analysis put the blame squarely on the malicious propaganda and incitement to violence spread by the Extremist press. In 1911, Daly, writing the first comprehensive report on the revolutionary movement in Bengal put together by the intelligence department, opened by mentioning the *Amrita Bazar Patrika* and alleging that

> the true policy of that paper was systematic opposition to all measures of Government, in a spirit of malignant hostility, rather than of honest public-spirited criticism. It lost no opportunity of attacking an European official, and of representing Europeans generally as tyrannical bullies, whose favourite diversion was kicking defenceless Indians.... It was the *Patrika*, I think, that first started the doctrine of retaliation, advising the children of the soil in dealing with Europeans to return frown for frown and blow for blow.[104]

Soon, journals such as *Yugāntar*, *Sandhyā*, and *Bande Mataram* were identified as the chief sources of "seditious" ideas. James Campbell Ker's magisterial survey of the early revolutionary movements has two whole chapters devoted to the contemporary pamphlet literature and nationalist press.[105] But officials were also aware of the difficulty in shutting down the circulation of this printed material. Initially, some faulted "the unwillingness of the Government to take any measures to suppress the audacity of the newspapers"[106] It was quickly discovered that if one paper was forced to close, another appeared in its place. Referring to *Yugāntar*, for instance, Charles Tegart, the most famous (or infamous, depending on one's perspective) counterterrorist police officer, reminded his audience at the Royal Empire Society in London: "In one year successive printers and publishers were five times successfully prosecuted, but the imprisonment of the individuals did not check the trouble, in fact aggravated it. Dummy printers and publishers were appointed from the junior ranks, who gloried in cheap martyrdom and each prosecution advanced the sales."[107] A new Press Act was put in force in 1910, giving the government sweeping powers to shut down, penalize, and confiscate presses charged with printing seditious material. The act served to moderate the tone of the newspapers, but did not stop the flow of young recruits into revolutionary groups.

The official criticism then turned to the state of education in Bengal. Chirol, the Indian correspondent for the *Times*, led the campaign. He complained bitterly about the superficiality of Western education in India, marked by mechanical imitation and cramming, far removed from the actual social and cultural world in which the student lived, and devoid of moral instruction. Secondary education in English, he thought, had expanded too quickly, and now most schoolteachers were Indian, not European. "From the point of view of mere instruction the results have been highly unsatisfactory. From the point of view of moral training and discipline and the formation of character they have been disastrous."[108] The more conservative among senior colonial officials concluded from this that the promotion of Western education in India had been a "grave political miscalculation." Lyall, introducing Chirol's book on the so-called anarchist movements in India, remarked that

> although education is a sovereign remedy for many ills ... yet an indiscriminate or superficial administration of this potent medicine may engender other disorders. It acts upon the frame of an antique society as a powerful dissolvent, heating weak brains, stimulating rash ambitions, raising inordinate expectations of which the disappointment is bitterly resented.[109]

Still, why should a superficial Western education turn young Bengalis from the propertied middle classes into bomb-throwing terrorists? Chirol provided the elements of a cultural-anthropological answer. It was, he said, that lethal combination of religion and modernity called "nationalism" that was the root of the problem.

> There are only two forces that aspire to substitute themselves for British rule.... One is the ancient and reactionary force of Brahmanism, which, having its roots in the social and religious system we call Hinduism, operates upon a very large section ...

of the population who are Hindus. The other is a modern and, in its essence, progressive force generated by Western education, which operates to some extent over the whole area of India, but only upon an infinitesimal fraction of the population recruited among a few privileged castes.... Though both these forces have developed of late years a spirit of revolt against British rule, neither of them has in itself sufficient substance to be dangerous. The one is too old, the other too young. But the most rebellious elements in both have effected a temporary and unnatural alliance on the basis of an illusory "nationalism" which appeals to nothing in Indian history, but is calculated and meant to appeal with dangerous force to Western sentiment and ignorance. It rests with us to break up that unnatural alliance.[110]

British officials in Bengal were fascinated by the presence of religious literature, especially the *Bhagavad Gītā*, in the libraries maintained by the revolutionary groups, the use of religious invocations in the initiation ceremonies for fresh recruits to the Anushilan Samiti, and most of all the seemingly ubiquitous appeal of what was described as the cult of the goddess Kālī. The portrayal of the purported Bengal anarchists as religious fanatics produced by some of the darkest, most mysterious strands in their culture was one way in which the official mind sought to resolve the paradox of Western education giving birth to terrorism: educated Bengalis, despite their knowledge of English, were still susceptible to the secret attractions of a savage religion. Consider this depiction by an ex-colonial writing under the unconvincing pseudonym of Moki Singh:

> Anarchism has a particularly objectionable religious accompaniment. While the initiate kneels at the feet of Mother Kali, represented in her wildest aspect, with matted hair pulled about her head, her bloodshot eyes glaring mercilessly down, her hands squeezing the last life blood out of a dummy man. Two bombs lie at her feet.... The exotic atmosphere bemuses the worshippers, leads them into a trance. Perhaps Mother Kali's hellish eyes have hypnotized them.... The doped struggling worshippers work themselves into a paroxysm of fanatical fervour.... The climax of the ceremony is reached; the anarchists claim another follower....
>
> We have them there, struggling against another depressing aftermath of primitive savagery, working once more from the bestiality that is the cornerstone of anarchism, until they again meet in another orgy.[111]

Once the terrorist had been identified as at core a religious fanatic, the moderating influence of Western education could only be of limited effectiveness. Although high-powered expert teams such as the Rowlatt committee recommended extensive educational reforms as a means to combat terrorism, they concluded that the only effective method was the use of punitive and preventive administrative powers against those most likely to conspire to commit violent acts against the state. The Rowlatt committee was not hopeful of achieving results merely by punishing the offenders:

> We may say at once that we do not expect very much from punitive measures. The conviction of offenders will never check such a movement as that which grew up in Bengal unless all the leaders can be convicted at the outset. Further, the real difficulties have been the scarcity of evidence.... The last difficulty is fundamental and cannot be remedied. No law can direct a court to be convinced when it is not.[112]

The committee considered the possibility of lowering the threshold for admissible evidence in sedition cases, but abandoned the idea because it might not be legally sustainable. The most promising option was preventive detention of potential offenders for which special powers were needed. The Defense of India rules enforced during World War I had given the government such powers, but they would lapse with the war's end. The Rowlatt committee recommended new "emergency" powers to deal with sedition, involving speedy trials, no right of appeal, and detention without trial of suspects.

> By those means alone [the Defense of India rules] has the conspiracy been paralysed for the present, and we are unable to devise any expedient operative according to strict judicial forms which can be relied upon to prevent its reviving, to check it if it does survive, or, in the last resort, to suppress it anew. This will involve some infringement of the rules normally safeguarding the liberty of the subject.[113]

The committee nonetheless was careful to add that the "interference with liberty" must not be penal in character: if suspects were to be detained, they should be kept in a special asylum and not in jail, and no one was to be convicted without a proper judicial trial. Detentions should be supervised by a periodic judicial review of each case. The emergency powers should be for a limited period only, to be renewed by a fresh notification by the government.[114]

Armed with these recommendations, the Imperial Legislative Council passed new laws in March 1919 to give the government special powers to curb seditious activities. The laws were condemned by virtually all sections of Indian opinion, from constitutional liberals to fire-eating revolutionaries. They were condemned for being arbitrary and excessive; indeed, they were condemned for being in violation of the law. Within a few days, Gandhi launched his first nationwide mass campaign against the so-called Rowlatt Act. Despite his fervent calls for nonviolent resistance to the government, the satyagraha was marked by considerable violence and bloodshed in most northern Indian cities.[115] The Rowlatt Act was never put into operation, and following the constitutional reforms in late 1919, was repealed.

That left the government with the conventional legal tool of punishing the offender. But how was revolutionary terrorism to be identified and proved as a crime, and the accused punished in a court of law? Some of the armed actions were merely plans that were never executed; others had been botched up. Most of the leaders, strategists, and ideologues were usually not directly associated with the actions, so how could they be charged with the crime? Most crucially, how could an individual motive be established for each single act committed by each individual offender? The fact was that the crimes in question were not ordinary criminal acts. The revolutionaries's crimes added up to a political of-fense—that of challenging the sovereign powers of the state. How was such a crime to be proved in court?

This is where the idea of conspiracy acquired the solid form of a powerful legal doctrine. With the rise of militant nationalist politics in twentieth-century India, conspiracy became the key legal concept in the construction of revolu-tionary politics as a crime. Leaders might not be present at the scene of an as-sassination, or a bomb could miss its target; plans for an insurrection may never bear fruit, or a revolutionary cell could restrict itself only to secret propaganda and recruitment. Yet all these would come under the umbrella of the most seri-ous political crime if a conspiracy could be proved. The proof of a conspiracy consisted in evidence of the existence of a party, group, or cell, leadership and propaganda, cadre recruitment, secret meetings and communications, the acqui-sition and storage of arms, secret training and indoctrination, and so on. Each of these activities could be proved in court by producing material evidence and the testimony of witnesses.

The conspiracy doctrine allowed these distinct and diverse activities by a large number of often-unconnected individuals to be pooled together in order to constitute a single criminal offense with a single motive shared by all the accused. Beginning with the Alipore conspiracy case of 1908, the history of political trials in British India is marked by a series of famous conspiracy cases each involving dozens—in some cases, hundreds—of accused. Leaders of the conspiracy were usually given the harshest sentences—death, life imprison-ment, or transportation to the Andaman Islands for life.

In this context, it is worth considering the implications of the general ten-dency in British imperial policy to maintain as strictly as possible the forms of legal propriety. The concern, on one level, was prompted largely by the super-visory powers exercised by the British Parliament over colonial policy. Democ-racy at home did not preclude the pursuit of imperialism abroad. But to make the exercise of imperial power in the colonies consistent with the enlightened claims of democratic civility at home, it was essential that colonial governments be seen to act in accordance with the best standards of the law. Colonial govern-ment, in other words, while being necessarily despotic, had to be a despotism under law. The use of state violence in late colonial India, even when it was aimed against rebels, outlaws, or terrorists, was never regarded as a war; it was always a police action that had to be carried out within the ambit of the law as proclaimed for all imperial subjects. When faced with threats such as that of terrorism, colonial governments would frequently complain, as in the report of the Rowlatt committee, of being hamstrung by the overly demanding requirements of the legal system and would ask for special powers to deal with an emergency.

But the effect of this pervasive legalism in British colonial governance was, paradoxically, the relative immunity of the body of positive law from nationalist critique. Extremist or moderate, violent or nonviolent, terrorist or Gandhian, Indian nationalists rarely questioned the positive content of the judicial and penal system built by the British colonial power in India. What they criticized was the legitimacy of the founding power that had made the law. The divine violence invoked in the sacrificial acts of revolutionary terrorists as well as those of Gandhian satyagrahis only sought to expose the myth of the lawmaking power of the colonial regime; it did not aspire to destroy the positive law of the state.

This explains the apparent contradiction of the new constituent power of a sovereign Indian people deciding in the aftermath of independence to preserve in their entireties the judicial system as well as the positive law designed by the colonial state. They were not, as imperial apologists would have it, the gifts of the British Empire to India.[116] Rather, they were seen as technologies of government in universal circulation that lacked, under conditions of imperial rule, a legitimate constituent power to promulgate them into the morally obligatory status of genuine law. This could only be done by the colonial regime's destruction, and the inauguration of sovereign and popular nationhood.

THE LATER PHASE

It remains for us here to briefly sketch the course of terrorism in Bengal in the 1920s and 1930s. The inauguration of constitutional reforms in 1919 led to the release of many revolutionary leaders held in detention. In a significant tactical shift, revolutionary groups, especially the Jugantar Party, decided to join the Swarajya Party of Chitta Ranjan Das, Bengal's preeminent Congress leader, and engage in open constitutional politics. It is said that there was a pact between the Jugantar leaders and Das; in return for political protection, the revolutionaries supplied cadres to Das to help him win support in the Congress district committees for his plan to contest elections and enter the newly formed provincial council.[117] In fact, from this time onward up to independence, the Congress organization in the districts, especially in eastern Bengal, and the provincial committee continued to be dominated by leaders with supposed terrorist links.

The 1920s, then, was a period of relative lull in terrorist activities in Bengal, although several Bengal revolutionaries played important roles in the spread of secret organizations in the United Provinces and Punjab that carried out several daring acts. But as soon as Gandhi's civil disobedience movement was launched in April 1930, there was an explosion of armed actions in Bengal. The most spectacular were the raids in Chittagong on the police and military armories along with the gutting of the telegraph office. The actions were planned for the Easter weekend in deliberate emulation of the Easter rising in Ireland in 1916. After the attacks, the raiders retreated to the hills and were hunted down four days later.[118]

The Chittagong revolutionaries—their leader Surya Sen, who was arrested three years later and hanged; Ambika Chakrabarti, Ganesh Ghosh, Ananta Singh, and Loknath Bal, who were all transported to the Andamans; and two women, Pritilata Wahdedar, who chose to swallow cyanide rather than surrender, and Kalpana Dutt, who spent nine years in prison—became stellar figures in the growing pantheon of revolutionary martyrs and heroes in Bengal. The Chittagong raids had an electrifying effect. "The younger members of all parties," an official report said,

> clamoured for a chance to emulate the Chittagong terrorists. Their leaders could no longer hope, nor did they wish, to keep them back, for the lesson of Chittagong had impressed itself on their minds no less than on those of their more youthful followers, and there seemed to be no reason why their over-cautious policy should be maintained. Recruits poured into the various groups in a steady stream, and the romantic appeal of the raid attracted into the fold of the terrorist party women and young girls, who from this time onwards are found assisting the terrorists as housekeepers, messengers, custodians of arms and sometimes as comrades.[119]

Assassination attempts against senior British officials came thick and fast. Francis Lowman, the inspector general of police, was shot dead in Dacca; Norman Simpson, the inspector general of prisons, was gunned down in his office inside the Writers' Buildings in Calcutta; and Tegart narrowly escaped death when his car was bombed on a Calcutta street. Ralph Reynolds Garlick, a district judge, was shot through the head in his courtroom in Alipore. Between 1931 and 1933, James Peddie, Robert Douglas, and Bernard Edward John Burge, three successive district magistrates of Midnapore, were assassinated. In December 1931, Charles Geoffrey Stevens, district magistrate of Tippera, was murdered in his bungalow by two young women, Suniti Chaudhuri and Shanti Ghosh. Two months later, Governor Stanley Jackson was delivering an address at the University of Calcutta's convocation when Bina Das, a fresh graduate, pulled out a pistol from within her academic robe and shot at him; she missed, and was overpowered and arrested. The next governor, John Anderson, introduced a tough regime of emergency laws with wide powers of search and detention. He was shot at in Darjeeling in 1934 and miraculously escaped unhurt.

With the systematic arrest and detention of their leaders, the revolutionaries now appeared to lose steam. The intelligence branch reported in 1937 that "the parties in most districts lack competent leadership and are disorganized, but recruitment is going on." In fact, although there appeared to be a vacuum in the planning of strategies and actions, the flow of young recruits continued unabated, with their ranks now swelled by women and in some cases Muslims. The intelligence reports noted that "the religious aspect" characteristic of the earlier life of the secret societies now seemed "to have been disregarded."[120] It was also said that in the Dacca District, 20 percent of high school students had been recruited by one revolutionary group alone, and that no more than 2 percent of students were progovernment.[121] It was in this period as well that the colonial government appeared to settle on a clearer definition of terrorism:

> Terrorism, as distinct from other revolutionary methods such as Communism or the Ghadr Movement, may be said to denote the commission of outrages of a comparatively "individual" nature. That is to say, the terrorist holds the belief that Indian independence can best be brought about by a series of revolutionary outrages calculated to instil fear into the British official classes and to drive them out of India.[122]

Curiously, it was in the mid-1930s that the Bengal revolutionaries too appeared to make serious choices between "individual terrorism" and other forms of organized revolutionary action. Mass nationalist mobilizations were now a familiar feature of Indian politics, and new questions about the economic and social future of the nation were being raised within the national movement. Confined to prisons and detention camps, the leaders of the revolutionary groups became acquainted with the new ideas of Marxism and possible role of the Communist Party in the anti-imperialist struggle. Many of them now renounced the politics of terrorism and assassination, and embraced the idea of sustained mass organization among workers and peasants. A considerable part of the leadership of the Left parties in Bengal at the time of independence, including the Communist Party, Revolutionary Socialist Party, and Forward Bloc, came from the ranks of the former nationalist revolutionary groups. Needless to say, the Congress Party that came to power in West Bengal after independence also contained many leaders with terrorist pasts. Now ranged on opposite sides of a new political divide, the former revolutionaries joined in giving birth to the new postcolonial orthodoxy: condemnation of the politics of terrorism while memorializing the sacrifice of the martyrs.

CHAPTER TEN

The Death and Everlasting Life of Empire

BHOLANATH CHANDRA (1822–1910) was a successful businessperson and observant traveler.[1] Although a prominent public figure in Bengal, he was never associated with nationalist political causes. Thus, he seemed somewhat unlikely to have initiated the process of the nationalist demolition of the narrative of the Black Hole of Calcutta.

The blow he dealt was small but telling. In a picturesque and often whimsical account of a journey by boat along the Hugli River, Chandra suddenly broached the subject of old Fort William and the Black Hole tragedy. On the latter, he said, he had "a very doubtful faith in its account."

> I have always questioned it to myself, how could 146 beings be squeezed into a room 18 feet square, even if it were possible to pack them like the seeds within a pomegranate.… Geometry contradicting arithmetic gives the lie to the story. It is little better than a bogey against which was raised an uproar of pity.[2]

The seeds of rational doubt were thus sown.[3] Historians with more explicitly nationalist motivations would soon reap a rich harvest.

A GIGANTIC HOAX

Akshaykumar Maitreya, in his *Sirājaddaulā*, published as a book in 1897, took up the cudgels in earnest. After first presenting Holwell's account of the event in some detail, Akshaykumar announced that the Black Hole deaths could not be regarded as a settled fact of history. There were several reasons to doubt Holwell's account. First, why is the event not mentioned by any Indian historian of the time, including those severely critical of Siraj? Second, if this was such a calamitous and traumatic event, then why do we not find any mention of it in any contemporary British account except for that of Holwell? Third, while reparations were extracted from Mir Jafar for every little damage inflicted on the British during Siraj's attack on Calcutta, why did the elaborate list of the defeated nawab's crimes and their compensation include not so much as a mention of the Black Hole deaths? Fourth, if the crime of the Black Hole was the principal reason for the war against Siraj, then why was Holwell's monument pulled down, and why was there no memorial to the tragedy in the capital of British India? Fifth, how could 146 people have been imprisoned in the Black Hole when, after reconciling the various accounts of the siege and subsequent surrender, it is certain that there were not that many people alive in the fort when it was captured? Indeed, Holwell was able to supply only 66 names, and that list included many now known to have not been among those who surrendered. As a matter of fact, there could have been no more than about 70 Europeans in the fort when it was captured, so how could 123 have died in the Black Hole and a further 23 survived the ordeal? Finally, Akshaykumar argued, whatever the true story of that night of June 20, 1756, there is no historical evidence at all that Siraj was in any way responsible for it. Even Holwell did not blame Siraj in his *Genuine Narrative*, instead inscribing the message of crime and retribution only on his return to Bengal following Siraj's defeat and death.[4]

As the turn of the century saw renewed interest and research among British scholars resident in Bengal, and several volumes of historical records such as those put together by Wilson and Hill were published, a mass of material became available to nationalist scholars keen to construct a "scientific" account, shorn of imperial mythology, of the British conquest of Bengal.[5] The weapons of modern European historiography would now be turned against imperialist history. In 1908, Nikhilnath Ray, a close associate of Akshaykumar, listed the key questions that would be asked on the subject by nationalist historians in the twentieth century:

1. Are the dimensions of the Black Hole chamber conclusively established? If so, how many people could have been accommodated within it in different positions [i.e., standing, sitting, or lying on the floor—as described by Holwell]?
2. Are the numbers of the dead and living among the inhabitants of the fort at the time of its capture and those imprisoned in the Black Hole conclusively established? Further, is it known how many of them were English and how many of other nationalities?
3. If the Black Hole deaths are a fact, was Siraj-ud-daulah responsible for it?
4. How was the significance of the Black Hole event discussed in India and in Europe?
5. Have similar events occurred elsewhere in the world? If so, how does the significance of the Black Hole deaths appear in comparison with those events?
6. What would be the correct conclusion on the facts and historical significance of the Black Hole deaths?[6]

Nikhilnath provided answers to these questions that would be reiterated, with large bodies of evidence and punctilious analysis, over the following decades. The outline for these answers had been already supplied by Akshaykumar.

The interesting addition that Nikhilnath made related to the event's historical significance.

> We do not believe that there ever occurred an event that could be called the Black Hole tragedy; what did occur was not of any great importance. For the few English officials used to a luxurious life, a night spent in captivity was probably traumatic. But there is no political significance attached to the event. In every country of the world, those defeated in battle are thrown into prison. Those injured in battle often die in captivity, and others suffer hardship.... What happened [in Calcutta] was something that happens everywhere between victors and vanquished.[7]

As we will see, Nikhilnath, an amateur historian of the early twentieth century, was anticipating the judgment of professional historians at the end of the century.

But even though Akshaykumar and Nikhilnath sought valiantly to employ the scientific methods of history writing introduced by German historians, their efforts had little impact on imperialist historiography since they wrote in Bengali. It was left to a district school teacher—an utterly marginal figure among the expatriate European community of Bengal—to make the most talked-about intervention.

James H. Little, a member of the Indian Education Service, was the headmaster of the Nawab Bahadur's Institution in Murshidabad who, in his spare time, was researching the family and business history of the famous banking house of the Jagat Seths. It is not known if he was in touch with Akshaykumar and his circle of amateur historians, but their names would soon become linked in the famous "Black Hole debate." In 1915, Little published an article in the historical journal *Bengal Past and Present* in which he announced that he was "prepared to prove that the Black Hole incident was a gigantic hoax."[8] His first line of argument seriously questioned Holwell's trustworthiness as the principal witness. The writer of the *Genuine Narrative* was, Little contended, extremely inaccurate with historical facts and utterly unscrupulous in inventing stories to serve his own ends. That Holwell had brought completely unfounded charges against Mir Jafar in order to replace him with Mir Qasim was a well-known fact in company circles. Further, in trying to establish himself as a scholar on Indian subjects after his return to Britain, Holwell had also claimed that he had procured "two very correct and valuable copies of the Gentoo Shastah," and had translated them himself, but the manuscripts were lost when Calcutta was captured in 1756. Little suggested that this was no more than an empty boast, since Holwell clearly did not have the knowledge of Sanskrit necessary to translate difficult religious or legal texts.

Moving to Holwell's narrative itself, Little pointed out Holwell's clear statement that Siraj had promised him that no harm would be done to the prisoners and that he had only given general orders that they should be secured for the night. How, then, could Holwell maintain that the guards on duty would so flagrantly disobey their nawab's orders and seek revenge for the deaths of their compatriots? Second, even if it were possible to tightly pack 146 persons into a cell of the presumed size of the Black Hole prison, it would have taken enormous effort on the part of the guards, especially in closing the door that opened into the cell. Yet there is no indication in Holwell's account that the prisoners resisted in any way being forcibly squeezed into the room. The anomaly is, of course, resolved if the number of prisoners was far less than the 146 claimed by Holwell.

The debate then became centered on the question of numbers. Diligently analyzing the various documents collected in Hill's volumes, Little came up with two lists of names of those who survived the siege and those who lost their lives. His conclusion was that there could not have been 146 prisoners in the Black Hole on the night of June 20, 1756; rather, there were probably only half as many. Tallying Holwell's own statements of those killed in the siege and those imprisoned, Little deduced with a flourish: "Therefore, Holwell cannot have his casualties and also his Black Hole victims. *Quod erat demonstrandum.*"

This fact, Little asserted, could be established with confidence. He next offered what he himself called a "theory" to explain the small number of survivors following the surrender, capture, and imprisonment of the fort's defenders. Little pointed to various available accounts to propose that the fighting did not end with Holwell's signal to surrender. When the nawab's troops stormed into the fort, they continued to shoot, and some of the defenders retaliated. When the Europeans were gathered together, the two sides kept on trading insults, and tensions were high. It is known that one of the Europeans fired a pistol, even though it supposedly had only powder and no shot, and some of the Indian troops fired back. Little's theory was that several of the defenders died in battle even after the formal surrender and it was only after Siraj's entry into the fort that hostilities actually ceased. Thus, Little's gloss on the Black Hole tragedy was quite different from the usual story about the hapless victims of an outrageous act of cruelty. On the contrary, it presented "to the British nation a band of heroes not unworthy in rank with those who held the trenches at Ypres or those who stormed the blood-stained heights of Gallipoli."

Little was not seeking to argue on behalf of an Indian nationalist cause; he was trying to remedy the self-seeking Holwell's condescending description of the Black Hole prisoners as a bunch of thoughtless creatures incapable of superior moral behavior. Realigning imperial history with the repository of archived facts, he was trying to reclaim the fall of Calcutta in 1756 as a tale of British heroism in the face of military adversity. Needless to say, it is significant that his attempt at historical revision was launched in the middle of the greatest imperialist war in history.

The Fallout

It is not easy to debunk well-established myths with theories and facts. Little's article provoked a storm of outraged reaction in the Anglo-Indian press, especially in the *Englishman* and *Statesman* of Calcutta as well as the *Pioneer* of Allahabad. From newspaper editors to history professors, British residents of India were scandalized that a cherished memory of the history of their empire in India should be so desecrated by one of their own kind. Apart from finding fault with Little's facts and reasoning, many correspondents questioned his loyalty to his country. The fact that he was only a schoolmaster in a small district town and a scholar of no standing did not help his credibility.

But the stir he had created was sufficient to persuade the Calcutta Historical Society, the new professional association of the modern variety of European scholars of India, to organize a debate in March 1916 on the Black Hole. Little was, not surprisingly, the principal speaker. He reiterated his argument, this time bolstered by citations from contemporary sources other than Holwell, that only a small number of people were actually imprisoned in the Black Hole since most of the besieged had been killed in the fighting. In support of his theory, Little cited a letter from Admiral Wilson to Siraj after Fort William had been retaken in which the British commander appears to be referring to certain killings following Siraj's capture of the fort in 1756. "He knew those men had been killed after the fort was formally surrendered by its governor and put the worst construction on it. I have no doubt he learned subsequently that the slaughter had been a terrible mistake and had been stopped by the Nawab himself." Little thus claimed that nothing resembling the horrible event described by Holwell ever took place, because the number of prisoners that night was relatively small.[9]

Edward Farley Oaten, professor of history at Presidency College in Calcutta, is well known in Bengal for an incident that took place only a few weeks before his participation in the Black Hole debate. In a speech at the college hostel, Oaten had remarked that just as the ancient Greeks had hellenized the barbarian races, so had the English come to India to civilize its people. The students protested to the college principal, who apparently did nothing about the matter, whereupon they decided to confront Oaten on the staircase and ended up physically assaulting him. On inquiry, it was found that the protest organizer was a student by the name of Subhas Chandra Bose, later to emerge as a major figure in nationalist politics. Subhas was expelled from the college, thus beginning a long series of confrontations with the British authorities in India—one of the last clashes being over the Black Hole.[10] But on this evening in March 1916, when Oaten spoke at the Calcutta Historical Society to raise doubts about Little's theory, he could not have known that one of the students who had attacked him would one day play a major part in removing the Black Hole monument from the city's central square.

Oaten began on a surprising note by claiming that he was "frankly prejudiced": he wanted to disbelieve the Black Hole story. "For the sake of our common humanity we ought to hope that the view which Mr Little is championing will finally triumph. I want to have a real excuse for relegating Holwell's Narrative to a museum of literary curiosities." But he did not think that Little had quite clinched the argument. Using the language of field warfare that must have become everyday parlance during World War I, Oaten remarked: "I am of opinion that Mr Little, though he has been able to gall the garrison with a very disturbing rifle and machine gun fire, has failed as yet to bring up those seven inch howitzers which the capture of most forts to-day seems to demand." The main difficulty with Little's theory, maintained Oaten, was not so much the admittedly suspect veracity of Holwell's testimony but instead how the survivors all conspired to uphold a false account of what had transpired that night, and in doing so, nevertheless ended up giving varied details of the imagined event. "[Little] omits to provide any adequate motive to explain why so many men should have joined in concocting and backing a story so singularly unheroic. For by the nature of things in the Black Hole the survivors were those who most successfully fought and trod their fellow creatures to death." Indeed, going by Little's demonstration of the maddening inconsistencies in the stories told by the Black Hole survivors, it appeared that "the most gigantic and successful hoax in history was successfully perpetrated by the most arrant set of clumsy bunglers imaginable." Oaten's conclusion was that Little's theory "of Englishmen resisting to the death and dying gloriously on the bastions" needed "more convincing testimony." It was hard to believe "that a secret, known on Mr Little's hypothesis to so many, could possibly have remained a secret for ever."[11]

Akshaykumar was also invited to join the debate. This in itself was remarkable, and a sign of the changing times, because it was probably the first occasion when an Indian historian whose research had been published only in Bengali was asked to contribute to the Calcutta Historical Society's proceedings. Speaking in English, Akshaykumar strongly supported Little, who was not, as alleged by the *Pioneer*, merely being an iconoclast: he, like the true modern historian, was destroying "an old fetish ... only to replace fiction by truth." Citing Lord Acton, he described the critical method of "the historians of the modern school in Europe" as one that prompts them, when they come on an interesting statement, to "begin by suspecting it." There were many reasons, said Akshaykumar, to interrogate the tradition of the Black Hole narrative as purveyed by historians since Orme. He reiterated the points he had already made in his Bengali writings twenty years before, bolstering them with evidence from recently published records and countering the explanations offered by Hill, retired professor of history at Presidency College, and Rushbrook Williams, professor of history at the University of Allahabad, both of whom had severely criticized Little. He disputed Williams's claim that the historical validity of the

Black Hole story could be established without fully accepting Holwell's account of it. Akshaykumar contended that the tale of the imprisonment of 146 persons and death of 123 "was the story of no one else but of Holwell"; hence "we cannot have the story of the Black Hole without Holwell, as we cannot have *Hamlet* without the Prince of Denmark." Not only that, but

> to support the current story, there must be evidence of the imprisonment of 146 and the death of 123. Who were they? That is the real question, which must legitimately demand to know the names of all. In the absence of evidence on that point, a true historian cannot go beyond saying that the story should be called "not to be proven."[12]

Compared to Little, Akshaykumar had superior skills as a historian, and these were supplemented by his training as a lawyer. He put together a far better case in demolishing the Black Hole tale than Little had been able to do. The key, once again, lay in the numbers—in the strong proof, that is, that 146 persons were simply not there to be put in prison. As a matter of fact, on the available evidence, no more than 65 or so could be accounted for as having been imprisoned that night. Akshaykumar also backed Little's theory of the continued fighting after the fort's formal surrender as "a welcome working hypothesis which agrees better with probable human conduct than the current story of the Black Hole." It was, of course, a hypothesis whose tenability or otherwise had nothing to do with the patent unacceptability of the received narrative itself. Little's theory was an example of how proper historical inquiry should proceed. By contrast, "the great body of unscholarly criticism" that had been raised against Little was "a general libel against the British love of truth."[13]

Buoyed by the stir he had created, Little appears to have overextended his enthusiastic razing of established myths. Referring to a *Narrative of a Journey* published in *Bengal Past and Present* in which an anonymous traveler to Calcutta in 1818 wrote about the Black Hole monument, Little sent a letter to the journal asking, "Did the author ... see the Holwell Monument?"[14] On being invited to contribute a longer article, Little surveyed the available evidence from 1789 to 1803, and concluded that no witnesses had said that they had seen the monument with their own eyes, and that many others who were in Calcutta during that time did not mention the monument at all.[15] This brought forth an angry response from Curzon himself from his home in England. He had little patience, he stated, "with these attempts to rewrite history in contempt of every rule of evidence." Listing a long series of textual and visual evidence from travelers, news reporters, and artists between 1760 and 1821 who had recorded the monument's existence in the ravelin of the old fort in front of its East Gate, on the southwest corner of the Writers' Building, Curzon poured scorn on Little's suggestion that just because some contemporary observers did not mention Holwell's column, it must not have existed at all.

With a similar treatment of evidence it would be easy to show a century hence that no such person as Mr Little had ever existed. Indeed, posterity will be inclined to believe that this was the case, on the double ground that no serious person could so treat history or travesty research, and that contemporary records were silent as to the presence in the first quarter of the twentieth century in Bengal of a super-wag of that name.[16]

This was something of a David-and-Goliath tussle—between an insignificant schoolmaster from a Bengal small town and the former viceroy of India, an arrogant English aristocrat, who with some luck, might have been prime minister of Britain. It is certainly significant that Curzon chose not to comment at all on the Black Hole debate itself and reserved his vitriol for the admittedly far-fetched case made by Little about the nonexistence of Holwell's monument. But then, Curzon had a personal reputation to defend, since he was the one who had ceremonially reinstalled the pillar at Dalhousie Square. He felt so strongly about it that he brought the matter up again in his book on British Indian government, complaining about "a school of native writers, supported by a solitary Englishman, who contended that no such incident as the Black Hole tragedy had ever occurred." Referring to his rejoinder, Curzon alleged that "no difficulty was experienced in shattering this preposterous fabric of perverted ingenuity and casuistical manipulation." He called it "the most barefaced instance known to me in history of the lengths to which political or racial partisanship, coupled with a sufficient lack of moral scruple, can be made to go. Nevertheless," he added, "I am disposed to think that both Holwell's Monument and mine will be found to have successfully survived the shock."[17] Supremely confident in the infallibility of his own judgment, Curzon was not aware that he had spoken too soon.

As it happened, the schoolmaster, even if he might have summoned the courage to reply to the former viceroy, never got a chance. Turning the pages of the issue of *Bengal Past and Present* in which Curzon's rejoinder was published, one suddenly comes on an obituary notice in which the editor, the archdeacon Walter Firminger, announced Little's death in the Presidency General Hospital in Calcutta on October 9, 1917. "A comparatively young man at the time of his death," Little had, Firminger noted, considerable literary abilities.

Had he enjoyed wider opportunities for research, and of consultation with fellow students, it may be believed that he, with his very considerable gifts, would have abandoned the kind of *tour de force* which has proved so seductive to literary men when they select history as a form of their labour.[18]

Little's reputation as a historian has not survived Firminger's condescension.[19] Yet neither has Curzon's claim to the historical truth survived the judgment of the residents of Calcutta. Public agitation in the city would soon be directed precisely against Curzon's reinstalled monument.

WE ARE KINGS OF THE COUNTRY, AND THE REST ARE SLAVES

Before we recount that story, let us note the rise of an entirely new public in the city of Calcutta. This development has a great deal to do, once again, with the game of football.

Although established as far back as 1891 in the poor neighbourhood of Kaiser Lane near Sealdah railway station, the Mohammedan Sporting Club was a relatively unknown entity until it won the second division league championship in 1933, thus gaining a promotion to Calcutta's premier league. What ensued was nothing less than a fairy tale.

But as is the case in most fairy tales, the miracle required much preparation. A. K. Aziz, the club's secretary from 1931 to 1934, was a dynamic leader with bold ideas. He decided to look beyond the immediate environs of Calcutta to seek new players for his team. Compared to the other Indian clubs such as Mohun Bagan and the recently promoted East Bengal, the club had only meager funds. Aziz decided that he would project Mohammedan Sporting Club as the leading football team of Indian Muslims and draw talented Muslim players from other parts of the country. He was hugely successful in his effort, recruiting Mohiuddin, Masoom, and the brothers Rahamat and Habib from Bangalore, Rashid from Vishakhapatnam, and Jumma Khan from Quetta.[20] He also acquired Samad, the wily old fox, from Eastern Bengal Railways. The following year, he got the goalkeeper Osman from Delhi.

Aziz also thought that the quaint practice of Indian footballers playing without boots was the principal reason why no Indian team had managed to win a single major trophy anywhere in India, save for the singular occasion of Mohun Bagan's victory in 1911. He decided to persuade all his players to wear boots. It was not easy to change so settled a practice. When his players complained that they felt uncomfortable with their feet wrapped in heavy leather, he ordered special light boots to be made for them. The result was magical. When Mohammedan Sporting beat Kalighat four to nil to take an unbeatable three-point lead over its nearest rivals Dalhousie and Mohun Bagan, and thus emerge as the first Indian team to win the Calcutta league—and in its first year in the championship—*Amrita Bazar Patrika* reported in its inimitable prose:

> The Mahomedans appeared in boots and Samad who made no exception had at once thousands of eyes set on him on being quite a novel sight. It is near about two decades he has been playing football and many were the occasions when he was discarded as a hopeless derelict on a wet day.

And the old juggler spread a regular revelation by the admirable way he reconciled his footwear. He ran with the easy grace of a stag, showed admirable precision in his shots and proved quite a wonder-man in his new equipage.

The report also pointed out what was so spectacularly new about the arrival of Mohammedan Sporting on the Maidan of Calcutta:

Clean, neat and delightfully scientific, the games of the victorious Mahomedan Sporting left an impress on the tournament and created new crowds for them. The popularity of the team increased with every match and eventually it became quite a feature with their games that the gates would be closed long before the appointed time to start....

The enclosure proved once again a mockery to the bulk of the throng who set their hearts on the match and presented themselves there.... The fort glacis easily scored a record of mammoth gathering that stood in tiers along the gradual slopes.[21]

This was when the song was coined somewhere along the streets of central Calcutta: "*Mohammedan Sporting tumko lakhon lakhon salam / ham ab deshka badshah bane, aur sab hai ghulam* [Mohammedan Sporting, a million salutes to you / We have now become kings of the country, all the rest are slaves]."

The dream run had only just begun, though. From 1934 to 1938, Mohammedan Sporting won the first division league an incredible five times in a row. Along the way, it also won the IFA Shield in 1937. It was without doubt the most popular football team among Muslims all over India. In Calcutta, it acquired a loyal following among not only the Muslim middle class as well as many Muslim students from eastern Bengal and Assam but also the poor Muslims of the city. They would throng around the club grounds every day that their team played, braving the monsoon sludge under their feet, and perching themselves on top of nearby electric poles or devising periscopes with reflecting mirrors in order to get a glimpse of the action from behind a wall of humanity. There were now three permanently fenced grounds on the Maidan, each with galleries on three sides and one side enclosed in barbed wire, allowing the crowds outside a view. The white stands on the west were for club members, while the green stands to the north and east were open to the public, at eight annas per seat in the enclosure with chairs and four annas in the wooden galleries—roughly equivalent to the price of a cinema ticket.[22]

Among the thousands of loyal supporters of Mohammedan Sporting who would pack the stands was a certain Jan Muhammad, who would from time to time raise the cry "Allah-u-akbar," bringing the entire crowd to its feet.[23] Almost every memoir of Muslim politicians and intellectuals who lived in Calcutta in the 1930s mentioned the electrifying effect on the Muslim public of the victories of Mohammedan Sporting on the football field.[24] Managers of

Figure 26. Spectators with periscopes outside Mohammedan Sporting grounds. *Photo: Ahmed Ali. Courtesy: Ahmed Ali and Centre for Studies in Social Sciences, Calcutta*

the jute factories in the northern suburbs and Howrah set up works committees among the predominantly Muslim workers to discuss the prospects of their favorite football club, and thus steer away from the more contentious topics of pay and working conditions.[25] In the districts of East Bengal, people would eagerly wait for Calcutta newspapers like *Azad* to arrive with news and photographs of the team that had made Muslims proud.[26] Their footballers became idols; fruit sellers, tea shops, and restaurants in and around New Market would serve them for free, and department stores such as Wachel Molla on Dharmatala Street would give them huge discounts. Kazi Nazrul Islam composed a paean to the victorious team:

> You have put the crown on the sunken head of India.
> You have shown that given a chance we can be invincible....
> Those feet that have so incredibly woven wonders with the football—
> May the power of all of India rise from those very feet.
> May those feet break our chains. And our fear, and our dread—
> May those feet kick them away! Allah-u-akbar![27]

Within a year or two of its winning the league, Mohammedan Sporting was also transformed into a favorite of the city's elite Muslims. Several members of the Dacca Nawab family became its patrons, and Khwaja Nazimuddin was elected the club's president. Prominent Muslim business families began to support the club. Subid Ali, a wealthy merchant, threw open the rooms of a building off Dharmatala Street for the accommodation of the team's players. After the formation of the coalition ministry led by Abul Kasem Fazlul Huq, several cabinet members would regularly watch important club matches. There is little doubt that the presence within the same enclosed space of supporters cutting across class lines, simultaneously experiencing the same visceral sensation of the rise and fall in the fortunes of their favorite team, lent an unprecedented collective identity to this new urban public.

When Mohammedan Sporting won its final fixture against Customs to win the league for the fifth time in 1938, "the match was watched by at least 50,000 persons including the sea of human heads that occupied the glacis of the fort." There were impromptu celebrations on the club grounds and also at Subid Ali Mansion. "Thousands of Mahomedan supporters marched in procession with band and rent the skies with tremendous shouts of jubilation.... A spontaneous Kabuli dancing recital was held under the skies on their ground, led by buglers."[28]

The dream run was broken in 1939, but for reasons that lay outside the football field. There was a buzz around the Maidan, circulating mostly among supporters of the Mohammedan Sporting and East Bengal clubs, that a conspiracy was afoot within the IFA to pave the way for Mohun Bagan to win the league that year, and this was revealed in particular by a series of shocking refereeing decisions. Midway through the league, Mohammedan Sporting dropped a point against Border Regiment when the latter equalized in the last minute from a doubtful penalty. Referee Gilson was stoned by an angry crowd, and Khwaja Nooruddin, the club's secretary, was hard-pressed to restrain the fans.[29] Mohammedan Sporting slipped to the fourth position in the league. A few days later, it lost to Customs, once again from a disputed penalty. When the referee Handyside was surrounded by an irate crowd, Nooruddin once more stepped in to tackle the situation.[30] On July 5, with only a few matches left, the Mohammedan Sporting, Kalighat, East Bengal, and Aryans clubs all announced that they would not participate anymore in the league unless the IFA took measures to redress their grievances, especially over the issue of bad refereeing.[31] In response, H. N. Nicholls, the IFA president from the Calcutta Football Club, took the unprecedented step of suspending the four clubs until the end of the calendar year for going to the press before the matter had been discussed in the governing body.[32]

But football and politics had, by this time, become deeply entangled in Calcutta. Nazimuddin, president of Mohammedan Sporting, was a prominent leader of the Muslim League and the home minister in the coalition government led by Fazlul Huq. Nalini Ranjan Sarker, president of East Bengal Club, was a former Congress leader and finance minister in the same government. At a meeting of the three rebel clubs (Aryans refused to join), it was agreed that they had no wish to leave the IFA unless forced, yet if that were to happen, they would form a new association. The IFA president was criticized for suggesting that the rebel clubs had tried to "belittle the achievement of Mohun Bagan." Nazimuddin said, "Any club especially an Indian club ought to feel proud of another Indian club achieving the coveted honours."[33] A few days later, it was reported that "the attitude taken by the IFA ... indicated that the door ... had been bolted against them [the rebel clubs]."[34]

Mohun Bagan won the league title for the first time in its history in July 1939. In August, the three rebel clubs—Mohammedan Sporting, East Bengal, and Kalighat—announced the formation of the Bengal Football Association. The meeting was convened by Jogesh Chandra Gupta, a Congress leader, and was attended by Nawab Habibullah of Dacca, the chief minister Fazlul Huq, and as many as four members of his cabinet—namely, Nazimuddin, Sarker, Bijay Prasad Singh Roy, and Husain Shaheed Suhrawardy. Abdul Momin, a prominent member of the Muslim League, said that the IFA was a "closed oligarchy" of twenty-two clubs, ostensibly with equal representation of seven members each from the European and Indian clubs. Nevertheless, there were only four European clubs that elected seven members to the governing body. There could be "no justification for such a heavy European representation."[35]

For the rest of the year, the new association could do little but organize friendly matches and go on tour to the districts. By the start of the season in 1940, things were patched up. Mohammedan Sporting won the league again that year. It also won the Rovers Cup in Bombay and the Durand Cup, played that year in Delhi instead of Simla. The following year, Mohammedan Sporting not only won the Calcutta league but the IFA Shield as well.

By then, however, the Muslim public in Calcutta was being mobilized for entirely new political futures.

SIRAJ, ONCE MORE ON STAGE

Girishchandra's *Sirājaddaulā* had been banned since 1910, even though its memory may have survived among the Swadeshi generation. But in 1938, in the new political climate created by the provincial coalition ministry of the Krishak Proja Party and Muslim League, headed by the immensely popular Fazlul Huq, the Natya Niketan theater decided to stage a new version of the Siraj and Palashi story. The new play was written by Sachin Sengupta, a young progressive writer, and produced by Nirmalendu Lahiri, also a popular actor, along with Satu Sen, who had revolutionized the Calcutta stage with electric lighting and modern stagecraft. An added attraction was the musical score and a set of songs written and set to tune by Kazi Nazrul Islam, the most popular composer in Bengal at the time. Bengal was ready for a revival of the Siraj story.

The Calcutta theater had gone through much change in the three decades since Girishchandra's plays were produced at the Minerva Theatre. With the modernization of the stage and lighting technology had come a new wave of plays that even when sticking to the familiar mythological or historical subjects, tried to eschew melodrama and adopt more realistic styles. A crucial impact was made here by the commanding presence of Sisir Kumar Bhaduri, who as actor and director, brought his considerable reputation as a scholar, teacher, and practitioner of sophisticated tastes to bear on his productions in the 1920s and 1930s. With him, the educated middle class of Bengal to a certain extent reclaimed its cultural hold on the Calcutta commercial stage. New companies such as the Art Theatre and Natya Niketan tried to introduce higher professional standards in their set designs, costumes, orchestral scores, and advertising. Performances were now put up on weekdays as well as on weekends, and a successful production could run for hundreds of nights.[36]

Sachin Sengupta's *Sirājaddaulā* had enough elements to remind one of Girish's play, even though it significantly toned down its excesses.[37] The exuberant slapstick was entirely removed, as was the web of magical causality. Karim Chacha was dimly recognizable in the mellowed-down jester Golamhosen, but the biting sarcasm and sardonic remarks were largely gone. The much-maligned Zahara was replaced by Aleya, a dancing girl who acts as a self-appointed spy on behalf of the country as well as Siraj, to whom she had bequeathed her heart. The vengeful and conspiring female character in the play, in deference to the historical facts, was Ghaseti Begam, Siraj's aunt. There were no speeches in verse, and other than at one or two specific moments, the dialogue was in unadorned everyday prose.

Fortunately for us, we do have a recording of an abridged version of the play initially released in an immensely popular boxed set of gramophone records.[38] Nirmalendu Lahiri portrays Siraj as calm, mature, and thoughtful; only in a few chosen moments when his words are meant to be directly addressed to the audience does he raise his voice to the stylized intonation of the traditional jatra-inspired speech. As in Girish's play, Siraj retains the quality of vulnerability, but even with his full knowledge and close analysis of the situation, is shown to be so completely surrounded by hostile forces that he has no means available for escape. Early in the play, Siraj confides to his wife:

SIRAJ: I have enemies on all sides, Lutfa. In the harem, in my palaces, in the city, in the villages—there is no end to Siraj's enemies. I have to be careful at every moment to defend myself. (I, 1)

In a crucial scene before the battle of Palashi, when his courtiers try to pin him down with allegations and complaints, Siraj fights back, producing evidence of their involvement in a conspiracy against him. Having silenced them, he then begs for their support in the coming conflict against the British.

SIRAJ: Bengal does not belong only to Hindus, or only to Muslims. Bengal is the motherland of both Hindus and Muslims—a garden of flowers. If I have wronged anyone, then I have wronged both Hindus and Muslims. If I have been hurt, then I have been hurt by both Hindus and Muslims. I have not been partial to anyone. (II, 1)

And then, in a rare lyrical passage (rendered in Nirmalendu's sonorous voice), Siraj reminds his ministers (as well as the audience) of the significance of the historical moment:

SIRAJ: Dark clouds have gathered over the sky of Bengal's destiny, her green fields are crisscrossed by streams of blood, the sun of the nation's fortune is sinking in the horizon. Only a tearful mother sits by the side of her sleeping child, counting the hours of the night. Who will give her hope? Who will give her assurance? Who will tell her, "We will stop this march of death even at the cost of our lives"? (II, 1)

The ministers pledge their full support in the impending battle. But in Palashi, when it becomes clear that Mir Jafar was acting to undermine the nawab's cause, Siraj quietly accepts the advice of his treacherous general. Answering the protests of a bewildered Golamhosen, the nawab says:

SIRAJ: … I can see that if you were the nawab, you would have given stern orders to Mirjafar. Of course, he would have refused to obey. You would have then put Mirjafar under arrest. Hearing the news, his soldiers would have rebelled. They would have attacked your camp and killed you. That would have put a quick end to your reign as nawab. So, my clever friend, do you understand now? [*Pats Golamhosen on the shoulder, walks away, and then returns*] I know everything, understand everything. But I am compelled to go along with Mirjafar. You and my friends get upset with me. I get upset with myself. But what can I do, Golamhosen? I have no choice—no choice at all. (II, 3)

When Siraj confirms Mir Jafar's proposal to suspend the battle for the night, he knows instantly the implications of the decision.

SIRAJ: Golamhosen, the battle is over!
GOLAMHOSEN: Then why are the cannons opening up again?
SIRAJ: I am telling you, Golamhosen, the battle is over. And so is my *nawabi*. (II, 3)

The defeat is so predictable that it is almost anticlimactic. It is Golamhosen who now explains its significance to Siraj:

GOLAMHOSEN: This defeat was necessary. My lord, foolish men don't realize the worth of their teeth while they still have them. In the same way, ignorant people don't realize the value of liberty while they have it. You gave Bengalis the opportunity of enjoying their independence by defying the suzerainty of Delhi; Bengalis did not appreciate the worth of what you gave them. Instead, the lure of sitting on the throne drove them to fight among themselves. They needed a big blow. Palashi has given them that blow. (III, 2)

In the play's final scene, we see the common people for the first time—they have been assembled by the villainous Miran to mock and heap insults on the captive Siraj before he is put to death. Siraj accepts their taunts:

SIRAJ: When I came to the throne, I had pledged to look after my subjects and protect their interests. But I have failed. That is why I have been humiliated. That is why I am the butt of your jokes.... If I had wanted to spend my days in peace, I need not have antagonized anyone. I could have conceded every unjust demand, thrown to the winds the honour and authority of my position, and given myself over to a life of luxury—I could have drowned myself in pleasure.... But I did not want to do that. Is that why you think I have done you wrong? (III, 3)

He continues:

SIRAJ: Even today—I know this well—if today I had not had to return having been defeated in the fields of Palashi, you would have welcomed me with open arms and rejoiced. But why was I defeated? Your Mirmadan gave his life, Mohanlal inflicted deadly bows on the enemy. And yet why do you stand defeated today? Why are you so helpless?

ONE FROM THE CROWD: My lord, we are weak.

SIRAJ: Thousands of soldiers stood inert like puppets on the fields of Palashi, while the hand of defeat crept up from behind and blackened our faces with the stain of disgrace. Who is accountable? Your nawab alone? Or the commander of your army? Where is he? Or your general Yarlatif? Your general Raidurlabh? Raja Rajballabh? The supremely wealthy Jagatseth? Call them to this darbar. Punish them. (III, 3)

His final call was to the people of Bengal:

SIRAJ: Then come, all my brothers, let us try once more to reclaim the jewel we lost at Palashi and put it back on the golden crown of Mother Bengal. (III, 3)

Even when the subject was historical, the immediate political context, we know, could never be far from the stage in Bengal. Siraj's constraints, helplessness, and having to pander to the dictates of his treacherous ministers were all strongly reminiscent of the unenviable position of Fazlul Huq, the most popular political leader of Bengal in 1938, hemmed in within the coalition party of which he was the head, but several of whose ministers, with the tacit help of the British bureaucracy, were plotting to remove him from power. While reviving the memory of the treachery that led to Siraj's defeat in Palashi, Sachin Sengupta's *Sirājuddaulā* made the allusions to Bengal's immediate predicament quite clear. Siraj's final cry of *bhāisab* (all my brothers) unmistakably echoes the oratorical voice of the embattled Fazlul Huq.

Endgames of Empire

Following the formation of the elected coalition ministry led by Fazlul Huq in 1937, there was a quite extraordinary convergence of political forces over the demand to remove the Holwell monument from Dalhousie Square. Of course, compared to the many contentious issues that faced the new government, such as the Krishak Proja Party's promise to abolish the entire Permanent Settlement system on which landlordism in Bengal was based or wipe out the peasants' debts, the monument had no more than symbolic value. Yet it took some agitation and considerable intrigue for something to happen.

The matter was first discussed by the Bengal ministry in 1938 when it was agreed that it would be proper "to obtain the consent of, or preferably a request from, the European Group in the legislature for its removal." Moreover, "the Monument being a protected monument and having, it was understood, been protected under orders from a previous Viceroy, the Bengal Government by itself would probably not be competent to remove it."[39] The intention, in short, was to stall for time. In 1939, the newly founded Muslim Renaissance Society, a cultural organization of Muslim intellectuals, declared July 3 (the day that the defeated nawab's corpse was paraded in Murshidabad in 1757) as Siraj-ud-daulah Day and formed a Siraj Memorial Committee with Habibullah Bahar, a prominent writer, editor, and former captain of Mohammedan Sporting Club, as chair.[40]

On that day, a meeting at Albert Hall addressed by major political leaders such as Abdel Halim Ghuznavi, Akram Khan, and Mozammel Huq urged the historians of Bengal to remove the stain on Siraj's character left by prejudiced foreign writers, and correct the history textbooks used in schools and colleges containing false, insulting allegations against Siraj. The meeting also urged the government to remove the Holwell monument and make arrangements to better preserve Siraj's tomb in Murshidabad. Several speakers noted the invaluable contribution of the late Akshaykumar Maitreya in presenting a correct historical picture of Siraj.[41] The *Mohammadī* pointed out that Bengal's liberty had been lost not because of the treachery of Umichand and Mir Jafar but rather because there was no national feeling among the people. Had there been a national feeling, the people would have made Siraj's fate their own and would have punished the traitors.[42] There were meetings in several district towns as well, especially in eastern Bengal, addressed by local Muslim and Hindu leaders. Official intelligence reports particularly highlighted the participation in a "nationalist" cause of prominent Muslim leaders of Bengal—the first time this had happened since the days of the Noncooperation and Khilafat movements in the early 1920s.

But this was hardly sufficient pressure to force the coalition government to stir a potential hornet's nest. Nothing might have happened in this matter if Subhas Chandra Bose, expelled from the Congress after his showdown with Gandhi and the working committee, had not decided in May 1940 to announce in Dacca that he would launch an agitation to demand the removal of Holwell's monument in Calcutta. Subhas was looking for new political allies and had just concluded a pact with the Muslim League to share seats in the Calcutta municipal body. He also traveled to Bombay to meet Mohammed Ali Jinnah. The Black Hole was an emotive issue whose appeal cut across the Hindu-Muslim divide.[43]

The action was to begin at the Holwell monument site on July 3, 1940, once again designated as Siraj-ud-daulah Day. At a crowded meeting at the Albert Hall on June 30 presided over by the young Muslim leader Muazzam Husain (Lal Mian), Subhas said that the issue had struck a chord among both Muslims and Hindus. He urged the youth of both communities to join in the demonstration. Abdul Waseq of the Muslim Students' League said that the Muslim students of Bengal had been demanding the removal of the objectionable monument for a long time, but the government had still not responded.[44] That same evening, Chief Minister Fazlul Huq issued a statement announcing that the government would make a decision by the end of the month; until then, no one should "force the issue by taking steps that may lead to the disturbance of the public peace."[45] Subhas immediately reacted by pointing out that Fazlul Huq had not indicated what decision would be announced then, and if indeed a decision is what was awaited, it should not take more than twenty-four hours to reach it. The premier's announcement, he said, was unsatisfactory and the protest would go ahead as planned.[46] On July 2, Subhas was arrested at his home under the Defense of India rules and detained without charges at Presidency jail.[47]

Behind the censored newspaper reports was hidden a story that typified the endgames of empire in India. John Herbert, the governor, reported to Victor

Hope, Lord Linlithgow, the viceroy, that "the agitation, though disingenuous, makes a strong appeal to Moslem sentiment and is one from which it is obviously difficult for any Moslem to dissociate himself." He emphasized that it was "only one phase of the consistent endeavours of Subhas Bose and the Forward Bloc to find some plank on which civil disobedience can be started with the assistance of Moslems." But there was another component that made the situation complicated and dangerous for the imperial power.

> There are elements in the ranks of the Muslims themselves who are prepared to follow Subhas Bose in these activities and in some cases probably even to instigate them. Among those who are prepared to follow him may be classed the most extreme left wing agrarian Muslims who either because of their radical views or because of their previous association with Congress or failure to achieve power in the present Government are not averse to embarrassing it. Among those who are probably prepared to instigate him I am inclined to place the Calcutta trio—Ispahani who is not a Bengali and whose commercial interests conflict with European interests, Siddiqui the present Mayor of Calcutta who has international connections … and Nooruddin a distant member of the Dacca Nawab family who has long been believed to have an anti-British bias. While the agrarian left wingers tended to owe allegiance more to the Congress than to the League, the urban trio are certainly in the League organisation, and although their loyalty to it may vary with their convenience, I have a strong feeling—but no proof—that they are in close contact with Jinnah and use their position in the League as well as their influence in Calcutta to bring pressure on Nazimuddin. It is this trio who were most prominent in the Football agitation—an affair which threatened to bring the police in possible conflict with Muslim masses on the one hand and Hindus on the other.

Herbert noted that there was only a fleeting convergence of interest among these varied political forces over the Holwell monument issue. "It may be that there is no greater common factor in their efforts than common antagonism to European vested interests and European obduracy."[48]

The need now was to "remove the immediate cause of conflict in which revolutionary Hindus and Muslims can be banded together against the Ministry and Europeans." Hence, Subhas had to be arrested and put out of action even though this was likely to anger some of the Muslim supporters of the ministry.

> Direct action [threatened by Bose] would necessarily involve a clash with the Police which, if allowed to develop under Subhas's leadership, would certainly not be limited to a few Hindu Satyagrahis since he would have Moslems with him, while on the other hand all chances of an amicable settlement with European feeling would be removed and Government would be likely to find itself between the cross fire of the Forward Bloc, Moslems and the Europeans.

With Subhas out of the way, Herbert proposed a solution to the Holwell monument issue:

> My own impression is that the British in Calcutta—although not necessarily else-where—might feel willing to themselves suggest the removal of the Monument provided that it was quite clear that far from acting under any threat their action was voluntarily undertaken for the sake of general goodwill.[49]

The action started on a low key during the afternoon of June 3 with a large police force stationed in Dalhousie Square and a small number of protesters. Four people were arrested.[50] Since they would not have been allowed to approach the highly secure zone around the Writers' Building in a procession, the demonstrators, usually ten to fifteen in number, mingled with the crowds emerging from offices in the evening rush hour and suddenly converge, hammer in hand, on the heavily guarded monument, where they would be arrested. Over the next few days, the demonstrations were carried out almost entirely by the Bengal Volunteers, a revolutionary group aligned with the Forward Bloc—that is, the suspended provincial committee of the Congress owing allegiance to Subhas.[51] Those arrested on the first few days were all Hindus, until on June 8, a Muslim and 5 Sikh agitators were also arrested.[52] The size of the demonstrations increased over the next few days, and 163, including a few women, were arrested in the first ten days.[53] One protester apparently even managed to slip through the police cordon, run up the steps, and strike a blow on the monument with a hammer, accompanied by shouts of "*Bande mataram*," before he was arrested.[54] Speaking in the legislative assembly, Fazlul Huq said that there was a feeling in the country that the Holwell monument should be removed, but "the only thing that stood in the way … was the satyagraha movement." He asserted that no government could tolerate such a movement in a time of war.[55]

The constraints on the coalition ministry were complicated. Uncertain of the position of the British bureaucracy and nonofficial European community on whose support in the legislature it vitally depended, Fazlul Huq's government was put into further difficulty by the troublesome but popular Subhas seizing the initiative. While for two years the government had sat on the demand voiced by many Muslim organizations, it could not now concede it without appearing to cave in to the opposition's pressure tactics. Within the government, although Fazlul Huq had come close to the Muslim League by moving the famous "Pakistan resolution" at Lahore in March 1940, Nazimuddin and the elite Muslim leaders of Calcutta treated him with suspicion for his espousal of radical peasant demands.

The Muslim student organizations, often with the covert and sometimes-open support of prominent Krishak Proja leaders, kept up their demand for the removal of the Holwell monument. They were joined by the Students' Federation, an organization of the Communist Party, which while supporting the demand, also resolved to cooperate with the Muslim students in their programs.[56] Abul Mansur Ahmad, a prominent Krishak Proja leader, later recounted that many Muslim intellectuals and students, who had been made aware by Girishchandra and Akshaykumar of the false representations of Siraj, were overjoyed when a major Hindu leader such as Subhas Bose took up the cause. Abul Mansur himself wrote enthusiastic editorials in the party organ *Dainik kṛṣak* supporting the agitation.[57]

On July 3, at a meeting called at the Town Hall to observe Siraj-ud-daulah Day, and following speeches by prominent political leaders such as Lal Mian, Syed Badruddoza, Shamsul Huda, and Niharendu Dutt-Mazumdar, the Muslim students present demanded that the government take no more than two weeks to make its decision.[58] Closely watching these developments, Governor Herbert sent a telegram to the viceroy on this meeting:

> It began quietly with thin attendance but swelled after close of football play on maidan…. General impression was that saner Muslims were inclined to be quiet, but Hindu followers of Subhas and some extreme Muslims were anxious to foment trouble…. Well known ex-terrorists and Forward Bloc Hindu agitators were prominent.[59]

A long letter published under the name "A Muslim" in the *Star of India*, a newspaper known to be close to the Muslim League, described the government's dillydallying as "shameful." The letter warned that there was a limit to the people's patience: "Muslims cannot for long allow their rightful place in this movement to be taken by others."[60] At another meeting at the Albert Hall on July 13, legislators Abdul Karim and Abdul Latif Biswas accused the government of dithering.[61] The next day, about 250 activists of the Muslim Students' League demonstrated in front of the chief minister's residence in Park Circus, forcing Fazlul Huq to appear before them in an attempt to pacify an important group of government supporters. When the students refused to disperse, Fazlul Huq left in a huff, and the police broke up the protest.[62] The chief minister was meant to address a meeting of Muslim students two days later at the Muslim Institute, but he declined to come. Annoyed, students then resolved to observe a day's strike on July 22.[63]

In the meantime, on July 16, the government issued an order under the Defense of India rules prohibiting the publication of any news or photograph concerning the ongoing protest over the Holwell monument. Raising the matter in the legislative assembly, dissident members of the Krishak Proja Party such as Jalaluddin Hashemy, Maniruzzaman Islamabadi, and Nausher Ali severely criticized the government for its "autocratic *zulm* [oppression]." The home minister, Nazimuddin, replied that the government could not allow the

Figure 27. Abul Kasem Fazlul Huq, photograph. *Courtesy: Amalendu Dey*

civil disobedience to go on since such movements were always followed by terrorism.[64]

Governor Herbert, not sufficiently familiar with the intricacies of Bengal politics, sought advice from Henry Twynam, who after many years of service in Bengal, had been appointed governor of the Central Provinces.

> This Subhas business is one of the most tiresome things one can imagine, because whatever may be the facts of the case he is now in jail and the great majority of agitators probably honestly believe that he is there because of his Holwell Monument agitation. The All-Bengal Muslim Students League have issued a handbill and are very stirred in the matter.... I am however far from happy about the situation gener-

ally.... I strongly suspect ... that [Fazlul Huq's] underlying motive is his desire to get away from League domination.... [Fazlul Huq] still hopes that some Forward Bloc elements might help him in a war policy. My own view is that Subhas cannot be trusted to back war aims.... Anyway, now that one can be wise after the event, I must say that I sincerely regret we were unable to take action, either in Bengal or elsewhere, before he had a chance of gaining advertisement and popular support on the Holwell Monument agitation. If only he could have been put out of the way some time in the middle of June, I do not think any serious situation could have arisen.[65]

In his reply, Twynam strongly recommended that Herbert not bank on Fazlul Huq's cooperation and instead put his trust in Nazimuddin to defend vital British interests in a time of war:

> I also agree that H. C. M.'s [Fazlul Huq's] underlying motive is to rid himself of League domination and so incidentally of Dacca Nawab family and work with people of his own kidney i.e. the Proja Party allied with leftists and even Congress Hindus. It seems to me that both in order to arrest this intrigue and on its own merits case for continued detention of Subhas is overwhelming and Nazimuddin should take full advantage of situation. I cannot express too strongly your conviction that Subhas cannot be trusted to back war aims as in anything that does not spell disaster to British. If H. C. M. professes to believe that the leopard Subhas will change its spots I regard it as convincing evidence of an intrigue to get rid of Nazimuddin and Company. The present Cabinet can I think be trusted to back Nazimuddin against HCM if former stands out for continued detention of Subhas and this seems to me the time to make stand against H. C. M.'s wrecking intrigue.[66]

The viceroy Linlithgow too reminded Herbert of his responsibility to defend imperial interests, if necessary even against the views of the elected provincial ministry: "But of course if you as Governor think that public security and the defence of India require it, you are bound, as I know you appreciate, to over-ride your Ministers without hesitation. Are you in fact satisfied that that point is not now being reached?"[67] The deliberations in the highest echelons of the colonial government regarding the state of politics in Bengal some two hundred years after Palashi were reminiscent of the dispatches of Watts or Scrafton on the intrigues in the court of Murshidabad. Indeed, the correspondence between Linlithgow and Herbert suggest the new imperial practices that were already being devised for the furtherance of imperial strategic and economic interests in a context of Indian self-government.

Pressed from all sides, Fazlul Huq made a statement in the legislative assembly declaring that nothing would please him more than to see Subhas out of prison and back in his proper position in the country's public life.[68] Herbert quickly wrote to Linlithgow, pointing out the underlying danger:

A real flutter was however caused by the CM remarking in Assembly that it would give him pleasure to see Subhas freed.... As you know, both the Chief Minister and Nazimuddin have been angling for Subhas's support, for opposite reasons.... There is still a popular feeling that Subhas Bose will shortly be released. I think that we are agreed that if this happened, he would come out on the crest of a wave of popular enthusiasm and with enhanced prestige.[69]

Having secured Linlithgow's concurrence, Herbert decided to unroll his planned solution to the immediate problem.[70] The crucial intervention was made by Percival J. Griffiths, retired civil servant and member of the central legislative assembly. Speaking on behalf of the European community, he said, "As far as I am aware no member of any community is opposed to the removal of the monument.... [T]his monument commemorates no event which is worth remembrance, and ... its existence is an offence to many of my Indian friends."[71] It was an indication of how much the old imperial idea had waned since the days of Curzon. Nonetheless, speaking in the Bengal legislative assembly, the European member C. W. Miles clarified that while many would have no objection to the monument's removal, "there would be whole-hearted antagonism to its demolition."[72]

The students of Islamia College organized a large demonstration on July 22, but were stopped by the police, leading to clashes that left many of the students wounded.[73] Things appeared to be getting out of hand. On July 23, Fazlul Huq announced in the legislative assembly that the government had decided "to take immediate steps to remove the Holwell monument."[74] He acknowledged "the unfailing sympathy which the European community have shown towards the question.... They have ever shown the utmost readiness to respond to Indian opinion and to help us in coming to a satisfactory solution."[75]

By the year's end, the Holwell monument was removed from Dalhousie Square to its present location in the cemetery of St. John's Church. The mythical history of empire could now be safely relinquished, clearing the way for a new era of imperial adjustment with indigenous governments on the subcontinent. At the same time, Linlithgow reiterated:

For the purposes of record, I might perhaps say that we may regard it now as a settled policy that he [Subhas] will not be released whatever the considerations of Bengal internal policy. And I regard it as most important (as I know you do too) that no pains should be spared to avoid that position being compromised by any action on the part of any Bengal Minister.[76]

When in December 1940 Herbert agreed to release Subhas on medical grounds and put him under house arrest, the governor quickly told the viceroy: "I am assured that the position is entirely satisfactory as far as it goes, but if he had died in jail the security of the Province would have been threatened.... I realize the anxious time you are having, and that the news must have been worrying in the form in which it arrived."[77] Hardly a month after his release, however, Subhas managed to evade his guards and escape from home, surfacing sometime later in Germany. But that, of course, is another story.[78] To continue along the parallel with the history of the British conquest of Bengal in the eighteenth century, 1943 saw yet another Bengal famine, almost of the same scale as that of 1769–70, and certainly one of the worst twentieth-century famines. The most cautious estimates put the death toll at somewhere around three million. It was brought about not by a crop failure but rather by the scorched-earth policy of the British fleeing from the threat of a Japanese invasion of eastern Bengal, the government's desperation to ensure food supplies to the army and Calcutta, and the resultant distortions in the food grains market.[79] And speaking of bloody revolutions, the fragile spirit of Hindu-Muslim fraternity was cruelly shattered in August 1946 by the Great Calcutta Killing, in which in the space of four or five days, several thousand people from both communities were slaughtered in the city in a frenzy of violence never seen in its relatively peaceful history since the time when Siraj laid siege to the old Fort William.[80] It is quite certain that there was considerable overlap between the public that celebrated the victories of the Mohun Bagan or Mohammedan Sporting clubs on the Maidan, the public that agitated for the removal of the Holwell monument, and the murderous public that went on a rampage on the streets and in the slums of Calcutta.

EMPIRE TODAY

In 1947, a US psychologist asked 115 senior college students in New York about the Black Hole incident. About one-third knew something about it, with most believing it to be "essentially true."[81] Today, it would be surprising to find one out of a hundred students anywhere in the world—even in Bengal—who knows anything about the Black Hole of Calcutta. What has changed?

One cannot blame the fickleness of popular memory for the obliteration of the Black Hole. The skepticism of scholars did in fact percolate slowly into the layers of public consciousness in Bengal. Tourist guides to Calcutta in the 1920s, for instance, routinely narrated the Black Hole story when describing the Holwell monument, plaques, and markings indicating the site of the old fort at Dalhousie Square.[82] But already one could hear the dissenting voice. A travel guide from 1921 authored by Hassan Suhrawardy, a doctor belonging to a notable Calcutta family, after complimenting Curzon for omitting the reference to Siraj's crimes in his inscription on the new monument, goes on to explain: "It is a physical impossibility to accommodate 146 persons in a space 18 feet by

15 feet even if they were packed like sardines laid one on top of another. That there was space to move about is proved by Holwell's statement.... It is indeed impossible that the incident as handed down to us for the purpose of rousing our historical ire could ever have taken place."[83]

The Black Hole debate had clearly not fallen on deaf ears. In 1948, the famous Indian historian Jadunath Sarkar, who had little sympathy for nationalist history, claimed that Holwell's story was an exaggeration and that the total number of prisoners in the Black Hole was probably sixty.[84] In 1958, Percival Spear, editing Vincent Smith's widely circulated textbook on Indian history for postcolonial times, added the following note on the Black Hole incident:

> We owe the traditional story of the Black Hole to the descriptive powers of J. Z. Holwell, the defender of Calcutta and a plausible but none too reliable man. For fifty years little notice was taken of the incident, but it then became convenient material for the compilers of an imperialist hagiology.... The emphasis upon the incident grew so great that the Black Hole became, along with Plassey and the Mutiny, one of the three things which every schoolboy knew about India.... The attempt to prove that the incident never occurred has not proved convincing, though the details of Holwell's account may well owe something to his imagination.... In my judgement something like the Black Hole incident as described by Holwell actually occurred, though the numbers involved and the details are not certain.[85]

In 1962, Brijen Gupta published what is considered the definitive historical work on the subject, taking into account every available piece of evidence, and came to the conclusion that the maximum number of persons confined in the Black Hole prison was sixty-four, of whom forty-three died and twenty-one survived. Among them were many who were seriously injured from the three-day battle.[86] The historians' consensus today can be gauged from the fact that the volume published in 1987 in the new *Cambridge History of India* on the conquest of Bengal, authored by the preeminent P. J. Marshall, does not even list the Black Hole in its index.[87] It is not worthy of even a mention. Has the star of empire, then, finally collapsed into a black hole?

One has reason to doubt it. Indeed, there are many reasons to think that the imperial impulse is still with us. Needless to say, the invasion and occupation of Afghanistan and Iraq by forces led by the United States in the last decade have rekindled memories of times when imperialism meant the annexation of colonial territories. Just as the occupation of Iraq or Afghanistan did not lead to direct colonial rule but rather the supervised creation of new sovereign constitutional regimes, though, so did the phase of decolonization after World War II *not* mean the end of the global practices of empire.[88] The second half of the twentieth century actually saw many attempts by scholars to make sense of a global order of empire without colonies.

In order to include both formal and informal modes of empire within a single conceptual frame, Charles Maier has defined empire as "a form of political organization in which the social elements that rule in the dominant state ... create networks of allied elites in regions abroad who accept subordination in international affairs in return for the security of their position in their own administrative unit."[89] Similarly, Michael Doyle has proposed that empires be defined as "relationships of political control imposed by some political societies over the effective sovereignty of other political societies."[90] This immediately begs the question of what one means by "political control."

It therefore is useful to begin by reiterating that imperial control works on the plane of *sovereignty*—its effects must be discerned from what it can or cannot do to the exercise of the sovereign powers of other states. Earlier in this book, we pointed out that imperial practices since the eighteenth century involved, even in the early days of European annexation of territories in the East, an assumption of formal equality between sovereign entities that could acquire or surrender territories and other privileges. By the nineteenth century, in the heyday of imperialism, the quality of sovereignty that demanded the recognition of formally equal status in the so-called family of nations became restricted to certain states of Europe and the Americas. It was in that period that a range of imperial practices were developed that involved varying degrees of intervention in the external and domestic powers of putatively sovereign political entities. There was thus, on the one hand, a normative assumption of formal equality in the relations between proper sovereign states such as the countries of Europe, and on the other hand, varying degrees of exception to that norm in the relations between imperial powers and entities of inferior status. It was in the context of that history of political practices that we defined the imperial power as the prerogative to declare the colonial exception. The formal equality of proper sovereign states ruled out the use of imperial practices of power in their mutual relations; they could only be employed in relations with inferior political entities. This was the normative foundation of the European states system in the eighteenth and nineteenth century so lauded by conservative theorists such as Schmitt.

We also saw, however, that by the early twentieth century, the idea had gained ground and become universally compelling that the sovereignty of the modern state truly resided only in the constituent body of a people-nation. Since the period of decolonization in the second half of the twentieth century, the status of formal equality of sovereign nation-states has been normatively established on a global scale and is embodied in international organizations such as the United Nations, at least in its General Assembly.[91] The old practices of imperial power, involving conquest and annexation of colonial territories, are no longer legitimate. Nevertheless, it is still our contention that *the most reliable definition of an imperial practice remains that of the privilege to declare the exception to the norm.*

Formal equality of status among sovereign nation-states constitutes the normative foundation of international practice. As we have seen in this book, from the time of Bentham's universal scheme for all governments, a common measure of comparison has given rise to two senses of the norm: the normal as the empirical average, and the normatively desirable. Interstate comparisons on a wide variety of economic, political, and social indicators are now commonplace, not only in the discourse of experts, but also in ordinary public discussion in the news media. Yet just as inequality of incomes is not in itself a violation of the right of equal citizenship in the modern state, so too inequality between nation-states is not in itself evidence of imperial domination by one or some nations over others. As such, the empirical deviation in the position of a state from the average or normal measure according to some economic or social indicator is not by itself a sign that its sovereignty is either respected or violated by other states. The exercise of power over the sovereignty of states occurs when a connection is established between the empirical and normative registers. That is when the empirical deviation is made the basis for declaring that the normative standard of relations between formally equal sovereign states must be suspended in a particular case and the nation-state in question must be declared an exception.

One of the key points of interest of this book was the close interweaving of the modern practices of imperial power with the modern discourses of political, economic, and legal knowledge. A claim we have made here is that modern imperial technologies of power emerged as an integral part of the philosophical discourse of the modern state—in fact, aligned for the most part with its most enlightened trends—and not as some external atavistic residue of archaic times when naked power was celebrated for its own sake. Hence, the enunciation of an imperial practice was almost always inextricably tied to its legal and moral justification.

It is interesting, of course, that it was precisely in the second half of the nineteenth century, when imperialism became an explicitly avowed policy objective of every recognized or aspiring great power, and the moral rhetoric of civilizing liberalism became somewhat unfashionable, that the language of realpolitik came to dominate the fields of foreign and colonial policy. But realist policies too required moral justification, even if it was only to assert that imperial interventions and acquisitions were in the national interest—that is, good for the metropolitan nation as a whole. Not surprisingly, then, the late nineteenth century was also when systematic critiques of empire were produced, claiming to show that those policies were actually in the interests of only some classes, whether feudal aristocrats, capitalist manufacturers, or financial oligarchs, and against the interests of the many.

The gap that was opened in the later nineteenth century between the avowed justifications of empire and its "real" reasons provided the invitation to many to investigate the underlying structural conditions in economy and society that led capitalist countries to pursue imperialist policies. As is evident, in this field, Marxist theories of imperialism have constituted a distinct tradition by itself.[92] When colonial empires came to an end in the second half of the twentieth century, and no one wanted to own up anymore to being an imperialist, Marxist scholars were prominent among those who argued that despite the formal disavowal of empires, there was in reality a neocolonialism or neoimperialism.[93] The key feature here was the emergence of a certain global division of labor between the advanced industrial manufacturing economies of the metropolitan First World and the underdeveloped, largely agrarian ones of the Third World supplying primary agricultural products and mineral raw materials.[94]

One influential line of argument here continued the Hilferding-Lenin theme, and focused on the monopoly corporate forms of industrial and financial capital, especially in the United States, where it was also deeply entwined with the defense and space research industry financed by the state. Paul Baran and Paul Sweezy held that in its new phase, state monopoly capital not only ensured the conditions of continued accumulation by monopoly capital, through the interventions of state agencies in the domestic economy, but also, with suitable foreign policy interventions, the continued competitive expansion of foreign markets and sources of raw materials, especially oil.[95] Tom Kemp and Harry Magdoff emphasized the structural power of monopoly corporate capital, particularly multinational firms, over the state in most Western countries, especially the United States. The state acted to promote the interests of multinationals in the underdeveloped world, by informal diplomatic means, if possible, or if necessary, even by the threat or use of force.[96] Over the last three decades, Noam Chomsky has indefatigably documented the effects on US foreign policy of this nexus between multinational corporations and the political elite.[97]

A second line of argument stressed the structural links of dependency between the advanced industrial economies of the center and the primary product economies of the global periphery, creating and perpetuating underdevelopment in the countries of Latin America, Africa, and Asia. André Gunder Frank made perhaps the most well-known statement of this position, to which Samir Amin added the interesting supplement that even though capitalist manufacture had been introduced in some Third World economies, the narrow specialization of such peripheral capitalism only perpetuated its structural dependence on the metropolitan economies.[98]

Significantly, most of these theories did not consider the clearly asymmetrical power relations between the USSR and its satellite countries, or indeed those between Russia and the other constituents of the Soviet federation, which were, in constitutional theory at least, self-determining nations with the right to secede from the union. Some claims were developed in the 1970s, with inspiration from the Chinese Cultural Revolution, of Soviet socialism being only a variant of state capitalism, and in its characteristic form of state monopoly, therefore being open to "social-imperialism."[99]

These theories of imperialism that were much in vogue in the 1960s and 1970s have been once more made obsolete by the ability of the capitalist order to adapt, and in fact restructure, itself in order to cope with the crises that have dotted its history. What changed decisively in the last two decades of the twentieth century was the emergence of a new mode of flexible production and accumulation coupled with the rapid expansion of the international financial markets. New developments in communications technology allowed for innovations in the management of production that could now disperse different components of the production process away from the centralized factory to smaller production and service units, often located in different parts of the world and sometimes even in the informal household sector. Alongside this, there was a huge rise in the speculative investment of capital in the international markets for stocks, bonds, and currencies.

These two developments jointly provided the basic economic push away from the old model of national economic autarky to one where global networks are acknowledged as exercising considerable power over national economies. It has meant that the emergent economies of Asia in particular have become the sites for rapid growth of industrial manufacturing, fueled by exports to the older capitalist economies of the West, while the latter have sought to profit from global financial speculation as well as a disorganized and dispirited working class at home. While large pockets of subsistence agriculture and poverty still remain in many countries of Asia, the main economic dynamic is now a rapidly growing, principally capitalist, modern industrial manufacturing sector that is quite diversified in its products and use of technology, and that supports the growth of modern financial, educational, and other tertiary sectors. Like capitalist growth in earlier historical periods, the recent growth in Asian economies is accompanied by the massive dissociation of primary producers from their means of labor—something that David Harvey has called "accumulation by dispossession."[100] What must be underlined, however, is that this transformation has been brought about everywhere in Asia, not only in China or India, but also in South Korea, Taiwan, Singapore, Malaysia, or Indonesia, by the direct, systematic, and active intervention of the postcolonial nation-state and its political leadership.

On the ideological front, the celebratory literature on globalization in the 1990s argued that the removal of trade barriers imposed by national governments, greater mobility of people, and the cultural impact of global information flows would make for conditions in which there would be a general desire globally for democratic forms of government and greater democratic values in social life. Free markets were expected to promote "free societies." As an extension of the fundamental liberal idea, it was assumed that in spite of differences in economic and military power, there would be respect for the autonomy of governments and peoples around the world, precisely because everyone was committed to the free and unrestricted flow of capital, goods, peoples, and ideas. Colonies and empires were clearly antithetical to this liberal ideal of the globalized society.

There was a second line of argument, however, that was also an important part of the globalization literature of the 1990s. It insisted that because of the new global conditions, it was not only possible but also necessary for the international community to use its power to protect human rights while promoting democratic values in countries under despotic and authoritarian rule. There could be no absolute protection afforded by the principle of national sovereignty to tyrannical regimes. Of course, the international community had to act through a legitimate international body such as the United Nations. Since this would imply a democratic consensus among the nations of the world (or at least a large number of them), international humanitarian intervention of this kind to protect human rights or prevent violence and oppression would not be imperial or colonial.

These two lines, both advanced within the discourse of liberal globalization, implied a contradiction. At one extreme, one could assert that democratic norms in international affairs meant that national sovereignty was inviolable except when there was a clear international consensus in favor of humanitarian intervention; anything less would be akin to imperialist meddling. At the other extreme, the claim might be that globalization had made national sovereignty an outdated concept. The peacekeeping requirements now necessitated something like an empire without a sovereign metropolitan center: a virtual empire representing an immanent global sovereignty. There would be no more wars, only police action. This is the contention presented eloquently, if unpersuasively, by Michael Hardt and Antonio Negri.[101]

It is hard to accept that the new globalized networks of production, exchange, and cultural flows have produced, as Hardt and Negri believe, the conditions of possibility for a new immanent, deterritorialized, and centerless Empire. The argument is not persuasive even for the 1990s—from the first Persian Gulf War to the war over Kosovo—when there was a relatively high level of consensus in the so-called international community for armed interventions to enforce international law and protect human rights. In the period after the invasion of Iraq, it has lost all credibility. Despite the rhetoric of a so-called global war against terror, the Bush administration's policies and those of each of its allies seemed to be perfectly explicable in terms of fairly old-fashioned calculations of ensuring national security and furthering national interests. Much of the resistance to US unilateralism, taking numerous forms from the diplomatic to the insurgent as well as cutting across ideological divides, also adopted the old logic of protecting the sovereign sphere of national power and frequently employed the old rhetoric of anti-imperialism. What then, if anything, has changed?

It is true that the era of globalization has seen the undermining of national sovereignty in critical areas of foreign trade, property, contract laws, and technologies of governance. There is an overwhelming pressure toward the uniformity of regulations and procedures in these areas, overseen, needless to say, by the major economic powers through new international economic institutions. It is also evident that the close connectedness of national economies through massive volumes of foreign trade and the interlocking of financial markets across the world have made the performance of individual economies as well as the policies of individual national governments a matter of global concern. Can one then presume that there exists something like a global agency of capital with its distinct interests acting through a consensus of views among at least the major capitalist powers? Or is there competition and conflict among the great powers, not unlike the situation before World War I, where international interventions of various kinds on the lesser powers are both common and legitimate? The answer, we suggest, lies in the variable and uncertain overlap between the economic and geopolitical interests of the three great power blocs today—the United States and Britain, the major powers of Europe, and China—all of them now fully integrated into the global circuits of capitalist production and exchange.

The situation has turned even more uncertain and unpredictable since 2008 because of the sudden emergence of a global financial crisis. The principal dynamic that drove consumption and growth in the world economy in the last two decades was provided by the predatory movements of speculative finance capital. The crisis has brought those movements to a screeching halt. This has resulted in not only recession and fears of large-scale unemployment in the advanced Western economies but also a severe slowdown in growth in the large developing economies dependent on exports to Western countries. We are witnessing, at least for the time being, a sudden retreat from the neoliberal ideologies that were dominant in the last two decades to a recourse to Keynesian policies of expanded state expenditure to stimulate demand and greater regulation of financial markets. On the other hand, the burden of huge budget deficits and massive external debts are threatening the financial collapse of national economies. Faced with these contradictory pressures, the sentiments of national autarky seem to be on the resurgence in many countries of Europe and North America.

Although there is much talk today of the current global financial crisis spelling the irreversible decline of the Western economies and the rise to dominance of the rapidly growing manufacturing economies of Asia, it is still too soon to make such predictions.[102] More crucially, one must not ignore the implications of the gap that will then be opened up between the declining economic influence of the United States and the European countries, and their continued overwhelming military dominance in the world. The economies of the United States and the countries of western Europe are no longer primarily driven by the strength and innovativeness of their manufacturing sectors, but by their ability to maintain financial dominance over the world economy. Despite staggering debts, the United States continues to enjoy worldwide confidence in its bonds and currency, because of the credibility of its political and military dominance. What sorts of political judgments can one expect those states to make in such a situation of asymmetry between their real economic capabilities and ambitions of global power?

This is the situation in which, we propose, our general definition of the imperial prerogative as the power to declare the exception is useful. Without discounting the specific and variable economic or geopolitical conditions that may sustain that prerogative, the definition grounds imperial practices on the political plane of national sovereignty. Equal rights of sovereignty constitute the norm. But exceptions are both plentiful and various. One exception is enshrined in the UN Security Council, which has five permanent members with veto power. The realist justification for this is that no collective security measure could be pragmatically expected to succeed if all the major powers of the world were not in agreement. This notion is perfectly in line with many realist justifications in history of the imperial privilege that claims more than what is entailed by the equal rights of sovereignty.

A plethora of exceptional practices, for instance, surround the place of Israel as the most recent European settler colony in Asia and the corresponding denial of the political rights of sovereign nationhood promised to Palestinians by the League of Nations mandate (every other mandated territory is now an independent nation-state and UN member). To cite another example, everyone agrees that nuclear proliferation is dangerous and should be stopped. Yet who decides that India may be allowed to have nuclear weapons, and also Israel, and maybe even Pakistan, but not North Korea or Iran? We all know that there are many brutally repressive regimes that are also sources of international terrorism, but who decided that it was not Saudi Arabia or Burma but rather Saddam Hussein's regime in Iraq that must be overthrown by force? US drones may be sent in to strike terrorist targets in Pakistan or Yemen without the willing approval of those states, but such action would be inconceivable if the terrorist targets were in, say, Russia or Spain. Public outrage over an oil spill in the Gulf of Mexico will induce the United States to demand that BP pay several billions of dollars to clean up the mess, while it would use diplomatic pressure, with the covert connivance of those in power in India, to ensure that Union Carbide pay no more than two thousand dollars for each of some twenty thousand persons killed in Bhopal in 1984 in the worst industrial disaster in history. Those who claim to decide on the exception do indeed arrogate to themselves the imperial prerogative.

Speaking of economic prerogatives, special concessions or privileges not given to other states, if extracted under diplomatic pressure in a situation where the nation-state concerned would not otherwise have granted it, would be a case of the use of the imperial prerogative. Free trade is ordinarily not characteristic of imperial domination, but it would be if it forcibly precludes a nation-state from imposing protective tariffs or restrictions on foreign capital if it wanted to. Lowering the credit ratings on the Greek or Irish economies, or insisting on spending cuts or administrative reforms as conditions for an international recovery package, need not mean the declaring of a colonial exception, yet it would if the same conditions were not dictated by international agencies to the United Kingdom even when the British debt situation is no better than the Greek or Irish. The criterion is, in all cases, the normative set of practices that apply between states that recognize one another's sovereignty as equal. Deviations from those norms are the marks of imperial practices of power.

Declaring an exception within the framework of normalization, we have seen, immediately opens up a pedagogical project. The imperial power must then take on the responsibility of educating, disciplining, and training the colony in order to bring it up to the norm. There have been only two forms of imperial pedagogy in history, as noted earlier: a pedagogy of violence, and a pedagogy of culture. The colony must either be disciplined by force or civilized by culture. We have seen both of these forms in recent times, long after the era of decolonization and the end of the cold war.

We should add that with the evident decline of US unilateralism following the end of the Bush presidency and advent of the global financial crisis, it is entirely conceivable that the imperial prerogative may now be shared among several new powers. There could well emerge regional hegemons claiming to declare the colonial exception within their own spheres of influence, and seeking to discipline deviant states by the instruments of violence and pedagogy. Germany could do this in Europe. And there is no reason to believe that a postcolonial democracy such as India would not harbor ambitions of playing such an imperial role, just as democracies of the nineteenth century had done. In some ways, that would resemble a structure of international politics familiar in the nineteenth-century imperial age of the balance of power.

Finally, there is one more possibility to worry about: the asymmetry between the economic troubles of the Western powers and their overwhelming military superiority could well open the field for a populist resurgence of imperialism, not unlike what was seen in the late nineteenth century. The economic decline of the once privileged is fertile ground for the ugly display of naked power. There are already signs of a growing populist politics in the United States and Western Europe seeking to defend the global privileges of the core body of citizens

Figure 28. Garbage dump at former paved site of Black Hole. *Photo: Abhijit Bhattacharya*

of those countries against the assertions of lesser powers and the intrusions of alien immigrants. That form of politics could claim increasing resort to preemptive strikes, the overthrowing of regimes, and the military occupation of other countries. In that case, within the general political definition of the imperial prerogative, we would see the use of imperial practices that were once quite ubiquitous, but in the wake of decolonization, rendered only temporarily obsolete.

The imperial prerogative to declare the exception has implied, ever since the nineteenth century, a range of alternative practices—from diplomatic pressure to secure differential concessions that would not otherwise be given, to the forcible occupation and annexation of territory. It is salutary to remember that all of those options remain open today, even though some are used more frequently than others. Just as we continue to live in the age of nation-states, so have we not transcended the age of empire.

AFTERWORD

Binay-Badal-Dinesh Bag is currently being given a facelift to restore its Victorian looks and make it more attractive to foreign tourists. The space between the General Post Office and Collectorate Building where Curzon had memoralized the site of the Black Hole prison has, however, turned into an unauthorized garbage dump, not by design, but instead because that is what usually happens to unutilized spaces in the densely populated city. On the pavement in front, the trunk of an ancient tree jutting out of a tiled rostrum is painted with oil and vermillion—a shrine dedicated to some roadside deity. Behind the General Post Office is located the rarely visited Philatelic Museum, which displays curiosities from the history of the post and telegraph services in India. On the floor of the museum office, reclining against the wall, is a black marble tablet that a historian will recognize as the plaque that Curzon had put up above his re-created site of the Black Hole prison. The inscription on it has faded, and a crack runs diagonally across its left side. An elderly gentleman in the museum office explains: "It used to be displayed on the wall of the Collectorate office. But Netaji Subhas Chandra wanted it removed. So he came in a demonstration and dealt a hammer blow that dislodged the plaque from the wall. You can still see the mark he left behind."

Unsurprisingly, the ground remains fertile for nationalist mythology.

Notes

CHAPTER 1. OUTRAGE IN CALCUTTA

1. Text of inscriptions in Holwell 1774, frontispiece. For a slightly different text of the inscription, probably incorporating corrections in the spellings of names, see Busteed 1888, 49.

2. For the most detailed account of Calcutta in this period, see Wilson 1906.

3. One careful estimate puts the population of the town in 1750 at 120,000. See Ray 1902.

4. Marshall 2000.

5. Bengal Public Consultations, Fort William, June 24, 1745, in Wilson 1906, 1:183; General Letter from Bengal to the Court, Fort William, January 31, 1746, in Wilson 1906, 1:185.

6. General Letter from the Court to Bengal, London, June 17, 1748, in Wilson 1906, 1:204–5.

7. As early as 1699, the court of directors in London was writing to Charles Eyre, the governor of the fort in Calcutta, that "the protected should pay an Acknowledgement to their Defenders.... We recommend to you the raising a standing Revenue by the Methods above mentioned ... well knowing that when they shall find the Impartiality and Mildness of the English Government, They shall be easily induced to betake themselves to your Protection, and in a short time render the Territory within your late Grant the most fflourishing Spott of Ground in Bengall" (Instructions from the Court to Sir Charles Eyre, London, December 20, 1699, in Wilson 1906, 1:47).

8. Nair 1990.

9. They added: "You cant be insensible the Mogull is daily drawing nearer his end which will very probably give birth to many Intestine Commotions before his Successor be quietly Settled in his Throne during which time all Rich Unfortified Places will be a tempting bait to those perfidious people" (General Letter from the Court to Bengal, London, November 29, 1700, in Wilson 1906, 1:48).

10. General Letter from the Court to Bengal, London, February 4, 1709, in Wilson 1906, 1:74–75. When the officials at Fort William wrote back saying that the fortifications had been made defensible "without alarming the Moors," the directors expressed satisfaction, reiterating: "Do all with the least noise and urge plausible reasons for what you do if enquiry is made about it" (Letter from Bengal to Court, Fort William, December 30, 1710, in Wilson 1906, 1:83; General Letter from the Court to Bengal, London, December 28, 1711, in Wilson 1906, 1:85).

11. Marshall 1976, 159, 181.

12. Ibid., 213–16.

13. Gupta 1962, 13.

14. Marshall 1998.

15. Marshall 1976, 60–63.

16. In 1727, for example, the governor of Fort William wrote to the directors in London that "every Company servant was free to improve his fortune in any way that he chose, either inland or by sea" (cited in ibid., 109).

17. Gupta 1962, 13.

18. Marshall 1976, 109–10.

19. General Letter from Bengal to the Court, Fort William in Calcutta, August 15, 1702, in Wilson 1906, 1:51–52.

20. Cited in Gupta 1962, 36.

21. Dodwell (1920) 1967.

22. Letter from the Court to the Governor of Fort William, London, June 17, 1748, in Wilson 1906, 1:205–12.

23. Letter from Orme to Clive, August 25, 1752, in Hill 1905, 1:xxxiii.

24. Letter from the Court to Scott, in Wilson 1906, 1:245–49; Additional Letter to Colonel Scott, London, December 15, 1752, in Wilson 1906, 1:245–49.

25. Gupta 1962, 38.

26. Cited in ibid., 39.

27. Scrafton (1763) 1770, 52.

28. Tabatabai (1902) 1986, 2:163.

29. Datta 1971, 9–11; Chaudhury 2000, 55–58. On the Rajballabh episode in particular, see R. Ray 1994, 24–25.

30. Drake to Fort William Council, January 17–25, 1757, in Hill 1905, 2:147. No copy of Drake's letter has been found, and there were allegations that Drake's later report to the council on the contents of his letter was not accurate. See Hill 1905, 1:l. Drake, it will be noticed, was only repeating an argument suggested by the directors in London from as far back as 1709.

31. Cited in Ali (1952) 1985, 63.

32. Chaudhury 2000, 45.

33. Datta 1971, 13.

34. R. Ray 1994, 29.

35. Letters from the Nawab to Coja Wajid, Rajmehal, May 28, 1756, Muxadabad, June 1, 1756, and on the way to Calcutta, in Hill 1905, 1:3–5; R. Ray 1994, 27–28. Francis Sykes, writing on behalf of William Watts, "who is in extream low spirits," specified that Siraj had demanded that "no *dusticks* be given to any of the black merchants" (Francis Sykes to Council, Fort William, Cossimbazar, June 4, 1756, in Hill 1905, 1:9–10). For more on this, see Chaudhury 2000, 54–55.

36. Letter from Nabob Mansoorel Muloch Serajah Dowlah Bahadur Hayabet Jung to the Gomasta of the English of the Trading House at Madras, in Hill 1905, 1:196.

37. Letter from Watts and Collet to Council at Fulta, Chandernagore, July 8, 1756, in Hill 1905, 1:61. The French merchants in Kasimbazar thought that the English had given in because of "faint-heartedness" and "cowardly behaviour" (Letter from M. Vernet and Council, Cossimbazar, to the Dutch Director and Council, Hugli, June 4, 1756, in Hill 1905, 1: 7–8; Letter from M. Vernet and Council, Cossimbazar, to M. La Tour at Patna, June 10, 1756, in Hill 1905, 1:16).

38. Letter from Council, Fort William, to Council, Fort St. George, June 8, 1756, in Hill 1905, 1:13–14.

39. Gupta 1962, 61–62.

40. An Account of the Capture of Calcutta by Captain Grant, July 13, 1756, in Hill 1905, 1:76.

41. William Tooke reported: "June 17th we caused all the *buzars* and *cajan* [*kacha*, meaning thatched] houses to the eastward to be burnt, as likewise to the southward, almost as far as Govinpoors where many of our people being detected plundering were instantly punished with dicapitation" (Narrative of the Capture of Calcutta from April 10, 1756, to November 10, 1756, by William Tooke, in Hill 1905, 1:257).

42. Narrative by Governor Drake, July 19, 1756, in Hill 1905, 1:139. Gobindaram was known as the "black zemindar," and from 1720 to 1756 was the chief official through whom the company collected rents in Black Town. He was reputed to have been both oppressive and fabulously wealthy, and Holwell dismissed him for his abuses.

43. Khan 1982, 120.

44. Narrative by Drake, July 19, 1756, in Hill 1905, 1:153.

45. Account by Grant, July 13, 1756, in Hill 1905, ed., 1:77, 84. Drake's narrative confirms this; see Hill 1905, 1:153. William Lindsay, a company official, reported that many soldiers had even "drawn bayonets on several of their officers" (William Lindsay to Robert Orme, off Fulta, July 1756, in Hill 1905, 1:166).

46. Account by Grant, July 13, 1756, in Hill 1905, 1:84.

47. Narrative by Drake, July 19, 1756, in Hill 1905, 1:141–42.

48. The French in Chandannagar heard that the English "have put all their money on the ships they have, on which also they have embarked all the women, and that in this state they are waiting for the Nawab" (Letter from Council, Chandernagore, to M. De La Bretesche, Patna, June 20, 1756, in Hill 1905, 22–24).

49. Account of the loss of Calcutta by Grey, Junior, June 1756, in Hill 1905, 1:107–8.

50. Hill 1905, 3:358.

51. Secret Consultations of the Dutch Council, Hugli, June 28, 1756, in Hill 1905, 1:37–38.

52. Letter to M. Demontorcin, Chandernagore, August 1, 1756, in Hill 1905, 1:180–81.

53. Letter from Council at Fulta to Council, Fort Saint George, off Fulta, July 13, 1756, in Hill 1905, 1:71–73.

54. Protest of the Late Inhabitants of Calcutta against Charles Manningham's Going to the Coast, off Fulta, July 10, 1756, in Hill 1905, 1:66.

55. Letter from Watts and Collet to Council at Fulta, Chandernagore, July 14, 1756, in Hill 1905, 1:97–98.

56. Letter from J. Z. Holwell to Councils, Bombay and Fort Saint George, Muxadavad, July 17, 1756, in Hill 1905, 1:109–16.

57. Lindsay to Orme, July 1756, in Hill 1905, 1:168. Clive, too, did not believe Holwell's story, remarking that "nothing but the want of a boat prevented his escape and flight with the rest" (cited in Edwardes 1969, 64).

58. Holwell's Minute on the Fulta Consultations, Fulta, August 13, 1756, in Hill 1905, 1:202–3.

59. Holwell's Minute and Dissent in Council at Fulta, August 20, 1756, in Hill 1905, 1:201–2.

60. Narrative by Tooke, in Hill 1905, 1:292–93, 298–99.

61. The contemporary historian Karam Ali ([1952] 1985, 64) writes: "Fakhr-ut-tujar [Khwaja Wajid] had said that the plunder of Calcutta would bring 3 *krors* [thirty million] of rupees to the Nawab's Government; it was indeed capable of yielding that amount, but the effects of the other traders, such as Muslims, Hindus, Armenians, were all plundered by the camp followers and the Nawab's only gain was a bad name. The Nawab's share [of the spoils] was specially dependent on the money in the factory. But the English sahibs loaded in their ships and took away with them all the money and valuable articles existing there."

62. Letter written from Chandernagore, July 3, 1756, in Hill 1905, 1:47–53.

63. Letter from Holwell, July 17, 1756, in Hill 1905, 1:112.

64. Letter from Holwell, August 3, 1756, in Hill 1905, 1:186.

65. Narrative by Tooke, in Hill 1905, 1:288–89.

66. Gupta 1962, 72–75.

67. Holwell 1758, 385.

68. Also included in Holwell 1774, 381–418. References to the *Genuine Narrative* are from this edition. Davis, a company servant in Bengal, had returned to Britain, leaving his private cotton trade in the hands of his friends Holwell and Edward Cruttenden. It was later alleged that his *banian* Nayanchand Mallik, using his "superior knowledge of the cotton trade," defrauded Davis of fifteen thousand rupees. The Mayor's Court in Calcutta dismissed Davis's complaint, but the decision was reversed on appeal to the council at Fort William. See *Edward Holden Cruttenden and John Zephania Holwell, Attorneys for, and on Behalf of, William Davis (Plaintiffs) v. Nian Mullick (Defendant), on Appeal against Decree of Mayor's Court to the President and Council of Fort William, and Further Cross-Appeal to His Majesty in Council, 1749*, Oriental and India Office Collections, British Library, London.

69. Holwell 1758, 392.

70. Ibid., 391.

71. Ibid., 389, 390.

72. Ibid., 393.

73. Ibid., 393.

74. Ibid., 394, 395.

75. Ibid., 395, 396.

76. Ibid., 399, 400.

77. Ibid., 397.

78. Ibid., 401.

79. Ibid., 401, 402.

80. Ibid., 404.

81. Ibid., 405, 406.

82. Ibid., 415, 416.

83. Ibid., 406.

84. Joseph 2004, 69.

85. I do not think, therefore, as Betty Joseph (ibid., 67) suggests, that Holwell writes from a position usually reserved for women and children in, for instance, North American captivity narratives. There is a fundamental difference between the image of the Native American "savage" and that of the despotic Moor.

86. For biographical details on Holwell, see Busteed 1888, 34–41.

87. Dirks 2006.

88. Letter from Council, Fort Saint George, to Colonel Clive, October 13, 1756, in Hill 1905, 1:233–34.

89. Letter from Select Committee, Fort Saint George, to the Select Committee, Fort William, October 13, 1756, in Hill 1905, 1:239–40.

90. Letter from Colonel Clive to the Secret Committee, London, Fort Saint George, October 11, 1756, in Hill 1905, 1:232–33.

91. Letter from Pierre Renault to le Marquis Dupleix, Chandernagore, August 26, 1756, in Hill 1905, 1:210–11.

92. Letter from M. Furnier to le Marquis Dupleix, Chandernagore, August 24, 1756, in Hill 1905, 1:205.

93. Clive to Secret Committee, October 11, 1756, in Hill 1905, 1:233.

94. Luke Scrafton ([1763] 1770, 58), active in Bengal both before and after the fall of Calcutta, speculated that Siraj probably held a low opinion of the armed strength of the English, and thought they would settle for peace "to carry on our trade like Armenians or his own subjects."

95. Letter from Select Committee, Fort William, to Select Committee, Fort Saint George, January 8, 1757, in Hill 1905, 2:93–94.

96. Letter from Clive to Pigot, Fort William, January 8, 1757, in Hill 1905, 2: 96–97.

97. Opinion of the Select Committee (Fort Saint George), September 29, 1756, in Hill 1905, 1:222.

98. Letter from Colonel Clive to Coja Wajid, January 21, 1757, in Hill 1905, 2:125.

99. Ali (1952) 1985, 71–72.

100. Datta 1971, 49–66; Gupta 1962, 101; Chaudhury 2000, 151.

101. For more on Khwaja Petrus, see Seth (1937) 1983, 327–47.

102. Letter from Scrafton to Walsh, Cossimbazar, April 9, 1757, in Hill 1905, 3:343.

103. Fort William Select Committee Proceedings of May 1, 1757, in Hill 1905, 2:370.

104. For Watts's own, highly self-congratulatory account of the secret negotiations, see Watts (1760) 1988.

105. For details on Rai Durlabh, see Mukhopadhyay 1974.

106. Clive was quite open about this. He wrote to the Select Committee at Fort William: "Enclosed you will receive the real and fictitious articles of Agreement, which you will please to sign; the Admiral promised me to do the same by the real one, but not the fictitious one; if he makes any scruple send it without and we will sign it for him in such manner that Omichund shall not discover it" (Clive to Select Committee, Fort William, Chandernagore, May 18, 1757, in Hill 1905, 2:387). For more details on Amirchand, see Sinha 1965, 241–47.

107. Karam Ali (1952) 1985, 76–77; Yusuf Ali 1982, 132–35. For Jadunath Sarkar's dramatic description of the battle, see Sarkar (1948) 1972, 487–95.

108. Clive to Jafar Ali Khan, Daudpur, June 24, 1757, in Hill 1905, 2:426–27.

109. Bandyopadhyay, Sengupta, and Das Biswas 2003, 643.

110. A hundred years ago, the historian Nikhilnath Ray ([1897] 1978, 143), writing about the cemetery, spoke of an otherworldly spirit of renunciation that enveloped the visitor to these somewhat-unkempt gardens that reminded him of the audacious attempt

by a ruler of Bengal to oust the enormously powerful British and his cruel end under the dirt of Khoshbagh.

Chapter 2. A Secret Veil

1. Seeley (1883) 1906, 179. Seeley also famously observed in his first course of lectures: "We seem, as it were, to have conquered and peopled half the world in a fit of absence of mind" (8).
2. Cited in Boxer 1981, 100.
3. Grotius 1916, 13.
4. Grotius 1950, 10.
5. For a discussion of the genealogy and significance of Grotius's arguments for the justification of European imperial expansion, see Tuck 1999, 78–108.
6. Cited in ibid., 119.
7. Ibid., 115–20.
8. Pearson 1987, 57–59.
9. Chaudhuri 1985, 63–64.
10. Chaudhuri 1978, 45.
11. Cited in Sutherland 1952, 3.
12. Chaudhuri 1978, 113.
13. Subrahmanyam 2005, 143–72.
14. Chaudhuri 1978, 121.
15. It is interesting to note that the image of the Dutch as ruthless in the pursuit of commercial gain entered into popular circulation in England in the late seventeenth century with the story of the alleged massacre in 1623 of twelve English traders by the Dutch on the Indonesian island of Amboina. John Dryden wrote a play, *Amboyna*, in 1673 in which the civility of the English, who valued gratitude, honor, heroism, and true religious faith, was contrasted with the brutality of the Dutch, who had no regard for reciprocity, faith, or justice. For a discussion, see Raman 2002, 189–236.
16. Cited in Sutherland 1952, 4.
17. Chaudhuri 1985, 95.
18. Chaudhuri 1978, 20.
19. Heckscher 1935, 1:436–55; Brewer 1988; Tilly 1990.
20. Cited in Heckscher 1935, 2:17, 18.
21. Cited in ibid., 2:29.
22. Cited in ibid., 2:29.
23. Colley 1992.
24. Scrafton (1763) 1770, 93.
25. For a summarization of a similar process of plunder in southern India in the same period, see Dirks 2006, 37–86.
26. Marshall 1976, 116.
27. Ibid., 117–18.
28. Cited in Kuiters 2002, 84.
29. Marshall 1976, 119, 120.
30. Cited in Kuiters 2002, 83.

31. Dirks 2006, 7–36.

32. Interestingly, it was Holwell, the temporary governor after Clive's departure, who led the move for a change of nawabs. It was openly alleged in company circles that Holwell had benefited little out of Mir Jafar, and so, "since that channel was stopped from whence it was expected some advantage would flow, it was necessary that another should be opened" (cited in Marshall 1976, 170). Holwell (1764) defended the "second revolution" in a pamphlet.

33. Marshall 1976, 126.

34. Cited in ibid., 155–56.

35. Cited in ibid., 168–69.

36. Letter from Court of Directors to Council in Bengal, February 19, 1766, in *FWIHC* 1949–58, 4:162–63.

37. Marshall 1976, 163.

38. Cited in Sutherland 1952, 297.

39. Sinha 1965, 224.

40. Cited in Forrest 1918, 2:176.

41. Cited in Marshall 1976, 130.

42. Clive to the Court of Directors, September 30, 1765, in *FWIHC* 1949–58, 4: 330–31.

43. Letter from Council in Bengal to Court of Directors, September 6, 1766, in *FWIHC* 1949–58, 426–29.

44. "Firmaun from the King Shah Aalum, Granting the Dewannee of Bengal, Bahar and Orissa, to the Company, Dated August 12th, 1765," in Forrest 1918, 2:287.

45. Clive to Thomas Rous, Madras, April 17, 1765, quoted in Forrest 1918, 2:256.

46. Pamphlet cited in Bowen 1991, 56.

47. Cited in ibid., 10.

48. For a discussion of this debate, see ibid., 48–66. For a detailed and critical review of the question of sovereignty in eighteenth-century British India, see Dirks 2006, 167–208.

49. For two recent discussions of the British historiography of India in the eighteenth century, with extended treatments of Orme, see Sen 2002; Dirks 2006, 245–84.

50. Cited in Dirks 2006, 247.

51. Orme 1778, 2:83–84, 79–80.

52. Ibid., 2:153–54.

53. Ibid., 2:70, 81–82.

54. Ibid., 2:75, 77.

55. Holwell 1767, 12–13.

56. Orme 1778, 2:185.

57. Ibid., 1:1–29.

58. Ibid., 1:5–6, 7–8.

59. Ibid., 29. The source for this expert observation is Bernier 1891, 200–38. Montesquieu ([1748] 1989, 234) cites the same observation in his discussion of the character of peoples living in southern climates.

60. Tuck 1999, 42, 67.

61. Montesquieu (1748) 1989 251–52. Montesquieu went on to contend that unlike northern Europeans, who conquered as free people, the Tartars, "Asia's natural conquerors,"

went to war only for their master. The conquerors themselves had become slaves. Hence, it was inescapable that "power should always be despotic in Asia" (282–83).

62. Koebner 1961.

63. Vattel 1916, 141.

64. For a critical discussion of these Spanish debates read in comparison with British and French ones, see Pagden 1995.

65. For an account of the tortuous theological and natural law arguments deployed in Spain to deny the right of the indigenous populations of America to their lands, see Pagden 1987.

66. Once again, see Pagden 1995. See also Armitage 2000, 97–99.

67. For an account of the different strands of argument going into this ideological construction, see Armitage 2000, 100–169.

68. See ibid., 173–98.

69. Wilson 1995, 189.

70. Armitage 2000, 175–76.

71. Tinker 1974.

72. Cited in Bowen 1991, 15.

73. Ibid., 16.

74. Cited in ibid., 24.

75. Forrest 1918, 2:179.

76. Bowen 1991, 31, 41–43.

77. For a well-summarized version of this story, see Dirks 2006, 37–86.

78. Cited in Marshall 1968, 26.

79. See especially Bowen 1991, 31–34.

80. Kumar 1983, 299–300.

81. Bowen 1991, 103–4.

82. Ibid., 119–30.

83. Bolts 1772. On the career of Bolts, see Kuiters 2002.

84. Bowen 1991, 95–96.

85. Dow 1772, 3:xxxix–cliv.

86. Foote 1778, 70.

87. Bolts 1772, 1:v, 1:213, 2:73, 2:123.

88. For an excellent discussion of Dow's intellectual connections to Enlightenment philosophy and mercantilist economic thinking, see Guha (1963) 1996, 12–36.

89. Travers 2007.

90. Dow 1772, 3:lxxi, lxxvii.

91. Ibid., 3:lxxxvi, xcvi.

92. For a list of pamphlets produced on this subject in Britain at this time, see Bowen 1991, 192–93.

93. Walpole to Seymour Conway, October 29, 1762, cited in Chaudhuri 1975, 277.

94. Cited in ibid., 395.

95. Hastings made several pleas to Parliament for a speedy conclusion of his trial—for instance, on the sixty-ninth day, May 23, 1791. See *History of the Trial* 1796, 67. Burke's phrases are repeated several times in the articles of impeachment presented by him to the House of Commons. See "Articles of Impeachment, 14, 21, 28 May 1787," in Burke 1991, 6:125–258.

96. Marshall 1965, 20.

97. "Speech on Nawab of Arcot's Debts," February 28, 1785, in Burke 1991, 5:543.

98. "Speech on Fox's India Bill," December 1, 1783, in Burke 1991, 5:403.

99. Speech by Warren Hastings in his Defense in the House of Commons on May 1, 1786, cited in Burke 1991, 6:348–49. Rosane Rocher (1983) speculates that these passages in Hastings's defense were actually composed by Nathaniel Brassey Halhed, a scholar of Indian languages.

100. "Opening of Impeachment," February 16, 1788, in Burke 1991, 6:345–46.

101. "Speech on Fox's India Bill," in Burke 1991, 5:401, 402.

102. Ibid., 5:430.

103. "Opening of Impeachment," February 16, 1788, in Burke 1991, 6:367–68.

104. *History of the Trial* 1796, Seventy-third day, June 2, 1791, 88, 98, 99, 101–2.

105. Dirks 2006, 207.

106. Marshall 2005, 128.

107. Arthur Lee to S. Adams, December 3, 1773, cited in Marshall 2005, 198.

108. Cited in ibid., 255–56, 201, 203.

109. For a discussion of the intellectual motivations of James Mill's *History*, see Majeed 1992, 123–200.

110. Mill (1817) 1858, 3:115–18.

111. Ibid., 3:130, 131, 135–36.

112. Ibid., 5:126. H. H. Wilson, editor of the 1858 edition of Mill's *History*, clearly bristled at Mill's taking Clive and Hastings to task, and added numerous footnotes refuting Mill. On Hastings, Wilson remarked, "Time has justified popular feelings" (154), and added a long note—virtually a small essay—defending him (194–200).

113. Thomas 1979, 101.

114. "Speech on Opening of Impeachment, 16 February 1788," in Burke 1991, 6:316–17.

115. Mill (1817) 1858, 2:342.

116. H. E. Busteed, "Site of Holwell's Monument," in Wilson 1906, 2:215–17.

117. Carey (1882) 1964, 46.

118. Blechynden (1905) 1978, 37.

119. Cotton (1909) 1980, 338–39.

120. *Calcutta Journal*, April 6, 1821, cited in Busteed 1888, 47.

CHAPTER 3. TIPU'S TIGER

1. Visram 1986; Fisher 2004.

2. Fisher 1996.

3. Emin (1792) 1918. For a discussion of his life in Britain, see Fisher 2004, 71–82. Another account that survives as a manuscript from this period is by Munshi Ismail, who lived in Kalna in Burdwan District and went to Britain in 1772–73. This travelogue is described in Digby 1989.

4. Although the original Persian manuscript of Ihtishamuddin's travelogue was never printed, several translations have been published over the years. The earliest is *Shigurf Namah i Velaët* (Ihtishamuddin 1827), which contains English and Urdu translations in

a single volume. A Bengali translation was published by Habibullah under the title *Bilāyetnāmā* (Ihtishamuddin 1981). A new English translation has been published by Kaiser Haq as *Wonders of Vilayet* (Ihtishamuddin 2001). The biographical and critical literature on Ihtishamuddin in Bengali is summarized in Ahmed 1985, 73–85.

5. For Ihtishamuddin's family history, see Zaman 2003, 16–23.

6. Firmaun from the King Shah Aalum, Dated August 12, 1765, in Forrest 1918, 2:287.

7. Ihtishamuddin 2001, 106. Michael Fisher (2004, 88) discovered from the records that the letter from Shah Alam did, in the end, reach the British monarch, but it did not have any effect.

8. Ihtishamuddin 2001, 28–29.

9. Ibid., 30.

10. Ibid., 50–51.

11. Ibid., 54–55.

12. Ibid., 129, 64, 74, 125.

13. Ibid., 125–26.

14. For a description of the exchange between Ihtishamuddin and Swinton, see Ihtishamuddin 2001, 138–42.

15. Salim (1903) 1975, 363–77; Ali (1952) 1985, 61–78. Abdus Salam (Salim [1903] 1975, 366n), the translator of Salim's *Riyaz*, also mentions two other contemporary Persian accounts—the *Ibrat-i-Arbab-i-Basr* and the *Tarikh-i-Mansuri*—neither of which apparently makes any mention of the Black Hole incident.

16. Tabatabai (1902) 1986, 2:190.

17. Khan 1982, 120–21.

18. See the biographical note by Abdus Subhan in his introduction to Khan 1982, 23–26.

19. Mukhopadhyay 1805.

20. Sarma 1808.

21. For a review of the eighteenth- and early nineteenth-century literature in Bengali on the rise of British power in Bengal, see Bhadra (1991) 2010.

22. Vidyalankar1835. The date of the event was, however, erroneously given as 1757. I am grateful to Gautam Bhadra for this reference.

23. Stewart 1813, 505n.

24. Khan 1982, 124–25.

25. Salim (1903) 1975, 363–64.

26. Tabatabai (1902) 1986, 2:188–89.

27. For a discussion of this, see Ray 1994, 63.

28. Subrahmanyam 1999, 253–65.

29. John Richards (1997), the historian of Mughal India, offers a somewhat-similar set of criteria for the "early modern" in order to attach the label to the Mughal period and thus make Indian history less detached from world history.

30. Pollock 2006.

31. Rao, Shulman, and Subrahmanyam 2001.

32. Bayly 1996, 82. Ali Ibrahim was the diwan of Mir Qasim from 1761 to 1764, an associate of Muhammad Reza Khan from 1765 to 1780, and chief magistrate of Benares from 1781 to 1793. His *Tarikh-i-Marhatta* was translated and included as the "Tarikh-i

Ibrahim Khan" in Elliott (1867–77) 2001, 8:257–97. There is a certain narrative objectivity in Ali Ibrahim's history, not unusual in other Indo-Persian histories of the period, but no significant historiographical or political reflections. It largely repeats a dominant Mughal common sense about the empire's decline and rise of the Marathas: "As [Mahrattas] undergo all sorts of toil and fatigue in prosecuting a guerilla warfare, they prove superior to the easy and effeminate troops of Hind, who for the most part are of more honourable birth and calling." For details on Ali Ibrahim's career and writings, see Khan 2002.

33. Dipesh Chakrabarty (2011) points out the imprecision and ambiguities that surround many of the current uses of early modern as a tool for periodizing Indian history.

34. Pomeranz 2000.

35. Singha 1988.

36. Sudipta Kaviraj (2005) argues that the so-called alternative modernities are better understood as alternative sequences of modernity.

37. Rao and Subrahmanyam 2008.

38. Cited in ibid., 46.

39. Alam 2004.

40. I have discussed this point at somewhat-greater length in a Bengali essay called "Nīti, netā, prajātantra," in Chattopadhyay 2005, 128–50. Also, Chatterjee 2011, 53–74.

41. Khan 2000; Chatterjee 1998.

42. I have used the four-volume edition of the 1788 translation published in 1902: Tabatabai (1902) 1986. The Persian original was first published by Nawal Kishore Press, Lucknow, in two volumes in 1866. I am grateful to Abhishek Kaicker for biographical details on Haji Mustafa.

43. Tabatabai (1902) 1986, 1:143.

44. Ibid., 2:560.

45. Ibid., 1:342.

46. Ibid., 1:21.

47. Ibid., 2:125–26.

48. Ibid., 2:192.

49. Ibid., 2:495.

50. Ibid., 2:402–3.

51. Letter from Court of Directors to the Council in Bengal, 26 April 1765, in *FWIHC* 1949–58, 4:96.

52. Tabatabai (1902) 1986, 3:76. Also unfortunately, nothing seems to be known about this early Indian visitor from Murshidabad to Britain.

53. Ibid., 3:124.

54. Ibid., 3:165ff.

55. Ibid., 3:181ff.

56. See Hasan 1969.

57. Khan 2000. Incidentally, as noted in chapter 2, Alexander Dow had already introduced the idea of a drain of wealth from Bengal to Britain. It is not impossible that Ghulam Husain, given his proximity to British officials, was familiar with these arguments.

58. See, for instance, Washbrook 1988.

59. Husain Ali Kirmani, *Nishan-i-Haidari*, trans. W. Miles, cited in Sinha (1941) 1959, 1. This important Persian source on Haidar was published as Khan 1842.

60. Captain Mathews, cited in Sinha (1941) 1959, 91.

61. Ibid., 91.

62. *Journal de M. le Marquis de Bussy*, cited in Ali 1982, 63.

63. Cited in Sinha (1941) 1959, 191.

64. Nair 2006.

65. Sinha (1941) 1959, 233.

66. Cited in Ali 1982, 122.

67. Ibid., 137.

68. Kausar 1980, 60–66, 175.

69. Napoléon to Tipu, January 26, 1799, cited in Jasanoff 2005, 164.

70. Maya Jasanoff (ibid., 153), however, reminds us—rightly—that it was the French connection that made Tipu such a potent threat to the British in India.

71. Jasanoff (ibid., 165) remarks: "Indeed, at every stage, Wellesley's actions anticipated his evidence to such an extent that it must be wondered how meaningful his evidence was."

72. For the most complete account of the diplomatic and military history of Tipu's reign, see Hasan (1951) 1971.

73. Habib 2001a, xxvii–xlvii.

74. Ibid., xxxv.

75. Stein 1985.

76. For a summary of Tipu's instructions to his revenue officials, see Iqbal Ghani Khan, "State Intervention in the Economy: Tipu's Orders to Revenue Collectors, 1792–97," in Habib 2001b, 66–81. For a summary of Tipu's regulations, titled *al Sirajiya*, see Stein 1989, 33–35. For another selection of Tipu's orders on various subjects, see Moienuddin 2000, 2–24. For a good description of the administration of land revenues in Mysore under Haidar and Tipu, see Guha 1985, 7–36.

77. Iqbal Husain, "The Diplomatic Vision of Tipu Sultan: Briefs for Embassies to Turkey and France, 1785–86," in Habib 2001b, 19–65.

78. Cited in Ali 1982, 123. For a summary account of trade and manufacture in Mysore under Tipu, see Guha 1985, 37–60.

79. For an examination of this aspect of Tipu's claims to legitimacy, see Brittlebank 1997.

80. Hasan (1951) 1971, 128–29; Ali 1982, 124–25; Brittlebank 1997, 70. The source of this suggestion seems to be an article by I. H. Qureshi, "The Purpose of Tipu Sultan's Embassy to Constantinople," first published in 1945 in the *Journal of Indian History*, and reprinted in Habib 2001a, 69–78.

81. Habib 2001b, xii.

82. Ibid., 49–51.

83. Schmitt 1985, 47–49.

84. Habib 2001a, xxiv–xxviii.

85. Habib 2001b, 36.

86. Hasan (1951) 1971, 331.

87. Cited in Teltscher 1998, 230–31.

88. Cited in Colley 2004, 298.

89. Edward Moor, *A Narrative of the Operations of Captain Little's Detachment*, cited in Teltscher 1998, 236.

90. Cited in Stein 1989, 20–21.

91. Stein 1985.

92. Sen 1977.

93. Guha 1985, 146. Guha also contends that many of the changes introduced by Haidar and Tipu in the field of agriculture and trade followed the prescriptions of an eighteenth-century Kannada text called *Atthavana tantra*. If this assertion is correct, it places military fiscalism in southern India within a somewhat-longer discursive genealogy.

94. It was found in Srirangapattana in 1799, and sent to London by Lord Wellesley as a present to the East India Company's court of directors. It was kept on public view in the company's offices on Leadenhall Street, where it attracted a lot of attention—John Keats wrote about the "Man-Tiger-Organ" in one of his poems—and created quite a din: "These shrieks and growls were the constant plague of the student busy at work in the Library of the old India House, when the Leadenhall Street public, unremittingly, it appears, were bent on keeping up the performance of the barbarous machine. No doubt that a number of perverse lections have crept in to the editions of our oriental works through the shock the tiger caused to the nerves of the readers taken unawares" (Archer 1959, 4).

95. See, for instance, Brittlebank 1997, 140–46.

96. Moienuddin 2000, 42–44.

97. Colley 2004, 265.

98. William Kirkpatrick, *Select Letters of Tippoo Sultaun*, x, cited in Teltscher 1998, 235.

99. Marshall 1991, 61.

100. Marshall 1991.

101. Cited in ibid., 62–63.

102. J. Moodie, *Remarks on the Most Important Military Operations of the English Forces on the Western Side of the Peninsula of Hindostan* (1788), cited in Teltscher 1998, 231.

103. Linda Colley (2004, 276) notes that thirteen hundred British prisoners were handed back as a result of the treaty of 1784, and an additional four hundred stayed on in Mysore until the 1790s.

104. James Bristow, *A Narrative of the Sufferings of James Bristow* (1794), cited in Teltscher 1998, 241.

105. For a recent analysis of British captivity accounts from eighteenth-century Mysore, see Colley 2004, 269–307.

106. Bayly 1989, 60.

107. Marshall 1991, 67, 69.

108. Officer of Colonel Baillie's Detachment 1788, 1:iv–vi.

109. It is worth noting that while the stories of Tipu's cruelty toward his prisoners were assimilated into a cause for the British nation, there were apparently a large variety of Europeans in Tipu's prisons. A prisoner's song quoted by Thomson goes, in part, as follows:

> You'd think we were far gone
> To hear but the jargon

Of nations so strangely combin'd;
　　We've Danes and we've Dutchmen,
　　You've scarce have seen such men,
And scarcely again will you find
　　We've Sawneys and Paddies,
　　And braw Highland laddies,
Free Britons in here too they ramm;
　　The Swiss and the Frenchman,
　　And leek-loving Welchman,
All chain'd in Seringapatam. (ibid., 2:294)

110. Ibid., 2:111. It is another matter that the specific purpose of this message was a request "to send us a few dozens of Tartar Emetic, and a list of country medicines, to be purchased in the Buzar" (ibid.).

111. Colley 2004, 303.

112. Marshall 1991, 72.

113. Wilks (1810) 1932, 2:768–69.

114. Khan (1814) 1972, chapter 22, 196. The original Persian account is now available as Khan 1983.

115. Khan (1810) 1972, 197.

116. Marshall 1991, 61.

117. Burke (1757) 2004, 109.

118. *Calcutta Gazette*, November 17, 1785, in Seton-Karr (1864) 1987, 173.

119. Cited in Nair 2004, 389.

120. Hickey 1925, 4:352–53.

121. Resolutions of Lord Minto, October 19, 1807, in *Extracts from Capt. Colin Mackenzie's Work*, 83–87, cited in Nair 2004, 369–72.

122. For an informative account of the Mysore family in Calcutta, see the chapter titled "Tippoo Sultan's Heirs in Kolkata," in Nair 2004, 359–427.

CHAPTER 4. LIBERTY OF THE SUBJECT

1. "Captain Barker's Report on a New Fort for Calcutta," Select Committee's Proceedings, May 2, 1757, in Long (1869) 1973, 119–21.

2. Mukhopadhyay (1915) 1985, 365.

3. Ghosh 1962, 389.

4. Letter from Council of Fort William to Court of Directors, January 10, 1758, in Long (1869) 1973, 151.

5. Datta 1991, 103.

6. Letter from Council to Court, August 20, 1757, in *FWIHC* 1949–58, 2:244.

7. Letter from Council to Court, December 29, 1759, in *FWIHC* 1949–58, 2:448.

8. Letter from Court to Council, December 31, 1760, in *FWIHC* 1949–58, 3:66.

9. Letter from Court to Council, April 1, 1760, in *FWIHC* 1949–58, 3:33.

10. The council president at Fort William announced to his colleagues that "having received intelligence of Mr. Brohier's intending privately to quit the settlement," he had

put him under arrest "till he knows the sentiments of the Board" (Select Committee's Proceedings, June 12, 1760, in Long [1869] 1973, 288).

11. Letter from Council to Court, January 16, 1761, in *FWIHC* 1949–58, 3:295–97.

12. Letter from Court to Council, September 30, 1761, in *FWIHC* 1949–58, 3: 114–15.

13. Select Committee's Proceedings, March 19, 1759, in Long (1869) 1973, 278–79.

14. Letter from Council to Court, November 12, 1761, in *FWIHC* 1949–58, 3: 372–73.

15. Select Committee's Proceedings, April 28, 1760, in Long (1869) 1973, 285.

16. Letter from Council to Court, December 19, 1763, in *FWIHC* 1949–58, 3:550.

17. For a brief outline of Polier's career, see Jasanoff 2005, 45–90. Also Alam and Alavi 2001.

18. Polier's pen-and-ink drawing is now in the British Library and is reproduced in Losty 1990, 39.

19. Letter from Court to Council, February 15, 1765, in *FWIHC* 1949–58, 4:79.

20. Letter from Council to Court, November 26, 1764, in *FWIHC* 1949–58, 4: 272–73.

21. Letter from Council to Court, February 2, 1769, in *FWIHC* 1949–58, 5:508.

22. Letter from Court to Council, March 16, 1768, in *FWIHC* 1949–58, 5:83.

23. Public Letter from Council to Court, January 25, 1770, in *FWIHC* 1949–58, 6:180.

24. Public Letter from Court to Council, March 25, 1772, in *FWIHC* 1949–58, 6: 145–46.

25. For a history of the new fort, see Chakrabarty, Chattopadhyay, and Das 1996.

26. Augustine 1999, 130.

27. Stavorinus 1798, 497–98.

28. Grandpré 1803, 268–72.

29. Fay (1817) 1908, 132.

30. Cited in Jasanoff 2005, 149–51.

31. For an account of the early printing presses in Calcutta, see Shaw 1981.

32. See Nair 1987.

33. *Hicky's Bengal Gazette*, July 15–22, 1780, reprinted in Nair 2001, 140.

34. *Bengal Gazette*, May 26–June 2, 1781, reprinted in Nair 2001, 172–73.

35. "The Printer's Soliloqui: A Parody of Hamlet's Soliloqui," *Bengal Gazette*, December 16–23, 1780, reprinted in Shaw 1981, frontispiece.

36. *Bengal Gazette*, November 18–25, 1780, quoted in Nair 2001, 42.

37. For an old account of Hicky's career, see "The Life and Death of the First Indian Newspaper," in Busteed 1888, 264–320. For a recent biographical essay, see Nair 2001.

38. For an account of Hicky's repeated petitions to senior government officials to provide him with a means of livelihood, see Barns 1940, 46–55.

39. Nair 2001, 6.

40. Mukhopadhyay 1988.

41. Ibid., 62–64.

42. Ibid., 78–83.

43. *Bengal Gazette*, no. 12 (1781), cited in Mukhopadhyay 1988, 84.

44. Cited in Mukhopadhyay 1988, 105.

45. *Bengal Gazette*, no. 39 (1781), cited in Mukhopadhyay 1988, 107.

46. *Bengal Gazette*, no. 35 (1780), cited in Mukhopadhyay 1988, 68.

47. *Bengal Gazette*, nos. 41 and 42 (1780), cited in Mukhopadhyay 1988, 89.

48. *Bengal Gazette*, nos. 31 and 42 (1780), cited in Mukhopadhyay 1988, 89.

49. On Duane's early life, see the sketch by his son William John Duane (1868).

50. Cited in Barns 1940, 65.

51. Cited in Clark 1905, 12. It is unlikely that the same Black Hole was still in use in 1794, because by then the old Fort William had been abandoned. But the "black hole" was "the usual name given officially by the British to any garrison lock-up normally used for confining drunken soldiers and [the practice] was not abandoned by the army until 1868" (Edwardes 1969, 65).

52. Barns 1940, 66.

53. Cited in Clark 1905, 54.

54. Cited in ibid., 50.

55. Cohen 1950.

56. For an account of Duane's prominent role in the partisan politics of the early decades of the United States, see Rosenfeld 1997. Curiously, Duane's brief experience of India would sometimes make its appearance in his columns, such as the following: "Toleration in religion, complete and perfect, was not known, except among the *Hindus*, in any part of the earth before our revolution" (*Aurora and General Advertiser* [Philadelphia], September 9, 1800).

57. Natarajan 1955, 8.

58. Cited in Barns 1940, 73.

59. Ibid., 74–75.

60. Cited ibid., 77.

61. Cited in Ahmed 1965, 61.

62. Turner 1930, 16.

63. Cited in Barns 1940, 93.

64. Cited in ibid., 95.

65. Cited in *Parliamentary Report on Mr. Buckingham's Claims* 1836, 8.

66. Cited in Turner 1930, 57.

67. Cited in ibid., 54.

68. Ibid., 32.

69. Cited in Barns 1940, 106.

70. Cited in ibid., 109.

71. Cited in Turner 1930, 68.

72. Cited in ibid., 71.

73. Proprietor of India Stock 1824, 43–44, 52.

74. "Conduct of Whigs and Tories in Mr. Buckingham's Case," in *Parliamentary Report on Buckingham's Claims* 1836, 77–80.

75. "Announcement of Mr. Buckingham's Resignation: To the Electors of Sheffield," in *Parliamentary Report on Buckingham's Claims* 1836, 85–88.

76. From the list in Natarajan 1955, 25.

77. From the list in Chanda 1987, 490–91.

78. Ahmed 1965, 70.

79. Ibid., 70. Although Roy is now officially recognized as having been born in 1772, some sources claim he was born in 1774.

80. Ibid., 71.

81. Ibid., 63. The signatories to this petition were Chandra Kumar Tagore, Dwarkanath Tagore, Rammohun Roy, Harachandra Ghose, Gauricharan Banerji, and Prasanna Kumar Tagore.

82. *Englishman,* January 3, 1835, cited in Ahmed 1965, 78.

83. For an account of Abu Taleb's life and the *Masir-i Talibi,* see Khan 1998, 95–100.

84. Khan (1814) 1972, 134–48, 156–57.

85. Ibid., 110–11.

86. Ibid., 105.

87. Ibid., 132–33.

88. Ibid., 121.

89. Ibid., 129.

90. Ibid., 130–31.

91. Ibid., 168.

92. Ibid., 164–66.

93. Ibid., 170–71, 177, 178.

94. Ibid., 157, 158–60.

95. Ibid., 342–51.

96. Ibid., 247–315.

97. Dalrymple 2002.

98. Jasanoff 2005.

99. Ghosh 2006, 9–10.

100. Hickey 1925, 3:276–77.

101. Mittra (1878) 1979; Sastri 1979.

102. *Friend of India,* cited in Mittra (1878) 1979, 75–77.

103. "A Brief Memoir of the Late Mr. David Drummond," *Oriental Magazine* 1, no. 6 (June 1843), reprinted in Mukhopadhyay 2004, 136–70.

104. For a list of "meritorious students" from the Durrumtollah Academy, see Mukhopadhyay 2004, 192–95.

105. Cited in "Durrumtollah Academy," *Calcutta Journal* 6, December 24, 1821, 331, reprinted in Mukhopadhyay 2004, 209–13.

106. Chaudhuri 2008a, xxi–lxxxi.

107. "From a Native Correspondent," *Calcutta Courier,* August 18, 1840, cited in Chaudhuri 2008a, lx.

108. "Freedom to the Slave," in Chaudhuri 2008a, 105–6.

109. *Calcutta Courier,* August 18, 1840.

110. Cited in Mittra (1878) 1979, 27–28.

111. See the poem "On the Abolition of Suttee" and the editorial note in Chaudhuri 2008a, 284–88.

112. Chattopadhyay 2005, 28–62.

113. Sinha (1862) 1991, 42n72; Sinha 2008.

114. Mukherjee 1977, especially 2–4.

115. Ibid., 60–85.

116. Chattopadhyay 2005, 157–67.

117. Bandyopadhyay 1987, 7.
118. For biographical details, see Bandyopadhyay (1940) 1982.
119. Bandyopadhyay 1987, 4.
120. Ibid., 1–30.
121. For an illuminating analysis of Bandyopadhyay's *Kalikātā kamalālay*, see Chattopadhyay, 141–50.

CHAPTER 5. EQUALITY OF SUBJECTS

1. "A Present to the Believers in One God: Being a Translation of *Tuhfatul muwahhiddin*," trans. Obaidullah El Obaide, in Roy 1906, 941–58.
2. I am using a more recent reprint of the Obaidullah translation: Mitter and Roy 1975.
3. Kissory Chand Mitter, "Rammohun Roy," *Calcutta Review*, 4, 8, reprinted in Mitter and Roy 1975, 25.
4. Mitter and Roy 1975, 5.
5. Ibid., 13.
6. Ibid., 10, 7.
7. Ibid., 15.
8. Ibid., 16.
9. Ibid., 7, 20.
10. Ibid., 21.
11. The 1883 edition has the title "Tuhfatul Muwahhiddin or a Gift to Deists." See ibid., 1.
12. Roy 1906, 941, 945, 957.
13. Lant Carpenter, "Biographical Sketch," in Carpenter (1866) 1976, 1.
14. The neighborhood of the old madrasa, north of the Chowk police station in Patna, is still known as Madrasa Mohalla. See Ahmed 1988, 71–87.
15. When John Digby's proposal to appoint Rammohan as the collector's diwan in Rangpur was turned down, Digby asked the Board of Revenue to refer to "the Cazy wul Cozzat in the Sudder Dewanny Adawlut, to the head Persian Moonshee of the College of Fort William, and to the other principal officers of these Departments for the character and qualifications of the man I have proposed" (Mr. Digby's Reply to the Letter of the Board of Revenue re: Rammohan Roy, January 31, 1810, in Chanda and Majumdar 1987, 43).
16. For details on these figures, see Khan 1998.
17. Seal (1924) 1972, 4.
18. Biswas 1983, 55–63.
19. Fani 1843, 1904.
20. Ray 1976, 22.
21. Biswas (1983, 575–98) reached this conclusion after a careful analysis of the evidence. Ajit Ray (1976, 74–75) is of the same opinion, and even proposes that the author might have been "a member of the staff either of the Sadar Dewani Adalat, or of the Persian department of the Fort William College in Calcutta."
22. Ray 1976, 69–74.

23. Biswas 1983, 584–85.

24. "Bhaṭṭācāryyer sahit bicār" (1817), in Ray 1973, 107–25. This tract was written in response to Mrityunjay Vidyalankar's attack on Rammohan in *Vedāntacandrikā*, reprinted in Ray 1973, 615–33.

25. "Gosvāmīr sahit bicār" (1818), in Ray 1973, 169–75.

26. "Cāri praśner uttar" (1822), in Ray 1973, 250–59; "Pathya pradān" (1823), in Ray 1973, 264–330; "Kāyasther sahit madyapān biṣayak bicār" (1828), in Ray 1973, 333–34.

27. "Cāri praśner uttar" (1822), in Ray 1973, 251.

28. For the best summary of each of Rammohan's polemical tracts, see Chattopadhyay (1881) 1972.

29. Majumdar (1941) 1983, 173–74.

30. Sen 1975; Sarkar 1975; De 1975.

31. Poddar 1982. See also Poddar 1970.

32. Sen 1975, 129.

33. Sarkar 1975, 59, 62.

34. Wakefield 1832.

35. Letter from John Jebb and James Pattison to the Right Hon. George Canning, February 27, 1818, in *Parliamentary Papers* 1832, 5:254.

36. Buckingham 1824a.

37. Sismondi 1825.

38. Buckingham's note to Say's essay, in Say 1824.

39. Crawfurd 1829, 16–17, 18–19.

40. Evidence of Major-gen. Sir J. Malcolm, in *Parliamentary Papers* 1832, 5:319.

41. Cited in Rosselli 1974, 195–96.

42. Evidence of Captain J. G. Duff, in *Parliamentary Papers* 1832, 5:487.

43. "Conduct of Europeans in India: The Following Paper Having Been Drawn Up by a Person in the Temporary Employ of the Board of Control," in *Parliamentary Papers* 1832, 5:343–70.

44. Crawfurd 1829, 42, 72–73.

45. Minute of Sir Charles Metcalfe, February 19, 1829, in *Parliamentary Papers* 1832, 5:274.

46. Minute of the Governor-general, May 30, 1829, in *Parliamentary Papers* 1832, 5:274–75, 278.

47. Rosselli 1974, 180–201.

48. Adam (1879) 1977, 16.

49. It is not true, however, that when in 1823, the Spanish liberals under General Rafael del Riego reissued the Cadiz constitution of 1812, they dedicated it to Rammohan, as Bayly (2007) has suggested, based on a misreading of the editors' supplementary notes to a recent edition of Rammohan's nineteenth-century biography by Sophia Dobson Collet ([1900] 1988, 165). The copy of this constitution now preserved in Calcutta appears to have been a presentation copy especially bound for Rammohan by the Real Compañia de Filipinas, the Spanish company that had a monopoly on the Cadiz-Manila trade, but was keen to see Indian trade opened with China and the East—a cause in which Rammohan supported the free traders.

50. *Calcutta Journal*, cited in Singh 1983, 1:281–82. The weekly paper *Mirat-ul-akhbar* was more ambivalent on the issue of Greek independence, hailing the end of Russian

incursions into Ottoman territory, and bemoaning the bloodshed and religious hatred spread by the Greek wars.

51. J.S. 1834.

52. Letter to William Rathbone, London, July 31, 1832, in Roy 1947, 91.

53. W. Scorsby, cited in Biswas 1983, 25.

54. Letter from Rammohun Roy to the Prince of Delhi, Heir Apparent, November 10, 1830, in Banerjee 1926, 23–24.

55. Letter to the Governor-general, Written Perhaps in September 1830, in Roy 1947, 117.

56. Letter to Charles William Wynn, April 16, 1832, in Roy 1947, 104. For Wynn's reply, see Singh 1983, 2–3:423. For a discussion on the possibility of Rammohan being elected to Parliament, see Zastoupil 2002.

57. "Native Newspapers: From the Prospectus: Mirat-ool-Ukhbar, No. 1," *Calcutta Journal*, April 24, 1822.

58. Tavakoli-Targhi 2001; Singh 1983, 1:305.

59. For the last editorial in the *Mirat*, on April 5, 1823, reproduced in Bengali translation, see Bandyopadhyay (1942) 1972, 55–57.

60. Memorial to the Honourable Sir Francis Macnaghten, Sole Acting Judge of the Supreme Court of Judicature at Fort William in Bengal, from Chunder Coomar Tagore, Dwarka Nauth Tagore, Rammohun Roy, Hurchunder Ghose, Gowree Churn Bonnerjee, and Prosunno Coomar Tagore, March 1823, in Roy 1947, 3–9; Appeal to the King in Council, 1823, in Roy 1906, 4:14–31.

61. Appeal to the King in Council, 26–27. Rammohan had made a similar point in the *Mirat* when, on publishing a selection of poems by Hafiz, the editorial note said that despite the unorthodoxy of the Sufi poet's religious views, he had never been persecuted by Muslims or any officer of the Islamic state. Cited in Singh 1983, 1:293–94.

62. Appeal to the King in Council, 29.

63. Letter to J. Crawford, August 18, 1828, in Roy 1947, 102–3.

64. "Opinion on Grant's Jury Bill," in Roy 1947, 35–39.

65. Majumdar (1941) 1983, 368–70.

66. "Questions and Answers on the Judicial System of India," in Roy 1906, 3:1138.

67. One of Rammohan's earliest surviving letters is a petition in 1809 to the governor-general complaining about Bhagalpur District magistrate Frederick Hamilton's "unmerited, wanton and capricious" bad behavior toward him. Rammohan referred to his own "birth, parentage and education," and sought redress for such conduct intended to "dishonour and degrade" natives "of caste and rank" (Letter to Lord Minto, April 12, 1809, in Roy 1906, 4:108–11).

68. Remarks by Rammohun Roy, on Settlement in India by Europeans, July 14, 1832, in *Parliamentary Papers* 1832, 5:341–43.

69. Ibid.

70. Evidence of Captain J. G. Duff, in *Parliamentary Papers* 1832, 5:487.

71. Evidence of Major-general Sir H. Worsley, in *Parliamentary Papers* 1832, 5:437.

72. *India Gazette*, June 25, 1832.

73. *Bengal Hurkaru*, reprinted in Majumdar (1941) 1983, 483–501.

74. Ramendra Mitra (1996) has written an entire book on Rammohan's position on the colonization question. Biswas (1983) defends Rammohan's role as the founder of

the Bengal renaissance, but only once mentions Rammohan's views on the settlement of Europeans without any comment on the debate over the subject.

75. Kling 1976, 73–93.
76. See Bagchi (1987) 2006, 278–86.
77. Kripalani 1981, 161–64.
78. *Bengal Hurkaru*, September 21, 1842.
79. Cited in Trevelyan (1876) 1978, 1–2:365.
80. Kissory Chand Mittra, *Memoir of Dwarkanath Tagore* (1870), cited in Kling 1976, 164.
81. Bayly 2007.
82. Zastoupil 2002.
83. "Untitled Poem," cited in Chaudhuri 2008a, 172–73.
84. Cited in *Bengal Hurkaru*, October 6, 1841.
85. See Chattopadhyay 1998.
86. Sarkar 1985, 18–36.
87. Thakur 1969, 103.

CHAPTER 6. FOR THE HAPPINESS OF MANKIND

1. Roberts 1927, 8.
2. Ibid., 13.
3. For a critical discussion of Macaulay's *History*, see Hall 2006.
4. Roberts 1927, 16.
5. Cited in Griffin 1965, 2–3.
6. Cited in ibid., 2.
7. Published separately, the essays on Clive and Hastings sold twice as well as the one on William Pitt, Lord Chatham, three times as well as that on Joseph Addison, and five times as well as that on Lord Byron. The demand kept increasing until the 1870s. For the sales details of Macaulay's essays, see Trevelyan (1876) 1978, 336n.
8. Morgan and Morgan 1927.
9. Young n.d.
10. Buller 1905.
11. Teltscher 1996.
12. "Lord Clive," *Edinburgh Review* (January 1840), in Macaulay (1907) 1946, 479.
13. Ibid., 486–87.
14. Ibid., 488–89.
15. Ibid., 489–90.
16. Ibid., 503, 504, 505.
17. Ibid., 505, 506.
18. Ibid., 506, 508.
19. Ibid., 508–9.
20. Ibid., 510.
21. Ibid., 510, 511.
22. Ibid., 512.
23. Ibid., 516–17.

24. Ibid., 524, 525, 526, 528–29.
25. Ibid., 531, 549, 526.
26. Ibid., 544, 545, 549.
27. "Minute Recorded in the General Department by Thomas Babington Macaulay, Law Member of the Governor-general's Council, Dated 2 February 1835," reprinted in Zastoupil and Moir 1999, 161–73.
28. Stokes 1959, especially 184–233.
29. Ibid., 225.
30. For new evaluations of Bentham's political thought, see Schofield 2006; Hart 1982; Hume 1981. For a general introduction to Bentham's thought, based on the new edition of his collected works, see Schofield 2009.
31. Bentham 2002, 322.
32. Hart 1976.
33. Boralevi 1984, 121–22.
34. Bentham 2002, 293, 312–13.
35. Bentham 1995, 24.
36. Lea Campos Boralevi (1984, 120–35) elucidates in some detail how Bentham employed this logic in his thinking on colonies.
37. Bentham 2002, 310–11.
38. Schofield 2006, 201.
39. Bentham (1789) 1907, chapter 16, § 4.
40. Bentham 1843, 171, 172. I am immensely grateful to Philip Schofield, director of the Bentham Project at University College London, for generously giving me access to the revised version of the specific work cited here, "Essay on the Influence of Time and Place in Matters of Legislation," which is to appear in a future volume of the *Collected Works*. I have accordingly amended where necessary the text of the essay that appears in Bentham 1843. Schofield has also confirmed that the essay was written by Bentham in 1780–82, and was intended to form a part of the *Principles of Morals and Legislation*.
41. Ibid., 172, 173–74, 177.
42. Ibid., 173.
43. Ibid., 171.
44. Hacking 1990, 160–69.
45. Bentham 1843, 174, 181.
46. Ibid., 178.
47. Letter from José del Valle to Jeremy Bentham, sometime in 1826, in Bentham 1998, 370; Letter from Jeremy Bentham to Rammohun Roy, mid-December 1827 and February 8, 1828, in Bentham 2006, 447–51.
48. Bentham 1998, 289.
49. John Bowring's Memoirs of Bentham [1809–10], cited in Bentham 1843, 10:450.
50. For a discussion of the claims and limitations of utilitarianism as a moral philosophy as well as a theory of public policy, see Sen and Williams 1982.
51. Krieger 1975, 39.
52. Ibid., 70.
53. Guha (1963) 1996.
54. Stokes 1959, xvi.
55. Ibid., xiv.

56. Pitts 2005; Muthu 2003.
57. Pitts 2005, 25–58.
58. Ibid., 103–62.
59. Mehta 1999.
60. *Second Treatise on Government* (1690), §§ 55–61, in Locke 1988, 304–9.
61. Mehta 1999, 48.
62. Ibid., 68.
63. Said 1978.
64. Iyer 1960.
65. Zastoupil 1994.
66. Dodson 2007, 82.
67. Zastoupil 1994, 130.
68. Mill 1963–91.
69. Cited in Zastoupil 1994, 97.
70. Ibid., 100, 153.
71. Urbinati 2007, 66–97.
72. Ibid., 81.
73. Maier 2006, 21.
74. Porter 2004.
75. Cited in Symonds 1986, 36. Richard Symonds also points out that during the high period of empire between 1880 and 1914, Oxford graduates outnumbered Cambridge ones in the Indian Civil Service by almost two to one. Of all British governors-general and viceroys in India, fifteen were from Oxford compared to five from Cambridge (ibid., 2). The Oxford Greats curriculum and efforts of Benjamin Jowett, the famous Greek scholar, as master of Balliol College are said to have been most influential in training Oxford graduates for colonial service.
76. Cited in ibid., 11.
77. Urbinati 2007, 95.
78. Ibid., 97.
79. For Wilson's career in the Asiatic Society, see Kejariwal 1988.
80. Mill (1817) 1858, 3:136–37.
81. Ibid., 118.

CHAPTER 7. THE PEDAGOGY OF VIOLENCE

1. Cited in Lee-Warner 1904, 1:124.
2. Maine 1888.
3. Anghie 2005, 59.
4. Alexandrowicz 1967, 154.
5. Ibid., 2.
6. In an earlier work (Chatterjee 1975), I discussed the transformation of the classical balance-of-power system.
7. Fisher 1993, xv.
8. Ibid., 18.
9. Malcolm 1826, 1, 11.

10. Westlake 1894, 81.

11. Ibid., 143.

12. Koskenniemi 2001, 131.

13. For an interesting discussion on the ambiguities of international law in the context of imperial China in the nineteenth century, see Liu 2004, especially 70–139.

14. Oppenheim 1912, 86. In the eighth edition of the book, edited by Hersch Lauterpacht, the passage was changed to: "Cession of territory made to an independent State by a State not yet recognised as such is ... a real cession and a concern of the Law of Nations, since such State becomes through the treaty of cession in some respects a State enjoying a certain position in international law" (Oppenheim 1955, 547–48). Clearly, in the age of the United Nations, the idea of some states being excluded from the family of nations was no longer legitimate.

15. Anghie 2005, 105.

16. Ibid., 71.

17. Lindley 1926, 182.

18. Lee-Warner 1894, 37–40.

19. Lauren Benton (2010, 222–78) calls this "quasi-sovereignty" and recognizes it as a pervasive feature of colonial empires.

20. Ramusack 2004, 48–131.

21. See Koskenniemi 2001, especially 413–509. A deeply committed universalist liberal jurist, Koskenniemi argues that international law was dead by the 1960s.

22. Mantena 2010.

23. Schmitt 2003.

24. Koskenniemi 2001, 491–92.

25. Goswami 2004.

26. See Menon 1956.

27. The East India Company sought to make metallic currency uniform throughout British India with the introduction of its rupee in 1835. In 1861, the government of India assumed the sole authority to issue paper currency. See Bagchi (1987) 2006, 206–7.

28. Fisher 1993, 22.

29. See, for example, the foreword by Bisheshwar Prasad in Prasad 1964, xv–xxxi.

30. Lee-Warner 1904, 2:109–10.

31. For an account of the decline and fall of the office of the vakil, see Fisher 1991, 272–81.

32. Dalhousie's minute of August 30, 1848, cited in Lee-Warner 1904, 2:116.

33. Cited in Jackson 1865, 35, 36.

34. Arnold 1862, 1:200.

35. Dalhousie's minute of March 27, 1851, cited in Lee-Warner 1904, 2:119.

36. Arnold 1862, 1:9.

37. Letter from Sir Charles Wood to Dalhousie, January 24, 1854, quoted in Lee-Warner 1904, 2:316.

38. Edwardes 1960, 13.

39. Marshall 1975.

40. Cited in *Dacoitee in Excelsis* 1857, 48.

41. Arthur Wellesley, "Memorandum on Marquess Wellesley's Government of India" (1806), reprinted in Fisher 1993, 178–82.

42. Edwardes 1960, 21.
43. Metcalf 1979, 40.
44. Pemble 1977, 9.
45. Cited in ibid., 63.
46. Cited in Stokes 1959, 34.
47. Jackson 1865, 24–25.
48. Arnold 1862, 1:365.
49. Sir Henry Elliot's Original Preface, reprinted in Elliot (1867–77) 2001, 1: xv–xvii.
50. Cited in Pemble 1977, 95.
51. Cited in Edwardes 1960. For a biography, see Edwardes 1958.
52. Marx 1979.
53. For a compilation of descriptions of Dalhousie's personality, see Rahim 1963, 3.
54. Trotter 1889, 165–66.
55. W. H. Sleeman to J. W. Hogg, Lucknow, October 28, 1852, in Sleeman 1858, 382.
56. J.G.A. Baird, ed., *Private Letters of the Marquess of Dalhousie* (London: William Blackwood, 1910), cited in Fisher 1993, 261.
57. Sleeman 1858.
58. Ibid., 386.
59. W. H. Sleeman to J. W. Hogg, Lucknow, October 28, 1852, in Sleeman 1858, 376–83.
60. W. H. Sleeman to Lord Dalhousie, Lucknow, September 1852, in Sleeman 1858, 370.
61. W. H. Sleeman to J. W. Hogg, Lucknow, January 2, 1853, in Sleeman 1858, 389.
62. W. H. Sleeman to J. W. Hogg, Lucknow, January 12, 1853, Sleeman 1858, 392; W. H. Sleeman to G. Buist, Lucknow, April 24, 1853, in Sleeman 1858, 396.
63. *Dacoitee in Excelsis* 1857, 104, 131.
64. The entire report is available in *Parliamentary Papers* 1856.
65. Ibid., 34.
66. Ibid., 46, 44.
67. *Dacoitee in Excelsis* 1857, 156.
68. Minute by Governor-General of India, June 18, 1855, in *Parliamentary Papers* 1856, 150, 184–87.
69. Governor-General of India to Court of Directors of the East India Company, Ootacamund, July 3, 1855, in *Parliamentary Papers* 1856, 1.
70. Cited in Lee-Warner 1904, 2:325.
71. Arnold 1862, 2:335–36.
72. Minute by Mr. Grant, August 7, 1855, in *Parliamentary Papers* 1856, 190.
73. Minute by John Peter Grant, November 22, 1854, in *Parliamentary Papers* 1856, 3.
74. Cited in Lee-Warner 1904, 2:324.
75. Minute by Mr. Peacock, August 22, 1855, in *Parliamentary Papers* 1856, 228.
76. Cited in Pemble 1977, 107.
77. Cited in ibid., 108.
78. Cited in Edwardes 1960, 175.

79. Court of Directors to Governor-General, November 21, 1855, in *Parliamentary Papers* 1856, 233-36.

80. Diary Entry by Dalhousie, January 9, 1856, cited in Lee-Warner 1904, 1:125.

81. Note of Interview between King of Oude and Outram, at Zurd Kothee Palace, February 4, 1856, in *Parliamentary Papers* 1856, 287–89.

82. Outram to Secretary, Government of India, Lucknow, February 7, 1856, in *Parliamentary Papers* 1856, 291.

83. Sinha (1862) 1991, 96. The song goes like this: "*Namakharamein mulk bigara / Ab hazrat jate landan ko / Mahal mahal mein begam royen / gali gali mein roye patharian.*" It is attributed to Wajid Ali, and was included, along with the more famous *Jab chhor chale lakhnau nagari*, in Lahiri (1905) 2001, 1007.

84. Minute by Governor-General, February 13, 1856, in *Parliamentary Papers* 1856, 300.

85. J.G.A. Baird, *Private Letters of Marquess of Dalhousie*, cited in Pemble 1977, 111.

86. *Dacoitee in Excelsis* 1857, 201.

87. Pemble 1977, 112.

88. For a history, see Mukherjee 1984.

89. For a discussion, see Metcalf 1964.

90. See Fisher 1991; Copland 1982; Mamdani 1996.

91. Stephen 1883.

92. Alfred Lyall, "Government of the Indian Empire," cited in Mantena 2010, 170.

93. Mantena 2010.

94. Ibid., 137.

95. Henry Sumner Maine, *Village-Communities in the East and the West: Six Lectures Delivered at Oxford* (1876), cited in Mantena 2010, 144, 145.

96. For a review of these colonial debates, see Guha 1999.

97. Mantena 2010, 173.

98. Ibid., 159.

99. Ibid., 112.

100. Ibid., 185.

101. Robinson and Gallagher 1961.

102. Fieldhouse 1973.

103. Maier 2006, 48.

104. Maine 1886, vii.

105. Stephen 1873, 26.

106. For an interesting collection of essays, see MacKenzie and Dunae 1984.

107. Chakravarty 2005, 6.

108. See, for instance, Thornton 1959; Hobsbawm 1987.

109. See, for example, Bartholomew 2006.

110. Cited in Filkins 2003.

111. Oldenburg 1984, 203.

112. Sharar (1913) 2001, 65–75.

113. Ibid., 71–72.

114. Ibid., 73.

115. Ibid., 74.

116. Mirza 1995, especially 53–75. I am grateful to Sonia Ahsan for her generous help in translating large sections of this book for me.
117. Ibid., 59.
118. Mitra 1990.
119. See Llewellyn-Jones 1985, especially 167–232.
120. Rosie Llewellyn-Jones (ibid., 189), the most recent scholar of Lucknow's historic architecture, states without any hesitation: "[The Qaisarbagh] is undoubtedly one of the most remarkable palace complexes ever created and had it not been especially singled out for destruction by the vengeful British and later neglected by the people of Lucknow it would have become one of the most celebrated structures in India. Post-1857 photographs show something of the virtuosity of the architect, the panache and fantastic vision translated into buildings that have a truly surreal quality."
121. For reproductions of some of these photographs, see Mirza 1995. Apparently, the foundations of the Rahas Manzil were discovered during World War II, and the New Theatre company used it as the location for a silent film, *Turki Hoor*. See Mirza 1995, 64.
122. Ibid., 72.
123. For a history, see Bakhle 2005.
124. Sharar (1913) 2001, 74–75.
125. Ibid., 75.

CHAPTER 8. THE PEDAGOGY OF CULTURE

1. Marshman 1844, 140.
2. Bandyopadhyay 1872, 22.
3. Ibid., 39.
4. Ray 1870, 43–44, 214.
5. Raychaudhuri 1876, i, 211.
6. On the Ilbert Bill controversy, see Sinha 1995.
7. Nurullah and Naik (1943) 1953, 297.
8. Seal 1970, 21–22.
9. Basu 1974.
10. Ibid., 105.
11. *Census of India, 1921*, 5.1:298, 394.
12. Basu 1974, 107.
13. Ibid., 80.
14. Computed from figures supplied in Seal 1970, 358.
15. Viswanathan 1990.
16. I have incorporated above a section from my essay "The Disciplines in Colonial Bengal" (Chatterjee 1995).
17. Andrew Sartori (2008) has correctly emphasized the crisis of early liberalism and rise of neo-Vedantic idealist nationalism in the later nineteenth century. Yet it is difficult to accept that this was due to the "misrecognition" by Bengali intellectuals of the true abstract subject of capitalist modernity.

18. Joyce 2003; Chatterjee 1993, 14–34.

19. By Order of the Most Noble the Governor of Fort William, C. T. Higgins, Offg. Town Major, July 7, 1821, cited in Banerjee 1989, 23.

20. C. S. Beverley, *Report on the Census of the Town of Calcutta* (1896), cited in Basu 1996, 71.

21. Banerjee 1989.

22. Rijaluddin 1982, 51, 61.

23. Sinha (1862) 1991, 35.

24. Ray (1886) 1984, 422.

25. Douglas Dewar, *In the Days of the Company* (1920), cited in Mitra 1967, 12.

26. Kling 1976, 49, 160.

27. For a list of visiting dramatic troupes, see Raychaudhuri 1972, appendix.

28. *What Is the Theatre?* 1842, 11.

29. Amritalal Basu, "Bhūbanmohan Niyogī," in Mitra 1982, 186.

30. Cited in Mitra 1967, 196–212.

31. For a discussion of the Baishnabcharan Addy episode, see Chatterjee 2007, 58–66.

32. For standard sources for this history, see Bandyopadhyay (1933) 1998; Das Gupta (1940) 2002, vols. 1–2.

33. Mitra 1982.

34. Bandyopadhyay (1933) 1998, 143.

35. The actor-producer Ahindra Chaudhuri (1962, 26–28) supplies a vivid portrait of his first visit to the theater as a child in the early years of the twentieth century.

36. For list of Shakespeare's plays in Bengali translation or adaptation, see Raychaudhuri 1972, appendix.

37. Cited in Bandyopadhyay (1933) 1998, 158.

38. The dominant choreographic style of the Bengali public theater was fashioned by imitating the styles of the Parsi theater, especially in the highly successful musicals *Ālibābā* (by Kshirodprasad Vidyavinode) and *Ābu hosen* (by Girishchandra Ghosh) in the first decade of the twentieth century. See Dhananjay Mukhopadhyay 1910, 65. The traveling Parsi theater was influential in developing the form of the popular melodrama. See Hansen 2002; Kapur 2006.

39. In consultations leading to the enactment of the Dramatic Performances Act in 1876 by the government of India, Richard Temple, lieutenant-governor of Bengal, declared that he would "try to prevent these plays being acted, even without law (though there may be difficulty)," but that he "would rather possess power by law to interfere" (Richard Temple to Lord Northbrook, Viceroy, Dacca, August 20, 1875, Govt. of India, Home Pub-B, November 1875, Nos. 251–54, "Proposed Introduction of a Bill to Empower the Govt. to Prohibit Certain Dramatic Performances" [National Archives of India], reproduced in Pandhe 1978, 7–9). The government argued that plays were being produced against which private prosecution for libel would be difficult and public prosecution for sedition unsuccessful: "If prevention is to be enforced there must be additional power given such as that conferred by the present Bill" (Home Public, August 1876, Nos. 97–112, "Bill to Empower the Government to Prohibit Certain Dramatic Performances" [National Archives of India], reproduced in Pandhe 1978, 100–101). For

reproductions of most of the archival documents on the deliberations leading up to the act, see Pandhe 1978; Bhattacharya 1989.

40. For a general survey of the nationalist theater in Bengal, see Chatterjee 2004.

41. Cited in Bandyopadhyay (1933) 1998, 150.

42. Dasi (1912) 1987, 50.

43. For the most reliable edition, see Sen 1959, 1–128.

44. Gangopadhyay (1927) 1977, 135–36.

45. Das Gupta (1940) 2002, 3:139; Datta 1941, 147.

46. An Irish doctor by the name of French Mullen who spent a lifetime in the colonial medical service in Bengal prepared a verse translation into English of the entire poem, which for reasons that are somewhat unclear, was never published. See Sen 1975, part 4, 82–87.

47. Chaudhuri 2008b. Lal Behari Day thought that the battle of Palashi was an unhappy choice as the subject of a national epic since it "reflects no lustre on the Bengali nation." But others have replied that Palashi was to the Bengali what Waterloo was to the French, as represented in the songs of Pierre-Jean de Béranger or in Victor Hugo's *Les Misérables*. See Palit 1973, 82.

48. Cited in Sen 1975, part 5, 249. Nabinchandra does not name the correspondent, but Chaudhuri (2008b, 6–7) has identified him as Chandranath Basu, the literary critic with strong Hindu revivalist views.

49. Sen 1975, part 5, 245–53.

50. F. A. Slack, Officiating Secretary to the Government of Bengal, to Babu Nobin Chandra Sen, Deputy Magistrate and Deputy Collector, Tippera, July 28, 1899, in Sen 1975, 433.

51. Cited in Sen 1975, 447.

52. Ibid., 445–47.

53. In his editor's introduction to *Palāśīr yuddha* (Sen 1959, iii–xvi), Sajanikanta Das provides a list of all the changes between the first edition of 1875 and the tenth edition of 1907.

54. For a discussion of the alterations to the text of *Palāśīr yuddha*, see Chaudhuri 2008b.

55. Maitreya (1897) 2006.

56. Akshaykumar appears to have been quite familiar with the new positivist methods of history writing elaborated in Germany by Leopold Ranke and transmitted in English principally by Lord Acton. For monograph that looks at Akshaykumar's historiography, see Haque 1991.

57. For a list of his publications, see Maitreya (1897) 2006, 33–42.

58. Ibid., 260.

59. Ibid., 151–52.

60. It is remarkable how, despite significant advances in academic history writing, the basic structure of the nationalist narrative of the British conquest of Bengal remains unaltered from Akshaykumar's day. See for instance, Gupta 1962; Chaudhury 2000.

61. Maitreya (1897) 2006, 242–50.

62. Akshaykumar's *Sirājaddaulā* has copious citations from both the English and Urdu translations of *Sair-ul mutakkhirin*.

63. Maitreya (1906) 2004.

64. Maitreya (1897) 2006, 242.

65. Ibid., 270.

66. *Palāśīr yuddha*, appendix, in Sen 1959, 128.

67. Maitreya (1897) 2006, 265.

68. For the debate in Bengal over the rival claims to truth of poetry and history, see Chaudhuri 2007.

69. Nabinchandra Sen to Girishchandra Ghosh, Rangoon, February 25, 1906, in Sen 1975, 537.

70. Nabinchandra Sen to Girishchandra Ghosh, Rangoon, March 23, 1906, in Sen 1975, 537–38.

71. Critics are generally unenthusiastic about Nabinchandra's handling of meter, noting that he was not especially innovative. On the other hand, they praise his confident use of the traditional payār and tripadī forms. See, for instance, Chattopadhyay 1978, 111–26. Apareschandra Mukhopadhyay ([1933] 1972, 11) testified that as an aspiring actor in the 1890s, he would accompany other members of his troupe to a secluded spot on the banks of the Hugli River and recite long passages aloud from *Palāśīr yuddha*.

72. Chattopadhyay 1994. Later critics alleged that Nabinchandra's Siraj was too cowardly, immoral, and passive to be a tragic hero. See, for instance, Mukhopadhyay 1966, 75.

73. See, for instance, Sastri 1975.

74. Nabinchandra Sen to Girishchandra Ghosh, February 25, 1906, in Sen 1975, 537.

75. This apocryphal anecdote is part of theater legend in Calcutta and is mentioned by many writers. See, for instance, Gupta 1963, vi.

76. Ibid., especially iii–viii.

77. Datta 1983.

78. Critics have, of course, noted the successful employment by Girishchandra of devices and styles from the popular jatra form in his mythological plays. See, most recently, Sengupta 1997, 195–98. But the historical plays based on modern narrative sources and realist theatrical conventions posed a different problem.

79. Das Gupta (1940) 2002, 4:42–43.

80. Ibid., 49.

81. Mukhopadhyay (1933) 1972, 92, 117–18. Since the average price of a ticket, even after allowing for the higher-priced box seats, was under a rupee, we may infer that the house was packed beyond capacity, with many having to settle for standing room.

82. Gangopadhyay (1927) 1977, 376. A major event marking the stage run of *Sirājaddaulā* was the visit to the theater by Bal Gangadhar Tilak, the foremost national leader of the so-called Extremist wing of the Congress. Das Gupta (1940) 2002, 4:47; Mukhopadhyay (1933) 1972, 92.

83. Preface to *Palāśīr prāyaścitta* (1906), in Bidyabinod 2001, 1.

84. Author's Preface (1905), in Ghosh 1973, 3–4.

85. Nabinchandra, while hugely appreciative of both *Sirājaddaulā* and *Mīr kāsim*, nevertheless asked: "But is there any proof that they were such *angels and patriots*? If so, it would be good if you could cite it in an appendix" (Nabinchandra Sen to Girishchan-

dra Ghosh, Rangoon, October 12, 1906, in Sen 1975, 539–40; emphasized words in English in the original).

86. Datta 1983, 98–100.

87. Kshetra Gupta, "Editor's Introduction," in Ghosh 1973, vii–lxxxiv. Debipada Bhattacharya, in his editorial introduction to Girishchandra's collected works, offers more or less the same judgment. See "Jīban-kathā" and "Sāhitya-sādhanā," in Ghosh 1969, xi–xxxiv and lxi–lxv.

88. Ghosh 1973, xxxiv–xlvi, l–lvi, xlvi–l, lxxiii–lxxvi. Asutosh Bhattacharya (1968, 288–89) thinks Zahara would have been more believable had she been portrayed consistently as a fantasy character, but the reference to a real historical character removes the ground for such an interpretation. Bhabanigopal Sanyal ("Introduction," in Ghosh 1975, lxxxvii) declares that Zahara is "unnatural and beyond credulity."

89. Ghosh 1973, xix–xxii. Praphullakumar Dasgupta (1977, 231–53), otherwise appreciative of Sirājaddaulā, agrees that Siraj's nationalism is overdrawn. Bhattacharya (1968, 281–83) admits the excess, yet argues that it was not inappropriate given the political circumstances of the Swadeshi movement.

90. Ghosh 1973, lx–lxvi.

91. Bhattacharya (1968, 290–92) upbraids Girishchandra for turning what could at best have been an ornamental character into the mainstay of his play, thus slowing down its pace with unnecessary commentary.

92. Ghosh 1973, xxviii, lxxix–lxxxi.

93. Mukhopadhyay 1910. I am grateful to Swapan Majumdar for the information that this was the nom de plume used by Byomkes, son of Ardhendusekhar Mustafi.

94. Ibid., 27–30.

95. Ibid., 32–33, 17, 39–50.

96. Ibid., 75.

97. Datta 1983, 258.

98. Mukhopadhyay (1933) 1972, 93–94, 95.

99. Ibid., 95–96.

100. Das 1993; also in Ray 1958, 241–42.

101. Upendranath used Durgadas as his pseudonym in the published text of Śarat-sarojinī. See Bandyopadhyay (1933) 1998, 213n. In fact, Upendranath, who was a rationalist and radical social reformer, probably anticipated trouble, because Śarat-sarojinī and Surendra-binodinī were first published in 1875 under the authorship of "the late Durgadas Das." Many of the appreciative reviews of the play regretted that such a promising dramatist was no more. The game of hide-and-seek between nationalist theater producers and the colonial government had begun. See the introduction by Mahadebprasad Saha in Das 1993, vii–xix. For details on the trial of Upendranath and Amritalal, see Bhattacharya 1989, 30–37.

102. E. V. Levinge to E. P. Chapman, August 20, 1910, reprinted in Bhattacharya 1989, 145–46.

103. Mukhopadhyay (1933) 1972, 91.

104. The main featured play in a theater was performed at this time only on Saturdays, and a successful play would run for twenty-five weeks. See ibid., 92–118.

105. S. L. Maddox to E. V. Levinge, June 21, 1910, reprinted in Bhattacharya 1989, 136.

106. Chief Secretary, Govt. of Bengal, to Commissioner of Police, Calcutta, January 25, 1911, reprinted in Bhattacharya 1989, 171.

107. Officiating Chief Secretary, Bengal, to Lt.-Governor of Bengal, November 7, 1910, reprinted in Bhattacharya 1989, 160.

108. Govt. of Bengal, Political Department, Report on the Native Papers in Bengal for the Week Ending the 25th June, 1910, quoted in Bhattacharya 1989, 125n.

109. Bhattacharya 1989, 177–78.

110. Cited in Chakrabarti 1992, 221.

111. Bhattacharya 1989, 553.

CHAPTER 9. BOMBS, SOVEREIGNTY, AND FOOTBALL

1. For his research, published posthumously, see Wilson 1906.

2. Busteed 1888, 564–73.

3. Ibid., 53n.

4. Ibid., 57.

5. I am grateful to Chitta Panda and Ghulam Nabi for their help in locating this object.

6. Busteed 1888, 73.

7. Curzon of Kedleston, "Introductory Letter," in Busteed 1888, v–vi.

8. Curzon's Message to the Calcutta Historical Society, cited in Firminger 1987.

9. Curzon 1925, 1:153.

10. These models are now kept in storage at the Victoria Memorial Hall in Calcutta.

11. Metcalf 2003.

12. Curzon 1925, 1:164–65.

13. Busteed 1888, 74.

14. See the remarkable tables in Clark 1936, 30–31.

15. I am drawing the argument from my earlier work *Arms, Alliances and Stability* (Chatterjee 1975, 135–52).

16. *Imperialism, the Highest Stage of Capitalism: A Popular Outline* (1916), in Lenin 1971, 1:727.

17. Gallagher and Robinson 1953.

18. Schumpeter (1919) 1951.

19. Hobson (1902) 1938.

20. Hilferding (1910) 1981.

21. Luxemburg (1913) 1951.

22. *Imperialism*, in Lenin 1971, 1:667–768.

23. "Preliminary Draft Theses on the National and the Colonial Questions" (July 1920), in Lenin 1971, 3:432–37; "Report of the Commission on the National and the Colonial Questions" (1921), in Lenin 1971, 3:465–69.

24. Cohen 1973, 63–65.

25. *Imperialism*, in Lenin 1971, 1:764.

26. "Report on the Party Programme" (March 1919), in Lenin 1971, 3:167–84.

27. See Manela 2007.

28. Lenin enunciated this as early as 1914. See "The Right of Nations to Self-determination," in Lenin 1971, 1:595–648.

29. *Covenant of the League of Nations* (Geneva: League of Nations, 1921), article 22, paragraphs 1–2.

30. For a discussion on this point, see Anghie 2005, 147–49.

31. Ibid., 148.

32. Ibid., 156.

33. Mitchell 2002.

34. Amiya Kumar Samanta (1995), as director of the Intelligence Branch of the West Bengal Police, compiled these reports in six large volumes.

35. Sarkar 1973, 474.

36. "Yet There Is Method in It," *Bande Mataram*, February 25, 1907, in Aurobindo 1973, 205–6.

37. "Many Delusions," *Bande Mataram*, April 5, 1907, in Aurobindo 1973, 234–37.

38. "Nationalism Not Extremism," *Bande Mataram*, April 26, 1907, in Aurobindo 1973, 296–99.

39. "Shall India Be Free?" *Bande Mataram*, April 29, 1907, in Aurobindo 1973, 305–8.

40. "The Need of the Moment," *Bande Mataram*, March 18, 1908, in Aurobindo 1973, 764–66.

41. "The Strength of the Idea," *Bande Mataram*, June 8, 1907, in Aurobindo 1973, 411–14.

42. "The Demand of the Mother," *Bande Mataram*, April 11, 1908, in Aurobindo 1973, 852–55.

43. The nationalist newspaper *Sandhyā*, in its characteristically direct style, had this to say about Kingsford: "On seeing the appearance of Magistrate Kingsford, one would take him to be a butcher. We do not know Mr. Kingsford's genealogy; if the facts about it were made public, perhaps it may become known that the Magistrate's father or grandfather, or somebody or other (related to him) was a butcher, otherwise how could his appearance be like that? And his understanding is like (his) appearance; as is the appearance so is the conduct" (official translation from *Sandhyā*, August 28, 1907, in *Seditious Newspaper Articles* [Calcutta: Government of Bengal, 1908], ex. 1339/1, reprinted in Samanta 1995, 4:628).

44. Cited in Heehs 1993, 165.

45. For the most recent and careful account of the Alipore conspiracy case, see Heehs 1993.

46. "List of Political Suspects, Corrected Up to the End of August 1912," reprinted in Samanta 1995, 5:457–666.

47. Intelligence Branch, CID, Bengal, *List of Persons Connected with the Revolutionary and Anarchical Movement in Bengal*, part 2, *Conviction Register*, reprinted in Samanta 1995, 5:667–773.

48. Hemchandra himself narrates the story in Kanungo (1928) 1997.

49. W. Sealy, *Connections with the Revolutionary Organization in Bihar and Orissa* (1917), paragraph 82, reprinted in Samanta 1995, 5:7–134.

50. *Notes on Outrages*, compiled by J. C. Nixon (1917), reprinted in Samanta 1995, 6:1–635.

51. Kanungo (1928) 1997.

52. Tripathi 1967, 117.

53. Sarkar 1973, 491–92.

54. Anderson 1983.

55. See, for instance, "Buyār yuddha: abyabasthita nā byabasthita?" *Yugāntar* 1, no. 41 (January 6, 1907), reprinted in Bandyopadhyay 2001, 263–67; "Buyar yuddha: ubhay pakṣer balābal o kṣetranīti," *Yugāntar* 1, no. 43 (January 20, 1907), reprinted in Bandyopadhyay 2001, 301–7.

56. "Biplab tattva (6)," *Yugāntar* 2, no. 3 (March 31, 1907), reprinted in Bandyopadhyay 2001, 405–6.

57. "Siḍisan o bideśī rājā," *Yugāntar* 2, no. 20 (July 30, 1907), reprinted in Bandyopadhyay 2001, 615–16.

58. Bandyopadhyay (1921) 1999, 26.

59. These were later published in 1907 as two separate booklets titled *Bartamān raṇanīti* and *Mukti kon pathe?* with the name of Abinash Chandra Bhattacharya, designated as the printer of *Yugāntar*, as their author. The pamphlets were soon prohibited. It is unlikely that Abinash Chandra was the author of these tracts.

60. "Yuddhai sṛṣṭir niyam" (in ten installments), *Yugāntar* 1, no. 30 (October 21, 1906) to *Yugāntar* 1, no. 39 (December 31, 1906), reprinted in Bandyopadhyay 2001, 91–93, 109–10, 123–25, 146–49, 162–65, 180–82, 224–28, 247–51, 290–92.

61. "Biplab tattva," *Yugāntar* 1, no. 42 (January 13, 1907), reprinted in Bandyopadhyay 2001, 280–82; "Biplab tattva (6)," *Yugāntar* 2, no. 3 (March 31, 1907), reprinted in Bandyopadhyay 2001, 406.

62. "Biplab tattva (7)," *Yugāntar* 2, no. 5 (April 14, 1907), reprinted in Bandyopadhyay 2001, 442. The installment dealing with public opinion is missing in this collection, but is available in English translation in *Seditious Newspaper Articles, 1906–1907* (Calcutta: Government of Bengal, 1908), ex. 1328/1, flag no. 13(b), reprinted in Samanta 1995, 4:576–79.

63. "Bartamān kartabya," *Yugāntar* 2, no. 4 (April 7, 1907), reprinted in Bandyopadhyay 2001, 416.

64. "Nūtan o purātan," *Yugāntar* 1, no. 47 (February 17, 1907), reprinted in Bandyopadhyay 2001, 353.

65. "Svarājya sthāpan," *Yugāntar* 1, no. 49 (March 3, 1907), reprinted in Bandyopadhyay 2001, 383. *Sandhyā*, as usual, was more direct: "It is a matter of great rejoicing that an excellent kind of bomb is being manufactured. This bomb is called the Kali Mai's boma, *i.e.* the bomb of Mother Kali. It is being experimented on, then it must be kept in every house.... A son is wanted from every family who must practise the virtue of a Kshatriya. Let them play with Kali Mai's bombs. Bom Kali, Kalkattawali" (official translation from *Sandhyā*, May 6, 1907, in *Seditious Newspaper Articles* [Calcutta: Government of Bengal, 1908], ex. 1338/1, reprinted in Samanta 1995, 4:611).

66. Tripathi 1967, 148.

67. Majumdar 1975, 156; see also 434–54.

68. F. C. Daly, *Note on the Growth of the Revolutionary Movement in Bengal* (1911), reprinted in Samanta 1995, 1:32–33.

69. Hemchandra offered a detailed account of the various plans laid to eliminate Naren. He also made the acerbic remark that the people's response to Kanailal's execution had nothing to do with their disapproval of traitors, because Naren's death did nothing to stop future revolutionaries from turning into approvers. See Kanungo (1928) 1997, 190–200.

70. Ibid., 202.
71. Heehs 1993, 192.
72. Daly, *Note*, in Samanta 1995, 1:44.
73. Chirol (1910) 1979, 97.
74. Chattopadhyay 1983, 236.
75. "Critique of Violence," in Benjamin 1979, 150.
76. Ibid., 150–51.
77. Pinney 2004.
78. Amin 1995.
79. Kolsky 2010.
80. Mangan 2001; Dimeo 2001.
81. Majumdar and Bandyopadhyay 2006, 18.
82. Advertisement in the *Indian Daily News*, June 8, 1889, reproduced in Arbi (1955) 2002, 38.
83. There was also an aura of Oriental magic surrounding the Indian preference for barefoot football. Karuna Bhattacharya (1942), a legendary player of the 1930s, wrote of the wondrous reception that greeted a visiting Indian team in Australia in 1938. The players' feet were closely inspected and photographed, and the pictures were published in newspapers. He was convinced that playing barefoot was the distinctly Indian style of football that ought not to be given up.
84. Cited in Basu 1980, 39.
85. "Football at Calcutta," *Bengalee*, July 30, 1911, reproduced in Arbi (1955) 2002, 125.
86. As a ten-year-old, Ahindra Chaudhuri went to the football grounds that day, but was unable to see most of the game except the last few minutes, when a kind gentleman pulled him up on top of a shipping box. For a graphic description of the proceedings outside the grounds, see Chaudhuri 1962, 42–43,
87. For a recent retelling of the story of Mohun Bagan's 1911 victory, see Basu 2003, 1–16. There is a curious anomaly in this story that indicates the predicament created by the event for many newspapers that normally did not carry any sports news. The Calcutta dailies *Amrita Bazar Patrika* and the *Statesman* published detailed reports of the match that described the first half as ending without a goal being scored. The *Bengalee*, on the other hand, reported that East Yorks was leading at halftime from Jackson's goal. This version has been carried into several later histories, including the one by Rakhal Bhattacharya.
88. Ganen Mallik, "I.F.A. Shield Tournament Final," *Amrita Bazar Patrika*, August 1, 1911; *Times* (London), July 31, 1911.
89. *Times*, July 31, 1911.
90. "The Immortal Eleven," *Amrita Bazar Patrika*, August 1, 1911.
91. Cited in "Manliness of the Bengalis," *Amrita Bazar Patrika*, August 8, 1911.
92. Ibid.
93. Cited in Arbi (1955) 2002, 23. The race angle appears even in the more didactic commentaries on football at this time. A 1928 article on the history of football in Britain, after declaring rather ruefully that football had become "the national game" of Bengalis and could not be eradicated as a foreign cultural import, nonetheless advised that Bengali spectators give up their habit of hurling filthy abuse at European teams. See Basu 1929. I am grateful to Kamalika Mukherjee for this reference.

94. *Amrita Bazar Patrika*, May 15, 1929.
95. Cited in *Amrita Bazar Patrika*, May 18, 1929.
96. Cited in *Amrita Bazar Patrika*, May 19, 1929.
97. "The Foot Ball Dead-Lock," *Amrita Bazar Patrika*, May 25, 1929.
98. *Amrita Bazar Patrika*, May 31, 1929.
99. "Scene in a Railway Train: European Fined for Assault," *Amrita Bazar Patrika*, August 8, 1911.
100. Many other people repeat this story, claiming to have heard it from Chatterjee. See, for example, Bandyopadhyay 1998, 34–35.
101. Upendranath (Bandyopadhyay, 1921] 1999, 18) mentions that after the failed attempt on the Bengal governor's train in late 1907, a government official told him knowledgeably that some Russian nihilists had arrived in India with the intention of spreading anarchy. Lord Curzon, in one of his telegrams to London in October 1905, remarked that "the agitation is now being conducted by methods of open terrorism," but this was before any bombs had been thrown; Curzon was referring to the movement of boycott of foreign goods, which often used methods of coercion and intimidation. See Chakrabarti 1992, 94–95.
102. Chakrabarti, 10.
103. Sedition Committee 1918, 26–27.
104. Daly, *Note*, in Samanta 1995, 1:3–4.
105. Ker (1917) 1973.
106. Daly, *Note*, in Samanta 1995, 1:15–16.
107. Tegart 1932, 12.
108. Chirol (1910) 1979, 215.
109. "Introduction by Sir Alfred Lyall," in Chirol (1910) 1979, xiii.
110. Chirol (1910) 1979, 324.
111. Singh 1938, 44–45.
112. Sedition Committee 1918, 197.
113. Ibid., 205.
114. Ibid., 206.
115. See Kumar 1971.
116. These apologists are not yet extinct. See, for instance, Ferguson 2002.
117. R.E.A. Ray, "Brief Note on the Alliance of Congress with Terrorism in Bengal" (1932), in Samanta 1995, 3:933–57. See also Jadugopal Mukhopadhyay (1956) 1983, 40–41.
118. For a recent account, see Chatterjee 1999.
119. Hale 1937, 34.
120. Cited in ibid., 60.
121. Ibid., 3–4.
122. Cited ibid., 1.

CHAPTER 10. THE DEATH AND EVERLASTING LIFE OF EMPIRE

1. Chunder 1869.
2. Chunder 1896.

3. Sarkar ([1948] 1972, 468–80) says, without attributing a source, that Bholanath "fenced an area 18 feet by 15, with bamboo stakes and counted the number of his Bengali tenants who could be crammed into it; the number was found to be much less than 146, and a Bengali villager's body occupies far less space than a British gentleman's."

4. Maitreya (1897) 2006, 179–91.

5. Wilson 1895–1917; Wilson 1906; Hill 1905.

6. Ray (1908) 2006.

7. Ibid., 332.

8. Little 1915.

9. Little 1916.

10. For details on the Oaten affair at Presidency College, see Gordon 1990, 48–50. A slightly different version appears in Bose 2011, 28–30.

11. Cited in Oaten 1916.

12. Maitra 1916.

13. In the same issue of *Bengal Past and Present*, an essay was published by Alfred Martineau (1916), who cited French documents from Pondicherry to show that the Black Hole incident was known to the French at Chandernagore. Martineau, however, did not entirely reject Little's theory but instead suggested that British heroism in times of war did not need such legends.

14. Letter from J. H. Little to W. K. Firminger, in *Bengal Past and Present* 14 (January–June 1917): 92–98.

15. Little 1917.

16. Curzon 1917.

17. Curzon 1925, 1:168–69, 176.

18. Firminger 1917.

19. The obituary note in the *Statesman* was in similar vein: "He sprang into fame a year or two ago when he published a paper challenging the authenticity of the Black Hole incident…. This startling thesis brought up all the big guns among Bengal archaeologists, and, in spite of the tearful support of the *Amrita Bazar Patrika*, Mr. Little was pounded until his batteries were badly damaged, though never completely silenced" ("Here and There," *Statesman*, October 11, 1917).

20. *Mohammedan Sporting Club, Calcutta: Football League Champions (1st Div.), 1934–1935: A Souvenir* (Calcutta, 1935), in Maharaja of Santosh Papers, Nehru Memorial Museum and Library, New Delhi.

21. "First Indian Win of the League," *Amrita Bazar Patrika*, July 6, 1934.

22. J. J. Headward, a private company, held a monopoly contract over the stands on the Maidan football grounds, maintaining the galleries and selling tickets. An unsuccessful attempt was made in 1935 by the IFA to take over the management of the stands. Petition from the IFA Council to Sir John Anderson, Governor, Maharaja of Santosh Papers, Nehru Memorial Museum and Library, New Delhi. The Headward monopoly lasted until the 1960s.

23. Waliullah 1967, 345.

24. See, for instance, Shamsuddin 1968, 165–68.

25. Chakrabarty 1989, 161.

26. Gafur 2000, 43.

27. Cited in ibid., 42–43.

28. "Hats Off to Mahomedan Sporting," *Amrita Bazar Patrika*, July 14, 1938.

29. *Amrita Bazar Patrika*, June 1, 1939.

30. *Amrita Bazar Patrika*, June 22, 1939.

31. "Football Crisis in Calcutta," *Amrita Bazar Patrika*, July 6, 1939.

32. *Amrita Bazar Patrika*, July 7, 1939.

33. Cited in *Amrita Bazar Patrika*, July 10, 1939.

34. *Amrita Bazar Patrika*, July 17, 1939.

35. *Amrita Bazar Patrika*, August 12, 1939.

36. For a description of these changes between the 1920s and 1940s, see Chaudhuri 1972, 118–31.

37. Sengupta (1938) 2001.

38. I currently have in my possession a copy of the 33⅓ rpm LP version released by His Master's Voice in 1970. I am grateful to Gautam Bhadra for loaning me this record, and Amlan Dasgupta and the Centre for Cultural Texts and Images at Jadavpur University for making me a usable copy. The dialogue of the recorded version diverges slightly from the 1938 printed text.

39. Letter from J. A. Herbert, Governor of Bengal, to the Marquis of Linlithgow, Viceroy, Dacca, July 4, 1940, file R/3/2/25, Bengal Governor's Secretariat Files, India Office Records.

40. Modabbir 1977, 70.

41. Ray and Chatterjee 2000, 20.

42. Motaher Hosen Chaudhuri, "Svādhīnatā, jātīyatā, sāmpradāyikatā," *Mohammadī* 13 (1939), 3, cited in Hossain 1994, 54.

43. For a discussion of the Holwell monument demonstrations in the context of Subhas's attempts to find an answer to the Hindu-Muslim question, see Chakrabarty 1990, 63–65.

44. "The Holwell Monument Removal Urged," *Amrita Bazar Patrika*, July 1, 1940; "Haloyel monument apasāraṇ: nāgarikgaṇer dābī," *Yugāntar*, July 1, 1940; "Demand for Removal of Holwell Monument," *Star of India*, July 3, 1940.

45. "Holwell Monument: Government Decision This Month," *Statesman*, July 2, 1940; "Holwell Monument: Government to Make Decision This Month," *Star of India*, July 2, 1940.

46. "Sj. Subhas Bose's Reply to Premier's Announcement," *Amrita Bazar Patrika*, July 2, 1940.

47. "Calcutta Arrest of Mr. S. C. Bose," *Statesman*, July 3, 1940; "Sj. Subhas Bose Arrested," *Amrita Bazar Patrika*, July 3, 1940.

48. Letter from Herbert to Linlithgow, Dacca, July 4, 1940, file R/3/2/25, Bengal Governor's Secretariat Files, India Office Records.

49. Ibid.

50. "4 Satyagrahis Arrested," *Amrita Bazar Patrika*, July 4, 1940; "Attempt on Holwell Monument," *Amrita Bazar Patrika*, July 5, 1940. Because of censorship, newspapers were forced to carry the daily official press release on the agitation with little additional news. Consequently, the reports published in the various newspapers were virtually identical.

51. For details on the alliance between the Bengal Volunteers and Forward Bloc, see Rakshit-ray 1966, 203–19.

52. "5 Sikhs and 1 Muslim Included: 18 Arrests," *Amrita Bazar Patrika*, July 9, 1940. Muhammad Modabbir (1977, 70–71) says that while the Forward Bloc kept supplying the demonstrators, the Siraj Memorial Committee was unable to mobilize any supporters because of its organizational weakness.

53. *Amrita Bazar Patrika*, July 14, 1940.

54. "Trouble over Holwell Monument," *Advance*, July 12, 1940.

55. "City Agitation Discussed by Assembly," *Statesman*, July 16, 1940; "Government Not to Be Coerced by Threat," *Star of India*, July 16, 1940.

56. "Haloyel manumenṭ sarāibār dābī samparke nīrabatā," *Yugāntar*, July 15, 1940.

57. Ahmad 1970, 204.

58. "Sirājaddaulā smṛti dibas: ṭāun haler sabhā," *Yugāntar*, July 4, 1940; "Serajuddowla Day Celebration: Huge Commemoration Meeting at Town Hall," *Star of India*, July 4, 1940.

59. Telegram from Governor to Viceroy, July 4, 1940, file R/3/2/25, Bengal Governor's Secretariat Files, India Office Records.

60. "Letter to the Editor: The Black Hole Tragedy," *Star of India*, July 10, 1940.

61. "Haloyel smṛtistambha apasāraṇ samparke nirdiṣṭa pratisruti dābī," *Yugāntar*, July 14, 1940.

62. "Haloyel manumenṭ sarāibār dābī samparke nīrabatā," *Yugāntar*, July 15, 1940.

63. "Muslim chātrasabhāy yog dite Miṣṭār Fajlul Hak 'asamartha,'" *Yugāntar*, July 17, 1940.

64. "Ban on News re. Holwell Monument Movement," *Advance*, July 19, 1940.

65. Letter from J. A. Herbert, Governor of Bengal, to H. J. Twynam, Governor, Central Provinces, July 13, 1940, file R/3/2/25, Bengal Governor's Secretariat Files, India Office Records.

66. Telegram from Twynam to Herbert, July 19, 1940, file R/3/2/25, Bengal Governor's Secretariat Files, India Office Records. Nazimuddin was a favorite of the Bengal bureaucracy, and Twynam predicted: "I have little doubt that we shall see him as the Chief Minister in Bengal in due course" (Sir H. Twynam to the Marquess of Linlithgow, June 24, 1942, in Mansergh 1971, 264–66).

67. Letter from Linlithgow to Herbert, July 16, 1940, file R/3/2/24, Bengal Governor's Secretariat Files, India Office Records.

68. "City Agitation Discussed by Assembly: Bengal Premier's Statement," *Statesman*, July 16, 1940.

69. Report from Herbert to Linlithgow, July 22, 1940, file R/3/2/32, Bengal Governor's Secretariat Files, India Office Records.

70. Linlithgow set down his terms as follows: "We agree that Central Government may withdraw notification under Ancient Monuments Protection Act provided following conditions are fulfilled: (1) Satyagraha movement must definitely be given up. (2) European Group must definitely agree to proposed action. (3) Your Ministers must understand future treatment of Subhas Bose is entirely outside these arrangements and is for future decision" (Telegram from Viceroy to Governor, August 7, 1940, file R/3/2/25, Bengal Governor's Secretariat Files, India Office Records).

71. Cited in "European M.L.A. and Holwell Monument," *Statesman*, July 7, 1940.

72. Cited in "City Agitation Discussed by Assembly."

73. "Lathi Charge on Islamia College Students," *Advance*, July 25, 1940.

74. Cited in "Holwell Monument to be Removed," *Star of India*, July 24, 1940.

75. "Holwell Monument to be Removed," *Amrita Bazar Patrika*, July 24, 1940.

76. Linlithgow to Herbert, Viceroy's Camp, Ganeshkhind, August 10, 1940, file R/3/2/24, Bengal Governor's Secretariat Files, India Office Records.

77. Herbert to Linlithgow, Governor's Camp, Bankura, December 9, 1940, file R/3/2/16, Bengal Governor's Secretariat Files, India Office Records.

78. For the subsequent career of Subhas Chandra Bose, see Bose 2011.

79. For the most recent historical account, see Mukherjee 2010. See also Greenough 1982. For an analytic study, see Sen 1981, 52–85. For an account of its effects, see Mahalanobis, Mukherjee, and Ghosh 1946.

80. Das 1991, 161–206.

81. Hartmann 1948.

82. See, for instance, Newell 1922; *Visitors' Guide to Calcutta* 1927.

83. Suhrawardy 1921, 49.

84. For his essay on the battle of Plassey, see Sarkar (1948) 1972, 487–95. Incidentally, though deeply skeptical of nationalist history, Sarkar (1987) acknowledged Akshaykumar's role in inaugurating "historical research in the modern spirit." Akshaykumar, he said, "broke new ground in his critical study of Siraj-ud-daulah's career." On Sarkar's relation to nationalist historiography, see Chakrabarty 2009.

85. Cited in Smith (1919) 1958, 479n.

86. Gupta 1962, 70–80. For a useful summary of the historical evidence on the Black Hole, see De 1970–71.

87. Marshall 1987.

88. For an analysis of decolonization in the British Empire as a new imperial strategy, see Louis and Robinson 1990. See also Louis 2006.

89. Maier 2006, 7.

90. Doyle 1986, 19.

91. For a recent discussion on the place of colonial empires in the formation of the United Nations, see Mazower 2009.

92. For one of the most useful surveys of this tradition, see Mommsen 1980.

93. For perhaps the earliest statement of a Marxist theory of neocolonialism, see Nkrumah 1965.

94. For a useful historical survey of this process, see Brown 1970.

95. Baran and Sweezy 1966.

96. Kemp 1967; Magdoff 1969; Magdoff 1979.

97. See, to mention a few, Chomsky 1978, 1993, 2004.

98. Frank 1969; Amin 1977.

99. See, for example, Bettelheim 1976.

100. Harvey 2003.

101. Hardt and Negri 2000.

102. Interestingly, scholars belonging to the old dependency school have made the strongest predictions along these lines. See Frank 1998; Arrighi 2008.

References

Archival Records

Bengal Governor's Secretariat Files, India Office Records, British Library, London
Centre for Studies in Social Sciences, Calcutta
Maharaja of Santosh Papers, Nehru Memorial Museum and Library, New Delhi
Oriental and India Office Collections, British Library, London

Published Government Records

Census of India, 1921, 5 (Bengal), 1. Calcutta: Central Publication Branch.
FWIHC (*Fort William-India House Correspondence [Public Series]*). 1949–58. 13 vols. New Delhi: National Archives of India.
Hale, H. W. 1937. *Terrorism in India, 1917–1936.* Simla: Government of India Press.
Hill, Samuel Charles, ed. 1905. *Bengal in 1756–1757: A Selection of Public and Private Papers Dealing with the Affairs of the British in Bengal during the Reign of Siraj-uddaula.* 3 vols. London: John Murray.
The History of the Trial of Warren Hastings, Esq. 1796. Part 4. London: J. Debrett.
Ker, James Campbell. (1917) 1973. *Political Trouble in India, 1907–1917.* Reprint, Calcutta: Editions Indian.
Long, J. (1869) 1973. *Selections from Unpublished Records of Government for the Years 1748 to 1767 Inclusive.* Reprint, Calcutta: Firma K. L. Mukhopadhyay.
Mansergh, Nicholas, ed. 1971. *The Transfer of Power, 1942–7.* Vol. 2. London: Her Majesty's Stationery Office.
Parliamentary Papers. 1832. House of Commons, *Report of the Select Committee on the Affairs of the East India Company.* 6 vols.
Parliamentary Papers: Papers Relating to Oude, Presented to Both Houses of Parliament by Command of Her Majesty. 1856.
Parliamentary Report on Mr. Buckingham's Claims to Compensation from the East India Company. 1836. London: C. Whiting.
Samanta, Amiya Kumar, ed. 1995. *Terrorism in Bengal: A Collection of Documents on Terrorist Activities from 1905 to 1939.* 6 vols. Calcutta: Government of West Bengal.
Sedition Committee. 1918. *Report.* Calcutta: Superintendent, Government Printing.
Wilson, Charles Robert, ed. 1895–1917. *Annals of the Early English in Bengal.* 3 vols. Calcutta: W. Thacker.
———, ed. 1906. *Old Fort William in Bengal: A Selection of Official Documents Dealing with Its History.* 2 vols. London: John Murray.

NEWSPAPERS

Advance (Calcutta)
Amrita Bazar Patrika (Calcutta)
Aurora and General Advertiser (Philadelphia)
Bengal Hurkaru (Calcutta)
Calcutta Journal (Calcutta)
India Gazette (Calcutta)
Star of India (Calcutta)
Statesman (Calcutta)
Times (London)
Yugāntar (Calcutta)

BOOKS AND ARTICLES IN EUROPEAN LANGUAGES

Adam, William. (1879) 1977. *A Lecture on the Life and Labours of Rammohun Roy, Delivered at Boston, USA, in 1848.* Edited by Rakhaldas Haldar. Reprint, Calcutta: Sadharan Brahmo Samaj.
Ahmed, A. F. Salahuddin. 1965. *Social Ideas and Social Change in Bengal, 1818–1835.* Leiden: E. J. Brill.
Ahmed, Qeyamuddin. 1988. "Patna-Azimabad (1540–1765): A Sketch." In *Patna through the Ages: Glimpses of History, Society, and Economy*, edited by Qeyamuddin Ahmed, 71–87. Patna: Janaki Prakashan.
Alam, Muzaffar. 2004. *The Languages of Political Islam in India, circa 1200–1800.* Delhi: Permanent Black.
Alam, Muzaffar, and Seema Alavi. 2001. *A European Experience of the Mughal Orient: The I'jaz-i Arsalani (Persian Letters, 1773–1779) of Antoine-Louis Henri Polier.* Delhi: Oxford University Press.
Alexandrowicz, Charles Henry. 1967. *An Introduction to the History of the Law of Nations in the East Indies.* Oxford: Oxford University Press.
Ali, B. Sheik. 1982. *Tipu Sultan: A Study in Diplomacy and Confrontation.* Mysore: Geetha Book House.
Amin, Samir. 1977. *Imperialism and Unequal Development.* New York: Monthly Review Press.
Amin, Shahid. 1995. *Event, Metaphor, Memory: Chauri Chaura, 1922–1992.* Delhi: Oxford University Press.
Anderson, Benedict. 1983. *Imagined Communities: Reflections on the Origin and Spread of Nationalism.* London: Verso.
Anghie, Antony. 2005. *Imperialism, Sovereignty, and the Making of International Law.* Cambridge: Cambridge University Press.
Archer, Mildred. 1959. *Tippoo's Tiger.* London: Victoria and Albert Museum.
Armitage, David. 2000. *The Ideological Origins of the British Empire.* Cambridge: Cambridge University Press.
Arnold, Edwin. 1862. *The Marquis of Dalhousie's Administration of British India.* 2 vols. London: Saunders, Otley.

Arrighi, Giovanni. 2008. *Adam Smith in Beijing: Lineages of the Twenty-First Century.* New York: Verso.

Augustine, M. L. 1999. *Fort William: Calcutta's Crowning Glory.* New Delhi: Ocean Books.

Aurobindo, Sri. 1973. *Bande Mataram: Early Political Writings.* Pondicherry: Sri Aurobindo Ashram.

Bagchi, Amiya Kumar. (1987) 2006. *The Evolution of the State Bank of India.* Vol. 1, *The Roots, 1806–1876.* Reprint, New Delhi: Penguin.

Bakhle, Janaki. 2005. *Two Men and Music: Nationalism in the Making of an Indian Classical Tradition.* New York: Oxford University Press.

Banerjee, Brajendranath. 1926. *Rajah Rammohun Roy's Mission to England: Based on Unpublished Sources.* Calcutta: N. M. Raychowdhury.

Banerjee, Sumanta. 1989. *The Parlour and the Streets: Elite and Popular Culture in Nineteenth-Century Calcutta.* Calcutta: Seagull Books.

Baran, Paul A., and Paul Sweezy. 1966. *Monopoly Capital.* New York: Monthly Review Press.

Barns, Margarita. 1940. *The Indian Press: A History of the Growth of Public Opinion in India.* London: George Allen and Unwin.

Bartholomew, Amy, ed. 2006. *Empire's Law: The American Imperial Project and the "War to Remake the World."* London: Pluto Press.

Basu, Aparna. 1974. *The Growth of Education and Political Development in India, 1898–1920.* Delhi: Oxford University Press.

Basu, Jaydeep. 2003. *Stories from Indian Football.* New Delhi: USB Publishers.

Bayly, Christopher A. 1989. *Imperial Meridian: The British Empire and the World, 1780–1830.* London: Longman.

———. 1996. *Empire and Information: Intelligence Gathering and Social Communication in India, 1780-1870.* Cambridge: Cambridge University Press.

———. 2007. "Rammohan Roy and the Advent of Constitutional Liberalism in India, 1800–30." *Modern Intellectual History* 4 (1): 25–41.

Benjamin, Walter. 1979. *One-Way Street and Other Writings.* Translated by Edmund Jephcott and Kingsley Shorter. London: New Left Books.

Bentham, Jeremy. (1789) 1907. *An Introduction to the Principles of Morals and Legislation.* Reprint, Oxford: Clarendon Press.

———. 1843. *The Works of Jeremy Bentham.* Edited by John Bowring. 10 vols. Edinburgh: William Tait.

———. 1995. *Colonies, Commerce, and Constitutional Law: Rid Yourselves of Ultramaria and Other Writings on Spain and Spanish America.* Edited by Philip Schofield. Oxford: Clarendon Press.

———. 1998. *"Legislator of the World": Writings on Codification, Law, and Education.* Edited by Philip Schofield and Jonathan Harris. Oxford: Clarendon Press.

———. 2002. *Rights, Representation, and Reform: Nonsense upon Stilts and Other Writings on the French Revolution.* Edited by Philip Schofield, Catherine Pease-Watkin, and Cyprian Blamires. Oxford: Clarendon Press.

———. 2006. *The Correspondence of Jeremy Bentham.* Edited by Luke O'Sullivan and Catherine Fuller. Vol. 12. Oxford: Clarendon Press.

Benton, Lauren. 2010. *A Search for Sovereignty: Law and Geography in European Empires, 1400–1900.* Cambridge: Cambridge University Press.

Bernier, François. 1891. *Travels in the Mogul Empire, A.D. 1656–1668*. Translated by Irving Brock. London: Archibald Constable.

Bettelheim, Charles. 1976. *Class Struggles in the USSR*. Translated by Brian Pearce. New York: Monthly Review Press.

Bhattacharya, Prabhat Kumar. 1989. *Shadow over Stage*. Calcutta: Barnali.

Blechynden, Kathleen. (1905) 1978. *Calcutta Past and Present*. Reprint, Calcutta: General Printers.

Bolts, William. 1772. *Considerations on India Affairs, Particularly respecting the Present State of Bengal and Its Dependencies*. 2 vols. London: Brotherton and Sewell.

Boralevi, Lea Campos. 1984. *Bentham and the Oppressed*. Berlin: Walter de Gruyter.

Bose, Sugata. 2011. *His Majesty's Opponent: Subhas Chandra Bose and India's Struggle against Empire*. Cambridge, MA: Harvard University Press.

Bowen, H. V. 1991. *Revenue and Reform: The Indian Problem in British Politics, 1757–1773*. Cambridge: Cambridge University Press.

Boxer, C. R. 1981. *João de Barros: Portuguese Humanist and Historian of Asia*. New Delhi: Concept.

Brewer, John. 1988. *The Sinews of Power: War, Money, and the English State, 1688–1783*. New York: Alfred A. Knopf.

Brittlebank, Kate. 1997. *Tipu Sultan's Search for Legitimacy: Islam and Kingship in a Hindu Domain*. Delhi: Oxford University Press.

Brown, Michael Barratt. 1970. *After Imperialism*. New York: Humanities Press.

Buckingham, James Silk. 1824. "Colonization of India." *Oriental Herald and Colonial Review* 1 (January–April): 275–84.

Buller, H. M. 1905. *Macaulay's Essay on Clive*. London: Macmillan.

Burke, Edmund. 1991. *The Writings and Speeches of Edmund Burke*. Edited by P. J. Marshall. 6 vols. Oxford: Clarendon Press.

———. (1757) 2004. *A Philosophical Enquiry into the Origin of Our Ideas of the Sublime and Beautiful and Other Pre-Revolutionary Writings*. Edited by David Womersley. Reprint, London: Penguin.

Busteed, Henry E. 1888. *Echoes from Old Calcutta: Being Chiefly Reminiscences of the Days of Warren Hastings, Francis, and Impey*. Calcutta: Thacker, Spink.

Carey, W. H. (1882) 1964. *The Good Old Days of Honourable John Company, Being Curious Reminiscences during the Rule of the East India Company from 1600 to 1858*. Edited by Amarendra Nath Mookerji. Reprint, Calcutta: Quins.

Carpenter, Mary. (1866) 1976. *The Last Days in England of the Rajah Rammohun Roy*. Edited by Swapan Majumdar. Reprint, Calcutta: Riddhi.

Chakrabarti, Hiren. 1992. *Political Protest in Bengal: Boycott and Terrorism, 1905–18*. Calcutta: Papyrus.

Chakrabarty, Bhaskar, Basudeb Chattopadhyay, and Suranjan Das. 1996. *Fort William: A Historical Perspective*. Calcutta: Sankar Mondal.

Chakrabarty, Bidyut. 1990. *Subhas Chandra Bose and Middle Class Radicalism: A Study in Indian Nationalism, 1928–1940*. London: I. B. Tauris.

Chakrabarty, Dipesh. 1989. *Rethinking Working Class History: Bengal, 1890–1940*. Princeton, NJ: Princeton University Press.

———. 2009. "Bourgeois Categories Made Global: Utopian and Actual Lives of Historical Documents in India." *Economic and Political Weekly* 44, no. 25 (June 20–26).

————. 2011. "The Muddle of Modernity." *American Historical Review* 116, no. 3 (June): 663–75.

Chakravarty, Gautam. 2005. *The Indian Mutiny and the British Imagination*. Cambridge: Cambridge University Press.

Chanda, Mrinal Kanti. 1987. *History of the English Press in Bengal, 1780–1857*. Calcutta: K. P. Bagchi.

Chanda, Rama Prasad, and Jatindra Kumar Majumdar, eds. 1987. *Raja Rammohun Roy: Letters and Documents*. Delhi: Anmol.

Chatterjee, Kumkum. 1998. "History as Self-Representation: The Recasting of a Political Tradition in Late Eighteenth-Century Eastern India." *Modern Asian Studies* 32 (4): 913–48.

Chatterjee, Manini. 1999. *Do and Die: The Chittagong Uprising, 1930–34*. New Delhi: Penguin Books India.

Chatterjee, Minoti. 2004. *Theatre beyond the Threshold: Colonialism, Nationalism, and the Bengali Stage, 1905–1947*. New Delhi: Indialog.

Chatterjee, Partha. 1975. *Arms, Alliances, and Stability: The Development of the Structure of International Politics*. Delhi: Macmillan.

————. 1993. *The Nation and Its Fragments: Colonial and Postcolonial Histories*. Princeton, NJ: Princeton University Press.

————. 1995. "The Disciplines in Colonial Bengal." In *Texts of Power: Emerging Disciplines in Colonial Bengal*, edited by Partha Chatterjee, 1–29. Minneapolis: University of Minnesota Press.

————. 2011. *Lineages of Political Society: Studies in Postcolonial Democracy*. Ranikhet: Permanent Black.

Chatterjee, Sudipto, 2007. *The Colonial Staged: Theatre in Colonial Calcutta*. London: Seagull Books.

Chattopadhyay, Basudeb. 1998. *The Town Hall of Calcutta: A Brief History*. Calcutta: Homage Trust.

Chattopadhyay, Swati. 2005. *Representing Calcutta: Modernity, Nationalism, and the Colonial Uncanny*. London: Routledge.

Chaudhuri, K. N. 1978. *The Trading World of Asia and the English East India Company, 1660–1760*. Cambridge: Cambridge University Press.

————. 1985. *Trade and Civilisation in the Indian Ocean: An Economic History from the Rise of Islam to 1750*. Cambridge: Cambridge University Press.

Chaudhuri, Nirad C. 1975. *Clive of India: A Political and Psychological Essay*. London: Barrie and Jenkins.

Chaudhuri, Rosinka. 2007. "History in Poetry: Nabinchandra Sen's *Palashir Yuddha* and the Question of Truth." *Journal of Asian Studies* 66, no. 4 (November): 897–918.

————. 2008a. *Derozio, Poet of India: The Definitive Edition*. Delhi: Oxford University Press.

————. 2008b. "The Politics of Poetry: An Investigation into Hindu-Muslim Representation in Nabinchandra Sen's *Palashir Yuddha*." *Studies in History* 24 (1): 1–25.

Chaudhury, Sushil. 2000. *The Prelude to Empire: Plassey Revolution of 1757*. New Delhi: Manohar.

Chirol, Valentine. (1910) 1979. *Indian Unrest*. Reprint, New Delhi: Light and Life.

Chomsky, Noam. 1978. *"Human Rights" and American Foreign Policy*. Nottingham: Spokesman Books.

———. 1993. *World Orders, Old and New.* New York: Columbia University Press.

———. 2004. *Hegemony or Survival: America's Quest for Global Dominance.* New York: Henry Holt.

Chunder, Bhola Nath. 1869. *The Travels of a Hindoo to Various Parts of Bengal and Upper India.* 2 vols. London: N. Trübner.

———. 1896. "Trip Down the Hughli, to Ulubaria, or Local Associations of Places on the Two Banks of Our River." *Calcutta University Magazine* (June): 50–82.

Clark, Allen C. 1905. *William Duane.* New York: Columbia Historical Society.

Clark, Grover. 1936. *The Balance Sheets of Imperialism.* New York: Columbia University Press.

Cohen, Benjamin J. 1973. *The Question of Imperialism: The Political Economy of Dominance and Dependence.* New York: Basic Books.

Cohen, Irving Seymour. 1950. "William Duane and the Republican Party, 1796–1802: A Study of an Editor in National Politics." Master's thesis, Columbia University.

Collet, Sophia Dobson. (1900) 1988. *The Life and Letters of Raja Rammohun Roy.* Edited by Dilip Kumar Biswas and Prabhat Chandra Ganguli. Reprint, Calcutta: Sadharan Brahmo Samaj.

Colley, Linda. 1992. *Britons: Forging the Nation, 1707–1837.* New Haven, CT: Yale University Press.

———. 2004. *Captives: Britain, Empire, and the World, 1600–1850.* New York: Random House.

Copland, Ian. 1982. *The British Raj and the Indian Princes: Paramountcy in Western India, 1857–1930.* Bombay: Orient Longman.

Cotton, H.E.A. (1909) 1980. *Calcutta Old and New.* Edited by N. R. Ray. Reprint, Calcutta: General Printers.

[Crawfurd, John]. 1829. *A View of the Present State and Future Prospects of the Free Trade and Colonization of India.* London: James Ridgway.

Curzon of Kedleston. 1917. "The True History of Holwell's Monument." *Bengal Past and Present* 15 (July–December): 11–24.

———. 1925. *British Administration in India.* 2 vols. London: Cassell.

Dacoitee in Excelsis; or, the Spoliation of Oude by the East India Company. 1857. 2nd ed. London: J. R. Taylor.

Dalrymple, William. 2002. *White Mughals: Love and Betrayal in Eighteenth-Century India.* London: HarperCollins.

Das, Suranjan. 1991. *Communal Riots in Bengal, 1905–1947.* Delhi: Oxford University Press.

Das Gupta, Hemendra Nath. (1940) 2002. *The Indian Stage.* 3 vols. Reprint, New Delhi: Munshiram Manoharlal.

Datta, Kalikinkar. 1971. *Siraj-ud-daulah.* Calcutta: Orient Longman.

De, Amalendu. 1970–71. "A Note on the Black Hole Tragedy." *Quarterly Review of Historical Studies* 10 (3–4): 141–64, 187–92.

De, Barun. 1975. "A Biographical Perspective on the Political and Economic Ideas of Rammohun Roy." In *Rammohun Roy and the Process of Modernization in India,* edited by V. C. Joshi, 136–48. Delhi: Vikas.

Digby, Simon. 1989. "An Eighteenth-Century Narrative of a Journey from Bengal to England: Munshi Ismail's *New History.*" In *Urdu and Mulsim South Asia: Studies in*

Honour of Ralph Russell, edited by Christopher Shackle, 49–65. London: School of Oriental and African Studies.

Dimeo, Paul. 2001. "Football and Politics in Bengal: Colonialism, Nationalism, Communalism." In *Soccer in South Asia: Empire, Nation, and Diaspora*, edited by Paul Dimeo and James Mills, 57–74. London: Frank Cass.

Dirks, Nicholas B. 2006. *The Scandal of Empire*. Cambridge, MA: Harvard University Press.

Dodson, Michael S. 2007. *Orientalism, Empire, and National Culture: India, 1770–1880*. Basingstoke, UK: Palgrave Macmillan.

Dodwell, Henry. (1920) 1967. *Dupleix and Clive: The Beginning of Empire*. Reprint, London: Frank Cass.

Dow, Alexander. 1772. *The History of Hindostan*. 3 vols. London, T. Becket and P. A. De Hondt.

Doyle, Michael W. 1986. *Empires*. Ithaca, NY: Cornell University Press.

Duane, William John. 1868. *Biographical Memoirs of William J. Duane*. Philadelphia: Claxton, Remsen and Heffelfinger.

Edwardes, Michael. 1958. *The Necessary Evil: John and Henry Lawrence and the Indian Empire*. London: Cassell.

———. 1960. *The Orchid House: Splendours and Miseries of the Kingdom of Oudh, 1827–1857*. London: Cassell.

———. 1969. *Plassey: The Founding of an Empire*. London: Hamish Hamilton.

Elliott, H. M. (1867–77) 2001. *The History of India, as Told by Its Own Historians*. Edited by John Dowson. 8 vols. Reprint, New Delhi: Low Price Publications.

Emin, Joseph. (1792) 1918. *Life and Adventures of Joseph Emin, An Armenian*. Reprint, Calcutta: Asiatic Society of Bengal.

Fay, Eliza. (1817) 1908. "Letter 15, May 22, 1780." In *Original Letters from India*. Reprint, Calcutta: Thacker, Spink.

Ferguson, Niall. 2002. *Empire: The Rise and Demise of the British World Order and the Lessons for Global Power*. New York: Basic Books.

Fieldhouse, David. 1973. *Economics and Empire, 1830–1914*. Ithaca, NY: Cornell University Press.

Filkins, Dexter. 2003. "Tough New Tactics by U.S. Tighten Grip on Iraq Towns." *New York Times*, December 7.

Firminger, Walter K. 1917. "Obituary Notice." *Bengal Past and Present* 15 (July–December): 36–37.

———. 1987. "Minutes of the Inaugural Meeting" (1907). Reprinted in *Bengal Past and Present* 106 (January–December): 7–14.

Fisher, Michael H. 1991. *Indirect Rule in India: Residents and the Residency System, 1764–1858*. Delhi: Oxford University Press.

———, ed. 1993. *The Politics of the British Annexation of India, 1757–1857*. Delhi: Oxford University Press.

———. 1996. *The First Indian Author in English: Dean Mahomed (1759–1851) in India, Ireland, and England*. Delhi: Oxford University Press.

———. 2004. *Counterflows to Colonialism: Indian Travellers and Settlers in Britain, 1600–1857*. Delhi: Permanent Black.

Foote, Samuel. 1778. *The Nabob: A Comedy in Three Acts as It Is Performed at the Theatre Royal in the Haymarket*. London: Colman.

Forrest, George. 1918. *The Life of Lord Clive.* 2 vols. London: Cassell.

Frank, André Gunder. 1969. *Capitalism and Underdevelopment in Latin America.* Harmondsworth, UK: Penguin.

————. 1998. *ReOrient: Global Economy in the Asian Age.* Berkeley: University of California Press.

Fraser, James Baillie. 1824. *Views of Calcutta and Environs.* London.

Gallagher, John, and Ronald Robinson. 1953. "The Imperialism of Free Trade." *Economic History Review* (2nd series) 6, no. 1 (August): 1–15.

Ghosh, Durba. 2006. *Sex and the Family in Colonial India: The Making of Empire.* Cambridge: Cambridge University Press.

Gordon, Leonard. 1990. *Brothers against the Raj.* New Delhi: Penguin.

Goswami, Manu. 2004. *Producing India: From Colonial Economy to National Space.* Chicago: University of Chicago Press.

Grandpré, Louis de. 1803. *A Voyage in the Indian Ocean and to Bengal.* Vol. 1. London: G. and J. Robinson.

Greenough, Paul R. 1982. *Prosperity and Misery in Modern Bengal: The Famine of 1943–1944.* New York: Oxford University Press.

Griffin, John R. 1965. *The Intellectual Milieu of Lord Macaulay.* Ottawa: University of Ottawa Press.

Grotius, Hugo. 1916. *The Freedom of the Seas.* Translated by Ralph van Deman Magoffin. New York: Oxford University Press.

————. 1950. *De iure praedae commentarius: Commentary of the Law of Prize and Booty.* Translated by Gwladys L. Williams. Vol. 1. Oxford: Clarendon Press.

Guha, Nikhiles. 1985. *Pre-British State System in South India: Mysore, 1761–1799.* Calcutta: Ratna Prakashan.

Guha, Ramachandra. 1999. *Savaging the Civilized: Verrier Elwin, His Tribals, and India.* Chicago: University of Chicago Press.

Guha, Ranajit. (1963) 1996. *A Rule of Property for Bengal: An Essay on the Idea of Permanent Settlement.* Reprint, Durham, NC: Duke University Press.

Gupta, Brijen K. 1962. *Sirajuddaullah and the East India Company, 1756–1757.* Leiden: E. J. Brill.

Habib, Irfan, ed. 2001a. *Confronting Colonialism: Resistance and Modernization under Haidar Ali and Tipu Sultan.* New Delhi: Tulika.

————, ed. 2001b. *State and Diplomacy under Tipu Sultan: Documents and Essays.* New Delhi: Tulika.

Hacking, Ian. 1990. *The Taming of Chance.* Cambridge: Cambridge University Press.

Hall, Catherine. 2006. "At Home with History: Macaulay and the *History of England.*" In *At Home with the Empire: Metropolitan Culture and the Imperial World*, edited by Catherine Hall and Sonya O. Rose. Cambridge: Cambridge University Press.

Hansen, Kathryn. 2002. "Parsi Theatre and the City: Locations, Patrons, Audiences." *Sarai Reader 02: The Cities of Everyday Life.* Delhi: SARAI.

Hardt, Michael, and Antonio Negri. 2000. *Empire.* Cambridge, MA: Harvard University Press.

Hart, H.L.A. 1976. "Bentham and the United States of America." *Journal of Law and Economics* 19:547–67.

———. 1982. *Essays on Bentham, Jurisprudence, and Political Theory*. Oxford: Oxford University Press.

Hartmann, George W. 1948. "The 'Black Hole' of Calcutta: Fact or Fiction?" *Journal of Social Psychology* 27 (February): 17–35.

Harvey, David. 2003. *The New Imperialism*. Oxford: Oxford University Press.

Hasan, Mohibbul. (1951) 1971. *History of Tipu Sultan*. Reprint, Calcutta: World Press.

Hasan, S. Nurul. 1969. "Zamindars under the Mughals." In *Land Control and Social Structure in Indian History*, edited by Robert Eric Frykenburg, 17–31. Madison: University of Wisconsin Press.

Heckscher, Eli. 1935. *Mercantilism*. Translated by Mendel Shapiro. Vol. 1. London: George Allen and Unwin.

Heehs, Peter. 1993. *The Bomb in Bengal: The Rise of Revolutionary Terrorism in India, 1900–1910*. Delhi: Oxford University Press.

Hickey, William. 1925. *Memoirs of William Hickey*. Edited by Alfred Spencer. 4 vols. London: Hurst and Blackett.

Hilferding, Rudolf. (1910) 1981. *Finance Capital: A Study of the Latest Phase of Capitalist Development*. Translated by Tom Bottomore. Reprint, London: Routledge and Kegan Paul.

Hobsbawm, Eric J. 1987. *The Age of Empire, 1875–1914*. London: Weidenfeld and Nicolson.

Hobson, John A. (1902) 1938. *Imperialism: A Study*. Reprint, London: Allen and Unwin.

Holwell, John Zephania. 1758. *A Genuine Narrative of the Deplorable Deaths of the English Gentlemen, and Others, Who Were Suffocated in the Black-Hole in Fort William, in Calcutta, in the Kingdom of Bengal; in the Night Succeeding the 20th Day of June, 1756*. London: A. Millar.

———. 1764. *An Address to the Proprietors of East India Stock; Setting Forth the Unavoidable Necessity and Real Motives for the Revolution in Bengal, in 1760*. London: T. Becket and P. A. de Hondt.

———. 1767. *An Address from John Zephania Holwell, Esq., to Luke Scrafton, Esq.: In Reply to the Pamphlet, Intitled, Observations on Mr. Vansittart's Narrative*. London: T. Becket and P. A. De Hondt.

———. 1774. *India Tracts*. London: T. Becket.

Hume, Leonard J. 1981. *Bentham and Bureaucracy*. Cambridge: Cambridge University Press.

Iyer, Raghavan. 1960. "Utilitarianism and All That: The Political Theory of British Imperialism in India." In *St. Antony's Papers: South Asian Affairs*, edited by Raghavan Iyer, 1:9–71. London: Chatto and Windus.

Jackson, Charles. 1865. *A Vindication of the Marquis of Dalhousie's Indian Administration*. London: Smith, Elder.

Jasanoff, Maya. 2005. *Edge of Empire: Lives, Culture, and Conquest in the East, 1759–1850*. New York: Vintage.

Joseph, Betty. 2004. *Reading the East India Company, 1720–1840: Colonial Currencies of Gender*. Chicago: University of Chicago Press.

Joyce, Patrick. 2003. *The Rule of Freedom: Liberalism and the Modern City*. London: Verso.

J.S. [James Sutherland]. 1834. "Reminiscences of Rammohun Roy." *Calcutta Literary Gazette* 9, no. 7 (February 1): 97–103.

Kapur, Anuradha. 2006. "Love in the Time of Parsi Theatre." In *Love in South Asia: A Cultural History*, edited by Francesca Orsini, 211–27. Cambridge: Cambridge University Press.

Kausar, Kabir. 1980. *Secret Correspondence of Tipu Sultan*. New Delhi: Light and Life.

Kaviraj, Sudipta. 2005. "An Outline of a Revisionist Theory of Modernity." *Archives européennes de sociologie* 46 (3): 497–526.

Kemp, Tom. 1967. *Theories of Imperialism*. London: Dobson.

Kejariwal, O. P. 1988. *The Asiatic Society of Bengal and the Discovery of India's Past, 1784–1838*. Delhi: Oxford University Press.

Khan, Gulfishan. 1998. *Indian Muslim Perceptions of the West during the Eighteenth Century*. Karachi: Oxford University Press.

Khan, Iqbal Ghani. 2000. "A Book with Two Views: Ghulam Husain Khan's 'An Overview of the Modern Times.'" In *Perspectives of Mutual Encounters in South Asian History, 1760–1860*, edited by Jamal Malik, 278–97. Leiden: Brill.

Khan, Shayesta. 2002. *A Biography of Ali Ibrahim Khan (circa 1740–1793)*. Patna: Khuda Bakhsh Oriental Public Library.

Kling, Blair B. 1976. *Partner in Empire: Dwarkanath Tagore and the Age of Enterprise in Eastern India*. Berkeley: University of California Press.

Koebner, Richard. 1961. *Empire*. Cambridge: Cambridge University Press.

Kolsky, Elizabeth. 2010. *Colonial Justice in British India: White Violence and the Rule of Law*. Cambridge: Cambridge University Press.

Koskenniemi, Martti. 2001. *The Gentle Civilizer of Nations: The Rise and Fall of International Law, 1870–1960*. Cambridge: Cambridge University Press.

Krieger, Leonard. 1975. *An Essay on the Theory of Enlightened Despotism*. Chicago: University of Chicago Press.

Kripalani, Krishna. 1981. *Dwarkanath Tagore: A Forgotten Pioneer: A Life*. New Delhi: National Book Trust.

Kuiters, Willem G. J. 2002. *The British in Bengal, 1756–1773: A Society in Transition Seen through the Biography of a Rebel, William Bolts (1739–1808)*. Paris: Les Indes Savantes.

Kumar, Dharma, ed. 1983. *The Cambridge Economic History of India*. Vol. 2. Cambridge: Cambridge University Press.

Kumar, Ravinder, ed. 1971. *Essays on Gandhian Politics: The Rowlatt Satyagraha of 1919*. Oxford: Clarendon Press.

Lee-Warner, William. 1894. *The Protected Princes of India*. London: Macmillan.

———. 1904. *The Life of the Marquis of Dalhousie*. 2 vols. London: Macmillan.

Lenin, Vladimir Ilyich. 1971. *Selected Works*. 3 vols. Moscow: Progress Publishers.

Lindley, Mark F. 1926. *The Acquisition and Government of Backward Territory in International Law*. London: Longmans, Green.

Little, James H. 1915. "The Black Hole: The Question of Holwell's Veracity." *Bengal Past and Present* 11 (July–December): 75–105.

———. 1916. "The Black Hole Debate." *Bengal Past and Present* 12 (January–June): 136–49.

———. 1917. "The Holwell Monument." *Bengal Past and Present* 14 (January–June): 270–90.

Liu, Lydia H. 2004. *The Clash of Empires: The Invention of China in Modern World Making*. Cambridge, MA: Harvard University Press.

Llewellyn-Jones, Rosie. 1985. *A Fatal Friendship: The Nawabs, the British, and the City of Lucknow*. Delhi: Oxford University Press.

Locke, John. 1988. *Two Treatises on Government*. Edited by Peter Laslett. Cambridge: Cambridge University Press.

Losty, Jeremiah P. 1990. *Calcutta, City of Palaces: A Survey of the City in the Days of the East India Company, 1690–1858*. London: British Library.

Louis, William Roger. 2006. *Ends of British Imperialism: The Scramble for Empire, Suez, and Decolonization*. London: I. B. Tauris.

Louis, William Roger, and Ronald Robinson. 1990. "The Imperialism of Decolonization." *Journal of Imperial and Commonwealth History* 22 (3): 462–511.

Luxemburg, Rosa. (1913) 1951. *The Accumulation of Capital*. Translated by Agnes Schwarzschild. London: Routledge.

Macaulay, Thomas Babington. (1907) 1946. *Critical and Historical Essays*. Vol. 1. Reprint, London: J. M. Dent.

MacKenzie, John M., and Patrick Dunae, eds. 1984. *Imperialism and Popular Culture*. Manchester, UK: Manchester University Press.

Magdoff, Harry. 1969. *The Age of Imperialism*. New York: Monthly Review Press.

———. 1979. *Imperialism: From the Colonial Age to the Present*. New York: Monthly Review Press.

Mahalanobis, P. C., Ramkrishna Mukherjee, and Ambika Ghosh. 1946. "A Sample Survey of the After-effects of the Bengal Famine of 1943." *Sankhya* 7 (4): 337–400.

Maier, Charles S. 2006. *Among Empires: American Ascendancy and Its Predecessors*. Cambridge, MA: Harvard University Press.

Maine, Henry Sumner. 1886. *Popular Government: Four Essays*. London: John Murray.

———. 1888. *International Law: The Whewell Lectures*. London: John Murray.

Maitra, Akshayakumar. 1916. "The Black Hole Debate." *Bengal Past and Present* 12 (January–June): 156-71.

Majeed, Javed. 1992. *Ungoverned Imaginings: James Mill's* The History of British India *and Orientalism*. Oxford: Clarendon Press.

Majumdar, Boria, and Kausik Bandyopadhyay. 2006. *Goalless: The Story of a Unique Footballing Nation*. New Delhi: Penguin India.

Majumdar, Jatindra Kumar, ed. (1941) 1983. *Rammohun Roy and Progressive Movements in India: A Selection from Records, 1775-1845*. Reprint, Calcutta: Brahmo Mission Press.

Majumdar, R. C. 1975. *History of the Freedom Movement in India*. Vol. 2. Calcutta: Firma K. L. Mukhopadhyay.

Malcolm, John. 1826. *The Political History of India from 1784 to 1823*. Vol. 1. London: John Murray.

Mamdani, Mahmood. 1996. *Citizen and Subject: Contemporary Africa and the Legacy of Late Colonialism*. Princeton, NJ: Princeton University Press.

Manela, Erez. 2007. *The Wilsonian Moment and the International Origins of Anticolonial Nationalism*. New York: Oxford University Press.

Mangan, J. A. 2001. "Soccer as Moral Training: Missionary Intentions and Imperial Legacies." In *Soccer in South Asia: Empire, Nation, and Diaspora*, edited by Paul Dimeo and James Mills, 41–56. London: Frank Cass.

Mantena, Karuna. 2010. *Alibis of Empire: Henry Maine and the Ends of Liberal Imperialism*. Princeton, NJ: Princeton University Press.

Marshall, P. J. 1965. *Impeachment of Warren Hastings*. London: Oxford University Press.

———. 1968. *Problems of Empire: Britain and India, 1757–1813*. London: Allen and Unwin.

———. 1975. "Economic and Political Expansion: The Case of Oudh." *Modern Asian Studies* 9 (4): 465–82.

———. 1976. *East Indian Fortunes: The British in Bengal in the Eighteenth Century*. Oxford: Clarendon Press.

———. 1987. *The New Cambridge History of India*. Vol. 2.2, *Bengal: The British Bridgehead, Eastern India, 1740–1828*. Cambridge: Cambridge University Press.

———. 1991. "'Cornwallis Triumphant': War in India and the British Public in the Late Eighteenth Century." In *War, Strategy, and International Politics*, edited by Lawrence Freedman, Paul Hayes, and Robert O'Neill, 57–74. Oxford: Clarendon Press.

———. 1998. "The British in Asia: From Trade to Dominion." In *The Oxford History of the British Empire*, edited by P. J. Marshall. Vol. 2, *The Eighteenth Century*. Oxford: Oxford University Press.

———. 2000. "The White Town of Calcutta under the Rule of the East India Company." *Modern Asian Studies* 34 (2): 307–31.

———. 2005. *The Making and Unmaking of Empires: Britain, India, and America, c.1750–1783*. Oxford : Oxford University Press.

Marshman, John C. 1844. *Outline of the History of Bengal*. 5th ed. Serampore: Baptist Mission Press.

Martineau, Alfred. 1916. "L'Episode du 'Black Hole': histoire ou légende?" *Bengal Past and Present* 12 (January–June): 32–37.

Marx, Karl. 1979. "The East India Question." *New York Daily Tribune*, July 25, 1853. In *Collected Works*, by Karl Marx and Frederick Engels, 12:198-200. Moscow: Progress Publishers.

Mazower, Mark. 2009. *No Enchanted Palace: The End of Empire and the Ideological Origins of the United Nations*. Princeton, NJ: Princeton University Press.

Mehta, Uday Singh. 1999. *Liberalism and Empire: A Study in Nineteenth-Century British Liberal Thought*. Chicago: University of Chicago Press.

Menon, V. P. 1956. *The Story of the Integration of the Indian States*. Calcutta: Orient Longmans.

Metcalf, Thomas R. 1964. *The Aftermath of Revolt: India, 1857–1870*. Princeton, NJ: Princeton University Press.

———. 1979. *Land, Landlords, and the British Raj: Northern India in the Nineteenth Century*. Berkeley: University of California Press.

———. 2003. "Monuments and Memorials: Lord Curzon's Creation of a Past for the Raj." In *Traces of India: Photography, Architecture, and the Politics of Representation, 1850–1900*, edited by Maria Antonella Pelizzari, 242–59. Montreal: Canadian Center for Architecture.

Mill, James. (1817) 1858. *The History of British India*. 5 vols. 5th ed. Reprint, London: James Madden.

Mill, John Stuart. 1963–91. "A Few Words on Non-Intervention." *The Collected Works of John Stuart Mill*, edited by John M. Robson, 21:109–24. Toronto: University of Toronto Press.

Mitchell, Timothy. 2002. *Rule of Experts: Egypt, Techno-politics, Modernity*. Berkeley: University of California Press.

Mitra, Rajyeshwar. 1990. "Music in Old Calcutta." In *Calcutta: The Living City*, edited by Sukanta Chaudhuri, 1:179–85. Calcutta: Oxford University Press.

Mitter, Kissory Chand, and Rammohun Roy. 1975. *Rammohun Roy and Tuhfatul Muwahhiddin*. Calcutta: K. P. Bagchi.

Mittra, Peary Chand. (1878) 1979. *A Biographical Sketch of David Hare*. Edited by Gouranga Gopal Sengupta. Reprint, Calcutta: Jijnasa.

Moienuddin, Mohammad. 2000. *Sunset at Srirangapatam: After the Death of Tipu Sultan*. Hyderabad: Orient Longman.

Mommsen, Wolfgang J. 1980. *Theories of Imperialism*. Translated by P. S. Falla. New York: Random House.

Montesquieu, Charles de Secondat. (1748) 1989. *The Spirit of the Laws*. Translated by Anne M. Cohler, Basia Carolyn Miller, and Harold Samuel Stone. Reprint, Cambridge: Cambridge University Press.

Morgan, R. M., and H. L. Morgan. 1927. *A Commentary and Questionnaire on Macaulay's Essay on Clive*. London: Pitman.

Mukherjee, Madhusree. 2010. *Churchill's Secret War: The British Empire and the Ravaging of India during World War II*. New York: Basic Books.

Mukherjee, Rudrangshu. 1984. *Awadh in Revolt, 1857–1858: A Study in Popular Resistance*. Delhi: Oxford University Press.

Mukherjee, S. N. 1977. *Calcutta: Myths and History*. Calcutta: Subarnarekha.

Mukhopadhyay, Subhas Chandra. 1974. *The Career of Rajah Durlabhram Mahindra (Rai-Durlabh): Diwan of Bengal, 1717–1770*. Varanasi: Manisha Prakashan.

Mukhopadhyay, Tarun Kumar. 1988. *Hicky's Bengal Gazette: Contemporary Life and Events*. Calcutta: Subarnarekha.

Muthu, Shankar. 2003. *Enlightenment against Empire*. Princeton, NJ: Princeton University Press.

Nair, Janaki. 2006. "Tipu Sultan, History Painting, and the Battle for 'Perspective.'" *Studies in History* 22, no. 1 (January–June): 97–143.

Nair, P. Thankappan. 1987. *A History of the Calcutta Press: The Beginnings*. Calcutta: Firma KLM.

———. 1990. "The Growth and Development of Old Calcutta." In *Calcutta: The Living City*, edited by Sukanta Chaudhuri, 1:10–23. Calcutta: Oxford University Press.

———. 2001. *Hicky and His Gazette*. Calcutta: S & T Book Stall.

———. 2004. *South Indians in Kolkata*. Calcutta: Punthi Pustak.

Natarajan, J. 1955. *History of Indian Journalism: Part II of the Report of the Press Commission*. Delhi: Publications Division.

Newell, H. A. 1922. *Calcutta, the First Capital of British India: An Illustrated Guide to Places of Interest with Map*. Calcutta: Caledonian Printing Company.

Nkrumah, Kwame. 1965. *Neo-colonialism, the Last Stage of Capitalism*. New York: International Publishers.

Nurullah, Syed, and J. P. Naik. (1943) 1953. *A History of Education in India (during the British Period)*. Reprint, Bombay: Macmillan.

Oaten, Edward F. 1916. "The Black Hole Debate." *Bengal Past and Present* 12 (January–June): 149–54.

An Officer of Colonel Baillie's Detachment [William Thomson]. 1788. *Memoirs of the Late War in Asia, with a Narrative of the Imprisonment and Sufferings of Our Officers and Soldiers*. London: J. Murray.

Oldenburg, Veena Talwar. 1984. *The Making of Colonial Lucknow, 1856–1877*. Princeton, NJ: Princeton University Press.

Oppenheim, Lassa. 1912. *International Law: A Treatise*. London: Longmans, Green.

———. 1955. *International Law: A Treatise*. Vol. 1, *Peace*. Edited by Hersch Lauterpacht. London: Longman, Green.

Orme, Robert. 1778. *A History of the Military Transactions of the British Nation in Indostan, from the Year MDCCXLV*. 2 vols. London: John Nourse.

Pagden, Anthony. 1987. "Dispossessing the Barbarian: The Language of Spanish Thomism and the Debate over the Property Rights of the American Indians." In *The Languages of Political Theory in Early-Modern Europe*, edited by Anthony Pagden, 79–98. Cambridge: Cambridge University Press.

———. 1995. *Lords of All the World: Ideologies of Empire in Spain, Britain, and France, c.1500–c.1800*. New Haven, CT: Yale University Press.

Palit, Indira. 1973. *Nabin Sen the Poet*. Calcutta: Prabhat.

Pandhe, Pramila, ed. 1978. *Suppression of Drama in Nineteenth Century India*. Calcutta: India Book Exchange.

Pearson, Michael N. 1987. *The Portuguese in India*. Cambridge: Cambridge University Press.

Pemble, John. 1977. *The Raj, the Indian Mutiny, and the Kingdom of Oudh, 1801–1859*. Sussex: Harvester Press.

Pinney, Christopher. 2004. *Photos of the Gods: The Printed Image and Political Struggle in India*. Delhi: Oxford University Press.

Pitts, Jennifer. 2005. *A Turn to Empire: The Rise of Imperial Liberalism in Britain and France*. Princeton, NJ: Princeton University Press.

Poddar, Arabinda. 1970. *Renaissance in Bengal: Quests and Confrontations, 1800–1860*. Simla: Indian Institute of Advanced Study.

Pollock, Sheldon. 2006. "Comparative Intellectual Histories of the Early Modern World." *International Institute of Asian Studies Newsletter* 43 (December): 1–13.

Pomeranz, Kenneth. 2000. *The Great Divergence: China, Europe, and the Making of the Modern World Economy*. Princeton, NJ: Princeton University Press.

Porter, Bernard. 2004. *Absent-minded Imperialists: Empire, Society, and Culture in Britain*. Oxford: Oxford University Press.

Prasad, Sri Nandan. 1964. *Paramountcy under Dalhousie*. Delhi: Ranjit Printers.

A Proprietor of India Stock [J. S. Sutherland]. 1824. *A Second Letter to Sir Charles Forbes, Bart., M. P., on the Suppression of Public Discussion in India, and the Banishment without Trial, of Two British Editors From That Country by the Acting Governor-general, Mr. Adam*. London.

Rahim, Muhammad Abdur. 1963. *Lord Dalhousie's Administration of the Conquered and Annexed States*. Delhi: S. Chand.

Raman, Shankar. 2002. *Framing "India": The Colonial Imaginary in Early Modern Culture*. Stanford, CA: Stanford University Press.

Ramusack, Barbara N. 2004. *The New Cambridge History of India*. Vol. 3.6, *The Indian Princes and Their States*. Cambridge: Cambridge University Press.

Rao, Velcheru Narayana, David Shulman, and Sanjay Subrahmanyam. 2001. *Textures of Time: Writing History in South India, 1600–1800*. Delhi: Permanent Black.

Rao, Velcheru Narayana, and Sanjay Subrahmanyam. 2008. "History and Politics in the Vernacular: Reflections on Medieval and Early Modern South India." In *History in the Vernacular*, edited by Raziuddin Aquil and Partha Chatterjee, 25–65. Delhi: Permanent Black.

Ray, A. K. 1902. "A Short History of Calcutta Town and Suburbs." Vol. 7, pt. 1, *Census of India 1901*. Calcutta: Commissioner of Census.

Ray, Ajit Kumar. 1976. *The Religious Ideas of Rammohun Roy: A Survey of His Writings on Religion Particularly in Persian, Sanskrit, and Bengali*. New Delhi: Kanak Publications.

Richards, John F. 1997. "Early Modern India and World History." *Journal of World History* 8 (2): 197–209.

Roberts, S. C. 1927. *Lord Macaulay: The Pre-eminent Victorian*. London: English Association.

Robinson, Ronald, and John Gallagher. 1961. *Africa and the Victorians: The Official Mind of Imperialism*. London: Macmillan.

Rocher, Rosane. 1983. *Orientalism, Poetry, and the Millennium: The Checkered Life of Nathaniel Brassey Halhed, 1751–1830*. Delhi: Motilal Banarsidass.

Rosenfeld, Richard N. 1997. *American Aurora: A Democratic-Republican Returns*. New York: St. Martin's Press.

Rosselli, John. 1974. *Lord William Bentinck: The Making of a Liberal Imperialist, 1774–1839*. Delhi: Thompson Press.

Roy, Rammohan. 1906. *The English Works of Raja Rammohun Roy*. Edited by Jogendra Chunder Ghose. Allahabad: Panini Office.

———. 1947. *The English Works of Raja Rammohun Roy*. Edited by Kalidas Nag and Debajyoti Barman. Part 4. Calcutta: Sadharan Brahmo Samaj.

Said, Edward W. 1978. *Orientalism*. London: Routledge and Kegan Paul.

Sarkar, Jadunath, ed. (1948) 1972. *History of Bengal*. Vol. 2, *Muslim Period, 1200–1757*. Reprint, Dhaka: University of Dacca.

———. 1987. "A Word to Research Workers in Indian History" (1948). Reprinted in *Bengal Past and Present* 106 (January–December): 158–62.

Sarkar, Sumit. 1973. *The Swadeshi Movement in Bengal, 1903–1908*. New Delhi: People's Publishing House.

———. 1975. "Rammohun Roy and the Break with the Past." In *Rammohun Roy and the Process of Modernization in India*, edited by V. C. Joshi, 46–68. Delhi: Vikas.

———. 1985. *A Critique of Colonial India*. Calcutta: Papyrus.

Sartori, Andrew. 2008. *Bengal in Global Concept History: Culturalism in the Age of Capital*. Chicago: University of Chicago Press.

Say, Jean-Baptiste. 1824. "Historical Essay on the Origin, Progress, and Probable Results of the Sovereignty of the English in India by Mons. J. B. Say." *Oriental Herald* 3, no. 11 (November): 348–60.

Schmitt, Carl. 1985. *Political Theology: Four Chapters on the Concept of Sovereignty.* Translated by George Schwab. Chicago: University of Chicago Press.

———. 2003. *The Nomos of the Earth in the International Law of the* Jus Publicum Europaeum. Translated by G. L. Ulmen. New York: Telos Press.

Schofield, Philip. 2006. *Utility and Democracy: The Political Thought of Jeremy Bentham.* Oxford: Oxford University Press.

———. 2009. *Bentham: A Guide for the Perplexed.* London: Continuum Books.

Schumpeter, Joseph A. (1919) 1951. *Imperialism and Social Classes.* Translated by Heinz Norden. Reprint, New York: Augustus M. Kelley.

Scrafton, Luke. (1763) 1770. *Reflections on the Government of Indostan, with a Short Sketch of the History of Bengal, from MDCCXXXVIIII to MDCCLVI.* Reprint, London: W. Strahan.

Seal, Anil. 1970. *The Emergence of Indian Nationalism: Competition and Collaboration in the Nineteenth Century.* Cambridge: Cambridge University Press.

Seal, Brajendra Nath. (1924) 1972. *Rammohun Roy: The Universal Man.* Reprint, Calcutta: Sadharan Brahmo Samaj.

Seeley, John R. (1883) 1906. *The Expansion of England: Two Courses of Lectures.* Reprint, London: Macmillan.

Sen, Amartya. 1981. *Poverty and Famines: An Essay on Entitlements and Deprivation.* Oxford: Clarendon Press.

Sen, Amartya, and Raymond Williams, eds. 1982. *Utilitarianism and Beyond.* Cambridge: Cambridge University Press.

Sen, Asok. 1975. "The Bengal Economy and Rammohun Roy." In *Rammohun Roy and the Process of Modernization in India,* edited by V. C. Joshi, 103–35. Delhi: Vikas.

———. 1977. "A Pre-British Economic Formation in India of the Late Eighteenth Century: Tipu Sultan's Mysore," in *Perspectives in Social Sciences: Historical Dimensions,* edited by Barun De, 46–119. Calcutta: Oxford University Press.

Sen, Sudipta. 2002. *A Distant Sovereignty: National Imperialism and the Origins of British India.* New York: Routledge.

Seth, Mesrovb Jacob. (1937) 1983. *Armenians in India: From the Earliest Times to the Present Day.* Reprint, Calcutta: Oxford and IBH.

Seton-Karr, W., ed. (1864) 1987. *Selections from Calcutta Gazettes.* Vol. 1. Reprint, Calcutta: Bibhash Gupta.

Shaw, Graham. 1981. *Printing in Calcutta to 1800.* London: Bibliographic Society.

Singh, Iqbal. 1983. *Rammohun Roy: A Biographical Inquiry into the Making of Modern India.* 3 vols. Bombay: Asia Publishing House.

Singh, Moki. 1938. *Mysterious India.* London: Stanley Paul.

Singha, Radhika. 1988. *A Despotism of Law: Crime and Justice in Early Colonial India.* Delhi: Oxford University Press.

Sinha, Mrinalini. 1995. *Colonial Masculinity: The "Manly Englishman" and the "Effeminate Bengali" in the Late Nineteenth Century.* Manchester, UK: Manchester University Press.

Sinha, Narendra Krishna. (1941) 1959. *Haidar Ali.* Reprint, Calcutta: A. Mukherjee.

———. 1965. *The Economic History of Bengal: From Plassey to the Permanent Settlement.* Vol. 1. Calcutta: Firma K. L. Mukhopadhyay.

Sismondi, Jean-Charles-Léonard de. 1825. "Article of M. Sismondi, on the Colonization of India." *Oriental Herald and Journal of General Literature* 4 (January–March): 227–35.

Sleeman, William H. 1858. *A Journey through the Kingdom of Oude, 1849–1850.* Vol. 2. London: Richard Bentley.

Smith, Vincent E. (1919) 1958. *The Oxford History of India.* Edited by Percival Spear. Reprint, London: Oxford University Press.

Stavorinus, John Splinter. 1798. *Voyages to the East-Indies.* Translated by Samuel Hull Wilcocke. Vol. 1. London: G. and J. Robinson.

Stein, Burton. 1985. "State Formation and Economy Reconsidered: Part One." *Modern Asian Studies* 19 (3): 387–413.

———. 1989. *Thomas Munro: The Origins of the Colonial State and His Vision of Empire.* Delhi: Oxford University Press.

Stephen, James Fitzjames. 1873. *Liberty, Equality, Fraternity.* London: Smith, Elder.

———. 1883. "Foundations of the Government of India." *Nineteenth Century* 70 (October): 541–68.

Stewart, Charles. 1813. *History of Bengal from the First Mohammedan Invasion until the Virtual Conquest of That Country by the English, A.D. 1757.* London: Black, Parry.

Stokes, Eric. 1959. *The English Utilitarians and India.* Oxford: Clarendon Press.

Subrahmanyam, Sanjay. 1999. *Penumbral Visions: Making Polities in Early Modern South India.* Delhi: Oxford University Press.

———. 2005. *Explorations in Connected History: Mughals and Franks.* Delhi: Oxford University Press.

Suhrawardy, Hassan. 1921. *Calcutta and Environs: An Illustrated Guide to Places of Interest and to Excursions in and around Calcutta.* Calcutta: E. I. Railway Press.

Sutherland, Lucy S. 1952. *The East India Company in Eighteenth-Century Politics.* Oxford: Clarendon Press.

Symonds, Richard. 1986. *Oxford and Empire: The Last Lost Cause.* London: Macmillan.

Tavakoli-Targhi, Mohamad. 2001. *Refashioning Iran: Orientalism, Occidentalism, and Historiography.* London: Palgrave.

Tegart, Charles. 1932. *Terrorism in India.* London: Royal Empire Society.

Teltscher, Kate. 1996. "'The Fearful Name of the Black Hole': Fashioning an Imperial Myth." In *Writing India, 1757–1990,* edited by Bart Moore-Gilbert, 30–51. Manchester, UK: Manchester University Press.

———. 1998. *India Inscribed: European and British Writing on India, 1600–1800.* Delhi: Oxford University Press.

Thomas, William. 1979. *The Philosophic Radicals: Nine Studies in Theory and Practice, 1817–1841.* Oxford: Clarendon Press.

Thornton, A. P. 1959. *The Imperial Idea and Its Enemies: A Study in British Power.* London: Macmillan.

Tilly, Charles. 1990. *Coercion, Capital, and European States, AD 900–1992.* Malden, MA: Blackwell.

Tinker, Hugh. 1974. *New System of Slavery: Export of Indian Labour Overseas, 1830–1920.* Oxford: Oxford University Press.

Travers, Robert. 2007. *Ideology and Empire in Eighteenth-Century India: The British in Bengal.* Cambridge: Cambridge University Press.

Trevelyan, George Otto. (1876) 1978. *The Life and Letters of Lord Macaulay.* 2 vols. Reprint, Oxford: Oxford University Press.

Tripathi, Amales. 1967. *The Extremist Challenge: India between 1890 and 1910.* Bombay: Orient Longman.

Trotter, Lionel I. 1889. *Life of the Marquis of Dalhousie.* London: W. H. Allen.

Tuck, Richard. 1999. *The Rights of War and Peace: Political Thought and the International Order from Grotius to Kant.* Oxford: Oxford University Press.

Turner, Ralph E. 1930. *The Relations of James Silk Buckingham with the East India Company, 1818–1836.* Pittsburgh: Ralph Turner.

Urbinati, Nadia. 2007. "The Many Heads of the Hydra: J. S. Mill on Despotism." In *J. S. Mill's Political Thought: A Bicentennial Reassessment,* edited by Nadia Urbinati and Alex Zakaras, 66–97. Cambridge: Cambridge University Press.

Vattel, Emerich de. 1916. *The Law of Nations or the Principles of Natural Law.* Translated by Charles G. Fenwick. Vol. 3. Washington, DC: Carnegie Institution.

Visitors' Guide to Calcutta. 1927. Calcutta: W. Newman.

Visram, Rozina. 1986. *Ayahs, Lascars, and Princes: Indians in Britain, 1700–1947.* London: Pluto Press.

Viswanathan, Gauri. 1990. *Masks of Conquest: Literary Study and British Rule in India.* London: Faber and Faber.

Wakefield, Edward Gibbon. 1832. *Plan of a Company to be Established for the Purpose of Founding a Colony in Southern Australia.* London: James Ridgway.

Washbrook, David A. 1988. "Progress and Problems: South Asian Economic and Social History, c.1720–1860." *Modern Asian Studies* 22 (1): 57–96.

Watts, William. (1760) 1988. *Memoirs of the Revolution in Bengal Anno Dom. 1757.* Edited by Bimal Kanti Ghosh. Reprint, Calcutta: K. P. Bagchi.

Westlake, John. 1894. *Chapters on the Principles of International Law.* Cambridge: Cambridge University Press.

What Is the Theatre? An Enquiry Suggested by Some Recent Circumstances. 1842. Calcutta: American Mission Press.

Wilks, Mark. (1810) 1932. *Historical Sketches of the South of India.* Vol. 2. Reprint, Mysore: Government Branch Press.

Wilson, Kathleen. 1995. *The Sense of the People: Politics, Culture, and Imperialism in England, 1715–1785.* Cambridge: Cambridge University Press.

Young, I. F. n.d. *Macaulay's Essay on Clive.* London: Normal Press.

Zaman, Shams N. 2003. *Mirza Shaikh Itesamuddin and His Travelogue: Shigurf Nama i Vilayet.* London: Shams N. Zaman.

Zastoupil, Lynn. 1994. *John Stuart Mill and India.* Stanford, CA: Stanford University Press.

———. 2002. "Defining Christians, Making Britons: Rammohun Roy and the Unitarians." *Victorian Studies* 45, no. 2 (Winter): 216–45.

Zastoupil, Lynn, and Martin Moir, eds. 1999. *The Great Indian Education Debate: Documents Relating to the Orientalist-Anglicist Controversy, 1781–1843.* Richmond, Surrey: Curzon Press.

BOOKS AND ARTICLES IN INDIAN LANGUAGES

Ahmad, Abul Mansur. 1970. *Āmār dekhā rājnītir pañcāś bachar.* Dhaka: Naoroz Kitabistan.

Ahmed, Waqil. 1985. *Bāṃlār muslim buddhijībi (1757–1800).* Dhaka: Bangla Academy.

Ali, Karam. (1952) 1985. *Muzaffar-namah.* In *Bengal Nawabs,* edited by Jadu Nath Sarkar. Reprint, Calcutta: Asiatic Society.

Arbi [Rakhal Bhattacharya]. (1955) 2002. *Kalkātār phuṭbal.* Edited by Sibram Kumar. Reprint, Calcutta: Prabhabati.

Bandyopadhyay, Angshuman, ed. 2001. *Agniyuger agnikathā: Yugāntar, 1906–1908.* Pondicherry: Sri Aurobindo Ashram.

Bandyopadhyay, Bhabanicharan. 1987. *Kalikātā kamalālay* (1823). In *Rasaracanāsamagra,* edited by Sanatkumar Gupta. Calcutta: Nabapatra.

Bandyopadhyay, Bijay Kumar, Saumitrasankar Sengupta, and Prakash Das Biswas, eds. 2003. *Murśidābād jelā gejeṭiyār.* Calcutta: West Bengal District Gazetteers.

Bandyopadhyay, Brajendranath. (1933) 1998. *Baṅgīya nāṭyaśālār itihās, 1795–1876.* Reprint, Calcutta: Bangiya Sahitya Parishat.

―――. *Bhabānīcaraṇ bandyopādhyāy.* (1940) 1982. Reprint, Calcutta: Bangiya Sahitya-Parishat.

―――. (1942) 1972. *Rāmmohan rāy.* Reprint, Calcutta: Bangiya Sahitya Parishat.

Bandyopadhyay, Kshetranath. 1872. *Śiśupāṭh bāṅgālār itihās, bargir hāṅgām haite larḍ narthbruker āgaman paryyanta.* Calcutta.

Bandyopadhyay, Santipriya. 1998. *Klāber nām mohanbāgān.* Calcutta: Aparna Book Distributors.

Bandyopadhyay, Upendranath. (1921) 1999. *Nirbāsiter ātmakathā.* Reprint, Calcutta: National Publishers.

Basu, Ajay. 1980. *Phuṭbale dikpāl.* Calcutta: Mandal Book House.

Basu, Ajitkumar. 1996. *Kalikātār rājpath samāje o saṃskṛtite.* Calcutta: Ananda.

Basu, Satyendrakumar. 1929. "Phuṭbal." *Māsik basumatī* 7, no. 2 (6): 993–1006.

Bhadra, Gautam. (1991) 2010. "Prāk-rāmmohan yuge kompānir śāsaner prati kayekjan bāṅgāli buddhijībir manobhāb." *Ākādemi patrikā* 4. Reprinted in *Nibandha baicitrer tin daśak,* edited by Anirban Mukhopadhyay, 95–126. Calcutta: Charchapad.

Bhattacharya, Asutosh. 1968. *Bāṃlā nāṭyasāhityer itihās.* Part 2. Calcutta: A. Mukherjee.

Bhattacharya, Karuna. 1942. "Asṭreliyāy bhāratīya phuṭbal dal." *Rammaśāl,* 390–95.

Bidyabinod, Kshirodprasad. 2001. *Kṣīrodprasād nāṭaksamagra.* Edited by Basabi Ray. Vol. 2. Calcutta: Sahitya Samsad.

Biswas, Dilipkumar. 1983. *Rāmmohan samīkṣa.* Calcutta: Saraswat Library.

Chattopadhyay, Bankimchandra. 1994. "Palāśīr yuddha." In *Baṅkim racanābalī,* edited by Jogeschandra Bagal, 2:831–33. Calcutta: Sahitya Samsad.

Chattopadhyay, Gita. 1983. *Bāṃlā svadeśī gān.* Delhi: University of Delhi Press.

Chattopadhyay, Nagendranath. (1881) 1972. *Mahātmā rājā rāmmohan rāy.* Reprint, Calcutta: Dey's.

Chattopadhyay, Partha. 2005. *Prajā o tantra.* Calcutta: Anustup.

Chattopadhyay, Santi. 1978. *Nabīncandra: sāhitya o sādhanā.* Calcutta: Jijnasa.

Chaudhuri, Ahindra. 1962. *Nijere hārāye khuñji.* Calcutta: Indian Associated.

―――. 1972. *Bāṅālir nāṭyacarcā.* Calcutta: Sankar Prakashan.

Das, Upendranath. 1993. *Śarat-sarojinī o surendra-binodinī*. Edited by Mahadebprasad Saha. Calcutta: Paschimbanga Natya Akademi.

Dasgupta, Praphullakumar. 1977. *Giriś nātya-sāhitya pariciti*. Calcutta: Sanyal and Company.

Dasi, Binodini. (1912) 1987. *Āmār kathā o anyānya racanā*. Edited by Saumitra Chattopadhyay and Nirmalya Acharya. Reprint, Calcutta: Subarnarekha.

Datta, Prankrishna. 1991. *Kalikātār itibṛtta o anyānya racanā*. Edited by Debashis Basu. Calcutta: Pustak Bipani.

Datta, Ramapati. 1941. *Raṅgālaye amarendranāth*. Calcutta: Harindranath Datta.

Datta, Utpal. 1983. *Giriś-mānas*. Calcutta: M. C. Sarkar.

[Fani, Muhammad Muin-al-Din Fani, or Mirza Muhsin Kashmiri Fani]. 1843. *The Dabistan or School of Manners*. Translated by David Shea and Anthony Troyer. 3 vols. Paris: Benjamin Duprat.

———. 1904. *Dabistan-i mazahib*. Kanpur: Nawal Kishor.

Gafur, Abdul. 2000. *Āmār kāler kathā*. Dhaka: Bangladesh Co-operative Book Society.

Gangopadhyay, Abinaschandra. (1927) 1977. *Giriścandra*. Edited by Swapan Majumdar. Reprint, Calcutta: Dey's.

Ghosh, Binay. 1962. "Ṭhākur-paribārer ādiparba o sekāler samāj." *Bisvabhāratī patrikā* 18 (4) (Baisakh 1369).

Ghosh, Girischandra. 1969. *Giriś racanābalī*. Edited by Rathindranath Ray and Debipada Bhattacharya. Vol. 1. Calcutta: Sahitya Samsad.

———. 1973. *Sirājaddaulā*. Edited by Kshetra Gupta. Calcutta: Sahitya Prakash.

———. 1975. *Sirājaddaulā*. Edited by Bhabanigopal Sanyal. Calcutta: Apurba.

Gupta, Jogendranath. 1963. *Mahākabi giriścandra*. Calcutta: University of Calcutta Press.

Haque, Fazlul. 1991. *Aitihāsik akṣaykumār maitreya: jīban o karma*. Dhaka: Muktadhara.

Hossain, Dilwar. 1994. *Mohammadī patrikāy muslim samāj*. Dhaka: Bangla Academy.

Ihtishamuddin, Mirza Shaikh. 1827. *Shigurf Namah i Velaët, or Excellent Intelligence concerning Europe; Being the Travels of Mirza Itesa Modeen, in Great Britain and France*. Translated from the original Persian manuscript into Hindoostanee, with an English version and notes, by James Edward Alexander. London: Parbury, Allen and Company.

———. 1981. *Bilāyetnāmā*. Translated by A.B.M. Habibullah. Dhaka: Muktadhara.

———. 2001. *The Wonders of Vilayet: Being the Memoir, Originally in Persian, of a Visit to France and Britain*. Translated by Kaiser Haq. London: Peepal Tree Press.

Kanungo, Hemchandra. (1928) 1997. *Bāṃlāy biplab pracesṭā*. Reprint, Calcutta: Chirayata.

Khan, Abu Taleb. (1814) 1972. *Travels of Mirza Abu Taleb Khan in Asia, Africa, and Europe during the Years 1799 to 1803*. Translated by Charles Stewart. Reprint, New Delhi: Sona Publications.

———. 1983. *Masir-e Tālebi: Safar nameh Mirza Abu Taleb Khan*. Edited by Hosein Khadive-Jam. Tehran: Islamic Revolution Publication.

Khan, Meer Hussein Ali. 1842. *The History of Hydur Naik Otherwise Styled Shams ul Moolk, Ameer ud Dowla, Nawaub Hyder Ali Khan Bahadoor*. Translated by W. Miles. London.

Khan, Yusuf Ali. 1982. *Ta'rikh-i-Bangala-i-Mahabatjangi*. Translated by Abdus Subhan. Calcutta: Asiatic Society.

Lahiri, Durgadas. (1905) 2001. *Bāṅgālīr gān*. Reprint, Calcutta: Paschimbanga Bangla Academy.

Maitreya, Akshaykumar. (1897) 2006. *Sirājaddaulā*. Reprint, Calcutta: Dey's.

———. (1906) 2004. *Mīr kāśim*. Reprint, Calcutta: Puthipatra.

———. 1982. *Bhāratśilper kathā*. Calcutta: Sahityalok.

Mirza, Kaukab Qadir Sajjad Ali. 1995. *Wajid Ali Shah ki adabi aur saqafati khidmat*. New Delhi: Taraqqi-yi Urdu Bureau.

Mitra, Amal. 1967. *Kalkātāy bideśī raṅgālay*. Calcutta: Prakash Bhaban.

Mitra, Arunkumar, ed. 1982. *Amṛtalāl basur smṛti o ātmasmṛti*. Calcutta: Sahityalok.

Mitra, Ramendra. 1996. *Rāmmohan o beṅgal harkarā: Briṭiś-bhārate iuropīya basatiprasaṅge*. Calcutta: Prima Publications.

Modabbir, Muhammad. 1977. *Sāṃbādiker rojnāmcā*. Dhaka: Barnamichhil.

Mukhopadhyay, Apareschandra. (1933) 1972. *Raṅgālaye triś batsar*. Edited by Swapan Majumdar. Reprint, Calcutta: Granthan.

Mukhopadhyay, Dhananjay. 1910. *Baṅgīya nāṭyaśālā (samālocanā)*. Calcutta.

Mukhopadhyay, Harisadhan. (1915) 1985. *Kalikātā sekāler o ekāler*. Edited by Nisithranjan Ray. Reprint, Calcutta: P. M. Bagchi.

Mukhopadhyay, Jadugopal. (1956) 1983. *Biplabī jībaner smṛti*. Reprint, Calcutta: Academic Publishers.

Mukhopadhyay, Nikhil. 1966. *Kabi nabīncandra*. Calcutta: Jatiya Sahitya Parishad.

Mukhopadhyay, Rajiblochan. 1805. *Mahārājā kṛṣṇacandra rāyasya caritra*. Srirampur: Baptist Mission Press.

Mukhopadhyay, Saktisadhan. 2004. *Kalkātār ādi ācārya ḍebhiḍ ḍrāmanḍ*. Calcutta: Punascha.

Nadvi, Mohammad Ilyas. 2004. *Tipu Sultan (A Life History)*. Translated by Mohammad Saghir Husain. New Delhi: Institute of Objective Studies.

Poddar, Arabinda. 1982. *Rāmmohan uttarpakṣa*. Calcutta: Uchcharan.

Rakshit-ray, Bhupendrakishor. 1966. *Sabār alakṣye*. Vol. 1. Calcutta: Bengal Publishers.

Ray, Amarendranath, ed. 1958. *Egāraṭi bāṃlā nāṭyagranther dṛśya-nidarśan*. Calcutta: University of Calcutta Press.

Ray, Debashish, and Chandan Chatterjee. 2000. *Haloyel manumen: apasāraṇ āndolan o prāsaṅgik*. Calcutta: Biswakosh Parishad.

Ray, Durgacharan. (1886) 1984. *Debgaṇer martye āgaman*. Reprint, Calcutta: Dey's.

Ray, Krishnachandra. 1870. *Bhāratbarṣer itihās, iṃrejdiger adhikārkāl*. Calcutta: J. C. Chatterjee.

Ray, Nikhilnath. (1897) 1978. *Aitihāsik citra: Murśidābād kāhinī*. Reprint, Calcutta: Puthipatra.

———. (1908) 2006. "Andhakūp-hatyā." *Aitihāsik citra* (October–December), reprinted in *Sirājaddaulā*, by Akshaykumar Maitreya, 322–32. Calcutta: Dey's.

Ray, Rajatkanta. 1994. *Palāśir ṣaḍayantra o sekāler samāj*. Calcutta: Ananda.

Ray, Rammohan. 1973. *Rāmmohan racanābalī*. Edited by Ajitkumar Ghosh. Calcutta: Haraf.

Ray, Rathindranath, and Debipada Bhattacharya, eds. 1969. *Giriś racanābalī*. Vol. 1. Calcutta: Sahitya Samsad.

Raychaudhuri, Kshirodchandra. 1876. *Samagra bhārater saṃkṣipta itihās*. Calcutta.

Raychaudhuri, Subir, ed. 1972. *Bilāti yātrā theke svadeśī thiyeṭār*. Calcutta: Jadavpur University.

Rijaluddin, Ahmad. 1982. *Hikayat Perintah Negeri Benggala*. Edited by C. Skinner. The Hague: Martinus Nijhoff.

Salim, Ghulam Hussain. (1903) 1975. *Riyazu-s-Salatin*. Translated by Abdus Salam. Reprint, Delhi: Idarah-i Adabiyat-i Delli.

Sarma, Mrityunjay. 1808. *Rājābali*. Srirampur: Baptist Mission Press.

Sastri, Sibnath. 1979. *Rāmtanu lāhiḍī o tatkālīn baṅgasamāj*. In *Racanāsamagra*. Calcutta: Saksarata Prakashan.

Sastri, Surendramohan. 1975. *Nabīncandrer kābya-samīkṣā*. Calcutta: Samskrita Pustak Bhandar.

Sen, Nabinchandra. 1959. *Nabīncandra-racanābalī*. Edited by Sajanikanta Das. Vol. 4. Calcutta: Bangiya Sahitya Parishat.

———. 1975. *Nabīncandra racanābalī*. Edited by Santikumar Dasgupta and Haribandhu Mukhati. Vol. 2. Calcutta: Dattachaudhuri.

Sengupta, Pradyot. 1997. *Bāṃlā nāṭak, nāṭyatattva o raṅgamaṇca prasaṅga*. Vol. 2. Calcutta: Barnali.

Sengupta, Sachindranath. (1938) 2001. *Sirājaddaulā: aitihāsik nāṭak*. Reprint, Calcutta: Dey's.

Shamsuddin, Abul Kalam. 1968. *Atīt diner smṛti*. Dhaka: Naoroz Kitabistan.

Sharar, Abdul Halim. (1913) 2001. *Lucknow: The Last Phase of an Oriental Culture*. Translated and edited by E. S. Harcourt and Fakhir Hussain. Reprint, Delhi: Oxford University Press.

Sinha, Kaliprasanna. (1862) 1991. *[Saṭīk] Hutom pyāñcār naksā*. Edited by Arun Nag. Reprint, Calcutta: Subarnarekha.

———. 2008. *The Observant Owl*. Translated by Swarup Roy. Delhi: Permanent Black.

Tabatabai, Ghulam Husain. (1902) 1986. *A Translation of the Seïr Mutaqherin; or View of Modern Times, being an History of India, from the Year 1118 to the Year 1194 (This Year Answers to the Christian Year 1781–82) of the Hedjrah*, by Seid-Gholam-Hossein-Khan. Vols. 1–4. Reprint, New Delhi: Inter-India Publications.

Thakur, Kshitindranath. 1969. *Dvārakānāth ṭhākurer jībanī*. Calcutta: Rabindrabharati University.

Vidyalankar, Gangagobinda, ed. 1835. *The Bengalee Annual Almanac, 1242*. Calcutta: Dinabandhu Press.

Waliullah, Muhammad. 1967. *Yugabicitrā*. Dhaka: Maola Brothers.

Index

Note: Page numbers in italic type indicate illustrations.